S0-ADG-483

GO!
with Microsoft®

Office 2007

Shelley Gaskin, Robert L. Ferrett, Alicia Vargas, and Carolyn McLellan

CUSTOM EDITION FOR TULSA COMMUNITY COLLEGE

Taken from:

GO! with Microsoft® Office 2007 Introductory, Third Edition
by Shelley Gaskin, Robert L. Ferrett, Alicia Vargas, and Carolyn McLellan

GO! with Windows Vista: Getting Started
by Shelley Gaskin and Robert L. Ferrett

Custom Publishing

New York   Boston   San Francisco
London   Toronto   Sydney   Tokyo   Singapore   Madrid
Mexico City   Munich   Paris   Cape Town   Hong Kong   Montreal

Cover Art: Courtesy of Photo Disc/Getty Images

Taken from:

GO! with Microsoft Office 2007 Introductory, Third Edition
by Shelley Gaskin, Robert L. Ferrett, Alicia Vargas, and Carolyn McLellan
Copyright © 2010, 2009, 2008 by Pearson Education, Inc.
Published by Prentice Hall
Upper Saddle River, New Jersey 07458

GO! with Windows Vista: Getting Started
by Shelley Gaskin and Robert L. Ferrett
Copyright © 2008 by Pearson Education, Inc.
Published by Prentice Hall
Upper Saddle River, New Jersey 07458

All rights reserved. No part of this book may be reproduced, in any form or by any means, without permission
in writing from the publisher.

This special edition published in cooperation with Pearson Custom Publishing.

All trademarks, service marks, registered trademarks, and registered service marks are the property of their respective
owners and are used herein for identification purposes only.

Printed in the United States of America

10 9 8 7 6 5 4 3 2 1

2009820024

CM

**Pearson
Custom Publishing**
is a division of

www.pearsonhighered.com

ISBN 10: 0-558-32103-8
ISBN 13: 978-0-558-32103-1

Contents in Brief

Table of Contents

Excel 2007

Chapter 9   Creating a Worksheet and Charting Data.........273

PowerPoint 2007

Chapter 15 Getting Started with Microsoft PowerPoint 2007 771

Letter from the Editor

Dear Instructors and Students,

The primary goal of the *GO!* Series is two-fold. The first goal is to help instructors teach the course they want in less time. The second goal is to provide students with the skills to solve business problems using the computer as a tool, for both themselves and the organization for which they might be employed.

The *GO!* Series was originally created by Series Editor Shelley Gaskin and published with the release of Microsoft Office 2003. Her ideas came from years of using textbooks that didn't meet all the needs of today's diverse classroom and that were too confusing for students. Shelley continues to enhance the series by ensuring we stay true to our vision of developing quality instruction and useful classroom tools.

But we also need your input and ideas.

Over time, the *GO!* Series has evolved based on direct feedback from instructors and students using the series. *We are the publisher that listens.* To publish a textbook that works for you, it's critical that we continue to listen to this feedback. It's important to me to talk with you and hear your stories about using *GO!* Your voice can make a difference.

My hope is that this letter will inspire you to write me an e-mail and share your thoughts on using the *GO!* Series.

Stephanie Wall
Executive Editor, *GO!* Series
stephanie_wall@prenhall.com

About the Authors

Shelley Gaskin, Series Editor, is a professor of business and computer technology at Pasadena City College in Pasadena, California. She holds a master's degree in business education from Northern Illinois University and a doctorate in adult and community education from Ball State University. Dr. Gaskin has 15 years of experience in the computer industry with several Fortune 500 companies and has developed and written training materials for custom systems applications in both the public and private sector. She is also the author of books on Microsoft Outlook and word processing.

Robert L. Ferrett recently retired as the director of the Center for Instructional Computing at Eastern Michigan University, where he provided computer training and support to faculty. He has authored or co-authored more than 70 books on Access, PowerPoint, Excel, Publisher, WordPerfect, and Word. Before writing for the GO! Series, Bob was a series editor and author for the Learn Series. He has a bachelor's degree in psychology, a master's degree in geography, and a master's degree in interdisciplinary technology from Eastern Michigan University. Bob's doctoral studies were in instructional technology at Wayne State University. For fun, Bob teaches a four-week computers and genealogy class and has written genealogy and local history books.

Alicia Vargas is a faculty member in Business Information Technology at Pasadena City College. She holds a master's and a bachelor's degree in business education from California State University, Los Angeles, and has authored several textbooks and training manuals on Microsoft Word, Microsoft Excel, and Microsoft PowerPoint.

Carolyn McLellan is the Dean of the Division of Information Technology and Business at Tidewater Community College in Virginia Beach, Virginia. She has an M.A. degree in Secondary Education from Regent University and a B.S. degree in Business Education from Old Dominion University. She taught for Norfolk Public Schools for 17 years in Business Education and served as a faculty member at Tidewater Community College for eight years teaching networking, where she developed over 23 new courses and earned the Microsoft Certified Trainer and Microsoft Certified System Engineer industry certifications. In addition to teaching, Carolyn loves to play volleyball, boogie board at the beach, bicycle, crochet, cook, and read.

Visual Walk-Through of the *GO!* System

The *GO!* System is designed for ease of implementation on the instructor side and ease of understanding on the student. It has been completely developed based on professor and student feedback.

The *GO!* System is divided into three categories that reflect how you might organize your course— **Prepare**, **Teach**, and **Assess**.

Prepare

NEW

Transition Guide

New to *GO!*–We've made it quick and easy to plan the format and activities for your class.

Syllabus Template

Includes course calendar planner for 8-,12-, and 16-week formats.

GO!

Because the GO! System was designed and written by instructors like yourself, it includes the tools that allow you to Prepare, Teach, and Assess in your course. We have organized the GO! System into these three categories that match how you work through your course and thus, it's even easier for you to implement.

To help you get started, here is an outline of the first activities you may want to do in order to conduct your course.

There are several other tools not listed here that are available in the GO! System so please refer to your GO! Guide for a complete listing of all the tools.

Prepare
1. Prepare the course syllabus
2. Plan the course assignments
3. Organize the student resources

Teach
4. Conduct demonstrations and lectures

Assess
5. Assign and grade assignments, quizzes, tests, and assessments

PREPARE

1. Prepare the course syllabus

A syllabus template is provided on the IRCD in the **go07_syllabus_template** folder of the main directory. It includes a course calendar planner for 8-week, 12-week, and 16-week formats. Depending on your term (summer or regular semester) you can modify one of these according to your course plan, and then add information pertinent to your course and institution.

2. Plan course assignments

For each chapter, an Assignment Sheet listing every in-chapter and end-of-chapter project is located on the IRCD within the **go01_gooffice2007intro_instructor_resources_by_chapter** folder. From there, navigate to the specific chapter folder. These sheets are Word tables, so you can delete rows for the projects that you choose not to assign or add rows for your own assignments—if any. There is a column to add the number of points you want to assign to each project depending on your grading scheme. At the top of the sheet, you can fill in the course information.

Transitioning to GO! Office 2007   Page 1 of 1

GO! with Microsoft Office 2007 Introductory
SAMPLE SYLLABUS (16 weeks)

I. COURSE INFORMATION

Course No.:   Semester:
Course Title: Credits:
Course Hours:

Instructor: Office:
Office Hours:
Email: Phone:

II. TEXT AND MATERIALS
Before starting the course, you will need the following:

 ➢ GO! with Microsoft Office 2007 Introductory by Shelley Gaskin, Robert L. Ferrett, Alicia Vargas, Suzanne Marks ©2007, published by Pearson Prentice Hall. ISBN 0-13-167990-6
 ➢ Storage device for saving files (any of the following: multiple diskettes, CD-RW, flash drive, etc.)

III. WHAT YOU WILL LEARN IN THIS COURSE
This is a hands-on course where you will learn to use a computer to practice the most commonly used Microsoft programs including the Windows operating system, Internet Explorer for navigating the Internet, Outlook for managing your personal information and the four most popular programs within the Microsoft Office Suite (Word, Excel, PowerPoint and Access). You will also practice the basics of using a computer, mouse and keyboard. You will learn to be an intermediate level user of the Microsoft Office Suite.

Within the Microsoft Office Suite, you will use Word, Excel, PowerPoint, and Access. Microsoft Word is a word processing program with which you can create common business and personal documents. Microsoft Excel is a spreadsheet program that organizes and calculates accounting-type information. Microsoft PowerPoint is a presentation graphics program with which you can develop slides to accompany an oral presentation. Finally, Microsoft Access is a database program that organizes large amounts of information in a useful manner.

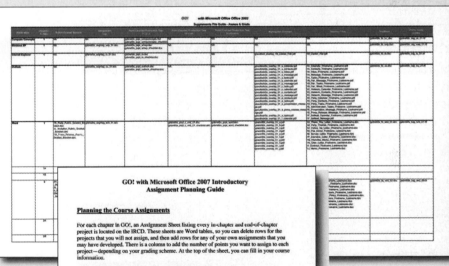

Assignment Sheet

One per chapter. Lists all possible assignments; add to and delete from this simple Word table according to your course plan.

File Guide to the *GO!* Supplements

Tabular listing of all supplements and their file names.

NEW

Assignment Planning Guide

Description of *GO!* assignments with recommendations based on class size, delivery mode, and student needs. Includes examples from fellow instructors.

Student Data Files

Music School Records discovers, launches, and and develops the careers of young artists in classical, jazz, and contemporary music. Our philosophy is to not only shape, distribute, and sell a music product, but to help artists create a career that can lats a lifetime. too often in the music industry, artists are forced to fit their music to a trend that is short-lived. Music School Records doesn't just follow trends, we take a long-term view of the music industry and help our artists develop a style and repertiore that is fluid and flexible and that will appeal to audiences for years and even decades.

The music industry is constantly changing, but over the last decade the changes have been enormous. New forms of entertainment such as DVDs, video games, and the Internet mean there are more competition for the leisure dollar in the market. New technologies give consomers more options for buying and listening to music, and they are demaning high quality recordings. Young consomers are comfortable with technology and want the music they love when and where they want it, no matter where they are or what they are doing.

Music School Records embraces new technologies and the sophisticated market of young music lovers. We believe that providing high quality recordings of truly talented artists make for more discerning listeners who will cherish the gift of music for the rest of their lives. The expertise of Music School Records includes:

- Insight into our target market and the ability to reach the desired audience
- The ability to access all current sources of music income
- A management team with years of experience in music commerce
- Innovative business strategies and artist development plans
- Investment in technology infrastructure for high quality recordings and business services
- Initiative and proactive management of artist careers

Online Study Guide for Students
Interactive objective-style questions based on chapter content.

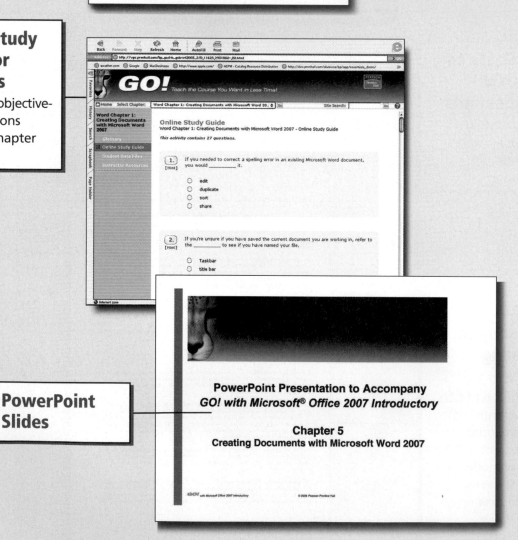

PowerPoint Slides

PowerPoint Presentation to Accompany
GO! with Microsoft® Office 2007 Introductory

Chapter 5
Creating Documents with Microsoft Word 2007

Teach

Student Textbook

Learning Objectives and Student Outcomes

Objectives are clustered around projects that result in student outcomes. They help students learn how to solve problems, not just learn software features.

Word 2007

chapter five

Creating Documents with Microsoft Word 2007

OBJECTIVES
At the end of this chapter you will be able to:

OUTCOMES
Mastering these objectives will enable you to:

1. Create and Save a New Document
2. Edit Text
3. Select, Delete, and Format Text
4. Print a Document

PROJECT 5A
Create, Edit, Save, and Print a Document

5. Navigate the Word Window
6. Add a Graphic to a Document
7. Use the Spelling and Grammar Checker
8. Preview and Print Documents, Close a Document, and Close Word
9. Use the Microsoft Help System

PROJECT 5B
Navigate the Word Window and Check Your Work

Word 237

Project-Based Instruction

Students do not practice features of the application; they create real projects that they will need in the real world. Projects are color coded for easy reference and are named to reflect skills the students will be practicing.

NEW

A and B Projects

Each chapter contains two instructional projects—A and B.

Music School Records

Music School Records was created to launch young musical artists with undiscovered talent in jazz, classical, and contemporary music. The creative management team searches internationally for talented young people, and has a reputation for mentoring and developing the skills of its artists. The company's music is tailored to an audience that is young, knowledgeable about music, and demands the highest quality recordings. Music School Records releases are available in CD format as well as digital downloads.

Getting Started with Microsoft Office Word 2007

A word processor is the most common program found on personal computers and one that almost everyone has a reason to use. When you learn word processing you are also learning skills and techniques that you need to work efficiently on a personal computer. You can use Microsoft Word to perform basic word processing tasks such as writing a memo, a report, or a letter. You can also use Word to complete complex word processing tasks, such as those that include sophisticated tables, embedded graphics, and links to other documents and the Internet. Word is a program that you can learn gradually, and then add more advanced skills one at a time.

Each chapter opens with a story that sets the stage for the projects the student will create; the instruction does not force the student to pretend to be someone or make up a scenario.

Each chapter has an introductory paragraph that briefs students on what is important.

Visual Summary

Shows students upfront what their projects will look like when they are done.

Objective

The skills the student will learn are clearly stated at the beginning of each project and color coded to match projects listed on the chapter opener page.

Project Summary

Stated clearly and quickly in one paragraph.

NEW

File Guide

Clearly shows students which files are needed for the project and the names they will use to save their documents.

KEY FEATURE

GO!

Teachable Moment

Expository text is woven into the steps—at the moment students need to know it—not chunked together in a block of text that will go unread.

NEW

Screen Shots

Larger screen shots.

Project 5A Application Letter

In Activities 5.1 through 5.11, you will create and make changes to a letter from John Diamond, Vice President of Creative Development, to William Hawken, an artist interested in becoming a client of Music School Records. Your completed document will look similar to Figure 5.1

For Project 5A, you will need the following file:

New blank Word document

You will save your document as
5A_Application_Letter_Firstname_Lastname

Music School Records

Figure 5.1
Project 5A—Application Letter

Objective 1
Create and Save a New Document

With a word processing program, you can type, *edit*—make changes to—move, and delete text or change the appearance of text. Because the documents that you create are stored electronically, they can be duplicated, printed, copied, and shared with others. In this project, you will become

Project 5A: Application Letter | **Word** 239

---

familiar with the parts of the Word window. Then you will create a document, edit and format text, and save your work.

Activity 5.1 Starting Word and Identifying Parts of the Word Window

Note — Comparing Your Screen With the Figures in This Textbook

Your screen will match the figures shown in this textbook if you set your screen resolution to 1024 × 768. At other resolutions, your screen will closely resemble, but not match, the figures shown. To view your screen's resolution, on the Windows desktop, right-click in a blank area, click Properties, and then click the Settings tab.

1. On the left side of the Windows taskbar, point to, and then click the **Start** button.

2. From the displayed **Start** menu, locate the **Word** program, and then click **Microsoft Office Word 2007**.

   The Word program may be located under All Programs or Microsoft Office or on the main Start menu.

   Print Layout view is the ideal view to use when you are learning Microsoft Word 2007 because you can see the document exactly the way it will look when it is printed.

3. If necessary, on the right side of the status bar, click the **Print Layout** button. If the ruler does not display, click the View tab, and then in the Show/Hide group, click the Ruler check box. Take a moment to study the parts of the Word screen shown in Figure 5.2 and described in the table in Figure 5.3.

Figure 5.2

240 **Word** | Chapter 5: Creating Documents with Microsoft Word 2007

Steps

Color coded to the current project, easy to read, and not too many to confuse the student or too few to be meaningless.

Sequential Pagination

No more confusing letters and abbreviations.

Microsoft Procedural Syntax

All steps are written in Microsoft Procedural Syntax to put the student in the right place at the right time.

End-of-Project Icon

All projects in the *GO! Series* have clearly identifiable end points, useful in self-paced or online environments.

(Textbook page 244)

Press Enter two more times.

In a business letter, insert two blank lines between the date and the inside address, which is the same as the address you would use on an envelope.

Type **Mr. William Hawken** and then press Enter.

The wavy red line under the proper name *Hawken* indicates that the word has been flagged as misspelled because it is a word not contained in the Word dictionary.

On two lines, type the following address, but do not press Enter at the end of the second line:

123 Eighth Street
Harrisville, MI 48740

Note — Typing the Address

Include a comma after the city name in an inside address. However, for mailing addresses on envelopes, eliminate the comma after the city name.

On the **Home tab**, in the **Styles group**, click the **Normal** button.

The Normal style is applied to the text in the rest of the document. Recall that the Normal style adds extra space between paragraphs; it also adds slightly more space between lines in a paragraph.

Press Enter. Type **Dear William** and then press Enter.

This salutation is the line that greets the person receiving the letter.

Type **Subject: Your Application to Music School Records** and press Enter. Notice the light dots between words, which indicate spaces and display when formatting marks are displayed. Also, notice the extra space after each paragraph, and then compare your screen with Figure 5.6.

The subject line is optional, but you should include a subject line in most letters to identify the topic. Depending on your Word settings, a wavy green line may display in the subject line, indicating a potential grammar error.

(Textbook page 264)

Note — Space Between Lines in Your Printed Document

The Cambria font, and many others, uses a slightly larger space between the lines than more traditional fonts like Times New Roman. As you progress in your study of Word, you will use many different fonts and also adjust the spacing between lines.

From the **Office** menu, click **Close**, saving any changes if prompted to do so. Leave Word open for the next project.

Another Way

To Print a Document

To print a document:

• From the Office menu, click Print to display the Print dialog box (to be covered later), from which you can choose a variety of different options, such as printing multiple copies, printing on a different printer, and printing some but not all pages.

• Hold down Ctrl and then press P. This is an alternative to the Office menu command, and opens the Print dialog box.

• Hold down Alt, press F, and then press P. This opens the Print dialog box.

End You have completed Project 5A

Teach (continued)

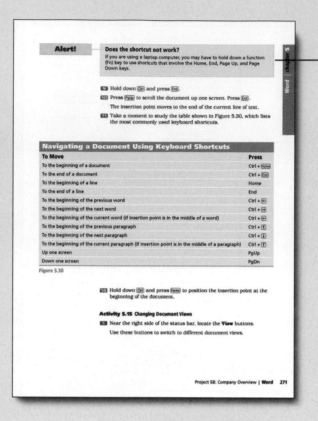

Alert box
Draws students' attention to make sure they aren't getting too far off course.

Another Way box
Shows students other ways of doing tasks.

More Knowledge box
Expands on a topic by going deeper into the material.

Note box
Points out important items to remember.

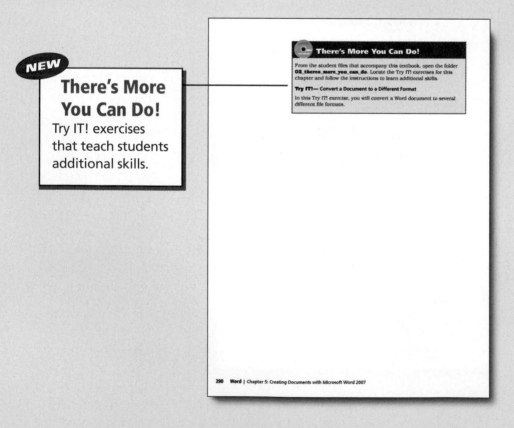

NEW

There's More You Can Do!
Try IT! exercises that teach students additional skills.

Teach (continued)

End-of-Chapter Material

Take your pick! Content-based or Outcomes-based projects to choose from. Below is a table outlining the various types of projects that fit into these two categories.

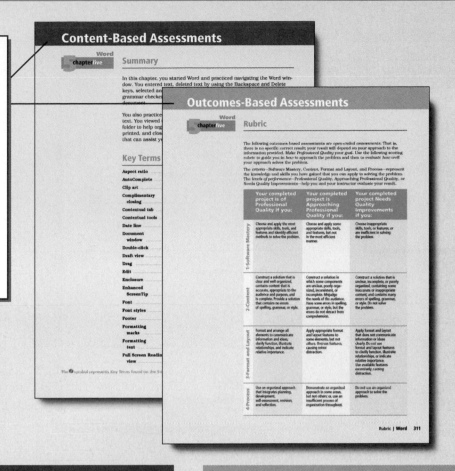

Content-Based Assessments
(Defined solutions with solution files provided for grading)

Project Letter	Name	Objectives Covered
N/A	Summary and Key Terms	
N/A	Multiple Choice	
N/A	Fill-in-the-blank	
C	Skills Review	Covers A Objectives
D	Skills Review	Covers B Objectives
E	Mastering Excel	Covers A Objectives
F	Mastering Excel	Covers B Objectives
G	Mastering Excel	Covers any combination of A and B Objectives
H	Mastering Excel	Covers any combination of A and B Objectives
I	Mastering Excel	Covers all A and B Objectives
J	Business Running Case	Covers all A and B Objectives

Outcomes-Based Assessments
(Open solutions that require a rubric for grading)

Project Letter	Name	Objectives Covered
N/A	Rubric	
K	Problem Solving	Covers as many Objectives from A and B as possible
L	Problem Solving	Covers as many Objectives from A and B as possible.
M	Problem Solving	Covers as many Objectives from A and B as possible.
N	Problem Solving	Covers as many Objectives from A and B as possible.
O	Problem Solving	Covers as many Objectives from A and B as possible.
P	You and GO!	Covers as many Objectives from A and B as possible
Q	GO! Help	Not tied to specific objectives
R	* Group Business Running Case	Covers A and B Objectives

* This project is provided only with the *GO! with Microsoft Office 2007 Introductory* book.

Teach (continued)

Objectives List

Most projects in the end-of-chapter section begin with a list of the objectives covered.

End of Each Project Clearly Marked

Clearly identified end points help separate the end-of-chapter projects.

Content-Based Assessments

 Word **Skills Review**

Project 5C — Receipt Letter

In this project, you will apply the skills you practiced from the Objectives in Project 5A.

Objectives: 1. *Create and Save a New Document;* **2.** *Edit Text;* **3.** *Select, Delete, and Format Text;* **4.** *Print a Document.*

In the following Skills Review, you will create and edit a follow-up letter from Jamal Anderssen, a production manager for Music School Records, to William Hawken, a recording artist who has submitted a demo CD with his application. Your completed letter will look similar to the one shown in Figure 5.49.

For Project 5C, you will need the following file:

New blank Word document

You will save your document as
5C_Receipt_Letter_Firstname_Lastname

Figure 5.49

Music School Records

September 20, 2009

Mr. William Hawken

Dear Mr. Hawken:

Subject: Receipt of Your CD

(Project 5C–Receipt Letter continues on the next page)

294 **Word** | Chapter 5: Creating Documents with Microsoft Word 2007

Content-Based Assessments

Word **Skills Review**

(Project 5C–Receipt Letter continued)

14. Save the changes you have made to your document. Press Ctrl + A to select the entire document. On the **Home tab**, in the **Font group**, click the **Font button arrow**. Scroll as necessary, and watch Live Preview change the document font as you point to different font names. Click to choose **Tahoma**. Recall that you can type T in the Font box to move quickly to the fonts beginning with that letter. Click anywhere in the document to cancel the selection.

15. Select the entire first line of text—*Music School Records*. On the Mini toolbar, click the **Font button arrow**, and then click **Arial Black**. With the Mini toolbar still displayed, click the **Font Size button arrow**, and then click **20**. With the Mini toolbar still displayed, click the **Bold** button.

16. Select the second, third, and fourth lines of text, beginning with *2620 Vine Street* and ending with the telephone number. On the Mini toolbar, click the **Font button arrow**, and then click **Arial**. With the Mini toolbar still displayed, click the **Font Size button arrow**, and then click **10**. With the Mini toolbar still displayed, click the **Italic** button.

17. In the paragraph beginning *Your demonstration*, select the text *Music School Records*. On the Mini toolbar, click the **Italic** button, and then click anywhere to deselect the text.

18. Click the **Insert tab**. In the **Header & Footer group**, click the **Footer** button,

and then click **Edit Footer**. On the **Design tab**, in the **Insert group**, click the **Quick Parts** button, and then click **Field**. In the **Field** dialog box, under **Field names**, scroll down and click to choose **FileName**, and then click **OK**. Double-click anywhere in the document to leave the footer area.

19. Click the **Page Layout tab**. In the **Page Setup group**, click the **Margins** button to display the Margins gallery. At the bottom of the **Margins gallery**, click **Custom Margins** to display the **Page Setup** dialog box. Near the top of the **Page Setup** dialog box, click the **Layout tab**. Under **Page**, click the **Vertical alignment arrow**, click **Center**, and then click **OK**.

20. From the **Office** menu, point to the **Print arrow**, and then click **Print Preview** to make a final check of your letter. Follow your instructor's directions for submitting this file. Check your *Chapter Assignment Sheet* or *Course Syllabus* or consult your instructor to determine if you are to submit your assignments on paper or electronically. To submit electronically, go to Step 22, and then follow the instructions provided by your instructor.

21. On the **Print Preview tab**, in the **Print group**, click the **Print** button. Collect your printout from the printer and submit it as directed.

22. From the **Office** menu, click **Exit Word**, saving any changes if prompted to do so.

End You have completed Project 5C

296 **Word** | Chapter 5: Creating Documents with Microsoft Word 2007

NEW

Rubric

A matrix that states the criteria and standards for grading student work. Used to grade open-ended assessments.

GO! with Help

Students practice using the Help feature of the Office application.

NEW

You and *GO!*

A project in which students use information from their own lives and apply the skills from the chapter to a personal task.

Teach (continued)

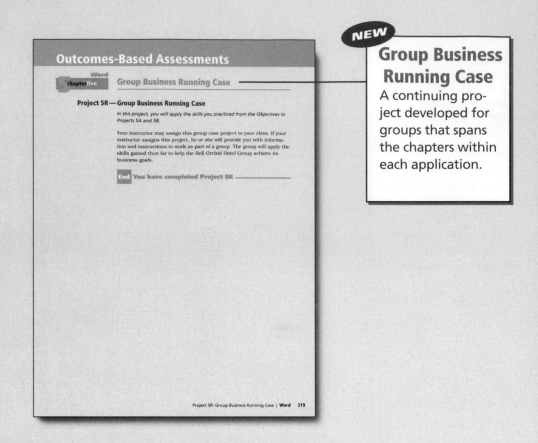

NEW

Group Business Running Case
A continuing project developed for groups that spans the chapters within each application.

Student CD includes:
- Student Data Files
- There's More You Can Do!
- Business Running Case
- You and *GO!*

xxvi   Visual Walk-Through

Companion Web site

An interactive Web site to further student leaning.

Online Study Guide

Interactive objective-style questions to help students study.

Annotated Instructor Edition

The Annotated Instructor Edition contains a full version of the student textbook that includes tips, supplement references, and pointers on teaching with the *GO!* instructional system.

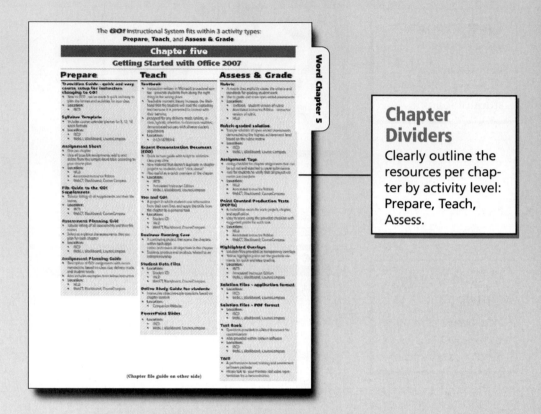

Chapter Dividers

Clearly outline the resources per chapter by activity level: Prepare, Teach, Assess.

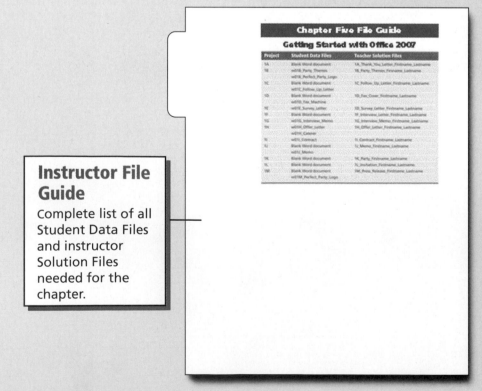

Instructor File Guide

Complete list of all Student Data Files and instructor Solution Files needed for the chapter.

Helpful Hints, Teaching Tips, Expand the Project

References correspond to what is being taught in the student textbook.

NEW

Full-Size Textbook Pages

An instructor copy of the textbook with traditional Instructor Manual content incorporated.

End-of-Chapter Concepts Assessments

contain the answers for quick reference.

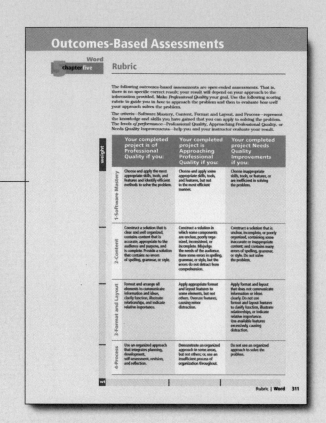

NEW

Rubric

A matrix to guide the student on how they will be assessed is reprinted in the Annotated Instructor Edition with suggested weights for each of the criteria and levels of performance. Instructors can modify the weights to suit their needs.

Assignment Tags

NEW

Scoring checklist for assignments. Now also available for Problem-Solving projects.

GO! with Microsoft® Office 2007

Assignment Tags for GO! with Office 2007
Word Chapter 5

Name:		Project:	5A	Name:		Project:	5B
Professor:		Course:		Professor:		Course:	
Task	Points	Your Score		Task	Points	Your Score	
Center text vertically on page	2			Insert the file w05B_Music_School_Records	4		
Delete the word "really"	1			Insert the Music Logo	4		
Delete the words "try to"	1			Remove duplicate "and"	2		
Replace "last" with "first"	1			Change spelling and grammar errors (4)	8		
Insert the word "potential"	1			Correct/Add footer as instructed	2		
Replace "John W. Diamond" with "Lucy Burrows"	2			Circled information is incorrect or formatted incorrectly			
Change entire document to the Cambria font	2						
Change the first line of text to Arial Black 20 pt. font	2						
Bold the first line of text	2						
Change the 2nd through 4th lines to Arial 10 pt.	2						
Italicize the 2nd through 4th lines of text	2						
Correct/Add footer as instructed	2						
Circled information is incorrect or formatted incorrectly							
Total Points	**20**	**0**		**Total Points**	**20**	**0**	
Name:		Project:	5C	Name:		Project:	5D
Professor:		Course:		Professor:		Course:	
Task	Points	Your Score		Task	Points	Your Score	
Add four line letterhead	2			Insert the file w05D_Marketing	4		
Insert today's date	1			Bold the first two title lines	2		
Add address block, subject line, and greeting	2			Correct spelling of "Marketting"	2		
Add two-paragraph body of letter	2			Correct spelling of "geners"	2		
Add closing, name, and title	2			Correct all misspellings of "allready"	2		
In subject line, capitalize "receipt"	1			Correct grammar error "are" to "is"	2		
Change "standards" to "guidelines"	1			Insert the Piano image	4		
Insert "quite"	1			Correct/add footer as instructed	2		
Insert "all"	1			Circled information is incorrect or formatted incorrectly			
Change the first line of text to Arial Black 20 pt. font	2						
Bold the first line of text	1						
Change the 2nd through 4th lines to Arial 10 pt.	2						
Italicize the 2nd through 4th lines of text	1						
Correct/add footer as instructed	2						
Circled information is incorrect or formatted incorrectly							
Total Points	**20**	**0**		**Total Points**	**20**	**0**	

Highlighted Overlays

Solution files provided as transparency overlays. Yellow highlights point out the gradable elements for quick and easy grading.

Music School Records

[20 point Arial Black, bold and underline]

2620 Vine Street
Los Angeles, CA 90028
323-555-0028

[10 point Arial, italic]

September 12, 2009

Mr. William Hawken
123 Eighth Street
Harrisville, MI 48740

[Text vertically centered on page]

[Body of document changed to Cambria font, 11 point]

Dear William:

Subject: Your Application to Music School Records

Thank you for submitting your application to Music School Records. Our talent scout for Northern Michigan, Catherine McDonald, is very enthusiastic about your music, and the demo CD you submitted certainly confirms her opinion.

[Word "really" deleted]

We discuss our applications from potential clients during the first week of each month. We will have a decision for you by the second week of October.

Yours Truly,

[Words "try to" deleted]

Lucy Burroughs

Point-Counted Production Tests (PCPTs)

A cumulative exam for each **project**, **chapter**, and **application**. Easy to score using the provided checklist with suggested points for each task.

GO! with Microsoft® Office 2007 Introductory

**Point-Counted Production Test—Project
for GO! with Microsoft® Office 2007 Introductory
Project 5A**

Instructor Name: _____
Course Information: _____

1. Start Word 2007 to begin a new blank document. Save your document as 5A_Cover_Letter_Firstname_Lastname Remember to save your file frequently as you work.

2. If necessary, display the formatting marks. With the insertion point blinking in the upper left corner of the document to the left of the default first paragraph mark, type the current date (you can use AutoComplete).

3. Press Enter three times and type the inside address:

   Music School Records
   2620 Vine Street
   Los Angeles, CA 90028

4. Press Enter three times, and type Dear Ms. Burroughs:

   Press Enter twice, and type Subject: Application to Music School Records

   Press Enter twice, and type the following text (skipping one line between paragraphs):

   I read about Music School Records in Con Brio magazine and I would like to inquire about the possibility of being represented by your company.

   I am very interested in a career in jazz and am planning to relocate to the Los Angeles area in the very near future. I would be interested in learning more about the company and about available opportunities.

   I was a member of my high school jazz band for three years. In addition, I have been playing in the local coffee shop for the last two years. My demo CD, which is enclosed, contains three of my most requested songs.

   I would appreciate the opportunity to speak with you. Thank you for your time and consideration. I look forward to speaking with you about this exciting opportunity.

5. Press Enter three times, and type the closing Sincerely, Press enter four times, and type your name.

6. Insert a footer that contains the file name.

7. Delete the first instance of the word *very* in the second body paragraph, and insert the word modern in front of *jazz*.

Copyright © 2008 Pearson Prentice Hall   Page 1 of 1

Test Bank

Available as TestGen Software or as a Word document for customization.

Chapter 5: Creating Documents with Microsoft Word 2007

Multiple Choice:

1. With word processing programs, how are documents stored?

   A. On a network

   B. On the computer

   C. Electronically

   D. On the floppy disk

   Answer: C   **Reference:** Objective 1: Create and Save a New Document   **Difficulty:** Moderate

2. Because you will see the document as it will print. _____ view is the ideal view to use when learning Microsoft Word 2007.

   A. Reading

   B. Normal

   C. Print Layout

   D. Outline

   Answer: C   **Reference:** Objective 1: Create and Save a New Document   **Difficulty:** Moderate

3. The blinking vertical line where text or graphics will be inserted is called the:

   A. cursor.

   B. insertion point.

   C. blinking line.

   D. I-beam.

   Answer: B   **Reference:** Objective 1: Create and Save a New Document   **Difficulty:** Easy

**Solution Files–
Application
and PDF
format**

Music School Records

Music School Records discovers, launches, and develops the careers of young artists in classical, jazz, and contemporary music. Our philosophy is to not only shape, distribute, and sell a music product, but to help artists create a career that can last a lifetime. Too often in the music industry, artists are forced to fit their music to a trend that is short-lived. Music School Records does not just follow trends, we take a long-term view of the music industry and help our artists develop a style and repertoire that is fluid and flexible and that will appeal to audiences for years and even decades.

The music industry is constantly changing, but over the last decade, the changes have been enormous. New forms of entertainment such as DVDs, video games, and the Internet mean there is more competition for the leisure dollar in the market. New technologies give consumers more options for buying and listening to music, and they are demanding high quality recordings. Young consumers are comfortable with technology and want the music they love when and where they want it, no matter where they are or what they are doing.

Music School Records embraces new technologies and the sophisticated market of young music lovers. We believe that providing high quality recordings of truly talented artists make for more discerning listeners who will cherish the gift of music for the rest of their lives. The expertise of Music School Records includes:

- Insight into our target market and the ability to reach the desired audience
- The ability to access all current sources of music income
- A management team with years of experience in music commerce
- Innovative business strategies and artist development plans
- Investment in technology infrastructure for high quality recordings and business services

pagexxxix_top.docx

Online Assessment and Training

my**it**lab is Prentice Hall's new performance-based solution that allows you to easily deliver outcomes-based courses on Microsoft Office 2007, with customized training and defensible assessment. Key features of my**it**lab include:

A *true* "system" approach: my**it**lab content is the same as in your textbook.
Project-based *and* skills-based: Students complete real-life assignments.
Advanced reporting *and* gradebook: These include student click stream data.
***No* installation required:** my**it**lab is completely Web-based. You just need an Internet connection, small plug-in, and Adobe Flash Player.

Ask your Prentice Hall sales representative for a demonstration or visit:

www.prenhall.com/myitlab

chapterone

Getting Started with Windows Vista

OBJECTIVES

At the end of this chapter you will be able to:

1. Get Started with Windows Vista
2. Use the Start Menu and Manage Windows
3. Resize, Move, and Scroll Windows

4. Create, Move, and Rename Folders
5. Copy, Move, Rename, and Delete Files
6. Find Files and Folders
7. Use Vista Help

OUTCOMES

Mastering these objectives will enable you to:

Project 1A
Familiarize Yourself with the Vista Interface

Project 1B
Work with Files and Folders

Windows Vista is the software that coordinates the activities of your computer's hardware. Windows Vista controls how your screen is displayed; how you open and close programs; and the startup, shutdown, and navigation procedures for your computer. It is useful to become familiar with the basic features of the Windows Vista operating system, especially working with the Start button and taskbar; opening, closing, moving, and resizing windows; and saving and managing files.

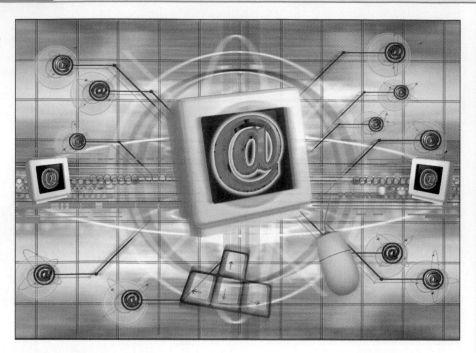

© Getty Images, Inc.

Getting Started with Windows Vista

Project 1A Familiarize Yourself with the Vista Interface

In Activities1.1 through 1.9, you will explore the Windows Vista screen and practice navigating Windows Vista. You will open, close, resize, and move windows, and you will open several windows at one time. The screens that you will be working with will look similar to Figure 1.1.

For Project 1A, you will need the following files:

No files needed for this project

Figure 1.1
Project 1A—Familiarize Yourself with the Vista Interface

Objective 1
Get Started with Windows Vista

Windows Vista is an *operating system*—software that controls the *hardware* attached to your computer, including its memory, disk drive space, attached devices such as printers and scanners, and the central processing unit. Windows Vista and earlier versions of Windows are similar; they use a *graphical user interface (GUI)*. A GUI uses graphics or pictures to represent commands and actions and enables you to see document formatting on the screen as it will look when printed on paper. *Windows*, when spelled with a capital *W*, refers to the operating system that runs your computer.

Starting Windows is an automatic procedure; you turn on your computer, and after a few moments the version of Windows installed on your computer displays. Some versions require that you log in, and some do not. If you are using a different version of Windows, some procedures used in this chapter may work differently. Windows Vista is available in several editions: Home Basic, Home Premium, Business, and Ultimate. For large institutions, there is also an Enterprise edition. For most tasks, the Home Premium, Business, and Ultimate editions work the same. The Business edition, however, does not support many multimedia features.

Alert!

Does your screen differ?

This chapter uses Windows Vista Home Premium Edition, and there are some differences between the look of this edition and the other editions. More importantly, the look of the screen will depend largely on the setting options that have been selected for your computer, and on the type of hardware installed in your computer—especially the video card and memory.

Activity 1.1 Exploring the Windows Vista Screen

In this activity, you will examine the different components of the Windows Vista screen.

1 Turn on your computer and wait for the **Windows** program to display, or follow the log-on instructions required for the computer you are using. For example, you might have to click a name on a Welcome screen, or enter a user ID or password. If this is your home computer and you are the only user, it is likely that you need do nothing except wait for a few moments. If you see the Welcome Center screen, examine its contents, and when you are done, click the red button with the X [X] in the upper right corner of the window.

The Windows *desktop*, which is the working area of the Windows Vista screen, displays. The working area is called a desktop because on it you can place electronic versions of things you have on your regular desk. The screen look will vary, depending on which version of Windows you are using and what you have on your own desktop.

Note — The Welcome Center

The **Welcome Center** window displays links to a number of topics, including upgrading Windows, connecting to the Internet, adding new users, and taking advantage of special offers from Microsoft. By default, the Welcome Center window displays every time you start your computer. If you clear the check box at the bottom of the window, you will skip this window at startup. If your Welcome Center does not display, and you would like to take advantage of any of its features, click the Start button, and then click Welcome Center.

2 Compare your Windows desktop with Figure 1.2 and then take a moment to study the Windows elements identified in the table in Figure 1.3.

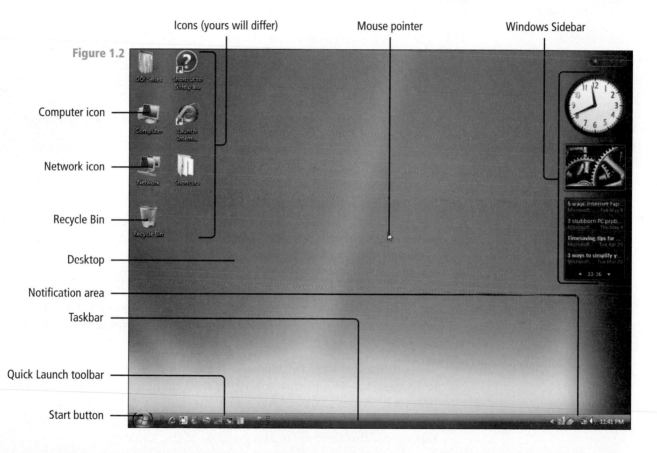

Figure 1.2

Labels: Icons (yours will differ), Mouse pointer, Windows Sidebar, Computer icon, Network icon, Recycle Bin, Desktop, Notification area, Taskbar, Quick Launch toolbar, Start button

Windows Screen Elements

Screen Element	Description
Computer icon	An icon that represents the computer on which you are working, and that provides access to the drives, folders, and files on your computer.
Desktop	The working area of the Windows Vista screen, consisting of program icons, a taskbar, a Sidebar, and a Start button.
Icon	A graphic representation of an object that you can select and open, such as a drive, a disk, a folder, a document, or a program.

(Continued)

(Continued)

Mouse pointer	The arrow, I-beam, or other symbol that moves when you move the mouse or other pointing device, and that indicates a location or position on your screen—also called the *pointer*.
Network icon	An icon that represents the network to which your computer is attached, and that provides access to the drives, folders, and files on your network.
Notification area	The area on the right side of the taskbar, formerly called the *system tray* or *status area*, where the clock and system notifications display. These notifications keep you informed about the processes that are occurring in the background, such as antivirus software checking, network connections, and other utility programs. Some notifications display only temporarily.
Quick Launch toolbar	An area to the right of the Start button that contains shortcut icons for commonly used programs.
Recycle Bin	A temporary storage area for files that you have deleted. Files can be either recovered or permanently removed from the Recycle Bin.
Start button	The button on the left side of the taskbar that is used to start programs, change system settings, find Windows help, or shut down the computer.
Taskbar	Displays the Start button and the name of any open documents. The taskbar may also display shortcut buttons for other programs.
Windows Sidebar	An area on the right side of the screen that displays useful gadgets, such as a clock, a stock market ticker, or a weather map.

Figure 1.3

3 Move the mouse across a flat surface to move the pointer on your screen. On the desktop, position the tip of the pointer in the center of the **Computer** icon—an action referred to as *pointing*. *Double-click*—press the left mouse button two times in rapid succession—using caution not to move the mouse. If the Computer icon is not visible, click Start, and then from the right side of the displayed Start menu, click Computer. Compare your screen with Figure 1.4, and then take a moment to study the **Computer** window elements in the table Figure 1.5.

The Computer window displays. A *window*—spelled with a lowercase *w*—is a rectangular box that displays information or a program. When a window is open, the name of the window is displayed—either in the status bar or in the title bar—and on a button on the taskbar at the bottom of the desktop.

Alert!

Does your screen differ?

Because the configuration of your Computer window depends on how it was last used, your window may not display all of the elements shown in Figure 1.4, in particular the menu bar, Details pane, Folders list, and Search box. Also, your Computer window may cover the entire screen.

Figure 1.4

Toolbar · Personal folders · Address bar · Menu bar · Details pane · Content pane · Search box · Close button

Command bar

Navigation pane

Folders list

Status bar

Window name in taskbar

Parts of a Window

Screen Element	Description
Address bar	A toolbar that displays the organizational path to the active file, folder, or window.
Close button	A shortcut button in a title bar that closes a window or a program.
Command bar	Area at the top of a window that includes the toolbar, menu bar, address bar, and search pane.
Content pane	Displays files and folders stored in the disk drive or folder that is currently selected in the Navigation pane.
Details pane	Displays details about the drive, folder, or file that is currently selected in the Content pane.
Folders list	Part of the Navigation pane that displays the drive and folder structure on the computer.
Menu bar	The bar near the top of a window that lists the names of menu categories.
Navigation pane	The pane on the left side of the Computer or Windows Explorer window that contains Personal folders and the Folders list.
Personal folders	The top part of the Navigation pane that displays folders associated with the current user.
ScreenTip	A small box, activated by pointing to a button or other screen object, that displays the name of or further information about the screen element.
Search box	A box in which you type a search word or phrase.

(Continued)

Status bar	A horizontal bar at the bottom of the document window that provides information about the current state of what you are viewing in the window, for example, the page number of a document. In some cases, the status bar also displays the name of the window.
Toolbar	A row of buttons that activate commands with a single click of the left mouse button.
Window name	The name of the window or program, displayed in the window status bar or title bar.

Figure 1.5

4 In the upper right corner of the **Computer** window title bar, point to, but do not click, the **Close** button ⊠, and then notice that the ScreenTip *Close* displays.

A **ScreenTip** is a small note, usually in a yellow box, that provides information about or describes a screen element.

5 **Click**—press the left mouse button one time—the **Close** button ⊠ to close the **Computer** window. Then, point to the **Computer** icon on the desktop and click the right mouse button—this action is known as a **right-click**. If the Computer icon does not display on your desktop, click the Start button 🔵, and then right-click Computer. Compare your screen with Figure 1.6.

A shortcut menu displays. A **menu** is a list of commands within a category. **Shortcut menus** list **context-sensitive commands**—commands commonly used when working with the selected object. On this shortcut menu, the Open command is displayed in bold because it is the default action that occurs when you double-click this icon.

Shortcut menu

Figure 1.6

Command in bold is the default action

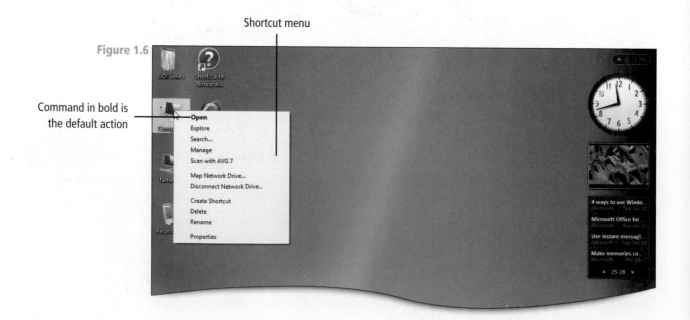

6 From the displayed shortcut menu, point to **Open** to highlight—select—the command, and then click one time. In the displayed **Computer** window, near the top of the **Content** pane, point to and then click the disk drive labeled **Local Disk (C:)**, and then notice the **Details** pane. Compare your screen with Figure 1.7.

The specifications of the *Local Disk*—the large disk drive inside your computer system, also referred to as the *hard drive*—are displayed in the Details pane. A *drive* is an area of storage that is formatted with the Windows file system, and that has a drive letter such as C, D, E, and so on.

Window
title

Close
button

Figure 1.7

Drive C: selected

Click to expand or hide
the Folders list

Details of the local disk

Alert!   **Is your Details pane missing?**

Recall that the configuration of your Computer window may vary, depending on how it was last configured. If your Details pane does not display, in the toolbar, click Organize, point to Layout, and then click Details Pane.

7 In the **Computer** window title bar, click the **Close** button .

More Knowledge

The Windows Aero User Interface

The screen you see in the figures in this book use the *Windows Aero* user interface. Windows Aero—which is an acronym for *A*uthentic, *E*nergetic, *R*eflective, *O*pen—features a three dimensional look, with transparent window frames, live previews of open windows, and multiple color schemes. This user interface is available with all but the most basic versions of Vista, but requires fairly substantial amounts of memory and powerful video cards. If your screen does not have the same look, your computer may not be capable of displaying the Aero interface.

Activity 1.2 Personalizing the Desktop

The Windows Vista desktop can be personalized to suit your needs and tastes. You can, for example, change the resolution of the monitor to make it easier to read, or to display more information. In this activity, you will change the screen saver and practice changing the desktop background.

1 Move the pointer to an open area of the desktop, and then right-click.

A shortcut menu displays commands that are available for your desktop.

2 From the displayed shortcut menu, move the pointer to the bottom of the list, and then click **Personalize**. Notice that the Personalization window displays, as shown in Figure 1.8.

Figure 1.8

Desktop Background options

Screen Saver options

Personalization window

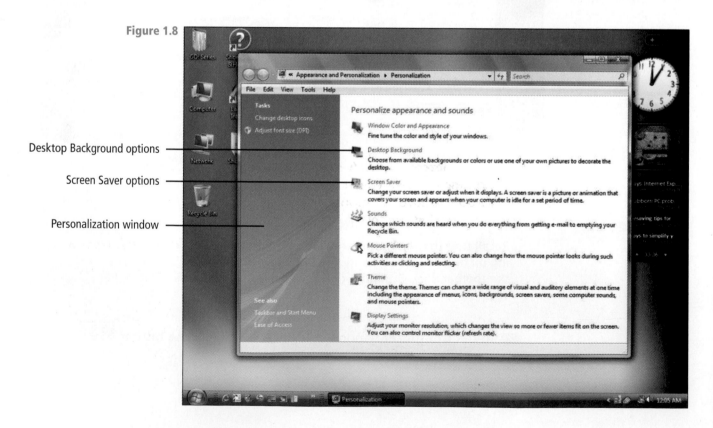

3 In the displayed **Personalization** window, click **Screen Saver**.

A *screen saver* is a picture or animation that displays on your screen after a set period of computer inactivity.

4 In the displayed **Screen Saver Settings** dialog box, click the **Screen saver box arrow**. From the displayed list, click **Aquarium**, and then compare your screen with Figure 1.9.

A *dialog box* is a box that asks you to make a decision about an individual object or topic. The Aquarium screen saver is selected, and a preview displays near the top of the dialog box. The default length of inactivity to trigger the screen saver is 15 minutes.

Figure 1.9

Preview of Aquarium screen saver

Screen saver box arrow

Selected screen saver

Period of inactivity before screen saver displays

5 In the **Screen Saver Settings** dialog box, click the **Preview** button to preview a full-screen version of the screen saver. When you are through, move the mouse to turn off the screen saver. At the bottom of the dialog box, click **OK**.

6 In the **Personalization** window, click **Desktop Background**.

The *desktop background* is the picture, pattern, or color that displays on the desktop.

7 In the displayed **Desktop Background** window, click the **Picture Location box arrow**, and then from the displayed list, click **Windows Wallpapers**. In the displayed list of desktop backgrounds, under **Light Auras**, click the first background, and then compare your screen with Figure 1.10. If this picture is not available, click another picture.

Windows Wallpaper group

Figure 1.10

Picture Location box arrow

Selected picture

Desktop background displays new picture

8 At the bottom of the **Desktop Background** window, click the **Cancel** button.

The Cancel button enables you to leave a window or dialog box without implementing the changes that you have made.

9 In the upper right corner of the **Personalization** window, click the **Close** button [X].

Activity 1.3 Adding and Removing Gadgets from the Windows Sidebar

The Windows Sidebar is located on the right side of the desktop, and is used to display dynamic programs—also known as *gadgets*—such as a currency converter, a calendar, or a clock. By default, a clock, a picture slideshow, and a news headlines box are displayed; your screen gadgets may be different.

1 In the **Windows Sidebar**, point to the **Clock** gadget. If the Clock gadget does not display, point to any other gadget. Notice that a set of tools displays to the right of the gadget, as shown in Figure 1.11.

The tool set is called the *gadget controls*, and includes a Move button in the shape of eight small dots, an Options button in the shape of a wrench, and a Close button.

Move button   Options button   Gadget   Close
                                  controls   button

Figure 1.11

Clock gadget

Alert! Is the Windows Sidebar missing?

If the last person to use the computer turned the Windows Sidebar off, it will remain off until turned back on. To turn on the Windows Sidebar, click the Start button, click All Programs, click Accessories, and then click Windows Sidebar.

2 In the **Windows Sidebar**, right-click in an open area. From the displayed shortcut menu, click **Add Gadgets**. Compare your screen with Figure 1.12.

Note — Removing a Gadget from the Windows Sidebar

To remove a gadget from the Windows Sidebar, right-click the gadget, and then from the displayed shortcut menu, click Close Gadget.

Figure 1.12

Available gadgets

Online link to other gadgets

3 Double-click the **Weather** gadget to place it in the Windows Sidebar. In the upper-right corner of the **Gadgets** dialog box, click the **Close** button ![Close button] .

4 Move the pointer over the **Weather** gadget, and then click the **Options** control—the button in the shape of a wrench.

5 In the **Weather** dialog box, click in the **Current Location** box. Type **Madison Wisconsin** and then press Enter. Compare your screen with Figure 1.13, and then from the displayed list, click **Madison, Wisconsin**. Under **Current location**, be sure *Madison, Wisconsin* displays.

Weather
dialog box   Selected city

Figure 1.13

6 In the **Weather** dialog box, click **OK** to confirm your selection. Notice that the current temperature and the name of the city display in the weather gadget.

7 If the Feed Headlines gadget does not display, use the techniques you just practiced to add it to the Windows Sidebar. Then, point to the **Feed Headlines** gadget, and click on one of the headlines.

More information displays in a pop-up window. You can click the story headline to see the full article.

8 On the desktop, click in any open area to close the headline.

More Knowledge
Use the Same Gadget More Than One Time

Some of the gadgets can be displayed multiple times. For example, if you are interested in the weather in two different locations, you can add two weather gadgets to the Windows Sidebar and keep an eye on two locations at one time.

Objective 2
Use the Start Menu and Manage Windows

Some programs and documents are available from the desktop. For most things, however, you will turn to the Start menu. The **Start menu** gives you access to all of the programs on your computer, and also enables you to change the way Windows operates, to access and configure your network, and to get help and support when it is needed. Once you have opened several programs, you can rearrange and resize the program windows to fit your needs.

Activity 1.4 Using the Start Menu

In this activity, you will use the Start menu to open an accessory program, and also to open the Computer window.

1 In the lower-left corner of the screen, on the left end of the taskbar, point to and then click the **Start** button 🪟 , and then compare your screen with Figure 1.14. Alternatively, press the Start button on your keyboard—a key with the Windows logo, often found to the left of the spacebar.

The left side of the Start menu contains three areas. At the bottom is the **All Programs** command, which takes you to a list of all of the programs you can access on the computer. Above *All Programs* is an area that contains the most recently opened programs. On the top left is the **pinned programs area**—an area reserved for programs that you want to display permanently, although you can also delete programs from this area. To delete a program from the pinned list, right-click the program, and then click *Remove From This List*.

On the top of the right side are links to your personal folders, while the bottom two sections give you access to many more features. *All Programs* and *Recent Items* display arrows, which indicate that a submenu is available for a command. A **submenu** is a second-level menu; the arrow indicates more items can be found related to the menu command.

Figure 1.14

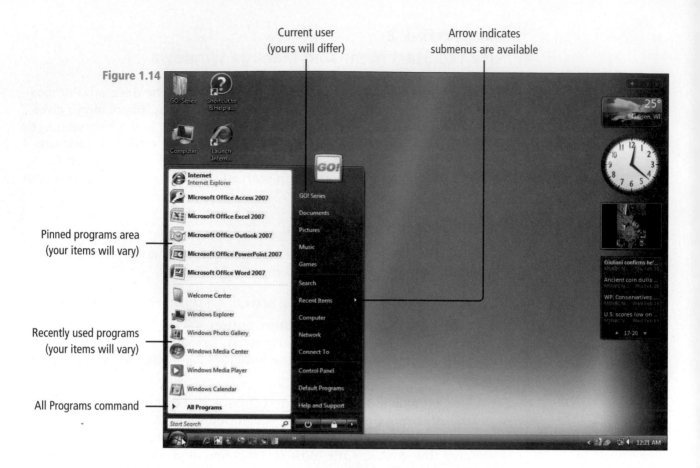

Current user
(yours will differ)

Arrow indicates
submenus are available

Pinned programs area
(your items will vary)

Recently used programs
(your items will vary)

All Programs command

Alert!

Is your taskbar hidden?

Some computers are set up to hide the taskbar when it is not in use. This adds more workspace to the desktop, and is particularly useful on portable computers with small screens. When the taskbar is hidden, move the pointer to the bottom of the screen, and it will display. However, in this chapter, it is assumed that the taskbar is displayed at all times.

To keep the taskbar displayed on your screen, find an open area on the taskbar, right-click, and then from the shortcut menu, click Properties. In the Taskbar and Start Menu Properties dialog box, on the Taskbar tab, locate the *Auto-hide the taskbar* check box. If the taskbar is hidden, there will be a check mark in the check box. To remove the Auto-hide feature, click the check box one time to clear—remove—the check mark. Note: If the Properties dialog box does not display when you right-click, try right-clicking over the clock on the far right side of the taskbar.

2 From the **Start** menu, point to, but do not click, the **All Programs** command. Compare your screen with Figure 1.15.

The All Programs submenu displays—displaying a portion of the contents found within All Programs—and the *All Programs* command changes to a *Back* command. Your menu will differ from the one shown in Figure 1.15 because your computer will have different programs installed. Folders in the menu contain more programs, or more folders, or some of each.

Figure 1.15

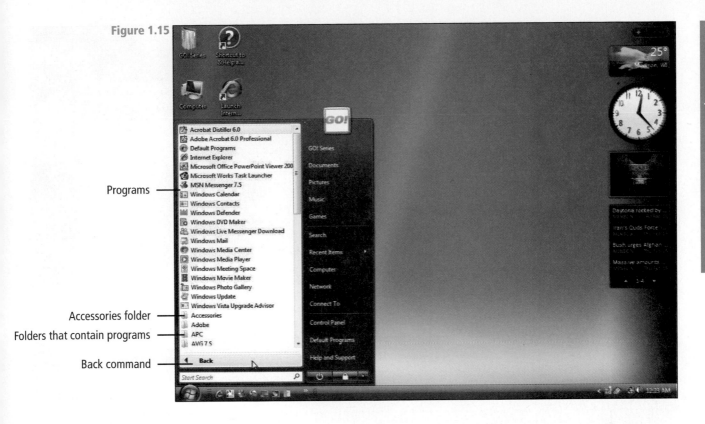

Programs

Accessories folder

Folders that contain programs

Back command

3 Click the **Accessories** folder, and then from the displayed list, click **Calculator**.

The Calculator window opens, and the Start menu closes. You can access the Accessories programs from the Start menu and use them while you are using other programs such as Microsoft Office. For example, you might want to make a quick calculation while you are typing a document in Microsoft Word. You can open the calculator, make the calculation, and then place the result in your Word document without closing Word.

4 Click the **Start** button again, and near the middle of the right side of the **Start menu**, click **Computer**. Compare your screen with Figure 1.16.

The Computer window opens, but the Calculator window is either partially or completely hidden, as shown in Figure 1.16. The buttons in the taskbar, however, indicate that two windows are open, and display the names of the windows. The darker button indicates the *active window*—the window in which the cursor movements, commands, or text entry occur when two or more windows are open.

Figure 1.16

Computer window hides
the Calculator window

Darker button indicates
the active window

Computer window button

Calculator
window button

5 Click the **Start** button ⊞, click **All Programs**, click **Accessories**, and then click **Welcome Center** to add a third open program to the desktop. Check the taskbar to confirm that three windows are open.

Activity 1.5 Adding Shortcuts to the Start Menu and the Desktop

There are programs that you will seldom use, and there are programs that you will use all the time. To make frequently used programs easily and quickly available, you can pin a shortcut to the program in the Start menu *pinned programs area,* or you can add a shortcut icon to the desktop.

1 Click the **Start** button ⊞, click **All Programs**, click **Accessories**, and then right-click **Calculator**.

2 From the displayed shortcut menu, click **Pin to Start Menu**. At the bottom of the **Start menu**, click the **Back** button, and notice that *Calculator* has been added to the pinned programs area, as shown in Figure 1.17.

Calculator program
pinned to Start menu

Figure 1.17

Pinned programs area

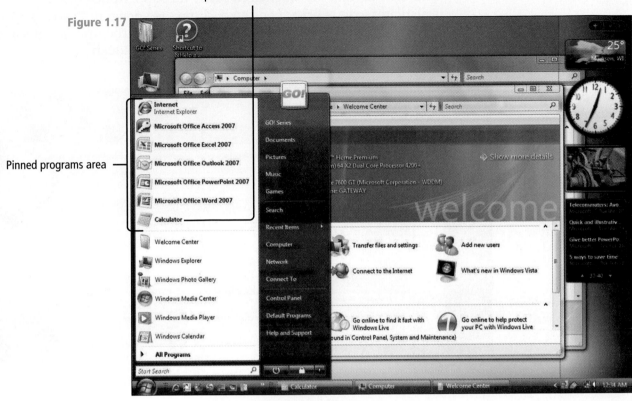

▣ Click the **Start** button 🔘, click **All Programs**, click **Accessories**, right-click **Calculator**, and then point to—but do not click—**Send To**. Notice the available commands on the *Send To* list, as shown in Figure 1.18.

Shortcut menu

Desktop (create
shortcut) command

Figure 1.18

Send To command

Project 1A: Familiarize Yourself with the Vista Interface | **Windows Vista**

4 From the displayed shortcut menu, click **Desktop (create shortcut)**, and then click in any open area of the desktop. Notice that a Calculator icon is placed on the desktop, as shown in Figure 1.19. Depending on the windows you have open, and the number of icons on your desktop, your Calculator icon may be hidden.

Figure 1.19

Calculator icon added
to the desktop

More Knowledge

Resizing the Taskbar

The taskbar can be resized to show more buttons, if necessary. Move the pointer to the top edge of the taskbar until it changes to a two-headed vertical arrow. Hold down the left mouse button and drag up until the taskbar displays all of the buttons for the open windows. You can also shrink the height of the taskbar down to the bottom of the screen. This can be done accidentally, and many new users panic when this happens, thinking the taskbar has disappeared. If you accidentally lose your taskbar, move the pointer to the very bottom of the screen. It will change to a vertical two-headed arrow, and you can drag the top of the taskbar back up to make it visible again.

Activity 1.6 Minimizing, Maximizing, and Restoring a Window

You can *maximize* a window, which enlarges the window to occupy the entire screen, and you can *restore* a window, which reduces the window to the size it was before being maximized. You can also *minimize* a window, which reduces the window to a button on the taskbar, removing it from the screen entirely without actually closing it. When you need to view the window again, you can click the taskbar button to bring it back into view.

1 With the **Welcome Center** window open as the top window, examine the three buttons in the upper right corner of the window. The left button is the **Minimize** button , the middle button is the **Maximize** button , and the right button is the **Close** button .

2 In the **Welcome** window, click the **Maximize** button . Alternatively, double-click in the bar at the top of the window. Notice that the window expands to cover the entire screen, and the Maximize button changes to a Restore Down button , as shown in Figure 1.20.

Maximize button changes to Restore Down button

Figure 1.20

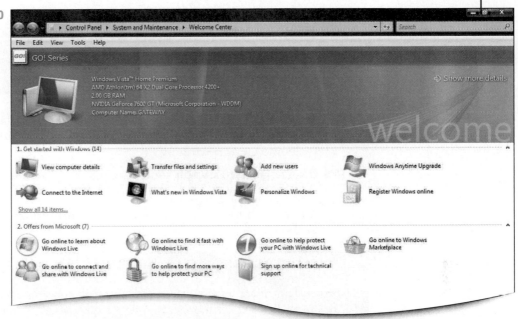

3 In the **Welcome** window, click the **Restore Down** button . Alternatively, double-click in the bar at the top of the window. Notice that the window resumes its former shape, size, and location.

4 In the **Welcome** window, click the **Minimize** button to display the Computer window. In the **Computer** window, click the **Minimize** button . Notice that the Calculator window, which had been hidden, now displays. Notice also that the two programs that you minimized are not closed—their buttons still display on the taskbar, as shown in Figure 1.21.

Figure 1.21

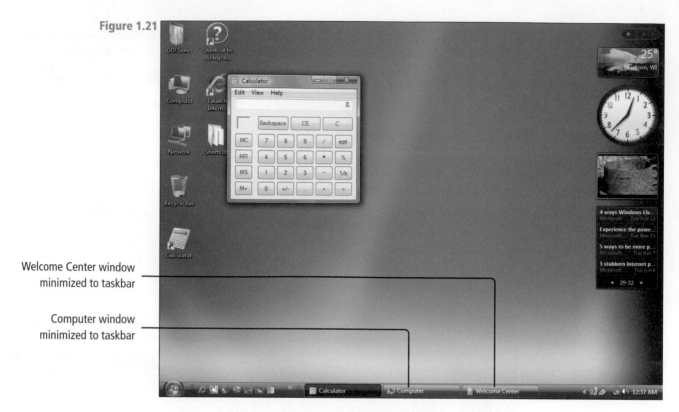

Welcome Center window
minimized to taskbar

Computer window
minimized to taskbar

> **5** In the taskbar, click the **Computer** button to restore the Computer window. Then, click the **Welcome Center** button to restore the Welcome Center window.

> **6** On the **Quick Launch** toolbar, click the **Show desktop** button . Compare your screen with Figure 1.22.

> All open windows on the desktop are minimized, including the Windows Sidebar.

Figure 1.22

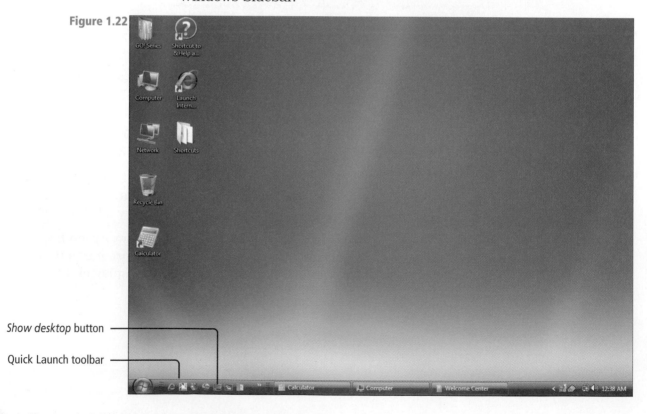

Show desktop button

Quick Launch toolbar

7 On the **Quick Launch** toolbar, click the **Show desktop** button again, and notice that all of the windows redisplay in their original locations. If you perform some action after you click the Show desktop button the first time, when you click it again, the windows will not redisplay—you will have to click the buttons for each window.

More Knowledge

Keeping More Than One Program Window Open at a Time

The ability to keep more than one window open at a time will become more useful as you become more familiar with Microsoft Office. For example, if you want to take information from two word processing documents to create a third document, you can open all three documents and use the taskbar to move among them, copying and pasting text from one document to another. Or, you could copy a chart from Excel and paste it into Word or take a table of data and paste it into PowerPoint. You can even have the same document open in two windows.

Objective 3
Resize, Move, and Scroll Windows

When a window opens on your screen, it generally opens in the same size and shape as it was when last used. If you are using more than one window at a time, you can increase or decrease the size of a window, or move a window so that you can see the information you need. As you work within a program, the information you create will likely grow larger than the screen can display. When the information in a window extends beyond the right or lower edges of the window, scroll bars display at the bottom and right. Using the *horizontal scroll bar*, you can move left and right to view information that extends beyond the left or right edge of the screen. Using the *vertical scroll bar*, you can move up and down to view information that extends beyond the top or bottom of the screen.

Activity 1.7 Previewing the Contents of the Taskbar

When you have a number of windows open, you may want to quickly review the contents of each document to determine which one to use.

1 On the taskbar, point to—but do not click—the **Computer** button, and then compare your screen with Figure 1.23.

A thumbnail of the window displays. A *thumbnail* is a miniature representation of a window or a file.

Figure 1.23

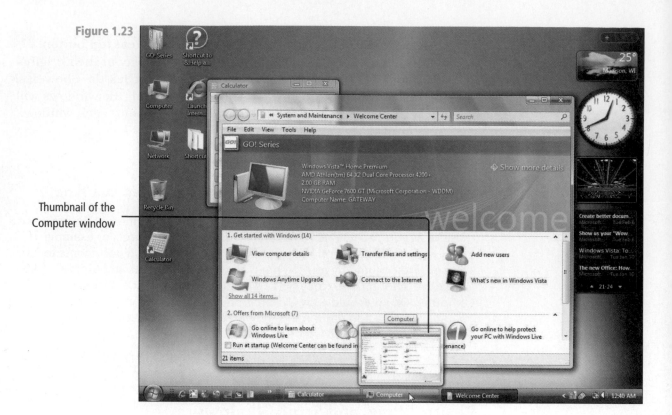

Thumbnail of the
Computer window

☐2 On the taskbar, point to—but do not click—the **Calculator** button. Move the pointer and point to the **Welcome Center** button.

☐3 Click the **Start** button 🔵 , click **All Programs**, click **Accessories**, and then click **WordPad**. If the WordPad window is maximized, click the Restore Down button 🔲 .

WordPad is a simple word processing program that comes with Vista, and generally opens maximized. Four programs are now open.

☐4 On the taskbar, click the **Switch between windows** button 🔳 , and then compare your screen with Figure 1.24.

The screen displays a visual representation of the windows that are open—called *Flip 3D*—including the desktop. The taskbar buttons, desktop icons, and Windows Sidebar gadget icons are all *dimmed*— displayed in a faded gray, which indicates that they are not currently available.

Figure 1.24

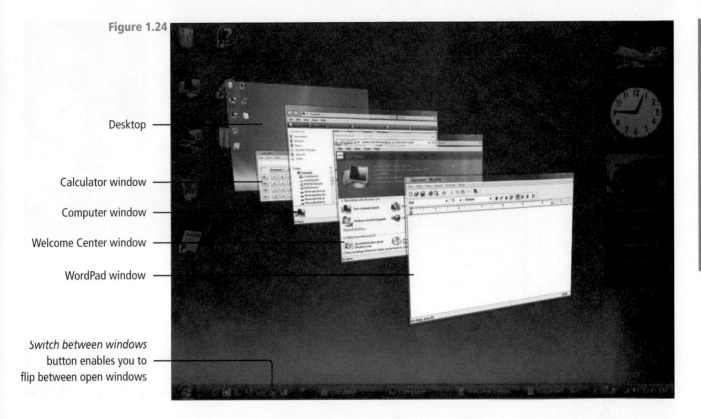

Desktop

Calculator window

Computer window

Welcome Center window

WordPad window

Switch between windows button enables you to flip between open windows

5 On the keyboard, press ←, and notice that the last item in the list moves to the front.

6 Take a moment to press ← and → to scroll through the open windows.

7 Move the **Calculator** window to the front, and then press Enter. Alternatively, move the pointer to the desired window and click one time.

All of the windows display again, with the Calculator window on top.

8 Click anywhere on any of the windows behind the Calculator window, and notice that the window becomes the active window.

To make a window active, you can click on any part of the window that is visible. Recall that on the taskbar, the button for the active window is darker than the buttons for the other windows.

Activity 1.8 Cascading and Stacking Windows

In this activity, you will practice several other methods of displaying windows.

1 Click the **Start** button , click **All Programs**, click **Accessories**, and then click **Paint**. If the Paint window opens maximized, click the Restore Down button .

Paint is a program included with Vista in which graphics are created or edited.

2 On the taskbar, right-click anywhere in an open area—any area that is not on a button. From the displayed shortcut menu, click **Show Windows Stacked**, and then compare your screen with Figure 1.25.

The windows are ***stacked***—Vista reduces the size of the windows and tries to fit them all onto the screen at one time.

Figure 1.25

Windows are stacked

3 On the taskbar, right-click anywhere in an open area, and then from the shortcut menu, click **Undo Show Stacked**.

The windows return to their original shape, size, and location.

4 On the taskbar, right-click anywhere in an open area, and then from the shortcut menu, click **Cascade Windows**. Compare your screen with Figure 1.26.

When you *cascade* the open windows, they line up in a diagonal line from the upper left corner of the screen downward.

Figure 1.26

Windows are cascaded

5 On the taskbar, right-click anywhere in an open area, and then from the shortcut menu, click **Undo Cascade**.

Activity 1.9 Resizing, Moving, Scrolling, and Closing Windows

In the following activity, you will resize and move the Computer window. You will also use the vertical scroll bar in the Computer window to view information that does not fit in the window.

1 On the **Quick Launch** toolbar, click the **Show desktop** button.

2 On the taskbar, click the **Computer** button to display the Computer window.

3 Move the pointer to the lower right corner of the window to display the diagonal resize pointer, and then compare your screen with Figure 1.27.

When the mouse pointer is in this shape, you can use it to change the size and shape of a window.

Figure 1.27

Diagonal resize pointer

4 Hold down the left mouse button, **drag**—move the mouse while holding down the left mouse button, and then release at the appropriate time—diagonally up and to the left until you see a scroll bar at the right side of the window, and then release the mouse button. Adjust as necessary so that the Computer window is the approximate size of the one shown in Figure 1.28.

Notice that a vertical scroll bar displays on the right side of the window. A scroll bar is added to the window whenever the window contains more than it can display.

Figure 1.28

Vertical scroll bar

Window is resized

5 At the top of the **Computer** window, point to a blank area to the left of the Minimize, Maximize, and Close buttons. Hold down the left mouse button, drag—hold down the left mouse button, move the mouse, and then release the mouse button—up until the top edge of the window is just below the top of the screen.

6 In the Computer window, at the bottom of the vertical scroll bar, point to the **down arrow** and click four times. Notice that information at the bottom of the window scrolls up so that you can see the folders and icons that were not visible before, as shown in Figure 1.29.

Window moved to the top of the screen   Vertical scroll bar down arrow   Vertical scroll bar up arrow

Figure 1.29

7 On the same scroll bar, point to the **up arrow**, and then click and hold down the left mouse button.

The list scrolls up to the top of the Content pane. You can click and hold down the left mouse button on the up or down scroll arrows to scroll rapidly through a long list of information.

8 Point to the scroll box, as shown in Figure 1.30, and then drag it downward.

The **scroll box** displays within the vertical and horizontal scroll bars and provides a visual indication of your location within the information displayed. It can also be used with the mouse to reposition the information on the screen. The size of the scroll box varies to indicate the relative size of the information. Moving the scroll box gives you more control as you scroll because you can see the information as it moves up or down in the window.

Vertical scroll box

Figure 1.30

Note — Moving a Screen at a Time

You can move up or down a screen at a time by clicking in the gray area above or below the vertical scroll box. You can also move left or right a screen at a time by clicking in the area to the left or right of a horizontal scroll box. The size of the scroll box indicates the relative size of the display to the whole document. If the scroll box is small, it means that the display is a small portion of the entire document.

9 On the taskbar, click the **Calculator** button to display the Calculator window.

The name of the window displays in the **title bar**—a bar at the top of the window that displays the Minimize, Maximize, and Close buttons, the program icon, the window name, and sometimes the name of a saved document. Not all windows have all of these elements. Recall that the Computer window has the program icon and window name in the status bar, rather than in the title bar.

10 In the **Calculator** window, move the pointer to an open area of the title bar, and then drag the window to the approximate location shown in Figure 1.31.

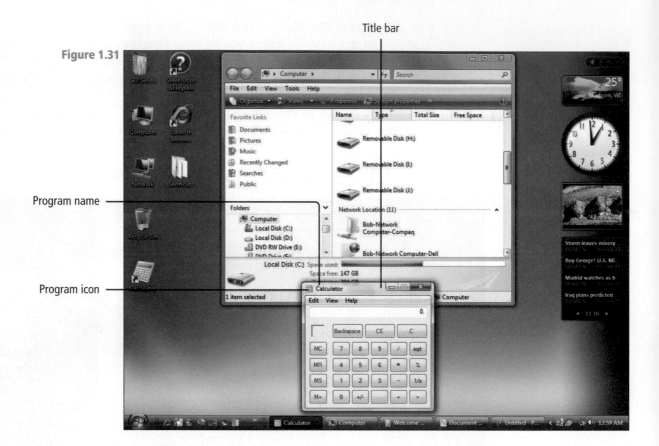

Title bar

Figure 1.31

Program name

Program icon

11 In the **Calculator** window title bar, click the **Close** button [X].

The program closes, and the Calculator taskbar button is removed.

12 On the taskbar, right-click the **Welcome Center** button, and from the displayed shortcut menu, click **Close**.

Use a shortcut menu to close a program without having to view the program window.

13 Use either procedure you have practiced to close the remaining open windows.

End **You have completed Project 1A**

Project 1B **Work with Files and Folders**

In Activities 1.10 through 1.19 you will create folders, and then copy, move, rename, and delete files and folders. You will use the Vista search features to search for files, and you will use Vista Help to get information on how to use the operating system. Finally, you will capture a copy of your computer screen, open a word processing program, and paste the screen in the document, which will look similar to Figure 1.32.

For Project 1B, you will need the following files:

43 sample files, and two folders containing 14 additional files

**You will save your document as
Captured_Screen_Firstname_Lastname**

Figure 1.32
Project 1B—Work with Files and Folders

Objective 4
Create, Move, and Rename Folders

Information that you create in a computer program is stored in the computer's memory, which is a temporary storage location. This data may be lost if the computer is turned off. To keep the information you create, you must save it as a file on one of the drives available to you. For example, a five-page term paper that you create in a word processing program such as Microsoft Word, when saved, is a *file*. Files can be stored directly on a drive, but more commonly are stored in a folder on the drive. A *folder* is a container for programs and files, and is represented on the screen by a picture of a common paper file folder.

Use folders to organize the location of your programs and files so that you can easily locate them for later use. Folders and files must be created and stored on one of the drives attached to your computer. Your available drives fall into three categories: 1) the non-removable hard drive, also called the local disk, inside the computer; 2) removable drives that you insert into the computer, such as a flash drive, an external hard drive, or a writable CD or DVD; or 3) a shared network drive connected to your computer through a computer network, such as the network at your college.

Activity 1.10 Opening and Navigating Windows Explorer

Windows Explorer is a program that enables you to create and manage folders, and manage copy, move, sort, and delete files. In the following activity, you will create a folder on one of the three types of drives available to you—the local disk (hard drive), a removable drive (USB flash drive, an external hard drive, or some other type of removable drive), or a network drive. If you are using a computer in a college lab, you may have space assigned to you on a shared network drive. You can create these folders on any drive that is available to you. For the rest of this chapter, a USB drive will be used.

1 Click the **Start** button 🔵 , click **All Programs**, click **Accessories**, and then click **Windows Explorer**.

The Computer windows opens, with the Folders list on the Navigation pane displayed, and the Documents folder expanded.

2 On the toolbar, click the **Organize** button, and then point to **Layout**. If the Details pane does not display at the bottom of your window, click Details Pane. If the Navigation pane does not display on the left side of your window, repeat the procedure and click Navigation Pane. If the Folders list does not display, at the bottom of the Navigation pane, click Folders.

3 In the upper right corner of the **Windows Explorer** window, click the **Maximize** button 🔲 to maximize the window, and then compare your screen with Figure 1.33. In the **Folders** list of the **Navigation** pane, use the vertical scroll bar to scroll up and down and examine the structure of the folders on your computer.

Figure 1.33

Organize button

Navigation pane

Folders list

Details pane

4 In the **Folders** list, scroll down, and then click **Computer**.

The Content pane displays a list of hard drives, removable storage devices, available network locations, and other devices connected to the computer.

5 In the **Folders** list, to the left of **Computer**, click the open triangle ▷. Notice that the triangle changes to a filled triangle pointing downward at an angle ◢.

The open triangle indicates that there are other folders and drives to be displayed. When you click the open triangle, the next level of folders and drives displays.

6 Insert your USB flash drive or other removable drive. If an action dialog box displays asking what you want Windows to do, click **Cancel**. Scroll down in the **Folders** list, and then click your removable drive—for this chapter, the removable drive name will be LEXAR MEDIA (K:). Compare your screen with Figure 1.34. Notice that the Content pane in the figure is empty; your storage device or drive may already contain files and folders.

Figure 1.34

Content pane is empty —

Flash drive —

More Knowledge

Computer Storage Devices

The hard drive (local disk) is usually identified on your computer by the notation C:\ (and sometimes D:\, E:\, and so on for additional drives). *Flash drives*—also known as *USB drives* or *thumb drives*—are small storage devices that plug into a computer Universal Serial Bus (USB) port, a connection between a computer and a peripheral device such as a printer, a mouse, a keyboard, or a USB drive.

You may also have access to files on another type of storage device, a *CD*—Compact Disc, or a *DVD*—Digital Video (or Versatile) Disc. CD and DVD drives are optical storage devices that come in two formats—read-only and read-write. If you are using files stored on a read-only CD or a DVD disc, you will need to open a file from the disc, and then save it to a writable drive, or copy a file to another disk and then open it.

Activity 1.11 Creating a New Folder

It is always a good idea to create a new folder when you have a new category of files to store. You do not need to create a new folder for each type of file, however. You can store many different kinds of files in the same folder.

1 With the removable drive selected, in an open area of the **Content** pane, right-click to display a shortcut menu, and then point to **New**. Compare your screen with Figure 1.35.

Figure 1.35

Create a new folder here

Shortcut menu

New command

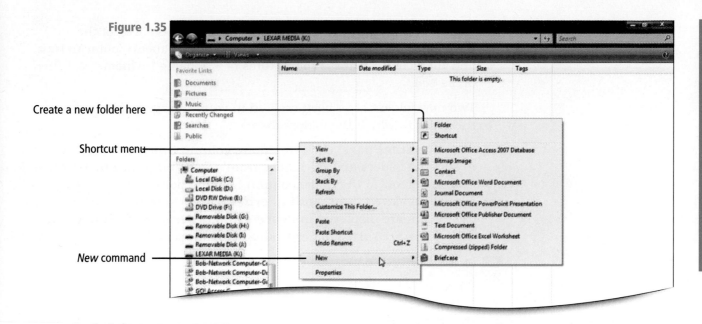

2 From the shortcut menu, click **Folder**.

A new folder—named *New Folder*—is created with the name of the folder displayed in the *edit mode*. Edit mode enables you to change the name of a file or folder, and works the same in all Windows programs.

3 With *New Folder* selected, substitute your name where indicated, and type **Word Documents of Firstname Lastname** and then press Enter. Click anywhere in the blank area of the Content pane to deselect the new folder and compare your screen with Figure 1.36.

Figure 1.36

Renamed folder

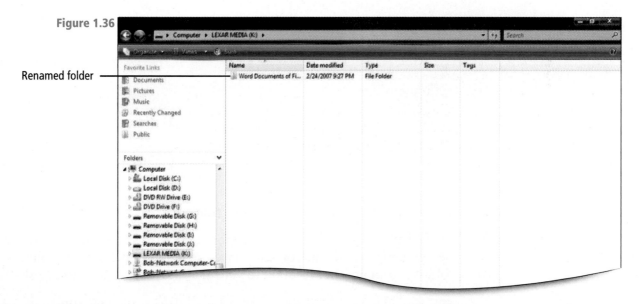

Another Way — **To Rename a Folder**

If you accidentally press Enter before you have a chance to name the folder, you can still rename it. Right-click the folder, click Rename from the shortcut menu, type a new name, and then press Enter. Alternatively, you can click the folder once, pause, and then click the folder again to activate edit mode.

4 With the removable drive still selected, in an open area of the **Content** pane, right-click to display a shortcut menu, point to **New**, and then click **Folder**. Type **Pictures of Firstname Lastname** and then press Enter.

Two new folders have been created in your storage location. Notice the order in which the folders display.

5 In the **Content** pane, click the **Name** column heading several times to sort the folders and file names from a to z and from z to a. Notice that the arrow in the Name column heading points up when the folders are displayed in ***ascending order*** (a to z), and points down when the folders are displayed in ***descending order*** (z to a). Stop when the folders are sorted in descending alphabetical order—from z to a.

6 In the **Content** pane, move the pointer to the line at the right of the

Name column heading to display the resize pointer ⊕, as shown in Figure 1.37. Drag the resize pointer to the right to make the column slightly wider than the longest folder name.

Name column heading with
arrow indicating sort order

Figure 1.37

Files in descending
alphabetical order

Resize pointer

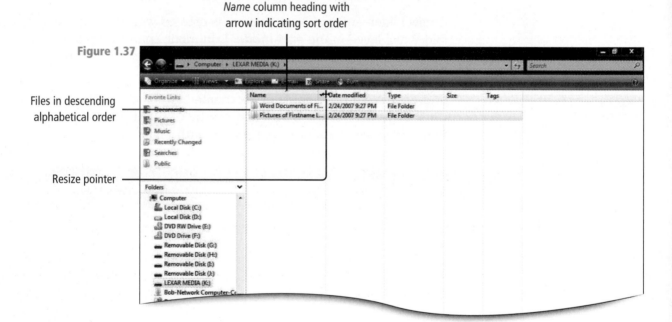

Activity 1.12 Moving and Renaming Folders

Your student files and folders are stored on a CD or another location chosen by your instructor. You can move the folders, including the files in the folders, from another location to your flash drive or other storage device.

1 Navigate to the location where your student files for this book are stored. They may be stored on a CD, in a course management system, on a hard drive, or on a shared network drive.

2 Locate and click the folder named **chapter_01_windows_vista**, and then compare your screen with Figure 1.38. If your files and folders do not display the way they display in the figure, on the toolbar, click the Views button, and then click Details.

There are two folders and a number of files in this folder. The total number of files and folders is displayed in the Details pane at the bottom of the screen. There are more files in the two folders, but they are not included in the totals in the Details pane—only the files and the folders currently displayed in the Content pane are counted.

Files

Figure 1.38

Folders

Student files for this chapter

Number of items in the selected folder

3 In the **Content** pane, move the pointer to the right border of the **Name** column heading to display the ⟷ pointer. Double-click to resize the border to the widest folder or file name. Repeat this procedure to display the full **Date modified** and **Type** column contents.

Note — Changing the Columns that Display in the Content Pane

If one or more of the columns displayed in Figure 1.38 do not display, right-click anywhere in the Content pane column titles, and then check the desired column.

4 In the **Folders** list, scroll as necessary to display your flash drive or other storage device. Be sure your student files and folders still display in the Content pane.

5 Locate the **XML Files** folder near the top of the **Content** pane. Click on the folder, hold the mouse button down, and drag the folder to the **Folders** list directly on top of your storage drive, as shown in

Figure 1.39. Notice that a folder displays attached to the pointer, and a ScreenTip says *Copy to LEXAR MEDIA (K:)*—your folder or drive name will vary.

Figure 1.39

ScreenTip indicates copy location

6 Release the mouse button.

7 Repeat the procedure you just practiced to copy the **Life Saving Service Drawings** folder to your storage area, and notice that a message box indicates the progress of the copy.

The message box displays because the size of the *Life Saving Service Drawings* folder is much larger than the size of the *XML Files* folder.

Figure 1.40

Message box indicates progress of the copy

8 In the **Folders** list, click the flash drive or other device where you are storing your files and folders. In the **Content** pane, right-click the **Life Saving Service Drawings** folder, and then from the displayed shortcut menu, click **Rename**.

9 With the folder name in edit mode, type **LSS Drawings** and then press Enter.

The folder name is changed. When text is selected, typing replaces all of the selected text.

Objective 5
Copy, Move, Rename, and Delete Files

Recall that Windows manages your data files because your files are stored on the drives attached to your computer. Copying files from one folder to another is a frequent data management task. For example, you might want to make a backup copy of important information, copy a file from a CD to a local disk, or copy information from your local disk drive to a removable drive. Copying files works the same regardless of the type of drive.

Performing other operations on files, such as deleting them or moving them, also works the same regardless of the type of drive. As you accumulate files, you will likely need to delete some to reduce clutter on your hard drive. You might also want to move documents into other folders on another drive to *archive* them—place them somewhere for long-term storage. Finally, you may want to change the names of file to make the names more descriptive. All of these tasks are functions of your Windows Vista operating system.

Activity 1.13 Copying Files

1 In the **Folders** list, scroll to the location where your student files for this book are stored. Locate and click the folder named **chapter_01_windows_vista** to display the files and folders in the folder.

2 In the **Folders** list, scroll as necessary to display your flash drive or other storage device. Be sure your student files and folders still display in the Content pane.

3 Near the top of the **Content** pane, locate the **BeachPicture** file, and then drag it to your storage device. Recall that dragging also includes releasing the mouse button at the destination location.

When you drag a file or folder from one device to another, it is copied, which means that the original file remains on the original drive, and a copy of the file is placed on the new drive. If you drag a file or folder to another place (such as a folder) on the *same* drive—for example, from one folder to another—the file or folder is moved and no longer resides in the original location.

4 Use the same procedure to move the **Budget** file to your storage device, and then in the **Folders** list, click your storage device. Click the **Name** column heading as necessary to sort the folder in ascending order—the arrow should be pointing up. Compare your screen with Figure 1.41.

The Content pane should display four folders—the two that you created, and the two that you copied. In addition, the two files that you copied should display below the folders. When you sort a folder in ascending order, the folders always display first.

Folders display first

Figure 1.41

Folders and files sorted in alphabetical order by Name

5 Display the files and folders in the **chapter_01_windows_vista** folder again. Click the **Agave Picture** file, hold down ⇧ Shift, and then click the **BBQ** file.

By holding down the Shift key, you select the two files you click and all of the files in between.

6 In the **Folders** list, scroll as necessary to display your storage area. Drag the selected files to your storage area.

7 Click the **Chef Hat** file, hold down Ctrl, and then click the **Food Pyramid** file, and then the **Grill Logo** file. Notice that by using the Control key, you can select several files that are not next to each other, as shown in Figure 1.42.

Figure 1.42

Selected files ——

8 Drag the selected files to your storage area.

9 In the **Content** pane, click the **Grill Menu** file, and then use the vertical scroll bar to scroll to the bottom of the pane. Hold down ⬆ Shift, and then click the **Waterride** file. In the Detail area, notice that the number of files and the total size of the selected files displays, as shown in Figure 1.43.

Selected files

Figure 1.43

Total size of selected files ——

Number of files selected ——

10 Drag the selected files to your storage area.

More Knowledge

File Extensions

The files you see may display three or four letters following the file name, such as *.docx*. These are *file extensions*, and most files have these extensions—although they may or may not display on your system. Files created by Microsoft Office programs have a standard set of extensions that identify the type of program used to create the file. For example, Microsoft Word documents end in *.doc* or *.docx*, Excel worksheets end in *.xls* or *.xlsx*, PowerPoint presentations end with *.ppt* or *pptx*, and so on.

Activity 1.14 Moving, Renaming, and Deleting Files

In the following activity, you will move files from one location on your removable drive to another location on the same drive. You will also rename and delete files.

1 In the **Folders** list, scroll as necessary and then click on your flash drive or other storage device.

Your storage device should display four folders at the top, and a total of 39 items in the folder, as displayed in the Details pane.

2 In the **Content** pane, click the **Type** column header to sort the files by file type. Move the pointer to the right border of the **Type** column heading to display the ⊕ pointer. Double-click to resize the border to the widest file type—*Microsoft Office PowerPoint Presentation*.

3 In the **Content** pane, use the wheel in the middle of your mouse to scroll down until you can see all of the *Microsoft Office Word Document* files. If you do not have a mouse wheel, use the vertical scroll bar.

4 Click the **Budget** file, hold down ⇧Shift, and then click the **Survey Letter** file to select all of the Word documents. Drag the selected files to the **Word Documents of Firstname Lastname** folder.

The files are moved to the new folder, and no longer display in their original location.

5 In the **Folders** list, click the **Word Documents of Firstname Lastname** folder, and then compare your screen with Figure 1.44.

Figure 1.44

Word files moved to different folder

6 In the **Folders** list, click on your flash drive or other storage device. Using the technique you just practiced, select the six **JPEG Images**, and then drag them to the **Pictures of Firstname Lastname** folder.

7 Select the **LSS-Crew Pulling Lifeboat** file and drag it to the **Pictures of Firstname Lastname** folder. Then, select all eight **Paintbrush Picture** files and drag them to the **Pictures of Firstname Lastname** folder.

Alert!

What if Paintbrush Picture file types do not display?

Paintbrush Picture file types may also be called something different, depending on the way files are associated with programs on your computer. These files are Windows Metafile images, and have a *.wmf* extension. There will be eight pictures with the same type displayed, including *Artist Picture*, *BBQ*, and so forth. If your file types differ, use these eight files in place of the Paintbrush Picture files.

---

8 In the **Folders** list, click the **Pictures of Firstname Lastname** folder, and then compare your screen with Figure 1.45.

Three kinds of picture files
moved to new folder

Figure 1.45

9 On the toolbar, click the **Views** button, and then click **Large Icons**.

Thumbnail images display for recognized file types, while the other files display a placeholder image.

10 In the **Content** pane, right-click the **Agave Picture** file, and then click **Rename**. Type **Agave Cactus** and then press Enter.

11 In the **Content** pane, right-click the **No Fire** file, and then click **Delete**. The **Delete File** message box displays, as shown in Figure 1.46.

Figure 1.46

Delete File message box
asks for confirmation of delete

12 In the **Delete File** message box, click **Yes** to send the file to the Recycle Bin.

13 In the upper left corner of the **Windows Explorer** window, click the **Back** button to move back to your main storage area. Alternatively, in the Folders list, click your storage location name.

14 In the **Content** pane, right-click the **XML Files** folder, and then click **Delete**. In the displayed **Delete Folder** message box, click **Yes**.

When you delete a folder, all files in the folder are also deleted.

Activity 1.15 Compressing Files

Some files may be too large to send quickly as an e-mail attachment. For example, files containing graphics tend to be quite large. Windows Vista includes a feature with which you can **compress**—reduce the file size of—one or more files into a single file that uses a *.zip* file extension. These files can then be uncompressed for editing on any other computer running Windows Vista. Many file types—such as Microsoft Office 2007 files, Adobe Acrobat files, and JPEG picture files—do not benefit much from file compression. However, compression is often used to combine many files into one file for easy distribution.

1 With your storage device selected, and three folders and ten files displayed in the **Content** pane, click the **Food Pyramid** file, hold down ⬆ Shift, and then click the second **Regulations** file. If your files are in a different order, select all ten files, but not the folders. Notice that the Details pane indicates that ten files are selected, with a total size of 582 KB.

2 In the **Content** pane, right-click any of the selected files, and then from the displayed shortcut menu, point to **Send To**. Compare your screen with Figure 1.47.

Figure 1.47

Compressed (zipped) Folder command

Project 1B: Work with Files and Folders | **Windows Vista**

3 From the displayed list, click **Compressed (zipped) Folder**.

The compressed folder displays the name of the file you right-clicked, but displays in edit mode so you can change the file name.

> ## Note — To Work with Third-Party Zip Programs
>
> If you are using a third-party zip program, such as WinZip™ or PKZIP™, you will need to use that program to complete this task—the procedure listed below may not work.

4 With the compressed folder name still in edit mode, type **Files of Firstname Lastname** and then press Enter. Notice that the compressed folder size is now just under 400 KB, or about two-thirds the size of the ten selected files. Compare your screen with Figure 1.48.

Compressed folder

Figure 1.48

File size reduced by about one-third

5 In the **Content** pane, double-click the **Files of Firstname Lastname** compressed folder. Compare your screen with Figure 1.49.

The files in the compressed folder are listed, along with their original sizes and their compressed sizes. The percent of space saved is indicated for each file. Some of the files show very little space savings, while in others the space saved is considerable. To extract the files from the compressed folder, click the *Extract all files* button on the toolbar. You can also open the files directly from the compressed folder.

Figure 1.49

Extract all files button

Files in compressed folder

Compressed file size
Original file size
Percent of space saved

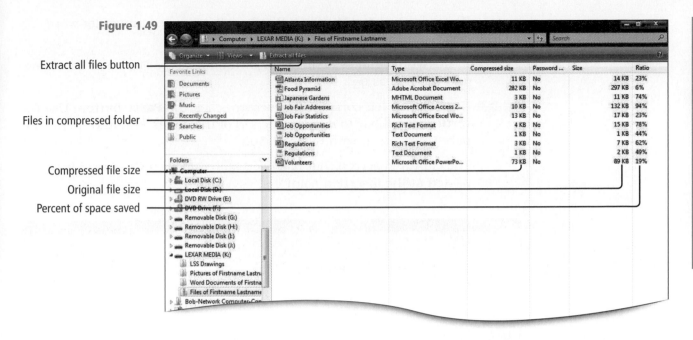

More Knowledge

Adding More Items to a Compressed Folder

You can add more files to an existing compressed folder by dragging files and dropping them on the compressed folder. You can drag the files to the folder from anywhere, and you can also drag folders into a compressed folder.

Activity 1.16 Capturing an Image of a Screen

Windows includes a screen capture utility so that you can capture an image of your screen and then print it or save it as a file. This can come in handy if you want to save something you found on a Web site, or if you need to document a screen problem or an error message.

1 In the upper left corner of the window, click the **Back** button to move back to your main storage area. Alternatively, in the Folders list, click your storage location name. Be sure that three folders, one compressed folder, and ten files are displayed in the **Content** pane.

If necessary, Maximize the Computer window.

2 On your keyboard, locate and press PrtScr.

The Print Screen key on your keyboard is commonly located near the right side of the top row of keys. This key captures an image of the entire screen and places it in a temporary storage area called the *Clipboard*. Items in the Clipboard can be placed in a document using the Paste command.

3 Click the **Start** button , click **All Programs**, and then locate and click **Microsoft Office Word 2007**. If necessary, Maximize the Word window.

If you do not have Microsoft Word available, open any other word processing program.

4 In the **Word** window, using your own name, type **Firstname Lastname** and then press Enter.

5 Near the top left corner of the screen, click the **Paste** button. Use the vertical scroll bar to move to the top of the document, and then compare your screen with Figure 1.50.

The captured screen that has been stored in your Clipboard is pasted at the insertion point.

Figure 1.50

Paste button

Captured screen

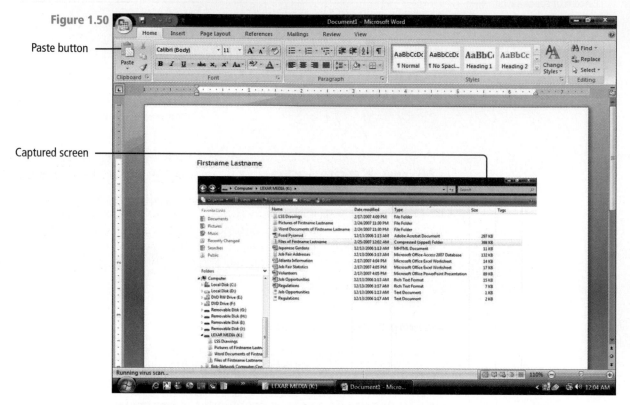

6 At the upper left corner of the Word window, click the **Office** button, and then click **Save As**. In the **Save As** dialog box, in the **Navigation** pane, click **Computer**. Locate and click your storage device. If you are using another storage area, click Documents and navigate to the location of your stored files.

7 Near the bottom of the **Save As** dialog box, in the **File Name** box, type **Captured Screen Firstname Lastname** and then at the bottom of the dialog box, click **Save**.

8 Check your *Course Syllabus* or *Chapter Assignment Sheet*, or ask your instructor, to determine if you are to submit a printed

or electronic copy of this file. To print, click the **Office** button, point to **Print**, and then click **Quick Print**. To submit electronically, using your college's course management system, consult your instructor's directions for saving and submitting the file.

9 Click the **Office** button, and then at the bottom right corner of the displayed list, click **Exit Word**.

Objective 6
Find Files and Folders

As you use a computer, you will likely accumulate a large number of files and folders. It's easy to forget where you stored a file, or what you named it. Windows Vista provides several search functions with which you can find files and folders. You can also add tags to files. *Tags* are custom file properties that help you find and organize your files. Tags are part of a file's *metadata*—items that record and display information about a file, such as a title, a rating, the file name, and the file size.

Activity 1.17 Adding Descriptions and Tags to Files

1 Be sure your storage device is selected, and three folders, one compressed folder, and eleven files are displayed in the **Content** pane. Also be sure the Details pane is open at the bottom of the window. If necessary, Maximize ▢ the Computer window. If your files display as a list, on the toolbar, click the Views button, and then click Large Icons.

2 In the **Navigation** pane, in the **Folders** list, click the **LSS Drawings** folder, and then click the file **LSS-Dragging Surfboat to Beach**.

3 In the **Details** pane, click in the **Tags** box—to the right of the word *Tags*. Type **LSS** and then press →. Type **LSS Boat** and then press →. Type **Surfboat** and then compare your screen with Figure 1.51. Notice on the left side of the Details pane that the file type for this file is JPEG—one of a number of image file types. If a pop-up box displays, ignore it.

When you add a tag, a semicolon immediately displays to the right of the insertion point. Semicolons separate multiple tags.

Figure 1.51

Selected file

Semicolons separate tags

New tags added

4 Press Enter to confirm the tags. Using the procedure you just practiced, add the same three tags to the **LSS-Surf Boat in High Surf** file. Notice on the left side of the Details pane that the file type for this file is JPEG.

5 Click the **LSS-Self-Righting Lifeboat with Sail** file. Notice that there is no place to add a tag.

This image is a bitmap image, which doesn't support tags. All Microsoft Office 2007 default file formats support tags, as do many other types of programs.

6 In the **Navigation** pane, in the **Folders** list, click the **Pictures of Firstname Lastname** folder, and then click the file **LSS-Charlotte NY Station**. Add the following tags: **LSS** and **LSS Boat** and **LSS Boat Ramp** and then press Enter.

7 In the **Details** pane, click the **Title** box, type **Life Saving Station at Charlotte, NY** and then press Enter.

8 In the **Content** pane, right click the **LSS-Charlotte NY Station** file, and then from the shortcut menu, click **Properties**. In the **Properties** dialog box, click the **Details tab**.

The items you entered in the Details pane display, and there are several other categories of tags that you can add, including a rating of the picture or document.

9 In the **Properties** dialog box, under **Description**, click the fourth **Rating** star from the left. Under **Origin**, click the **Copyright** box, type **Public Domain** and then compare your screen with Figure 1.52.

Figure 1.52

Selected file

Title added

Rating tag

New tags added

Copyright information

10 At the bottom of the **Properties** dialog box, click **OK** to close the dialog box.

Activity 1.18 Finding Files and Folders and Creating a Search Folder

1 In the **Folders** list, click your storage location name. Be sure your storage device is selected, and three folders, one compressed folder, and eleven files display in the **Content** pane.

2 Near the upper right corner of the window, click in the **Search** box, type **J** and then in the **Content** pane, examine the results of your search, as shown in Figure 1.53.

The program found all files and folders that contain the letter *J*, along with all file types that contain the letter *J*—in this case, all JPEG image files. A *Search Results* folder displays in the Folders list.

File types containing the letter *J*

First letter to search for   Search box

Figure 1.53

Files containing the letter *J*

3 Type the letter **P** and examine the search results. Notice that the only files, folders, or file types in your storage device that contain the consecutive letters *JP* are the JPEG image files.

4 Press ⟵Bksp, and notice that the search results again display all files, folders, and file types that contain the letter *J*.

5 Now type **ob** to complete the word *Job*. Notice that five files display, as shown in Figure 1.54.

Figure 1.54

Search term

Files that contain the letters *Job*

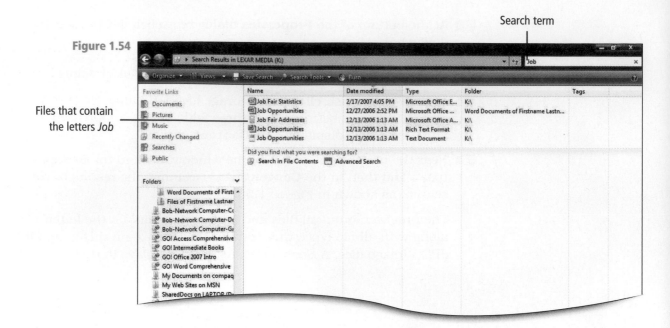

6 Press ⟨←Bksp⟩ three times, type **LSS** and then notice that files and folders from various locations display in the Content pane.

7 Press ⟨Spacebar⟩, type **boat** and then notice that only one file or folder meets this search condition, even though you added *LSS Boat* as a tag to several files. Also notice that the file that was found had both search words, but they do not have to be next to each other.

When you enter a word or phrase in the Search box, only the file names, folder names, and file types are searched.

8 In the **Navigation** pane, in the **Folders** list, right-click your storage device, and then from the shortcut menu, click **Search**. On the right side of the menu bar, click the **Advanced Search arrow**.

The Advanced Search enables you to search for tags, authors, or names. It also enables you to search for the date the file was created or last saved.

Note — Searching Document Contents

If you conduct a search from the Search box and do not find what you need, you can also search for documents that contain key words or phrases *in the document*. To search for document contents, in the Content pane, at the bottom of the search results, click Search in File Contents.

9 In the **Tags** box, type **LSS Boat** and then click the **Search** button. Notice that all of the files with LSS Boat tags display in the search results, as shown in Figure 1.55.

Figure 1.55

Search term in *Tags* box

Save Search button

Files that include *LSS Boat* tag

10 On the toolbar, click the **Save Search** button. In the displayed **Save As** dialog box, click **Save**.

A ***search folder*** is saved on your computer—not on your removable storage device. A search folder retains all of the search conditions you specified during your search, and re-creates the search every time you click the search folder. As you add more pictures with the *LSS Boat* tag to your removable storage device, the search folder will find them. It is important to remember that the search folder will only search the location you specified—it will not search the rest of the computer.

11 Close [X] the Search Results dialog box.

12 In the **Navigation** pane, in the **Folders** list, scroll up and locate the **Searches** folder. Click the open triangle to the left of **Searches**, and then notice that your search is saved there, as shown in Figure 1.56.

Figure 1.56

New search folder ——
Saved search ——

More Knowledge

Using Wildcards in Searches

When you are searching for a particular type of file, you can specify the extension by using a wildcard, followed by the extension. A **wildcard** takes the place of one or more characters in a search. For example, if you wanted to search for all of your Excel 2007 files in the Document folder, select the folder, and then type *.*xlsx* in the Search box. All files with the *.xlsx* extension will display. If you want to display all your Excel files, including older versions (with the *.xls* extension), type *.*xls*. This search will locate all *.xls* and *.xlsx* files. Similarly, you can search for all files beginning with *Fun* by typing *Fun**, which will return all files with those first three letters, including *Fundamentals of Business* and *Fun with Trombones.*

Objective 7
Use Vista Help

There will be times that you can't figure out how to make Vista do what you want it to do. Microsoft offers a robust Help system that enables you to read instructions on topics of your choice, and in some cases even walks you through the steps to accomplish a task. Help is available both installed on your computer and online.

Activity 1.19 Using Vista Help

1 With **Windows Explorer** open, on the right side of the toolbar, click the **Get help** button 🔞 .

The Windows Help and Support dialog box displays, with some general topics of interest, a Search box, and a link to Online Help.

2 In the displayed **Windows Help and Support** dialog box, in the **Search** box, type **Quick Launch toolbar** and then press Enter. Compare your screen with Figure 1.57.

Several topics associated with the Quick Launch toolbar display.

Figure 1.57

Search term

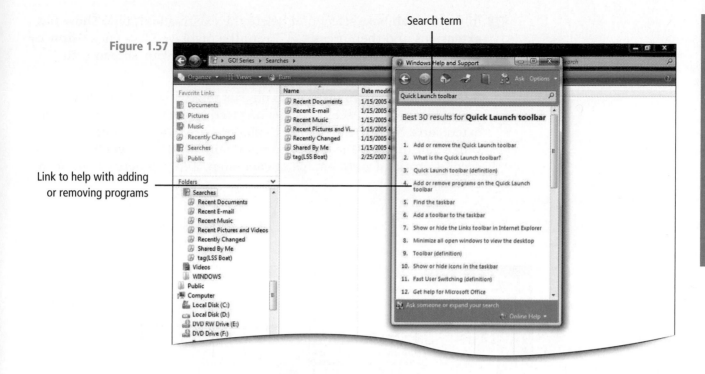

Link to help with adding or removing programs

▣ In the list of associated topics, click **Add or remove programs on the Quick Launch toolbar**, and notice the help that is available.

The green text indicates links to definitions; the blue text indicates that the text can be expanded to display more information.

▣ In the **Windows Help and Support** dialog box, click the blue text **To add a program icon to the Quick Launch toolbar** to expand the topic. In the paragraph below the topic title, click the green text *Quick Launch toolbar*, and then compare your screen with Figure 1.58.

Figure 1.58

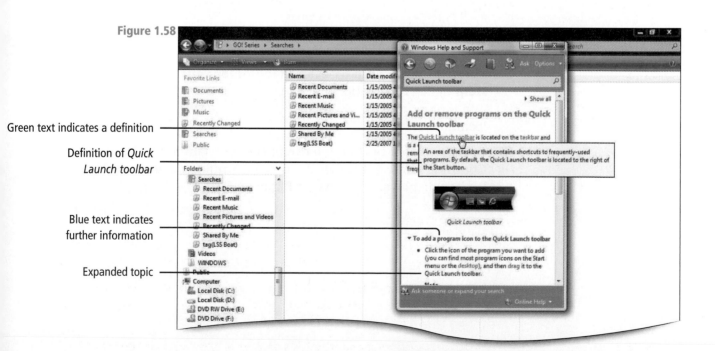

Green text indicates a definition

Definition of *Quick Launch toolbar*

Blue text indicates further information

Expanded topic

5 In the **Search** box, select and delete the existing text, type **Show file extensions** and then press ⏎. From the displayed list, click **Show or hide file name extensions**, and then compare your screen with Figure 1.59.

There are three ways to get help on this topic. If you scroll down the dialog box, you will see the steps involved in showing—or hiding—file extensions. Near the top of the dialog box are two other options. One walks you through the steps automatically, while you watch. The second—*guided help*—stops at each step, and you actually perform the steps.

Walks you through the
process automatically

Stops at each step and
lets you perform the step

Figure 1.59

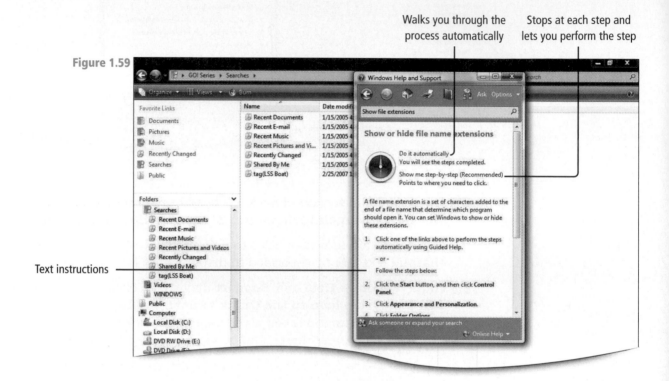

Text instructions

6 Click **Show me step-by-step (Recommended)**. In the first **Guided Help** dialog box, notice that the first step is to click the Start button, and that everything else on the screen is gray except the correct location.

7 Click the **Start** button to move to the next **Guided Help** dialog box. Continue moving through the process until the **Folder Options** dialog box displays, as shown in Figure 1.60.

Folder Options
dialog box

Next step displays in the
Guided Help dialog box

Figure 1.60

Next step is highlighted

Screen is gray

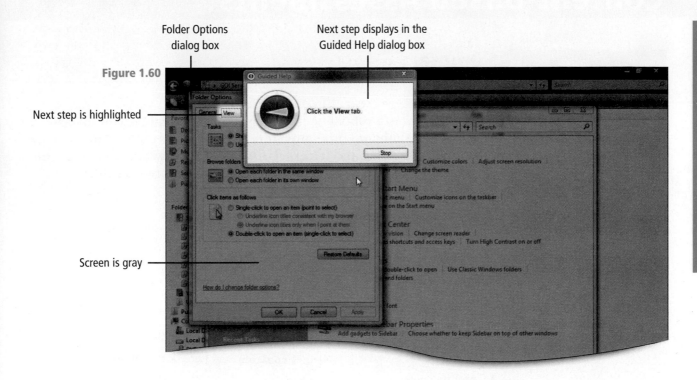

8 Unless you want to turn the file extensions on or off, in the **Guided Help** dialog box, click **Stop**, and then click **Exit**. **Close** all remaining dialog boxes and windows.

More Knowledge
Printing Help

If you wish to print the help topic for future reference, on the toolbar, click the Print button, or click the Options button, and then click Print.

End **You have completed Project 1B** ⎯⎯⎯⎯⎯

Content-Based Assessments

Summary

Windows Vista is a robust operating system that enables you to easily locate information and programs. It enables you to create, rename, move, copy, and delete files and folders. You can add key words and other information to the files to make searching easier and more accurate.

Key Terms

Active window

Address bar

Aero

All Programs

Archive

Ascending order

Cascade

CD

Click

Clipboard

Close button

Command bar

Compress

Computer icon

Content pane

Context-sensitive command

Descending order

Desktop

Desktop background

Details pane

Dialog box

Dimmed

Double-click

Drag

Drive

DVD

Edit mode

File extension

Flash drive

Folder

Folders list

Flip 3D

Gadget

Gadget controls

Graphical user interface (GUI)

Guided help

Hard drive

Horizontal scroll bar

Icon

Local disk

Maximize

Menu

Menu bar

Metadata

Minimize

Mouse pointer

Navigation pane

Network icon

Notification area

Operating system

Paint

Personal folders

Pointing

Pointer

Quick Launch toolbar

Recycle Bin

Restore

Right-click

Screen saver

ScreenTip

Scroll box

Search box

Search folder

Shortcut menu

Stacked

Start button

Start menu

Status area

Submenu

System tray

Tags

Taskbar

Thumb

Thumbnail

Title bar

Toolbar

USB drive

Vertical scroll bar

Welcome Center

Wildcard

Window name

Windows Aero

Windows Explorer

Windows Sidebar

WordPad

Content-Based Assessments

Matching

Match each term in the second column with its correct definition in the first column. Write the letter of the term on the blank line in front of the correct definition.

_____ **1.** The Vista user interface that features a three-dimensional look, with transparent window frames, live previews of open windows, and multiple color schemes.

_____ **2.** The pane on the left side of the Computer or Windows Explorer window that contains Personal folders and the Folders list.

_____ **3.** Displays information about the drive, folder, or file selected in the Content pane.

_____ **4.** A set of instructions that coordinates the activities of your computer.

_____ **5.** A computer interface that shows documents as they will look in their final form and uses icons to represent programs.

_____ **6.** Part of the Navigation pane that displays the drive and folder structure on the computer.

_____ **7.** Displays the Start button and the name of any open documents; it may also display shortcut buttons for other programs.

_____ **8.** Command at the bottom of the Start menu that takes you to all available programs on your computer.

_____ **9.** To remove the window from the screen without closing it.

_____ **10.** To increase the size of a window to fill the screen.

_____ **11.** The bar at the right side of a window that enables you to move up and down to view information that extends beyond the top and bottom of the screen.

_____ **12.** The bar at the bottom of a window that enables you to move left and right to view information that extends beyond the left and right edges of the screen.

_____ **13.** Move the mouse pointer while holding down the left mouse button, and then release at the appropriate time.

_____ **14.** Work that you save and store on a drive, such as a Word document or a PowerPoint presentation.

_____ **15.** A program that enables you to create and manage folders, and manage copy, move, sort, and delete files.

A All Programs

B Details pane

C Drag

D File

E Folders list

F Graphical user interface

G Horizontal scroll bar

H Maximize

I Minimize

J Navigation pane

K Operating system

L Taskbar

M Vertical scroll bar

N Windows Aero

O Windows Explorer

Content-Based Assessments

Fill in the Blank

Write the correct word in the space provided.

1. The files and folders stored in the selected disk drive or folder are displayed in the _____ pane.

2. The working area of the Windows Vista screen—consisting of program icons, a taskbar, a Sidebar, and a Start button—is the _____.

3. A graphic representation—often a small image on a button that enables you to run a program or program function—is a(n) _____.

4. The arrow, I-beam, or other symbol that shows the location or position of the mouse on your screen is the mouse _____.

5. The _____ area is an area on the right side of the taskbar that keeps you informed about processes that are occurring in the background, such as antivirus software, network connections, and other utility programs.

6. Custom file properties such as names, places, and descriptions that are added to files are called _____.

7. You can activate a(n) _____ menu by placing the pointer over an object and clicking the right mouse button.

8. An area to the right of the Start button that contains shortcut icons for commonly used programs is the _____ _____ toolbar.

9. The button on the left side of the taskbar that is used to start programs, change system settings, find Windows help, or shut down the computer is called the _____ button.

10. An area on the right side of the screen, the Windows _____ displays useful dynamic programs, such as a clock, a stock market ticker, or a weather window.

11. A dynamic program—such as a clock, a stock market ticker, or a weather window—that display on the desktop is a(n) _____.

12. A small storage device that plugs into a computer USB port; also called a thumb drive or a USB drive, is commonly known as a(n) _____ drive.

13. The three or four characters to the right of the period in a file name, the file _____ can be hidden or displayed.

14. You can _____ a file or files to reduce the size of the files or combine files to make them easier to send.

15. When you copy an item, it is stored in the _____, a temporary storage area in Windows.

chapterfive

Creating Documents with Microsoft Word 2007

OBJECTIVES

At the end of this chapter you will be able to:

1. Create and Save a New Document
2. Edit Text
3. Select, Delete, and Format Text
4. Print a Document

OUTCOMES

Mastering these objectives will enable you to:

PROJECT 5A

Create, Edit, Save, and Print a Document

5. Navigate the Word Window
6. Add a Graphic to a Document
7. Use the Spelling and Grammar Checker
8. Preview and Print Documents, Close a Document, and Close Word
9. Use the Microsoft Help System

PROJECT 5B

Navigate the Word Window and Check Your Work

Music School Records

Music School Records was created to launch young musical artists with undiscovered talent in jazz, classical, and contemporary music. The creative management team searches internationally for talented young people, and has a reputation for mentoring and developing the skills of its artists. The company's music is tailored to an audience that is young, knowledgeable about music, and demands the highest quality recordings. Music School Records releases are available in CD format as well as digital downloads.

© Steve Mercer / Getty Images, Inc.—Taxi

Getting Started with Microsoft Office Word 2007

A word processor is the most common program found on personal computers and one that almost everyone has a reason to use. When you learn word processing you are also learning skills and techniques that you need to work efficiently on a personal computer. You can use Microsoft Word to perform basic word processing tasks such as writing a memo, a report, or a letter. You can also use Word to complete complex word processing tasks, such as creating sophisticated tables, embedding graphics, and linking to other documents and the Internet. Word is a program that you can learn gradually, and then add more advanced skills one at a time.

Project 5A Application Letter

In Activities 5.01 through 5.11, you will create and make changes to a letter from Lucy Burroughs, Vice President of Creative Development, to William Hawken, an artist interested in becoming a client of Music School Records. Your completed document will look similar to Figure 5.1.

For Project 5A, you will need the following file:

New blank Word document

You will save your document as
5A_Application_Letter_Firstname_Lastname

Music School Records
2620 Vine Street
Los Angeles, CA 90028
323-555-0028

September 12, 2009

Mr. William Hawken
123 Eighth Street
Harrisville, MI 48740

Dear William:

Subject: Your Application to Music School Records

Thank you for submitting your application to Music School Records. Our talent scout for Northern Michigan, Catherine McDonald, is very enthusiastic about your music, and the demo CD you submitted certainly confirms her opinion.

We discuss our applications from potential clients during the first week of each month. We will have a decision for you by the second week of October.

Yours truly,

Lucy Burroughs

5A_Application_Letter_Firstname_Lastname

Figure 5.1
Project 5A—Application Letter

Objective 1
Create and Save a New Document

With a word processing program, you can type, *edit*—make changes to—move, and delete text or change the appearance of text. Because the documents that you create are stored electronically, they can be duplicated, printed, copied, and shared with others. In this project, you will become familiar with the parts of the Word window. Then you will create a document, edit and format text, and save your document.

Activity 5.01 Starting Word and Identifying Parts of the Word Window

1 On the left side of the Windows taskbar, point to, and then click the **Start** button 🏁.

2 From the **Start** menu, locate the **Word** program, and then click **Microsoft Office Word 2007**.

> The Word program may be located under All Programs or Microsoft Office or on the main Start menu.

3 If necessary, on the right side of the status bar, click the Print Layout button 🗏. If the ruler does not display, click the View tab, and then in the Show/Hide group, select the Ruler check box. Take a moment to study the parts of the Word screen shown in Figure 5.2 and described in the table in Figure 5.3.

Figure 5.2

Office button · Title bar · Vertical scroll bar · Scroll box · Ribbon · Quick Access Toolbar (yours may display a different array of buttons) · Ruler · Insertion point · Word document window · View options · Print Layout button · Status bar

	Description
	Indicates, with a blinking vertical line, where text or graphics will be inserted.
Office button	Displays a list of commands related to things you can do *with* a document, such as opening, saving, printing, or sharing.
Quick Access Toolbar	Displays buttons to perform frequently used commands with a single click.
Ribbon	Organizes commands on tabs, and then groups the commands by topic for performing related document tasks.
Ruler	Displays the location of margins, indents, columns, and tab stops for the selected paragraph(s).
Scroll box	Provides a visual indication of your location in a document. It can also be used with the mouse to drag a document up and down to reposition the document.
Status bar	Displays, on the left side, the page number, word count, and the Proof button. On the right side, displays buttons to control the look of the window.
Title bar	Displays the name of the document and the name of the program. The Minimize, Maximize/Restore Down, and Close buttons are grouped on the right side of the title bar.
Vertical scroll bar	Enables you to move up and down in a document to display text that is not visible.
View options	Contains buttons for viewing the document in Print Layout, Full Screen Reading, Web Layout, Outline, or Draft views, and also displays controls to Zoom Out and Zoom In.
Word document window	Displays the active document.

Figure 5.3

Alert!

Does your screen differ?
The appearance of the screen can vary, depending on various settings that were established when Office 2007 was installed. Additionally, the Quick Access Toolbar can display any combination of buttons.

Activity 5.02 Beginning a New Document and Displaying Formatting Marks

When you start Word, you need only start typing to create a new document.

Note — Comparing Your Screen with the Figures in This Textbook
Your screen will match the figures shown in this textbook if you set your screen resolution to 1024 × 768. At other resolutions, your screen will closely resemble, but not match, the figures shown. To view your screen's resolution, on the Windows desktop, right-click in a blank area, click Personalize, and then click Display Settings.

1 On the title bar, notice that *Document1* displays.

Word displays the file name of a document in both the title bar at the top of the screen and on a button in the Windows taskbar at the lower edge of the screen. New unsaved documents display *Document* followed by a number.

2 In the displayed blank document, determine if a paragraph symbol (¶) displays in the upper left corner of the document, as shown in Figure 5.4. If you do *not* see the paragraph symbol, on the Ribbon, on the Home tab, in the Paragraph group, click the Show/Hide ¶ button ¶.

When you press Enter, Spacebar, or Tab on your keyboard, characters display in your document to represent these keystrokes. These characters do not print and are referred to as *formatting marks* or *nonprinting characters*. These marks will display throughout this instruction.

Figure 5.4
Default document name
Show/Hide ¶ button
Paragraph symbol
No Spacing style button

3 Click the **Show/Hide ¶** button ¶ to turn off the display of nonprinting characters. Then, click the **Show/Hide ¶** button ¶ one more time to turn it on again.

The Show/Hide ¶ button is referred to as a *toggle button*—you can click the button one time to turn it on and click it again to turn it off.

4 On the **Home tab**, in the **Styles group**, click the **No Spacing** style button.

By default, Word adds spacing after each paragraph. The No Spacing button applies a style to the text that removes extra spacing. A *style* is a set of formatting characteristics—such as line spacing, space after paragraphs, font, and font style—that can be applied to text, paragraphs, tables, or lists.

Activity 5.03 Entering Text and Inserting Blank Lines

Business letters follow a standard format and contain the following parts: the current date—the *date line*; the name and address of the person receiving the letter—the *inside address*; a greeting—the *salutation*; an optional subject—the *subject line*; the body of the letter; a closing line—the *complimentary closing*; and the *writer's identification*, which includes the name or job title (or both) of the writer. Some letters also include the initials of the person who prepared the letter, and a list of *enclosures*—documents included with the letter.

1 With the insertion point blinking in the upper left corner of the document, to the left of the default first paragraph mark, type **Music School Records** and then press Enter.

> The first paragraph is complete and the insertion point is positioned at the beginning of the next line. A paragraph is created when you press Enter. Thus, a paragraph can be a single line or a blank line.

2 Type the following and press Enter after each line:

> **2620 Vine Street**
> **Los Angeles, CA 90028**
> **323-555-0028**

3 Press Enter five times, type **Sept** and then compare your screen with Figure 5.5.

> A ScreenTip displays *September (Press ENTER to Insert)*. This feature, called ***AutoComplete***, assists you in typing. After you type the first few characters, AutoComplete suggests commonly used words and phrases to enter. A ***ScreenTip*** is a small note, activated by pointing to a button or other screen object, which displays information about a screen element.

Figure 5.5

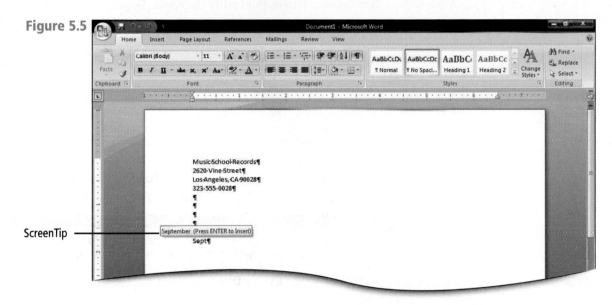

ScreenTip

4 To finish the word *September*, press Enter. Press Spacebar, type **12, 2009** and then press Enter. If you are completing this activity during the month of September, AutoComplete may offer to fill in the current date. To ignore the suggestion, continue typing as indicated.

5 Press Enter two times.

6 Type **Mr. William Hawken** and then press Enter.

> The wavy red line under the proper name *Hawken* indicates that the word has been flagged as misspelled because it is a word not contained in the Word dictionary.

7 On two lines, type the following address, but do not press Enter at the end of the second line:

> **123 Eighth Street**
> **Harrisville, MI 48740**

Note — Typing the Address

Include a comma after the city name in an inside address. However, for mailing addresses on envelopes, eliminate the comma after the city name.

8 On the **Home tab**, in the **Styles group**, click the **Normal** button.

> Word applies the Normal style to the text in the remainder of the document. Recall that the Normal style adds extra space between paragraphs; it also adds slightly more space between lines in a paragraph.

9 Press Enter. Type the salutation **Dear William:** and then press Enter.

10 Type **Subject: Your Application to Music School Records** and press Enter. Notice the light dots between words, which indicate spaces and display when formatting marks are displayed. Also, notice the extra space below each paragraph, and then compare your screen with Figure 5.6.

> The subject line is optional, but it is good practice to include a subject line in most letters to identify the topic. Depending on your Word settings, a wavy green line may display in the subject line, indicating a potential grammar error.

Note — Locating the Subject Line

According to *The Gregg Reference Manual*, Tenth Edition (William A. Sabin, McGraw Hill/Irwin, Boston, 2005), the subject line is placed between the salutation and the body of the letter. *Business Communication Process and Product*, Fourth Edition (Mary Ellen Guffey, South-Western College Publishing, Boston, 2003) indicates, "Although experts suggest placing the subject line 1 blank line below the salutation, many businesses actually place it above the salutation. Use whatever style your organization prefers."

Figure 5.6

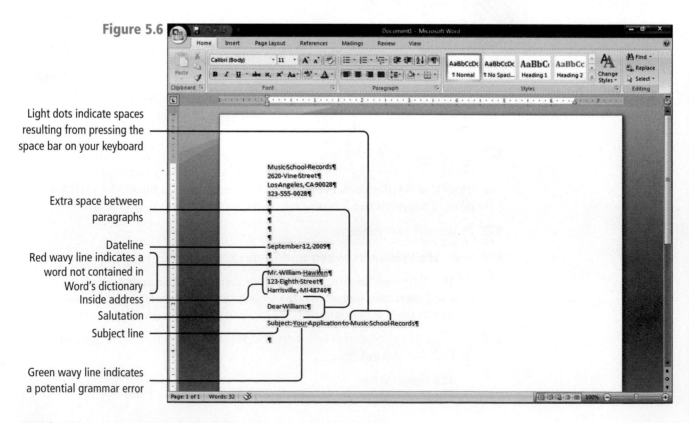

Light dots indicate spaces resulting from pressing the space bar on your keyboard

Extra space between paragraphs

Dateline

Red wavy line indicates a word not contained in Word's dictionary

Inside address

Salutation

Subject line

Green wavy line indicates a potential grammar error

Activity 5.04 Creating Folders for Document Storage and Saving a Document

In the same way that you use file folders to organize your paper documents, Windows uses a hierarchy of electronic folders to keep your electronic files organized. Changes that you make to existing documents, such as changing text or typing in new text, are not permanently saved until you perform a Save operation.

1 In the upper left corner of your screen, click the **Office** button ⬜, and from the menu, point to the words **Save As**—not the Save As arrow—and click.

2 In the **Save As** dialog box, in the **Navigation** pane, click **Computer** to view a list of available drives, as shown in Figure 5.7. If you are saving your files on your hard drive, in the Navigation pane, click Documents.

Figure 5.7

Your list of available drives will differ

New Folder button

Displays documents on the hard drive

Displays a list of storage devices

Navigation pane

3 Navigate to the location in which you will be storing your folders and projects for this chapter—for example, a USB flash drive, a shared drive on a network, the Documents folder on your computer's hard drive, or the drive designated by your instructor or lab coordinator.

4 In the **Save As** dialog box, on the toolbar, click the **New Folder** button. With **New Folder** displayed in edit mode, type **Word Chapter 5** as shown in Figure 5.8, and then press Enter. If the new folder is not displayed in edit mode, right-click the words *New Folder*, and then from the shortcut menu, click Rename and type the new folder name.

A **shortcut menu** is a context-sensitive menu that displays commands relevant to the selected object. The new folder name displays in the Address bar, indicating that the folder is open and ready to store your document. The folder is currently empty.

Figure 5.8

New folder name
in edit mode

5 In the lower portion of the **Save As** dialog box, locate the **File name** box. If necessary, select or delete the existing text, and then in the **File name** box, using your own first and last names, type **5A_Application_ Letter_Firstname_Lastname** being sure to include the underscore— ⬆Shift + - —instead of spaces between words, as shown in Figure 5.9.

The Microsoft Windows operating system recognizes file names with spaces. However, some Internet file transfer programs do not. To facilitate sending your files over the Internet, in this textbook you will be instructed to save files using an underscore instead of a space.

Figure 5.9

Underscore characters
in file name

6 In the lower portion of the **Save As** dialog box, click the **Save** button. The file extension *.docx* may or may not display, depending on your Word settings.

Word saves your file on the storage device that you selected in the *Word Chapter 5* folder with the new file name. The new file name also displays in the title bar.

7 As you type the following text, press Spacebar only one time at the end of a sentence: **Thank you for submitting your application to Music School Records. Our talent scout for Northern Michigan, Catherine McDonald, is really very enthusiastic about your music, and the demo CD you submitted certainly confirms her opinion.** Press Enter.

As you type, the insertion point moves to the right, and when it approaches the right margin, Word determines whether or not the next word in the line will fit within the established right margin. If the word does not fit, Word will move the whole word down to the next line. This feature, called ***wordwrap***, enables you to type without having to press Enter to end a line. Press Enter *only* when you reach the end of a paragraph.

> **Note** — **Spacing Between Sentences**
>
> Although you may have learned to press Spacebar two times at the end of a sentence, now it is common practice to space only one time between sentences.

8 Type **We discuss our applications from clients during the last week of each month. We will try to have a decision for you by the second week of October.**

9 Press Enter. Type **Yours truly,** and then press Enter two times.

10 Type **John W. Diamond** and then compare your screen with Figure 5.10.

As you reach the bottom of the screen, the page scrolls up to enable you to read what you are typing.

Figure 5.10

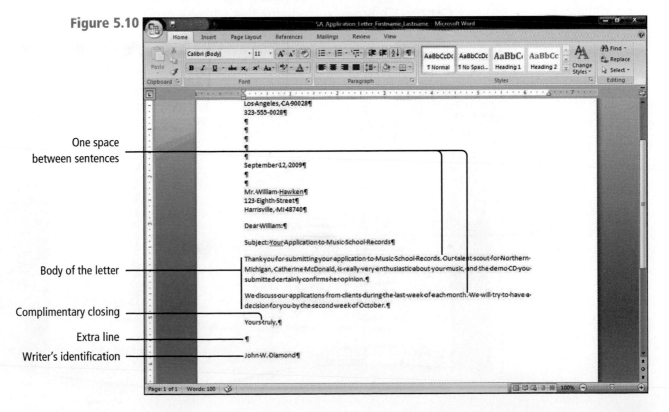

One space between sentences

Body of the letter

Complimentary closing

Extra line

Writer's identification

11 On the Ribbon, click the **Page Layout tab**. In the **Page Setup group**, click the **Margins** button to display the Margins gallery, as shown in Figure 5.11.

A *gallery* displays a list of potential results.

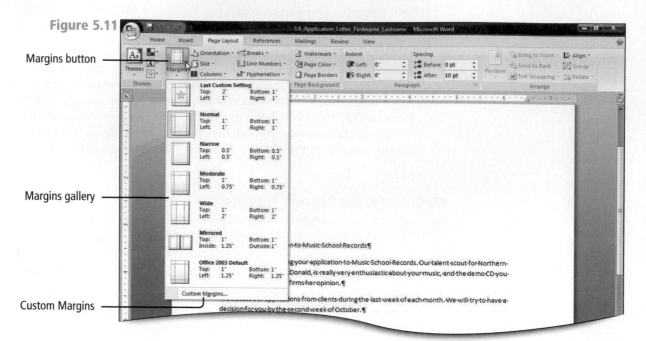

Figure 5.11

Margins button

Margins gallery

Custom Margins

12 At the bottom of the **Margins gallery**, click **Custom Margins** to display the **Page Setup** dialog box.

13 Near the top of the **Page Setup** dialog box, click the **Layout tab**. Under **Page**, click the **Vertical alignment arrow**, and then click **Center**. Compare your dialog box with Figure 5.12.

Figure 5.12

Layout tab

Center

14 In the lower right corner of the **Page Setup** dialog box, click **OK**. Notice that the text is centered vertically on the page, which makes the letter more visually appealing.

15 On the **Quick Access Toolbar**, click the **Save** button 💾 to save the changes you have made to the letter since your last save operation.

> ### More Knowledge — Letter Placement
>
> According to *The Gregg Reference Manual*, Tenth Edition, a one-page letter typed on blank stationery may be centered vertically in this manner. If you are using letterhead stationery, leave at least a 0.5-inch space between the letterhead and the first element typed. Always consult trusted references when deciding on the proper formats for your personal and professional documents.

Objective 2
Edit Text

When you change text or formatting in a document, you are editing the text. Two commonly used editing tools are the Delete key and the Backspace key. The Backspace and Delete keys on your keyboard remove text from the screen one character at a time. Backspace removes a character to the left of the insertion point; Delete removes a character to the right of the insertion point.

Activity 5.05 Editing Text with the Delete and Backspace Keys

1 Using the vertical scroll bar, scroll as necessary to view the paragraph beginning *Thank you*. In the middle of the second line of the paragraph, click to position your insertion point to the left of the *v* in the word *very* and then press ⌫ Bksp. Compare your screen with Figure 5.13.

Word removes the space between the words *really* and *very*.

Figure 5.13

Insertion point

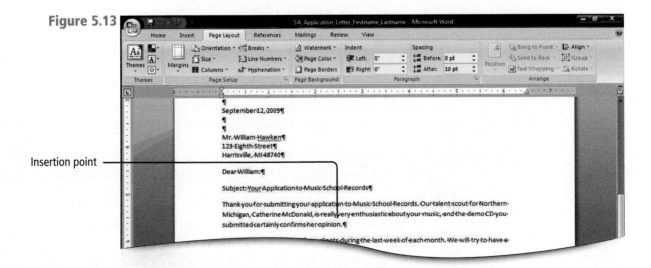

2 With the insertion point between the two words, press ⌫Bksp six times.

The word *really* is removed. Be sure there is only one dot—recall that dots are the formatting marks that indicate spaces—between *is* and *very*. You can see that when editing text, it is useful to display formatting marks.

3 In the paragraph beginning *We discuss*, in the first line, locate the phrase *try to* and then click to position the insertion point to the left of the word *to*.

4 Press ⌫Bksp four times to remove the word *try* and the extra space. Press Delete three times, and then compare your screen with Figure 5.14.

The word *to* at the right of the insertion point is removed, along with the space following the word. Be sure there is only one dot (space) between *will* and *have*.

Figure 5.14

One space

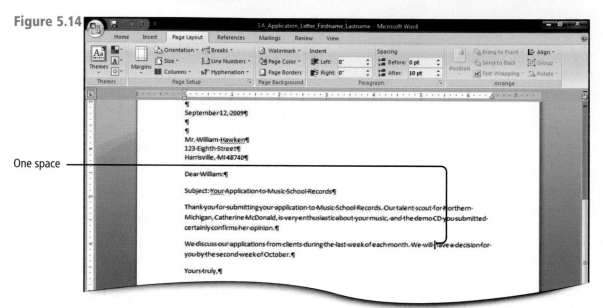

5 On the **Quick Access Toolbar**, click the **Save** button.

Activity 5.06 Inserting New Text

When you place the insertion point in the middle of a word or sentence and start typing, the existing text moves to the right to make space for your new keystrokes. This is called ***insert mode*** and is the default setting in Word.

1 In the paragraph beginning *We discuss*, in the first line, click to place the insertion point to the left of the letter *c* in the word *clients*.

2 Type **potential** and then press Spacebar.

As you type, the existing text moves to the right to make space for your new keystrokes.

3 In the last line of the document, click to place the insertion point to the left of *John W. Diamond*.

4 Type **Lucy Burroughs** and then press Delete until the name *John W. Diamond* is removed. Compare your screen with Figure 5.15.

Figure 5.15

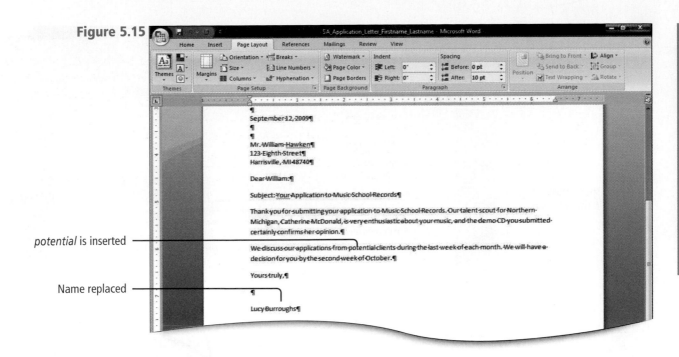

potential is inserted ————

Name replaced ————

5 **Save** 💾 the changes you have made to your document.

Objective 3
Select, Delete, and Format Text

Selecting text refers to highlighting, by dragging with your mouse, areas of text so that the text can be edited, formatted, copied, or moved. Word recognizes a selected area of text as one unit, to which you can make changes. ***Formatting text*** is the process of setting the overall appearance of text by changing the text layout, color, shading, emphasis, or font characteristics.

Activity 5.07 Selecting and Deleting Text

1 In the paragraph beginning *Thank you*, position the ⌶ pointer to the left of *Thank*, hold down the left mouse button, and then drag to the right to select the first sentence including the ending period and its following space, as shown in Figure 5.16. Release the mouse button.

> The first sentence of the paragraph is selected, and a Mini toolbar displays above and to the right of the selected text. ***Dragging*** is the technique of holding down the left mouse button and moving over an area of text. Selected text is indicated when the background changes to a light blue or gray.

> The ***Mini toolbar*** displays buttons that are commonly used with the selected object. When you move the pointer away from the Mini toolbar, it fades from view. Selecting text may require some practice. If you are not satisfied with your result, click anywhere and begin again.

Figure 5.16

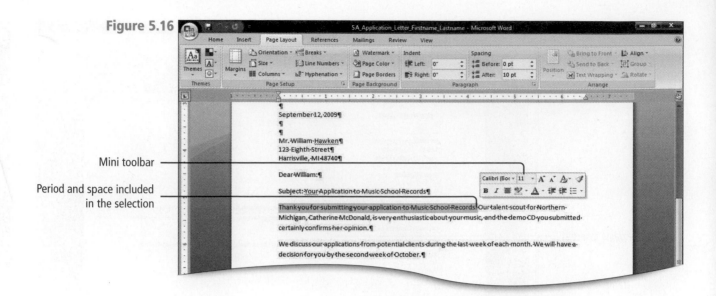

Mini toolbar

Period and space included in the selection

2 Click anywhere in the document to deselect the sentence. Then, in the same sentence, move the pointer over the word *Music* and **double-click**—click the left mouse button two times in rapid succession.

> The entire word is selected and the Mini toolbar displays. Double-clicking takes a steady hand. The speed of the two clicks is not difficult (although you only have about a second between clicks), but you must hold the mouse perfectly still between the two clicks.

3 Click anywhere in the document to deselect the word *Music*. Then, in the paragraph that begins *We discuss*, point to the word *last* and double-click. Type **first** and notice that when you type the first letter, the selected word is deleted.

4 In the paragraph beginning *Thank you*, point to the word *Music*, and then triple-click the left mouse button.

> The entire paragraph is selected. You can triple-click anywhere in a paragraph to select the entire paragraph.

5 Hold down [Ctrl] and press [A] to select the entire document, as shown in Figure 5.17.

> Holding down [Ctrl] and typing a letter to perform a command is called a **keyboard shortcut**. There are many keyboard shortcuts for selecting text. Take a moment to study the shortcuts shown in the table in Figure 5.18.

Figure 5.17

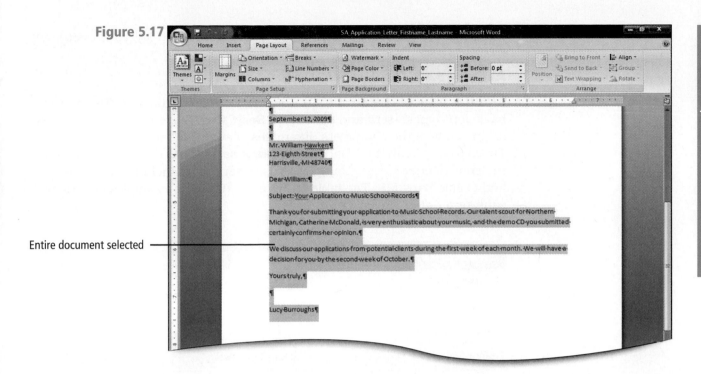

Entire document selected

Selecting Text in a Document

To Select	Do This
A portion of text	Click to position the insertion point at the beginning of the text you want to select, hold down ⟨⇧ Shift⟩, and then click at the end of the text you want to select. Alternatively, hold down the left mouse button and drag from the beginning to the end of the text you want to select.
A word	Double-click the word.
A sentence	Hold down ⟨Ctrl⟩ and click anywhere in the sentence.
A paragraph	Triple-click anywhere in the paragraph; or, move the pointer to the left of the line, into the margin area. When the pointer displays, double-click.
A line	Move the pointer to the left of the line. When the pointer displays, click one time.
One character at a time	Position the insertion point to the left of the first character, hold down ⟨⇧ Shift⟩, and press → or ← as many times as desired.
A string of words	Position the insertion point to the left of the first word, hold down ⟨⇧ Shift⟩ and ⟨Ctrl⟩, and then press ← or → as many times as desired.
Consecutive lines	Position the insertion point to the left of the first word, hold down ⟨⇧ Shift⟩ and press ↑ or ↓.
Consecutive paragraphs	Position the insertion point to the left of the first word, hold down ⟨⇧ Shift⟩ and ⟨Ctrl⟩ and press ↑ or ↓.
The entire document	Hold down ⟨Ctrl⟩ and press Ⓐ. Alternatively, move the pointer to the left of any line in the document. When the pointer displays, triple-click.

Figure 5.18

6 Click anywhere to cancel the text selection. **Save** 🖫 your document.

Activity 5.08 Changing Font and Font Size

A *font* is a set of characters with the same design and shape. There are two basic font types—serif and sans serif. *Serif fonts* have extensions or lines on the ends of the characters. Examples of serif fonts include Cambria, Times New Roman, and Garamond. *Sans serif fonts* do not have lines on the ends of characters. Examples of sans serif fonts include Calibri, Arial, and Comic Sans MS. The table in Figure 5.19 shows examples of serif and sans serif fonts.

Examples of Serif and Sans Serif Fonts	
Serif Fonts	**Sans Serif Fonts**
Cambria	Calibri
Times New Roman	Arial
Garamond	Comic Sans MS

Figure 5.19

1 Hold down Ctrl and press A to select the entire document.

2 Click the **Home tab**, and then in the **Font group**, click the **Font button arrow**. At the top of the **Font gallery**, under **Theme Fonts**, point to—but do not click—**Cambria**. Notice that the font in the document changes to a preview of the Cambria font, as shown in Figure 5.20.

> This is an example of *Live Preview*—a technology that shows the results of applying editing or formatting changes as you point to selections in a gallery or list. Here, Live Preview changes the selected text to the Cambria font, even though you did not click the font name.

> A *theme* is a predefined set of colors, fonts, lines, and fill effects that look good together and that can be applied to your entire document or to specific items—for example, to a paragraph or table. As you progress in your study of Word, you will use more theme features.

Figure 5.20
Font button arrow
Theme Fonts
Live Preview displays the document in the chosen font
List of fonts

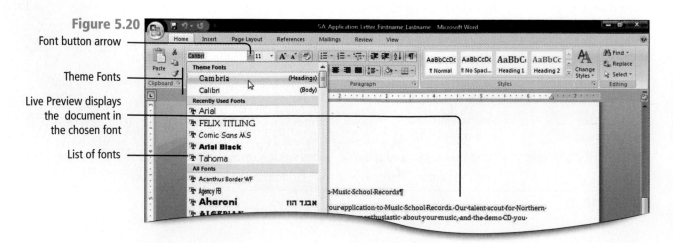

3 Click **Cambria** to apply the font to the entire document. On the **Home tab**, in the **Font group**, click the **Font Size button arrow** `12 ▾`, click **12**, and then click anywhere to cancel the selection.

> Fonts are measured in *points*, with one point equal to 1/72 of an inch. A higher point size indicates a larger font size. For large amounts of text, font sizes between 10 point and 12 point are good choices. Headings and titles are often formatted by using a larger font size. The word *point* is abbreviated as *pt*.

4 Scroll up, and then move the pointer into the left margin area, slightly to the left of the first line of the document—*Music School Records*. When the ⌐ pointer displays, click one time to select the entire first line of text.

5 On the Mini toolbar, click the **Font button arrow**, scroll down if necessary, and then click **Arial Black**.

6 With the Mini toolbar still displayed, click the **Font Size button arrow** `12 ▾`, and then click **20**.

7 Position the ⌐ pointer to the left of the second line of the document—*2620 Vine Street*. Drag down to select the second, third, and fourth lines of the document, ending with the telephone number.

8 On the Mini toolbar, click the **Font button arrow**, and then click **Arial**. With the Mini toolbar still displayed, click the **Font Size button arrow** `12 ▾`, and then click **10**. Click anywhere to cancel the selection, and then compare your screen with Figure 5.21.

Figure 5.21

20 point Arial Black font
10 point Arial font

Note — Moving Quickly in a Long List

The list of available fonts is frequently very long. You can move quickly to any font by typing the first (or even first and second) letter of the font after you click the Font button arrow.

9 **Save** 🖫 the changes you have made to your document.

Activity 5.09 Adding Emphasis to Text

Font styles emphasize text and are a visual cue to draw the reader's eye to important text. Font styles include bold, italic, and underline, although underline is not commonly used for emphasis.

1 Point anywhere in the first line of text—*Music School Records*—and triple-click to select the paragraph. Then, on the Mini toolbar, click the **Bold** button **B** to apply bold emphasis to the paragraph that forms the first line of the letterhead.

2 On the **Home tab**, in the **Font group**, click the **Underline** button **U** .

Another Way

— To Apply Font Styles

Use the keyboard shortcuts of Ctrl + B for bold, Ctrl + I for italic, or Ctrl + U for underline.

---

3 Position the pointer to the left of the second line of the document— *2620 Vine Street*. Drag down to select the second, third, and fourth lines of the document, ending with the telephone number.

4 On the Mini toolbar, click the **Italic** button **I** to apply italic emphasis to the paragraphs that form the remainder of the letterhead. Click anywhere to cancel the selection.

5 From the **Office** menu , point to **Print**, and then click **Print Preview**. Compare your screen with Figure 5.22.

The Ribbon displays the Print Preview ***program tab***, which replaces the standard set of tabs when you switch to certain authoring modes or views, including Print Preview. Print Preview displays the entire page and enables you to see what the document will look like when printed.

Note — Viewing Keyboard Shortcuts

The key combinations for Ctrl keyboard shortcuts are identified in the ScreenTip for each button. The Alt keyboard shortcuts are displayed by pressing and then releasing the Alt key.

Figure 5.22

Print Preview program tab

Close Print Preview button

Bold, underlined text

Text with italic emphasis

Document displayed in Print Preview

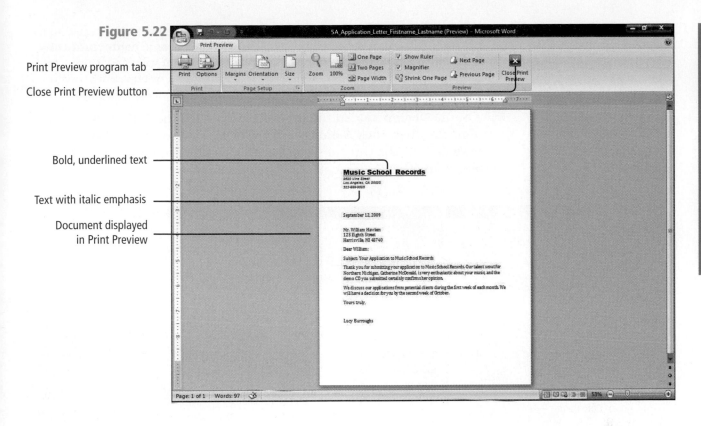

On the **Print Preview tab**, in the **Preview group**, click the **Close Print Preview** button, and then **Save** 🖫 your changes.

Objective 4
Print a Document

Information in headers and footers helps identify a document when it is printed. A *header* is information that prints at the top of every page; a *footer* is information that prints at the bottom of every page.

Activity 5.10 Accessing Headers and Footers

1️⃣ Click the **Insert tab**, and then, in the **Header & Footer group**, click the **Footer** button.

Another Way

To Open a Footer
Scroll to the bottom of the page, right-click near the bottom edge of the page, and then click Edit Footer to open the footer area.

2️⃣ At the bottom of the **Footer gallery**, click **Edit Footer**.

The footer area displays with the insertion point blinking at the left edge of the footer area. Because the footer area is active, the contextual tools *Header & Footer Tools* display and add contextual tabs—in this instance the Design tab—next to the standard tabs on the Ribbon.

Contextual tools enable you to perform specific commands related to the active area or selected object, and display one or more ***contextual tabs*** that contain related ***groups*** of commands that you will need. Contextual tools display only when needed for a selected area or object; when you deselect the area or object, the contextual tools no longer display.

3 On the **Design tab**, in the **Insert group**, click the **Quick Parts** button, and then click **Field**. In the **Field** dialog box, under **Field names**, use the vertical scroll bar to examine the items that you can insert in a header or footer, as shown in Figure 5.23.

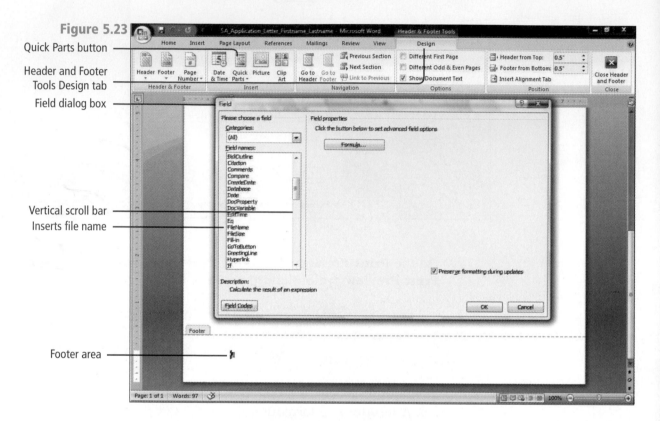

Figure 5.23
Quick Parts button
Header and Footer Tools Design tab
Field dialog box
Vertical scroll bar
Inserts file name
Footer area

4 In the **Field names** list, scroll as necessary to locate and click **FileName**, and then click **OK**.

The file name displays in the Footer area. The file extension *.docx* may or may not display, depending on your Windows settings.

5 Double-click anywhere in the document to close the footer area. Alternatively, in the Close group, click the Close Header and Footer button. Scroll down until you can see the footer, and then compare your screen with Figure 5.24.

The footer displays in gray. Because it is a proper name and is likely not in Word's dictionary, your name in the footer may display with wavy red lines.

Figure 5.24

File name inserted in the footer

6 **Save** 🖫 your document.

More Knowledge — Moving to the Header or Footer

To quickly edit an existing header or footer, double-click in the header or footer area. This will display the Header & Footer contextual tools and place the insertion point at the beginning of the header or footer.

Activity 5.11 Printing a Document

1 Check your *Chapter Assignment Sheet* or *Course Syllabus*, or consult your instructor, to determine if you are to submit your assignments on paper or electronically. To submit electronically, go to Step 3, and then follow the instructions provided by your instructor.

2 Click the **Office** button 🔘, point to the **Print arrow**, and then click **Quick Print**.

> One copy of your document prints on the default printer connected to your system. The formatting marks that indicate spaces and paragraphs do not print.

3 From the **Office** menu 🔘, click **Close**, saving any changes if prompted to do so. Leave Word open for the next project.

Another Way

To Print a Document

To print a document:

- From the Office menu, click Print to display the Print dialog box, from which you can choose a variety of different options, such as printing multiple copies, printing on a different printer, and printing some but not all pages.

- Hold down Ctrl, and then press P. This is an alternative to the Office menu command, and opens the Print dialog box.

- Press and release Alt, press F, and then press P to open the Print dialog box.

End **You have completed Project 5A** ————————————————

Project 5B **Company Overview**

In Activities 5.12 through 5.23, you will create a document that describes the mission of Music School Records. You will add a graphic image to the document, and insert text from another document. Your completed document will look similar to Figure 5.25.

For Project 5B, you will need the following files:

w05B_Music_School_Records
w05B_Music_Logo

You will save your document as
5B_Company_Overview_Firstname_Lastname

Figure 5.25
Project 5B—Company Overview

Objective 5
Navigate the Word Window

Most Word documents are longer than the Word window—some are wider than the window. Use the scroll bars to *navigate*—move around in—a document.

Activity 5.12 Opening and Closing an Existing Document

1 If necessary, **Start** 🔲 Word. From the **Office** menu 🔲, click **Open**.

2 Navigate to the location where the student files for this textbook are stored, which may be on a CD that came with your textbook or in some other location designated by your instructor.

3 Locate **w05B_Music_School_Records** and click to select it. Then, in the lower right corner of the **Open** dialog box, click the **Open** button.

4 If necessary, on the Home tab, in the Paragraph group, click the Show/Hide ¶ button 🔲 to display the nonprinting characters.

> The document displays in the Word window. This text will be inserted into a new document in Activity 5.13.

5 From the **Office** menu 🔲, click **Close** to close the document and leave Word open.

Activity 5.13 Inserting Existing Text into a New Document

1 From the **Office** menu 🔲, click **New** to display the **New Document** dialog box. Notice that the *Blank document* button is selected by default. Compare your screen with Figure 5.26.

Figure 5.26

New Document dialog box —

Blank document button —

Create button —

2 In the lower right corner of the **New Document** dialog box, click **Create** to create a new document. Type **Music School Records** and then press Enter.

3 Click the **Insert tab**. In the **Text group**, click the **Object button arrow**, and then click **Text from File**.

Alert!

Did the Object dialog box display?

If the Object dialog box displays, then you clicked the Object *button* instead of the Object *button arrow*. Close the Object dialog box, and then in the Text group, click the Object button arrow, as shown in Figure 5.27. Click *Text from File*, and then continue with Step 4.

4 In the **Insert File** dialog box, navigate to your student files. Locate **w05B_Music_School_Records**, click to select it, and then in the lower right corner, click the **Insert** button. Compare your screen with Figure 5.27.

A copy of the text from the w05B_Music_School_Records document is inserted into the blank document, the last page of the three-page document displays, and the insertion point displays at the end of the inserted text. The original w05B_Music_School_Records document remains intact. The page number, total number of pages in the document, and number of words in the document display in the status bar.

Figure 5.27

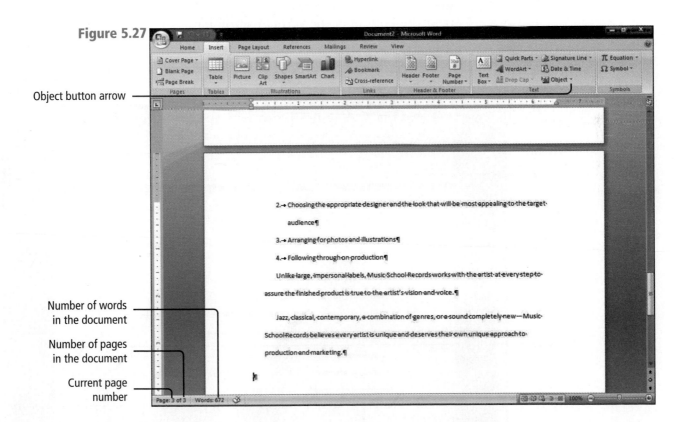

Object button arrow

Number of words in the document

Number of pages in the document

Current page number

5 Press ⌫Bksp to delete the blank line at the end of the document. On the **Quick Access Toolbar**, click **Save** 🖫. In the **Save As** dialog box, navigate to your **Word Chapter 5** folder.

> Recall that because this is a new unnamed document—*Document2* or some other number displays in the title bar—the *Save As* dialog box displays so that you can name and designate a storage location for the document. The first line of text in the document displays in the *File name* box.

6 In the **File name** box, delete any existing text. Using your own name, type **5B_Company_Overview_Firstname_ Lastname** and then click **Save**.

7 On the **Insert tab**, in the **Header & Footer group**, click the **Footer** button. At the bottom of the **Footer gallery**, click **Edit Footer**.

8 On the **Design tab**, in the **Insert group**, click the **Quick Parts** button, and then click **Field**. In the **Field** dialog box, under **Field names**, locate and click **FileName**, and then click **OK**.

9 Double-click anywhere in the document to close the footer area. **Save** 🖫 your document.

Activity 5.14 Navigating a Document

1 At the right of your screen, in the vertical scroll bar, locate the **up scroll arrow** ▲ at the top of the scroll bar, as shown in Figure 5.28. Then, click the **up scroll arrow** ▲ five times. Notice that the document scrolls up one line at a time. Also, notice that the scroll box is near the bottom of the vertical scroll bar.

Figure 5.28

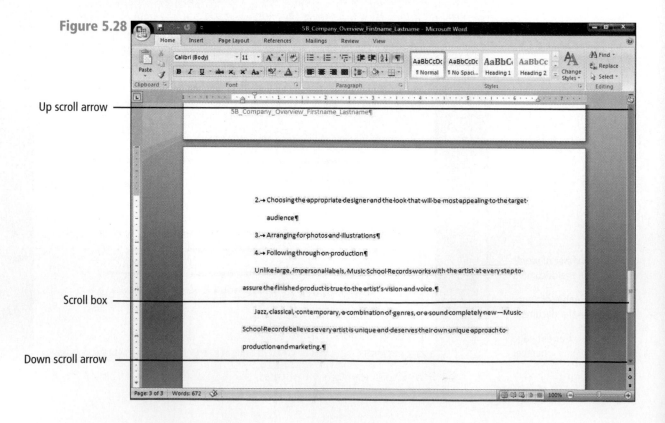

Up scroll arrow

Scroll box

Down scroll arrow

2 Point to the **up scroll arrow** ▲ again. Click and hold down the mouse button for several seconds.

The document text scrolls up continuously, one line at a time.

3 At the top of the vertical scroll bar, point to the **up scroll arrow** ▲, and then click and hold down the mouse button until you have scrolled to the beginning of the document. As you do so, notice that the scroll box moves up in the scroll bar.

4 Near the top of the vertical scroll bar, point to the **scroll box**, and then press and hold down the left mouse button. Compare your screen with Figure 5.29.

A ScreenTip displays, indicating the page number. The page number and total number of pages in the document display in the status bar—in this instance, page 1 of 3 pages.

Figure 5.29

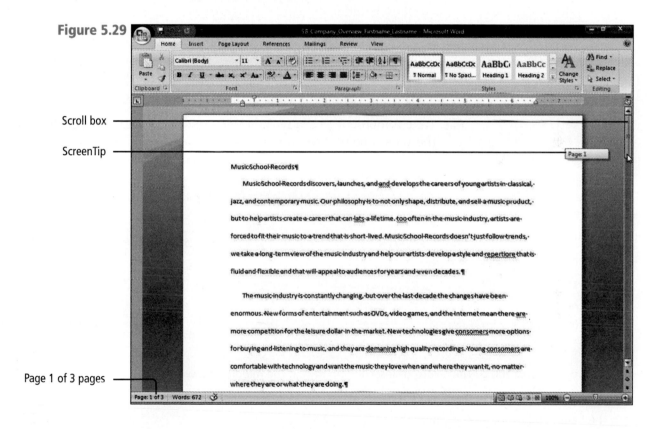

Scroll box

ScreenTip

Page 1 of 3 pages

5 Drag the **scroll box** slowly down to the bottom of the scroll bar. As you do so, notice that the ScreenTip changes as each new page reaches the top of the screen.

6 Release the mouse button, and then click in the dark area just above the scroll box.

The document scrolls up one screen. This is a quick way to scan a document.

7 Practice clicking in the area above and below the scroll box.

Another Way

To Scroll Through a Document

If your mouse has a small wheel button between the left and right mouse buttons, you can scroll up and down in the document by rotating the wheel.

8 On your keyboard, hold down Ctrl and press Home.

The beginning of the document displays, and the insertion point moves to the left of the first word in the document. In this document, Word has flagged some spelling, grammar, and contextual errors (red, green, and blue wavy lines), which you will correct in Activity 5.19.

Alert!

Does the shortcut work?

If you are using a laptop computer, you may have to hold down a function Fn key to use shortcuts that involve the Home, End, Page Up, and PgDn keys.

9 Hold down Ctrl and press End.

10 Press PgUp to scroll the document up one screen. Press End.

The insertion point moves to the end of the current line of text.

11 Take a moment to study the table shown in Figure 5.30, which lists the most useful keyboard shortcuts.

Navigating a Document Using Keyboard Shortcuts

To Move	Press
To the beginning of a document	Ctrl + Home
To the end of a document	Ctrl + End
To the beginning of a line	Home
To the end of a line	End
To the beginning of the previous word	Ctrl + ←
To the beginning of the next word	Ctrl + →
To the beginning of the current word (if insertion point is in the middle of a word)	Ctrl + ←
To the beginning of the previous paragraph	Ctrl + ↑
To the beginning of the next paragraph	Ctrl + ↓
To the beginning of the current paragraph (if insertion point is in the middle of a paragraph)	Ctrl + ↑
Up one screen	PgUp
Down one screen	PgDn

Figure 5.30

12 Hold down [Ctrl] and press [Home] to position the insertion point at the beginning of the document.

Activity 5.15 Changing Document Views

1 Near the right side of the status bar, locate the **View** buttons.

Note — Viewing Documents

There are five ways to view your document on the screen. Each view is useful in different situations.

- *Print Layout view* displays the page borders, margins, text, and graphics as they will look when you print the document. Because Word users commonly prefer this view for most tasks, it is the default view.
- *Full Screen Reading view* creates easy-to-read pages that fit on the screen to increase legibility. This view does not represent the pages as they would print. Each screen page is labeled with a screen number, rather than a page number.
- *Web Layout view* shows how the document will look when saved as a Web page and viewed in a Web browser.
- *Outline view* shows the organizational structure of your document by headings and subheadings and can be collapsed and expanded to look at individual sections of a document.
- *Draft view* simplifies the page layout for quick typing, and shows a little more text on the screen than the Print Layout view. Graphics, headers, and footers do not display.

---

2 Click the **Draft** button 📄, and then examine the document display.

3 Click the **Full Screen Reading** button 📖.

Text displays in a side-by-side format, and can be read like a book.

4 Near the upper right corner of the screen, click the **Close** button to display the document in Print Layout view.

Activity 5.16 Using the Zoom Slider

To *zoom* means to increase or decrease the viewing area of the screen. You can zoom in to look closely at a particular section of a document, and then zoom out to see an entire page on the screen. You can also zoom to view multiple pages on the screen.

1 On the right side of the status bar, just to the right of the View buttons, drag the **Zoom slider** to the right until you have zoomed to approximately 150%, as shown in Figure 5.31.

Figure 5.31

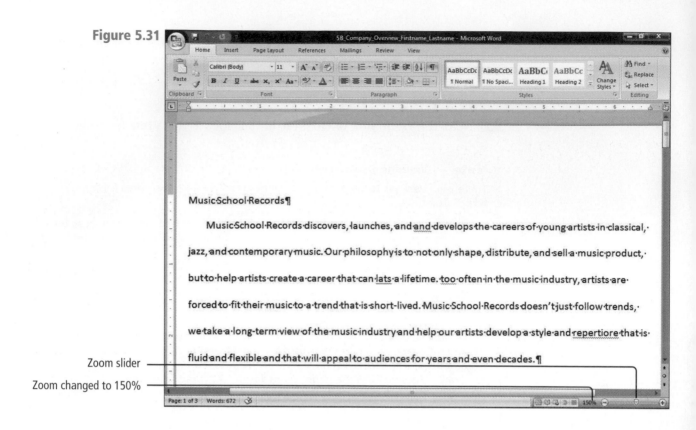

Zoom slider

Zoom changed to 150%

2 Drag the **Zoom slider** to the left until you have zoomed to approximately 40%, as shown in Figure 5.32. Notice that as the pages get smaller, multiple pages display.

Figure 5.32

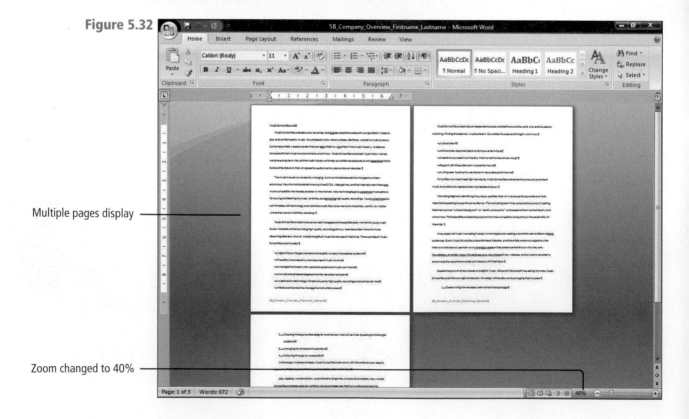

Multiple pages display

Zoom changed to 40%

3 Drag the **Zoom slider** to the right until you have zoomed to a page size with which you are comfortable—typically 100%.

> As you work on various documents, adjust the zoom to best display the document.

Another Way

To Change the Zoom

You can click the page percentage label to the right of the View buttons to open the Zoom dialog box. Here you can specify the exact page percentage you want, stretch the page to the width of the screen, or display several pages at once.

Activity 5.17 Splitting Windows and Arranging Panes

You can split the Word screen so that you can look at two different parts of the same document at the same time. You can also view two documents side by side and make comparisons between the two.

1 Press [Ctrl] + [Home] to move the insertion point to the beginning of the document. Click the **View tab**, and then, in the **Window group**, click the **Split** button. Compare your screen with Figure 5.33.

> A **split bar** displays near the middle of the document area, with a move pointer ⊕ on the bar. The split bar indicates the location of the border between the windows.

Figure 5.33

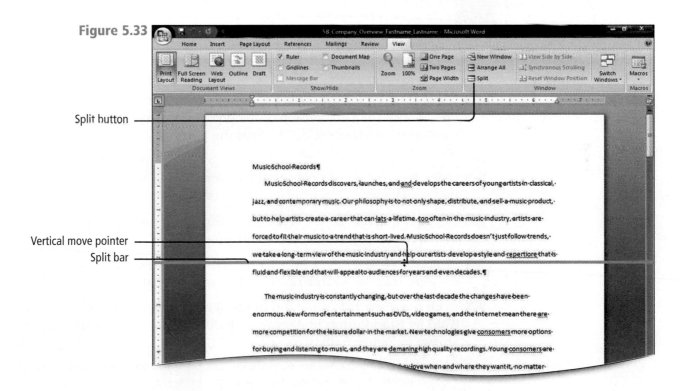

Split button

Vertical move pointer

Split bar

2 Drag the split bar slightly below the fifth line of text—including the title—that contains the phrase *that is short lived*, and then click to position the split bar.

3 Notice that both the top and bottom halves of the screen display rulers, and two different parts of the same document display in the two document windows, as shown in Figure 5.34. If you don't see the rulers, on the View tab, in the Show/Hide group, select the Ruler check box.

Figure 5.34

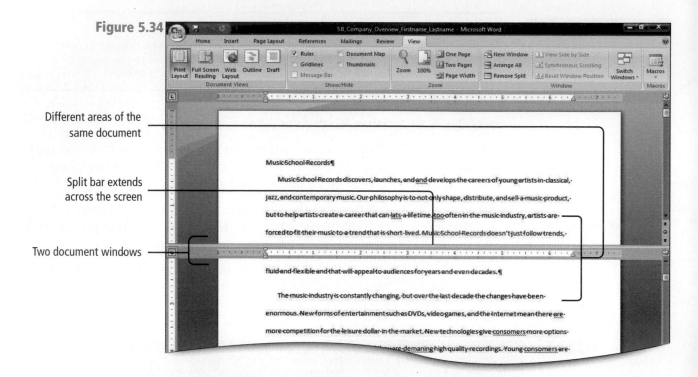

Different areas of the same document

Split bar extends across the screen

Two document windows

4 Using the top vertical scroll bar, scroll down and up in the top window. Notice that the portion of the document displayed in the top window moves independently from the portion of the document displayed in the bottom window.

5 Using the bottom vertical scroll bar, scroll up and down in the bottom widow.

6 On the **View tab**, in the **Window group**, click the **Remove Split** button to return to a single document window.

7 From the **Office** menu 🗔, click **Open**. Locate and open the **5A_Application_Letter** document that you created in Project 5A.

8 Click the **View tab**, and then in the **Window group**, click the **View Side by Side** button to display both documents at the same time, as shown in Figure 5.35.

With two documents open, you can edit both at the same time, or move text or objects between the documents.

Figure 5.35

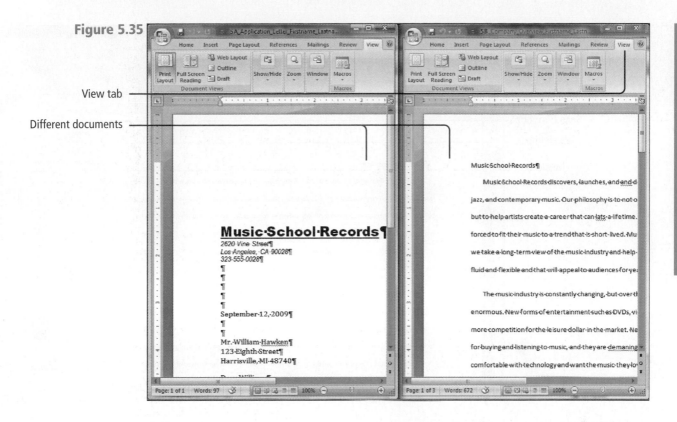

View tab

Different documents

9 On the title bar of the document on the left, click the **Close** button ✕ to close the letter. Notice that the **5B_Company_Overview** window is maximized when the other window is closed.

Objective 6
Add a Graphic to a Document

Clip art images—predefined graphics included with Microsoft Office or downloaded from the Web—can make your document more interesting and visually appealing.

Activity 5.18 Inserting Clip Art

1 Press Ctrl + Home to move the insertion point to the beginning of the document. Press Spacebar three times, and then press ← three times to move the insertion point back to the beginning of the line.

2 Click the **Insert tab**, and then in the **Illustrations group**, click the **Clip Art** button.

3 In the **Clip Art** task pane, in the **Search for** box, type **Music** and then in the **Search in** box, be sure **All collections** is selected. Click the **Results should be arrow**, and then clear all the check boxes except **Clip Art**.

4 Click **Go**, and then compare your screen with Figure 5.36. If necessary, scroll up to view the first displayed music images.

Figure 5.36

Search for box

Search in box

Music logo

---

5 Click the **music logo** clip art image. Notice that the image displays over the text.

Alert!	**Are you unable to find the right image?**
	If the music logo image does not display in the Clip Art task pane, close the task pane. Then, from the Illustrations group, click the Picture button. Navigate to your student files, click the w05B_Music_Logo file, and then click Insert. If you use the student file, you will not need to format the image. Go to Step 8.

6 Right-click the image, and then from the shortcut menu, click **Format AutoShape**. In the **Format AutoShape** dialog box, on the **Layout tab**, under **Wrapping style**, click **In line with text**, which will treat the clip art image as a text character.

7 In the **Format AutoShape** dialog box, click the **Size tab**. Under **Scale**, click the **Lock aspect ratio** check box. In the **Height** box, select the current value, and then type **30** to reduce the image to 30 percent of its original size. Compare your dialog box with Figure 5.37.

The ***aspect ratio*** of an object is the relationship of its height to its width. If you lock the aspect ratio, changing either the height or width of an object will resize the object proportionally.

Figure 5.37

Layout tab

Size tab

New size of object

Lock aspect ratio check box

8 At the bottom of the **Format AutoShape** dialog box, click **OK**, and then click anywhere in the document to deselect the image. Compare your screen with Figure 5.38.

Figure 5.38

Task pane Close button

Inserted clip art image

9 **Close** ⊠ the **Clip Art** task pane, and then **Save** 🖫 your document.

Objective 7
Use the Spelling and Grammar Checker

Word compares your typing to words in the Word dictionary and compares your phrases and punctuation to a list of grammar rules. Words that are not in the Word dictionary are marked with a wavy red underline. Phrases and punctuation that differ from the grammar rules are marked with a wavy green underline. A list of grammar rules applied by a computer program can never be exact, and a computer dictionary cannot contain all known words and proper names; thus, you will need to check any words flagged by Word with wavy underlines.

Word also places a wavy blue underline under a word that is spelled correctly but used incorrectly, such as the misuse of *their*, *there*, and *they're*. However, Word will not flag the word *sign* as misspelled, even though you intended to type *sing a song* rather than *sign a song*, because both are legitimate words contained within Word's dictionary.

Activity 5.19 Checking Individual Spelling and Grammar Errors

One way to check spelling and grammar errors flagged by Word is to right-click the flagged word or phrase, and then from the shortcut menu, choose a suitable correction or instruction.

1 Scan the text on the screen to locate green, red, and blue wavy underlines.

Note — Activating Spelling and Grammar Checking

If you do not see any wavy red, green, or blue lines under words, the automatic spelling and/or grammar checking has been turned off on your system. To activate the spelling and grammar checking, display the Office menu, click Word Options, and then in the list, click Proofing. Under *When correcting spelling in Microsoft Office programs*, select the first four check boxes. Under *When correcting spelling and grammar in Word*, select the first four check boxes, and then click the Writing Style arrow and click Grammar & Style. Under *Exceptions for*, clear both check boxes. To display the flagged spelling and grammar errors, click the Recheck Document button, and then close the dialog box.

---

2 In the first line of the paragraph that begins *Music School Records discovers*, locate the word *and* with the wavy red underline. Point to the word and **right-click**—click the right mouse button—to display a shortcut menu, as shown in Figure 5.39.

A shortcut menu displays under the Mini toolbar. Word identified a duplicate word, and provides two suggestions—*Delete Repeated Word* or *Ignore*. The second option is included because sometimes the same word will be correctly used two times in succession.

Figure 5.39

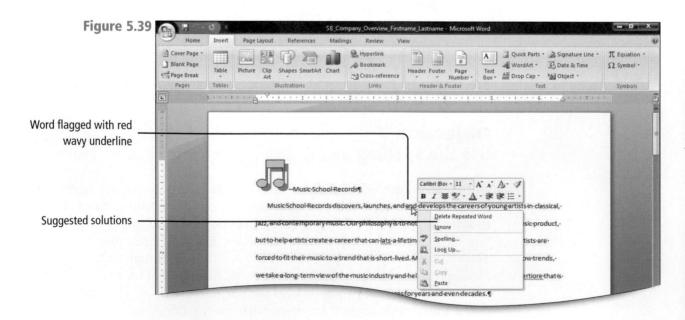

Word flagged with red wavy underline

Suggested solutions

3 From the shortcut menu, click **Delete Repeated Word** to delete the duplicate word.

4 In the third line of the same paragraph, locate and right-click the misspelled word *lats*, and then compare your screen with Figure 5.40.

In this instance, Word identifies a misspelled word. Suggested replacements are shown at the top of the shortcut menu.

Figure 5.40

Suggested replacements

Word flagged with
wavy red underline

5 At the top of the shortcut menu, click **last** to replace the misspelled widow.

6 In the third line of the same paragraph, locate and right-click the word *too* that has a wavy green underline.

The wavy green underline indicates a grammar error; in this instance, a word at the beginning of a sentence that should be capitalized.

7 From the shortcut menu, click **Too** to capitalize the word.

8 Scroll down to view the bottom of **Page 2**. In the paragraph beginning *A key aspect*, notice that two words have wavy blue underlines.

The wavy blue underline indicates a word that is recognized by the dictionary, but may be the wrong form of the word—in this instance *there* is incorrectly used instead of *their*, and *too* is used instead of *to*.

9 In the paragraph beginning *A key aspect*, right-click *there*, and then from the shortcut menu, click **their**. In the same paragraph, right-click *too*, and then from the shortcut menu, click **to**.

10 **Save** your document.

Activity 5.20 Checking Spelling and Grammar in an Entire Document

Initiating the spelling and grammar checking feature from the Ribbon displays the Spelling and Grammar dialog box, which provides more options than the shortcut menus.

1 Scan the document to locate red, green, and blue wavy underlines. Notice the 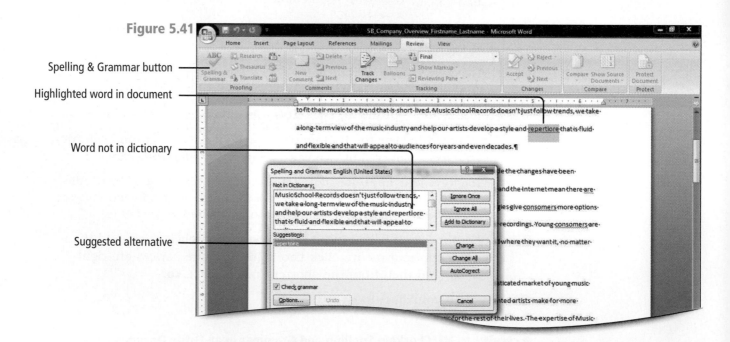 icon in the status bar, which indicates that the document contains flagged entries that need to be addressed.

2 Press Ctrl + Home to move the insertion point to the beginning of the document. Click the **Review tab**, and then in the **Proofing group**, click the **Spelling & Grammar** button to begin to check the document.

The first suggested error may be a potential grammar error—using a passive voice.

Alert!

Do your spelling and grammar selections differ?

The errors that are flagged by Word depend on the Proofing settings. Not all of the potential errors listed in this activity may appear in your spelling and grammar check. Your document may also display errors not noted here. If you encounter flagged words or phrases that are not included here, click the Ignore Once button to move to the next potential error.

3 If a *passive voice* error is flagged, in the **Spelling and Grammar** dialog box, click the **Ignore Once** button. If necessary, point to the title bar of the dialog box, and then drag the dialog box out of the way so you can see the misspelled word *repertiore*, which is selected. Compare your screen with Figure 5.41.

Under *Not in Dictionary*, the misspelled word displays in red, and under *Suggestions*, a suggested change is presented.

Figure 5.41

Spelling & Grammar button

Highlighted word in document

Word not in dictionary

Suggested alternative

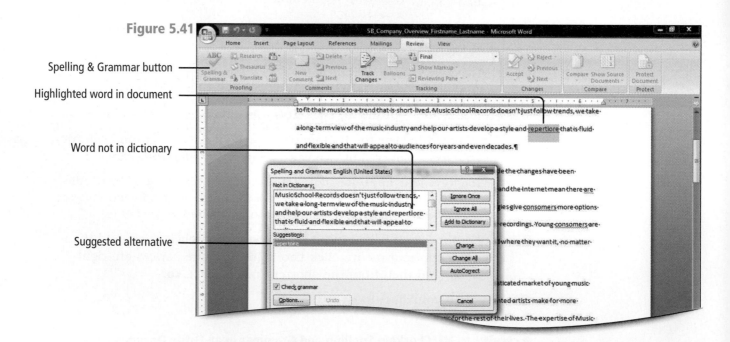

4 Take a moment to study the spelling and grammar options available in the **Spelling and Grammar** dialog box, as shown in the table in Figure 5.42.

Spelling and Grammar Dialog Box Buttons

Button	Action
Ignore Once	Ignores the identified word one time, but flags it in other locations in the document.
Ignore All	Discontinues flagging any instance of the word anywhere in the document.
Add to Dictionary	Adds the word to a custom dictionary, which can be edited. This option does not change the built-in Office dictionary.
Change	Changes the identified word to the word highlighted under Suggestions.
Change All	Changes every instance of the word in the document to the word highlighted under Suggestions.
AutoCorrect	Adds the flagged word to the AutoCorrect list, which will subsequently correct the word automatically if misspelled in any documents typed in the future.
Ignore Rule (Grammar)	Ignores the specific rule used to determine a grammar error and removes the green wavy line.
Next Sentence (Grammar)	Moves to the next identified error.
Explain (Grammar)	Displays the rule used to identify a grammar error.
Options	Displays the Proofing section of the Word Options dialog box.

Figure 5.42

5 If necessary, under **Suggestions**, select **repertoire**, and then click the **Change** button. Compare your screen with Figure 5.43.

The correction is made and the next identified error is highlighted, which is a contraction use error. Under *Contraction Use*, the entire sentence displays, with the contraction *doesn't* displayed in green. The suggested replacement—*does not*—displays in the Suggestions box.

Alert!

Did your spelling and grammar checker miss the Contraction Use error?

Recall that because of the settings on your computer, your spelling and grammar selections may differ. If you do not see a Contraction Use error, you have Grammar checking turned on, but not Style checking. When the Spelling check is done, go back and make this change manually.

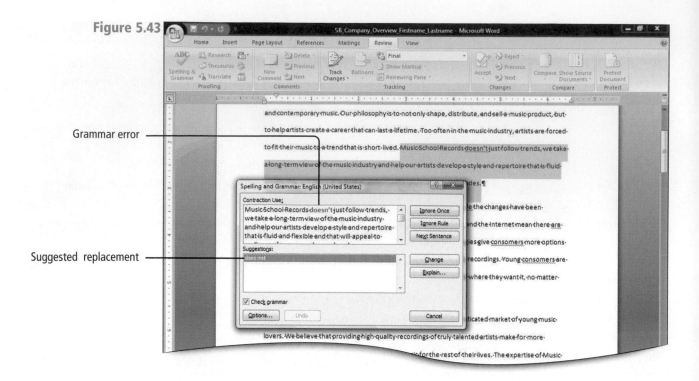

Figure 5.43

Grammar error

Suggested replacement

6 Under **Suggestions**, be sure **does not** is selected, and then click the **Change** button.

The correction is made and the next identified error is highlighted, which is a grammar error. Under *Comma Use*, the entire sentence displays. The suggested change is to add a comma.

7 Under **Suggestions**, be sure **decade** is selected, and then click the **Change** button.

The error is corrected, and the next potential error displays—a Subject-Verb Agreement grammar error.

8 Under **Suggestions**, be sure **is** is selected, and then click the **Change** button.

The error is corrected, and the next potential error displays. The word *consomers* is misspelled in two successive sentences.

9 Under **Suggestions**, be sure **consumers** is selected, and then click the **Change All** button to change all instances of the misspelled word.

10 Continue to the end of the document. Change *demaning* to **demanding**, and then click **Ignore Once** for any other marked words or phrases.

A message indicates that the spelling and grammar check is complete.

11 Click **OK** to close the dialog box, and then **Save** 🖫 your changes.

Alert!

Does the Readability Statistics box display?

If, on your computer, Word is configured to display readability statistics, a Readability Statistics dialog box displays. Readability statistics include character, word, paragraph, and sentence counts, along with reading level statistics. After reviewing the information, click OK to close the dialog box.

Objective 8
Preview and Print Documents, Close a Document, and Close Word

To ensure that you are getting the result you want, it is useful to display Print Preview from time to time while creating your document. Then, before printing, make a final preview to be sure the document layout is what you intended.

Activity 5.21 Previewing and Printing a Document

1 Press Ctrl + Home to move the insertion point to the beginning of the document. From the **Office** menu , point to **Print**, and then click **Print Preview**.

One or more pages of your document display exactly as they will print. The formatting marks, which do not print, are not displayed. The size of the preview depends on the zoom level used the last time the Print Preview window was opened.

2 In the **Print Preview** window, move the mouse pointer anywhere over the document. Notice that the pointer becomes a magnifying glass with a plus in it, indicating that you can magnify the view, as shown in Figure 5.44.

If you are viewing multiple pages, you may have to click on a page before the magnifying glass displays.

Figure 5.44

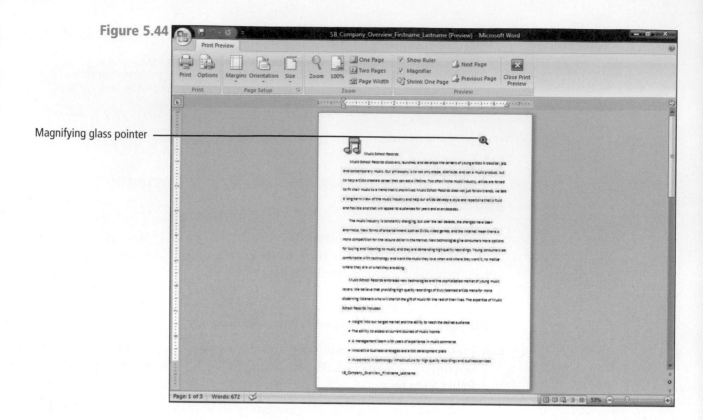

Magnifying glass pointer

3 Move the 🔍 pointer over the upper portion of the first page of the document and click one time.

The top portion of the document magnifies, making it easier to read. The pointer changes to a magnifying glass with a minus sign.

4 Click anywhere on the document to zoom out. On the right side of the status bar, drag the **Zoom slider** to the left until you can see all three pages, as shown in Figure 5.45. Notice that the footers display on the bottom of each page.

Figure 5.45

One Page button

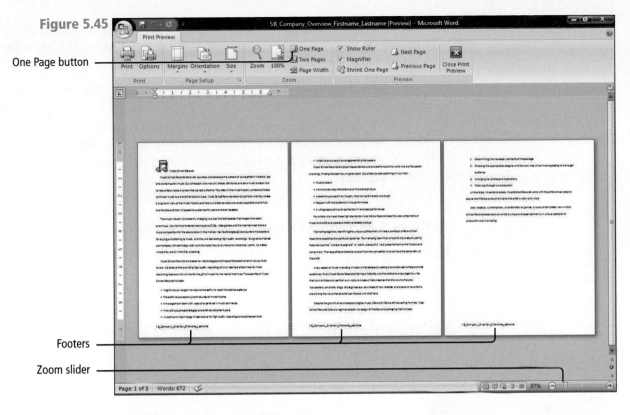

Footers

Zoom slider

5 On the **Print Preview tab**, in the **Zoom group**, click the **One Page** button to display a single page of the document.

6 In the **Preview group**, click the **Close Print Preview** button.

7 From the **Office** menu , click **Print**, and then compare your screen with Figure 5.46.

The Print dialog box displays. Here you can specify which pages to print and how many copies you want. Additional command buttons for Options and Properties provide more printing choices. The printer that displays will be the default printer that is selected for your computer.

Figure 5.46

Selected printer

Number of copies

Current page option
Pages to print

8 In the **Print** dialog box, under **Copies**, change the number of copies to 2 by typing **2** in the text box, or by clicking the **spin box up arrow**.

> A *spin box* is a small box with upward- and downward-pointing arrows that enables you to move—spin—through a set of values by clicking.

9 Under **Page range**, click the **Current page** option button, and then, at the bottom of the **Print** dialog box, click **OK** if you want to print two copies of the first page. If you do not want to print, click **Cancel**.

Activity 5.22 Closing a Document and Closing Word

1 Check your *Chapter Assignment Sheet* or *Course Syllabus* or consult your instructor to determine if you are to submit your assignments on paper or electronically. To submit electronically, go to Step 3, and then follow the instructions provided by your instructor.

2 From the **Office** menu 🗐, click **Print**. At the bottom of the **Print** dialog box, click **OK**.

3 From the **Office** menu 🗐, click **Close**, saving any changes if prompted to do so.

4 At the far right of the title bar, click the **Close** button ![X] to exit the Word program.

Objective 9
Use the Microsoft Help System

As you work with Word, you can get assistance by using the Help feature. You can type key words and phrases and Help will provide you with information and step-by-step instructions for performing tasks.

Activity 5.23 Getting Help

Word Help is available on your computer, online at the Microsoft Web site, and on your screen with enhanced ScreenTips.

1 **Start** Word. Click the **Page Layout tab**, and then in the **Page Setup group**, point to—but do not click—the **Hyphenation** button.

> The ScreenTip for this button has more information than just the name. This is called an *Enhanced ScreenTip*, and is part of the Microsoft Office 2007 Help system.

2 Move your pointer to the right side of the Ribbon and click the **Microsoft Office Word Help** button ⓘ. In the **Word Help** dialog box, click the **Search button arrow**, and then under **Content from this computer**, click **Word Help**.

> This search for Help will be restricted to the Help installed on your computer. Depending on your Word settings, the *Table of Contents* on the left of the Word Help dialog box may not display.

3 To the left of the **Search** button, click in the **Type words to search for** box, type **save a file** and then press Enter. Notice that a list of related topics displays, as shown in Figure 5.47. Your list may differ.

Figure 5.47

Search button arrow

Type words to search for box

Help button

Search results

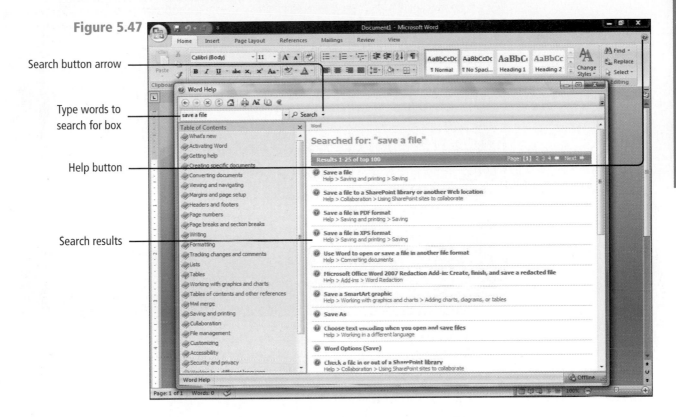

4 From the list, point to, and then click **Save a file**.

5 Under **What do you want to do?** click **Save a file to another format (Save As command)**—the wording for this topic may vary. Notice that step-by-step instructions are given, as shown in Figure 5.48.

Figure 5.48

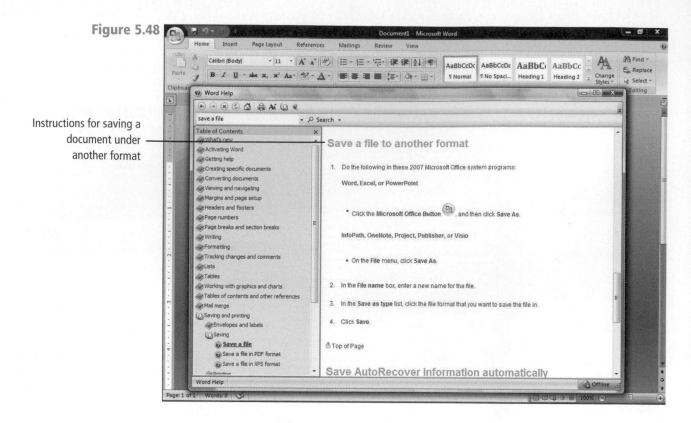

Instructions for saving a
document under
another format

6 In the upper right corner of the Word Help window, click the **Close**
button ▣. From the **Office** menu ▣, click **Exit Word** to close the
Word program.

End You have completed Project 5B ——————————

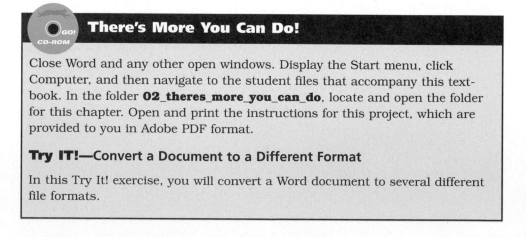

There's More You Can Do!

Close Word and any other open windows. Display the Start menu, click
Computer, and then navigate to the student files that accompany this textbook. In the folder **02_theres_more_you_can_do**, locate and open the folder
for this chapter. Open and print the instructions for this project, which are
provided to you in Adobe PDF format.

Try IT!—Convert a Document to a Different Format

In this Try It! exercise, you will convert a Word document to several different
file formats.

Content-Based Assessments

Summary

In this chapter, you started Word and practiced navigating the Word window. You entered text, deleted text by using the Backspace and Delete keys, selected and replaced text, and inserted text. The spelling and grammar checker tools were demonstrated, and an image was added to a document.

You also practiced changing font style and size and adding emphasis to text. You viewed the header and footer areas, and created a chapter folder to help organize your files. Each document was saved, previewed, printed, and closed. Finally, the Help program was introduced as a tool that can assist you in using Word.

Key Terms

Aspect ratio 36	Group 22	Salutation 6
AutoComplete 7	Header 21	Sans serif fonts 18
Clip art 35	Insert mode 14	ScreenTip 7
Complimentary closing 6	Insertion point 5	Scroll box 5
	Inside address 6	Selecting text 15
Contextual tab 22	Keyboard shortcut 16	Serif font 18
Contextual tools 22	Live Preview 18	Shortcut menu 9
Date line 6	Mini toolbar 15	Spin box 46
Document window 5	Navigate 26	Split bar 33
Double-click............16	Nonprinting characters 6	Status bar 5
Draft view 31		Style 6
Drag 15	Office button 5	Subject line 6
Edit 4	Outline view 31	Text Format ....●
Enclosure 6	Point 19	Theme 18
Enhanced ScreenTip 46	Print Layout view 31	Title bar..................5
	Program tab 20	Toggle button 6
Font 18	Pt. 19	Vertical scroll bar........5
Font styles 20	Quick Access Toolbar 5	View options.............5
Footer 21		Web Layout view 31
Formatting marks 6	Ribbon 5	Wordwrap 11
Formatting text.........15	Right-click..............38	Writer's identification 6
Full Screen Reading view..........31	Rich Text Format ....●	Zoom...................31
Gallery 12	Ruler 5	

The ● symbol represents Key Terms found on the Student CD in the 02_theres_more_you_can_do folder for this chapter.

Content-Based Assessments

Matching

Match each term in the second column with its correct definition in the first column. Write the letter of the term on the blank line in front of the correct definition.

_____ **1.** The location in the Word window, indicated by a blinking vertical line, where text will be inserted when you start to type.

_____ **2.** In the Word window, the location of the Minimize, Maximize/Restore Down, and Close buttons.

_____ **3.** A button that represents the command to reveal nonprinting characters.

_____ **4.** The action that takes place when the insertion point reaches the right margin and automatically moves down and to the left margin of the next line.

_____ **5.** The process of setting the overall appearance of the text within the document.

_____ **6.** To hold down the left mouse button and move the mouse pointer over text to select it.

_____ **7.** A set of characters (letters and numbers) with the same design and shape.

_____ **8.** A unit of measure to describe the size of a font.

_____ **9.** A font type, such as Calibri or Arial, that does not have lines on the ends of characters.

_____ **10.** A font type, such as Cambria or Times New Roman, that has extensions or lines on the ends of the characters.

_____ **11.** The term that refers to pressing one or more keys to navigate a window or execute commands.

_____ **12.** This feature changes the selected text when the pointer points to a button or list item to display what the text will look like if the button or list item is clicked.

_____ **13.** A reserved area for text and graphics that displays at the bottom of each page in a document or section of a document.

_____ **14.** A view that simplifies the page layout for quick typing and can show more text on a smaller screen.

_____ **15.** A context-sensitive list that displays when you click the right mouse button.

A Draft

B Drag

C Font

D Footer

E Formatting

F Insertion point

G Keyboard shortcut

H Live Preview

I Point

J Sans serif

K Serif

L Shortcut menu

M Show/Hide

N Title bar

O Wordwrap

Content-Based Assessments

Fill in the Blank

Write the correct word in the space provided.

1. Microsoft Word 2007 is a word _____ program that you can use to perform tasks such as writing a memo, a report, or a letter.

2. Located at the bottom of the Word window, the bar that provides information such as page number and word count is referred to as the _____ bar.

3. Within the scroll bar, dragging the _____ _____ downward causes the document on your screen to move up.

4. A toolbar above the Ribbon and to the right of the Office button, which can be customized by adding frequently used buttons, is called the _____ _____ _____.

5. Characters that display on the screen to show the location of paragraph marks, tabs, and spaces but that do not print are called _____ marks.

6. If you point to a button on the Ribbon, a _____ displays the name of the button.

7. In a business letter, the address of the recipient is called a _____ address.

8. When you select text, the _____ toolbar displays buttons that are commonly used with the selected object.

9. Before text can be edited, changed, formatted, copied, or moved, it must first be _____.

10. To add emphasis to text, use the _____ or _____ or _____ command, each of which has a button on the Ribbon.

11. The view that displays the page borders, margins, text, and graphics is the _____ _____ view.

12. The View buttons are located on the right side of the _____ bar.

13. To enlarge or decrease the viewing area of the document, use the _____ _____ on the status bar.

14. Graphic images, of which some are included with Word, that can be inserted in the document are called _____ art.

15. To display a shortcut menu, click the _____ mouse button.

Skills Review

Project 5C—Receipt Letter

In this project, you will apply the skills you practiced from the Objectives in Project 5A.

Objectives: 1. *Create and Save a New Document;* **2.** *Edit Text;* **3.** *Select, Delete, and Format Text;* **4.** *Print a Document.*

In the following Skills Review, you will create and edit a follow-up letter from Jamal Anderssen, a production manager for Music School Records, to William Hawken, a recording artist who has submitted a demo CD with his application. Your completed letter will look similar to the one shown in Figure 5.49.

For Project 5C, you will need the following file:

New blank Word document

You will save your document as
5C_Receipt_Letter_Firstname_Lastname

Figure 5.49

Music School Records
2620 Vine Street
Los Angeles, CA 90028
323-555-0028

September 22, 2009

Mr. William Hawken
123 Eighth Street
Harrisville, MI 48740

Dear Mr. Hawken:

Subject: Receipt of Your CD

I received your demo CD yesterday. Thank you for following our submission and recording guidelines so carefully. Everything is quite satisfactory, and we will be able to duplicate the CD and send it to our internal reviewers.

Your demonstration CD will not be circulated outside *Music School Records*. You retain all rights to your material until such time as a contract is finalized.

Best regards,

Jamal Anderssen
Production Manager

5C_Receipt_Letter_Firstname_Lastname

(Project 5C–Receipt Letter continues on the next page)

Content-Based Assessments

(Project 5C–Receipt Letter continued)

1. **Start** Word. If necessary, on the Ribbon, in the **Paragraph group**, click the **Show/Hide ¶** button to display the formatting marks. In the status bar, use the **Zoom slider** to adjust the page width to display both the left and right page edges.

2. On the **Home tab**, in the **Styles group**, click the **No Spacing** style. With the insertion point blinking in the upper left corner of the document to the left of the default first paragraph mark, type **Music School Records** and then press Enter. Type the following text and press Enter after each line:

   2620 Vine Street
   Los Angeles, CA 90028
   323-555-0028

3. Press Enter five more times. Begin typing today's date and let AutoComplete assist in your typing by pressing Enter when the ScreenTip displays. Press Enter four times. Type the inside address on three lines:

   Mr. William Hawken
   123 Eighth Street
   Harrisville, MI 48740

4. On the **Quick Access Toolbar**, click the **Save** button. In the **Save As** dialog box, navigate to your **Word Chapter 5** folder. In the **File name** box, using your own first and last names, type **5C_Receipt_Letter_Firstname_Lastname** and then click **Save**.

5. On the **Home tab**, in the **Styles group**, click the **Normal** style. Press Enter, type the salutation **Dear Mr. Hawken:** and then press Enter.

6. Type **Subject: receipt of Your CD** and then press Enter. Then, using just one space following the periods at the end of sentences, type the following text:

   I received your demo CD yesterday. Thank you for following our submission and recording standards so carefully.

   Everything is satisfactory, and we will be able to duplicate the CD and send it to our internal reviewers.

7. Press Enter to begin a new paragraph, and then type the following:

   Your demonstration CD will not be circulated outside Music School Records. You retain the rights to your material until such time as a contract is finalized.

8. Press Enter, type the closing **Best regards,** and then press Enter two times.

9. On the **Quick Access Toolbar**, click the **Save** button to save your changes. On the **Home tab**, in the **Styles group**, click the **No Spacing** style. Finish the letter by typing the writer's identification on two lines:

   Jamal Anderssen
   Production Manager

10. If necessary, drag the vertical scroll box to the top of the scroll bar to view the upper portion of the document. In the *Subject* line, position the insertion point to the left of *receipt*, and then press Del. Type **R** to capitalize *Receipt*.

11. In the paragraph beginning *I received*, double-click the word **standards** to select it, and then type **guidelines**

12. In the same paragraph, position the insertion point to the left of the word *satisfactory*. Type **quite** and then press Spacebar one time.

13. In the paragraph beginning *Your demonstration*, click to position the insertion point to the left of *rights*, press ←Bksp four times. Type **all** and then press Spacebar to change the phrase to *retain all rights*.

14. **Save** your changes. Press Ctrl + A to select the entire document. On the **Home**

(Project 5C–Receipt Letter continues on the next page)

(Project 5C–Receipt Letter continued)

tab, in the **Font group**, click the **Font button arrow**. Scroll as necessary, and watch Live Preview change the document font as you point to different font names. Click to choose **Tahoma**. Click anywhere in the document to cancel the selection.

15. Select the entire first line of text—*Music School Records*. On the Mini toolbar, click the **Font button arrow**, and then click **Arial Black**. With the Mini toolbar still displayed, click the **Font Size button arrow**, and then click **20**. With the Mini toolbar still displayed, click the **Bold** button.

16. Select the second, third, and fourth lines of text, beginning with *2620 Vine Street* and ending with the telephone number. On the Mini toolbar, click the **Font button arrow**, and then click **Arial**. With the Mini toolbar still displayed, click the **Font Size button arrow**, and then click **10**. With the Mini toolbar still displayed, click the **Italic** button.

17. In the paragraph beginning *Your demonstration*, select the text *Music School Records*. On the Mini toolbar, click the **Italic** button, and then click anywhere to deselect the text.

18. Click the **Insert tab**. In the **Header & Footer group**, click the **Footer** button, and then click **Edit Footer**. On the

Design tab, in the **Insert group**, click the **Quick Parts** button, and then click **Field**. In the **Field** dialog box, under **Field names**, scroll down and click to choose **FileName**, and then click **OK**. Double-click anywhere in the document to leave the footer area.

19. Click the **Page Layout tab**. In the **Page Setup group**, click the **Margins** button to display the Margins gallery. At the bottom of the **Margins gallery**, click **Custom Margins** to display the **Page Setup** dialog box. Near the top of the **Page Setup** dialog box, click the **Layout tab**. Under **Page**, click the **Vertical alignment arrow**, click **Center**, and then click **OK**.

20. From the **Office** menu, point to **Print**, and then click **Print Preview** to make a final check of your letter. Check your *Chapter Assignment Sheet* or *Course Syllabus* or consult your instructor to determine if you are to submit your assignments on paper or electronically. To submit electronically, go to Step 22, and then follow the instructions provided by your instructor.

21. On the **Print Preview tab**, in the **Print group**, click the **Print** button. Click **OK**, and then **Close Print Preview**.

22. From the **Office** menu, click **Exit Word**, saving any changes if prompted to do so.

End **You have completed Project 5C** ———————

Content-Based Assessments

Skills Review

Project 5D — Marketing

In this project, you will apply the skills you practiced from the Objectives in Project 5B.

Objectives: 5. *Navigate the Word Window;* **6.** *Add a Graphic to a Document;* **7.** *Use the Spelling and Grammar Checker;* **8.** *Preview and Print Documents, Close a Document, and Close Word;* **9.** *Use the Microsoft Help System.*

In the following Skills Review, you will edit a document that details the marketing and promotion plan for Music School Records. Your completed document will look similar to Figure 5.50.

For Project 5D, you will need the following files:

New blank Word document
w05D_Marketing
w05D_Piano

You will save your document as
5D_Marketing_Firstname_Lastname

Figure 5.50

(Project 5D–Marketing continues on the next page)

Content-Based Assessments

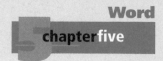
(Project 5D–Marketing continued)

1. **Start** Word and be sure a new blank document is displayed. If necessary, on the Ribbon, in the Paragraph group, click the Show/Hide ¶ button to display the formatting marks. In the status bar, use the Zoom slider to adjust the page width to display both the left and right page edges.

2. On the **Quick Access Toolbar**, click the **Save** button. In the **Save As** dialog box, navigate to your **Word Chapter 5** folder. In the **File name** box, using your own first and last names, type **5D_Marketing_ Firstname_Lastname** and then click **Save**.

3. Click the **Insert tab**. In the **Header & Footer group**, click the **Footer** button to display the Footer gallery. At the bottom of the **Footer gallery**, click **Edit Footer**. On the **Design tab**, in the **Insert group**, click the **Quick Parts** button, and then click **Field**. In the **Field** dialog box, under **Field names**, scroll down and click **FileName**, and then click **OK**. Double-click anywhere in the document to leave the footer area.

4. Click the **Insert tab**. In the **Text group**, click the **Object button arrow**, and then click **Text from File**. In the **Insert File** dialog box, navigate to your student files. Locate and select **w05D_Marketing**, and then click the **Insert** button to insert the text.

5. Press ⌐←Bksp⌐ to remove the blank line at the end of the document. Use the vertical scroll bar to examine the document. When you are finished, press ⌐Ctrl⌐ + ⌐Home⌐ to move to the beginning of the document.

6. **Save** your document. Move the ⌐↗⌐ pointer into the margin area to the left of the title *Music School Records* and drag down to select the title, the blank line, and the second title that begins *International Marketting*. Be sure to include the blank

line between the two titles. On the Mini toolbar, click the **Bold** button. Click anywhere in the document to deselect the text.

7. In the second title line, notice that the word *Marketting* is marked as misspelled. Right-click *Marketting*, and from the shortcut menu, click **Marketing**. In the first line of the paragraph that begins *The growing global*, right-click *geners*, and from the shortcut menu, locate and click **genres**.

8. Click the **Review tab**, and then, in the **Proofing group**, click the **Spelling & Grammar** button to open the **Spelling and Grammar** dialog box. The first word flagged is *allready*. Notice that this word is misspelled several times in the document.

9. In the **Spelling and Grammar** dialog box, click the **Change All** button to correct all occurrences of this misspelled word. The next potential error—a subject-verb agreement problem—is highlighted. Notice that two suggested corrections are listed. If necessary, click **is a growing demand**, and then click the **Change** button.

10. If a Passive Voice error is identified next, click Ignore Once. In the paragraph that begins *The Internet will be key*, another potential grammar problem is highlighted. Click the **Ignore Once** button to leave the sentence the way it was written. Ignore other grammar errors, and then correct the spelling error for the word *Millenium*. Continue to click the **Ignore Once** button until you reach the end of the document. When a message box tells you the check is complete, click **OK**.

11. Press ⌐Ctrl⌐ + ⌐Home⌐ to move to the beginning of the document, and then press ⌐Enter⌐ to add a blank line. Click to position the insertion point in the new blank line.

(Project 5D–Marketing continues on the next page)

Content-Based Assessments

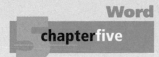

Word

chapterfive   Skills Review

(Project 5D–Marketing continued)

12. Click the **Microsoft Office Word Help** button. In the **Word Help** dialog box, click the **Search button arrow**, and then under **Content from this computer**, click **Word Help**. In the **Type words to search for** box, type **graphic file types** and then press ⏎. In the search results, click **Types of media files you can add** and examine the list of graphic file types that can be added to a Word document.

13. **Close** the **Word Help** window, and then click the **Insert tab**. In the **Illustrations group**, click the **Picture** button. In the **Insert Picture** dialog box, navigate to the student files that accompany this text-book, click the **w05D_Piano** file, and then click **Insert**.

14. **Save** your changes. Check your *Chapter Assignment Sheet* or *Course Syllabus* or consult your instructor to determine if you are to submit your assignments on paper or electronically. To submit electronically, go to Step 16, and then follow the instructions provided by your instructor.

15. From the **Office** menu, point to **Print**, and then click **Print Preview** to make a final check of your document. On the **Print Preview tab**, in the **Print group**, click the **Print** button, and from the **Print** dialog box, click **OK**. Then, in the **Preview group**, click the **Close Print Preview** button.

16. From the **Office** menu, click **Close**. At the right end of the title bar, click the **Close** button to close Word.

End **You have completed Project 5D** ──────────────

Content-Based Assessments

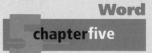
Mastering Word

Project 5E—Contract

In this project, you will apply the skills you practiced from the Objectives in Projects 5A and 5B.

Objectives: 2. *Edit Text;* **3.** *Select, Delete, and Format Text;* **4.** *Print a Document;* **5.** *Navigate the Word Window;* **7.** *Use the Spelling and Grammar Checker;* **8.** *Preview and Print Documents, Close a Document, and Close Word.*

In the following Mastering Word project, you will edit a contract between a client and Music School Records. Your completed document will look similar to Figure 5.51.

For Project 5E, you will need the following file:

w05E_Contract

You will save your document as
5E_Contract_Firstname_Lastname

Figure 5.51

The Second Party is required to present an individualized promotional plan for the Artist in the Chicago Metropolitan Area. Upon approval of the plan, Music School Records will release the above-mentioned products and allow access to the Artist. The Second Party ... implementation and sales figures to

... e Second Party will be paid an amount
... ago Metropolitan Area during the
... e year after the contract has been

... ubject to renewal and/or revision at

's fees.
Los Angeles, County of Los Angeles,

...: _____

...: _____

Contract for Services

PARTIES TO THE CONTRACT
The First Party's name is Music School Records, a Corporation.

The Second Party's name is **Evie Chardan**, an individual proprietor.

WHO HAS TO DO WHAT
Music School Records and **Evie Chardan** agree to the following:
Music School Records will provide the Second Party various marketing materials and recordings of **Evie Chardan** (the Artist) for the purposes of publicizing and promoting the Artist to music stores in the Chicago metropolitan area.

The materials provided by Music School Records may include printed brochures, promotional CDs, pre-loaded digital music players, advertising copy, Artist fact sheets, photographs, and press clips. Also available as requested will be low-value promotional items such as buttons, stickers, and other trinkets.

Music School Records will also provide, with proper notice and approval of venue, access to the Artist for press conferences, interviews, media appearances, and performances. All such personal appearances will be subject to Music School Records' contract with the Artist.

Music School Records is responsible for the accuracy of all printed materials. Music School Records is also

The Second Party will take all legally required actions and professionally appropriate care in protecting the copyrights of Music School Records and the Artist. The Second Party is responsible for the health and safety of the Artist while at appearances arranged by the Second Party. If the Artist is a minor, the Second Party will follow all applicable laws relating to care and work of a minor.

The Second Party will be responsible for writing/producing and releasing press clips (print, audio and video) following any promotional events. The Second Party is responsible for the accuracy of such releases and clips. Other promotional actions are expected to include, but are not limited to:

• Announcements and listings in local press entertainment calendars
• Arrangement of and public service announcements for charity events
• Mailings, faxes, and phone calls to local press, club owners, music store managers, etc.
• Any necessary local Web presence

5E_Contract_Firstname_Lastname

(Project 5E–Contract continues on the next page)

Content-Based Assessments

(Project 5E–Contract continued)

1. Locate and open the document **w05E_ Contract**. **Save** the document in your **Word Chapter 5** folder as **5E_Contract_ Firstname_Lastname** and then add the file name to the footer. Display formatting marks, display the ruler, and set the page width to a comfortable size for you.

2. If necessary, move to the beginning of the document, type **Contract for Services** and press Enter. Select *Contract for Services*, change the **Font Size** to **18** points, and apply **Bold** emphasis.

3. Use the **Spelling and Grammar** checker to correct the errors in the document. There are several misspellings of the word *responsibel* and a subject-verb agreement error—*are* instead of *is*. Ignore all other flagged items.

4. Locate the three headings in uppercase letters. Select each one and add **Bold** emphasis. Recall that when you select the text, the Mini toolbar displays with the Bold button on it.

5. Locate the black lines in the document that represent blanks to be filled in. In the line beginning *The Second Party's name*, select the long line, but not the comma following it. Type **Evie Chardan** and notice that as you type, your typing will be displayed in bold. On the next two long lines, use the same technique to type **Evie Chardan** again.

6. On **Page 2**, in the paragraph beginning *For services provided*, select the line and type **12** Select the line following *This agreement will be in force for*, type **2** and then delete *months/* so that the sentence reads *in force for 2 years*.

7. **Save** your changes. At the end of the contract, under *Signed*, select the text *Music School Records*, and then on the Mini toolbar, change the font size to **10** and add **Bold** emphasis. **Save** your changes. **Preview** the document and then print or submit electronically as directed by your instructor. **Close** the document, and then **Exit** Word.

End **You have completed Project 5E** _____

Content-Based Assessments

Project 5F—Invitation

In this project, you will apply the skills you practiced from the Objectives in Projects 5A and 5B.

Objectives: 1. *Create and Save a New Document;* **2.** *Edit Text;* **3.** *Select, Delete, and Format Text;* **4.** *Print a Document;* **5.** *Navigate the Word Window;* **6.** *Add a Graphic to a Document;* **7.** *Use the Spelling and Grammar Checker;* **8.** *Preview and Print Documents, Close a Document, and Close Word.*

In the following Mastering Word project, you will create a new letter to a talent agent, and then insert and edit text from a file. Your completed document will look similar to Figure 5.52.

For Project 5F, you will need the following files:

New blank Word document
w05F_Invitation
w05F_Letterhead

You will save your document as
5F_Invitation_Firstname_Lastname

Figure 5.52

> **Music School Records**
>
> **2620 Vine Street**
>
> **Los Angeles, CA 90028**
>
> **323-555-0028**
>
> **Musicschoolrecords.com**
>
> September 30, 2009
>
> Ms. Caroline Westbrook
> Artists' Workshop Agency
> 249 Fifth Avenue #2700
> New York, NY 10001
>
> Dear Ms. Westbrook:
>
> Thank you for the introduction to your client, Ms. Evie Chardan. Our representatives were very impressed with the quality of Ms. Chardan's music, stage presence, and obvious rapport with the young audience for which she performed. It is certainly our pleasure to invite Ms. Chardan to consider a recording contract with **Music School Records.**
>
> Upon your approval, we will draft a standard contract for your and Ms. Chardan's attorneys' review. The contract will be subject to the laws of California and will include language outlining the term of the contract, guaranteed minimum payments per year, and obligations of the artist and **Music School Records.** As part of the standard contract we do require a period of exclusivity regarding the artist's recording, and this period is subject to negotiation.
>
> Please call me as soon as possible to confirm your client's agreement to draft the contract. We are looking forward to working with you again and playing a key role in the development of Ms. Chardan's career.
>
> Sincerely,
>
> John Diamond
> Assistant Vice President, Creative Development
>
> 5F_Invitation_Firstname_Lastname

(Project 5F–Invitation continues on the next page)

Content-Based Assessments

Mastering Word

(Project 5F–Invitation continued)

1. **Start** Word and be sure a new blank document is displayed. Display formatting marks, display the ruler, and be sure your screen displays both the left and right document edges. **Save** the document in your **Word Chapter 5** folder as **5F_Invitation_Firstname_Lastname** Open the document footer and add the file name.

2. Locate and insert the file **w05F_ Letterhead**. Be sure the insertion point is positioned at the second blank line below the letterhead, and then type the current date. Using the skills you practiced in Project 5A, be sure the address style is set to **No Spacing**, and then add the following inside address:

> **Ms. Caroline Westbrook**
> **Artists' Workshop Agency**
> **249 Fifth Avenue #2700**
> **New York, NY 10001**

3. Change the style back to **Normal**, press Enter, and then type **Dear Ms. Westbrook:** Press Enter, and then locate and insert the file **w05F_Invitation**. Add the following paragraph at the end of the document:

> **Please call me as soon as possible to confirm your client's agreement to draft the contract. We are looking forward to working with you again and playing a key role in the development of Ms. Chardan's career.**

4. Using appropriate spacing, add the complimentary closing **Sincerely,** and then add the following writer's identification:

> **John Diamond**
> **Assistant Vice President, Creative Development**

5. **Save** your changes. Be sure grammar errors are flagged in the document. In the paragraph beginning *Thank you*, in the second sentence, correct the grammar error *was*, and then type **very** between *were* and *impressed*. In the third line of the same paragraph, add **certainly** between *It is* and *our pleasure*. In the last sentence of the same paragraph, change *sign* to **consider**

6. Use the **Spelling & Grammar** checker to correct the errors in the document. There is one error—the misspelled word *qualty*. Ignore all other flagged items.

7. At the end of the paragraph beginning *Thank you for the introduction*, locate the text *Music School Records* and add **Bold** emphasis. In the paragraph beginning *Upon your approval*, add **Bold** emphasis to *Music School Records*.

8. Select the entire document. Change the **Font** to **Cambria**. **Save** your changes.

9. **Preview** the document and then print or submit electronically as directed by your instructor. **Close** the file, and then **Exit** Word.

 End **You have completed Project 5F**

Word
chapterfive

Mastering Word

Project 5G — Fax Cover

In this project, you will apply the skills you practiced from the Objectives in Projects 5A and 5B.

Objectives: 1. *Create and Save a New Document;* **2.** *Edit Text;* **3.** *Select, Delete, and Format Text;* **4.** *Print a Document;* **5.** *Navigate the Word Window;* **6.** *Add a Graphic to a Document;* **7.** *Use the Spelling and Grammar Checker;* **8.** *Preview and Print Documents, Close a Document, and Close Word.*

In the following Mastering Word project, you will create a cover sheet for a facsimile (fax) transmission. When sending a fax, it is common practice to include a cover sheet with a note describing the pages that will follow. Your completed document will look similar to Figure 5.53.

For Project 5G, you will need the following files:

New blank Word document
w05G_Fax_Cover
w05G_Fax_Machine

**You will save your document as
5G_Fax_Cover_Firstname_Lastname**

Figure 5.53

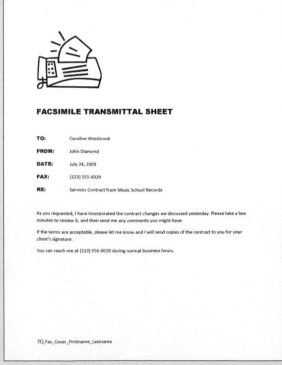

(Project 5G–Fax Cover continues on the next page)

Content-Based Assessments

(Project 5G–Fax Cover continued)

1. **Start** Word and be sure a new blank document is displayed. Display formatting marks and rulers, and be sure your screen displays both the left and right document edges. **Save** the document in your **Word Chapter 5** folder as **5G_Fax_Cover_Firstname_Lastname** Open the document footer and add the file name to the footer.

2. Move the insertion point to the top of the document. Press [Enter] two times, and then move back to the top of the document. From your student files, insert the **w05G_Fax_Machine** picture. Press [Ctrl] + [End]. Press [CapsLock], type **FACSIMILE TRANSMITTAL SHEET** and then press [Enter] two times. Press [CapsLock] again.

3. Locate and insert the file **w05G_Fax_Cover**. Move to the blank line at the end of the document, and then type **You can reach me at (323) 555-0029 during normal business hours. Save** your document.

4. Select the text *FACSIMILE TRANSMITTAL SHEET*. Change the **Font Size** to **16**, and the **Font** to **Arial Black**. Change the font of the line headings *TO:*, *FROM:*, *DATE:*, *FAX:*, and *RE:* to **Arial Black**.

5. In the paragraph that begins *As you requested*, select and delete the text *on the telephone*. In the same paragraph, replace the phrase *look it over* with **review it** and, in the same sentence, add an **s** to *comment*.

6. There are several grammar and spelling errors that need to be corrected. Use the **Spelling & Grammar** checker to correct the duplicate or misspelled words. In the paragraph beginning *If the term are*, select the **terms are** suggested change. **Save** your changes.

7. Use [Ctrl] + [Home] to navigate to the beginning of the document. Proofread the fax cover to be sure you have made all necessary corrections.

8. **Preview** the document, and then print or submit electronically as directed by your instructor. **Close** the document, and **Exit** Word.

End **You have completed Project 5G**

Content-Based Assessments

Mastering Word

Project 5H — *GO!* Fix It

In this project, you will construct a solution by applying any combination of the skills you practiced from the Objectives in Projects 5A and 5B.

> **For Project 5H, you will need the following files:**
>
> w05H_Approval_Letter
> w05H_Music_Logo

You will save your document as
5H_Approval_Letter_Firstname_Lastname

From the student files that accompany this textbook, locate and open the file **w05H_Approval_Letter**, and then save the file in your chapter folder as **5H_Approval_Letter_Firstname_Lastname**

This document contains errors that you must find and correct. Read and examine the document, and then edit to correct the errors that you find. Types of errors could include:

- Spelling, grammar, punctuation, and usage errors such as text case, repeated text, subject-verb agreement, and meaning.

- Content errors such as missing or incorrect text.

- Paragraph formatting and positioning errors such as wordwrap, sentence spacing, missing text, or unnecessary text or blank lines.

- Page setup errors such as margins, orientation, layout, or alignment.

Things you should know to complete this project:

- Displaying formatting marks will assist in locating spacing errors.

- The name Hawken and the name HawkenDove are spelled correctly.

- Set the Word Proofing Options so that when correcting spelling and grammar in Word, Grammar & Style is selected.

- There are no errors in the fonts or font sizes.

- A logo graphic is missing in the letterhead. From your student files, insert the logo graphic **w05H_ Music_Logo** to the left of *Music School Records* followed by one space. Format the logo graphic using wrapping style In line with text. For the size, modify the scale height to 50% and select the lock aspect ratio.

- Spacing following the inside address should change to Normal style.

Save your document, add the file name to the footer, and then submit as directed.

End **You have completed Project 5H**

Outcomes-Based Assessments

Rubric

The following outcomes-based assessments are *open-ended assessments*. That is, there is no specific correct result; your result will depend on your approach to the information provided. Make *Professional Quality* your goal. Use the following scoring rubric to guide you in *how* to approach the problem and then to evaluate *how well* your approach solves the problem.

The *criteria*—Software Mastery, Content, Format and Layout, and Process—represent the knowledge and skills you have gained that you can apply to solving the problem. The *levels of performance*—Professional Quality, Approaching Professional Quality, or Needs Quality Improvements—help you and your instructor evaluate your result.

	Your completed project is of Professional Quality if you:	Your completed project is Approaching Professional Quality if you:	Your completed project Needs Quality Improvements if you:
1-Software Mastery	Choose and apply the most appropriate skills, tools, and features and identify efficient methods to solve the problem.	Choose and apply some appropriate skills, tools, and features, but not in the most efficient manner.	Choose inappropriate skills, tools, or features, or are inefficient in solving the problem.
2-Content	Construct a solution that is clear and well organized, contains content that is accurate, appropriate to the audience and purpose, and is complete. Provide a solution that contains no errors of spelling, grammar, or style.	Construct a solution in which some components are unclear, poorly organized, inconsistent, or incomplete. Misjudge the needs of the audience. Have some errors in spelling, grammar, or style, but the errors do not detract from comprehension.	Construct a solution that is unclear, incomplete, or poorly organized; contains some inaccurate or inappropriate content; and contains many errors of spelling, grammar, or style. Do not solve the problem.
3-Format and Layout	Format and arrange all elements to communicate information and ideas, clarify function, illustrate relationships, and indicate relative importance.	Apply appropriate format and layout features to some elements, but not others. Overuse features, causing minor distraction.	Apply format and layout that does not communicate information or ideas clearly. Do not use format and layout features to clarify function, illustrate relationships, or indicate relative importance. Use available features excessively, causing distraction.
4-Process	Use an organized approach that integrates planning, development, self-assessment, revision, and reflection.	Demonstrate an organized approach in some areas, but not others; or, use an insufficient process of organization throughout.	Do not use an organized approach to solve the problem.

Outcomes-Based Assessments

Problem Solving

Project 5I — Services

In this project, you will construct a solution by applying any combination of the skills you practiced from the Objectives in Projects 5A and 5B.

For Project 5I, you will need the following file:

New blank Word document

You will save your document as
5I_Services_Firstname_Lastname

Using the information provided, compose a form letter from Lucy Burroughs—Vice President of Creative Services—that explains the services offered by the company. Music School Records is located at 2620 Vine Street, Los Angeles, CA 90028, (323) 555-0028. The tone of the letter should be positive and sales-oriented. The letter should answer the question, *Why do I need this service?* As you write the letter, use the information in Project 5B that describes the company. The letter should contain three paragraphs—an introductory paragraph, a second paragraph describing the services offered, and a closing paragraph.

The letter should include the appropriate business letter components, and should be in the proper business format. Add the file name to the footer. Check the letter for spelling or grammar errors. Save the letter as **5I_Services_Firstname_Lastname** and submit it as directed.

End **You have completed Project 5I** ———————————

Outcomes-Based Assessments

Problem Solving

Project 5J — Survey Form

In this project, you will construct a solution by applying any combination of the skills you practiced from the Objectives in Projects 5A and 5B.

For Project 5J, you will need the following file:

New blank Word document

You will save your document as
5J_Survey_Form_Firstname_Lastname

In Project 5J, you will create a brief survey form to be filled out by potential clients of Music School Records. The purpose of the survey form is to do a quick screening of applicants to be sure they are a match for the company before they talk to a field representative or send in a demo recording.

The target audience will be high school and college students, and young performers already working in their field. The form should include information that may be important to a screening committee, including the client's:

- Place of residence

- Current school (if any)

- Type of talent (instrument, voice)

- Genre of music

- Professional experience (if any)

- Awards and other types of public recognition

Include any other topics you feel would be helpful in a brief survey form. The form should list the topics down the left side of the page, and should leave three or four blank lines between each so the person filling out the form will have enough space to write.

Add the file name to the footer. Check the survey form for spelling or grammar errors. Save the document as **5J_Survey_Form_Firstname_Lastname** and submit it as directed.

End **You have completed Project 5J** ——————

Outcomes-Based Assessments

Problem Solving

Project 5K — Holidays

In this project, you will construct a solution by applying any combination of the skills you practiced from the Objectives in Projects 5A and 5B.

For Project 5K, you will need the following files:

New blank Word document
w05K_Musical_Score

**You will save your document as
5K_Holidays_Firstname_Lastname**

In Project 5K, you will write a memo to announce the days that Music School Records will be closed for holidays in the upcoming year. Use a memo format that you like. If you are unsure of what should be contained in the memo heading, search *memo format* on the Internet. Most memos have at least four lines at the top—Date, To, From, and Subject.

The memo should be from Mahadevan Ropa, Vice President for Business Development, to all employees at the Los Angeles office. Include an opening paragraph that mentions the reason for the memo, and then identify seven or eight holidays for which the office will be closed. Choose any typical holidays that you want to include. If you are not sure of the dates of holidays, or which ones to include, search the Web, using as search terms the year and the word *holidays*.

Add the file name to the footer. Check the memo for spelling or grammar errors. Add the **w05K_Musical_Score** image where appropriate. Save the document as **5K_Holidays_Firstname_Lastname** and submit it as directed.

 You have completed Project 5K ————————

More on your Student CD

The instructions for the following additional end-of-chapter projects are on your student CD in the folder 03_additional_end_of_chapter_projects.

Content-Based Assessments

Project L Mastering Word

Apply the skills you practiced in Project A.

Project M Mastering Word

Apply the skills you practiced in Project B.

Project N Business Running Case

Apply the skills you practiced in Projects A and B while helping an entrepreneur with the daily tasks of running a business.

In each chapter, this project focuses on applying the skills you have practiced in Projects A and B to a business. The project related to this business runs throughout the textbook. You will see how the Office applications relate to the day-to-day operation of a small business called Nelson Architectural Planning.

Outcomes-Based Assessments

Project O Problem Solving

Construct a solution by applying any combination of the skills you practiced from Projects A and B.

Project P Problem Solving

Construct a solution by applying any combination of the skills you practiced from Projects A and B.

Project Q You and GO!

Construct a solution that applies to your own life by applying any combination of the skills you practiced from Projects A and B.

Project R GO! with Help

Practice using Microsoft Office's Help Feature.

Project S Group Business Running Case

Work as part of a group to apply the skills you have gained thus far to help the Bell Orchid Hotel Group achieve its business goals.

Multimedia

The following multimedia accompany this textbook:

Companion Web site
www.prenhall.com/go

An interactive Web site designed to reinforce and test your understanding of the skills in this chapter.

AV-EDDs

In the folder in the front of this book you will find videos that demonstrate the objectives of the A and B projects in this chapter. These may help you understand how to complete the projects in this book.

Video Podcasts

In the folder in the front of this book are videos that can be played on your iPod, MP3 player, or computer. These videos demonstrate how to complete the more challenging objectives in this textbook.

chaptersix

Formatting and Organizing Text

OBJECTIVES

At the end of this chapter you will be able to:

1. Change Document and Paragraph Layout
2. Change and Reorganize Text
3. Create and Modify Lists

4. Insert and Format Headers and Footers
5. Insert Frequently Used Text
6. Insert and Format References

OUTCOMES

Mastering these objectives will enable you to:

PROJECT 6A
Format Text and Use Lists

PROJECT 6B
Create a Research Paper

GHS Law Partners

GHS Law Partners specializes in patent and intellectual property law and government contracts, serving clients in the e-commerce, computer technology, pharmaceutical, and health care fields. The firm researches and prepares patents, litigates intellectual property infringement, handles licensing disputes, and prepares appeals. In the growing area of government contracts, the firm counsels its clients regarding United States government policymaking and prepares contracts according to government procurement policies. The firm's experienced staff of attorneys includes many who have formerly worked as prosecutors, federal court law clerks, and United States patent inspectors and procurement contract attorneys.

© Christine Balderas / Courtesy of www.istockphoto.com

Formatting and Organizing Text

Typing text is just the beginning of the process of creating an effective, professional looking document. Microsoft Word provides many tools for formatting paragraphs and documents. For example, there are tools to create shortcuts for entering commonly used text, and quick ways to copy, cut, and move text. Word also provides tools that enable you to create specialized formats, such as footnotes, bulleted and numbered lists, and indented paragraphs.

In this chapter, you will edit a seminar announcement, and then you will create and format a research paper.

Project 6A Seminar

In Activities 6.01 through 6.15, you will edit an announcement from GHS Law Partners about an upcoming Intellectual Property Seminar. Your completed document will look similar to Figure 6.1.

For Project 6A, you will need the following file:

w06A_Seminar

You will save your document as
6A_Seminar_Firstname_Lastname

GHS Law Partners
Intellectual Property Seminar for Business Attorneys

July 12, 2009
Atlanta, GA
Draft Announcement

GHS Law Partners will present its fifth annual Intellectual Property Seminar for Business Attorneys in Atlanta, GA, on July 12, 2009. This event is intended for attorneys who want to expand their knowledge of intellectual property in order to better serve their clients. Intellectual property law affects every kind of business and clients' rights, obligations, and strategies. GHS Law Partners believes that sharing knowledge and expertise in this area of law enhances the business climate and improves the ability of business-focused firms to serve their diverse client base.

Some states confer Continuing Legal Education credits for this seminar. Each attendee will receive a complete set of all seminar materials along with an Intellectual Property textbook written by one of our partners. Audio tapes and DVDs of selected sessions will also be available.

The three morning sessions will focus on copyrights:

1. Introduction to Copyrights
2. Copyright FAQs
3. Current Issues in Copyrights

Lunch will feature a panel discussion of GHS attorneys and other trademark experts. Among the topics discussed will be:

™ Use of trademarks
™ Trademark enforcement
™ Avoiding dilution of trademark

The four afternoon sessions will cover patents:

1. Patent Basics
2. Understanding Trade Secrets and Patent Protection
3. Current Issues in Patents
4. Business Considerations in Patents and Trademarks

Questions and discussion are encouraged at all sessions, and attendees are reminded that such discussions should be kept confidential to protect the wide array of clients represented by the group.

Registration will open on April 1, 2009, and is limited to 400 attendees. Discounted rates are available at several nearby hotels. A "dine-around" dinner will be arranged at several local restaurants for those who want to participate.

If you would like a brochure containing much more detailed information about the topics to be covered in the upcoming Intellectual Property Seminar, contact Melissa Rosella at (404) 555-0022. You can also register online at www.ghslaw.com/ipseminar.

6A_Seminar_Firstname_Lastname

Figure 6.1
Project 6A—Seminar

Objective 1
Change Document and Paragraph Layout

Document layout includes *margins*—the space between the text and the top, bottom, left, and right edges of the paper. Paragraph layout includes line spacing, indents, and tabs. In Word, the information about paragraph formats is stored in the paragraph mark at the end of a paragraph. When you press the Enter key, the new paragraph mark contains the formatting of the previous paragraph, unless you take steps to change it.

Activity 6.01 Setting Margins

You can change each of the four page margins—top, bottom, left, and right—independently.

> **Note — Comparing Your Screen with the Figures in This Textbook**
>
> Your screen will match the figures shown in this textbook if you set your screen resolution to 1024 × 768. At other resolutions, your screen will closely resemble, but not match, the figures shown. To view your screen's resolution, on the Windows desktop, right-click in a blank area, click Personalize, and then click Display Settings.

1 **Start** Word. From your student files, locate and open the document **w06A_Seminar**.

2 From the **Office** menu ⊙, display the **Save As** dialog box, and then navigate to the location where you are saving your files. On the toolbar, click the **New Folder** button. Name the new folder **Word Chapter 6** and then press ⏎.

3 In the **File name** box, delete the existing text. Using your own name, type **6A_Seminar_Firstname_Lastname** and then click **Save**. If necessary, display formatting marks.

4 Click the **Page Layout tab**. In the **Page Setup group**, click the **Margins** button, and then at the bottom of the **Margins gallery**, click **Custom Margins**.

5 In the **Page Setup** dialog box, press ⟨Tab⟩ as necessary to select the value in the **Left** box, and then, with *1.25″* selected, type **1**

> This action will change the left margin to 1 inch on all pages of the document. You do not need to type the inch (″) mark.

6 Press ⟨Tab⟩ to select the measurement in the **Right** box, type **1** and then compare your screen with Figure 6.2. Notice that the new margins will be applied to the entire document.

Figure 6.2

New left margin

New right margin

Margins applied to entire document

Word | Chapter 6

7 Click **OK** to apply the new margins and close the dialog box. If the ruler below the Ribbon is not displayed, at the top of the vertical scroll bar, click the **View Ruler** button. Compare your screen with Figure 6.3.

Figure 6.3

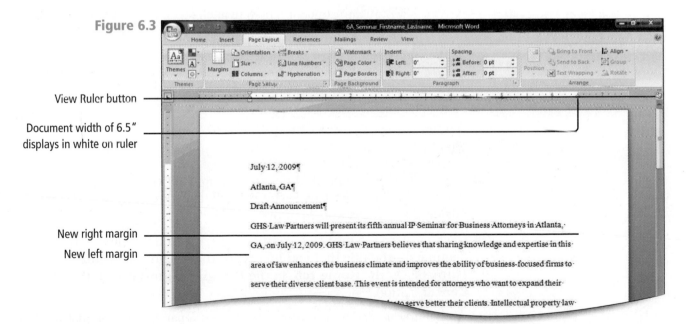

View Ruler button

Document width of 6.5″ displays in white on ruler

New right margin
New left margin

8 Scroll to view the bottom of **Page 1**. Near the bottom edge of the page, right-click, and then click **Edit Footer** to display the footer area.

This shortcut provides a quick way to display either the footer or header area. Because the insertion point is in the footer area, *Header & Footer Tools* displays, and the Design tab is added to the standard tabs on the Ribbon.

9 On the **Design tab**, in the **Insert group**, click the **Quick Parts** button, and then click **Field**. In the **Field** dialog box, under **Field names**, locate and click **FileName**, and then click **OK**.

10 Double-click anywhere in the document to close the footer area. **Save** 🔲 your document.

Activity 6.02 Aligning Text

Alignment is the placement of paragraph text relative to the left and right margins. Most paragraph text uses *left alignment*—aligned at the left margin, leaving the right margin uneven. Three other types of paragraph alignment are available: *center alignment*—centered between the left and right margins; *right alignment*—aligned on the right margin; and *justified alignment*—text aligned on both the left and right margins. Examples are shown in the table in Figure 6.4.

Paragraph Alignment Options		
Alignment	**Button**	**Description and Example**
Align Text Left	▤	Align Text Left is the default paragraph alignment in Word. Text in the paragraph aligns at the left margin, and the right margin is uneven.
Center	▤	Center alignment aligns text in the paragraph so that it is centered between the left and right margins.
Align Text Right	▤	Align Text Right is used to align text at the right margin. Using Align Text Right, the left margin, which is normally even, is uneven.
Justify	▤	The Justify alignment option adds additional space between words so that both the left and right margins are even. Justify is often used when formatting newspaper-style columns.

Figure 6.4

1 Press Ctrl + Home to place the insertion point at the beginning of the document. Type **GHS Law Partners Intellectual Property Seminar for Business Attorneys** and then press Enter.

2 Click to place the insertion point anywhere in the first line of the document—the title that you just typed that begins *GHS Law Partners*. On the **Home tab**, in the **Paragraph group**, click the **Center** button ▤.

> The first paragraph is centered. To format a paragraph, you just need to have the insertion point somewhere in the paragraph.

3 Move the mouse pointer into the left margin area to the left of the second line of text that begins *July 12* until the ▨ pointer displays. Drag down to select that line and the two lines following it, ending with *Draft Announcement*, and then on the Mini toolbar, click the **Center** button 📃. Compare your screen with Figure 6.5.

> A paragraph consists of a paragraph mark and all the text in front of it. To format multiple paragraphs, they must all be selected.

Figure 6.5

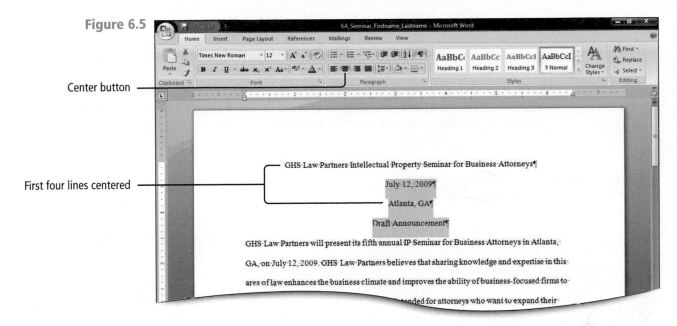

Center button

First four lines centered

4. Move the 🔏 pointer into the left margin area to the left of the fifth line of text that begins *GHS Law Partners will present*. Then, drag down to select this line of text and the next eight lines of text— including the line that ends *will also be available*.

5. In the **Paragraph group**, click the **Justify** button 📃, and then compare your screen with Figure 6.6.

> Both the left and right edges of the paragraphs are even. The other paragraphs are not affected.

Figure 6.6

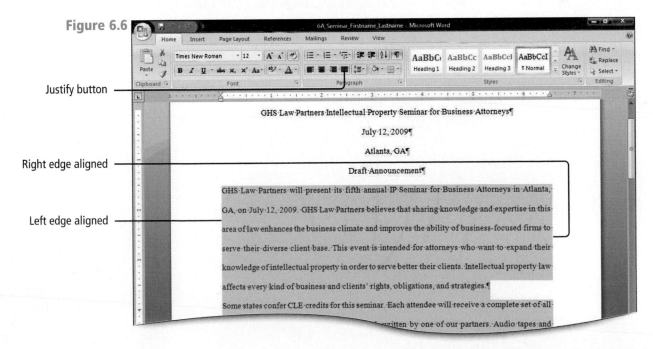

Justify button

Right edge aligned

Left edge aligned

6 Because justified text is better used in narrow columns, with the text still selected, in the **Paragraph group**, click the **Align Text Left** button ▤. Click anywhere in the document to deselect the text. **Save** 🖫 the document.

Activity 6.03 Changing Line Spacing

Line spacing is the distance between lines of text in a paragraph. A single-spaced paragraph of 12-point text accommodates six lines in a vertical inch. If you double-space the same text, each line will be 24 points high—12 points of text, 12 points of space—and will accommodate only three lines in a vertical inch as shown in the table in Figure 6.7.

Line Spacing Options	
Spacing	**Example**
Single (1.0)	Most business documents are single-spaced. This means that the spacing between lines is just enough to separate the text.
Multiple with 1.15 line spacing	The default line spacing in Microsoft Word 2007 is 1.15, which is equivalent to single spacing with an extra 1/6 line added between lines.
Double (2.0)	Many college research papers and reports, and many draft documents that need space for notes, are double-spaced; there is space for a full line of text between each document line.

Figure 6.7

1 Press [Ctrl] + [Home]. In the left margin area, display the 🔁 pointer and drag down to select the first four lines of text—the four centered title lines.

2 In the **Paragraph group**, click the **Line spacing** button ‡≣▾, and then compare your screen with Figure 6.8.

A check mark next to 2.0 indicates that the selected paragraphs are double-spaced.

Figure 6.8

Line spacing button

Double-spacing

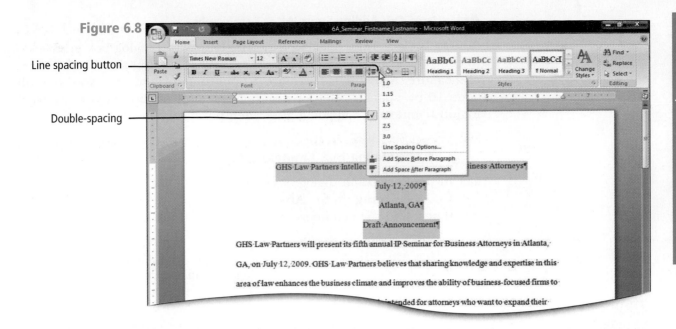

3 In the **Line spacing** list, click **1.0** to change the line spacing of the first four paragraphs.

4 Click to place the insertion point in the paragraph that begins *GHS Law Partners will present*. In the **Paragraph group**, click the **Line spacing** button, and then click **1.0**. Compare your screen with Figure 6.9.

The first five paragraphs of the document are single-spaced.

Figure 6.9

First five paragraphs of the document are single-spaced

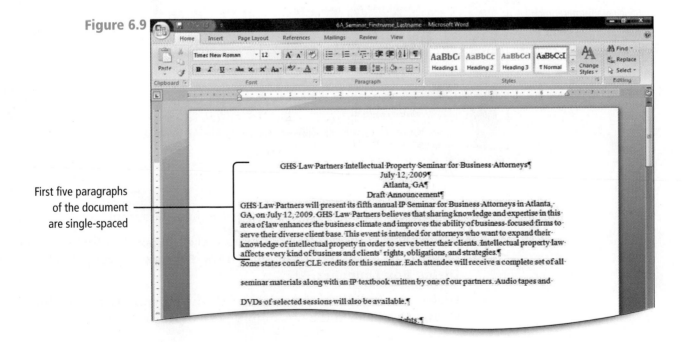

5 **Save** the changes you have made to your document.

Activity 6.04 Adding Space After Paragraphs

Adjusting paragraph spacing from the Paragraph dialog box enables you to control the space before or after paragraphs using points as the unit of measure. Recall that there are 72 points per inch. The Word default adds 10-pt. spacing after each paragraph. The document you are working on has no extra spacing after each paragraph.

1 Press Ctrl + Home. In the lower right corner of the **Paragraph group**, click the **Dialog Box Launcher** ▣.

2 In the **Paragraph** dialog box, click the **Indents and Spacing tab**. Under **Spacing**, in the **After** spin box, click the **up spin arrow** two times, and then compare your screen with Figure 6.10.

> The value in the box changes from 0 pt to 12 pt. A ***spin box*** is a small box with upward- and downward-pointing arrows that lets you move (spin) through a set of values by clicking. The up and down arrows, called ***spin box arrows***, increment the point size by six points at a time.

Figure 6.10

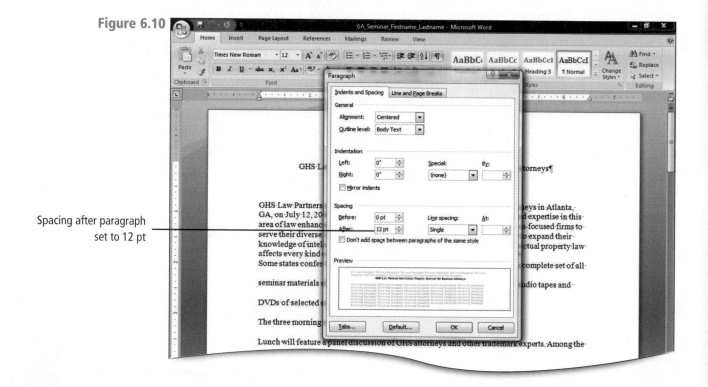

Spacing after paragraph set to 12 pt

3 Click **OK** to add a 12-pt space after the first paragraph.

4 In the *Draft Announcement* paragraph, click to position the insertion point anywhere in the paragraph. In the **Paragraph group**, click the **Dialog Box Launcher** ▣.

5 Under **Spacing**, in the **After** box, click the **up spin arrow** one time to change the value in the box from *0 pt* to **6 pt**. Click **OK**.

Another Way **To Add Spacing Before and After Paragraphs**

You can also change the spacing before and after paragraphs using the Ribbon. Click the Page Layout tab, and then in the Paragraph group, use the Spacing buttons.

6 In the paragraph beginning *GHS Law Partners will present*, click to position the insertion point anywhere in the paragraph. In the **Paragraph group**, display the **Paragraph** dialog box. Under **Spacing**, set **After** to **6 pt**, and then click **OK**. Compare your screen with Figure 6.11.

Figure 6.11

12 pt. spacing after the first paragraph

6-pt. spacing after each paragraph

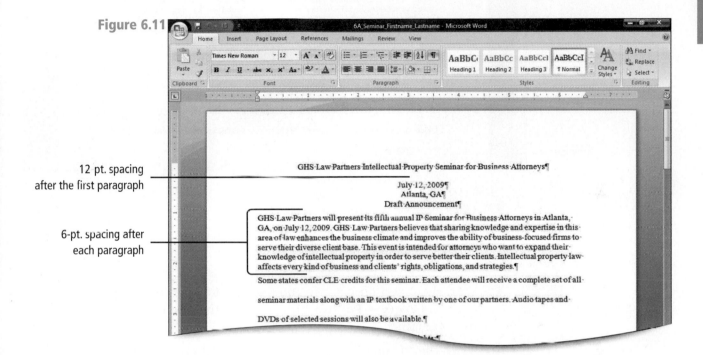

7 **Save** 🖫 the changes you have made to your document.

Activity 6.05 Using the Format Painter

Use the ***Format Painter*** to copy the formatting of specific text or of a paragraph and then apply it in other locations in your document.

1 Click anywhere in the paragraph that begins *GHS Law Partners will present*. On the **Home tab**, in the **Clipboard group**, click the **Format Painter** button 🖌. Position the pointer anywhere in the paragraph that begins *Some states confer*, and then compare your screen with Figure 6.12.

The pointer takes the shape of a paintbrush, and contains the formatting information from the paragraph where the insertion point is positioned. Instructions on how to turn the Format Painter off display in the status bar.

Figure 6.12

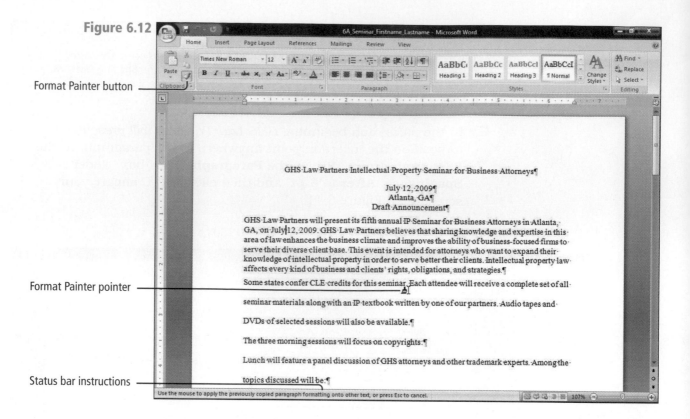

Format Painter button

Format Painter pointer

Status bar instructions

2 Click the ▲I pointer one time.

The paragraph formatting from the original paragraph—single-spacing, 6-pt space after the paragraph—is copied to this paragraph. The Format Painter is no longer active.

3 With the insertion point in the recently formatted paragraph, double-click the **Format Painter** button 🖌 to use the Format Painter multiple times.

4 Move the ▲I pointer to the paragraph that begins *The three morning sessions*, and then click one time.

The paragraph formatting from the original paragraph is copied to this paragraph, and the Format Painter remains active.

5 Move the ▲I pointer to the paragraph that begins *Lunch will feature*, and then click one time.

6 Using the **down scroll arrow**, locate and click in the paragraph that begins *The four afternoon sessions*. Use the Format Painter to change the formatting of the last three paragraphs, starting with the paragraph that begins *Registration will open*. Compare your screen with Figure 6.13.

Figure 6.13

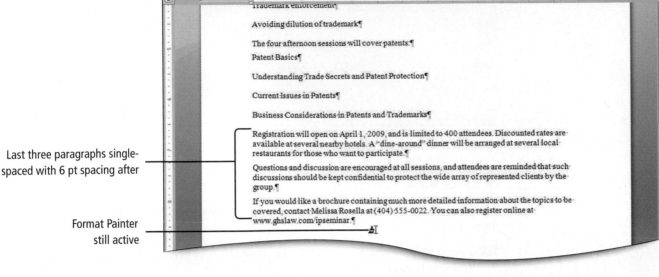

Last three paragraphs single-spaced with 6 pt spacing after

Format Painter still active

Alert!

Did you click the wrong paragraph?

If you accidentally click in one of the other paragraphs while scrolling down, click the Undo button to undo the formatting. Clicking the Undo button turns off the Format Painter, so you will need to click in the paragraph with the desired formatting again, and then turn the Format Painter on again to format the last paragraphs.

7 In the **Clipboard group**, click the **Format Painter** button to turn the command off. Alternatively, press Esc to turn off the Format Painter feature.

8 **Save** your document.

Objective 2
Change and Reorganize Text

Changing and reorganizing text is accomplished using Word features such as the Find and Replace dialog box and the **Office Clipboard**, a temporary storage area that holds text. You can **copy** text to the Office Clipboard, which leaves the original text in place, or **cut** text, which removes it from its original location. Then, you can **paste**—insert—the contents of the Office Clipboard in a new location. The keyboard short-cuts for these commands are shown in the table in Figure 6.14.

Keyboard Shortcut for Editing Text

Keyboard Shortcut	Action
Ctrl + X	Cut text or graphic and move it to the Office Clipboard.
Ctrl + C	Copy text or graphic to the Office Clipboard.
Ctrl + V	Paste the contents of the Office Clipboard.
Ctrl + Z	Undo an action.
Ctrl + Y	Redo an action.
Ctrl + F	Find text.
Ctrl + H	Find and replace text.

Figure 6.14

Activity 6.06 Finding and Replacing Text

Finding and then replacing text is a quick way to make the same change more than one time in a document.

1 Press Ctrl + Home to position the insertion point at the beginning of the document.

> When you initiate a find operation or a find-and-replace operation, the search begins from the location of the insertion point and proceeds to the end of the document.

2 On the **Home tab**, in the **Editing group**, click the **Find** button. In the **Find and Replace** dialog box, in the **Find what** box, type **CLE** which is an acronym for *Continuing Legal Education*.

3 In the **Find and Replace** dialog box, click the **Find Next** button to select the first occurrence of *CLE*.

4 In the **Find and Replace** dialog box, click **Cancel**. Press Ctrl + Home.

5 In the **Editing group**, click the **Replace** button.

6 If necessary, in the **Find and Replace** dialog box, in the **Find what** box, type **CLE** and then in the **Replace with** box, type **Continuing Legal Education**

7 Click the **More** button to expand the dialog box, and then under **Search Options**, select the **Match case** and **Find whole words only** check boxes. Click **Find Next**, and then compare your screen with Figure 6.15.

> By searching for whole words only, you will avoid changing the search text if it occurs in the middle of a word—for example, *CLEVELAND*. By matching case, you not only instruct the program to look for text in the same case, but also to replace text using the same case as the text in the Replace with box.

Figure 6.15

Find what box

Replace with box

Match case check box

Find whole words only check box

First instance of found text

8 In the **Find and Replace** dialog box, click the **Replace** button.

The text is replaced, and a message indicates that Word has finished searching the document.

9 Click **OK**. In the **Find what** box, type **IP** and in the **Replace with** box, type **Intellectual Property**

10 Click **Replace All**.

A message displays, indicating that two replacements have been made.

11 Click **OK** to close the message box. Clear the two **Search Options** check boxes, click the **Less** button, and then click **Close**. **Save** 🖫 your document.

Activity 6.07 Cutting, Copying, and Pasting Text

Use the Cut command to move text out of the document to the Office Clipboard—the temporary storage location for text or graphics. Then, use the Paste command to paste the contents of the Office Clipboard to the new location. The Copy command places a copy of selected text on the Office Clipboard, which you can then paste to another location.

1 Near the end of the document, locate the paragraph that begins *Questions and discussion*, and then double-click to select the word *represented*.

2 On the **Home tab**, in the **Clipboard group**, click the **Cut** button 🔏. Alternatively, right-click the selected text and click Cut from the shortcut menu; or, press Ctrl + X.

The selected text is removed from the document and moved to the Office Clipboard.

Note — The Difference Between Using Delete, Backspace, and Cut

When you use the Cut command to remove text, it is moved to the Office Clipboard and can be pasted into the same—or a different—document. When you use Delete or Backspace to remove text, the text is not moved to the Office Clipboard. The only way you can retrieve text removed with Delete or Backspace is by using the Undo command.

3 In the same line of text, click to position the insertion point between *clients* and *by*. In the **Clipboard group**, click the **Paste** button. Alternatively, right-click and then click Paste from the menu, or press Ctrl + V. Adjust the spacing before and after the word if necessary.

The text is placed at the insertion point, but also remains on the Office Clipboard. The Paste Options button displays below the pasted word.

4 Point to the **Paste Options** button until its ScreenTip *Paste Options* displays, click the button, and then compare your screen with Figure 6.16.

The displayed list provides commands related specifically to the Paste command. You can determine whether you want to format the pasted text the same as the surrounding text or retain its original formatting.

Figure 6.16

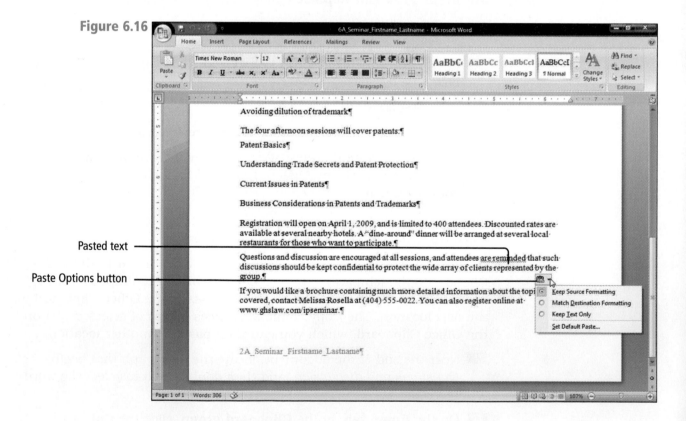

Pasted text

Paste Options button

5 Click anywhere in the document to close the **Paste Options** menu and retain the same formatting. Alternatively, press Esc to cancel its display.

6 Position the pointer in the paragraph that begins *Registration will open*, and then triple-click to select the entire paragraph.

7 In the **Clipboard group**, click the **Cut** button ✂. Locate the paragraph that begins *If you would like* and position the insertion point at the beginning of that paragraph. In the **Clipboard group**, click the **Paste** button to paste the text in the new location.

Alert!

Did the Clipboard task pane open?

The Clipboard task pane may display on your screen depending on the options that have been set for the Office Clipboard on your computer. If the task pane opens, click the Close button on the task pane title bar.

---

8 Press Ctrl + Home. In the first title line, select *Intellectual Property Seminar*. In the **Clipboard group**, click the **Copy** button 📋. Press Ctrl + End to move to the end of the document.

9 In the last paragraph, locate the word *covered* and position the insertion point between the word and the following comma. Press Spacebar, type **in the upcoming** and then press Spacebar. In the **Clipboard group**, click the **Paste** button, and then compare your screen with Figure 6.17.

The copied text is inserted in the new location, but is not removed from the original location. The Paste Options button displays below the pasted text.

Figure 6.17

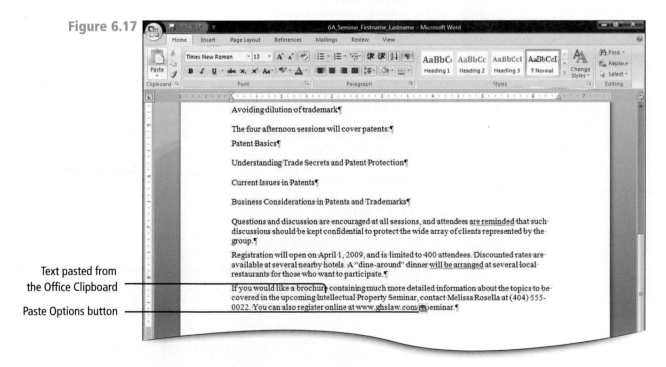

Text pasted from the Office Clipboard

Paste Options button

10 **Save** 💾 the changes you have made to your document.

Activity 6.08 Moving Text to a New Location

Another method of moving text is the ***drag and drop*** technique, which uses the mouse to drag selected text from one location to another. This method is useful if the text to be moved is on the same screen as the destination location.

1 Press Ctrl + Home. In the fifth line of the paragraph that begins *GHS Law Partners will present*, locate and select *better*.

2 Point to the selected word to display the pointer as shown in Figure 6.18.

Figure 6.18

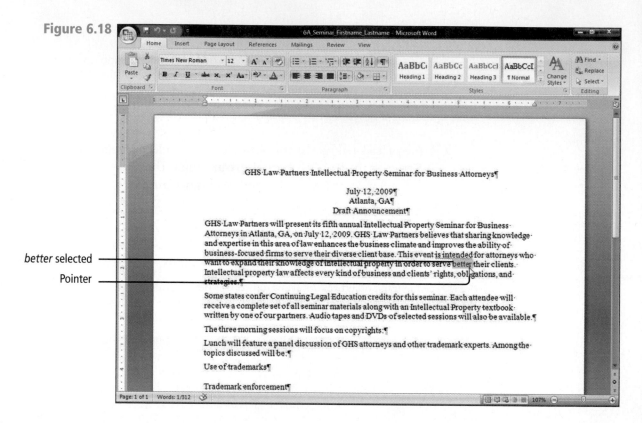

better selected

Pointer

3 Hold down the left mouse button and drag to the left until the dotted vertical line that floats next to the pointer is positioned to the left of the word *serve* in the same line, and then release the left mouse button.

4 Click anywhere to deselect the text, and then compare your screen with Figure 6.19.

> The word is moved to the insertion point location. The vertical line of the pointer assists you in dropping the moved text in the place where you want it. The small box attached to the pointer indicates that there is text attached to the pointer.

Figure 6.19

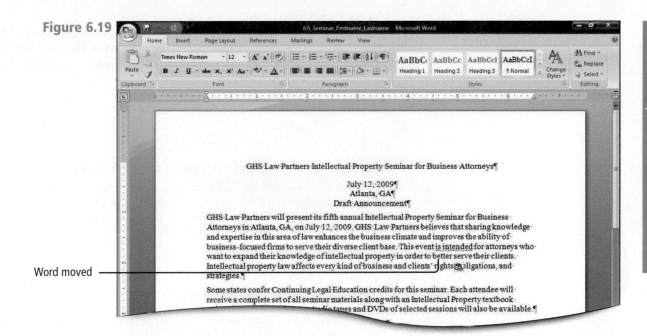

Word moved

5 In the same paragraph, point to the second sentence—the one that begins *GHS Law Partners believes*. Hold down Ctrl and click one time to select the entire sentence.

6 Point to the selected sentence to display the ⬙ pointer, and then drag down to the end of the paragraph and position the vertical line to the right of the period at the end of *obligations, and strategies*, as shown in Figure 6.20.

Figure 6.20

Pointer with text attached

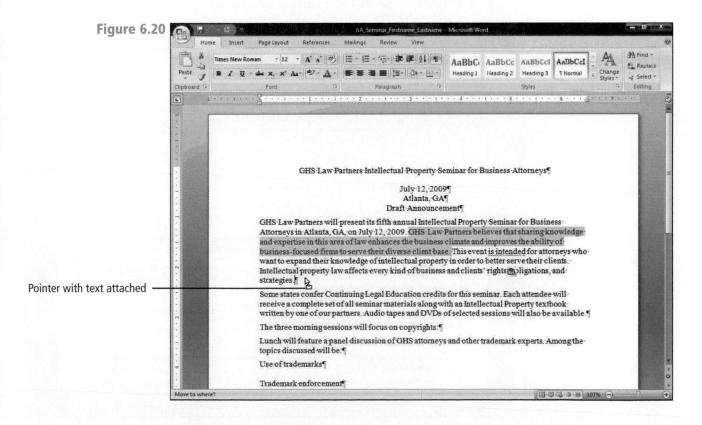

7 Release the mouse button, and click anywhere in the document to deselect the text. The sentence you moved becomes the last sentence in the paragraph. Notice that a space was automatically added before the sentence.

8 **Save** 🔲 the changes you have made to your document.

> **More Knowledge — Drag and Drop Using the Right Mouse Button**
>
> You can also drag and drop using the right mouse button. Select the text, point to the selected text and hold the right mouse button down, and then drag to a new location. A shortcut menu displays, giving you the option of moving the text to the new location, copying the text to the new location, or creating a link.

Activity 6.09 Undoing and Redoing Changes

You can undo one or more actions that you made to an active document. An Undo action can be reversed with the Redo command.

1 In the fourth paragraph, *Draft Announcement*, double-click *Draft* to select it, and then press [Delete].

2 On the **Quick Access Toolbar**, click the **Undo** button 🔄.

The word you deleted returns to its original location.

3 On the **Quick Access Toolbar**, click the **Undo** button 🔄 two times. The sentence you dragged and dropped returns to its original location, and the words *serve* and *better* are switched back to their original locations, as shown in Figure 6.21.

Figure 6.21

Undo button ——

Deleted word restored ——

Moves undone ——

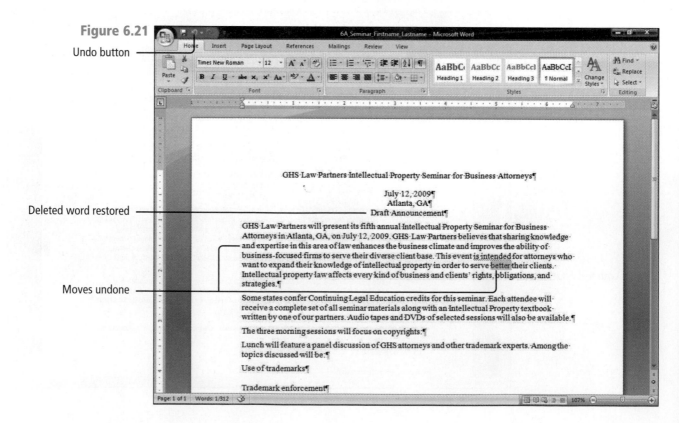

4 On the **Quick Access Toolbar**, click the **Redo** button ↻ two times. The words are switched back, and the sentence moves back to the end of the paragraph. Notice that clicking the Undo and Redo buttons changes one action at a time.

5 On the **Quick Access Toolbar**, click the **Undo button arrow** ↺ ⌄.

A list of changes displays showing all of the changes made since you last opened your document. From the displayed list, you can click any of the actions and undo it, but all of the changes above the one you select will also be undone.

6 Click anywhere in the document to close the Undo button list without undoing any other actions.

Activity 6.10 Inserting Nonbreaking Spaces and Hyphens

When you want to keep two words together regardless of where they fall in a paragraph, use a **nonbreaking space**, which will wrap both words even if only the second word would normally wrap to the next line. For example, if the words *Mt. McKinley* fall at the end of a line so that *Mt.* is on one line and *McKinley* moves to the next, inserting a nonbreaking space will treat the two words as one so that they are not split between two lines. Similarly, you may have a hyphenated term, such as a postal code with the four-digit extension. If you want that term to be treated as one entity, use a nonbreaking hyphen.

1 Press Ctrl + End to move to the end of the document. Locate the paragraph that begins *If you would like*, and then click to position the insertion point at the end of the second line.

2 In the telephone number, delete the hyphen. While holding down both Ctrl and ⇧ Shift, press - one time.

The hyphen is replaced with a **nonbreaking hyphen**; the telephone number will not break at the hyphen if you edit the paragraph. The nonbreaking hyphen is indicated by a slightly longer, slightly higher line than a standard hyphen, but prints as a normal hyphen.

3 At the end of the second line, after the telephone number area code, delete the space. While holding down both Ctrl and ⇧ Shift, press Spacebar one time. Compare your screen with Figure 6.22.

This combination of keys inserts a nonbreaking space. The result of inserting the nonbreaking space and nonbreaking hyphen is that the telephone number is treated as one word, so when Word applies its word-wrapping rules, the number is kept together on the same line. The nonbreaking space is indicated by an open circle rather than the dot normally used to indicate a space, but prints as a normal space.

Figure 6.22

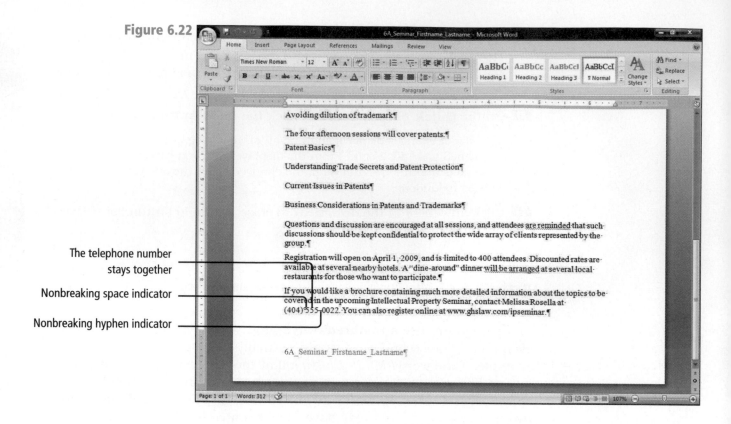

The telephone number stays together

Nonbreaking space indicator

Nonbreaking hyphen indicator

4 In the same sentence, locate and select the word *Seminar*, and then press Delete. Notice that the telephone number moves to the previous line as one word.

5 On the **Quick Access Toolbar**, click the **Undo** button ↺ to reinsert the deleted word. **Save** 💾 your changes.

Activity 6.11 Entering a Line Break

You can end a line of text with a ***manual line break***, which moves the insertion point to the next line without creating a new paragraph.

1 Press Ctrl + Home to move to the beginning of the document. Position the ⟑ pointer in the left margin area, and then select the first four lines of text—the four centered title lines.

2 On the Mini toolbar, click the **Bold** button **B**, click the **Font Size button arrow** `12 ▾`, and then click **14**.

3 In the first title line, notice the 12-point spacing after the first paragraph. Then, select the space between *Partners* and *Intellectual* and press Delete.

4 Hold down ⇧ Shift, and then press Enter. Compare your screen with Figure 6.23.

> By using a manual line break, the 12-pt spacing after the paragraph is not inserted because a new paragraph is not created; rather, a new line within the same paragraph is created. The bent arrow at the end of the first line indicates an inserted line break.

Figure 6.23

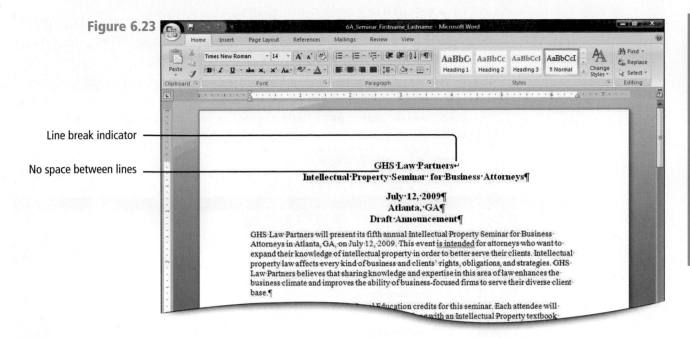

Line break indicator

No space between lines

Save your changes.

Objective 3
Create and Modify Lists

Word displays lists of information in two ways. A *bulleted list* uses *bullets*, which are text symbols such as small circles or check marks, to introduce each piece of information. *Numbered lists* use consecutive numbers or letters to introduce each item in a list. Use bulleted lists when the items in the list can be displayed in any order; use numbered lists for items that have definite steps, a sequence of actions, or are in chronological order.

Activity 6.12 Creating a Bulleted List

1 Locate the *Use of trademarks* paragraph, and then move the pointer into the left margin area to display the pointer. Drag down to select this paragraph and the next two paragraphs.

2 On the Mini toolbar, click the **Bullets** button . Alternatively, on the Home tab, in the Paragraph group, click the Bullets button.

The default bullet is a large, round, black dot. Your bullet symbols may differ, depending on which bullets were most recently used on your computer.

3 With the bulleted list still selected, in the **Paragraph group**, click the **Increase Indent** button one time. Click anywhere in the document to deselect the text.

The bulleted list indents another 0.25 inch to the right.

4 Move the pointer into the left margin area to the left of the *Use of trademarks* paragraph until the ⬈ pointer displays. Then, drag down to select this paragraph and the next paragraph.

5 In the **Paragraph group**, click the **Line spacing** button 〔≣▾〕, and notice that the items are double-spaced. Click **1.0** to single-space the selected text, click anywhere in the document to deselect the text, and then compare your screen with Figure 6.24.

6 **Save** 💾 your changes.

Figure 6.24

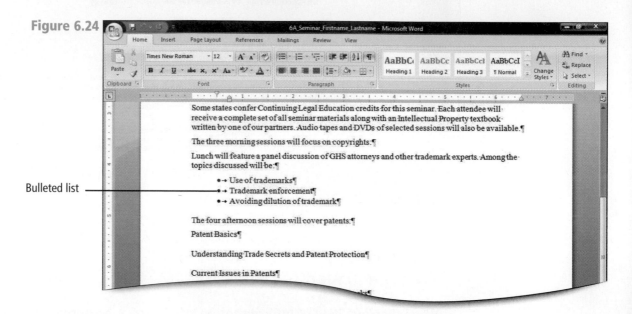

Bulleted list

Activity 6.13 Using AutoFormat to Create a Numbered List

In the previous activity, you created a list using existing text. In this activity, you will create a new list. Because the list items are the names of sessions in sequential order, you will number the items using Word's Numbering command.

1 Locate the paragraph that begins *The three morning sessions*, and then position the insertion point at the end of that paragraph. Press 〔Enter〕 to create a blank line.

> Until you change it, your newly created paragraph will retain the formatting of the previous paragraph, because formatting information is stored in the paragraph mark.

2 From the **Office** menu 🔘, in the lower right corner click **Word Options**. In the list on the left side of the **Word Options** dialog box, click **Proofing**. Under **AutoCorrect options**, click the **AutoCorrect Options** button.

3 In the **AutoCorrect** dialog box, click the **AutoFormat As You Type tab**, and then compare your screen with Figure 6.25.

> *AutoFormat As You Type* is a Word feature that anticipates formatting based on what you type.

Figure 6.25

AutoFormat As You Type tab

Automatic numbered
lists check box

4 Under **Apply as you type**, if it is not selected, select the **Automatic numbered lists** check box, and then click **OK**. At the bottom of the **Word Options** dialog box, click **OK**.

5 Type **1.** and press Spacebar. Be sure to type the period after the number.

Word determines that this paragraph is the first item in a numbered list and formats the new paragraph accordingly. The space after the number changes to a tab, and the AutoCorrect Options button displays to the left of the list item.

6 Click the **AutoCorrect Options** button, and then compare your screen with Figure 6.26.

From the displayed list, you can remove the automatic formatting here, or stop using the automatic numbered lists option in this document. You also have the option to open the AutoCorrect dialog box to *Control AutoFormat Options*.

Figure 6.26

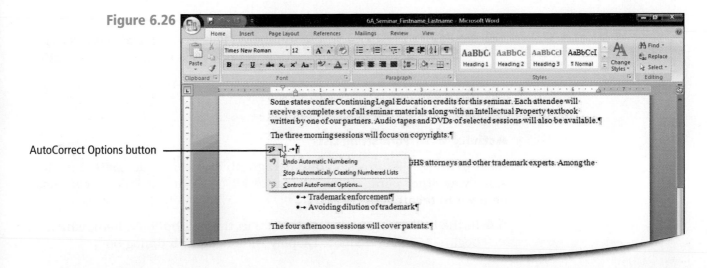

AutoCorrect Options button

7 Click the **AutoCorrect Options** button to close the menu without selecting any of the commands. Type **Introduction to Copyrights** and press Enter. Notice that the second number and a tab are added to the next line.

8 Type **Copyright FAQs** and press Enter. Type **Current Issues in Copyrights** and press Enter. Compare your screen with Figure 6.27.

Figure 6.27

Numbered list

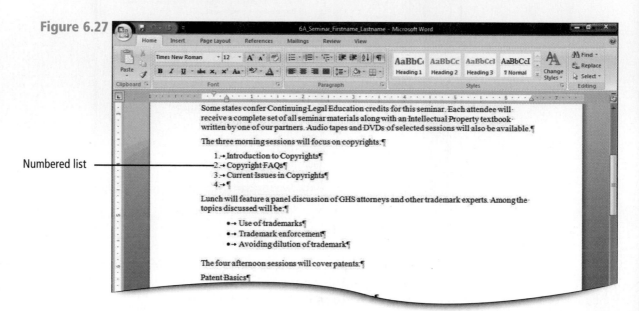

9 Press ←Bksp to turn off the list. Then, press ←Bksp as necessary to remove the blank line.

More Knowledge — To End a List

When you end a list and press Enter, the next line will be formatted as a list item. To turn the list off, you can press ←Bksp, click the Numbering or Bullets button, or press Enter a second time. Both list buttons—Numbering and Bullets—act as *toggle buttons*; that is, clicking the button one time turns the feature on, and clicking the button again turns the feature off.

---

10 Select all three items in the numbered list. In the **Paragraph group**, click the **Increase Indent** button 🔲 one time to move the list 0.25 inch to the right.

11 **Save** 🔲 your document.

Activity 6.14 Formatting Lists

Each item in a list is a separate paragraph and can be formatted in the same way other paragraphs are formatted. The Format Painter can also be used to create lists.

1 In the bulleted list, click anywhere in the last bulleted item, which begins *Avoiding dilution*. Display the **Paragraph** dialog box.

2 Under **Spacing**, click the **Line spacing arrow**, and then click **Single**. Under **Spacing**, in the **After** spin box, click the **up spin arrow** one time to add **6pt** spacing, and then click **OK**. Compare your screen with Figure 6.28.

The last item in the bulleted list now has the same formatting as the last item in the numbered list.

Figure 6.28

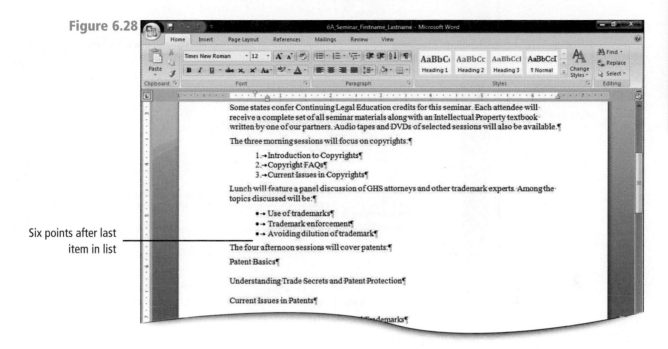

Six points after last item in list

3 In the first item of the numbered list, click anywhere to place the insertion point. In the **Clipboard group**, click the **Format Painter** button.

4 Move the pointer to the *Patent Basics* one-line paragraph, and then click one time. Notice that the *Patent Basics* paragraph takes on the formatting characteristics of the first item in the numbered list, and the numbering continues with the number 4. Also notice that the Format Painter pointer no longer displays.

5 In the **Clipboard group**, double-click the **Format Painter** button. Use the pointer to change the paragraph beginning *Understanding Trade*.

The Format Painter pointer still displays. When you double-click the Format Painter button, it remains active until you turn it off.

6 Use the pointer to change the paragraphs that begin *Current Issues* and *Business Considerations*. Then, in the **Clipboard group**, click the **Format Painter** button to turn it off. Alternatively, press Esc to turn off the Format Painter.

7 Move to **item number 4** in the list—*Patent Basics*—and then right click. Notice that the shortcut menu contains list formatting commands, as shown in Figure 6.29.

Figure 6.29

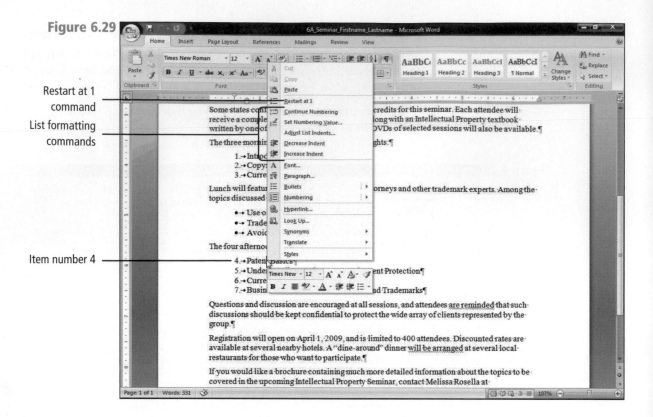

Restart at 1 command

List formatting commands

Item number 4

8 From the shortcut menu, click **Restart at 1**. Notice that the numbering is restarted for the second numbered list.

9 **Save** your document.

More Knowledge — Using Multiple Levels in a Numbered List

If your numbered list contains two levels of information, type all of the list entries using automatic numbering. When you have completed the list, select the items that are at the lower level and click the Increase Indent button. The top level will retain the *1, 2, 3* format, while the lower level will use an *a, b, c* format.

Activity 6.15 Customizing Bullets

You can use any symbol from any font on your computer for your bullet character.

1 Select the three bulleted points, and then right-click anywhere in the selected text. From the shortcut menu, point to **Bullets**, and then compare your screen with Figure 6.30.

A gallery displays showing recently used bullets and a library of popular bullet shapes. The bullets that display in your gallery may differ.

Figure 6.30

Bullets gallery

Bullets command

Bulleted list

2 At the bottom of the **Bullets gallery**, click **Define New Bullet**. In the **Define New Bullet** dialog box, click the **Symbol** button.

3 In the **Symbol** dialog box, be sure *Symbol* displays in the **Font** box. Scroll to the bottom of the list of symbols, and then in the third row from the bottom, click the trademark (TM) symbol, as shown in Figure 6.31.

Figure 6.31

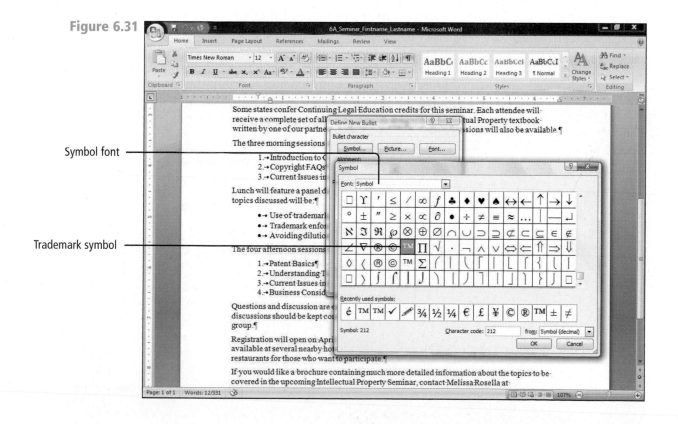

Symbol font

Trademark symbol

4 At the bottom of the **Symbol** dialog box, click **OK**. At the bottom of the **Define New Bullet** dialog box, click **OK**. Click anywhere to deselect the list. Notice that the bullets change to a trademark symbol, as shown in Figure 6.32. **Save** 🖫 your document.

Figure 6.32

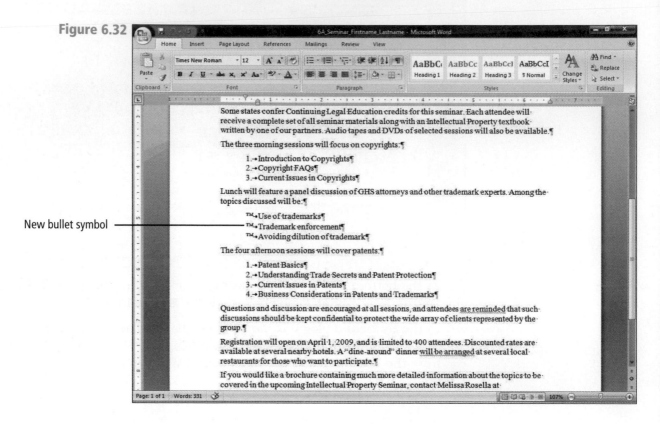

New bullet symbol ———————

5 From the **Office** menu 🔘, point to **Print**, and then click **Print Preview** to make a final check of your document. Check your *Chapter Assignment Sheet* or *Course Syllabus* or consult your instructor to determine if you are to submit your assignments on paper or electronically. To submit electronically, go to Step 7, and then follow the instructions provided by your instructor.

6 On the **Print Preview tab**, in the **Print group**, click the **Print** button. Click **OK**, **Close** the **Print Preview** window and submit your printout as directed.

7 **Close** your document, and then **Exit** Word.

End **You have completed Project 6A** —————————

Project 6B Law Overview

In Activities 6.16 through 6.24, you will edit a research paper, which contains an overview of intellectual property law. This paper was created by a student intern of GHS Law Partners, and will later be modified for inclusion in an information packet for potential clients. Your completed document will look similar to Figure 6.33.

For Project 6B, you will need the following file:

w06B_Law_Overview

You will save your document as
6B_Law_Overview_Firstname_Lastname

Figure 6.33
Project 6B—Law Overview

Objective 4
Insert and Format Headers and Footers

Text that you insert into a header or footer displays on every page of a document. Within a header or footer, you can add automatic page numbers, dates, times, the file name, and pictures.

Activity 6.16 Inserting and Formatting Page Numbers

1 **Start** Word. From your student files, locate and open the document **w06B_Law_Overview**. If necessary, display the formatting marks. Be sure all document margins are set to **1"**. **Save** the file in your **Word Chapter 6** folder as **6B_Law_Overview_Firstname_Lastname**

Note — Standard Styles for Research Papers

When you write a research paper or a report for college or business, you will need to follow a format prescribed by one of the standard style guides. The two most commonly used styles are those created by the *Modern Language Association (MLA)* and the *American Psychological Association (APA)*; there are several others. This project uses the MLA style.

---

2 Press Ctrl + A. Right-click the selected text, and then click **Paragraph**. In the **Paragraph** dialog box, under **Spacing**, click the **After down spin arrow** two times to set the space after to **0**. Click the **Line spacing arrow**, and then click **Double**. Click **OK**.

> The MLA style uses 1-inch margins and double spacing throughout the document, with no extra space between paragraphs.

3 Press Ctrl + Home. Type **Mary Cowling** and press Enter, and then type **Henry Kim** and press Enter. Type **Business Law** and press Enter, and then type **October 1, 2009** and press Enter.

> The first line in an MLA research paper is the name of the author; the second is the name of the person for whom the report is prepared—for example, your course professor. The third line contains the name of the class, and the fourth line contains the date.

4 Type **Intellectual Property Overview** and then press Enter. Press ↑ to place the insertion point in the line you just typed. In the **Paragraph group**, click the **Center** button ▤, and then compare your screen with Figure 6.34.

Figure 6.34

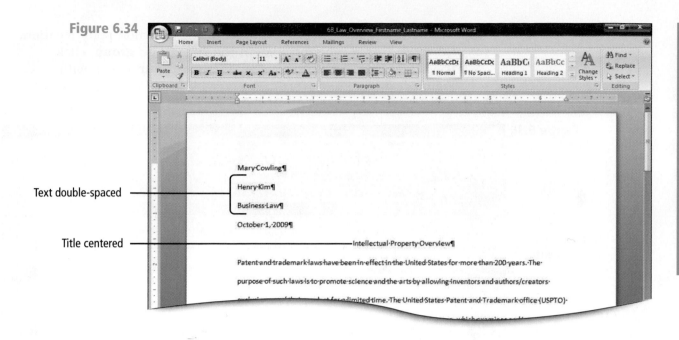

Text double-spaced

Title centered

5 Move the pointer to the top edge of **Page 1** and right-click. Click **Edit Header**, in the header area, type **Cowling** and then press Spacebar.

6 On the **Design tab**, in the **Insert group**, click the **Quick Parts** button, and then click **Field**. In the **Field** dialog box, under **Field names**, locate and click **Page**. Under **Field properties**, click the first page number style—**1, 2, 3**. Compare your screen with Figure 6.35.

Figure 6.35

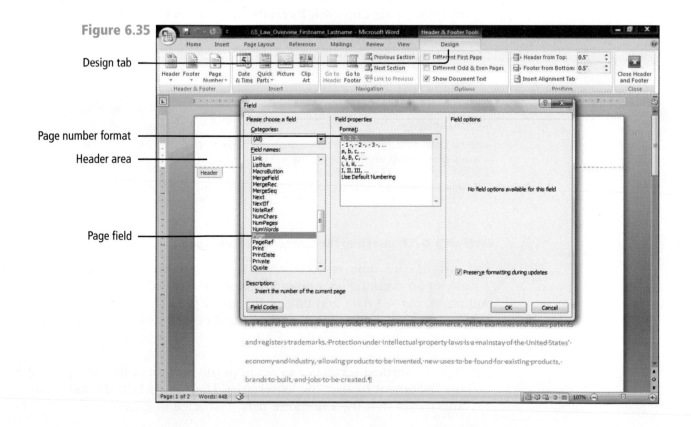

Design tab

Page number format

Header area

Page field

7 Click **OK** to place the page number at the insertion point location. Click the **Home tab**, and then in the **Paragraph group**, click the **Align Text Right** button . Compare your screen with Figure 6.36.

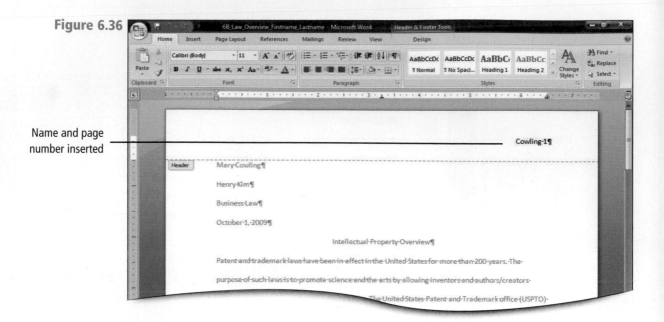

Figure 6.36

Name and page number inserted

8 Click the **Design tab**, and then in the **Navigation group**, click the **Go to Footer** button. In the **Insert group**, click the **Quick Parts** button, and then click **Field**. In the **Field** dialog box, under **Field names**, locate and click **FileName**, and then click **OK**.

9 Double-click anywhere outside the footer area, and then press Ctrl + Home. **Save** your changes.

More Knowledge — Suppressing the Page Number on the First Page of a Document

Some style guidelines may require that the page number on the first page be hidden from view—suppressed. To hide the information contained in the header and footer areas on Page 1 of a document, double-click in the header or footer area. On the Design tab, in the Options group, select the Different First Page check box.

Activity 6.17 Inserting the Current Date and Time

The current date, time, or both can be inserted anywhere in a document. When you are working on a research paper, which will likely be revised several times, put the date and time in the footer to help identify the various revisions you will make. Then, remove the date and time before submitting the paper.

1 Use the vertical scroll bar to scroll to the bottom of the first page of the document to view the footer area. Double-click in the footer area, and notice that the **FileName** field is shaded in gray.

2 Click to position the insertion point to the right of the file name, and then press Enter to move the insertion point to the next line.

3 On the **Design tab**, in the **Insert group**, click the **Date & Time** button.

4 In the **Date and Time** dialog box, locate and click the date and time format that displays the date in a *10/01/2009 4:43 PM* (or *AM*) format, as shown in Figure 6.37.

Figure 6.37
Date & Time button

Selected format
(your date and
time will vary)

Note — Automatically Update the Date

At the bottom of the Date and Time dialog box, you can select the *Update automatically* check box to have Word update the date every time you open the document.

---

5 In the **Date and Time** dialog box, click **OK**. Double-click anywhere outside the footer area, and then press Ctrl + Home.

6 **Save** 🖫 your changes.

Objective 5
Insert Frequently Used Text

AutoCorrect corrects common spelling errors as you type. When you type a word incorrectly, for example *teh*, Word automatically changes it to *the*. You can add words that you frequently misspell to the AutoCorrect list. You can also add shortcuts to phrases you type often. Another type of frequently used text includes various symbols, such as the trademark symbol ™ or copyright symbol ©.

Activity 6.18 Recording AutoCorrect Entries

You can add words that you frequently misspell to the AutoCorrect list for automatic correction.

1 From the **Office** menu 🔘, click **Word Options**. In the **Word Options** list, click **Proofing**, and then under **AutoCorrect options**, click the **AutoCorrect Options** button.

2 In the **AutoCorrect** dialog box, click the **AutoCorrect tab**. Under **Replace**, type **intellectaul** and under **With**, type **intellectual** Compare your screen with Figure 6.38.

> If another student has already added this AutoCorrect entry, the Add button will change to a Replace button.

Figure 6.38

intellectaul and *intellectual* added to the AutoCorrect list

Replace or Add button

3 Click **Add**. If the entry already exists, click Replace instead, and then click Yes. Click **OK** two times to close the dialog boxes.

4 Near the top of the document, locate the paragraph beginning *Patent and trademark laws*, and then click to position the insertion point at the beginning of the paragraph. Scroll to the end of the document, hold down ⇧Shift, and then click to the right of the last paragraph mark. Scroll up to see the top of the document.

5 Right-click the selected text and click **Paragraph**. On the **Indents and Spacing tab**, under **Indentation**, click the **Special arrow**, and then click **First line**. Under **Indentation**, in the **By** box, be sure *0.5"* displays. Compare your screen with Figure 6.39.

> ***Indenting***—moving the beginning of the first line of a paragraph to the right or left of the rest of the paragraph—provides visual cues to the reader to help break the document up and make it easier to read. The MLA style uses 0.5-inch indents at the beginning of the first line of every paragraph.

Figure 6.39

Indentation will be applied to the *First line* of the paragraph

First line will be indented 0.5 (one-half) inch

☐6 Click **OK**. Near the top of the document, locate the paragraph beginning *Patent and trademark laws*, and then click to position the insertion point at the beginning of the paragraph.

☐7 Press [Enter], and then press [↑] to place the insertion point in the blank line. Type **Patents, copyrights, and trademarks are all examples of protections of** and then press [Spacebar].

☐8 Type **intellectaul** and watch the screen as you press [Spacebar]. Notice that the misspelled word is automatically corrected.

☐9 Click in the corrected word, and then notice the blue line that displays under the word. Move the pointer over the blue line until the **AutoCorrect Options** button displays, and then click the button. Compare your screen with Figure 6.40.

Figure 6.40

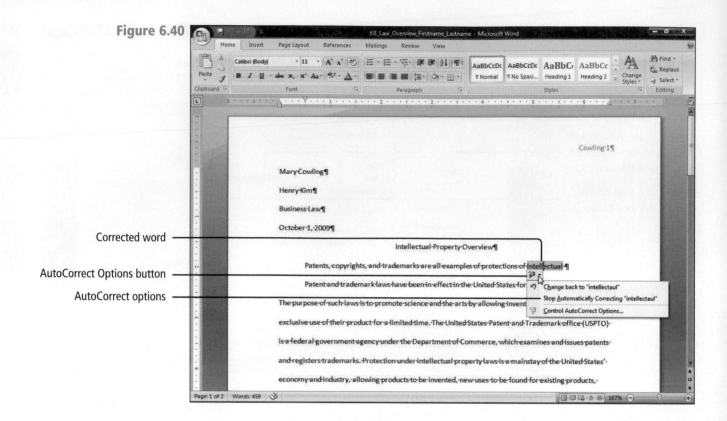

Corrected word

AutoCorrect Options button

AutoCorrect options

10 Click anywhere in the document to close the **AutoCorrect Options** menu without selecting a command. Locate the word *intellectual* that you just corrected and position the insertion point at the end of that line. Type **property (IP).** and then press ⏐Spacebar⏐.

11 Type the remainder of the paragraph, and then compare your screen with Figure 6.41.

Intellectual property has many definitions, but is usually considered to be information having commercial value and original products of the mind. Intellectual property isn't tangible, but can be protected by the law. Intellectual property is not an item that was invented, but the thought process and plans that allowed the item to be invented and manufactured. Intellectual property is not the clothing that is sold in stores, but rather the brand name that represents the quality and style of the clothing.

Figure 6.41

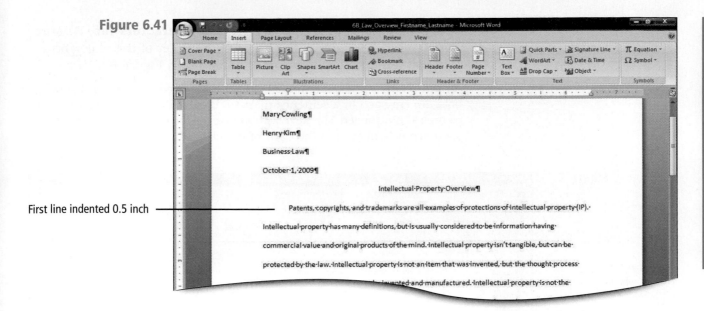

First line indented 0.5 inch

12 Save 🖫 your changes.

> ### More Knowledge — AutoCorrect Shortcuts
>
> The AutoCorrect replacement is most commonly used to correct spelling errors, but it can also be used to expand shortcut text into longer words or phrases. In the Replace box, type a shortcut phrase, and type the full phrase in the With box. When setting up an AutoCorrect shortcut, it is best not to use shortcut text that is an actual word or a commonly used abbreviation. For example, if you type both *GHS* and *GHS Law Partners* frequently, you may want to add ghsx (or just ghx) as an AutoCorrect shortcut for the text *GHS Law Partners*.

Activity 6.19 Inserting Symbols

There are many symbols that are used occasionally, but not often enough to put on a standard keyboard. These symbols can be found on, and inserted from, the Symbols group on the Insert tab.

1 Use the vertical scroll bar to move down in the document to display the bottom half of **Page 1**.

2 In the paragraph that begins *Patent is defined*, in the second line, locate the word *novel*, and then place the insertion point just to the right of the word. Press [Delete] two times to remove the space and the left parenthesis.

3 Click the **Insert tab**, and then in the **Symbols group**, click the **Symbol** button. At the bottom of the **Symbol gallery**, click **More Symbols**.

4 In the **Symbol** dialog box, click the **Special Characters tab**. Be sure the **Em Dash** is selected. In the lower right corner of the dialog box, click **Insert**, and then compare your screen with Figure 6.42.

> An *em dash* is the default symbol in the list of commonly used symbols. An em dash in a sentence marks a break in thought, similar to a comma but stronger. The keyboard shortcuts for inserting the commonly used symbols display to the right of the character name.

Figure 6.42

Inserted em dash

Keyboard shortcuts

Em dash

5 If necessary, drag the dialog box out of the way so you can see the third line of the same paragraph. With the **Symbol** dialog box still open, to the right of *in a publication*, remove the right parenthesis, the comma, and the space; and then click the **Insert** button again. At the bottom of the **Symbol** dialog box, click **Close**.

6 Press Ctrl + Home to move to the beginning of the document. Place the insertion point to the right of the title text *Intellectual Property Overview*, type **(c)** and then compare your document with Figure 6.43.

> Your typed text *(c)* changes to the copyright symbol ©. Although this symbol is available from the Symbol gallery, it is also included in Word's AutoCorrect list. The parentheses are necessary for AutoComplete to insert a Copyright symbol. If you point to the copyright symbol, the AutoCorrect Options button displays, which enables you to remove the copyright symbol and display *(c)* instead.

Figure 6.43

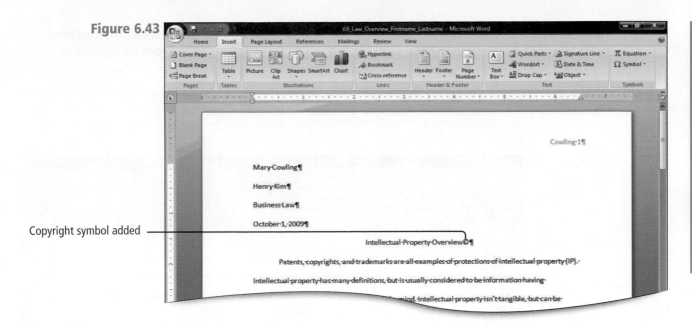

Copyright symbol added

Word | Chapter 6

7 **Save** 📄 your changes.

Objective 6
Insert and Format References

Reports frequently include information taken from other sources, and these must be credited. Within report text, numbers mark the location of *references*—information that has been taken from another source. The numbers refer to *footnotes*—references placed at the bottom of the page containing the reference, or *endnotes*—references placed at the end of a document or chapter. When footnotes or endnotes are included in a report, a page listing the references is included. Such a list is commonly titled *Works Cited*, *Bibliography*, *Sources*, or References.

Activity 6.20 Inserting Footnotes

Footnotes can be added as you type the document or after the document is complete. Footnotes do not need to be entered in order, and if one footnote is removed, Word renumbers the remaining footnotes automatically.

1 Scroll to view **Page 2** and locate the paragraph that begins *Copyrights protect*. At the end of the paragraph, position the insertion point following the period.

2 Click the **References tab**, and then in the **Footnotes group**, click **Insert Footnote**.

Word creates a footnote in the footnote area at the bottom of the page, and adds a footnote number to the text at the insertion point location. Footnote 1 displays at the top of the footnote area, and the insertion point moves to the right of the number. A short blank line is added just above the footnote area. You do not need to type the footnote number.

3 Type **According to the United States Copyright Office, abstractions, such as an idea for a book or movie, are not subject to copyright law.** Compare your screen with Figure 6.44.

This is an explanatory footnote, giving additional information that does not fit well in the body of the report. The new footnote is single-spaced, even though the document text is double-spaced.

Figure 6.44

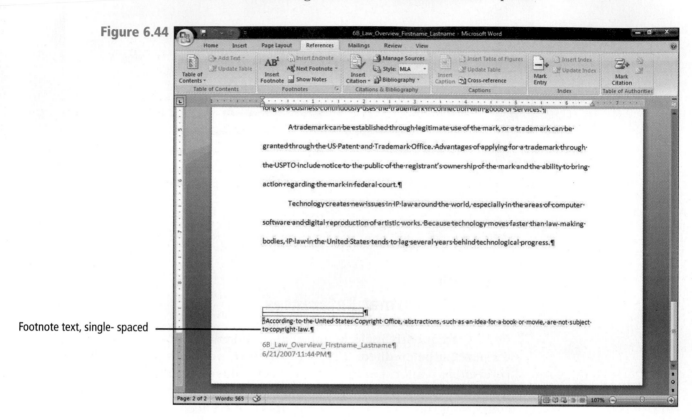

Footnote text, single- spaced

4 Press [Ctrl] + [Home] to move to the beginning of the document. Locate the paragraph that begins *Patents, copyrights.* At the end of the paragraph, position the insertion point following the period.

This sentence refers to the *protections* of intellectual property, and the report's author wants to clarify the scope of protections by adding a reference.

5 In the **Footnotes group**, click the **Insert Footnote** button. Type **There is no set of international intellectual property laws, although many countries have reciprocal copyright, trademark, and patent agreements with the United States.** Notice that the footnote you just added is the new footnote *1*, while the other footnote is renumbered as footnote *2*.

6 **Save** 💾 your changes.

More Knowledge — Using Symbols Rather Than Numbers for Notes

Instead of using numbers to designate footnotes, you can use standard footnote symbols. The seven traditional symbols, available from the Footnote and Endnote dialog box, in order, are * (asterisk), † (dagger), ‡ (double dagger), § (section mark), || (parallels), ¶ (paragraph mark), and # (number or pound sign). This sequence can be continuous (this is the default setting), or can begin anew with each page.

Activity 6.21 Modifying a Footnote Style

Microsoft Word contains built-in paragraph formats called *styles*, which can be applied to a paragraph with one command. The default style for footnote text is a single-spaced paragraph that uses a 10-point Calibri font and no indents. MLA style specifies double-spaced text in all areas of a research paper—including footnotes. According to the MLA style, footnotes must also be indented 0.5 inch.

1 Scroll to view the bottom of **Page 1** and right-click anywhere in the footnote text. From the shortcut menu, click **Style**. Compare your screen with Figure 6.45.

> The Style dialog box displays, listing the styles currently in use in the document, in addition to some of the word processing elements that come with special built-in styles. Because you right-clicked on the footnote text, the selected style is the Footnote Text paragraph style.

Figure 6.45

All styles selected

Elements with special built-in styles

Footnote Text paragraph style

Modify button

2 In the **Style** dialog box, click the **Modify** button. In the **Modify Style** dialog box, locate the small Formatting toolbar in the center of the dialog box, click the **Font Size button arrow**, click **11**, and then compare your screen with Figure 6.46.

Figure 6.46

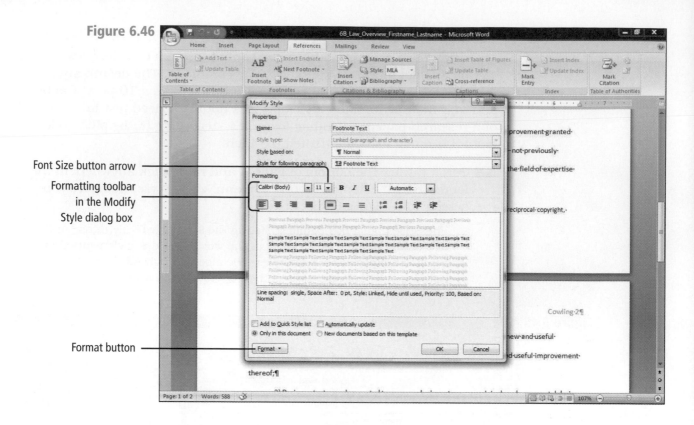

Font Size button arrow

Formatting toolbar
in the Modify
Style dialog box

Format button

---

3 In the lower left corner of the dialog box, click the **Format** button, and then click **Paragraph**. In the **Paragraph** dialog box, under **Indentation**, click the **Special arrow**, and then click **First line**.

4 Under **Spacing**, click the **Line spacing button arrow**, and then click **Double**. Compare your dialog box with Figure 6.47.

Figure 6.47

First line indent

Line spacing set to *Double*

---

5 Click **OK** to close the **Paragraph** dialog box, click **OK** to close the **Modify Style** dialog box, and then click **Apply** to apply the new style and close the **Style** dialog box. Compare your screen with Figure 6.48.

> Your inserted footnotes are formatted with the new Footnote Text paragraph style; any new footnotes that you insert will also use this format.

Figure 6.48

First line indented

Footnote text double-spaced

6 Scroll to view the bottom of **Page 2** to confirm that the new format was also applied to the second footnote, and then **Save** your document.

Activity 6.22 Adding Citations

When writing a long research paper, you will likely reference numerous books, articles, and Web sites. Some of your research sources may be referenced many times, others only one time. References to sources within the text of your research paper are indicated in an *abbreviated* manner. However, as you enter a reference for the first time, you can also enter the *complete* information about the source. Then, when you have finished your paper, you will be able to automatically generate the list of sources that must be included at the end of your research paper.

1 On **Page 2** of the document, locate the paragraph that begins *Copyrights protect*, and then position the insertion point at the end of the paragraph, but before the period. Click the **References tab** to begin the process of inserting a citation.

> A *citation* is a list of information about a source, usually including the name of the author, the full title of the work, the year of publication, and other publication information.

2 In the **Citations & Bibliography group**, click the **Style button arrow**, and then click **MLA** to insert a reference using MLA style.

3 Click the **Insert Citation** button, and then click **Add New Source**. Be sure **Book** is selected as the **Type of Source**. Add the following information, and then compare your screen with Figure 6.49:

Author:	**Schechter, Roger E.; Thomas, John R.**
Title:	**Intellectual Property: The Law of Copyrights, Patents and Trademarks**
Year:	**2003**
City:	**St. Paul, MN**
Publisher:	**West Publishing Company**

Figure 6.49

Insert Citation button on the Ribbon

Source type

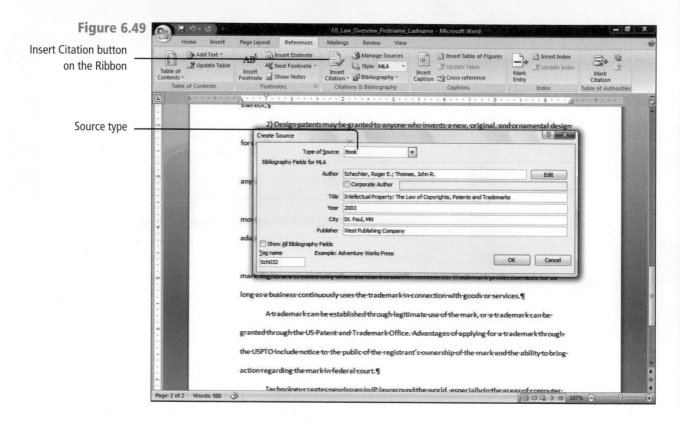

In the MLA style, references to items on the Works Cited page are placed in *parenthetical references*—references that include the last name of the author or authors and the page number in the referenced source, which you add to the reference. No year is indicated, and there is no comma between the name and the page number.

4 Click **OK** to insert the reference. Click to select the reference, and notice that a small box surrounds the reference and an arrow displays in the lower right corner of the box. Click this **Citation Options arrow**, and then from the list of options, click **Edit Citation**.

5 In the **Edit Citation** dialog box, under **Add**, in the **Pages** box, type **2** to indicate that you are citing from page 2 of this source. Compare your screen with Figure 6.50. Notice that the citation wraps from one line to the next, so the citation box also wraps between lines.

Figure 6.50

Word | Chapter 6

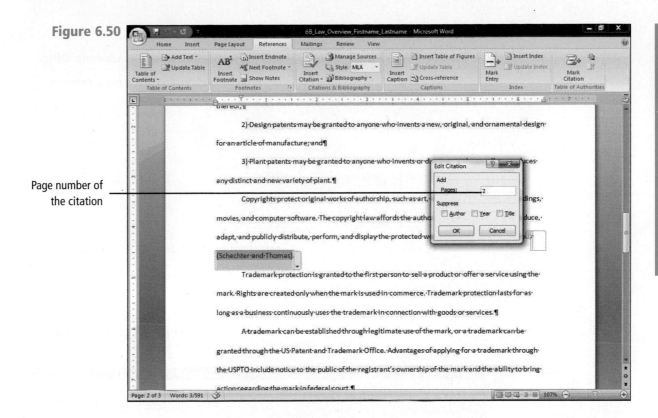

Page number of
the citation

6B_Law_Overview_Firstname_Lastname - Microsoft Word

2) Design patents may be granted to anyone who invents a new, original, and ornamental design for an article of manufacture; and¶

3) Plant patents may be granted to anyone who invents or di...uces any distinct and new variety of plant.¶

Copyrights protect original works of authorship, such as art, ...dings, movies, and computer software. The copyright law affords the autho...duce, adapt, and publicly distribute, perform, and display the protected we...

(Schechter and Thomas).

Trademark protection is granted to the first person to sell a product or offer a service using the mark. Rights are created only when the mark is used in commerce. Trademark protection lasts for as long as a business continuously uses the trademark in connection with goods or services.¶

A trademark can be established through legitimate use of the mark, or a trademark can be granted through the US Patent and Trademark Office. Advantages of applying for a trademark through the USPTO include notice to the public of the registrant's ownership of the mark and the ability to bring action regarding the mark in federal court.¶

Edit Citation dialog box contents:
Add
Pages: 2
Suppress
☐ Author ☐ Year ☐ Title
OK   Cancel

Page: 2 of 3   Words: 3/591   107%

6 Click **OK** to display the page number of the citation. In the next paragraph, which begins *Trademark protection*, position the insertion point at the end of the paragraph, but before the period.

7 In the **Citations & Bibliography group**, click the **Insert Citation** button, and then click **Add New Source**. Be sure **Book** is selected as the **Type of Source**, and then add the following information:

Author:	**Stim, Richard W.**
Title:	**Trademark Law**
Year:	**2000**
City:	**Stamford, CT**
Publisher:	**Thomson Delmar Learning**

8 Click **OK**. Click to select the reference, click the **Citation Options arrow**, and then click **Edit Citation**. In the **Edit Citation** dialog box, under **Add**, in the **Pages** box, type **4** to indicate that you are citing from page 4 of this source. Click **OK**.

9 On the same page, locate the paragraph that begins *3) Plant patents*. At the end of that sentence, click to position the insertion point before the period. In the **Citations & Bibliography group**, click the **Insert Citation** button, and then click **Add New Source**. Click the **Type of Source arrow**, scroll down, and select **Web site** from the list. Under **Bibliography Fields for MLA**, click to select the **Corporate Author** check box.

10 Type the following information:

Corporate Author:	**United States Patent and Trademark Office**
Name of Web Page:	**General Information Concerning Patents**
Year:	**2005**
Month:	**March**
Day:	**22**
Year Accessed:	**2009**
Month Accessed:	**October**
Day Accessed:	**11**
URL:	**http://www.uspto.gov/web/offices/pac/doc/general/index.html#patent**

11 Click **OK**, and then compare your screen with Figure 6.51.

A parenthetical reference is added. Because the cited Web page has no page numbers, only the author name is used in the parenthetical reference.

Figure 6.51

Parenthetical references

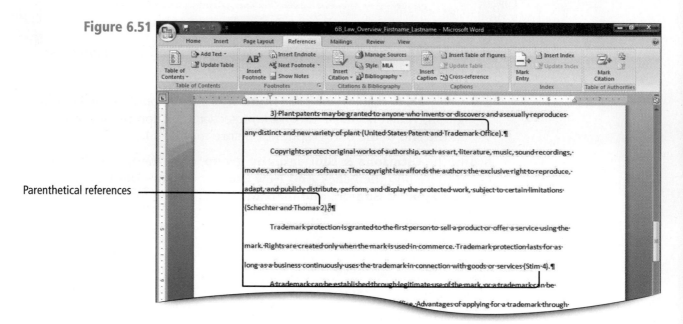

12 On the **References tab**, in the **Citations & Bibliography group**, click the **Manage Sources** button, and then compare your screen with Figure 6.52.

The Source Manager dialog box displays. You may have fewer sources, more sources, or different sources. Other citations on your computer display in the Master List box. The citations for the current document display in the Current List box. If you use the same sources regularly, you can copy sources from your Master List to the current document.

Figure 6.52

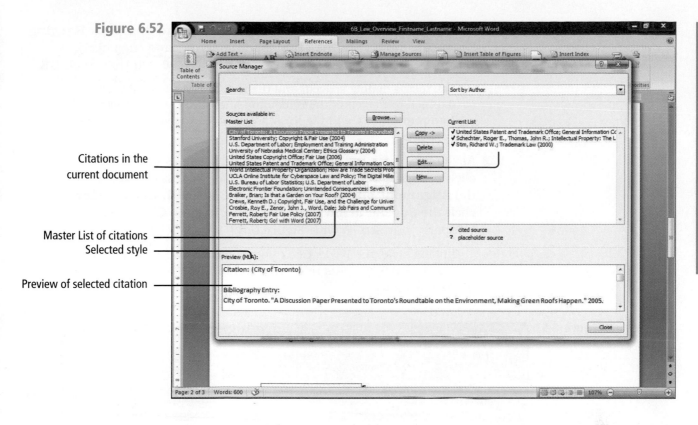

Citations in the current document

Master List of citations
Selected style

Preview of selected citation

13 At the bottom of the **Source Manager** dialog box, click **Close**. **Save** your changes.

Activity 6.23 Creating a Reference Page

It is common to include, at the end of a report, a list of each source referenced. *Works Cited* is the reference page heading used in the MLA style guidelines. Other styles may refer to this page as a *Bibliography* (Business Style) or *References* (APA Style).

1 Press Ctrl + End to move the insertion point to the end of the document. Press Ctrl + Enter to insert a manual page break.

2 Type **Works Cited** and then press Enter. On the **References tab**, in the **Citations & Bibliography group**, be sure **MLA** displays in the **Style** box.

3 In the **Citations & Bibliography group**, click the **Bibliography** button, and then click **Insert Bibliography**.

The bibliography displays as a field, and the field links to the Source Manager for the citations. The references display alphabetically by author name.

4 In the bibliography, move the pointer to the left of the first entry—beginning *Schechter, Roger*—to display the ↗ pointer. Drag down to select all three references. Right-click the selected text, and then click **Paragraph**.

5 Under **Indentation**, click the **Special arrow**, and then click **Hanging**. Under **Spacing**, click the **Line spacing arrow**, and then click **Double**. Under **Spacing**, in the **After** box, type **0** and then click **OK**.

> The text is double-spaced, and the first line of each entry extends 0.5 inch to the left of the remaining lines of the entry. This is called a *hanging indent*, and the lines are double-spaced according to MLA guidelines.

6 At the top of the last page, right-click the *Works Cited* title, and then click **Paragraph**. In the **Paragraph** dialog box, under **General**, click the **Alignment arrow**, and then click **Centered**. Under **Indentation**, click the **Special arrow**, and then click **(none)**. Click **OK**, and then compare your screen with Figure 6.53.

> In MLA style, the *Works Cited* title is aligned and centered. The first line indent of 0.5 inch was removed to center the title between the left and right margins.

Figure 6.53

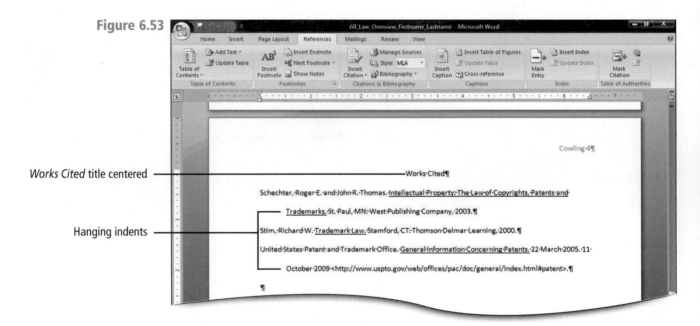

Works Cited title centered

Hanging indents

7 **Save** your document.

Activity 6.24 Managing Document Properties

Document properties refer to the detailed information about your Word document file that can help you identify or organize your electronic files. Document property information is stored in the *Document Information Panel*, and can include the document title, the name of the author, the subject of the document, and keywords that will help you search for the document in your computer system.

1 From the **Office** menu 🔵, point to **Prepare**, and then click **Properties** to display the **Document Information Panel**.

2 In the **Author** box, type your name, if necessary.

3 In the **Title** box, type **Intellectual Property Law**

4 In the **Keywords** box, type **copyright, patent, trademark** and then compare your screen with Figure 6.54. Notice that not all boxes need to be filled in.

Figure 6.54

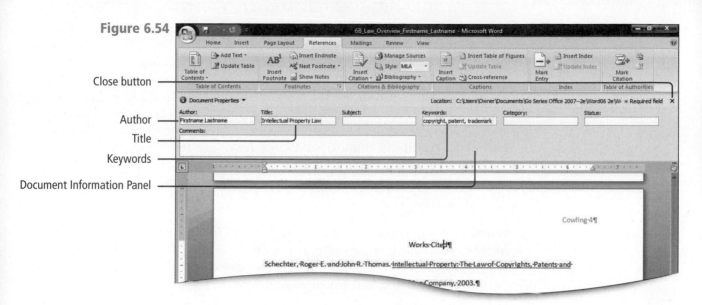

Close button

Author

Title

Keywords

Document Information Panel

5 On the right side of the **Document Information Panel**, click the **Close** button ☒, **Save** 🖫 your document.

6 From the **Office** menu 🏛, point to **Print**, and then click **Print Preview** to make a final check of your research paper. Check your *Chapter Assignment Sheet* or *Course Syllabus* or consult your instructor to determine if you are to submit your assignments on paper or electronically. To submit electronically, go to Step 8, and then follow the instructions provided by your instructor.

7 On the **Print Preview tab**, in the **Print group**, click the **Print** button, click **OK**, and then click **Close Print Preview**.

8 From the **Office** menu 🏛, click **Exit Word**, saving any changes if prompted to do so.

End **You have completed Project 6B**

There's More You Can Do!

Close Word and any other open windows. Display the Start menu, click Computer, and then navigate to the student files that accompany this textbook. In the folder **02_theres_more_you_can_do**, locate and open the folder for this chapter. Open and print the instructions for this project, which are provided to you in Adobe PDF format.

Try IT!—Add a Custom Entry to the Quick Part Gallery

In this Try It! exercise, you will add a custom entry to the Quick Part gallery.

Content-Based Assessments

Summary

You can change the format of pages by setting different margins, and change the format of paragraphs by changing indents, line spacing, and the spacing after paragraphs. To apply formats from one paragraph to others, use the Format Painter. You can also format paragraphs by creating numbered and bulleted lists and modifying the bullets.

Use commands such as Cut and Paste, or techniques such as the drag-and-drop operation, to move and copy text. Use the Find and Replace dialog box to locate text that you want to modify. Some formatting in Word can be performed automatically using AutoCorrect and AutoComplete.

When creating reports, use the header and footer areas to add page numbers or to insert the date, time, or file name. Reports also require adding footnotes or endnotes and a reference page to list other sources of information cited within the report.

Key Terms

The 🌐 symbol represents Key Terms found on the Student CD in the 02_theres_more_you_can_do folder for this chapter.

Content-Based Assessments

Matching

Match each term in the second column with its correct definition in the first column by writing the letter of the term on the blank line in front of the correct definition.

_____ **1.** The most commonly used text alignment, where text is aligned at the left margin, leaving the right margin uneven.

_____ **2.** The alignment of text centered between the left and right margins.

_____ **3.** Text that is aligned on both the left and right margins.

_____ **4.** The distance between lines of text in a paragraph.

_____ **5.** A small box with upward- and downward-pointing arrows that let you move rapidly through a set of values.

_____ **6.** A Word tool with which you can copy the formatting of specific text, or of a paragraph, to text in another location in the document.

_____ **7.** A temporary storage area that holds text or graphics that have been cut or copied, and that can subsequently be placed in another location in the document or in another Office program.

_____ **8.** The action of removing selected text from a document and moving it to the Office Clipboard.

_____ **9.** A small button that displays beneath pasted text, and lets you determine how the information is pasted into your document.

_____ **10.** Text symbols such as small circles or check marks used to introduce items in a list.

_____ **11.** A Word feature that automatically corrects common typing and spelling errors as you type, such as changing _teh_ to _the_.

_____ **12.** The word processing name for a long dash in a sentence that marks a break in thought, similar to a comma but stronger.

_____ **13.** In a report or research paper, references placed at the bottom of a report page containing the source of the reference.

_____ **14.** A term used to describe a list of referenced works placed at the end of a research paper or report when using the MLA style.

_____ **15.** An indent style in which the first line of a paragraph extends to the left of the remaining lines; this indent style is commonly used for bibliographic entries.

A AutoCorrect

B Bullets

C Center alignment

D Cutting

E Em dash

F Footnotes

G Format Painter

H Hanging indent

I Justified alignment

J Left alignment

K Line spacing

L Office Clipboard

M Paste Options

N Spin box

O Works Cited

Content-Based Assessments

Fill in the Blank

Write the correct answer in the space provided.

1. The space between the text and the top, bottom, left, and right edges of the paper is known as the _____.

2. The placement of paragraph text relative to the left and right margins is known as the _____.

3. When you paste text, the text is moved from the _____ _____ and placed where the insertion point is positioned.

4. The keyboard shortcut used to copy text is Ctrl + _____.

5. When you drag text and then drop it in another location, the text is _____ from one place to another.

6. When you click the Redo button, it reverses the action of the _____ button.

7. To keep two words together as one unit, so that Word does not split them at the end of a line, insert a _____ space.

8. To move the insertion point to the next line without pressing Enter and without creating a new paragraph, insert a manual _____ _____.

9. A list of items with each item introduced by a consecutive number to indicate definite steps, a sequence of actions, or chronological order is a _____ list.

10. In a report or research paper, a reference placed at the end of a report is called an _____.

11. If you need to add ™ or ® or © to a document, display the _____ dialog box.

12. A set of formatting characteristics that can be applied to a paragraph with one shortcut command is known as a _____.

13. In the MLA report style, references placed in parentheses within the report text that includes the last name of the author or authors and the page number in the referenced source, are called _____ _____.

14. A list of information about a reference source, usually including the name of the author, the full title of the work, the year of publication, a Web address, and other publication information, is called a _____.

15. The detailed information about a document that can help you identify or organize your files, including author name, title, and keywords, is called the Document _____.

Content-Based Assessments

Project 6C—Patent Search

In this project, you will apply the skills you practiced from the Objectives in Project 6A.

Objectives: 1. *Change Document and Paragraph Layout;* **2.** *Change and Reorganize Text;* **3.** *Create and Modify Lists.*

In the following Skills Review, you will edit a document describing the patent search process performed by GHS Law Partners. Your completed document will look similar to the one shown in Figure 6.55.

For Project 6C, you will need the following file:

w06C_Patent_Search

You will save your document as 6C_Patent_Search_Firstname_Lastname

Figure 6.55

(Project 6C–Patent Search continues on the next page)

Content-Based Assessments

Skills Review

(Project 6C–Patent Search continued)

1. **Start** Word. Locate and open the file **w06C_Patent_Search**, and then **Save** the file in your **Word Chapter 6** folder as 6C_Patent_Search_Firstname_Lastname Display formatting marks and rulers.

2. Click the **Page Layout tab**, click the **Margins** button, and then at the bottom of the **Margins gallery**, click **Custom Margins**. In the **Page Setup** dialog box, press Tab as necessary to select the value in the **Left** box. With *1.25"* selected, type **1** and then press Tab. In the **Right** box, change the value from *1.25"* to **1** and then click **OK**.

3. Click the **Insert tab**. In the **Header & Footer group**, click the **Footer** button, and then click **Edit Footer**. On the **Design tab**, in the **Insert group**, click the **Quick Parts** button, and then click **Field**. In the **Field** dialog box, under **Field names**, locate and click **FileName**, and then click **OK**. Double-click anywhere in the document to close the footer area. **Save** your document.

4. Select the first line of the document. On the Mini toolbar, click the **Center** button, and then click the **Bold** button.

5. Right-click anywhere in the paragraph beginning *GHS Law Partners conducts patent*, and then from the shortcut menu, click **Paragraph**. In the **Paragraph** dialog box, under **Indentation**, click the **Special arrow**, and then click **First line**. Under **Spacing**, in the **After** box, click the **up spin arrow** to change the spacing from *10 pt* to **12 pt**. Under **Spacing**, click the **Line spacing arrow**, and then click **Single**. Click **OK** to close the Paragraph dialog box.

6. With the insertion point in the paragraph beginning *GHS Law Partners conducts patent*, in the **Clipboard group**, double-click the **Format Painter** button. Move the [AI] pointer to the paragraph beginning *The search process* and click one time. Use the **Format Painter** to format the paragraph that begins *GHS Law Partners conducts three*, the paragraph beginning *GHS Law Partners employs*, and the last paragraph in the document, beginning *GHS Law Partners can also*. In the **Clipboard group**, click the **Format Painter** button again to turn it off.

7. **Save** your changes. Press Ctrl + Home. On the right side of the **Home tab**, in the **Editing group**, click the **Replace** button. In the **Find and Replace** dialog box, in the **Find what** box, type **USPTO** and in the **Replace with** box, type **United States Patent and Trademark Office**

8. In the **Find and Replace** dialog box, click the **More** button, and then under **Search Options**, if necessary, select the **Match case** check box. Click **Find Next** to find the first instance of *USPTO*, and then click the **Replace** button. **Close** the dialog box.

9. In the fourth line of the document, double-click to select the word *already*, and then in the **Clipboard group**, click the **Cut** button. Move the pointer to the right of the next word in the sentence—*patented*—and then click the **Paste** button. In the next paragraph, beginning *The search process*, locate and select the last sentence, beginning *Patents are grouped*. In the **Clipboard group**, click the **Cut** button. Move the insertion point to the beginning of the same paragraph, and then click the **Paste** button. Adjust spacing at the end of the pasted sentence as necessary.

10. In the fifth paragraph beginning *Examine the patent*, select the entire paragraph, including the paragraph mark. Drag the

(Project 6C–Patent Search continues on the next page)

Content-Based Assessments

Skills Review

(Project 6C–Patent Search continued)

paragraph down to the beginning of the paragraph beginning *GHS Law Partners employs*. In the same paragraph, select *Examine* and replace it with **Study**

11. On the **Quick Access Toolbar**, click the **Undo** button to remove *Study* and replace it with *Examine*. Click the **Undo** button one more time to move the paragraph back to its original location, and then click the **Redo** button to move it back to its new location.

12. Near the top of **Page 2**, in the paragraph beginning *Appl. No.: 737838*, select the space before *2000*. Hold down Ctrl and ⇧ Shift, and then press Spacebar to add a nonbreaking space. Use the same procedure to add a nonbreaking space between *December* and *14* to keep the date together if the line is edited.

13. Press Ctrl + Home. Right-click the title, and then click **Paragraph**. Under **Spacing**, in the **After** box, click the **up spin arrow** two times to change the value in the box from *10 pt* to **18 pt**. Click the **Line spacing arrow**, and then click **Single**. Click **OK**. In the title, click to the left of **Patent**, and then remove the space between *Partners* and *Patent*. Hold down ⇧ Shift and press Enter to enter a manual line break. **Save** your document.

14. In the middle of **Page 1**, point to the left of the paragraph beginning *Organize the search*, and then drag down to select the next four lines, including the line beginning *Examine the patent*. On the **Home**

tab, in the **Paragraph group**, click the **Numbering** button.

15. Below the numbered list, select the two paragraphs that begin *Reference section* and *Abstract*. In the **Paragraph group**, click the **Bullets** button. Use the same procedure to add bullets to the four paragraphs near the end of the document beginning *Field and background* and ending with *Inventor's description*.

16. On **Page 1**, below the second bulleted point, point to the left of the paragraph beginning *United States Patent*, and then drag down to select the text through the paragraph beginning *Appl. No.*– the line above the second part of the bulleted list. In the **Paragraph group**, click the **Increase Indent** button two times. **Save** your document.

17. From the **Office** menu, point to **Print**, and then click **Print Preview** to make a final check of your document. Check your *Chapter Assignment Sheet* or *Course Syllabus* or consult your instructor to determine if you are to submit your assignments on paper or electronically. To submit electronically, go to Step 19, and then follow the instructions provided by your instructor.

18. On the **Print Preview tab**, click the **Print** button, click **OK**, and then click **Close Print Preview**.

19. From the **Office** menu, click **Exit Word**, saving any changes if prompted to do so.

End You have completed Project 6C ——————————

Content-Based Assessments

Skills Review

Project 6D — Copyright Law

In this project, you will apply the skills you practiced from the Objectives in Project 6B.

Objectives: 4. *Insert and Format Headers and Footers;* **5.** *Insert Frequently Used Text;* **6.** *Insert and Format References.*

In the following Skills Review, you will edit a short research paper about the Digital Millennium Copyright Act. This paper was written by an intern at GHS Law Partners. Your completed document will look similar to Figure 6.56.

> ### For Project 6D, you will need the following files:
>
> New blank Word document
> w06D_Copyright_Law
>
> **You will save your document as**
> **6D_Copyright_Law_Firstname_Lastname**

Figure 6.56

(Project 6D–Copyright Law continues on the next page)

Content-Based Assessments

Skills Review

(Project 6D–Copyright Law continued)

1. **Start** Word and be sure a new blank document is displayed. Display formatting marks and rulers. Be sure all margins are set to **1** inch.

2. On the **Quick Access Toolbar**, click the **Save** button. In the **Save As** dialog box, navigate to your **Word Chapter 6** folder. Name your file **6D_Copyright_Law_Firstname_Lastname** and then click **Save**.

3. Type **Yvan LaFleur** and press [Enter], and then type **Henry Kim** and press [Enter]. Type **Business Law** and press [Enter], and then type **October 21, 2009** and press [Enter]. Click the **Home tab**, and then in the **Paragraph group**, click the **Center** button, type **Digital Millennium Copyright Act** and press [Enter]. Then, in the **Paragraph group**, click the **Align Text Left** button.

4. Click the **Insert tab**. In the **Header & Footer group**, click **Header**, and then click **Edit Header**. In the header area, type **LaFleur** and then press [Spacebar]. On the **Design tab**, in the **Insert group**, click the **Quick Parts** button, and then click **Field**. In the **Field** dialog box, under **Field names**, locate and click **Page**. Under **Field properties**, click the first page number style—**1, 2, 3**—and then click **OK**. Click the **Home tab**, and then in the **Paragraph group**, click the **Align Text Right** button.

5. Click the **Design tab**, and then in the **Navigation group**, click the **Go to Footer** button. In the **Insert group**, click the **Quick Parts** button, and then click **Field**. In the **Field** dialog box, under **Field names**, locate and click **FileName**, and then click **OK**. Press [Enter] to create a new line in the footer.

6. In the **Insert group**, click the **Date & Time** button. In the **Date and Time** dialog box, locate and click the date and time

format that displays the date in a *November 14, 2009* format. Click **OK**. Double-click anywhere in the document to close the footer area. **Save** your changes.

7. Press [Ctrl] + [End]. Click the **Insert tab**. In the **Text group**, click the **Object button arrow**, and then click **Text from File**. Navigate to your student files, select **w06D_Copyright_Law**, and then click **Insert**. Press [←Bksp] to remove the empty paragraph at the end of the document. Press [Ctrl] + [A] to select the entire document. On the **Home tab**, in the **Paragraph group**, click the **Line spacing** button, and then click **2.0**. Click the **Page Layout tab**, and then in the **Paragraph group**, click the **After down spin arrow** to set the space after to **0**. Click anywhere in the document to deselect the text.

8. From the **Office** menu, click **Word Options**. Click **Proofing**, and then under **AutoCorrect options**, click the **AutoCorrect Options** button. In the **AutoCorrect** dialog box, under **Replace**, type **intruzion** and under **With**, type **intrusion** and then click **OK** two times to close both dialog boxes.

9. Locate the last bulleted item near the end of the document, and then click to place the insertion point to the right of the space after *computer*. Watch the screen as you type **intruzion** and then press [Spacebar] to see the AutoCorrect feature work.

10. On **Page 1**, locate the bulleted item that begins *Limits liability*. In the first line, select the two hyphens. On the **Insert tab**, in the **Symbols group**, click the **Symbol** button, and then click **More Symbols**. In the **Symbol** dialog box, click the **Special Characters tab**. Be sure the **Em Dash** is selected, and then click **Insert**. Repeat this procedure to replace the two hyphens

(Project 6D–Copyright Law continues on the next page)

(Project 6D—Copyright Law continued)

in the second line of the same bulleted item with an em dash. **Close** the **Symbol** dialog box.

11. Scroll to view the middle of **Page 2**, locate the first bulleted item that begins *Jeopardizing*, and then position the insertion point following the last quotation mark. Click the **References tab**, and then in the **Footnotes group**, click the **Dialog Box Launcher**. In the **Footnote and Endnote** dialog box, under **Location**, be sure **Footnotes** is selected. Under **Format**, in the **Custom mark** box, type an asterisk (*) and then click **Insert**. Type **See GHS Law Partners internal memorandum** *The Changing Face of Fair Use*.

12. At the bottom of **Page 2**, right-click the footnote text, and then from the shortcut menu, click **Style**. In the **Style** dialog box, click **Modify**, change the **Font Size** to **11**, and then click **OK**. **Close** the **Style** dialog box.

13. In the middle of **Page 2**, in the paragraph that begins *This federal statute*, at the end of the first sentence, click to place the insertion point before the period. Click the **References tab**. In the **Citations & Bibliography group**, be sure **MLA** style is selected, click the **Insert Citation** button, and then click **Add New Source**. Click the **Type of Source arrow**, and then click **Book**. Add the following book citation:

Author:	Stim, Richard W.
Title:	Patent, Copyright & Trademark: An Intellectual Property Desk Reference, 8th Edition
Year:	2006
City:	Berkeley, CA
Publisher:	NOLO

14. Click **OK**. If prompted to Update an existing reference, click Yes. Click to select the

reference, click the **Citation Options arrow**, and then click **Edit Citation**. In the **Edit Citation** dialog box, under **Add**, in the **Pages** box, type **227** and then click **OK**. **Save** your document.

15. Move to the top of the document. In the paragraph beginning *In 1998*, in the last line of the paragraph, place the insertion point after the word *Policy*, but before the comma. In the **Citations & Bibliography group**, click the **Insert Citation** button, and then click **Add New Source**. Click the **Type of Source arrow**, and then scroll down and select **Web site** from the list. Under **Bibliography Fields for MLA**, select the **Corporate Author** check box. Type the following information:

Corporate Author:	UCLA Online Institute for Cyberspace Law and Policy
Name of Web Page:	The Digital Millennium Copyright Act
Year:	2001
Month:	February
Day:	8
Year Accessed:	2009
Month Accessed:	November
Day Accessed:	14

16. Click **OK**. If you are prompted to update an existing reference, click Yes.

17. Move to **Page 2** and locate the paragraph beginning *This federal statute*. At the end of the last sentence, after *unintended consequences*, place the insertion point before the comma. In the **Citations & Bibliography group**, click the **Insert Citation** button, and then click **Add New Source**. Under **Type of Source**, be sure **Web site** is selected. Under **Bibliography Fields for MLA**, select the **Corporate**

(Project 6D—Copyright Law continues on the next page)

(Project 6D–Copyright Law continued)

Author check box. Type the following information:

Corporate Author:	**Electronic Frontier Foundation**
Name of Web Page:	**Unintended Consequences: Seven Years under the DMCA**
Year:	**2006**
Month:	**April**
Day:	**13**
Year Accessed:	**2009**
Month Accessed:	**November**
Day Accessed:	**14**
URL:	**http://www.eff.org/ IP/DMCA/?f= unintended_ consequences.html**

18. Click **OK**. If you are prompted to update an existing reference, click Yes.

19. **Save** your document. Press Ctrl + End. Hold down Ctrl and press Enter to insert a manual page break. Type **Works Cited** and press Enter. On the **References tab**, in the **Citations & Bibliography group**, be sure **MLA** displays in the **Style** box.

20. In the **Citations & Bibliography group**, click the **Bibliography** button, and then click **Insert Bibliography** to insert the citations you typed earlier. Select the three references, right-click the selected text, and then click **Paragraph**.

21. Under **Indentation**, click the **Special arrow**, and then click **Hanging**. Under

Spacing, click the **Line spacing button arrow**, and then click **Double**. Under **Spacing**, in the **After** box, type **0** and then click **OK**.

22. Right-click the *Works Cited* title, and then click **Paragraph**. In the **Paragraph** dialog box, under **General**, click the **Alignment arrow**, and then click **Centered**. Under **Indentation**, click the **Special arrow**, and then click **(none)**. Click **OK**.

23. From the **Office** menu, point to **Prepare**, and then click **Properties**. In the **Document Information Panel**, in the **Author** box, type your name, and in the **Title** box, type **Digital Millennium Copyright Act** On the right side of the **Document Information Panel**, click the **Close** button.

24. From the **Office** menu, point to **Print**, and then click **Print Preview** to make a final check of your document. Check your *Chapter Assignment Sheet* or *Course Syllabus* or consult your instructor to determine if you are to submit your assignments on paper or electronically. To submit electronically, go to Step 26, and then follow the instructions provided by your instructor.

25. On the **Print Preview tab**, click the **Print** button, click **OK**, and then click **Close Print Preview**.

26. From the **Office** menu, click **Exit Word**, saving any changes if prompted to do so.

End You have completed Project 6D

Project 6E — Disputes

In this project, you will apply the skills you practiced from the Objectives in Projects 6A and 6B.

Objectives: 1. *Change Document and Paragraph Layout;* **2.** *Change and Reorganize Text;* **3.** *Create and Modify Lists;* **4.** *Insert and Format Headers and Footers;* **5.** *Insert Frequently Used Text;* **6.** *Insert and Format References.*

In the following Mastering Word project, you will edit an internal document on domain name disputes for GHS Law Partners. Your completed document will look similar to Figure 6.57.

For Project 6E, you will need the following file:

w06E_Disputes

You will save your document as
6E_Disputes_Firstname_Lastname

Figure 6.57

(Project 6E–Disputes continues on the next page)

Content-Based Assessments

Mastering Word

(Project 6E–Disputes continued)

1. Locate and open the file **w06E_Disputes**. **Save** the file in your **Word Chapter 6** folder as **6E_Disputes_Firstname_Lastname** and then add the file name to the footer. Display formatting marks and rulers.

2. Select the document title, increase the **Font Size** to **14** points, and add **Bold** emphasis. Select all of the text in the document, change the **Font** to **Cambria**, change the **Line Spacing** to **1.0**, and then add **6 pt.** spacing after each paragraph.

3. Change the top margin to **1.5** inches and the other margins to **1** inch. Open the document header, type **INTERNAL DISTRIBUTION ONLY** and then **Center** the header. Change the header font to **Cambria**.

4. Near the top of the document, in the paragraph beginning *Because Web sites*, select the first sentence of the paragraph and move it to the end of the same paragraph.

5. In the paragraph that begins *Registering a Web site*, locate the two hyphens (--) after the word *cybersquatting*, and then replace the hyphens with an **em dash**.

6. **Save** your changes. Use the **Find and Replace** dialog box to locate the second occurrence of *World Intellectual Property Organization*, replace it with **WIPO** and then remove the word *the* preceding WIPO.

7. Near the bottom of **Page 1**, select the three paragraphs that begin with *Whether*. Change the selected paragraphs to a numbered list, and **Increase Indent** one time.

8. At the end of the third item in the list, after the period following *bad faith*, insert the following footnote:

http://www.wipo.int/about-ip/en/studies/publications/domain_names.htm

9. At the bottom of **Page 1**, at the end of the paragraph beginning *The policy defines*, insert the following footnote:

http://www.icann.org/udrp/udrp-policy-24oct99.htm

10. Modify the **Footnote** style to use the **Cambria** font, and **11** point font size.

11. **Save** your changes. **Preview** the document, and then **Print** it, or submit it electronically as directed. **Close** the file, and then **Exit** Word.

End **You have completed Project 6E** ─────────

Content-Based Assessments

Project 6F—Trademarks

In this project, you will apply the skills you practiced from the Objectives in Projects 6A and 6B.

Objectives: 1. *Change Document and Paragraph Layout;* **2.** *Change and Reorganize Text;* **3.** *Create and Modify Lists;* **4.** *Insert and Format Headers and Footers;* **5.** *Insert Frequently Used Text;* **6.** *Insert and Format References.*

In the following Mastering Word project, you will edit a handout on trademarks and commercial identifiers prepared by GHS Law Partners. Your completed document will look similar to Figure 6.58.

For Project 6F, you will need the following files:

New blank Word document
w06F_Trademarks

You will save your document as
6F_Trademarks_Firstname_Lastname

Figure 6.58

GHS LAW PARTNERS

GHS LAW PARTNERS

Trademarks and Commercial Identifiers

Trademarks—also known as commercial identifiers or marks—can be words, phrases, logos, symbols, or images. Sometimes a trademark is made up of two or more of these. You can look at just about any product and see one or more trademarks. A trademark is used to identify a product as being unique to the company that owns it, so therefore trademarks are extremely valuable to their owners. A trademark can be identified with a company to indicate quality, flavor, scent, innovation, or any number of "ideas" that a company wishes to express.

Exclusive rights to a mark are partially established through commercial use, such as:

- Entering the mark on state or county records
- Applying the mark to signs and promotional materials
- Using the mark on letterhead, business cards, and Web sites

Marks can also be registered with the United States Patent and Trademark Office (USPTO), which gives companies more leverage should a dispute arise over a mark. The mark will return a result during trademark searches, discouraging others from trying to claim the mark as their own, and registration puts the burden of proof of originality on any infringer.

A company may hold hundreds of trademarks. Microsoft provides a Web page listing its many trademarked names for games, software, fonts, brands, etc., along with information on how to cite each name. Microsoft also provides a page titled "General Microsoft Trademark Guidelines," that provides very specific instructions on referencing Microsoft trademarks and logos in any kind of publication.

Some trademarked names become so common in the language that they can become generic. This can be financially harmful to a company because the word or phrase is no longer necessarily associated with its creator. Some common name brands that have become generic include:

- ™ Jacuzzi for hot tub
- ™ Xerox for copiers
- ™ Band-Aid for adhesive
- ™ AstroTurf for artificial grass

Skilled intellectual property attorneys like those at GHS Law Partners are helpful to companies at every stage in the trademark process. In the design phase, our attorneys perform thorough searches for similar phrases or logos, preventing resources from being spent on an idea unlikely to achieve registration. Once design is complete, GHS Law Partners assists in the preparation and filing of the registration application and work with the USPTO to resolve objection and answer questions. After

6F_Trademarks_Firstname_Lastname
11/24/2009 6:00 PM

(Project 6F–Trademarks continues on the next page)

Content-Based Assessments

(Project 6F–Trademarks continued)

1. **Start** Word and be sure a new blank document is displayed. Display formatting marks and rulers. Change the top margin to **2** inches and the other margins to **1** inch.

2. Type **Trademarks and Commercial Identifiers** and press Enter. Select the title and increase the **Font Size** to **14 pt**, add **Bold** emphasis, and **Center** the title. **Save** the file in your **Word Chapter 6** folder as **6F_Trademarks_Firstname_Lastname** and then add the file name to the footer. With the footer open, insert a blank line under the **FileName** field, and then insert the **Date** field in the format *6/26/2009 5:15 PM*. **Close** the footer.

3. Place the insertion point in the blank line below the title. Locate and insert the file **w06F_Trademarks**. Remove the blank line at the end of the document. Select all of the text in the document—including the title—change the line spacing to **1.0**, and add **18 pt** spacing after each paragraph.

4. Open the document header, type **GHS LAW PARTNERS** and then **Center** the header. Select the header text and change the font to **Arial Black**, **28 pt**.

5. Near the top of **Page 2**, at the end of the second line, position the insertion point after the word *generic*. Display the **Footnote and Endnote** dialog box, and then change the footnote mark from a number to an asterisk (*). Insert a footnote and type **If infringements or disputes arise, we handle all details from cease and desist letters (which often end the case) through litigation.**

6. **Save** your changes and move to the beginning of the document. Use the **Find and Replace** dialog box to find the word **allow** and then replace it with **enable**

7. Near the top of the document, in the paragraph beginning *Trademarks, also known as*, delete the comma and space after *Trademarks* and insert an **em dash**. In the same line, after *marks*, delete the comma and space and insert an **em dash**.

8. Near the bottom of **Page 1**, select the four lines of trademarked names, beginning with *Xerox*. Change the selected paragraphs to a bulleted list, and increase the indent one time. With the bullets still selected, right-click any of the list items, display the **Define New Bullet** dialog box, and then change the bullet type to a trademark symbol (™).

9. Near the top of **Page 1**, select the three lines beginning with *Entering the mark* and ending with *Using the mark*. Change the selected paragraphs to a bulleted list using black dots for bullets, and increase the indent one time.

10. In the bottom bulleted list, select the fourth bullet point—beginning with *Jacuzzi*—and move it up so it becomes the first bullet point.

11. **Save** your changes. **Preview** the document, and then **Print** it, or submit it electronically as directed. **Close** the file, and then **Exit** Word.

End **You have completed Project 6F**

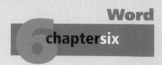

Word

chaptersix

Mastering Word

Project 6G — Fair Use

In this project, you will apply the skills you practiced from all the Objectives in Projects 6A and 6B.

Objectives: 1. *Change Document and Paragraph Layout;* **2.** *Change and Reorganize Text;* **3.** *Create and Modify Lists;* **4.** *Insert and Format Headers and Footers;* **5.** *Insert Frequently Used Text;* **6.** *Insert and Format References.*

In the following Mastering Word project, you will edit a report on fair use of copyrighted material, created by summer intern Clara Madison for GHS Law Partners. Your completed document will look similar to Figure 6.59.

> ### For Project 6G, you will need the following files:
>
> New blank Word document
> w06G_Fair_Use
>
> **You will save your document as**
> **6G_Fair_Use_Firstname_Lastname**

Figure 6.59

(Project 6G–Fair Use continues on the next page)

(Project 6G–Fair Use continued)

1. **Start** Word and be sure a new blank document is displayed. Display formatting marks and rulers. If necessary, change all document margins to **1** inch. **Save** the document as **6G_Fair_Use_Firstname_Lastname** Open the document footer and add the file name to the footer.

2. Move to the document header. In the header area, type **Madison** and then add a space and the page number, using the **1, 2, 3** format. Right align the header text.

3. Move to the beginning of the document. Type the following, pressing Enter after each line:

   Clara Madison
   Henry Kim
   Business Law
   December 17, 2009
   Fair Use of Copyrighted Materials

4. Center the last paragraph you typed—*Fair Use of Copyrighted Materials*. In the blank line below the centered title, insert the **w06G_Fair_Use** file. Delete the blank line at the end of the document. Select all of the document text. Set the **Line Spacing** to **2**, and the space **After** to **0**.

5. Select the inserted text, but not the five lines at the beginning of the document that you typed. Open the **Paragraph** dialog box, add a **0.5** inch first line indent.

6. Near the top of **Page 1**, select the four paragraphs, starting with the paragraph beginning *The purpose and character*. Create a numbered list from the selected paragraphs. Decrease the indent of the numbered list until it is aligned with the left margin of the document. Display the **Paragraph** dialog box, and set the **Special** indentation to **First line**. Set the **First line** indent to **0.5** inches.

7. Near the middle of **Page 2**, select the two paragraphs starting with the paragraph

beginning *You use a very small excerpt*. Create a bulleted list from the selected paragraphs. Decrease the indent of the bulleted list until it is aligned with the left margin of the document. Modify the paragraph formatting using the procedure in Step 6.

8. Move to the end of the document. In the second-to-last paragraph, beginning with *Laws governing*, locate and select the three periods between *availability* and *many*. Display the **Symbol** dialog box, and from the **Special Characters tab**, insert an **Ellipsis** (...).

9. In the last paragraph of the document, move the first sentence—beginning with *With cases constantly*—to the end of the paragraph.

10. Display the **Find and Replace** dialog box, use it to replace **make the determinations into** with **determine** and then **Save** your document.

11. Near the top of **Page 1**, in the fourth item in the numbered list, position the insertion point to the left of the period. Insert the following **Web site** citation, using **MLA** style. Be sure to select the **Corporate Author** check box:

Corporate Author:	**United States Copyright Office**
Name of Web Page:	**Fair Use**
Year:	**2006**
Month:	**January**
Day:	**31**
Year Accessed:	**2009**
Month Accessed:	**June**
Day Accessed:	**6**
URL:	**http://www. copyright.gov/fls/ fl102.html**

(Project 6G–Fair Use continues on the next page)

(Project 6G–Fair Use continued)

12. **Save** your document. On **Page 2**, at the end of the second bullet point, use the same procedure to add the following **Web site** citation:

Corporate Author:	**Stanford University**
Name of Web Page:	**Copyright & Fair Use**
Year:	**2004**
Year Accessed:	**2009**
Month Accessed:	**June**
Day Accessed:	**8**
URL:	**http://fairuse. stanford.edu/ Copyright_and_Fair_ Use_Overview/ chapter9/9-d.html**

13. **Save** your document. At the end of the second-to-last paragraph of the document, locate the long quotation, which begins *"Copyright is among,"* and position the insertion point to the right of the second quotation mark. Add the following **Book** citation:

Author:	**Crews, Kenneth D.**
Title:	**Copyright, Fair Use, and the Challenge for Universities**

Year:	**1993**
City:	**Chicago, IL**
Publisher:	**University of Chicago Press**

14. Add the page number **2** to the citation.

15. **Save** your document. Move to the end of the document and insert a manual page break. Type **Works Cited** and press Enter. **Center** the *Works Cited* title and remove the first line indent. Position the insertion point in the blank line below *Works Cited*.

16. On the **References tab**, click the **MLA** style, and then insert a **Bibliography**. Select the bibliography field, and then display the **Paragraph** dialog box. Double-space the selected text, and then add a hanging indent.

17. **Save** your changes. **Preview** the document, and then **Print** it, or submit it electronically as directed. **Close** the file, and then **Exit** Word.

End **You have completed Project 6G**

Mastering Word

Project 6H — *GO!* Fix It

In this project, you will construct a solution by applying any combination of the skills you practiced from the Objectives in Projects 6A and 6B.

For Project 6H, you will need the following file:

w06H_Garageman

You will save your document as
6H_Garageman_Firstname_Lastname

Locate and open the file **w06H_Garageman**, and then save it in your chapter folder as **6H_Garageman_Firstname_Lastname**

This short research paper, which was written for GHS Law Partners by their intern, Yvan LeFleur, contains errors that you must find and correct. Read and examine the document, and then edit to correct the errors that you find. Types of errors may include:

- Spelling, grammar, punctuation, and usage errors such as text case, repeated text, subject-verb agreement, and meaning.
- Content errors such as missing or incorrect data, text, pictures, hyperlinks, or other objects.
- Font formatting and positioning errors such as font used, style, size, color, underline style, effects, font character spacing, text effects, special characters, and styles.
- Paragraph formatting and positioning errors such as indents and spacing, tabs, line and page breaks, wordwrap, sentence spacing, missing text or unnecessary text or blank lines, or errors in footnotes or endnotes or references.
- Page setup errors such as margins, orientation, layout, or alignment.

Things you should know to complete this project:

- The research paper should conform to the MLA formatting style that was covered in Project 6B.
- The AutoFormat feature in Word may cause paragraph indents to shift position when lists are reformatted. An easy way to correct this problem is to select the text and then drag the indent marker(s) on the ruler to the correct position.
- Numbered lists are used in this project, instead of bulleted lists, to allow easier identification of individual items.
- There are no errors in the citation on the reference page.
- Save the changes you have made, add the file name to the footer, and then submit it as directed.

 End **You have completed Project 6H** ———————————

Outcomes-Based Assessments

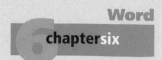

Rubric

The following outcomes-based assessments are *open-ended assessments*. That is, there is no specific correct result; your result will depend on your approach to the information provided. Make *Professional Quality* your goal. Use the following scoring rubric to guide you in *how* to approach the problem and then to evaluate *how well* your approach solves the problem.

The *criteria*—Software Mastery, Content, Format and Layout, and Process—represent the knowledge and skills you have gained that you can apply to solving the problem. The *levels of performance*—Professional Quality, Approaching Professional Quality, or Needs Quality Improvements—help you and your instructor evaluate your result.

	Your completed project is of Professional Quality if you:	Your completed project is Approaching Professional Quality if you:	Your completed project Needs Quality Improvements if you:
1-Software Mastery	Choose and apply the most appropriate skills, tools, and features and identify efficient methods to solve the problem.	Choose and apply some appropriate skills, tools, and features, but not in the most efficient manner.	Choose inappropriate skills, tools, or features, or are inefficient in solving the problem.
2-Content	Construct a solution that is clear and well organized, contains content that is accurate, appropriate to the audience and purpose, and is complete. Provide a solution that contains no errors of spelling, grammar, or style.	Construct a solution in which some components are unclear, poorly organized, inconsistent, or incomplete. Misjudge the needs of the audience. Have some errors in spelling, grammar, or style, but the errors do not detract from comprehension.	Construct a solution that is unclear, incomplete, or poorly organized; contains some inaccurate or inappropriate content; and contains many errors of spelling, grammar, or style. Do not solve the problem.
3-Format and Layout	Format and arrange all elements to communicate information and ideas, clarify function, illustrate relationships, and indicate relative importance.	Apply appropriate format and layout features to some elements, but not others. Overuse features, causing minor distraction.	Apply format and layout that does not communicate information or ideas clearly. Do not use format and layout features to clarify function, illustrate relationships, or indicate relative importance. Use available features excessively, causing distraction.
4-Process	Use an organized approach that integrates planning, development, self-assessment, revision, and reflection.	Demonstrate an organized approach in some areas, but not others; or, use an insufficient process of organization throughout.	Do not use an organized approach to solve the problem.

Outcomes-Based Assessments

Word
chaptersix
Problem Solving

Project 6I — Seminar

In this project, you will construct a solution by applying any combination of the skills you practiced from the Objectives in Projects 6A and 6B.

For Project 6I, you will need the following file:

New blank Word document

You will save your document as 6I_Seminar_Firstname_Lastname

College students are often asked to write research papers and presentations that involve information gathered from many sources. GHS Law Partners has been asked by the local college to conduct a seminar for faculty members that covers the topic of how students use the intellectual property of others. In this Problem Solving project, you will create a one-page document that outlines the topic.

Your document should consist of an introduction to the law firm and the topic, followed by a list of definitions of terms, including—but not limited to—*intellectual property, copyright, fair use,* and *plagiarism.* Add a footnote indicating your source for the definitions. Then, add a list of the topics to be covered in the order in which they will be presented. You might include topics such as quotations, downloaded pictures from the Web, and how to cite sources. Add a title to the document, and format the text appropriately. You may want to do some research on the Web or in your school library on such topics as copyrights, plagiarism, and citing sources to develop your topics.

Add the file name to the footer. Check your document for spelling and grammar errors. Save the document as **6I_Seminar_Firstname_Lastname** and submit it as directed.

End **You have completed Project 6I** ————————————

Outcomes-Based Assessments

chaptersix

Problem Solving

Project 6J—Evaluation

In this project, you will construct a solution by applying any combination of the skills you practiced from the Objectives in Projects 6A and 6B.

For Project 6J, you will need the following file:

New blank Word document

You will save your document as
6J_Evaluation_Firstname_Lastname

In this project, you will write a letter that summarizes the categories and the criteria to be used in a job performance evaluation for summer interns. The letter should be addressed to Andrea Smith, 1884 Bullpen Dr., Black River, GA 30366, and should be from Michael Scott, the Office Manager of the law firm, GHS Law Partners.

Be sure to

- Use the letter style you practiced in Chapter 5.
- Research the topic in your library or on the Web. There are many sites that discuss the types of criteria used when rating employee performance. (Hint: Search for *employee evaluation* or *job evaluation*.)
- Divide the criteria into two or three categories. Introduce the categories, and then add a short list of criteria under each category.
- Use at least one special bullet symbol for a list.

Add the file name to the footer. Check the letter for spelling and grammar errors. Save the document as **6J_Evaluation_Firstname_Lastname** and submit it as directed.

End **You have completed Project 6J** ———————

Outcomes-Based Assessments

Word
chaptersix
Problem Solving

Project 6K—Trademarks

In this project, you will construct a solution by applying any combination of the skills you practiced from the Objectives in Projects 6A and 6B.

For Project 6K, you will need the following file:

New blank Word document

You will save your document as
6K_Trademarks_Firstname_Lastname

When a company has a very recognizable name that is used for a product, they often get protection for that name from the U.S. Patent and Trademark Office. Microsoft, for example, has a long list of trademarks, logos, and trade names, including Microsoft Windows® and MapVision™. To view the list, use a Web browser and go to *www.microsoft.com*. At the bottom of the Microsoft home page, click **Trademarks**. Notice that some of the items use the Registered® symbol, and some use the Trademark™ symbol.

Write a 400 to 600 word research paper (about two pages long) that identifies the similarities and differences between items that are identified as *registered* and those identified as *trademarked*. Your paper should follow MLA style guidelines, or other style guidelines as directed by your instructor. Use at least two references, and include a Works Cited page. Detailed information about writing in the MLA style can be found in your college library and also online. Include at least one list, two symbols, and one informational endnote or footnote. Save the research paper as **6K_Trademarks_Firstname_Lastname** and then create a footer that contains the file name. Submit the document as directed.

End **You have completed Project 6K** ————————————

More on your Student CD

The instructions for the following additional end-of-chapter projects are on your student CD in the folder 03_additional_end_of_chapter_projects.

Content-Based Assessments

Project L Mastering Word

Apply the skills you practiced in Project A.

Project M Mastering Word

Apply the skills you practiced in Project B.

Project N Business Running Case

Apply the skills you practiced in Projects A and B while helping an entrepreneur with the daily tasks of running a business.

In each chapter, this project focuses on applying the skills you have practiced in Projects A and B to a business. The project related to this business runs throughout the textbook. You will see how the Office applications relate to the day-to-day operation of a small business called Nelson Architectural Planning.

Outcomes-Based Assessments

Project O Problem Solving

Construct a solution by applying any combination of the skills you practiced from Projects A and B.

Project P Problem Solving

Construct a solution by applying any combination of the skills you practiced from Projects A and B.

Project Q You and GO!

Construct a solution that applies to your own life by applying any combination of the skills you practiced from Projects A and B.

Project R GO! with Help

Practice using Microsoft Office's Help Feature.

Project S Group Business Running Case

Work as part of a group to apply the skills you have gained thus far to help the Bell Orchid Hotel Group achieve its business goals.

Multimedia

The following multimedia accompany this textbook:

Companion Web site
www.prenhall.com/go

An interactive Web site designed to reinforce and test your understanding of the skills in this chapter.

AV-EDDs

In the folder in the front of this book you will find videos that demonstrate the objectives of the A and B projects in this chapter. These may help you understand how to complete the projects in this book.

Video Podcasts

In the folder in the front of this book are videos that can be played on your iPod, MP3 player, or computer. These videos demonstrate how to complete the more challenging objectives in this textbook.

7 chapterseven

Using Graphics and Tables

OBJECTIVES

At the end of this chapter you will be able to:

1. Insert and Format Graphics
2. Set Tab Stops
3. Insert and Modify Text Boxes and Shapes

4. Create a Table
5. Format a Table

OUTCOMES

Mastering these objectives will enable you to:

PROJECT 7A
Insert and Modify Graphics and Set Tab Stops

PROJECT 7B
Create and Format a Table

Memories Old and New

Professional and amateur artists, photographers, students, teachers, and hobbyists have made Memories Old and New one of Chicago's fastest-growing art, photography, and scrapbooking supply stores. The store carries a wide variety of premium art supplies, such as paints, pencils, cutting and framing tools, and brushes. Local photographers are featured in the small gallery, and photo restoration services and supplies are offered. For scrapbookers, the store provides the newest and highest quality books, papers, stencils, and archival supplies. Scrapbooking classes are also offered to assist customers in adding principles of art and design to their projects.

© David Young-Wolff PhotoEdit Inc.

Using Graphics and Tables

Adding graphics enhances the effectiveness of documents. Digital images, such as those obtained from a digital camera or a scanner, can be inserted into documents. You can also create your own graphic objects by using the Drawing tools.

Tab stops are useful to horizontally align text and numbers. Use the Tab key to move text to specific tab stop locations on a line. You can set and specify the alignment of your own tab locations.

Tables present data effectively and efficiently. The row and column format of a table makes information easy to find and easy to read. A table also helps the reader organize and categorize the data. The Word table feature has tools with which you can format text, change column width and row height, and change the background for all or part of a table. You can also modify the table's borders and lines.

Project 7A **Photography Flyer**

In Activities 7.01 through 7.14, you will create a flyer for an upcoming exhibition of photographs by photographer Annie DeCesare at Memories Old and New. Your completed document will look similar to Figure 7.1.

For Project 7A, you will need the following files:

New blank Word document

w07A_Photography_Flyer
w07A_Machine
w07A_Ore_Cart
You will save your document as
7A_Photography_Flyer_Firstname_Lastname

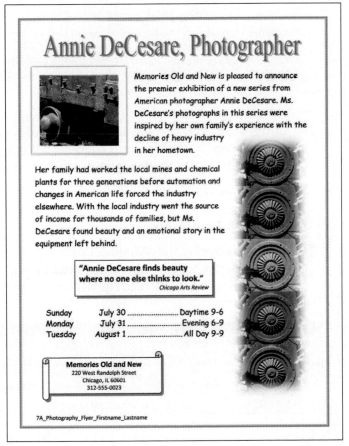

Figure 7.1
Project 7A—Photography Flyer

Objective 1
Insert and Format Graphics

Graphics include pictures, clip art, charts, and *drawing objects*—shapes, diagrams, lines, and so on. You can modify drawing objects by changing their color, pattern, border, and other characteristics. Graphics that you insert in a document convey information in a way that plain text cannot. For additional visual interest, you can convert text to an attractive graphic format; add, resize, move and format pictures; and provide a finishing touch to your document by adding a page border.

Activity 7.01 Formatting Text Using WordArt

WordArt is a gallery of text styles with which you can create decorative effects, such as shadowed or mirrored text.

> **Note — Comparing Your Screen with the Figures in This Textbook**
>
> Your screen will match the figures shown in this textbook if you set your screen resolution to 1024 × 768. At other resolutions, your screen will closely resemble, but not match, the figures shown. To view your screen's resolution, on the Windows desktop, right-click in a blank area, click Personalize, and then click Display Settings.

1 **Start** Word, and display formatting marks and rulers. Display the **Page Setup** dialog box, and then set all margins to **.75″**. On the **Home tab**, in the **Styles group**, click the **No Spacing** button.

2 Type **Annie DeCesare, Photographer** and then press Enter. Notice that the last name is flagged as a spelling error. Right-click *DeCesare*, and then click **Ignore All**.

3 Without selecting the paragraph mark at the end, select the first line of text. Click the **Insert tab**. In the **Text group**, click the **WordArt** button, and then notice the ScreenTip *WordArt style 8* shown in Figure 7.2.

Figure 7.2

WordArt button ⎯

WordArt style 8 ⎯

Selected text ⎯

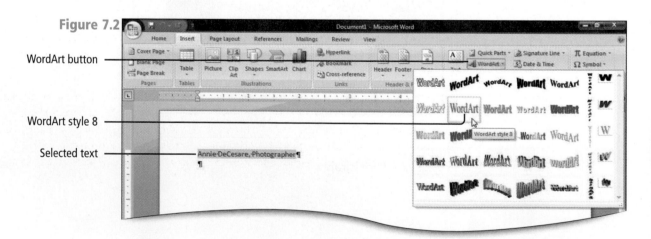

4 Click **WordArt style 8**, and then compare your screen with Figure 7.3.

> The Edit WordArt Text dialog box displays, and the selected text displays in the Text box. The default font size is 36 point.

Figure 7.3

Word | Chapter 7

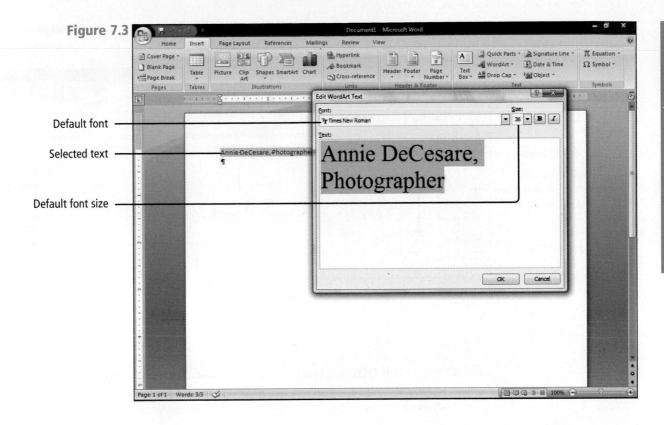

Default font

Selected text

Default font size

5 At the bottom of the **Edit WordArt Text** dialog box, click **OK**.

The WordArt contextual tools display on the Ribbon. The WordArt object displays *sizing handles*—small dark boxes with which you can manually change its size.

6 On the **Format tab**, in the **Size group**, click the **Shape Height button up spin arrow** 3.5" as necessary to change the height of the WordArt to **0.7"**. Click the **Shape Width button up spin arrow** 6" as necessary to change the width of the WordArt to **6.5"**.

7 In the **Arrange group**, click the **Position** button, and then under **With Text Wrapping**, in the top row of the gallery, point to the second button to display the ScreenTip *Position in Top Center with Square Text Wrapping*, and then click the button. Compare your screen with Figure 7.4.

The WordArt is centered between the left and right margins, and positioned at the top of the document. The *anchor* symbol indicates the paragraph to which the WordArt is attached and the corner sizing handles display as circles. Additionally, a *rotate handle* to rotate the WordArt and an *adjustment handle* to drag parts of the object into various positions display.

Figure 7.4

Position button

Shape Height up spin arrow

Shape Width up spin arrow

Rotate handle

Anchor indicates paragraph to which the WordArt is attached

Adjustment handle

Sizing handles

Annie DeCesare, Photographer

8 From the **Office** menu 🔘, display the **Save As** dialog box, and then navigate to the location where you are saving your files. Click the **New Folder** button. Name the new folder **Word Chapter 7**

9 In the **File name** box, using your own name, type **7A_Photography_ Flyer_Firstname_Lastname** and then click **Save**.

Activity 7.02 Inserting Pictures from Files

1 Press Ctrl + End. Click the **Insert tab**. In the **Text group**, click the **Object button arrow**, and then click **Text from File**. Locate and **Insert** the file **w07A_Photography_Flyer**.

2 Delete the blank line at the end of the document. If necessary, right-click any words flagged with wavy underlines and ignore all suggested corrections.

3 In the paragraph beginning *Memories Old and New*, click to position the insertion point at the beginning of the paragraph. On the **Insert tab**, in the **Illustrations group**, click the **Picture** button. From your student data files, **Insert** the file **w07A_Ore_Cart**. Compare your screen with Figure 7.5.

> Word inserts the picture as an ***inline object***; that is, the picture is positioned directly in the text at the insertion point, just like a character in a sentence. Sizing handles surround the picture.

> The round corner sizing handles resize the graphic proportionally. The square sizing handles resize a graphic vertically or horizontally only; sizing with these will distort the graphic. A rotate handle, with which you can rotate the graphic to any angle, displays above the top center sizing handle.

4 **Save** 🖫 your document.

Figure 7.5

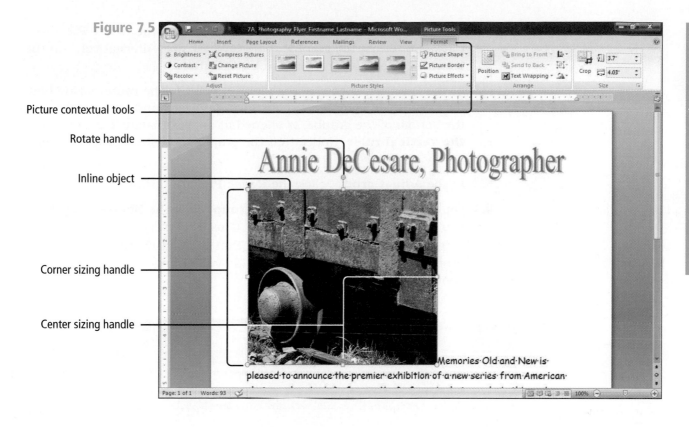

Picture contextual tools

Rotate handle

Inline object

Corner sizing handle

Center sizing handle

Activity 7.03 Resizing a Graphic

1 If necessary, click to select the ore cart picture.

2 On the lower edge of the picture, point to the center square sizing handle until the ⬍ pointer displays. Drag upward until the bottom of the graphic is aligned at approximately **2 inches on the vertical ruler**. Notice that the height of the graphic is resized, but the width remains unchanged, as shown in Figure 7.6.

Figure 7.6

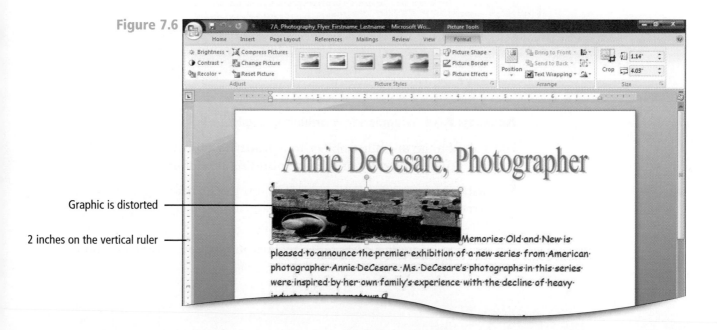

Graphic is distorted

2 inches on the vertical ruler

3 On the **Format tab**, in the **Adjust group**, click the **Reset Picture** button to return the graphic to its original size. Alternatively, on the Quick Access Toolbar, click the Undo button.

4 At the lower left corner of the picture, point to the round sizing handle until the ⬈ pointer displays. Drag upward and to the right until the bottom of the graphic is aligned at approximately **2 inches on the vertical ruler**. Notice that the graphic is resized proportionally and not distorted.

5 In the **Adjust group**, click the **Reset Picture** button.

6 On the **Format tab**, in the **Size group**, click the **Shape Height button spin box down arrow** ⬚ 3.5" ⬚ as necessary to change the height of the picture to **2"**. Notice that the picture resizes proportionally—the width adjusts as you change the height—as shown in Figure 7.7.

Figure 7.7

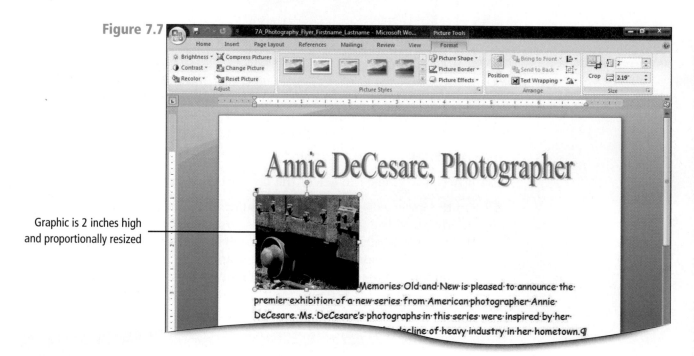

Graphic is 2 inches high and proportionally resized

7 Save 💾 your document.

Activity 7.04 Wrapping Text Around a Graphic

You can change an inline object to a **_floating object_**—a graphic that can be moved independently of the surrounding text characters.

1 With the **ore cart** picture selected, on the **Format tab**, in the **Arrange group**, click the **Text Wrapping** button to display the Text Wrapping gallery, as shown in Figure 7.8.

> **_Text wrapping_** refers to the manner in which text displays around an object.

Figure 7.8

Text Wrapping gallery

2 From the **Text Wrapping gallery**, click **Square**.

Square text wrapping ensures that all four edges of the surrounding text will be straight. To wrap text around an irregularly shaped object use the Tight text wrap format.

3 Click to the left of *M* in the first line of the paragraph that begins *Memories Old and New* to deselect the picture. Click the **Insert tab**. In the **Illustrations group**, click the **Picture** button. Locate and **Insert** the file **w07A_Machine**.

The inserted picture becomes the first character in the paragraph and the text is forced down in the document.

4 On the **Format tab**, in the **Arrange group**, click the **Text Wrapping** button, and then click **Square**. Compare your screen with Figure 7.9.

The text wraps around the second graphic.

Figure 7.9

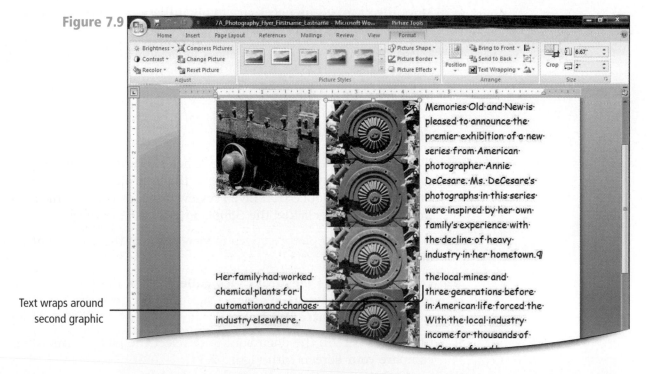

Text wraps around second graphic

5 **Save** your document.

Activity 7.05 Moving a Graphic

1 Point to the **machine** picture to display the 🔯 pointer.

> The Move pointer displays a four-way arrow, and enables you to move a floating object anywhere in the document.

2 Drag the picture to the right until the right edge of the picture aligns at approximately **7 inches on the horizontal ruler**, and then drag downward until the top edge of the picture aligns at approximately **2.5 inches on the vertical ruler**. Compare your screen with Figure 7.10.

Figure 7.10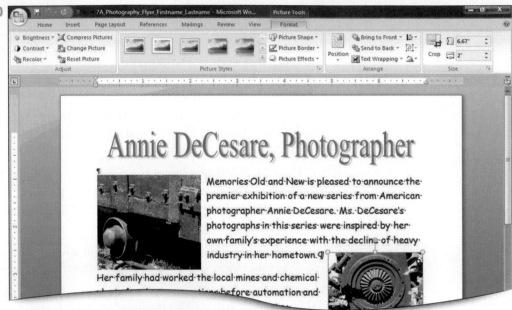

3 Move the graphics as necessary to align them in approximately the same position as those shown in Figure 7.10.

> Recall that you can nudge an object in small increments by pressing the arrow keys.

4 **Save** 🖫 your document.

Activity 7.06 Applying Picture Styles

1 Click to select the **ore cart** picture. Click the **Format tab**, and then in the **Picture Styles group**, point to the first picture style—**Simple Frame, White**. Notice that Live Preview displays the graphic as it would look if you clicked the *Simple Frame, White* button.

2 Point to the other picture styles to view some of the styles that are available.

3 To the right of the **Picture Styles gallery**, click the **More** button ▼ to display more available styles. Click the second button in the first row—**Beveled Matte, White**.

4 Click anywhere in the document to deselect the picture, and then compare your screen with Figure 7.11.

Figure 7.11

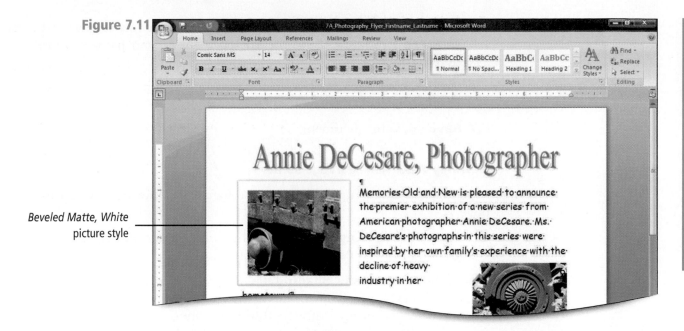

Beveled Matte, White picture style

5 Click to select the **w07A_Machine** picture. On the **Format tab**, in the **Picture Styles group**, click the **Picture Effects** button. In the **Picture Effects gallery**, point to **Soft Edges**, and then click **25 Point**.

6 Click anywhere in the document to deselect the picture, and then compare your screen with Figure 7.12.

> The Soft Edges feature fades the edges of the picture. The number of points you choose determines how far the fade goes inward from the edges of the picture. Recall that a point is 1/72 of an inch.

Figure 7.12

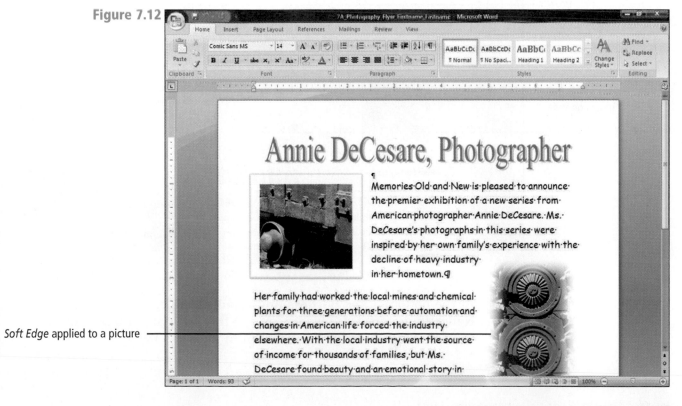

Soft Edge applied to a picture

7 From the **Office** menu 🔘, point to the **Print button arrow**, and then click **Print Preview** to see the arrangement of your pictures in relation to the text.

8 On the **Print Preview tab**, in the **Preview group**, click the **Close Print Preview** button.

9 **Save** 🖫 your document.

Activity 7.07 Adding a Page Border

Page borders frame a page and help to focus the information on the page.

1 Click the **Page Layout tab**, and then in the **Page Background group**, click the **Page Borders** button.

2 In the **Borders and Shading** dialog box, under **Setting**, click **Box**. Under **Style**, scroll down the list about a third of the way and click the heavy outer line with the thin inner line—check the **Preview** area to be sure the heavier line is the nearest to the edges of the page.

3 Click the **Color arrow**, and then under **Theme Colors**, in the fifth column, click the first color—**Blue, Accent 1**. Compare your screen with Figure 7.13.

Figure 7.13

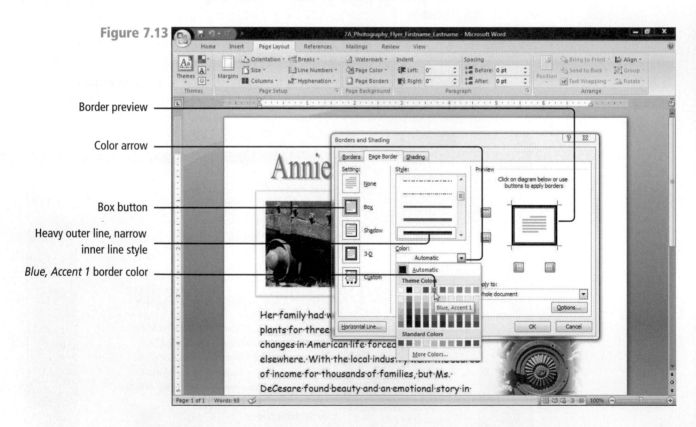

Border preview
Color arrow
Box button
Heavy outer line, narrow inner line style
Blue, Accent 1 border color

4 At the bottom of the **Borders and Shading** dialog box, click **OK**. Notice that a border is placed around the page, about 0.5 inches in from the edge of the page, as shown in Figure 7.14.

Figure 7.14

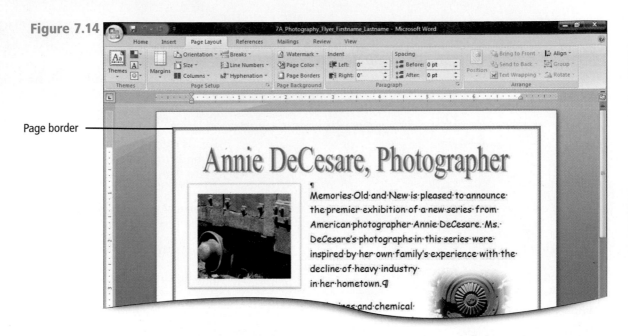

Page border

5 **Save** your document.

Objective 2
Set Tab Stops

Tab stops mark specific locations on a line of text; use tab stops to indent and align text. Press Tab to move to tab stops. In the following activities, you will use tab stops to format a short table of dates and times.

Activity 7.08 Setting Tab Stops and Using Click and Type

1 Take a moment to study the tab alignment options shown in Figure 7.15 and described in the table in Figure 7.16.

Left Tab   Center Tab   Right Tab   Decimal Tab   Bar Tab

Figure 7.15

Tab Alignment button

Aligned right

Aligned center

Aligned left

Aligned on the decimal point

Bar tab added

Tab Alignment Options

Type	Tab Alignment Button Displays	Description
Left	⌞	Text is left aligned at the tab stop and extends to the right.
Center	⊥	Text is centered around the tab stop.
Right	⌟	Text is right aligned at the tab stop and extends to the left.
Decimal	⊥·	The decimal point aligns at the tab stop.
Bar	│	A vertical bar is inserted in the document at the tab stop.
First Line Indent	▽	Indents the first line of a paragraph.
Hanging Indent	⊔	Indents all lines but the first in a paragraph.

Figure 7.16

2 Scroll to the bottom of the document and click anywhere in the last paragraph. Position the pointer below the text and near the left margin to display the I≡ pointer, as shown in Figure 7.17.

This is one of several *click and type pointers*; a series of pointers with lines attached in various arrangements to depict alignment. In this instance, the pointer displays left aligned horizontal lines. The shape attached to the pointer indicates what type of formatting will be applied if you double-click at the pointer location on the page.

Figure 7.17

Click and type pointer ——

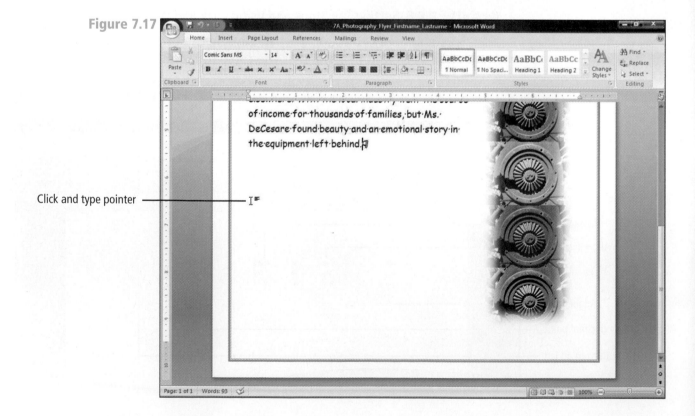

Alert!

What if the click and type pointer does not display?

If you move the pointer around the blank area of the document and do not see the click and type pointer, click the Office button, and then click Word Options. Click Advanced, and then under *Editing options*, select the *Enable click and type* check box.

3 With the [I⁼] pointer displayed at approximately **7 inches on the vertical ruler** and at the left margin, double-click to place the insertion point. Notice that the insertion point is positioned at the left margin.

> Because you cannot type in a blank area of a document without some type of paragraph formatting in place, click and type inserts blank lines without having to press [Enter] numerous times—and uses the formatting of the nearest paragraph above.

> If you double-click the click and type pointer near the horizontal middle of the document, a center tab is inserted; if you double-click near the right margin, a right tab is inserted.

4 To the left of the horizontal ruler, point to the **Tab Alignment** button and notice the *Left Tab* ScreenTip. Click the **Tab Alignment** button [L] one time, move the mouse pointer away, and then point to the button again to display the next ScreenTip—*Center Tab*. Repeat this process to cycle through and view the ScreenTip for each of the types of tab stops, and then stop at the **Left Tab** button [L].

5 Move the pointer into the horizontal ruler, click at **0.5 inches on the horizontal ruler**, and then compare your screen with Figure 7.18.

> A left tab stop displays on the ruler for the paragraph containing the insertion point. By default, tab stops are set every half inch, but they do not display on the ruler. When you customize a tab by clicking on the ruler, the custom tab stop overrides default tab stops that are to the left of the custom tab. A tab stop is part of a paragraph's format and thus the information about tab stops is stored in the paragraph mark.

Figure 7.18

Left alignment tab at 0.5 inch

Insertion point

6 Click the **Tab Alignment** button 🄻 two times to display the **Right Tab** button 🄐. Point to **2.25 inches on the horizontal ruler**, and then click one time to insert a right tab stop at this position in the paragraph.

7 Click the **Tab Alignment** button 🄐 six times to display the **Center Tab** button 🄗. Click at **3.5 inches on the horizontal ruler**, and then click again at **4.5 inches**. Notice that two center tab stops display on the ruler, as shown in Figure 7.19.

Figure 7.19

Right alignment tab

Center alignment tabs

Tabs set only for the line in
which the insertion point
is positioned

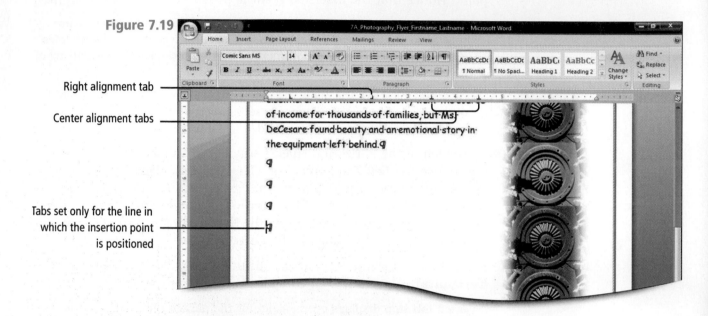

8 **Save** 🄳 your document.

Activity 7.09 Formatting and Removing Tab Stops

Recall that tab stops are a form of paragraph formatting, and thus, the information about them is stored in the paragraph mark to which they were applied.

1 On the **Home tab**, in the **Paragraph group**, click the **Dialog Box Launcher** 🄐. If necessary, change the spacing *After* to 0, and the *Line Spacing* to Single, and then click **OK**.

2 Point to any of the tab markers on the ruler, double-click to display the **Tabs** dialog box, and then compare your screen with Figure 7.20.

The tabs you just added to the ruler display under *Tab stop position*. In the Tabs dialog box, you have more flexibility in adding, removing, and formatting tab stops.

Figure 7.20

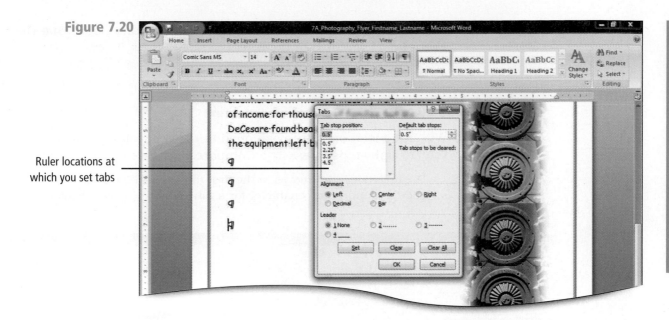

Ruler locations at
which you set tabs

3 Under **Tab stop position**, click **3.5"**, and then at the bottom of the **Tabs** dialog box, click the **Clear** button.

> The cleared tab stop will be removed when you click OK to close the dialog box.

4 If necessary, under **Tab stop position**, click **4.5"**. Under **Alignment**, click the **Right** option button. Under **Leader**, click the **2** option button. Near the bottom of the **Tabs** dialog box, click **Set**, and then compare your screen with Figure 7.21.

> The Set button saves the change. The tab stop at 4.5 inches changes to a right tab and displays a ***leader character***. Leader characters create a solid, dotted, or dashed line that fills the space to the left of a tab character. A leader character draws the reader's eyes across the page from one item to the next. When the character used for the leader is a dot, this is commonly referred to as a ***dot leader***.

Figure 7.21

Selected tab stop
Tab stop will be cleared
when the dialog box closes
Tab stop changed
to right alignment
Dot leader

5 At the bottom of the **Tabs** dialog box, click **OK**, and notice that the changes are reflected in the ruler.

6 **Save** 🖫 your document.

Activity 7.10 Using Tab Stops to Enter Text

1 With the insertion point positioned at the beginning of the line with the new tab stops, press ⌨Tab. Compare your screen with Figure 7.22.

> The insertion point moves to the first tab stop, which is at 0.5 inches, and the nonprinting character for a tab—a small arrow—displays.

Figure 7.22

Tab stop

Nonprinting character indicating that the Tab key was pressed

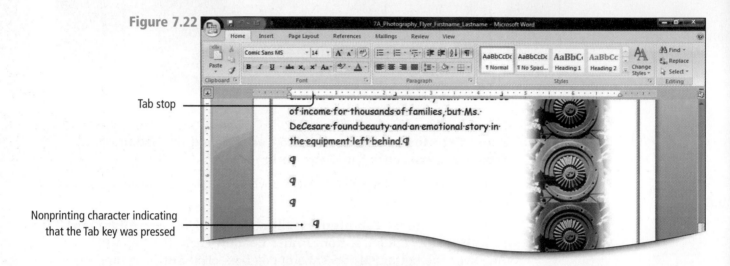

2 Type **Sunday** and notice that the left edge of the text remains aligned with the tab stop. Press ⌨Tab, and then type **July 30**

> The insertion point moves to the tab stop at 2.25 inches, and the text moves to the left of the right tab mark.

3 Press ⌨Tab, type **Daytime 9 - 6** and then press ⌨Enter. Compare your screen with Figure 7.23. Look at the ruler, and notice that the formatting of the previous paragraph, including tab stops, is copied to the new paragraph.

> A dot leader is added, helping to draw your eyes across the page to the next item. Depending on your Word settings, when you type a hyphen surrounded by spaces, the hyphen may change to a longer dash.

Note — Using Dot Leaders

It is sometimes tempting to hold down ⸬ on the keyboard to create a string of dots. This is not a good idea for several reasons. The periods, because of proportional spacing, may be spaced differently between rows. The periods will not line up, and, most importantly, the column on the right side of the string of periods may look lined up on the screen, but will be crooked when printed. If you need a string of dots, always insert a tab stop with a dot leader.

Figure 7.23

Tab stops included
in new paragraph

Dot leader

4 Type the following—first pressing Tab one time to indent each line—to complete the exhibition schedule. Click **Save** 💾, and then compare your screen with Figure 7.24:

Monday	**July 31**	**Evening 6 - 9**
Tuesday	**August 1**	**All Day 9 - 9**

Figure 7.24

Another Way ── **To Create an Indent**

If the items in the first column of a list are indented the same amount using a left-aligned tab, you can save keystrokes by indenting the paragraph instead. You can do this on the Home tab by clicking the Increase Indent button in the Paragraph group, or by setting Indentation in the Paragraph dialog box. You can also drag the Left Indent marker from the left side of the ruler and position it at the desired location. When you are finished typing the list, you can drag the marker back to the left margin position. When you use an indent at the beginning of the paragraph for a tabbed list, it is not necessary to press Tab before you type the first item in the list.

Activity 7.11 Moving Tab Stops

If you are not satisfied with the arrangement of your text after setting tab stops, you can reposition the text by moving tab stops.

1 Move the pointer into the left margin area, to the left of the first line of tabbed text. When the ⌐ pointer displays, drag downward to select the three lines of tabbed text.

> By selecting all of the paragraphs, changes you make to the tab stops will change all three lines simultaneously.

2 With the three lines of tabbed text selected, point to the horizontal ruler and position the pointer so the tip of the pointer arrow is touching the **0.5-inch tab stop**. When you see the *Left Tab* ScreenTip, drag the tab stop mark to the left to **0.25 inches on the ruler**, and then release the mouse button.

Note — Selecting Tab Stop Marks

Selecting and moving tab stop marks on the horizontal ruler requires fairly exact mouse movement. The tip of the pointer must touch the tab mark. If you miss the mark by even a little, you will probably insert another tab stop. One way to tell if you are in the right position to move a tab stop on the ruler is to look for a ScreenTip showing the tab type. To remove an accidental tab stop when you are trying to select an existing one, click the Undo button and try again. Alternatively, you can drag the unwanted tab stop marker below the ruler and release the mouse button.

---

3 In the horizontal ruler, point to the **4.5-inch tab stop** until you see the *Right Tab* ScreenTip. Drag the tab stop mark to the right to **4.75 inches on the horizontal ruler**. Compare your screen with Figure 7.25.

Figure 7.25

Tab stop at 0.25 inch

Tab stop at 4.75 inches

Selected text moved

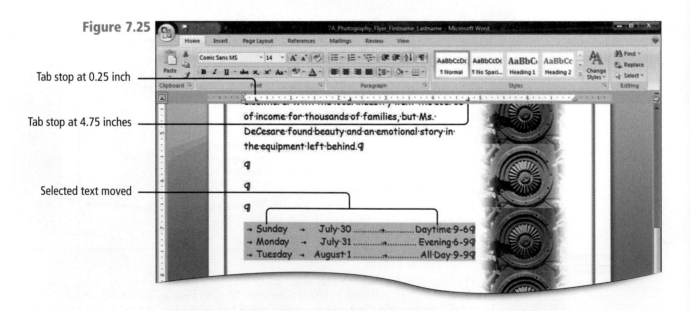

4 Click anywhere to deselect the text, and then **Save** 🖫 your document.

Objective 3
Insert and Modify Text Boxes and Shapes

In addition to graphics such as pictures and clip art you can also add predefined shapes and text boxes to documents. The *drawing canvas* feature provides a work area for complex drawings; however, when inserting and formatting simple drawing objects, it is not necessary to activate the drawing canvas.

Activity 7.12 Inserting a Text Box

A *text box* is a movable, resizable container for text or graphics. A text box is useful to give text a different orientation from other text in the document because a text box can be placed anywhere in the document in the manner of a floating object.

1 Scroll down to display the bottom edge of the document. Click the **Insert tab**, and then from the **Text group**, click the **Text Box** button. At the bottom of the **Text Box gallery**, click **Draw Text Box**.

2 Position the ⊞ pointer at the left margin and at approximately **5.5 inches on the vertical ruler**. Drag down and to the right to create a text box approximately **1.25 inches** high and **4 inches** wide.

3 In the **Size group**, use the spin arrows to set the height and width precisely at **1.3** and **4** inches. Compare your screen with Figure 7.26. If you are not satisfied with your result, click the Undo button and try again.

Figure 7.26

Width of text box

Height of text box

Text box

4 With the insertion point displayed in the text box, click the **Home tab**. In the **Styles group**, click the **No Spacing** style to remove the space *After* paragraphs and change the line spacing to *Single*.

5 Include the quotation marks as you type **"Annie DeCesare finds beauty where no one else thinks to look."** and then press Enter. Type **Chicago Arts Review**

6 In the text box, select the quote, including both quotation marks and the paragraph mark. On the Mini toolbar, click the **Font Size button arrow**, and then click **16**. With the text still selected, on the Mini toolbar, click the **Bold** button **B**.

7 In the text box, select *Chicago Arts Review*, and then on the Mini toolbar, click the **Italic** button **I**. In the **Paragraph group**, click the **Align Text Right** button. Click anywhere outside the text box, and then compare your screen with Figure 7.27.

Figure 7.27

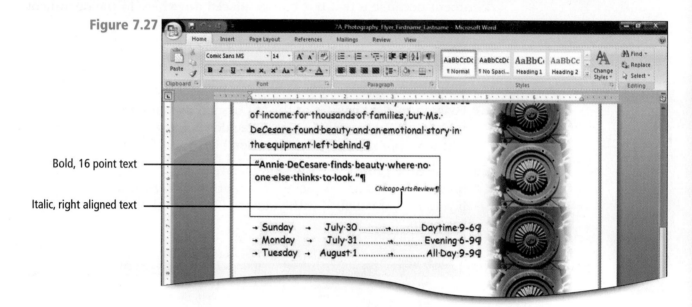

Bold, 16 point text

Italic, right aligned text

8 **Save** your document.

Activity 7.13 Moving, Resizing, and Formatting a Text Box

1 Click anywhere inside the text box to select the box. Click the **Format tab**. In the **Size group**, change the **Height** of the text box to **0.9"** and the **Width** to **3.5"**.

2 Point to one of the text box borders until the pointer displays. Drag the text box down and to the right until it is centered in the same approximate location as the one shown in Figure 7.28. Position the right edge at approximately **4.5 inches on the horizontal ruler**, and the top edge at approximately **5.75 inches on the vertical ruler**.

Because the rulers show the size of the text box, but not the location of the text box relative to the rest of the document, you will likely need to deselect the text box, check the position, and then move the box again.

Figure 7.28

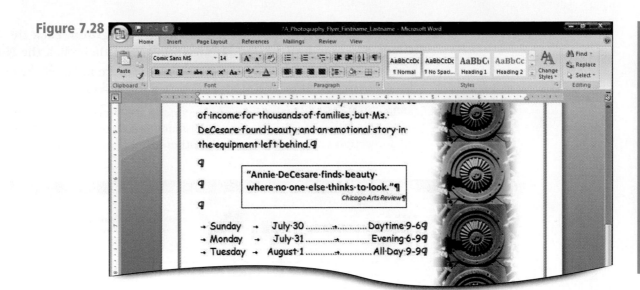

3 If necessary, select the text box. On the **Format tab**, in the **Shadow Effects group**, click the **Shadow Effects** button.

4 In the **Shadow Effects gallery**, under **Drop Shadow**, in the first row, point to the fourth shadow—**Shadow Style 4**. Notice that Live Preview displays a shadow around the text box, as shown in Figure 7.29.

Because the default shadow on the WordArt is down and to the right, it is good design to create a text box shadow in the same direction.

Figure 7.29

Shadow Effects gallery

Shadow Style 4

Live Preview displays the shadow

5 Click **Shadow Style 4**. In the **Shadow Effects group**, click the **Nudge Shadow Left** button two times, and then click the **Nudge Shadow Up** button two times. Click anywhere in the document to deselect the text box, and then compare your screen with Figure 7.30.

The Nudge Shadow buttons enable you to apply precision formatting to your shadows; in this instance you made the shadow more subtle and in proportion to the shadows on the other graphic on the page.

Figure 7.30

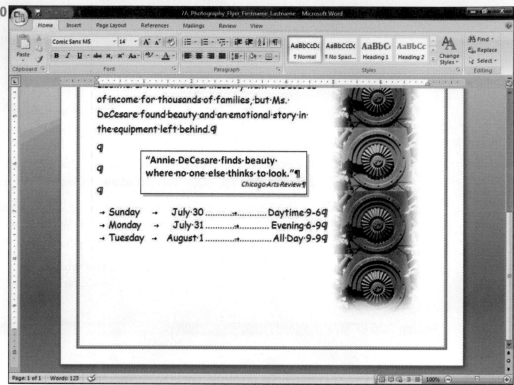

6 **Save** your document.

Activity 7.14 Inserting a Predefined Shape

Shapes are predefined drawing objects such as stars, banners, arrows, and callouts. More than 150 predefined Shapes are available with Word.

1 Click the **Insert tab**, and then in the **Illustrations group**, click the **Shapes** button to display the Shapes gallery, as shown in Figure 7.31.

Figure 7.31

Horizontal Scroll button

2 From the **Shapes gallery**, under **Stars and Banners**, in the second row, click the second shape—**Horizontal Scroll**.

3 Move the ⊞ pointer near the left margin at approximately **8 inches on the vertical ruler**. Using both the horizontal and vertical rulers as guides, drag down and to the right to create a banner approximately **1 inch** high and **3 inches** wide.

4 In the **Size group**, use the **Shape Height** and **Shape Width spin box arrows** to set the **Height** to **1.2"** and the **Width** to **3"**. Compare your screen with Figure 7.32. If you are not satisfied with your result, undo your changes and begin again.

Figure 7.32

Banner 1.2 inches high and 3 inches wide

5 Right-click the banner, and then from the shortcut menu, click **Add Text**. Click the **Home tab**. In the **Styles group**, click the **No Spacing** style button to remove the space *After* paragraphs and change the line spacing to *Single*.

6 Type the following text, pressing ⏎ after each line except the last line:

Memories Old and New
220 West Randolph Street
Chicago, IL 60601
312-555-0023

7 In the banner, select the first line of text—*Memories Old and New*—and then on the Mini toolbar, click **Bold** [B]. Click the **Font Size button arrow**, and then click **14**.

8 Select all of the text in the banner, and then on the Mini toolbar, click the **Center** button [≡]. If necessary, adjust the height of the banner to accommodate the text.

9 Click the **Format tab**, and then in the **Shadow Effects group**, click the **Shadow Effects** button. Use the technique you practiced with the text box to apply **Shadow Style 4**.

10 Nudge the shadow **Up** two times and to the **Left** two times. Click outside of the banner to deselect it, and then compare your screen with Figure 7.33.

Figure 7.33

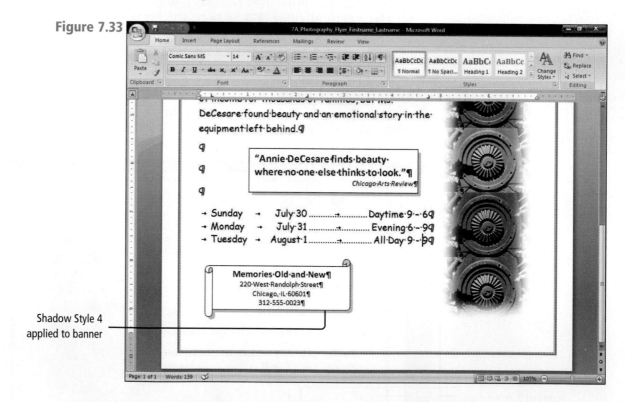

Shadow Style 4 applied to banner

11 Add the file name to the footer, and then display the **Print Preview** window to make a final check of your document. **Save** [💾] your document, and then submit the document as directed.

12 **Close** your document, and then **Exit** Word.

End You have completed Project 7A

Project 7B **Price List**

In Activities 7.15 through 7.24, you will create a price list for framed and unframed prints by photographer Annie DeCesare at Memories Old and New. Your completed document will look similar to Figure 7.34.

For Project 7B, you will need the following file:

w07B_Price_List

You will save your document as 7B_Price_List_Firstname_Lastname

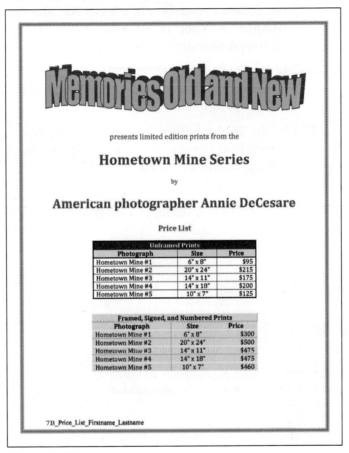

Figure 7.34
Project 7B—Price List

Objective 4
Create a Table

The table feature in Word has largely replaced the use of tabs because of its flexibility and ease of use. *Tables* contain rows and columns in which you can organize data. You can create an empty table, and then fill in the *cells*—the boxes created at the intersections of columns and rows. You can also convert existing text to a table provided the text is properly formatted.

Activity 7.15 Creating a Table and Entering Text

1 **Start** Word, display the formatting marks and rulers, and then from your student files, locate and open the file **w07B_Price_List**. From the **Office** menu 🅑, click **Save As**, and then navigate to your **Word Chapter 7** folder. In the **File name** box, type **7B_Price_List_Firstname_Lastname** and press Enter.

2 In the three blank lines under *Price List*, click in the middle blank line. Click the **Insert tab**, and then in the **Tables group**, click the **Table** button.

3 In the **Table gallery**, in the fifth row, point to the second square. Notice that the size of the table—*2x5*—displays at the top of the gallery, as shown in Figure 7.35.

Figure 7.35

Table size

Preview of inserted table

4 Click one time, and then compare your screen with Figure 7.36.

A table with five rows and two columns displays at the insertion point location, and the insertion point displays in the upper left cell. The table fills the width of the page, from the left margin to the right margin. Table Tools display on the Ribbon, and add two contextual tabs—*Design* and *Layout*.

Figure 7.36

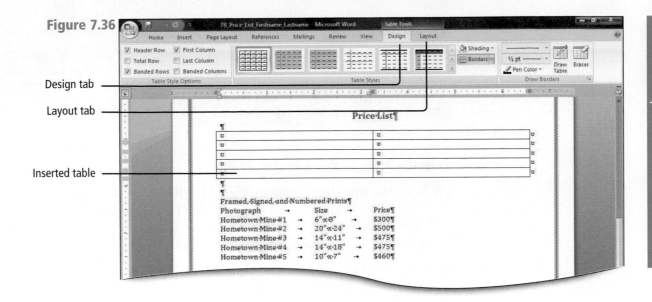

Design tab

Layout tab

Inserted table

5 Type **Unframed Prints** and then press Tab to move to the second cell in the first row of the table.

Use Tab—rather than Enter—to move from cell to cell in a Word table. Pressing Enter creates an additional line in the same cell, similar to the way you add a new line in a document. If you press Enter by mistake, press ←Bksp to remove the extra line.

6 Press Tab again to move to the first cell in the second row. Type **Hometown Mine #1** and press Tab. Type **$95** and press Tab.

7 Type the following to complete the table, but do not press Tab after the last item. Compare your screen with Figure 7.37.

Hometown Mine #2	$215
Hometown Mine #3	$175
Hometown Mine #4	$200

Figure 7.37

8 **Save** the document.

More Knowledge — Navigating in a Table

You can move to a previous cell in a table by pressing ⇧Shift + Tab. This action selects the contents of the previous cell. The selection moves back one cell at a time each time you press Tab while holding down ⇧Shift. You can also use the up or down arrow keys to move up or down a column. The left and right arrow keys, however, move the insertion point one character at a time within a cell.

Activity 7.16 Adding a Row to a Table

1 With the insertion point in the last cell in the table, press Tab to add a new row to the bottom of the table. Type **Hometown Mine #5** and press Tab. Type **$125** and then, in the second row of the table, click anywhere to position the insertion point.

2 Click the **Layout tab**, and then in the **Rows & Columns group**, click the **Insert Above** button to insert a new row.

3 In the new row, type **Photograph** and press Tab.

When the entire row is selected, text that you type automatically begins in the cell on the left.

4 Type **Price** and then compare your table with Figure 7.38.

Figure 7.38

New rows

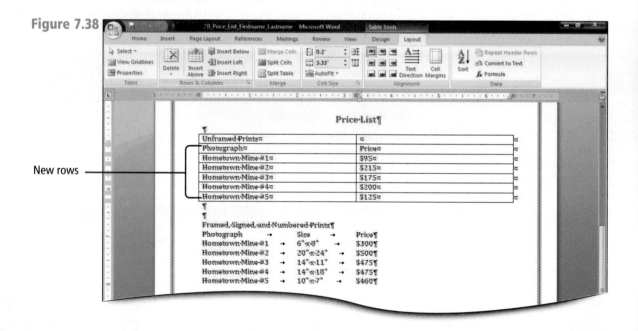

5 Save your document.

Activity 7.17 Changing the Width of a Table Column

1 In the first column of the table, point to the right boundary until the pointer displays, as shown in Figure 7.39.

Figure 7.39

Resize pointer

2 Drag the boundary to the left until the first column's right boundary aligns at approximately **2 inches on the horizontal ruler**; use the horizontal ruler as a guide. If only one row resizes, click the Undo button and begin again.

3 Drag the right boundary of the second column to **2.75 inches on the horizontal ruler**. Compare your table with Figure 7.40.

4 **Save** your document.

Figure 7.40

Columns resized

Activity 7.18 Adding a Column to a Table

You can add a column to a Word table in a manner similar to inserting a row.

1 In the first column of the table, click anywhere in the column to position the insertion point. On the **Layout tab**, in the **Rows & Columns group**, click the **Insert Right** button.

2 In the new column, click to place the insertion point in the second row. Type **Size** and press ↓.

3 From the **Office** menu 🏢, click the **Word Options** button, and then click **Proofing**. Under **AutoCorrect options**, click the **AutoCorrect Options** button. On the **AutoFormat tab**, under **Replace**, clear the **"Straight quotes" with "smart quotes"** check box.

4 On the **AutoFormat As You Type tab**, under **Replace as you type**, clear the **"Straight quotes" with "smart quotes"** check box, and then click **OK** two times.

5 Complete the column with the following information; the text may be too wide for the cell, and wrap to the next line in the same cell.

> **6" × 8"**
> **20" × 24"**
> **14" × 11"**
> **14" × 18"**
> **10" × 7"**

Note — Using Straight Quotes Versus Smart Quotes

When you type a quotation mark in Word, one of two characters displays—a straight quote (") or a smart quote ("). *Straight quotes* consist of two straight lines, and are used for inch marks. *Smart quotes*, which have rounded sides and are more decorative, are often used for quotations. By default, when you type a quotation mark, Word's AutoCorrect feature automatically changes it to a smart quote. However, many computers will have this AutoCorrect feature turned off. The single quote mark works the same way, where a smart single quotation mark is used as an apostrophe for contractions and possessive words, while the straight single quotation mark is used for foot marks in measurements.

---

6 Drag the right boundary of the third column to **4 inches on the horizontal ruler**.

> If you try to resize the middle column first, the right border of the table will remain fixed, thus decreasing the width of the column on the right.

7 Drag the right boundary of the second column to **3 inches on the horizontal ruler**, and then compare your screen with Figure 7.41.

Figure 7.41

New column inserted ———

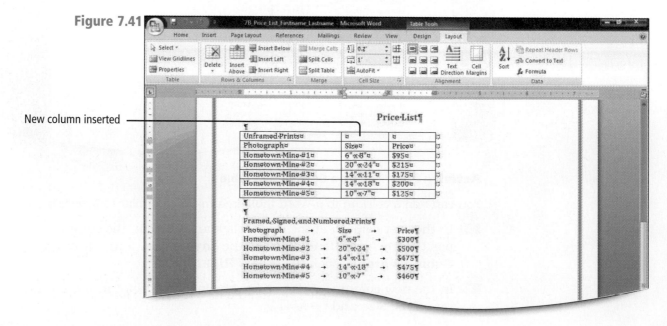

8 Save 🖫 your document.

More Knowledge — Using Tabs in Tables

You can add tabs to a table column; doing so lets you indent items within a table cell. The easiest way to add a tab is to click on the ruler to set the location within a column. Then you can drag the tab stop indicator to change the location of the tab within the column or add the hanging indent marker so multiple lines in a list are evenly indented. To move to the tabbed location within the cell—and not to the next cell—press Ctrl + Tab.

Activity 7.19 Converting Text to Tables

The Insert Table feature is useful if you are beginning a new table, but Word also provides a tool that enables you to convert existing text to a table. The text must be marked using *separator characters*—usually tabs or commas that separate the text in each line. When you convert text to a table, you can have Word optimize the column widths at the same time.

1 Scroll as necessary to view the lower portion of the document. In the block of text at the end of the document, beginning with *Framed* and continuing to the end of the document, notice the tab marks, as shown in Figure 7.42.

> Tab marks can act as separator characters for the purpose of converting text to a table.

Figure 7.42

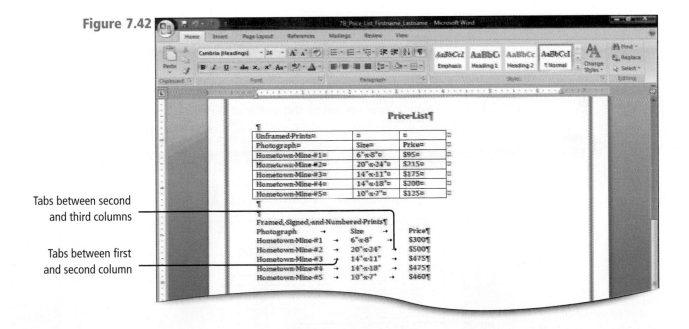

Tabs between second and third columns

Tabs between first and second column

2 Click to position the insertion point to the left of the word *Framed*, hold down ⇧Shift, and then click at the end of the last line, after *$460*. Be sure you include the paragraph mark to the right of *$460*.

3 With the text selected, click the **Insert tab**. In the **Tables group**, click the **Table** button, and then click **Convert Text to Table**.

4 In the **Convert Text to Table** dialog box, under **Table size**, click the **Number of columns up spin arrow** to change the number of columns to **3**. Then, under **AutoFit behavior**, click the **AutoFit to contents** option button.

The AutoFit to contents option instructs Word to evaluate the contents of the columns and choose appropriate column widths for each column.

5 Under **Separate text at**, click the **Tabs** option button. Compare your dialog box with Figure 7.43.

Figure 7.43

Three columns

Column width adjusts to fit contents

Separator type

6 At the bottom of the **Convert Text to Table** dialog box, click **OK**. Click anywhere in the document to deselect the table. Click **Save**, and then compare your table with Figure 7.44.

The columns are set to the width of the widest item in each column.

Figure 7.44

Three columns—column widths adjust to fit contents

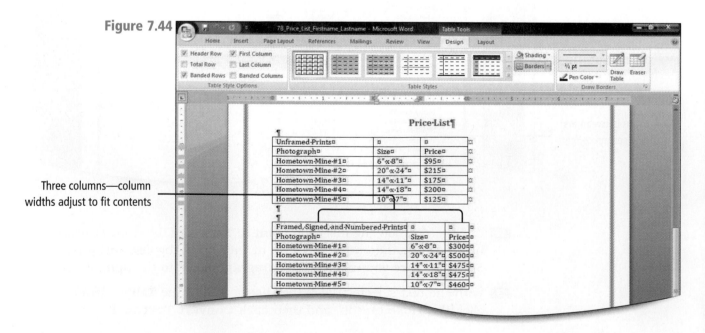

More Knowledge — Formatting Text for Easy Conversion to a Table

To format text that will eventually be converted to a table, separate the columns using a separator character. Tabs and commas are the most commonly used separators, but you can specify some other marks, including dashes, dollar signs, or colons. Word will not recognize a mixture of tabs and commas as separators in the same block of text.

Objective 5
Format a Table

You can format tables to make them more attractive and easier to read. When you type numbers, for example, they line up on the left of a column instead of on the right. With Word's formatting tools, you can shade cells, format the table borders and grid, align text, and center the table between the document margins. All of these features make a table more inviting to the reader.

Activity 7.20 Formatting Text in Cells and Shading Cells

1 In the upper table, click anywhere in the cell containing the word *Photograph*, hold down the left mouse button, and then drag to the right to select all three cells in the second row. On the Mini toolbar, click **Bold** B and **Center** ☰. Compare your screen with Figure 7.45.

Figure 7.45

Bold, centered text

2 In the second column, click in the cell containing *6" × 8"*, and then drag down to select the third cell through the seventh cell. On the Mini toolbar, click **Center** ☰.

3 In the third column, click in the cell containing *$95*, and then drag down to select the third cell through the seventh cell. On the **Home tab**, in the **Paragraph group**, click the **Align Text Right** button ☰. Compare your screen with Figure 7.46.

Figure 7.46

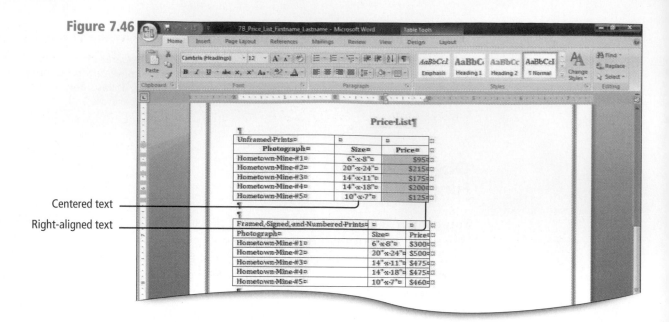

Centered text ———

Right-aligned text ———

---

4 In the upper table, click anywhere in the cell containing the *Unframed Prints*, and then drag to the right to select all three cells in the first row. Click the **Design tab**, and then in the **Table Styles group**, click the **Shading button arrow**.

5 In the **Shading gallery**, near the bottom of the fourth column, point to—but do not click—**Dark Blue, Text 2, Darker 25%**. Compare your screen with Figure 7.47.

Figure 7.47

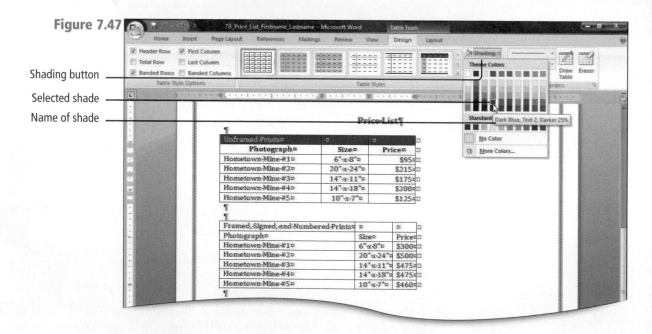

Shading button ———

Selected shade ———

Name of shade ———

---

6 Click to apply *Dark Blue, Text 2, Darker 25%*.

7 In the upper table, click anywhere in the cell containing the word *Photograph*, and then drag to the right to select all three cells in the second row. On the **Design tab**, in the **Table Styles group**, click the **Shading button arrow**.

8 In the **Shading gallery**, click the second button in the fourth column—**Dark Blue, Text 2, Lighter 80%**. Click anywhere in the table to deselect the cells, and then compare your screen with Figure 7.48.

Figure 7.48

Shades applied ———

9 **Save** the document.

Activity 7.21 Changing the Table Border

You can modify or remove the border from an entire table, a selected cell, or individual boundaries of a cell.

1 In the upper table, click anywhere in the cell containing the word *Photograph*, and then drag to the right to select all three cells in the second row.

2 On the **Design tab**, in the **Table Styles group**, click the **Borders button arrow**, and then click **Borders and Shading**.

3 In the **Borders and Shading** dialog box, under **Setting**, click the **Custom** button. Click the **Width arrow**, and then click **1 1/2 pt**. In the **Preview** area, click the bottom border of the preview diagram. Notice that the Preview area displays a bottom border that is heavier than the side or top borders, as shown in Figure 7.49.

The Custom setting enables you to change the characteristics of individual border lines, rather than change all of the borders at one time.

Figure 7.49

Thicker bottom border ———

Custom button ———

Line width ———

4 Click **OK** to change the bottom border of the selected cells. Click any-where in the upper table, and then click the **Layout tab**. In the **Table group**, click the **Select** button, and then click **Select Table**.

5 Click the **Design tab**, and then in the **Table Styles group**, click the **Borders** button. In the **Borders and Shading** dialog box, under **Setting**, click the **Custom** button, if necessary. Click the **Width arrow**, and then click **1 1/2 pt**. In the **Preview** area, click the four outside borders, and then click **OK**.

6 Click anywhere in the document to deselect the table, and then com-pare your screen with Figure 7.50.

Figure 7.50

Thicker cell border ———

Thicker outside border ———

7 **Save** your document.

Activity 7.22 Centering a Table

1 Click anywhere in the upper table, and then click the **Layout tab**. In the **Table group**, click the **Select** button, and then click **Select Table**.

2 Click the **Home tab**, and then in the **Paragraph group**, click the **Center** button ▤.

Another Way ── **To Center a Table**

You can center a table without selecting the table first. Right-click anywhere in the table, and then, from the shortcut menu, click Table Properties. In the Table Properties dialog box, on the Table tab, under Alignment, click Center. The Table Properties dialog box also enables you to wrap text around a table in the same way you wrap text around a graphic.

---

3 Click anywhere in the document to deselect the table, and then compare your screen with Figure 7.51.

Figure 7.51

Table centered horizontally on the page

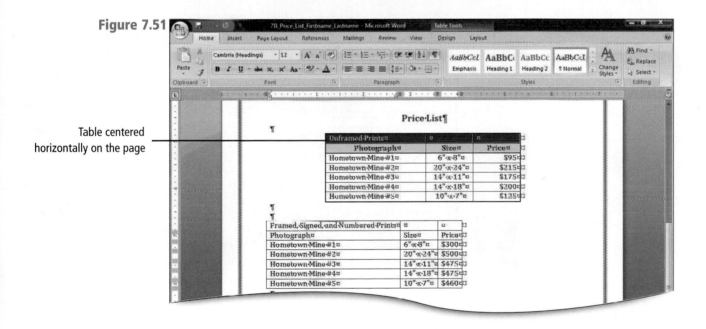

4 **Save** 🖫 your document.

Activity 7.23 Merging Cells

The title of a table typically spans two or more columns. In this activity, you will merge cells so that you can position the table title across the columns.

1 In the upper table, click anywhere in the cell containing the word *Unframed Prints*, and then drag to the right to select all three cells in the first row.

2 Click the **Layout tab**, and then in the **Merge group**, click the **Merge Cells** button.

> The cells are merged, and the borders between the cells in the top row are removed.

3 Select the text in the top cell—**Unframed Prints**. On the Mini toolbar, click **Bold** **B** and **Center** .

Another Way ── **To Align Text in a Table**

You can use shortcut menus to align text in a table. Right-click the cell, point to Cell Alignment from the shortcut menu, and then from the Cell Alignment gallery that displays, click the alignment style you want. You can choose from both vertical and horizontal cell alignment options using the Cell Alignment gallery.

4 Click anywhere in the document to deselect the table, and then compare your screen with Figure 7.52.

Figure 7.52

Text is merged across three cells

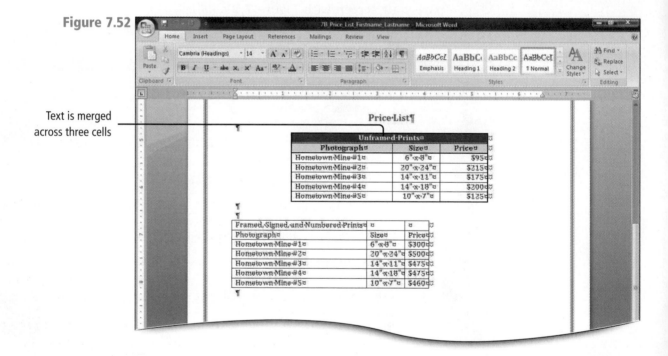

5 **Save** your document.

Activity 7.24 Applying a Predefined Format to a Table

Word includes a number of built-in table formats with which you can quickly give your table a professional design. This is accomplished by applying a *Table Style*—a predefined set of formatting characteristics, including font, alignment, and cell shading.

1 In the lower table, click anywhere to position the insertion point within the table—you need not select the entire table to use Table Styles.

2 Click the **Design tab**. In the **Table Styles group**, point to the second Table Style—**Table 3D effects 1**—and notice that Live Preview displays the table the way it would look if you clicked that style, as shown in Figure 7.53.

Figure 7.53

Table 3D effects 1 style

Live Preview displays the table style

3 In the **Table Styles group**, click the **More** button. Scroll down to view the available table styles, and then point to several of the styles in the gallery. Click anywhere in the document to close the gallery.

4 In the **Table Styles group**, point to the third style—**Table 3D effects 2**—and click to apply the style. Click the **Layout tab**. In the **Table group**, click the **Select** button, and then click **Select Table**.

5 Click the **Design tab**. In the **Table Styles group**, click the **Shading button arrow**, and then in the second row, click the fourth color— **Dark Blue, Text 2, Lighter 80%**.

6 Right-click the table, and then from the shortcut menu, click **Table Properties**. In the **Table Properties** dialog box, on the **Table tab**, under **Alignment**, click **Center**.

7 Point to the **Table Properties** dialog box title bar, and then drag the dialog box up and to the right so that you can see most of the lower table. In the **Table Properties** dialog box, click the **Column tab**. Under **Size**, click the **Next Column** button to select the first column, as shown in Figure 7.54.

Figure 7.54

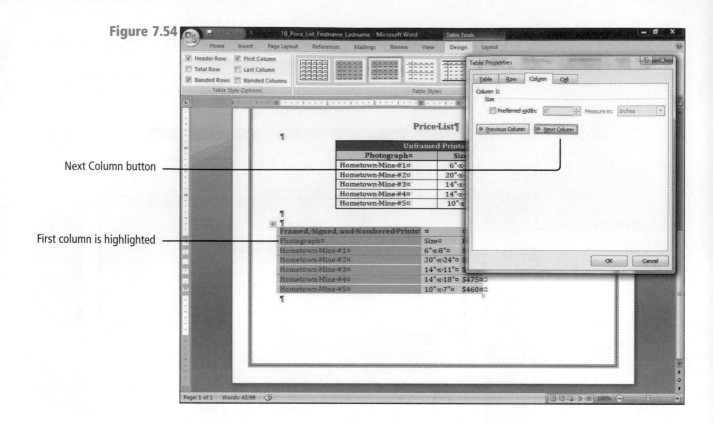

Next Column button

First column is highlighted

8 With the first column selected, select the **Preferred width** check box, select the text in the **Preferred width** box, type **2** and then click the **Next Column** button. Use the same procedure to make the second and third columns **1.1** inches wide, and then click **OK**.

9 Point to the first cell of the top row and drag to the right to select all three cells. Click the **Layout tab**. In the **Merge group**, click the **Merge Cells** button. In the **Alignment group**, click the **Align Center** button ▣.

10 In the second row of the table, select all three cells, and then on the Mini toolbar, click **Bold** ▣ and **Center** ▣.

11 In the second column, click in the cell containing *6″ × 8″*, and then drag down to select the third cell through the seventh cell. On the Mini toolbar, click the **Center** button ▣.

12 In the third column, click in the cell containing *$300*, and then drag down to select the third cell through the seventh cell. Click the **Home tab**, and then in the **Paragraph group**, click the **Align Text Right** button ▣. Click anywhere in the document to deselect the cells, and then compare your screen with Figure 7.55.

Figure 7.55

Right-aligned text

Centered text

13 From the **Office** menu 🔘, click the **Word Options** button, and then click **Proofing**. Under **AutoCorrect options**, click the **AutoCorrect Options** button. On the **AutoFormat tab**, under **Replace**, select the **"Straight quotes" with "smart quotes"** check box. Repeat this procedure on the **AutoFormat As You Type tab**, and then click **OK** two times.

14 Add the file name to the footer, and then **Save** 💾 your document. Submit the document as directed.

15 **Close** your document, and then **Exit** Word.

End You have completed Project 7B ————————

There's More You Can Do!

Close Word and any other open windows. Display the Start menu, click Computer, and then navigate to the student files that accompany this textbook. From the CD that came with your book, open the folder **02_theres_more_you_can_do**, locate and open the folder for this chapter. Open and print the instructions for this project, which are provided to you in Adobe PDF format.

Try IT! — Create a Chart

In this Try It! exercise, you will insert a chart into a Word document.

Content-Based Assessments

Summary

Many graphic elements can be inserted into a Word document, including clip art, pictures, and basic shapes created with Word's drawing tools. Text can also be converted into a graphic format using WordArt.

An effective way to present information is with a tabbed list or a table. A variety of tabs can be used, such as left-aligned, decimal, centered, or right-aligned. Leader characters, such as a solid, dotted, or dashed line, can be used to fill the space created by using a tab stop.

Tables present information in a format of rows and columns. Tables can be formatted to display the information in a manner that emphasizes certain parts of the table. Text in a table can be formatted using both the Table contextual tools and Table Styles. Existing text can be converted to a table format.

Key Terms

The ⊙ symbol represents Key Terms found on the Student CD in the 02_theres_more_you_can_do folder for this chapter

Content-Based Assessments

Matching

Match each term in the second column with its correct definition in the first column by writing the letter of the term on the blank line in front of the correct definition.

_____ **1.** A gallery of text styles with which you can create decorative effects, such as shadowed or mirrored text.

_____ **2.** An object or graphic that can be moved independently of the surrounding text.

_____ **3.** An object or graphic inserted in a document that acts like a character in a sentence.

_____ **4.** Small circles in the corners of a selected graphic with which you can resize the graphic proportionally.

_____ **5.** A movable, resizable container for text or graphics.

_____ **6.** A handle on a selected graphic that can be dragged to rotate the graphic to any angle.

_____ **7.** The symbol that indicates the paragraph to which an object is attached.

_____ **8.** Predefined drawing shapes, such as stars, banners, arrows, and callouts, included with Microsoft Office, that can be inserted into documents.

_____ **9.** Characters that form a solid, dotted, or dashed line that fills the space used by a tab character.

_____ **10.** A character used to identify column placement in text; usually a tab or a comma.

_____ **11.** A mark on the ruler that indicates the location where the insertion point will be placed when you press the Tab key.

_____ **12.** The text select (I-beam) pointer with various attached shapes that indicate which formatting will be applied when you double-click—such as a left-aligned, centered, or right-aligned tab stop.

_____ **13.** The rectangular box in a table formed by the intersection of a row and column.

_____ **14.** Rows and columns of text or numbers used to organize data and present it effectively.

_____ **15.** A command that applies one of a number of built-in table formats—resulting in a table with a professional design.

A Anchor

B Cell

C Click and type pointer

D Corner sizing handles

E Floating object

F Inline object

G Leader characters

H Rotate handle

I Separator character

J Shapes

K Tab stop

O Table

N Table Style

L Text box

M WordArt

Content-Based Assessments

Fill in the Blank

Write the correct answer in the space provided.

1. An _____ symbol indicates the paragraph to which an object is attached.

2. When a graphic is selected, _____ _____ display around the edge of the graphic.

3. To align text to the contours of an irregularly shaped graphic, choose _____ Text Wrapping.

4. A banner is an example of a predefined _____ that can be inserted into a document.

5. Tab stops are a form of paragraph formatting and are stored in the _____ mark.

6. The tab alignment option that centers text around a tab stop is the _____ tab.

7. A series of dots following a tab that serve to guide the reader's eyes is known as a dot _____.

8. To move text aligned with tabs, select the text and drag the _____ _____ on the ruler.

9. To move from cell to cell across a table as you enter text, press _____.

10. To create a table in Word, click the _____ button on the Insert tab.

11. When you press ⟨Tab⟩ with the insertion point in the last cell in a table, a new _____ is added to the table.

12. On the Table Tools Design tab, click the _____ button to add gray or color to a table cell.

13. To set the alignment of a table on a page, display the Table tab of the _____ _____ dialog box.

14. A predefined set of table formatting characteristics, including font, alignment, and cell shading is called a Table _____.

15. To combine two or more cells into one cell, use the _____ _____ button on the Layout tab.

Content-Based Assessments

Project 7C—Creative Supplies

In this project, you will apply the skills you practiced from the Objectives in Project 7A.

Objectives: 1. *Insert and Format Graphics;* **2.** *Set Tab Stops;* **3.** *Insert and Modify Text Boxes and Shapes.*

In the following Skills Review, you will create a flyer for Memories Old and New that describes the range of products available at the store. Your completed flyer will look similar to the one shown in Figure 7.56.

For Project 7C, you will need the following files:

New blank Word document
w07C_Art_Supplies
w07C_Supplies

You will save your document as
7C_Creative_Supplies_Firstname_Lastname

Figure 7.56

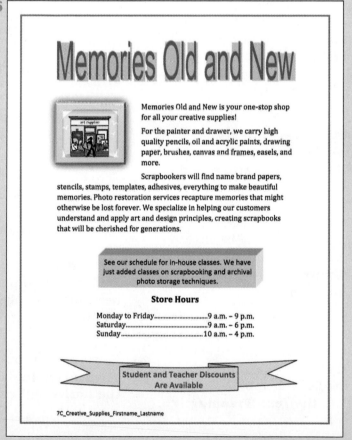

(Project 7C–Creative Supplies continues on the next page)

(Project 7C–Creative Supplies continued)

1. **Start** Word and display formatting marks and rulers. From the **Page Layout tab**, display the **Page Setup** dialog box, set the **Top** and **Bottom** margins to **1"**, the **Left** and **Right** margins to **1.25"**, and then click **OK**.

2. Type **Memories Old and New** and then press Enter two times. Select the text you just typed, but do not select the paragraph mark. Click the **Insert tab**. In the **Text group**, click the **WordArt** button. From the **WordArt gallery**, in the second row, click the second style—**WordArt style 8**. Click **OK**.

3. On the **Format tab**, in the **Size group**, click the **Shape Height button up spin arrow** as necessary to change the height of the WordArt to **1"**. Click the **Shape Width button up spin arrow** as necessary to change the width of the WordArt to **6"**. Display the **Save As** dialog box, navigate to your **Word Chapter 7** folder, **Save** the document as **7C_Creative_Supplies_Firstname_Lastname** and then add the file name to the footer.

4. **Close** the footer area. Press Ctrl + End. Click the **Insert tab**. From the **Text group**, click the **Object button arrow**, and then click **Text from File**. Locate and insert the file **w07C_Supplies**. In the paragraph beginning *Scrapbookers*, click to position the insertion point at the beginning of the paragraph. In the **Illustrations group**, click the **Picture** button. Locate and insert **w07C_Art_Supplies**.

5. On the **Format tab**, in the **Size group**, click the **Shape Height spin box down arrow** as necessary to change the height of the picture to **1.4"**. With the graphic still selected, on the **Format tab**, in the **Arrange group**, click the **Text Wrapping** button. From the **Text Wrapping gallery**, click **Square** to wrap the text around the graphic.

6. Point anywhere in the **w07C_Art_Supplies** graphic to display the ⬚ pointer, and then drag the graphic up until the top edge of the graphic is aligned with the top edge of the paragraph beginning *Memories Old and New*. Be sure the left side of the graphic is aligned with the left side of the text.

7. With the graphic still selected, on the **Format tab**, in the **Picture Styles group**, click the third picture style—**Metal Frame**. Move the picture as necessary to match Figure 7.56.

8. Click anywhere in the document to deselect the graphic. Click the **Page Layout tab**, and then in the **Page Background group**, click the **Page Borders** button. In the **Borders and Shading** dialog box, under **Setting**, click **Box**. Click the **Color arrow**, and then in the last column of colors, click the fifth button—**Orange, Accent 6, Darker 25%**. Click the **Width arrow**, click **3 pt**, and then click **OK**. **Save** your document.

9. Scroll to display the lower half of the document on your screen, and then click in the blank line at the end of the document. Move the ⬚ pointer on your screen to position it at approximately **6.5 inches on the vertical ruler** and at the left margin, double-click to place the insertion point. If necessary, change the Font to Cambria, and the Font Size to 14. Type **Store Hours** and press Enter.

10. Be sure the **Tab Alignment** button displays a **Left tab**. Click on **4 inches on the horizontal ruler**. Double-click the tab

(Project 7C–Creative Supplies continues on the next page)

Content-Based Assessments

(Project 7C–Creative Supplies continued)

stop you just added to the ruler. In the **Tabs** dialog box, under **Tab stop position**, click to select the lower **4"**. Under **Alignment**, click the **Right** option button. Under **Leader**, click the **2** option button to add a dot leader. Click the **Set** button, and then click **OK**.

11. Display the **Paragraph** dialog box. Under **Indentation**, click the **Left spin box up arrow** to change the left margin indent to **1"**. Under **Spacing**, click the **After down spin arrow** two times to change the spacing to **0**. Click the **Line spacing arrow**, click **Single**, and then click **OK**.

12. Type the following text, pressing Tab after the days of the week, and Enter after the time:

Monday to Friday	9 a.m. – 9 p.m.
Saturday	9 a.m. – 6 p.m.
Sunday	10 a.m. – 4 p.m.

13. Select the text *Store Hours*. On the Mini toolbar, click the **Bold** and **Center** buttons. Click the **Font Size button arrow**, and then click **16**. Select the three lines of tabbed text. Point to the horizontal ruler and position the pointer so the tip of the pointer arrow is touching the **4-inch tab stop**. When you see the *Right Tab* ScreenTip, drag the tab stop mark to the right to **5 inches on the ruler**. Click anywhere in the document to deselect the text.

14. Click the **Insert tab**, and then in the **Text group**, click the **Text Box** button. At the bottom of the **Text Box gallery**, click **Draw Text Box**. Move the ⊞ pointer to the left margin at **5 inches on the vertical ruler**. Using both the horizontal and vertical rulers as guides, drag down and to the right to create a text box approximately **1 inch** high and **3 inches** wide—then use the spin arrows in the **Size group** to size the text box precisely.

15. With the insertion point displayed in the text box, type **See our schedule for in-house classes. We have just added classes on scrapbooking and archival photo storage techniques.**

16. In the text box, select all of the text. On the Mini toolbar, click the **Font Size button arrow**, and then click **14**. If necessary, click the Font button arrow, and then click Calibri. Click the **Center** button. Display the **Paragraph** dialog box. Change the spacing **After** to **0** and the **Line spacing** to **Single**.

17. With the text box still selected, on the **Format tab**, in the **Size group**, click the **Shape Width button up spin arrow** as necessary to change the width of the text box to **4"**. Click the **Shape Height button down spin arrow** as necessary to change the height of the text box to **0.8"**.

18. Point to one of the text box borders until the 🔀 pointer displays. Drag the text box down and to the right until the left edge is at approximately **1 inch on the horizontal ruler**, and the top edge is at approximately **5.5 inches on the vertical ruler**. Use Figure 7.56 as a guide. On the **Format tab**, in the **3-D Effects group**, click the **3-D Effects** button. Under **Parallel**, click the first button—**3-D Style 1**. Click anywhere in the document to deselect the text box. **Save** your document.

19. Click the **Insert tab**, and then in the **Illustrations group**, click the **Shapes** button. In the **Shapes gallery**, under **Stars and Banners**, in the first row, click the last button—**Curved Down Ribbon**.

20. Move the ⊞ pointer to the left margin at **8 inches on the vertical ruler**. Using both the horizontal and vertical rulers as guides, drag down and to the right to

(Project 7C–Creative Supplies continues on the next page)

Content-Based Assessments

(Project 7C–Creative Supplies continued)

create a banner approximately **0.8 inch** high and **6 inches** wide—then use the spin box arrows in the **Size group** to size the banner precisely. Center the banner between the left and right border, and between the tabbed list and the bottom border.

21. Right-click the banner. From the shortcut menu, click **Add Text**. Type **Student and Teacher Discounts Are Available** Select the banner text. On the Mini toolbar, click the **Bold** button, and then click the **Center** button. Click the **Font Color button arrow**, and then in the last column, click the last button—click **Orange, Accent 6, Darker 50%**. Click the **Font Size button**

arrow, and then click **16**. On the **Home tab**, in the **Paragraph group**, click the **Line spacing button arrow**, and then click **1.0**.

22. On the **Format tab**, in the **Text Box Styles group**, click the **Shape Fill arrow**, and then in the last column, click the third button—**Orange, Accent 6, Lighter 60%**. Click to deselect the banner, and then **Save** your document.

23. Display the **Print Preview** to make a final check of your document. Submit your document as directed.

24. **Close** your document, and then **Exit** Word.

End You have completed Project 7C

Content-Based Assessments

Skills Review

Project 7D—Sales Figures

In this project, you will apply the skills you practiced from the Objectives in Project 7B.

Objectives: 4. *Create a Table;* **5**. *Format a Table.*

In the following Skills Review, you will edit a memo about the recent photography exhibition at Memories Old and New. You will create and format a table, convert text to a table, and then AutoFormat the table. Your completed document will look similar to Figure 7.57.

For Project 7D, you will need the following file:

w07D_Sales_Figures

**You will save your document as
7D_Sales_Figures_Firstname_Lastname**

Figure 7.57

To: Henry Smith
          Bill Masterson

From: Sharon Nguyen, Manager

Date: March 12, 2009

Subject: Winter Exhibition Sales Results

This year's winter photography exhibition was a big success, with attendance and sales surpassing last year's event. Extended hours and increased promotion in the store and local media ads clearly made a difference.

2009 Exhibition		
Day	Attendees	Increase
Opening Night	300	60
Saturday	250	40
Sunday	220	30
Monday	130	-10
Tuesday	90	50
Closing	270	70

Gross Photograph Sales		
Day	2009	2008
Opening Night	$20,320	$15,600
Saturday	$18,500	$10,000
Sunday	$17,680	$10,900
Monday	$5,850	$6,000
Tuesday	$4,900	$3,200
Closing	$19,700	$17,800

Planning for next year's ad buys is already under way in order to secure space and rates. At the next staff meeting I will present a plan and budget for next year's winter exhibit, including further increasing in-store promotional activities.

7D_Sales_Figures_Firstname_Lastname

(Project 7D–Sales Figures continues on the next page)

Content-Based Assessments

(Project 7D–Sales Figures continued)

1. **Start** Word. From your student files, locate and open the document **w07D_Sales_Figures**, and display formatting marks and rulers. In the three blank lines under the paragraph beginning *This year's winter*, click in the middle blank line. Click the **Insert tab**, and then in the **Tables group**, click the **Table** button. In the **Table gallery**, in the sixth row of squares, point to the second square, and then click to insert a **2x6** table.

2. Type **2009 Exhibition** and then press ↓ to move to the first cell in the second row. Type **Opening Night** and press ⟦Tab⟧. Type **300** and press ⟦Tab⟧.

3. Type the following to complete the table, but do not press ⟦Tab⟧ after the last item.

Saturday	250
Sunday	220
Monday	130
Tuesday	90

4. From the **Office** menu, display the **Save As** dialog box, and then navigate to your **Word Chapter 7 folder**. In the **File name** box, type **7D_Sales_Figures_Firstname_Lastname** and press ⟦Enter⟧. Add the file name to the footer area.

5. Position the insertion point in the last cell in the table, and then press ⟦Tab⟧ to add a new row to the bottom of the table. Type **Closing** and press ⟦Tab⟧. Type **270** and then in the second row of the table, click anywhere to position the insertion point. Click the **Layout tab**, and then in the **Rows & Columns group**, click the **Insert Above** button to insert a new row. Type **Day** and press ⟦Tab⟧. Type **Attendees**

6. In the first column of the table, move the pointer to the right boundary until the ⟦+⟧ pointer displays. Drag the boundary to the left until the first column's right boundary

aligns at approximately **1.5 inches on the horizontal ruler**. If only one row resizes, click the Undo button and begin again. In the second column, drag the right boundary to **2.5 inches on the horizontal ruler**. **Save** your document.

7. In the second column of the table, click anywhere in the column to position the insertion point. On the **Layout tab**, in the **Rows & Columns group**, click the **Insert Right** button. In the new column, click to place the insertion point in the second row. Type **Increase** and press ↓.

8. Complete the column with the following information:

60
40
30
–10
50
70

9. In the second row, click anywhere in the first cell, and then drag to the right to select all three cells in the second row. On the Mini toolbar, click the **Bold** and **Center** buttons.

10. In the second column, click in the cell containing *300*, and then drag down and to the right to select the third cell through the eighth cell of the second and third columns, ending with *70*. Click the **Home tab**, and then in the **Paragraph group**, click the **Align Text Right** button.

11. Select all three cells in the first row. Click the **Design tab**, and then in the **Table Styles group**, click the **Shading** button. Under **Theme Colors**, click the third button in the first row—**Tan, Background 2**.

12. Click the **Layout tab**, and then in the **Merge group**, click the **Merge Cells** button. Select the text in the top cell—**2009 Exhibition**. On the Mini toolbar, click the

(Project 7D–Sales Figures continues on the next page)

Content-Based Assessments

(Project 7D–Sales Figures continued)

Bold and **Center** buttons. **Save** the document.

13. Click anywhere in the table to deselect the cells. On the **Design tab**, in the **Table Styles group**, click the **Borders button arrow**, and then click **Borders and Shading**. In the **Borders and Shading** dialog box, under **Setting**, click **Box**. Click the **Width arrow**, and then click **3 pt**. In the **Apply to** box, be sure that **Table** is indicated, and then click **OK**.

14. Click the **Layout tab**. In the **Table group**, click the **Select** button, and then click **Select Table**. Click the **Home tab**, and then in the **Paragraph group**, click the **Center** button. **Save** the document.

15. In the block of text near the end of the document, beginning with *Gross Photograph Sales*, click to position the insertion point to the left of the word *Gross*, hold down ⇧Shift, and then click after the paragraph mark at the end of the line beginning *Closing*—after *$17,800.*

16. With the text selected, click the **Insert tab**. In the **Tables group**, click the **Table** button, and then click **Convert Text to Table**. In the **Convert Text to Table** dialog box, under **Table size**, click the **Number of columns up spin arrow** to change the number of columns to **3**.

17. Under **AutoFit behavior**, click the **AutoFit to contents** option button. Then, under **Separate text at**, click the **Tabs** option button. At the bottom of the **Convert Text to Table** dialog box, click **OK**.

18. Click anywhere to position the insertion point in the lower table. On the **Design tab**, in the **Table Styles group**, click the **More** button. Under **Built-In**, in the first row, click the fifth table style—**Table Classic 2**. Right-click the table, and then from the shortcut menu, click **Table**

Properties. In the **Table Properties** dialog box, on the **Table tab**, under **Alignment**, click **Center**.

19. Drag the dialog box so that you can see most of the lower table. In the **Table Properties** dialog box, click the **Column tab**. Under **Size**, click the **Next Column** button until the first column of the lower table is highlighted. Select the **Preferred width** check box, and then in the box to the right, click the spin box arrows as necessary to set the **Preferred width** to **1.5"**. Click the **Next Column** button. Use the same procedure to make the second and third columns **1"** wide, and then click **OK**.

20. In the lower table, point to the first cell of the top row and drag to the right to select all three cells. Click the **Layout tab**, and then in the **Merge group**, click the **Merge Cells** button. In the **Alignment group**, click the **Align Center** button.

21. In the second row of the table, select the second and third cells, and then on the Mini toolbar, click the **Bold** and **Center** buttons. In the second row, in the first cell, select the text *Day*, and then on the Mini toolbar, click the **Center** button.

22. In the second column, click in the cell containing *$20,320*, and then drag down and to the right to select the third cell of the second column through the eighth cell of the third column—*$17,800*. Click the **Home tab**, and then in the **Paragraph group**, click the **Align Text Right** button.

23. Display the **Print Preview** to make a final check of your document. **Save** your changes, and then submit your document as directed.

24. **Close** your document, and then **Exit** Word.

End **You have completed Project 7D**

Content-Based Assessments

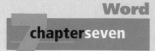

Mastering Word

Project 7E — Photo Enhancement

In this project, you will apply the skills you practiced from the Objectives in Projects 7A and 7B.

Objectives: 1. *Insert and Format Graphics;* **3.** *Insert and Modify Text Boxes and Shapes;* **4.** *Create a Table;* **5.** *Format a Table.*

In the following Mastering Word project, you will create a handout that describes the photo enhancement services offered by Memories Old and New. Your completed document will look similar to Figure 7.58.

For Project 7E, you will need the following files:

w07E_Photo_Enhancement
w07E_Chess

You will save your document as 7E_Photo_Enhancement_Firstname_Lastname

Figure 7.58

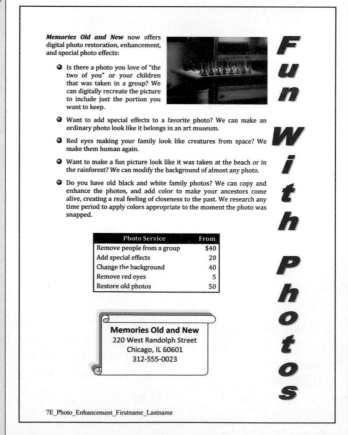

(Project 7E–Photo Enhancement continues on the next page)

Content-Based Assessments

(Project 7E–Photo Enhancement continued)

1. Locate and open the file **w07E_Photo_Enhancement**. **Save** the file in your chapter folder as **7E_Photo_Enhancement_Firstname_Lastname** and then add the file name to the footer. Display formatting marks and rulers.

2. Position the insertion point at the beginning of the document. **Insert** a **Fun With Photos** vertical **WordArt** title using **WordArt style 12**—in the second row, the sixth style. Set the **Width** to **9 inches** and the **Height** to **.8 inch**. Note that with a vertical WordArt, the Width setting is actually the height.

3. Add **Square** text wrapping, and then drag the WordArt title so that the upper right corner is at **0 inches on the vertical ruler** and **6.5 inches on the horizontal ruler**.

4. Position the insertion point at the beginning of the document. **Insert** the picture **w07E_Chess**, and change the **Width** to **2.5 inches**. Change the **Text Wrapping** to **Square**, and then position left edge of the picture at **3 inches on the horizontal ruler**, and the top edge of the picture level with the top edge of the text.

5. Click to place the insertion point in the blank line at the end of the document, and then press Enter. **Insert** a **2x6 Table**, and then add the following text:

Photo Service	From
Remove people from a group	$40
Add special effects	20
Change the background	40
Remove red eyes	5
Restore old photos	50

6. Display the **Table Properties** dialog box and **Center** the table horizontally on the page. Click the **Column tab**, and then set the first column to **2.5 inches** wide, and set the width of the second column to **.6**

inch wide. In the second column of the table, format the cells that contain numbers with the **Align Text Right** command.

7. In the first row, apply **Center** and **Bold** to both cells. Select the first row of the table, display the **Shading gallery**, and the second color in the first row—**Black, Text 1** shading. **Save** your work.

8. Click to place the insertion point anywhere in the table and display the **Borders and Shading** dialog box. Click **Box**, and then change the line width to **1 1/2 pt**.

9. Press Ctrl + End. Display the **Shapes gallery**. Under **Stars and Banners**, click the first shape in the second row—**Vertical Scroll**. Starting at **7.25 inches on the vertical ruler**, and at **1 inch on the horizontal ruler**, draw a bevel that is **3 inches** wide by **1.5 inches** high. Use the **Size** buttons to make the measurements exact.

10. Right-click on the bevel, click **Add Text**, and type the following:

Memories Old and New
220 West Randolph Street
Chicago, IL 60601
312-555-0023

11. **Center** the bevel text, change the **Font** to **Calibri**, and increase the **Font Size** to **14**. If necessary, remove any spacing *After* the paragraphs, and set the *Line Spacing* to Single.

12. Select the first line of text in the bevel, apply **Bold**, and then change the **Font Size** to **16**. Display the **Shadow Effects gallery**, and then under **Additional Shadow Styles**, click **Shadow Style 16**. **Nudge Shadow Left** two clicks and **Nudge Shadow Up** two clicks.

(Project 7E–Photo Enhancement continues on the next page)

Content-Based Assessments

Mastering Word

(Project 7E–Photo Enhancement continued)

13. Move the bevel so that it is centered horizontally under the table, with the top edge at about **7.25 inches on the vertical ruler**. Add a **Box** page border to the document, using a **1 1/2 pt** line width and the default black color.

14. **Preview** the document, and then print it, or submit it electronically as directed. **Save** your changes. **Close** the file, and then **Exit** Word.

 End **You have completed Project 7E** ——————————————

Content-Based Assessments

Project 7F—Photo Restoration

In this project, you will apply the skills you practiced from the Objectives in Projects 7A and 7B.

Objectives: 1. *Insert and Format Graphics;* **2**. *Set Tab Stops;* **3**. *Insert and Modify Text Boxes and Shapes.*

In the following Mastering Word project, you will create a handout about photograph restoration services available at Memories Old and New. Your completed document will look similar to Figure 7.59.

For Project 7F, you will need the following files:

w07F_Original
w07F_Photo_Restoration
w07F_Quick_Restore

**You will save your document as
7F_Photo_Restoration_Firstname_Lastname**

Figure 7.59

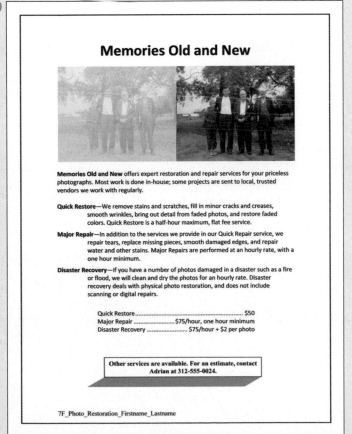

(Project 7F–Photo Restoration continues on the next page)

Content-Based Assessments

Mastering Word

(Project 7F–Photo Restoration continued)

1. Locate and open the file **w07F_Photo_Restoration**. **Save** the file in your chapter folder as **7F_Photo_ Restoration_Firstname_Lastname** and then add the file name to the footer. Display formatting marks and rulers.

2. Position the insertion point in the blank line under the title. Locate and **Insert** the picture **w07F_Original**. Reduce the **Width** of the picture to **3 inches**, and then change the **Text Wrapping** of the picture to **Square**.

3. Click to position the insertion point in the blank line under the title, and then **Insert** the **w07F_Quick_Restore** picture. Format this second picture in the same manner you formatted the first picture. Move the second picture to the right of (and touching) the first picture—use Figure 7.59 as a guide.

4. Press Ctrl + End. Insert a **Right tab stop** at **5 inches on the horizontal ruler**. Display the **Paragraph** dialog box and set the **Left Indentation** to **1 inch**. Display the **Tabs** dialog box. Add a **dot leader** to the tab stop at **5 inches on the horizontal ruler**. Type the following text, pressing Tab between the service and the price:

Quick Restore	$50
Major Repair	$75/hour, one hour minimum
Disaster Recovery	$75/hour + $2 per photo

5. **Save** your changes. **Draw** a **Text Box** that is aligned with the left margin, with the top edge at **8 inches on the vertical ruler**. Use the **Size** buttons to change the **Width** to **4"** and the **Height** to **.5"**.

6. In the text box, type **Other services are available. For an estimate, contact Adrian at 312-555-0024.** Select all of the text in the text box, and use the Mini toolbar to **Center** the text and add **Bold** emphasis.

7. With the insertion point in the text box, display the **Shadow Effects gallery**. Under **Perspective Shadow**, add a **Shadow Style 8** shadow effect to the text box. Drag the text box to center it horizontally on the page, and position the top edge at about **7.75 inches on the vertical ruler**, as shown in Figure 7.59.

8. Add a **Box** page border, using a **1 1/2 pt** line width and the default black color.

9. **Save** your document. **Preview** the document, and then print it, or submit it electronically as directed. **Close** the file, and then **Exit** Word.

End You have completed Project 7F ————————

Content-Based Assessments

Mastering Word

Project 7G—Student Days

In this project, you will apply the skills you practiced from all the Objectives in Projects 7A and 7B.

Objectives: 1. *Insert and Format Graphics;* **2**. *Set Tab Stops;* **3**. *Insert and Modify Text Boxes and Shapes;* **4**. *Create a Table;* **5**. *Format a Table.*

In the following Mastering Word Assessment, you will create a flyer for the Student Days celebration at Memories Old and New. Your completed document will look similar to Figure 7.60.

For Project 7G, you will need the following files:

New blank Word document
w07G_Student_Artist

**You will save your document as
7G_Student_Days_Firstname_Lastname**

Figure 7.60

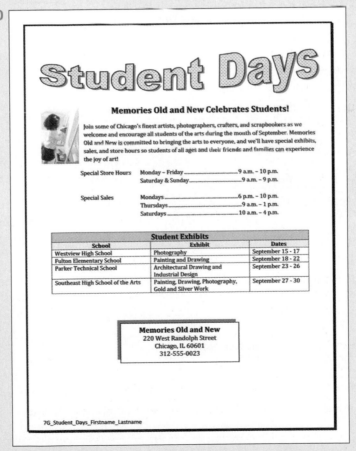

(Project 7G–Student Days continues on the next page)

Content-Based Assessments

(Project 7G–Student Days continued)

1. **Start** Word and be sure a new blank document is displayed. Display formatting marks and rulers. **Save** the document in your chapter folder as **7G_Student_Days_Firstname_Lastname** and add the file name to the footer. Change all four document margins to **.75 inch**. Change the **Font** to **Cambria** and be sure the **Font Size** is set to **11**.

2. **Insert** a **Student Days** WordArt title, using the fifth style in the fourth row—**WordArt style 23**. Change the **WordArt** size to **7 inches** wide and **1.5 inches** high.

3. Click to the right of the WordArt title, and then press Enter. Type **Memories Old and New Celebrates Students!** and press Enter. Select the text you just typed, **Center** the text, apply **Bold** emphasis, and then change the **Font Size** to **16**.

4. Position the insertion point in the blank line below the title you just typed, press Enter, and then type the following text:

   Join some of Chicago's finest artists, photographers, crafters, and scrapbookers as we welcome and encourage all students of the arts during the month of September. Memories Old and New is committed to bringing the arts to everyone, and we'll have special exhibits, sales, and store hours so students of all ages and their friends and families can experience the joy of art!

5. Press Enter. Insert a **Left tab stop** at **2.5 inches on the horizontal ruler**. Insert a **Right tab stop** at **6 inches on the horizontal ruler**. Display the **Tabs** dialog box. Add a **dot leader** to the tab stop at **6 inches**. Type the following text, pressing Tab between entries, and press Enter at the end of each line, including the last line. In the lines with no text in the first column, press Tab. Leave the third line blank:

Special Store Hours	Monday - Friday	9 a.m. - 10 p.m.
	Saturday & Sunday	9 a.m. - 9 p.m.
Special Sales	Mondays	6 p.m. - 10 p.m.
	Thursdays	9 a.m. - 1 p.m.
	Saturdays	10 a.m. - 4 p.m.

6. Starting with the text that begins *Special Store Hours*, select the text from that point to the end of the document, but do not include the blank line at the end of the document. Display the **Paragraph** dialog box, set the **Left Indentation** to **1 inch**, and set the **Spacing After** to **0**.

7. Press Ctrl + End, and then press Enter. Display the **Paragraph** dialog box and set the **Spacing After** to **0**. Insert a **3x6** table, and then add the following text:

Student Exhibits		
School	Exhibit	Dates
Westview High School	Photography	September 15 - 17
Fulton Elementary School	Painting and Drawing	September 18 - 22
Parker Technical School	Architectural Drawing and Industrial Design	September 23 - 26
Southeast High School of the Arts	Painting, Drawing, Photography, Gold and Silver Work	September 27 - 30

(Project 7G–Student Days continues on the next page)

Content-Based Assessments

(Project 7G–Student Days continued)

8. Display the **Table Properties** dialog box and **Center** the table. Click the **Column tab**, and then set the first two columns to **2.5 inches** wide, and the third column to **1.5 inches** wide.

9. In the first row, merge the three cells, and then **Center** and **Bold** *Student Exhibits*, and change the **Font Size** to **14**. **Center** and **Bold** the text in the three cells in the second row of the table.

10. Select the first row of the table. On the **Design tab**, display the **Shading gallery**, and add the fourth color in the last column—**Orange, Accent 6, Lighter 40%** shading. Select the second row of the table, display the **Shading gallery**, and add the second shade in the last column—**Orange, Accent 6, Lighter 80%**. **Save** your work.

11. Place the insertion point to the left of the paragraph that begins *Join some of Chicago's*, and then from your student files, insert the picture **w07G_Student_Artist**. Change the **Height** of the picture to **1.4 inches**, and then apply **Square Text Wrapping**. Move the picture to the position shown in Figure 7.60 at the beginning of this project.

12. **Save** your changes. **Draw** a **Text Box** that is aligned with the left margin, with the top edge at **7.0 inches on the vertical ruler**. Use the **Size** buttons to change the **Height** to **1"** and the **Width** to **3"**. Select the paragraph mark in the text box, display the **Paragraph** dialog box, and then set the space **After** to **0** and the **Line Spacing** to **Single**. In the text box, type:

Memories Old and New
220 West Randolph Street
Chicago, IL 60601
312-555-0023

13. Select all of the text in the text box and **Center** the text. Change the **Font Size** to **12**. Select the top line of text in the text box, add **Bold** emphasis, and change the **Font Size** to **14**. Display the **Shadow Effects gallery**, and under **Drop Shadow**, click the first style—**Shadow Style 1**. Drag to center the text box under the table.

14. Add a **Shadow** page border, using a **2 1/4 pt** line width and the default black color.

15. **Preview** the document, and then print it, or submit it electronically as directed. **Save** your changes. **Close** the file, and then **Exit** Word.

End You have completed Project 7G ——————————————————————

Project 7H—*GO!* Fix It

In this project, you will apply the skills you practiced from the Objectives in Projects 7A and 7B.

For Project 7H, you will need the following file:

w07H_Digital_Dog_Flyer

**You will save your document as
7H_Digital_Dog_Flyer_Firstname_Lastname**

In this project, you will edit a flyer for a workshop on digital pet photography that is being prepared for Memories Old and New. From the student files that accompany this textbook, open the file **w07H_Digital_ Dog_Flyer**, and then save the file in your chapter folder as **7H_Digital_ Dog_Flyer_Firstname_Lastname**

This document contains errors that you must find and correct. Read and examine the document, and then edit to correct the errors that you find. Types of errors could include:

- Spelling, grammar, punctuation, and usage errors such as text case, repeated text, subject-verb agreement, and meaning.

- Content errors such as missing or incorrect text, pictures, or other objects.

- Font formatting and positioning errors such as font used, style, size, color, underline style, effects, font character spacing, text effects, special characters, and styles.

- Paragraph formatting and positioning errors such as indents and spacing, tabs, line and page breaks, wordwrap, sentence spacing, missing text, unnecessary text, or blank lines

- Image or object formatting and positioning errors relating to color, lines, size, scale, layout, positioning, or picture control.

- Page setup errors such as margins, orientation, layout, or alignment.

To complete the project you should:

- Be aware that there are no errors in sentence or paragraph spacing.

- Reformat the picture style of the dog image by using *Metal Frame*.

- Modify the words *Pet Photos?* in the title by applying WordArt style 9 with 36 pt font size.

- Format the Horizontal Scroll shape by applying Shadow Style 4.

(Project 7H–*GO!* Fix It continues on the next page)

Word

chapterseven

Mastering Word

(Project 7H–*GO!* Fix It continued)

- Modify the table by merging cells, aligning text in the first row and in the second column, and by applying Table Style *Linear Up Gradient - Dark.*

- Center the table horizontally on the page.

Save the changes you have made, add the file name to the footer, and then submit as directed.

 End You have completed Project 7H ————————————

Outcomes-Based Assessments

Rubric

The following outcomes-based assessments are *open-ended assessments*. That is, there is no specific correct result; your result will depend on your approach to the information provided. Make *Professional Quality* your goal. Use the following scoring rubric to guide you in *how* to approach the problem, and then to evaluate *how well* your approach solves the problem.

The *criteria*—Software Mastery, Content, Format and Layout, and Process—represent the knowledge and skills you have gained that you can apply to solving the problem. The *levels of performance*—Professional Quality, Approaching Professional Quality, or Needs Quality Improvements—help you and your instructor evaluate your result.

	Your completed project is of Professional Quality if you:	Your completed project is Approaching Professional Quality if you:	Your completed project Needs Quality Improvements if you:
1-Software Mastery	Choose and apply the most appropriate skills, tools, and features and identify efficient methods to solve the problem.	Choose and apply some appropriate skills, tools, and features, but not in the most efficient manner.	Choose inappropriate skills, tools, or features, or are inefficient in solving the problem.
2-Content	Construct a solution that is clear and well organized, contains content that is accurate, appropriate to the audience and purpose, and is complete. Provide a solution that contains no errors of spelling, grammar, or style.	Construct a solution in which some components are unclear, poorly organized, inconsistent, or incomplete. Misjudge the needs of the audience. Have some errors in spelling, grammar, or style, but the errors do not detract from comprehension.	Construct a solution that is unclear, incomplete, or poorly organized; contains some inaccurate or inappropriate content; and contains many errors of spelling, grammar, or style. Do not solve the problem.
3-Format and Layout	Format and arrange all elements to communicate information and ideas, clarify function, illustrate relationships, and indicate relative importance.	Apply appropriate format and layout features to some elements, but not others. Overuse features, causing minor distraction.	Apply format and layout that does not communicate information or ideas clearly. Do not use format and layout features to clarify function, illustrate relationships, or indicate relative importance. Use available features excessively, causing distraction.
4-Process	Use an organized approach that integrates planning, development, self-assessment, revision, and reflection.	Demonstrate an organized approach in some areas, but not others; or, use an insufficient process of organization throughout.	Do not use an organized approach to solve the problem.

Outcomes-Based Assessments

Problem Solving

Project 7I—Books

In this project, you will apply the skills you practiced from the Objectives in Projects 7A and 7B.

For Project 7I, you will need the following file:

New blank Word document

**You will save your document as
7I_Books_Firstname_Lastname**

Memories Old and New carries an extensive line of books and periodicals for artists, photographers, students, teachers, and hobbyists. They have recently begun stocking a full line of scrapbooking books. In this project, you will create a flyer that includes a table of popular scrapbooking books for sale in the store.

To complete this assignment:

- Include a WordArt title, either with the name of the store, or the topic that is covered in the flyer.

- Write an opening paragraph introducing the topic.

- Create a table that consists of books on scrapbooking. The table should use at least three columns, including the author's name, the title of the book, and the book price. You should include at least six books in the table—use an online book dealer to search for appropriate titles.

- Format the table with a title that spans all of the columns and include a heading for each column. The title and column headings should be formatted distinctively.

- Include a text box with instructions for placing orders by phone.

- Include a shape with the name, address, and phone number of the store.

Add the file name to the footer. Check the flyer for spelling or grammar errors. Save the document as **7I_Books_Firstname_Lastname** and submit it as directed.

End **You have completed Project 7I** ————————————

Outcomes-Based Assessments

Problem Solving

Project 7J—Restoration Class

In this project, you will construct a solution by applying any combination of the skills you practiced from the Objectives in Projects 7A and 7B.

For Project 7J, you will need the following files:

New blank Word document
w07J_McArthur

You will save your document as
7J_Restoration_Class_Firstname_Lastname

Memories Old and New offers extensive photo restoration and photo recovery services. They also offer Beginner, Intermediate, and Advanced level classes on basic restoration techniques, using popular photograph manipulation software. Each level consists of two sessions that are four hours in length. Each session costs $50, and all six sessions can be taken for $250.

Create a flyer that can be handed out to customers in the store, and that contains information about the photo restoration classes. The flyer should include a decorative title, an introductory paragraph about Memories Old and New and photo restoration, and information about the classes. Format the information using a table, or using tab stops and dot leaders. You will need to include at least one text box with the name and address of the company, and one photo. If you have one or two old family photos that you would like to include, use those. Otherwise, use **w07J_McArthur**, which is included with your student files. Add a Picture Style or a Picture Effect to make the picture more visually interesting. The address information for Memories Old and New can be found in Activity 7.14.

Add the file name to the footer. Check the flyer for spelling or grammar errors. Save the document as **7J_Restoration_Class_Firstname_Lastname** and submit it as directed.

End **You have completed Project 7J** ————————————

Outcomes-Based Assessments

Problem Solving

Project 7K—Flower Show

In this project, you will construct a solution by applying any combination of the skills you practiced from the Objectives in Projects 7A and 7B.

For Project 7K, you will need the following files:

New blank Word document
w07K_Flower1
w07K_Flower2
w07K_Flower3
w07K_Flower4
w07K_Flower5
w07K_Flower6

**You will save your document as
7K_Flower_Show_Firstname_Lastname**

Memories Old and New is heavily involved in community activities. Every year, the neighborhood's small botanical garden—The Northwest Chicago Botanical Garden—sponsors a flower show, and solicits local businesses to participate and to help defray the expenses of the event. In return, participating companies receive good publicity. This year, Memories Old and New has agreed to create the event flyers.

In this project, you will create a flyer advertising the event. This year's event runs from May 20 to May 25. Admission is free, and the hours are from 10 a.m. until 7 p.m. on May 20–22; 10 a.m. until 5 p.m. on May 23; and Noon to 5 p.m. on May 24–25. On the flyer, the abbreviated name of the garden—NWC Botanical Garden—should display as a decorative title. One or two paragraphs are necessary to describe the details of the event, which include a flower show and flower sale, and activities for children. A table or tabbed list is necessary to convey information about dates and times. Include at least two pictures in the flyer. You can use any flower pictures you'd like, including the six that are included with your student files. Resize the pictures as necessary, and apply special effects to the pictures that enhance the overall design of the flyer. Add a banner indicating that Memories Old and New provided the flyers and that provides information about the company. Add an appropriate page border.

Save the flyer as **7K_Flower_Show_Firstname_Lastname** and then create a footer that contains file name. Submit the document as directed.

End You have completed Project 7K ————————

More on your Student CD

The instructions for the following additional end-of-chapter projects are on your student CD in the folder 03_additional_end_of_chapter_projects.

Content-Based Assessments	
Project L Mastering Word	Apply the skills you practiced in Project A.
Project M Mastering Word	Apply the skills you practiced in Project B.
Project N Business Running Case	Apply the skills you practiced in Projects A and B while helping an entrepreneur with the daily tasks of running a business. In each chapter, this project focuses on applying the skills you have practiced in Projects A and B to a business. The project related to this business runs throughout the textbook. You will see how the Office programs relate to the day-to-day operation of a small business called Nelson Architectural Planning.

Outcomes-Based Assessments	
Project O Problem Solving	Construct a solution by applying any combination of the skills you practiced from Projects A and B.
Project P Problem Solving	Construct a solution by applying any combination of the skills you practiced from Projects A and B.
Project Q You and GO!	Construct a solution that applies to your own life by applying any combination of the skills you practiced from Projects A and B.
Project R GO! with Help	Practice using Microsoft Office's Help Feature.
Project S Group Business Running Case	Work as part of a group to apply the skills you have gained thus far to help the Bell Orchid Hotel Group achieve its business goals.

Multimedia

The following multimedia accompany this textbook:

Companion Web site *www.prenhall.com/go*	An interactive Web site designed to reinforce and test your understanding of the skills in this chapter.
AV-EDDs	In the folder in the front of this book you will find videos that demonstrate the objectives of the A and B projects in this chapter. These may help you understand how to complete the projects in this book.
Video Podcasts	In the folder in the front of this book are videos that can be played on your iPod, MP3 player, or computer. These videos demonstrate how to complete the more challenging objectives in this textbook.

9 chapternine

Creating a Worksheet and Charting Data

OBJECTIVES

At the end of this chapter you will be able to:

1. Create, Save, and Navigate an Excel Workbook
2. Enter and Edit Data in a Worksheet
3. Construct and Copy Formulas, Use the Sum Function, and Edit Cells
4. Format Data, Cells, and Worksheets
5. Close and Reopen a Workbook
6. Chart Data
7. Use Page Layout View, Prepare a Worksheet for Printing, and Close Excel

8. Design a Worksheet
9. Construct Formulas for Mathematical Operations
10. Format Percentages and Move Formulas
11. Create a Pie Chart and a Chart Sheet
12. Use the Excel Help System

OUTCOMES

Mastering these objectives will enable you to:

PROJECT 9A
Create a Worksheet and Chart Data

Project 9B
Perform Calculations and Make Comparisons by Using a Pie Chart

Rio Rancho Auto Gallery

Rio Rancho Auto Gallery is a one-stop shop for car enthusiasts. The auto sales group sells a wide variety of manufacturer-certified preowned cars, cars that have passed rigorous inspection as determined by the manufacturers and that meet strict mileage and condition standards. The retail department sells automotive accessories such as custom wheels and performance parts, gadgets, gifts, books, magazines, and clothing, including branded items from major manufacturers. To complete the package, the company also offers auto financing and repairs and service.

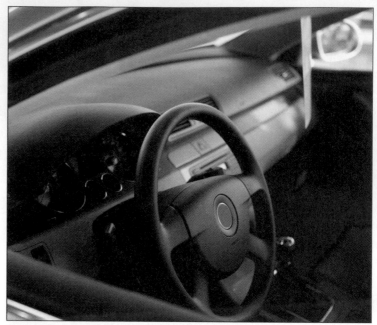

© Jan Tyler / Courtesy of www.istockphoto.com

Creating a Worksheet and Charting Data

With Microsoft Office Excel 2007, you can create and analyze data organized into columns and rows. After you have entered data in a worksheet, you can perform calculations, analyze the data to make logical decisions, and create a visual representation of the data in the form of a chart. In addition to its worksheet capability, Excel can manage your data, sort your data, and search for specific pieces of information.

In this chapter, you will create and modify Excel workbooks. You will practice the basics of worksheet design, create a footer, enter and edit data in a worksheet, and save, preview, and print your work. You will construct formulas to perform calculations, automatically complete text, use Excel's spelling tool, create a chart, and access Excel's Help feature.

Project 9A **Auto Sales**

In Activities 9.01 through 9.17, you will construct an Excel worksheet for Sandy Cizek, the Auto Sales Manager for Rio Rancho Auto Gallery. The worksheet will display the first quarter sales of vehicle types for the current year, and will include a chart to visually represent the worksheet. Your completed worksheet will look similar to Figure 9.1.

For Project 9A, you will need the following file:

New blank Excel workbook

You will save your workbook as
9A_Auto_Sales_Firstname_Lastname

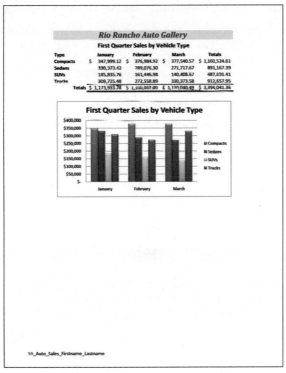

Figure 9.1
Project 9A—Auto Sales

Objective 1
Create, Save, and Navigate an Excel Workbook

When you start Excel, a new blank **workbook** displays. A workbook contains one or more pages called **worksheets**. A worksheet—also called a **spreadsheet**—is the primary document that you use in Excel to store and work with data. A worksheet is always stored in a workbook.

A worksheet is formatted as a pattern of uniformly spaced horizontal and vertical lines. This grid pattern of the worksheet forms vertical columns and horizontal rows. The intersection of a column and a row forms a small box referred to as a **cell**.

Activity 9.01 Starting Excel and Naming and Saving a Workbook

In this activity, you will start Excel and use the first worksheet in the workbook to prepare a report of quarterly auto sales.

Note — Comparing Your Screen with the Figures in This Textbook

Your screen will match the figures shown in this textbook if you set your screen resolution to 1024 × 768. At other resolutions, your screen will closely resemble, but not match, the figures shown. To view your screen's resolution, on the Windows desktop, right-click in a blank area, click Personalize, and then click Display Settings.

1 On the Windows taskbar, click **Start** 🟢. Locate and open Excel. Compare your screen with Figure 9.2 and study the parts of the Excel window described in the table in Figure 9.3.

Figure 9.2

Quick Access Toolbar (yours might display a different array of buttons) • Formula Bar • Title bar • Workbook-level buttons • Help button • Program-level buttons

Ribbon • Office button • Name Box • Worksheet grid • View options • Status bar

Parts of the Excel Window

Screen Part	Description
Formula Bar	Displays the value or formula contained in the active cell; also permits entry or editing of values or formulas.
Help button	Displays the Help window.
Name Box	Displays the name of the selected cell, table, chart, or object.
Office button	Displays a list of commands related to things you can do *with* a workbook, such as opening, saving, printing, or sharing.
Program-level buttons	Minimize, restore, or close the Excel program.
Quick Access Toolbar	Displays buttons to perform frequently used commands with a single click. Frequently used commands in Excel include Save, Undo, and Redo. For commands that *you* use frequently, you can add additional buttons here.
Ribbon	Groups the commands for performing related workbook tasks.
Status bar	Displays, on the left side, the current cell mode, page number, and worksheet information. On the right side, displays buttons to control how the window looks; when numerical data is selected, common calculations such as Sum and Average display.
Title bar	Indicates the name of the current workbook and the program name.
View options	Contain buttons for viewing the workbook in Normal view, Page Layout view, or Page Break Preview, and also displays controls for Zoom Out and Zoom In to increase or decrease the number of rows and columns displayed.
Workbook-level buttons	Minimize or restore the displayed workbook.
Worksheet grid	Displays the columns and rows that intersect to form the worksheet's cells.

Figure 9.3

2 In the upper left corner of your screen, click the **Office** button ; on the menu, point to **Save As**. Compare your screen with Figure 9.4.

Figure 9.4

Office button

Save As command

Office menu

3 Click **Save As**. In the **Save As** dialog box, if necessary, click Browse Folders to display the Navigation pane.

4 In the **Navigation pane**, click **Computer** to view a list of the drives available to you, and then navigate to the drive on which you will store your folders and workbooks for this textbook—for example, a USB flash drive such as the one shown in Figure 9.5. If you are saving your files on your hard disk drive, in the Navigation pane, click Documents or the location of your choice.

Figure 9.5

Address bar displays path to your selected drive

New Folder button

Navigation pane expanded

5 On the **Save As** dialog box toolbar, click the **New Folder** button. With *New Folder* selected, type **Excel Chapter 9** and then press Enter.

> Windows creates the *Excel Chapter 9* folder and makes it the active folder in the Save As dialog box. At the bottom of the Save As dialog box, in the File name box, *Book1* displays as the default file name.

6 In the **File name** box, type **9A_Auto_Sales_Firstname_Lastname** Compare your screen with Figure 9.6.

Figure 9.6

Your folder name

File name with your name and underscores between words

7 In the lower right corner of the **Save As** dialog box, click **Save**; or press Enter.

Windows saves the file in the new folder with the new name. The workbook redisplays, and the new name displays in the title bar.

Activity 9.02 Navigating a Worksheet and a Workbook

1 Take a moment to study Figure 9.7 and the table in Figure 9.8 to become familiar with the Excel workbook window.

Figure 9.7

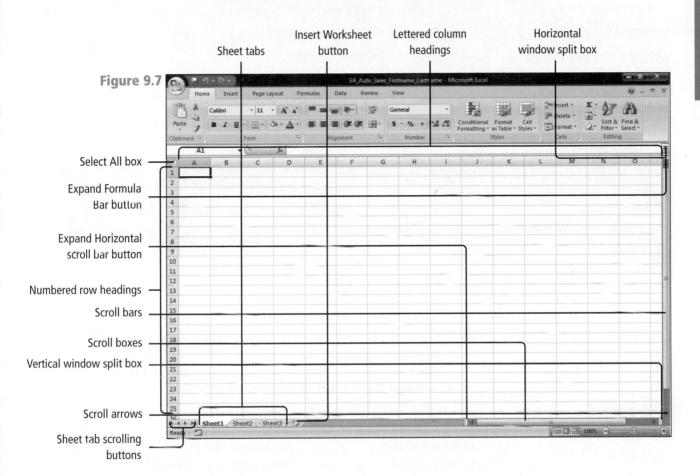

Excel Workbook Window Elements

Workbook window element	Description
Expand Formula Bar button	Increases the height of the Formula Bar to display lengthy cell content.
Expand horizontal scroll bar button	Increases the width of the horizontal scroll bar.
Horizontal window split box	Splits the worksheet into two horizontal views of the same worksheet.
Insert Worksheet button	Inserts an additional worksheet into the workbook.
Lettered column headings	Indicate the column letter.
Numbered row headings	Indicate the row number.
Scroll arrows	Scroll one column or row at a time.
Scroll bars	Scroll the Excel window up and down or left and right.
Scroll boxes	Move the position of the window up and down or left and right.
Select All box	Selects all the cells in a worksheet.
Sheet tab scrolling buttons	Display sheet tabs that are not in view; used when there are more sheet tabs than will display in the space provided.
Sheet tabs	Identify the worksheets in a workbook.
Vertical window split box	Splits the worksheet into two vertical views of the same worksheet.

Figure 9.8

2 In the horizontal scroll bar, point to, and then click the **right scroll arrow**.

The workbook window shifts so that column A moves out of view. The number of times you click one of the arrows on the horizontal scroll bar determines the number of columns by which the window shifts—either to the left or to the right.

3 In the horizontal scroll bar, click the **right scroll arrow**, and then hold down the left mouse button until the columns begin to scroll rapidly to the right; release when you begin to see pairs of letters as the column headings.

The workbook window moves rapidly. This technique also works for the left scroll arrow and for the two vertical scroll arrows.

4 In the horizontal scroll bar, click the **left scroll arrow** to shift one column. Then, in the horizontal scroll bar, point to the **horizontal scroll box**.

5 Hold down the left mouse button, *drag* the box to the left to display **column A**, and then notice that *ScreenTips* with the column letters display as you drag. Release the mouse button.

> You can drag to move something from one location on the screen to another; the action of dragging includes releasing the mouse button at the desired time or location. ScreenTips display useful information when you perform various mouse actions such as pointing to screen elements or dragging.

> Use the scroll boxes in this manner to move various parts of the worksheet into view. Scroll boxes change in size to indicate how the visible portion of the worksheet compares to the total amount of the worksheet in use.

6 Use the techniques you just practiced to scroll the worksheet to position **column Z** near the center of your screen.

> Column headings to the right of column Z use two letters starting with AA, AB, AC, and so on through ZZ. After that, columns begin with three letters beginning with AAA. This pattern is used to provide a total of 16,384 columns. The last column available is column XFD.

7 Near the lower left of the screen, click the **Sheet2 tab**.

> The second worksheet in the workbook displays and becomes the active worksheet. Column A displays at the left.

8 Click the **Sheet1 tab**.

> The first worksheet in the workbook becomes the active worksheet. A workbook consists of one or more worksheets. By default, new workbooks contain three worksheets. When you save a workbook, the worksheets are contained within it and do not have separate file names.

9 In the vertical scroll bar, point to, and then click the **down scroll arrow** one time.

> Row 1 moves out of view. The number of times you click the arrows on the vertical scroll bar determines the number of rows shifted either up or down. You can drag the vertical scroll box to scroll downward in a manner similar to the technique used in the horizontal scroll bar.

10 In the vertical scroll bar, point to, and then click the **up scroll arrow**.

> Row 1 comes back into view. The maximum number of rows on a single Excel worksheet is 1,048,576.

11 Use the skills you just practiced to scroll horizontally to display **column A**.

Activity 9.03 Selecting Parts of a Worksheet

In this activity, you will *select* both individual cells and groups of cells. Selecting refers to highlighting, by clicking or dragging with your mouse, one or more cells so that the selected cells can be edited, formatted, copied, or moved. Selected cells are indicated by a dark border, and Excel treats the selected *range*—two or more cells on a worksheet that are adjacent or nonadjacent—as a single unit so you can make the same change, or combination of changes, to more than one cell at a time.

In Excel, text or numbers in a cell are referred to as *data*. Before you enter data into a worksheet, you must select the location in the worksheet where you want the data to display. You can select one or more cells of data to which you can apply Excel's formatting, features, and functions.

1 In **Sheet 1**, move the mouse pointer over—*point* to—the cell at the intersection of **column A** and **row 3**, and then click. Compare your screen with Figure 9.9.

> A black border surrounds the cell, indicating that it is the *active cell*. The active cell is ready to receive data or be affected by the next Excel command.
>
> A cell is identified by the intersecting column letter and row number, which forms the *cell reference*. A cell reference is also referred to as a *cell address*. The cell reference displays in the *Name Box*. You can use lowercase or uppercase letters to indicate columns; uppercase letters are commonly used.

Figure 9.9

Cell A3 is selected

Cell address displays in the Name Box

Active cell

2 Press ↓ three times, and then look at the cell address in the **Name Box**.

> Cell A6 becomes the active cell. Pressing one of the four direction arrow keys relocates the active cell. The cell address of the active cell always displays in the Name Box.

3 Point to cell **B2** and drag down to select cells **B2**, **B3**, **B4**, and **B5**, and then continue to drag across to cell **C5** and release the left mouse button. Alternatively, drag diagonally from cell B2 to C5. If you are not satisfied with your result, click anywhere and begin again. Compare your screen with Figure 9.10.

> The eight cells, B2 through B5 and C2 through C5 are selected. This range of cells is referred to as *B2:C5*. When you see a colon (:) between two cell references, the range includes all the cells between the two cell references.

> The cell references used to indicate the range are the upper left cell and the lower right cell—in this instance, B2 and C5. When you select a range of cells, the cells are bordered by a thick black line, and the cells change color except for the first cell in the range, which displays in the Name Box.

Selected range B2:C5

Figure 9.10

Name Box always indicates address of the first cell in range

First cell selected but not highlighted

Black border surrounds selected range

4 At the left edge of the worksheet, point to **3** to display the ➡ mouse pointer, and then click the **row 3** heading to select the entire row.

> A **row** is a horizontal group of cells in a worksheet. Beginning with number 1, a unique number identifies each row—this is the **row heading**, located at the left side of the worksheet. All the cells in the row are selected, including those that are out of view.

5 In the upper left corner of **Sheet1**, point to the letter **A** to display the ⬇ pointer, and then click one time.

> Column A is selected. A **column** is a vertical group of cells in a worksheet. Beginning with the first letter of the alphabet, A, a unique letter identifies each column—this is called the **column heading**. All the cells in the column are selected, including those that are out of view.

6 Click in the **Name Box**; notice that the cell reference *A1* moves to the left edge and is highlighted in blue.

> In any Windows program, text highlighted in blue in this manner will be replaced by your typing.

7 Type **d4:f6** and then compare your screen with Figure 9.11.

Figure 9.11

Range typed in Name Box— OK to type lowercase or uppercaseletters

8 Press [Enter] to select the range. Then, click in the **Name Box**, type **b2:b8,e2:e8** press [Enter], and compare your screen with Figure 9.12.

> Two ***nonadjacent ranges***—ranges that are not next to each other—are selected. Ranges of cells that are not ***adjacent***—next to each other—can be selected by typing the ranges into the Name Box separated by a comma.

Figure 9.12

Name Box displays the first cell in the second range

Selected ranges B2:B8 and E2:E8

9 Select the range **C3:C5**, notice that the previously selected cells are deselected, and then hold down [Ctrl] and select the range **E3:E5**.

> Use either technique to select cells that are nonadjacent. A range of cells can be adjacent or nonadjacent. Recall that a range of cells that is nonadjacent can be indicated by separating the ranges with a comma. In this instance, the selected ranges can be referred to as *c3:c5,e3:e5*.

10 At the upper left corner of your worksheet, locate, and then click the **Select All** box—the small box above **row heading 1** and to the left of **column heading A** to select all of the cells in the worksheet. Then, point to any cell on your worksheet and click to cancel the selection.

Objective 2
Enter and Edit Data in a Worksheet

Anything you type into a cell is *cell content*. Cell content can be one of two things—either a *constant value*—referred to simply as a *value*—or a *formula*. The most commonly used values are text values and number values, but a value can also include a date or a time of day. A formula is an equation that performs mathematical calculations on values in your worksheet.

Values in a cell can be *edited*—changed—or cleared from the cell. Text values usually provide information about number values in other worksheet cells. For example, a title such as *Quarterly Auto Sales* gives the reader an indication that the data in the worksheet relates to information about sales of autos during a three-month period.

Activity 9.04 Entering Text, Using AutoComplete, Filling a Series with Auto Fill, and Using Spelling Checker and Undo to Correct Typing Errors

To enter text in a cell, select the cell and type. In this activity, you will enter a title for the worksheet and titles for the rows and columns that will identify the types of vehicles purchased and the monthly sales amount for each vehicle type.

1 Click the **Sheet1 tab**, if necessary, so that **Sheet 1** is the active sheet. Click cell **A1**, type **Rio Rancho Auto Gallery** and then press Enter.

After you type data in a cell, you must confirm the entry to store it in the cell. One way to do this is to press the Enter key, which typically moves the selection to the cell below to facilitate entry in a column of cells. You can also use other keyboard movements, such as Tab, or one of the arrow keys on your keyboard.

2 Look at cell **A1** and notice that the text does not fit; the text spills over and displays in cells **B1** and **C1** to the right.

If text is too long for a cell and the cells to the right are empty, the text will display. If the cells to the right contain other data, only the text that will fit in the cell will display. Cell A2 is the active cell, as indicated by the black border surrounding it.

3 In cell **A2**, type **Monthly Sales by Vehicle Type** and then press Enter. In cell **A3**, type **Type** and then press Enter. Compare your screen with Figure 9.13.

Figure 9.13

Text too long for cell spills into adjacent cells if the adjacent cells are empty

Cell A4 active cell

4 In cell **A4**, type **Sedans** and then press Enter.

The text is left aligned in the cell and the selection moves to cell A5. **Left alignment**—characters align at the left edge of the cell—is the default for text values. Information about how a cell is formatted is stored with the cell.

5 In cell **A5**, type **S** and notice that the text from the previous cell displays.

Excel assists you in typing. If the first characters you type in a cell match an existing entry in the column, Excel fills in the remaining characters for you. This feature, called **AutoComplete**, speeds your typing. AutoComplete assists only with alphabetic values; it does not assist with numeric values.

6 Continue typing the remainder of the row title, **UVs** and press Enter.

As soon as the entry you are typing differs from the previous value, the AutoComplete suggestion is removed.

7 Without correcting the spelling error, in cell **A6**, type **Truks** and then press Enter. Then, in cell **A7**, type **Convertibles** and press Enter. In cell **A8**, type **Totals** and press Enter.

8 Click cell **B3** to make it the active cell. Type **J** and notice that when you begin to type in a cell, on the **Formula Bar**, the **Cancel** and **Enter** buttons become active, as shown in Figure 9.14.

Figure 9.14

Enter button

Cancel button

Formula Bar

Completed text
entry (SUVs)

9 Continue to type **anuary** and then on the **Formula Bar**, click the **Enter** button ✓ to keep cell **B3** the active cell.

Click this Enter button to confirm the entry and maintain the current cell as the active cell. This is convenient if you want to take further action on the cell. If you mistakenly press Enter, reselect the cell.

10 With **B3** as the active cell, locate the small black square in the lower right corner of the selected cell.

You can drag the **fill handle**—the small black square in the lower right corner of a selected cell—to adjacent cells to fill the cells with values based on the first cell or cells in the series.

11 Point to the fill handle until the ⊞ pointer displays, hold down the left mouse button, drag to the right to cell **F3**, and as you drag notice the ScreenTips *February*, *March*, *April* and *May*. Release the left mouse button, point to the **Auto Fill Options** button that displays, and then compare your screen with Figure 9.15.

> Excel's ***Auto Fill*** feature can generate a ***series*** of values into adjacent cells, based on the value of other cells. A series is a group of things that come one after another in succession. For example, *January*, *February*, *March*, and so on, is a series. Likewise, *1st Qtr*, *2nd Qtr*, *3rd Qtr*, and *4th Qtr* form a series.

Figure 9.15

Series of months completed

Auto Fill Options button

12 To the right of and below the filled data, point to, and then click the **Auto Fill Options** button.

> The Auto Fill Options button displays just below a filled selection after you fill data in a worksheet. When you click the button, a list displays with options to fill the data. The list of options varies depending on the content you are filling, the program you are filling from, and the format of the data you are filling.

> *Fill Series* is selected, indicating the action that was taken. Because the options are related to the current task, the button is referred to as being ***context sensitive***.

13 Click in any cell to cancel the display of the Auto Fill Options list.

> The list no longer displays; the button will display until you perform some other screen action.

14 Hold down Ctrl, and then press Home to make cell **A1** the active cell.

> This type of action is a ***keyboard shortcut***, which is an individual keystroke or a combination of keys pressed simultaneously to either perform an Excel command or move to another location on your screen.

15 Take a moment to study the table in Figure 9.16 to become familiar with additional keyboard shortcuts with which you can navigate the Excel worksheet.

Keyboard Shortcuts to Navigate the Excel Screen	
To Move the Location of the Active Cell:	**Press:**
Up, down, right, or left one cell	⬆, ⬇, ➡, ⬅
Down one cell	Enter
Up one cell	⇧ Shift + Enter
Up one full screen	Page Up
Down one full screen	PageDown
Left one full screen	Alt + Page Up
Right one full screen	Alt + PageDown
To column A of the current row	Home
To the last cell in the last column of the active area (the rectangle formed by all the rows and columns in a worksheet that contain entries)	Ctrl + End
To cell A1	Ctrl + Home
Right one cell	Tab
Left one cell	⇧ Shift + Tab

Figure 9.16

16 With cell **A1** active, click the **Review tab**, and then in the **Proofing group**, click the **Spelling** button. Alternatively, press F7—the keyboard shortcut for the Spelling command. Compare your screen with Figure 9.17.

Figure 9.17

Spelling dialog box

Word indicated as *Not in Dictionary*

Alert!

Does a message display asking if you want to continue checking at the beginning of the sheet?

If a message displays asking if you want to continue checking at the beginning of the sheet, click Yes. The Spelling command begins its checking process with the currently selected cell and moves to the right and down. Thus, if your active cell was a cell after A6, this message may display.

17 In the **Spelling** dialog box, under **Not in Dictionary**, notice the word *Truks*.

The spelling tool does not have this word in its dictionary. Under *Suggestions*, Excel provides a list of suggested spellings.

18 Under **Suggestions**, click **Trucks**, and then click the **Change** button.

Truks, a typing error, is changed to *Trucks*. A message box displays *The spelling check is complete for the entire sheet*. Because the spelling check begins its checking process starting with the currently selected cell, it is good practice to return to cell A1 before starting the Spelling command.

Note — Words Not in the Dictionary Are Not Necessarily Misspelled

Many proper nouns or less commonly used words are not in the dictionary used by Excel. If Excel indicates a correct word as *Not in Dictionary*, you can choose to ignore this word or add it to the dictionary. You may want to add proper names that you expect to use often, such as your own last name, to the dictionary.

19 Correct any other errors you may have made. When the message displays, *The spelling check is complete for the entire sheet*, click **OK**.

20 Point to cell **A5**, and then **double-click**—click the left mouse button two times in rapid succession while keeping the mouse still. Compare your screen with Figure 9.18.

The insertion point displays in the text in cell A5, and the text also displays in the Formula Bar.

Figure 9.18

Cell content displays in the Formula Bar

Insertion point displays inside the cell

21 Move the mouse pointer away from the cell so that you have a clear view, and then using the ⌦, ⌫, or arrow keys as necessary, edit the text and change it to **Vans** Confirm the change by pressing ⏎.

22 On the **Quick Access Toolbar**, click the **Undo** button ↺. Alternatively, you can press ⌃ + Ⓩ on the keyboard to reverse (undo) the last action.

> *SUVs* is restored and *Vans* is deleted—your action was undone.

More Knowledge — AutoCorrect Also Assists in Your Typing

AutoCorrect assists in your typing by automatically correcting and formatting some text as you type. Excel compares your typing to a list of commonly mistyped words and when it finds a match, it substitutes the correct word. For example, if you type *monday*, Excel will automatically correct to *Monday*. To view the AutoCorrect options, display the Office menu. At the lower right, click Excel Options; on the left, click Proofing, and then click the AutoCorrect Options button.

Activity 9.05 Aligning Text and Adjusting the Size of Columns and Rows

Data in a cell can be aligned at the left, at the right, or centered. You can make columns wider or narrower and make rows taller or shorter.

1 In the **column heading area**, point to the vertical line between **column A** and **column B** to display the ➕ pointer, press and hold down the left mouse button, and then compare your screen with Figure 9.19.

> A ScreenTip displays information about the width of the column.

Figure 9.19

ScreenTip

Pointer

Dotted line indicates
column divider is selected

2 Drag to the right and release the mouse button when the number of pixels indicated in the ScreenTip reaches **90 pixels**, which is wide enough to display the longest row title in cells A4 through A7—the worksheet title in A1 will span more than one column and still does not fit in column A. If you are not satisfied with your result, click the Undo button and begin again.

The default width of a column is 64 **pixels**. A pixel, short for **picture element**, is a point of light measured in dots per square inch on a screen. Sixty-four pixels equals 8.43 characters, which is the average number of digits that will fit in a cell using the default **font**—a set of characters with the same design, size, and shape.

The default font in Excel is Calibri, and the default **font size**—the size of characters in a font measured in **points**—is 11. There are 72 points in an inch, with 10 or 11 points being a typical font size in Excel. Point is usually abbreviated as **pt**.

3 Click cell **A8**. Click the **Home tab**, and then in the **Alignment group**, click the **Align Text Right** button ⊞.

The row title aligns at the right side of the cell to distinguish it from the other row titles in the column. Text can be aligned at the center, left, or right of a cell. By default, text values align at the left.

4 Select the range **B3:F3**, and then with your pointer positioned anywhere over the selected range, **right-click**—click the right mouse button—to display a **shortcut menu** and a **Mini toolbar**—both of which display commands most commonly used in the context of selected text of this type.

5 On the Mini toolbar, click the **Center** button ⊞ and notice that the shortcut menu no longer displays. Then, move the mouse slightly below the Mini toolbar and notice that the Mini toolbar fades so that you can see the result of your formatting.

6 Move the pointer back into the Mini toolbar, and then notice that it displays and once again becomes a functioning toolbar.

The column titles *January – May* align in the center of each cell. A shortcut menu offers the most commonly used commands relevant to the selected area and thus is context sensitive. You can also press ⇧Shift + F10 to display a shortcut menu.

7 Click any cell to cancel the selection and close the Mini toolbar. In the **row heading area**, point to the boundary between **row 1** and **row 2** until the ⊞ pointer displays. Drag downward, release the mouse button when the height of **row 1** is **28 pixels**, and then compare your screen with Figure 9.20.

The row height increases. Row height is measured in points or in pixels. Points are the units in which font size is measured and pixels are units of screen display. The default height of a row is 15.00 points or 20 pixels.

Figure 9.20

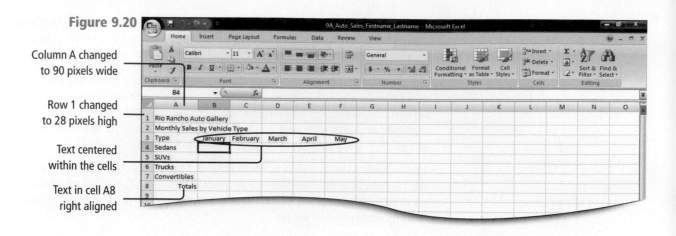

Column A changed to 90 pixels wide

Row 1 changed to 28 pixels high

Text centered within the cells

Text in cell A8 right aligned

8 On the **Quick Access Toolbar**, click **Save** 🖫 to save the changes you have made to your workbook; alternatively, press Ctrl + S.

Activity 9.06 Entering Numbers

To type number values, you can use either the number keys across the top of your keyboard or the number keys and Enter on the numeric keypad. Try to develop some proficiency in touch control of the numeric keypad. In this activity, you will enter the sales amounts for Rio Rancho Auto Gallery.

1 Click cell **B4**, type **330373.42** and then on the **Formula Bar**, click the **Enter** button ✔ to maintain cell **B4** as the active cell. Compare your screen with Figure 9.21.

By default, number values align at the right edge of the cell. The default *number format*—a specific way in which Excel displays numbers—is the *general format*. The general format has no specific characteristics—whatever you type in the cell will display, with the exception that trailing zeros to the right of a decimal point will not display. For example, if you type *125.50* the cell will display *125.5* instead.

Number values that are too long to fit in the cell do *not* spill over into the unoccupied cell to the right in the same manner as text values. Rather, the number is rounded. However, the entire number still exists and displays in the Formula Bar.

Data that displays in a cell is referred to as the ***displayed value***. Data that displays in the Formula Bar is referred to as the ***underlying value***. The number of digits or characters that display in a cell—the displayed value—depends on the width of the column.

Figure 9.21

Cell content, in full, displays in Formula Bar

Display of number does not extend into occupied cells, number is rounded

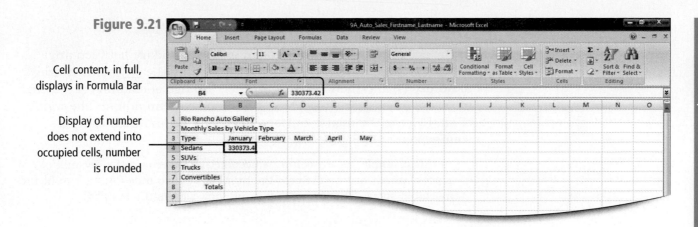

2 Enter the remaining sales figures for *Sedans* and *SUVs* in the months of January through May, as shown in the following table. Press Tab to simultaneously confirm your entry and move across the row, and then press Enter at the end of a row to move to the next row. Notice that as you type, if the column is too narrow to display all of the decimal places in a number, the display of the number will be rounded to fit the available space. When finished, compare your screen with Figure 9.22.

> *Rounding* is a procedure in which you determine which digit at the right of the number will be the last digit displayed and then increase it by one if the next digit to its right is 5, 6, 7, 8, or 9.

> Recall that trailing zeros to the right of a decimal point will not display. So for example, if you type 289076.30, the cell will display 289076.3 and if you type 297467.00, the cell will display 297467.

> Calculations performed on numbers in Excel will always be based on the underlying value, not the displayed value.

	January	February	March	April	May
Sedans	330373.42	289076.30	271717.67	326243.00	297467.00
SUVs	185835.76	163446.98	140408.67	247780.87	189756.00

Figure 9.22

Values entered for Sedans and SUVs

3 Click in the **Name Box**, type **b:f** and then press Enter.

4 In the **column heading area**, point to the boundary between any two of the selected column headings to display the ✛ pointer, drag to **50** pixels, and then notice that when a range of columns is selected in this manner, adjusting the width of one column adjusts the width of all. Release the mouse button, click cell **C5**, and then compare your screen with Figure 9.23.

> In this example, as the columns become narrower and the decimal places cannot fit into the cell, the numbers are rounded further to fit the available space. The underlying value, however, is unchanged.

Figure 9.23

Cell content, in full, displays in Formula Bar; displays underlying value

Display of numbers does not extend into occupied cells; rounded to 163447

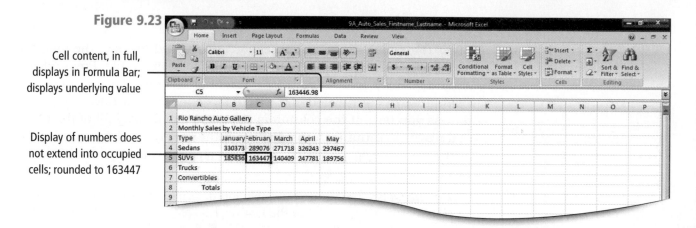

5 On the **Quick Access Toolbar**, click the **Undo** button ↺ to restore the column widths to 64 pixels. Click in any cell to deselect the columns.

6 In the **column heading area**, point to the right boundary of **column D**, and then drag the right column border to the left to set the width of **column D** to **30 pixels**. Then, click cell **D5** and compare your screen with Figure 9.24.

> If a cell width is too narrow to display the entire number, Excel displays a series of # symbols instead; displaying only a portion of a whole number would be misleading. The underlying values remain unchanged and are displayed in the Formula Bar for the selected cell. The underlying value also displays in the ScreenTip if you point to a cell containing ###.

Figure 9.24

Underlying value displays in the Formula Bar

Pound signs indicate cell is too narrow to display the number

Point to a cell containing ### to display underlying value in a ScreenTip

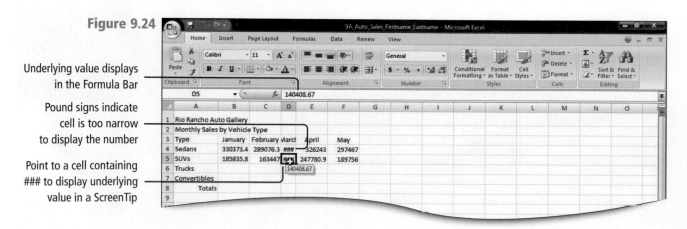

7 On the **Quick Access Toolbar**, click the **Undo** button 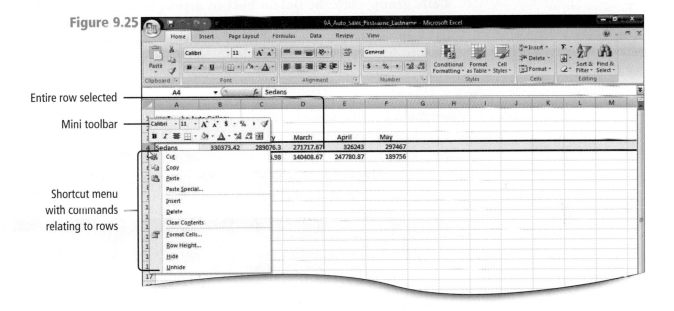 to restore column **D** to a width of 64 pixels. Select **columns B:F**. In the **column heading area**, point to the boundary between any two of the selected column headings to display the ⊞ pointer, and then drag to **85** pixels.

> Recall that in the default general number format, trailing zeros to the right of a decimal point do not display regardless of the column width.

8 Click any cell to cancel the selection, and then **Save** your workbook.

Activity 9.07 Inserting and Deleting Rows and Columns, and Using the Insert Options Button

In this activity, you will insert a new row to record sales for the vehicle type *Compacts* and delete the *Convertibles* vehicle type.

1 Point to the **row 4** heading, and then right-click to simultaneously select the row and display the shortcut menu and the Mini toolbar. Compare your screen with Figure 9.25.

> You can right-click row numbers or column headings to simultaneously select and display a context-sensitive shortcut menu and the Mini toolbar.

Figure 9.25

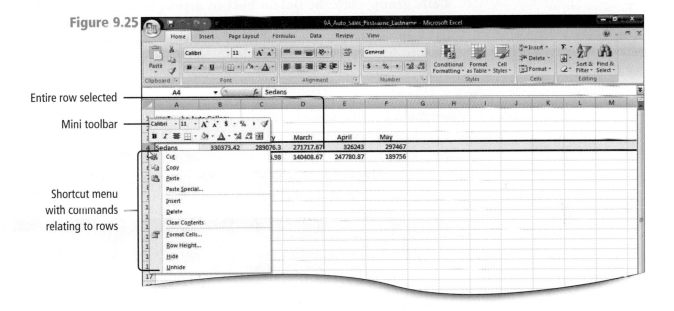

Entire row selected

Mini toolbar

Shortcut menu with commands relating to rows

2 On the shortcut menu, click **Insert**.

> Excel inserts a new row 4 above the selected row, and the existing rows shift down one row. Additionally, the Insert Options button displays.

Note — Insert Columns by Using the Same Shortcut Menu Technique

Use a similar technique to insert a new column in a worksheet. That is, from the column heading area, right-click to simultaneously select the column and display the context-sensitive shortcut menu. Click Insert to insert a new column and shift the remaining columns to the right. Alternatively, select the column, and then on the Ribbon, in the Cells group, click the Insert button or the Insert button arrow for additional options.

---

3 Point to the **Insert Options** button 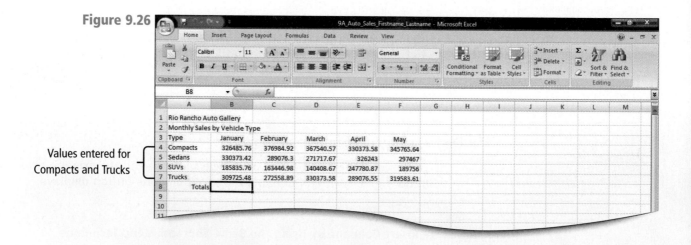 to display its ScreenTip and its arrow, and then click the button to display a list of options.

From this menu, you can format the new row like the row above or the row below, or you can leave it unformatted. The default is *Format Same As Above*.

4 Click **Format Same As Below**.

The new row is formatted, using the format from the row of data *below* instead of the row of column titles above, which are centered. The Insert Options button remains visible until you perform another screen action.

5 Click cell **A4**, type **Compacts** and then press Tab. Enter the values for *Compacts* for each month, as shown in the following table. Use Tab to confirm each entry and move the active cell across the row.

Type	January	February	March	April	May
Compacts	326485.76	376984.92	367540.57	330373.58	345765.64

6 From the **row heading area**, select **row 8**. On the Ribbon, in the **Cells group**, click the **Delete button arrow**, and then click **Delete Sheet Rows**. Alternatively, click the Delete button on the Ribbon; or, right-click the row 8 heading to simultaneously select the row and display a shortcut menu, and then from the shortcut menu, click Delete.

7 Enter the remaining sales figures for *Trucks* as follows, and then compare your screen with Figure 9.26.

Type	January	February	March	April	May
Trucks	309725.48	272558.89	330373.58	289076.55	319583.61

Figure 9.26

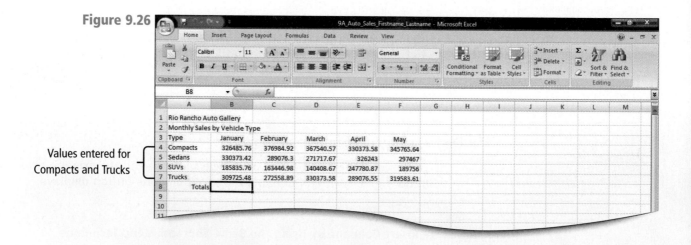

Values entered for Compacts and Trucks

8 **Save** your workbook.

Objective 3
Construct and Copy Formulas, Use the Sum Function, and Edit Cells

Excel performs calculations on numbers; that is why you use Excel. If you make changes to the numbers, Excel automatically *re*-calculates. This is one of the most powerful and valuable features of Excel. You can arrange data in a format of columns and rows in other programs—in a word processing program, for example—and even perform simple calculations. Excel, however, performs complex calculations on numbers.

Recall that a cell contains either a constant value or a formula. Recall also that a formula is an equation that performs mathematical calculations on values in other cells, and then places the result in the cell containing the formula. You can create your own formulas, or you can use one of Excel's prewritten formulas called a ***function***. A function is a prewritten formula that takes one or more values, performs an operation, and then returns a value or values.

Activity 9.08 Constructing a Formula, Using the Sum Function, and Editing Numbers in Cells

In this activity, you will sum the sales of vehicles by month and by type and use various methods to edit numbers within a cell.

1 Click cell **B8** to make it the active cell and type **=**

> The equal sign (=) displays in the cell with the insertion point blinking, ready to accept more data.
>
> All formulas begin with the = sign, which signals Excel to begin a calculation. The Formula Bar displays the = sign, and the Formula Bar Cancel and Enter buttons display.

2 At the insertion point, type **b4** and then compare your screen with Figure 9.27.

> A list of Excel functions that begin with the letter *B* may briefly display—as you progress in your study of Excel, you will use functions of this type. A blue border with small corner boxes surrounds cell B4, which indicates that the cell is part of an active formula. The color used in the box matches the color of the cell reference in the formula.

Figure 9.27

Your typing displays in Formula Bar

Cell outlined in the same color as the cell reference in the formula

Formula started in the active cell

3 At the insertion point, type **+** and then type **b5** Alternatively, use the ⊞ key on your numeric keypad, which does not require the ⇧ Shift key.

> A border of another color surrounds cell B5, and the color matches the color of the cell reference in the active formula. Recall that when typing cell references, it is not necessary to use uppercase letters.

4 At the insertion point, type **+b6+b7** and then press Enter.

> The result of the formula calculation—*1152420.42*—displays in the cell.

5 Click cell **B8** again to make it the active cell, and then look at the **Formula Bar**. Compare your screen with Figure 9.28.

> The formula adds the values in cells B4 through B7, and the result of adding the values in those cells displays in cell B8. Although cell B8 displays the *result* of the formula, the formula itself displays in the Formula Bar. This is referred to as the ***underlying formula***. Always view the Formula Bar to be sure of the exact content of a cell—*a displayed number may actually be a formula.*

Figure 9.28

Underlying formula displays in the Formula Bar

Result of the formula displays in the active cell

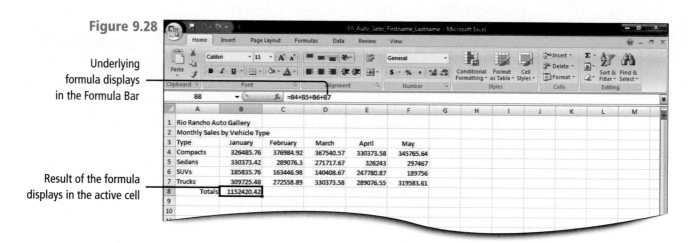

6 To change the value in cell B4, click cell **B4**, type **347999.12** and then watch cell **B8** as you press Enter.

> Excel recalculates the formula and displays *1173933.78*. Excel formulas *recalculate* if you change values in a cell that is referenced in the formula. It is not necessary to delete the old value in a cell; selecting the cell and typing a new value replaces the old value with your new typing.

7 In cell **C8**, type **=** to signal the beginning of a formula. Then, point to cell **C4**, click one time, and compare your screen with Figure 9.29.

> The reference to the cell, C4, is added to the active formula. A moving border surrounds the referenced cell, and the border color and the color of the cell reference in the formula are color-coded to match.

Figure 9.29

The cell referred to outlined with a moving border

Formula with cell reference created by pointing and clicking

8 At the insertion point, type **+** and then click cell **C5**. Repeat this process to complete the formula to add cells **C4** through **C7**, and then press Enter.

The result of the formula calculation—*1102067.09*—displays in the cell. This method of constructing a formula is the ***point and click method***. Constructing a formula by using the point and click method is convenient when the referenced cells are not adjacent to one another.

9 Point to cell **C6**, and then double-click to place the insertion point within the cell. Use the arrow keys to move the insertion point to the left or right of *3*, and then use either Del or ←Bksp to delete the *3* and then type **1** Watch cell **C8** as you press Enter and then notice the recalculation of the formula.

10 Click cell **D8**. On the **Home tab**, in the **Editing group**, click the **Sum** button Σ ▾. Alternatively, use the keyboard shortcut Alt + =; or, on the Formulas tab, in the Function Library group, click the AutoSum button. Compare your screen with Figure 9.30.

Sum is an Excel function—a prewritten formula. A moving border surrounds cells D4:D7, and *=SUM(D4:D7)* displays in cell D8.

The = sign signals the beginning of a formula, *SUM* indicates the type of calculation that will take place (addition), and *(D4:D7)* indicates the range of cells on which the sum operation will be performed. A ScreenTip provides additional information about the action.

Figure 9.30

ScreenTip with additional
information on the SUM function   Sum button on the Ribbon

Underlying formula
displays in Formula Bar

Moving border surrounds
the range selected by Sum

Formula generated by
the Sum function

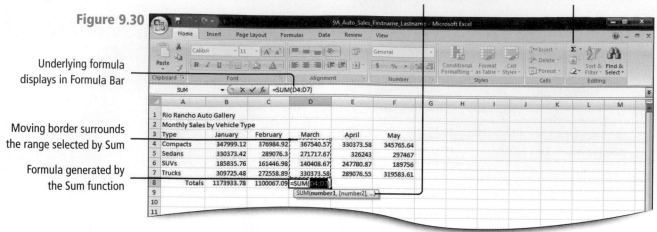

11 Look at the **Formula Bar**, and notice that the formula also displays there. Then, look again at the cells surrounded by the moving border.

When you activate the Sum function, Excel first looks *above* the active cell for a range of cells to sum. If no range is above the active cell, Excel will look to the *left* for a range of cells to sum. If the proposed range is not what you want to calculate, you can select a different group of cells.

12 Press Enter to view the sum of March sales—*1110040.49*—in cell **D8**.

Because the Sum function is frequently used, it has its own button in the Editing group on the Ribbon. A larger version of the button also displays on the Formulas tab in the Function Library group. As you progress in your study of Excel, you will use additional Excel functions. This button is also referred to as *AutoSum*.

13 Click cell **D4**, and then click in the **Formula Bar** to position the insertion point there. Change the number *6* to **7** so that the value is *377540.57*, and then press Enter to recalculate the formula.

The total for March is recalculated to *1120040.49*. You can edit cells in the Formula Bar or inside the cell itself.

14 Select the range **E4:F8**, look at the status bar at the lower right of your screen, and then compare your screen with Figure 9.31.

By selecting a range of cells and including the empty cells at the bottom of each column, you can apply the Sum function to sum several columns at once; the formula for adding each column will be placed in the empty cells at the bottom of each column.

Additionally, when you select a range of cells containing numbers, Excel displays the result of applying the Average, Count, or Sum functions in the status bar. You can see that if you averaged the numbers of the selected cells, the result would be 293255.7813; if you counted the cells in the selection that contain values (text or numbers), the result would be 8, and if you added the numbers in the selected cells, the total would be 2346046.25.

Figure 9.31

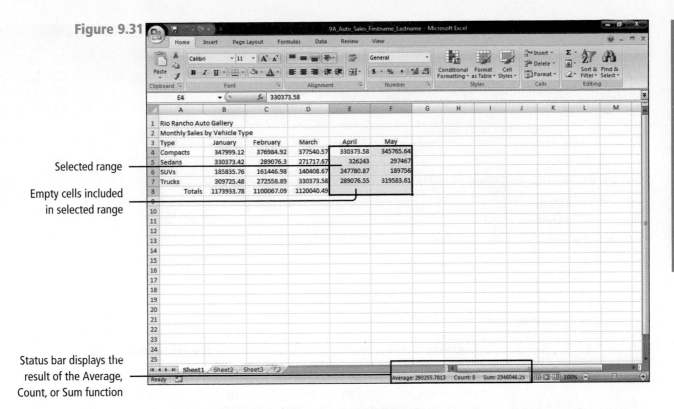

Selected range

Empty cells included
in selected range

Status bar displays the
result of the Average,
Count, or Sum function

More Knowledge — Multiple Status Bar Calculations

When numerical data is selected, three calculations display in the status bar by default—Average, Count, and Sum. You can display a total of six of these calculations on the status bar by adding the Numerical Count (the number of cells within the selection that contain numbers), Minimum, and Maximum functions to the status bar. To add additional calculations, right-click the status bar and select the calculations you want to display.

15 In the **Editing group**, click the **Sum** button $\boxed{\Sigma \cdot}$ or press $\boxed{Alt}$ + $\boxed{=}$.

Excel places the Sum formula in cells E8 and F8 and a result displays in cells E8 and F8 indicating the sums *1193474* and *1152572.25*. Recall that in the General number format, trailing zeros do not display.

16 Click cell **E8**, and then notice the formula in the **Formula Bar**. Click cell **F8** to view the formula in the **Formula Bar**. Compare your screen with Figure 9.32.

The cells display the result of the calculated function, which is a formula that Excel has prewritten and named.

Figure 9.32

Formula indicated
in Formula Bar

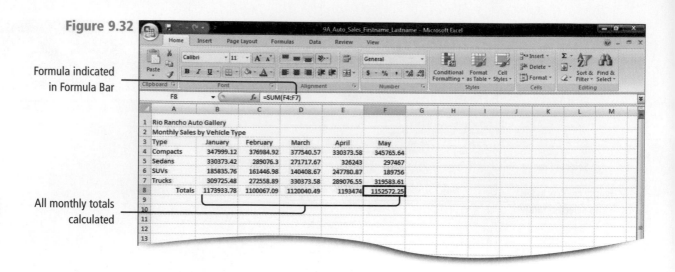

All monthly totals
calculated

17 **Save** 🖫 your workbook.

Activity 9.09 Copying a Formula by Using the Fill Handle

Excel provides a quick method—called copying formulas—to create formulas without typing, pointing and clicking, or using a command from the Ribbon. When you copy a formula from one cell to another, Excel adjusts the cell references to fit the new location of the formula. In this activity, you will delete the columns that do not relate to the first quarter, and then copy formulas.

1 From the **column heading area**, select **columns E:F**. In the **Cells group**, click the **Delete button arrow**, and then click **Delete Sheet Columns**. Alternatively, click the Delete button; or, right-click over the selected columns to display the shortcut menu and click Delete.

> Only the monthly sales for the first quarter of the year—January through March—display.

2 Click cell **E4**, hold down (Alt), and then press (=). Compare your screen with Figure 9.33.

> The (Alt) + (=) keyboard shortcut is the fastest way to apply the Sum function. Recall that Excel first looks above the selected cell for a proposed range of cells to sum, and if no data is detected, Excel then looks to the left and proposes a range of cells to sum.

Figure 9.33

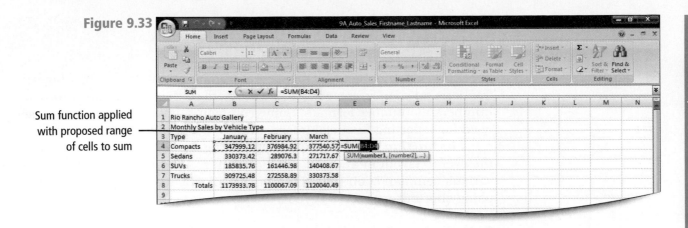

Sum function applied
with proposed range
of cells to sum

3 On the **Formula Bar**, click the **Enter** button ✓ to keep cell **E4** active.

> The total dollar amount of *Compacts* sold in the quarter is *1102525*. In cells E5:E8, you can see that you need a formula similar to the one in E4, but one that refers to the cells in row 5, row 6, and so forth.

4 With cell **E4** active, point to the fill handle in the lower right corner of the cell until the ➕ pointer displays. Then, drag downward through cell **E8**. Compare your screen with Figure 9.34.

Figure 9.34

Rows 4 – 8 summed

Auto Fill Options button

5 Click cell **E5**, look at the **Formula Bar**, and notice the formula *=SUM(B5:D5)*. Click cell **E6**, look at the **Formula Bar**, and then notice the formula *=SUM(B6:D6)*.

> In each row, Excel copied the formula but adjusted the cell references *relative to* the row number. This is called a ***relative cell reference***— a cell reference based on the relative position of the cell that contains the formula and the cells referred to.

> The calculation is the same, but it is performed on the cells in that particular row. Use this quick method to insert numerous formulas into spreadsheets.

6 **Save** 💾 your workbook.

Objective 4
Format Data, Cells, and Worksheets

Excel has many options for displaying numbers—think of percentages, fractions, or money. Recall that Excel refers to the various ways to write numbers as number formats. Some common number formats are those used for reporting financial information like monthly sales.

Formatting is the process of specifying the appearance of cells and the overall layout of a worksheet. Formatting is accomplished through various commands on the Ribbon, many of which are also available by using shortcut menus or keyboard shortcuts.

Activity 9.10 Formatting Financial Numbers, Using Column AutoFit, and Using Format Painter

The General format is the default format for a number that you type in a cell. Unless you apply a different number format to a cell, Excel will use the General format. The General format displays a number exactly as you type it—with three exceptions, as noted in the table in Figure 9.36.

1 Click cell **B4** so that a cell with a number value is selected. On the **Home tab**, in the **Number group**, point to the **Dialog Box Launcher** button ⬚ in the lower right corner, as shown in Figure 9.35.

A ScreenTip displays what the result of clicking the button will be. A **Dialog Box Launcher** displays in some groups on the Ribbon and opens a related dialog box providing additional options and commands related to that group.

Figure 9.35

Dialog Box Launcher button

Number group on the Home tab

ScreenTip indicates what will display

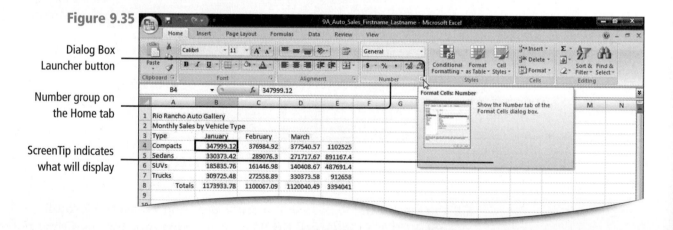

2 Click the **Dialog Box Launcher** button ⬚, and then in the **Format Cells** dialog box, on the **Number tab** under **Category**, click each category. As you do so, look at the **Sample** box to view the effect that each number format will have on the selected cell, and then take a moment to study the information about each number format in the table in Figure 9.36.

Excel Number Formats

Number Format	Description
General	The General format is the default format for a number that you type in a cell. The General format displays a number exactly as you type it—with three exceptions:
	1. Extremely long numbers may be abbreviated to a shorthand version of numbers called scientific notation; Excel will still use the underlying value in any calculations.
	2. Trailing zeros will not display in the General format.
	3. A decimal fraction entered without a number to the left of the decimal point will display with a zero.
Number	Number format is used for the general display of non-currency numbers. The default format has two decimal places, and you may choose to check the option for using a comma as a thousand separator. Negative numbers can display in red, be preceded by a minus sign, be enclosed in parentheses, or display both in red and in parentheses.
Currency	Currency format is used for general monetary values—the U.S. dollar sign is the default symbol. The default format has two decimal places.
Accounting	Accounting format lines up the currency symbols and decimal points in a column. It is similar to Currency format with two differences—the dollar sign (or other currency symbol) always displays at the left edge of the cell, rather than flush against the first number. Thus, both dollar signs and numbers are vertically aligned in the same column. Also, Accounting format adds a blank space equal to the width of a closing parenthesis on the right side of positive values to ensure that decimal points align if a column has both positive and negative numbers. The default format has two decimal places.
Date	Date format provides many common ways to display dates. The default format is month, day, and year, separated by a slash. The year displays as four digits by default, but may be changed in the Control Panel to a two-digit display. Formats that begin with an asterisk are subject to change by regional date and time settings specified in the Control Panel.
Time	Time format provides many common ways to display time; formats are subject to change in the manner described above for dates.
Percentage	Percentage format multiplies the cell value by 100 and displays the result with a percent sign. The default format has two decimal places.
Fraction	Fraction format displays fractional amounts as actual fractions rather than as decimal values.
Scientific	Scientific format displays numbers in scientific (exponential) notation. This is useful for extremely large numbers. The default format has two decimal places.
Text	Text format treats a number as if it were text. The number is left-aligned like text.
Special	Special formats used primarily with database functions such as postal codes, telephone numbers, and taxpayer ID numbers.
Custom	Custom format is used to create your own number format.

Figure 9.36

3 In the **Format Cells** dialog box, click **Cancel**. Hold down Ctrl, select the nonadjacent ranges **B4:E4** and **B8:E8**, and then in the **Number group**, click the **Accounting Number Format** button $ ▾ . Compare your screen with Figure 9.37.

Columns B through D are not wide enough to accommodate the newly formatted numbers and thus display # symbols.

The **Accounting Number Format** button formats the number with the default Accounting format that uses the U.S. dollar sign. That is, it applies a thousand comma separator where appropriate, inserts a fixed U.S. dollar sign aligned at the left edge of the cell, applies two decimal places, and leaves a small amount of space at the right edge of the cell to accommodate a parenthesis for negative numbers.

Figure 9.37

Accounting Number Format button in Number group

Accounting Number Format applied to selected cells

Cells too narrow for newly formatted numbers display # signs

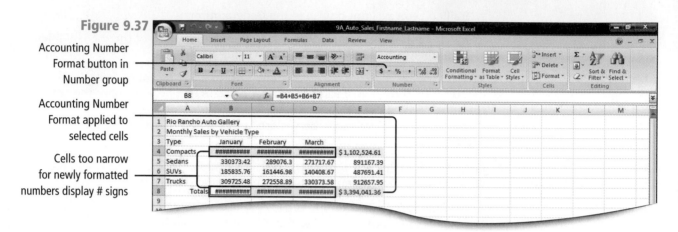

Note — Showing Fewer Decimal Places

Many financial documents do not display values with cents because either it is unnecessary to be completely precise or it not feasible to determine the exact number. To decrease the number of decimal places and round to the nearest whole dollar amount, select the cells, and then on the Home tab of the Ribbon, in the Number group, click the Decrease Decimal button two times to show a less precise value by showing fewer decimal places. Alternatively, on the Home tab, in the Styles group, click the Cell Style button, and then under Number Format, click *Currency [0]*.

---

4 Select **column B**. In the **Cells group**, click the **Format** button, and then from the menu, click **AutoFit Column Width**.

The width of the column adjusts to accommodate the longest entry, which is the formatted total in cell B8.

5 Select **columns C:E**. In the **column heading area**, point to the right boundary of any of the selected columns to display the ⊞ pointer, and then double-click.

This is an alternative method to apply the AutoFit Column Width command. Each column width adjusts to accommodate the longest entry in its column.

6 Select the range **B5:B7**, and then in the **Number group**, click the **Comma Style** button .

The **Comma Style** inserts thousand comma separators where appropriate and applies two decimal places. Comma Style also leaves space at the right to accommodate a parenthesis for negative numbers.

7 Click cell **B5**. In the **Clipboard group**, click the **Format Painter** button 🖌. With the 🖌 pointer, select the range **C5:E7**, and then compare your screen with Figure 9.38.

Use *Format Painter* to copy the *formatting* of one cell to other cells—there are numerous methods to apply formatting to cells.

When preparing worksheets with financial information, the first row of dollar amounts and the total rows of dollar amounts are formatted in the Accounting Number Format; that is, with thousand comma separators, dollar signs, two decimal places, and space at the right to accommodate a parenthesis for negative numbers, if any. Rows that are not the first row or the total row should be formatted with the Comma Style.

Figure 9.38

Cells in selected range formatted with the Comma Style

Cells formatted with the Accounting Number Format

Accounting Number Format aligns dollar sign at left edge of cell

Space allowed for a parenthesis when number is negative

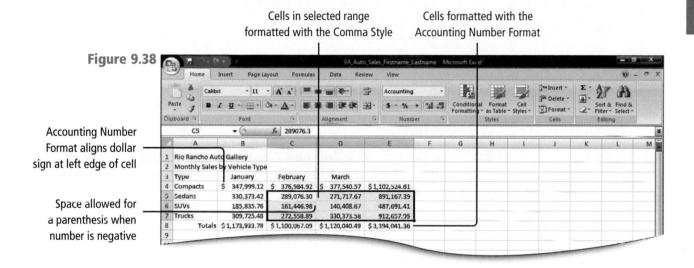

Note — Double-Click Format Painter to Copy Formatting to Multiple Selections

Double-clicking the Format Painter button causes it to remain active until you click the button again, or press Esc, to turn it off. Use this technique to copy cell formatting to two or more cells that are not adjacent.

8 Select the range **B8:E8**. In the **Font group**, click the **Borders button arrow** 🔲▾ to display a gallery of commonly used border styles. Compare your screen with Figure 9.39.

A *gallery* displays a list of potential results. The Borders button displays the most recently used border style; clicking the button, rather than the arrow, applies the most recently used style as indicated by the button.

Figure 9.39

Borders arrow

Top and Double
Bottom Border

9 From the list, click **Top and Double Bottom Border**. Click any empty cell to deselect the range, and then compare your screen with Figure 9.40.

This is a common way to apply borders to financial information. The single border indicates that calculations were performed on the numbers above, and the double border indicates that the information is complete.

Figure 9.40

Top border

Double bottom border

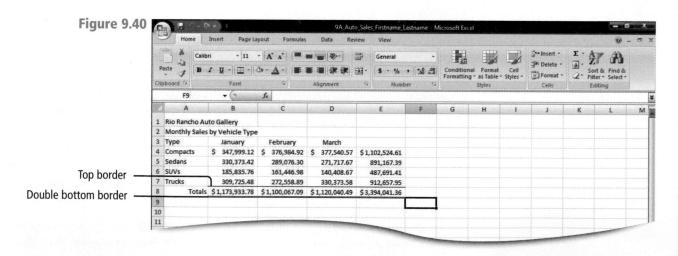

10 **Save** your workbook.

Note — Using Negative Numbers in a Worksheet

You can see a small amount of space to the right of each of the formatted number cells. The formats you applied allow this space in the event parentheses are needed to indicate negative numbers. If your worksheet contains negative numbers, display the Format Cells dialog box and select from among various formats to accommodate negative numbers. As you progress in your study of Excel, you will practice formatting negative numbers.

Activity 9.11 Formatting Text and Using Merge and Center

Use techniques similar to other Office programs to change fonts; you can add emphasis by using bold, italic, and underline, and align text in the center, or at the left or right edge of a cell. In this activity, you will format the worksheet's title and subtitle to increase their visibility and inform the reader of the worksheet's purpose.

1 Select the range **A1:E1**, and then in the **Alignment group**, click the **Merge & Center** button.

The Merge & Center command joins the selected cells into one larger cell and centers the contents in the new cell; cells A1:E1 can no longer be selected individually because they are merged into cell A1.

2 Select the range **A2:E2**, right-click over the selection, and then on the Mini toolbar, click the **Merge & Center** button.

3 Click cell **A1**. In the **Font group**, click the **Font button arrow**.

4 At the top of the list, under **Theme Fonts**, point to **Cambria**, and notice *(Headings)* to the right.

A *theme* is a predefined set of colors, fonts, lines, and fill effects that look good together and that can be applied to your entire workbook or to specific items—for example, to a chart or table.

Cambria is a *serif* font—a font that includes small line extensions on the ends of the letters to guide the eye in reading from left to right. In the default theme, *Cambria* is the suggested font for headings, and *Calibri* is the suggested font for the body of the worksheet.

5 Click **Cambria** to apply the font. With cell **A1** still selected, in the **Font group**, click the **Font Size button arrow**, and then point to **14**, and then **16**, and then **18**, and notice how the text expands as you point to each size. Click **18**.

This is *Live Preview*—a technology that shows the results of applying an editing or formatting change as you point to the items presented in the gallery or list.

6 With cell **A1** active, in the **Font group**, click **Bold**.

The Bold *font style* is applied to your text. Font styles are used to emphasize text by using bold, italic, and underline.

7 With cell **A1** still selected, in the lower right corner of the **Font group**, click the **Dialog Box Launcher** to display the **Font tab** of the **Format Cells** dialog box. Notice that *Cambria* is selected and that a preview of the font is also displayed under **Preview**.

8 Under **Font style**, click **Bold Italic**, and then notice that the Preview changes to reflect your selection.

9 Click the **Color arrow**. Under **Theme Colors**, in the fourth column, point to the first box to display the ScreenTip *Dark Blue, Text 2*, and then in that column of colors, click the next to last color—**Dark Blue, Text 2, Darker 25%**—as shown in Figure 9.41.

From the Format Cells dialog box, you can apply multiple formats at one time in this manner.

Figure 9.41

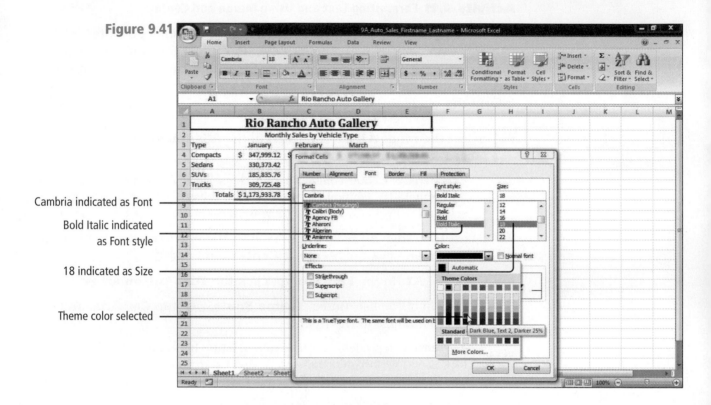

Cambria indicated as Font

Bold Italic indicated as Font style

18 indicated as Size

Theme color selected

10 Click **OK**. With cell **A1** still active, in the **Font group**, click the **Underline** button .

From the Ribbon, you can apply some common formats such as this one. The Underline button places a single underline under the *contents* of a cell. The Bold, Italic, and Underline buttons on the Ribbon are **toggle buttons**, which means that you can click the button one time to turn the formatting on and click it again to turn it off.

11 With cell **A1** selected, in the **Font group**, click the **Underline** button again to turn off Underline.

The Underline font style is removed from the text, but the Bold and Italic font styles remain.

12 With cell **A1** selected, in the **Font group**, click the **Fill Color button arrow** . Under **Theme Colors**, in the fourth column, click the second color—**Dark Blue, Text 2, Lighter 80%**.

The background of the cell—its *fill color*—changes. If your printer does not print in color, the colors will print as shades of gray, so select light colors to provide better contrast. Colors are especially distinctive if your workbook will be viewed on a screen.

13 Point to cell **A2**, right-click, on the Mini toolbar, click the **Increase Font Size** button A˄ two times, and as you click, notice that the new Font Size number displays on both the Ribbon and the Mini toolbar. Then, on the Mini toolbar, click the **Bold** button B.

14 Move the mouse pointer slightly away so that the Mini toolbar fades, view your formatting, and then click any cell to cancel the selection and close the Mini toolbar.

15 Double-click cell **A2** and edit the word *Monthly* to change it to **First Quarter** Press Enter.

16 Select **row 2**, and in the **row heading area**, drag the lower border of **row 2** down to increase the row height to **35 pixels**.

17 Select cell **A2**, and then in the **Alignment group**, click the **Middle Align** button ≡ to align the text vertically in the cell.

18 In cell **E3**, type **Totals** and then press Enter. Select the nonadjacent ranges **A3:E3** and **A4:A8** and apply **Bold** B emphasis.

19 **Save** 💾 your workbook, click any cell, and then compare your screen with Figure 9.42.

> The text in cell E3 is centered because the centered format continues from the adjacent cell. The same formatting will be applied to adjacent cells until two cells are left blank, and then the formatting is not continued.

Figure 9.42

Column title added

Monthly changed to First Quarter

Formatting applied to worksheet title and subtitle

Column and row titles in bold

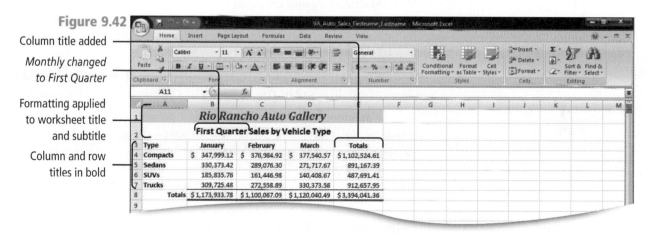

Objective 5
Close and Reopen a Workbook

You can save and close a workbook and then reopen it later to continue working. For example, at this point in this project, you may want to close the workbook and continue working later.

Activity 9.12 Closing and Reopening an Existing Workbook

1 To close the workbook, from the **Office** menu 🔵, click **Close**; if there are changes to be saved, Excel will prompt you to save before closing.

2 In the upper right corner of your screen, click the **Close** button ⊠ to exit Excel. Alternatively, from the Office menu, click Exit Excel. Or, to simultaneously close your workbook and close the Excel program, from the Office menu in the lower right corner, click Exit Excel.

3 To reopen the workbook, start Excel, and then display the **Office** menu ⊕. From the list of **Recent Documents**, click your workbook name if it displays. Alternatively, click the Open button and navigate to your storage location, select your workbook, and then click Open.

Objective 6
Chart Data

A *chart* is a graphic representation of data in a worksheet. Data presented as a chart is easier to understand than a table of numbers.

Activity 9.13 Charting Data

In this activity, you will create a column chart showing the monthly sales of vehicles by type during the first quarter. The chart will enable Sandy Cizek, the Auto Sales Manager, to see a pattern of overall monthly sales and a pattern of monthly sales by vehicle type.

1 Select the range **A3:E8**. Click the **Insert tab**, and then in the **Charts group**, click **Column** to display a gallery of Column chart types.

Various *chart types* are used to chart data in a way that is meaningful to the reader—common examples are column charts, pie charts, and line charts. A *column chart* is useful for illustrating comparisons among related numbers.

2 From the gallery of column chart types, under **2-D Column**, point to the first chart to display the ScreenTip *Clustered Column*, and then click to select it. Compare your screen with Figure 9.43.

A column chart displays in the worksheet, and the charted data is bordered by colored lines. Because the chart object is selected—surrounded by a border and displaying sizing handles—*contextual tools* named *Chart Tools* display and add *contextual tabs* next to the standard tabs on the Ribbon.

Contextual tools display only when needed for a selected object; when you deselect the object, the contextual tools no longer display.

Figure 9.43

Cells outlined in blue represented in chart columns

Cells outlined in green represent the legend

Chart Tools indicates that tools for selected object added to the Ribbon

Chart Tools contextual tabs added to standard Ribbon tabs

Cells outlined in purple represent category labels

Clustered column chart displays in the worksheet

Border and sizing handles indicate chart is selected

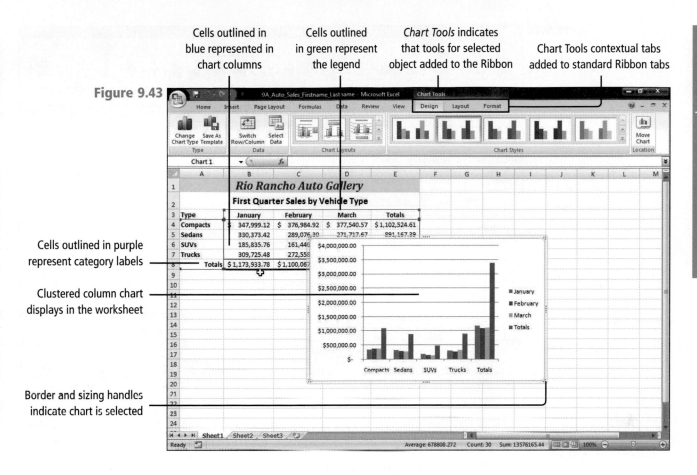

3 Point to the top border of the chart to display the ⊕ pointer, hold down the left mouse button, and then drag the upper left corner of the chart just inside the upper left corner of cell **A10**, approximately as shown in Figure 9.44.

Based on the data in your worksheet, Excel constructs a column chart and adds *category labels*—the labels that display along the bottom of the chart to identify the category of data. This area is referred to as the *category axis* or the *x-axis*. Excel uses the row titles as the category names.

On the left, Excel includes a numerical scale on which the charted data is based; this is referred to as the *value axis* or the *y-axis*. On the right, a *legend*, which identifies the patterns or colors that are assigned to the categories in the chart, displays.

Figure 9.44

Legend

Totals included as a category

Value axis, also called y-axis (based on total quarterly sales)

Category axis, also called x-axis

Category labels

4 On the Ribbon, locate the three contextual tabs that are active under **Chart Tools—Design**, **Layout**, and **Format**.

When a chart is selected, Chart Tools become available and these three tabs—Design, Layout, and Format—provide commands for working with the chart. When the chart is not selected, the Chart Tools do not display.

5 Point to the lower right corner of cell **E8** to display the ⬉ pointer, and then notice that the blue border surrounding the group of charted cells becomes thicker and brighter in color. Compare your screen with Figure 9.45.

You can adjust the chart by selecting a different group of cells to chart. On this chart, Sandy Cizek, the Auto Sales Manager, wants to see only the sales by month and not the total sales for the quarter.

When charting data, typically, you should *not* include totals—include only the comparable data.

Figure 9.45

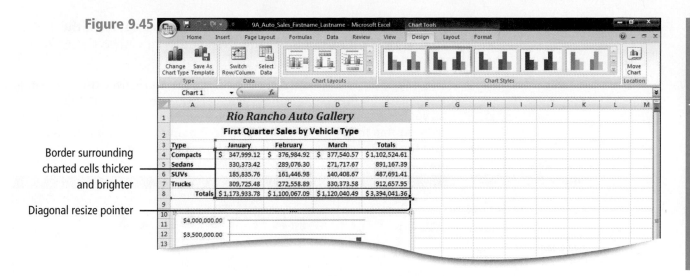

Border surrounding charted cells thicker and brighter

Diagonal resize pointer

6 Drag the ↖ pointer up and to the left until only the monthly dollar amounts in the range **B4:D7** are surrounded by the blue border. Release the left mouse button and notice the changes in your chart. Compare your screen with Figure 9.46.

> Each of the 12 cells bordered in blue is referred to as a ***data point***—a value that originates in a worksheet cell. Each data point is represented in the chart by a ***data marker***—a column, bar, area, dot, pie slice, or other symbol in a chart that represents a single data point.

> Related data points form a ***data series***; for example, there is a data series for *January*, for *February*, and for *March*. Each data series has a unique color or pattern represented in the chart legend.

Figure 9.46

Only sales figures for January, February, and March display

Each value in the selected range is a data point

Totals no longer included in the charted data

Data markers (columns) represent each data point

Color for each data series defined in legend

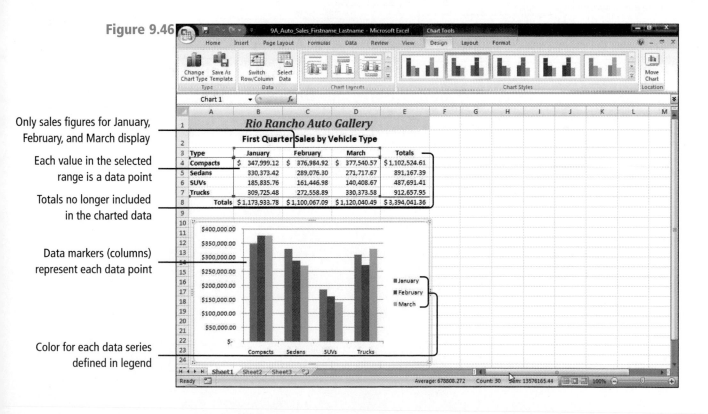

7 On the **Design tab** of the Ribbon, in the **Data group**, click the **Switch Row/Column** button, and then compare your chart with Figure 9.47.

> You can easily change the categories of data from the row titles, which is the default, to the column titles. Whether you use row or column titles as your category names depends on how you want to view your charted data. In this instance, the Sales Manager wants to see monthly sales and the breakdown of vehicle type within each month.

Figure 9.47

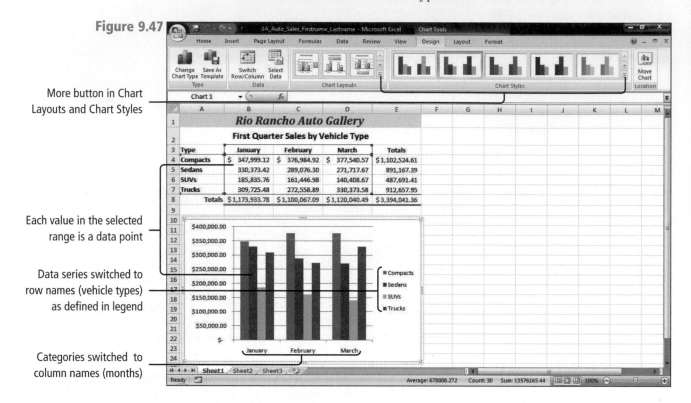

More button in Chart Layouts and Chart Styles

Each value in the selected range is a data point

Data series switched to row names (vehicle types) as defined in legend

Categories switched to column names (months)

8 On the **Design tab** of the Ribbon, in the **Chart Layouts group**, locate, and then click the **More** button ⬇, and then compare your screen with Figure 9.48.

> From the *Chart Layouts gallery*, you can select a predesigned *chart layout*—the combination of chart elements you want to display, which can include a title, legend, labels for the columns, and the table of charted cells.

Figure 9.48

Chart Layouts gallery

9 Click several different layouts to see the effect on your chart, and then using the ScreenTips as your guide, locate and click **Layout 1**.

10 In the chart, point to the text *Chart Title*, right-click, and then click **Edit Text**. Delete the text, and then type **First Quarter Sales by Vehicle Type**

11 Click in a white area *inside* the chart to deselect the chart title, but leaving the chart itself selected. On the **Design tab**, in the **Chart Styles group**, point to, and then click the **More** button , and then compare your screen with Figure 9.49.

> The **Chart Styles gallery** displays. Here you can select from an array of predefined **chart styles**—the overall visual look of the chart in terms of its graphic effects, colors, and backgrounds. For example, you can have flat or beveled columns, colors that are solid or transparent, and backgrounds that are dark or light.

Figure 9.49

Chart Styles gallery

Title added to chart

12 Click several different styles to see the effect on your chart, and then using the ScreenTips as your guide, locate and click **Style 26**.

> This style uses a white background, formats the columns by using theme colors, and applies a slightly beveled effect to the columns.

> With this clear visual representation of the data, Mr. Cizek can see that sales of compact cars have risen in each month of the quarter. He can also see that sales of sedans and SUVs have declined steadily in each month of the quarter. Finally, Mr. Cizek can see that truck sales declined slightly, and then rose again in March.

13 In your chart, notice that the values on the **value axis** include two decimal places. Then, on the Ribbon, click the **Layout tab**. In the **Axes group**, click the **Axes** button, point to **Primary Vertical Axis**, and then compare your screen with Figure 9.50.

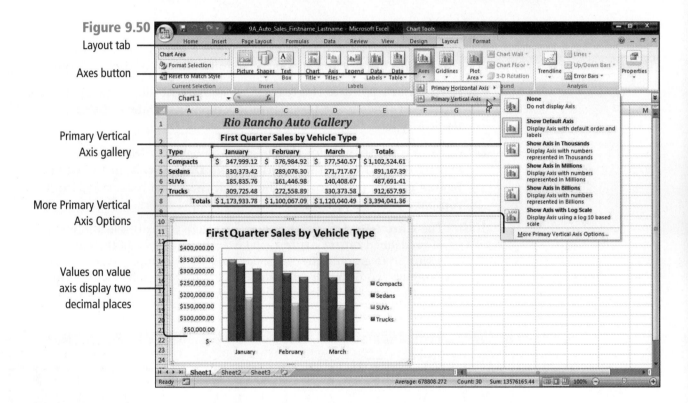

Figure 9.50
Layout tab
Axes button
Primary Vertical Axis gallery
More Primary Vertical Axis Options
Values on value axis display two decimal places

14 At the bottom of the gallery, click **More Primary Vertical Axis Options** to display the **Format Axis** dialog box.

15 In the dialog box, in the column at the left, click **Number**, and then in the **Decimal places** box, delete the existing number, type **0** and then click **Close**.

> The decimal places are removed from the value axis, resulting in a less cluttered look, and the value axis area of the chart is selected.

16 Click any cell to deselect the chart, and notice that the *Chart Tools* no longer display on the Ribbon. Compare your screen with Figure 9.51.

> Contextual tabs related to contextual tools in Office 2007 programs display when an object is selected, and then are removed from view when the object is deselected.

Figure 9.51

Chart Tools removed
from view when
chart not selected

Decimal places removed
from value axis

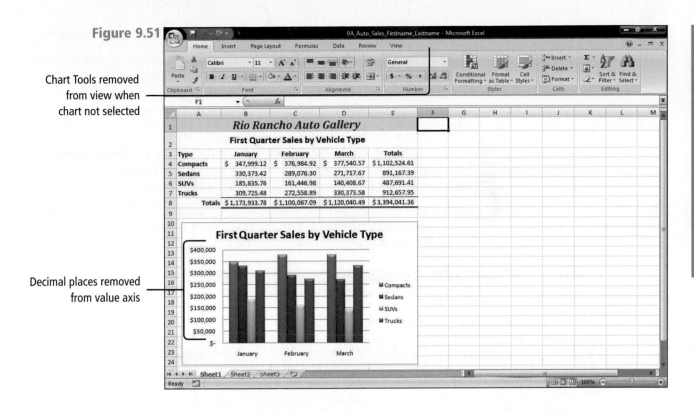

17 **Save** 💾 your workbook.

More Knowledge — A Chart Can Occupy a Separate Sheet in the Workbook

When a chart displays as an object within the worksheet, it is referred to as an *embedded chart*. With the chart selected, on the Design tab of the Ribbon, the last button —Move Chart—creates a new workbook sheet and places the chart on a separate workbook sheet. An embedded chart is useful when you want to view or print a chart on the same page as its source data.

Objective 7
Use Page Layout View, Prepare a Worksheet for Printing, and Close Excel

Before you print a worksheet, use *Page Layout view* and the commands on the Page Layout tab to prepare your data for printing. In Page Layout view, you can use the rulers to measure the width and height of data, set margins for printing, hide or display the numbered row headings and the lettered column headings, and change the *page orientation*—the position of data on the paper.

In *portrait orientation*, the paper is taller than it is wide. In *landscape orientation*, the paper is wider than it is tall. In Page Layout view, you can also add *headers* or *footers* which are text, page numbers, graphics, and formatting that print at the top (header) or bottom (footer) of every page of a worksheet. Finally, using Print Preview, you can see how the data and chart are centered on the page and if everything fits onto one page.

Activity 9.14 Changing Views, Creating a Footer and Using Print Preview

For each of your projects in this textbook, you will create a footer containing your name and the project name. This will make it easy for you to identify your printed documents in a shared printer environment such as a lab or classroom, or if you or your instructor view your completed work electronically.

1 On the Ribbon, click the **Insert tab**, and then in the **Text group**, click **Header & Footer** to switch to **Page Layout view** and open the **Header area**. Compare your screen with Figure 9.52.

> In this view, you can see the edges of the paper of multiple pages, the margins, and the rulers. You can also insert a header or footer by typing in the areas indicated and using the Header & Footer Tools.

Figure 9.52

Go to Footer button

Rulers

Header area open and selected

Margin

Edge of pages

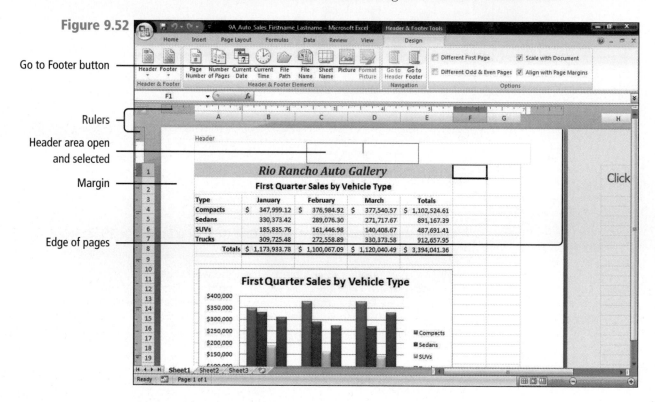

2 In the **Navigation group**, click the **Go to Footer** button to move to the bottom of the page and open the **Footer area**, and then click just above the word *Footer* to place the insertion point in the left section of the **Footer area**.

> The Header and Footer areas have three distinct sections—left, center, and right.

3 On the Ribbon, in the **Header & Footer Elements group**, click the **File Name** button to add the name of your file to the footer—*&[File]* displays in the left section of the **Footer area**. Then, click in a cell just above the footer to exit the **Footer area** and view your file name.

> The Header & Footer Tools are removed from view. In Page Layout vew, you can also type a header or footer directly into the areas indicated, but use this technique to automatically insert the file name.

4 Scroll up to view your chart, click the upper right corner of the chart to select it, and then check to see if the chart is centered under the data in the cells. If necessary, point to the **right resize handle** to display the ↔ pointer, as shown in Figure 9.53.

Figure 9.53

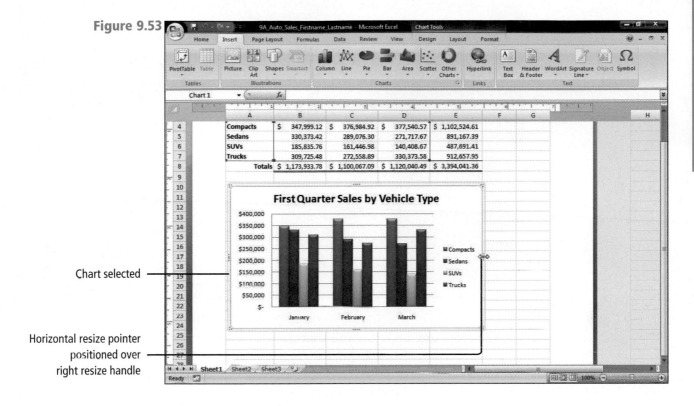

Chart selected

Horizontal resize pointer positioned over right resize handle

5 Drag the right border of the chart until it is almost even with the right border of **column E**, and then click any cell to deselect the chart. Be sure the left and right borders of the chart are just slightly inside the left border of **column A** and the right border of **column E**—adjust as necessary.

6 Click any cell to deselect the chart. Click the **Page Layout tab**, in the **Page Setup group**, click the **Margins** button, and then at the bottom of the **Margins gallery**, click **Custom Margins**. In the **Page Setup** dialog box, under **Center on page**, select the **Horizontally** check box.

This action will center the data and chart horizontally on the page, as shown in the Preview area.

7 In the lower right corner of the **Page Setup** dialog box, click **OK**. In the upper left corner of your screen, click the **Office** button 🏢, on the menu, point to the **Print button**, and then click **Print Preview**. Alternatively, press Ctrl + F2 to view the Print Preview. Compare your screen with Figure 9.54.

The Ribbon displays the Print Preview program tab, which replaces the standard set of tabs when you switch to Print Preview.

Figure 9.54

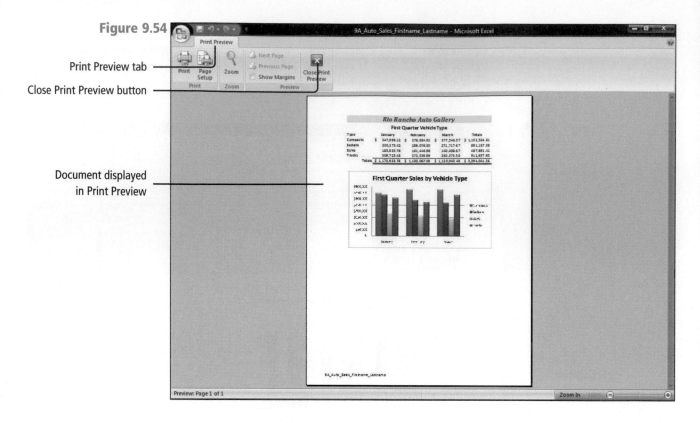

Print Preview tab

Close Print Preview button

Document displayed
in Print Preview

8 Note any adjustments that need to be made, and then on the Ribbon, click the **Close Print Preview** button. On the right side of the status bar, click the **Normal** button ⊞ to return to Normal view, and then press Ctrl + Home to return to cell **A1**.

> *Normal view* maximizes the number of cells visible on your screen and keeps the column letters and row numbers closer. The vertical dotted line between columns indicates that as currently arranged, only the columns to the left of the dotted line will print on the first page. The exact position of the vertical line will depend on your default printer setting—yours may fall elsewhere.

9 **Save** 💾 your workbook.

Activity 9.15 Deleting Unused Sheets in a Workbook

By default, each new Excel workbook contains three blank worksheets. Although it is not necessary to delete unused sheets, doing so saves storage space and removes any doubt that additional information is in the workbook.

1 At the bottom of your worksheet, click the **Sheet2 tab** to display Sheet 2 and make it the active worksheet.

2 Hold down Ctrl, and then click the **Sheet3 tab**. With both sheets selected (tab background is white, not blue, on the selected sheets), display the **Home tab**. In the **Cells group**, click the **Delete button arrow**, and then click **Delete Sheet**. Alternatively, point to either of the selected sheet tabs, right-click, and then click Delete to delete the sheets.

> Excel deletes the two unused sheets from your workbook. If you attempt to delete a worksheet with data, Excel will display a warning and permit you to cancel the deletion.

3 **Save** 🖫 your workbook.

Activity 9.16 Printing a Worksheet

1 Check your *Chapter Assignment Sheet* or *Course Syllabus*, or consult your instructor, to determine if you are to submit your assignments on paper or electronically. To submit electronically, follow the instructions provided by your instructor.

2 From the **Office** menu 🔘, click the **Print** button. In the **Print** dialog box, under **Print range**, verify that the **All** option button is selected. Under **Print what**, verify that **Active sheet(s)** is selected, and then under **Copies**, verify that the **Number of copies** is **1**. Compare your screen with Figure 9.55.

Figure 9.55

Print dialog box
Your default printer

Print all pages

Print currently
active worksheet

One copy

3 Click **OK** to print your worksheet, and then **Save** 🖫 your workbook.

Alert!

Is your printed result centered horizontally?

If your worksheet does not appear to be centered horizontally on the page, reduce the width of the chart by a small amount so that its borders fall slightly inside the left and right columns with which they are aligned.

Activity 9.17 Displaying, Printing, and Hiding Formulas

When you place a formula in a cell, the cell displays the results of the formula. Recall that this value is called the displayed value. You can view and print the underlying formulas in the cells. When you do so, a formula often takes more horizontal space to display than the result of the calculation. Thus, the landscape orientation is usually a better choice than portrait orientation to fit the formulas on one page. In this activity, you will print the formulas in Sheet1 in landscape orientation and then close the workbook without saving the changes.

1 Because you will make some temporary changes to your workbook, on the **Quick Access Toolbar**, click the **Save** button 🖫 to be sure that you have saved your work up to this point.

2 Hold down Ctrl, press ⌐ (usually located below Esc), and then compare your screen with Figure 9.56. Alternatively, on the Formulas tab, in the Formula Auditing group, click the Show Formulas button.

The Ctrl + ⌐ keyboard shortcut acts like a toggle; that is, pressing the two keys once displays the formulas, and pressing the two keys again hides the formulas.

Figure 9.56

Dotted line shows page break

Underlying formulas displayed

3 From the **column heading area**, select columns **A:E**. Point to the column heading boundary between any two of the selected columns and double-click to AutoFit the selected columns.

4 Display the **Page Layout tab**. In the **Page Setup group**, click the **Orientation** button, and then click **Landscape**. In the **Scale to Fit group**, click the **Dialog Box Launcher** button 🖫 to display the **Page tab** of the **Page Setup** dialog box.

5 Under **Scaling**, click the **Fit to** option button, and then in the lower right corner, click the **Print Preview** button—this is another point from which you can display the Print Preview.

Scaling adjusts the size of the printed worksheet to fit on the page, and is convenient for printing formulas. Although it is not always the case, formulas frequently take up more space than the actual data.

6 Click **Close Print Preview**. Check your *Chapter Assignment Sheet* or *Course Syllabus*, or consult your instructor, to determine if you are to submit your printed formulas on paper or electronically. To submit electronically, follow the instructions provided by your instructor.

7 From the **Office** menu 🖫, click the **Print** button. In the **Print** dialog box, under **Print range**, verify that the **All** option button is selected. Under **Print what**, verify that **Active sheet(s)** is selected, and then under **Copies**, verify that the **Number of copies** is **1**.

8 Click **OK** to print your worksheet. From the **Office** menu 🔵, click **Close**, and when prompted, click **No** so that you do *not* save the changes you made—displaying formulas, changing column widths and orientation, and scaling—to print your formulas.

9 In the upper right corner of your screen, click the **Close** button 🅇 to close Excel.

End You have completed Project 9A ――――――――――

Project 9B Safety Products

In Activities 9.18 through 9.25, you will create a workbook for Arthur Potempa, the Retail Sales Manager for Rio Rancho Auto Gallery. One of the retail areas in the Auto Gallery carries an inventory of safety products. Mr. Potempa wants to calculate the retail value of the inventory of safety products and then, using a pie chart, display how each item's retail value contributes to the total retail value. Your completed worksheet and chart will look similar to Figure 9.57.

For Project 9B, you will need the following file:

New blank Excel workbook

You will save your workbook as
9B_Safety_Products_Firstname_Lastname

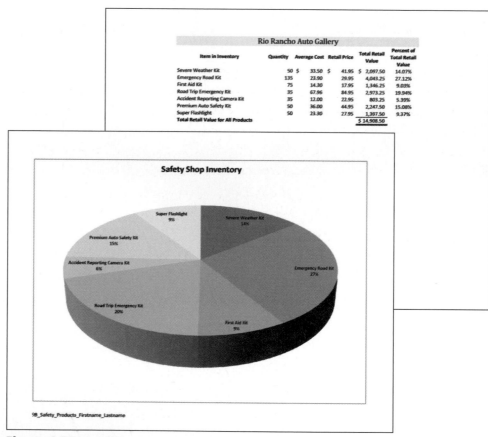

Figure 9.57
Project 9B—Safety Products

Objective 8
Design a Worksheet

Make your worksheet useful to the reader by using good design techniques, such as: use rows rather than columns for the most abundant data; consider how the worksheet will look on paper; and, arrange the data so that it is easily charted.

Activity 9.18 Setting Column Widths and Creating Row and Column Titles

The worksheet title is typically placed in the first row and centered above the columns of data.

1 **Start** Ⓔ **Excel**. From the **Office** menu Ⓑ, click **Close** to close the open workbook but leave the Excel program open.

2 Display the **Office** menu Ⓑ again and click **New**. In the **New Workbook** dialog box, under **Blank and recent**, click **Blank Workbook**, and then in the lower right corner, click the **Create** button. Alternatively, press Ctrl + N.

> With Excel open, these are techniques you can use to begin a new workbook.

3 From the **Office** menu Ⓑ, display the **Save As** dialog box, navigate to your **Excel Chapter 9** folder, and then in the **File name** box, replace the existing text with **9B_Safety_Products_Firstname_Lastname** and then click **Save**.

4 Click cell **A2**, type **Item in Inventory** and press Tab. In cell **B2**, type **Quantity** and press Tab.

5 In cell **C2**, type **Average Cost** and press Tab. In cell **D2**, type **Retail Price** and press Tab.

6 In cell **E2**, type **Total Retail Value** and press Tab. In cell **F2**, type **Percent of Total Retail Value** and press Enter.

7 In cell **A3**, type **Severe Weather Kit** and press Enter. Type the remaining row titles in cells **A4:A9**, and then compare your screen with Figure 9.58.

> **Emergency Road Kit**
>
> **First Aid Kit**
>
> **Accident Reporting Camera Kit**
>
> **Premium Auto Safety Kit**
>
> **Super Flashlight**
>
> **Total Retail Value for All Products**

Figure 9.58

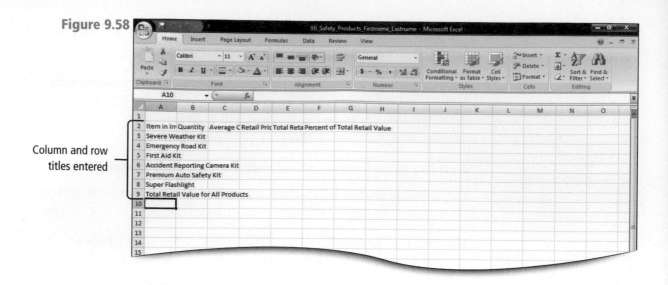

Column and row titles entered

8 Right-click cell **A9** and on the Mini toolbar, click **Bold** B.

9 Select **columns A:F**, position the ⬌ pointer over the right boundary of any of the selected column heading letters, and then double-click to apply **AutoFit Column Width**. Alternatively, click the Format button arrow, and then click AutoFit Column Width.

10 Click cell **A1** and type **Rio Rancho Auto Gallery** and then on the **Formula Bar**, click the **Enter** button ✓. Select the range **A1:F1**, and then right-click over the selection.

11 On the Mini toolbar, click the **Merge & Center** button ⊞▾, change the **Font** to **Cambria**, and then change the **Font Size** to **16**.

12 With cell **A1** selected, click the **Fill Color arrow** 🎨▾. In the seventh column of colors, click the third color—**Olive Green, Accent 3, Lighter 60%**.

13 Click anywhere to deselect cell **A1**, **Save** 💾 your workbook, and then compare your screen with Figure 9.59.

> Formatting the worksheet title with a different font, font size, and fill color distinguishes it visually from the worksheet data.

Figure 9.59

Column widths adjusted

Worksheet title entered
and formatted

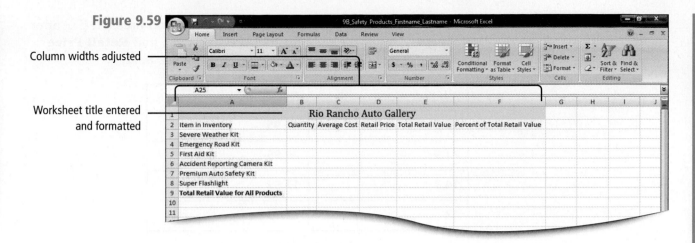

Activity 9.19 Entering Data by Range

In this activity, you will enter data by first selecting a range of cells; this is a time-saving technique, especially if you use the numeric keypad to enter the numbers.

1 Select the range **B3:D8**, type **50** and then press Enter.

The first value displays in cell B3 and cell B4 becomes the active cell.

2 Beginning in cell **B4** and pressing Enter after each entry, type the following, and then compare your screen with Figure 9.60:

135

75

35

50

50

After you enter the last value and press Enter, the active cell moves to the top of the next column within the selected range. Selecting the range in this manner—before you enter data—saves time because it confines the movement of the active cell to the selected range.

Figure 9.60

Active cell moves
to the next column

3 From the following table, beginning in cell **C3** and pressing ⌷Enter⌷ after each entry, enter the data for the **Average Cost** and **Retail Price** columns. Then compare your screen with Figure 9.61.

Average Cost	Retail Price
33.5	**41.95**
23.9	**29.95**
14.3	**17.95**
12	**22.95**
36	**44.95**
23.3	**27.95**

Recall that the default number format for cells is the *General* number format, in which numbers display exactly as you type them and trailing zeros do not display, even if you type them.

Figure 9.61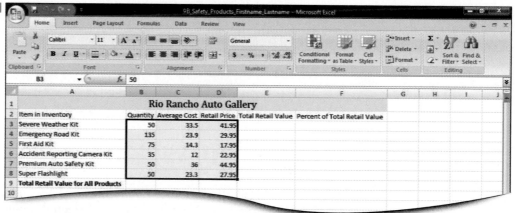

4 **Save** 💾 your workbook.

Objective 9
Construct Formulas for Mathematical Operations

Operators are symbols with which you can specify the type of calculation you want to perform in a formula.

Activity 9.20 Using Arithmetic Operators

1 In cell **E3**, type **=b3*d3** and press ⌷Enter⌷.

The *Total Retail Value* of all *Severe Weather Kit* items in the shop— 2097.5—equals the *Quantity* (50) times the *Retail Price* (selling price) of 41.95. In Excel, the asterisk (*) indicates multiplication.

2 Take a moment to study the symbols you will use to perform basic mathematical operations in Excel, as shown in the table in Figure 9.62—these are referred to as ***arithmetic operators***.

Symbols Used in Excel for Arithmetic Operators

Operator Symbol	Operation
+	Addition
-	Subtraction (also negation)
*	Multiplication
/	Division
%	Percent
^	Exponentiation

Figure 9.62

3 Click cell **E3**.

You can see that in cells E4:E8, you need a formula similar to the one in E3, but one that refers to the cells in row 4, row 5, and so forth. Recall that you can copy formulas and the cell references will change *relative to* the row number.

4 With cell **E3** selected, position your pointer over the fill handle in the lower right corner of the cell until the **+** pointer displays. Then, drag down through cell **E8** to copy the formula.

5 Select the range **C3:E3**, right-click over the selection, and then on the Mini toolbar, click the **Accounting Number Format** button **$ ▾**.

6 Select the range **C4:E8**, right-click over the selection, and then on the Mini toolbar, click the **Comma Style** button **,**.

7 Click cell **E9**, in the **Editing group**, click the **Sum** button **Σ ▾**, and then press Enter. Click **Save** and compare your screen with Figure 9.63.

Your result is *$11,935.25*. The Accounting Number Format is automatically applied to cell E9. The format of the cell containing the formula is the same as the format of the cells used in the formula. If the formula references a range of cells and those cells contain a mix of formats, the format from the cell in the upper left corner of the range is applied.

Excel | chapter 9

Figure 9.63

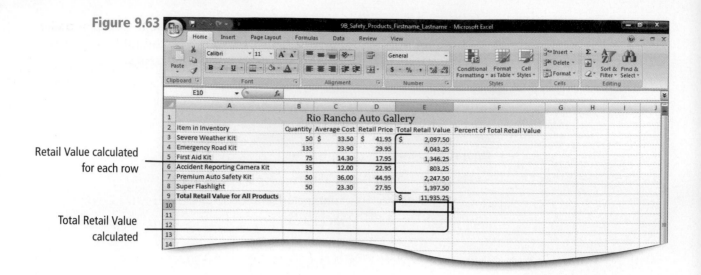

Retail Value calculated
for each row

Total Retail Value
calculated

Activity 9.21 Copying Formulas Containing Absolute Cell References

A relative cell reference refers to cells by their position in relation to the cell that contains the formula. An **absolute cell reference**, on the other hand, refers to a cell by its *fixed* position in the worksheet, for example, the total in cell E9.

A relative cell reference automatically adjusts when a formula is copied. An absolute cell reference does *not* adjust; rather, it remains the same when the formula is copied—and there are times when you will want to do this.

1 Click cell **F3**, type = and then click cell **E3**. Type / and then click cell **E9**.

> The formula =E3/E9 indicates that the value in cell E3 will be divided by the value in cell E9. Why? Because Mr. Potempa wants to know the percentage by which each product's Total Retail Value makes up the Total Retail Value for All Products. Arithmetically, the percentage is computed by dividing the *Total Retail Value* for each product by the *Total Retail Value for All Products*. The result will be a percentage expressed as a decimal.

Workshop

Calculate a Percentage if You Know the Total and the Amount

Using the equation *amount/total = percentage*, you can calculate the percentage by which a part makes up a total—with the percentage formatted as a decimal.

For example, if on a quiz you score 42 points correctly out of 50, your percentage of correct answers is 42/50 = 0.84 or 84%.

2 Press [Enter]. Click cell **F3** and notice that the formula displays in the **Formula Bar**. Then, point to cell **F3** and double-click.

The formula, with the two referenced cells displayed in color and bordered with the same color, displays in the cell. This is the *range finder*, and is useful for verifying formulas or quickly positioning the insertion point within the cell to perform editing directly in the cell.

3 Press [Enter] to redisplay the result of the calculation in the cell, and notice that approximately 17% of the total retail value of the inventory is made up of Severe Weather Kits.

4 Click cell **F3** again, and drag the fill handle down through cell **F8**. Compare your screen with Figure 9.64.

Each cell displays an error message—*#DIV/0!* and a green triangle in the upper left corner of each cell indicates an error has been found. Like a grammar checker, Excel uses rules to check for formula errors and flags them in this manner. Additionally, the Auto Fill Options button displays, from which you can select formatting options for the copied cells.

Figure 9.64

Error messages

Green triangles indicate errors

Auto Fill Options button

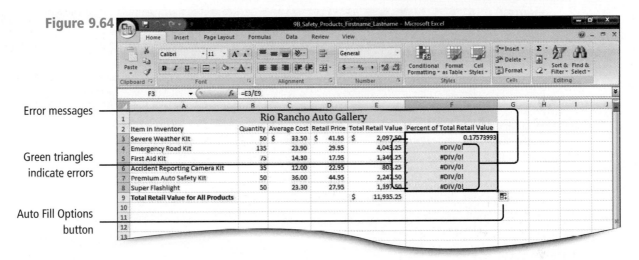

5 Click cell **F4**, and to the left of the cell, point to the **Error Checking** button to display its ScreenTip—*The formula or function used is dividing by zero or empty cells.*

In this manner, Excel suggests the cause of an error.

6 Look at the **Formula Bar** and examine the formula.

The formula is *=E4/E10*. The cell reference to *E4* is correct, but the cell reference following the division operator (/) is *E10*, and E10 is an *empty* cell.

7 Click cell **F5**, point to the **Error Checking** button ![icon], and in the **Formula Bar** examine the formula.

> Because the cell references are relative, Excel attempts to build the formulas by increasing the row number for each equation. In this particular calculation, however, the divisor must always be the value in cell E9—the *Total Retail Value for All Products.*

8 Point to cell **F3**, and then double-click to have the range finder display the cell's formula and place the insertion point within the cell.

9 Within the cell, be sure the insertion point is blinking to the right of *E9*, and then press F4. Alternatively, edit the formula so that it indicates =E3/$E$9 Compare your screen with Figure 9.65.

> Dollar signs ($) display in an absolute cell reference. The use of the dollar sign to denote an absolute reference is not related in any way to whether or not the values you are working with are currency values. It is simply the symbol used by Excel to denote an absolute cell reference.

Figure 9.65

Edited formula with dollar signs denoting an absolute cell reference

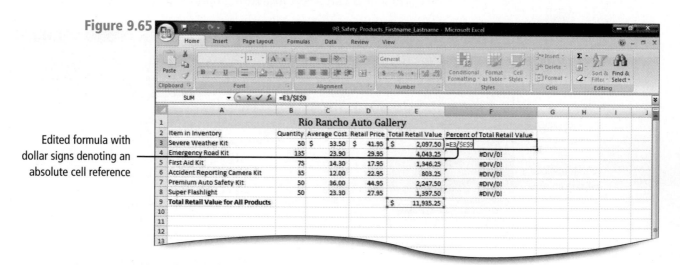

10 On the **Formula Bar**, click the **Enter** button ![icon] so that **F3** is still the active cell. Then, drag the fill handle to copy the formula down through cell **F8**. Compare your screen with Figure 9.66.

Figure 9.66

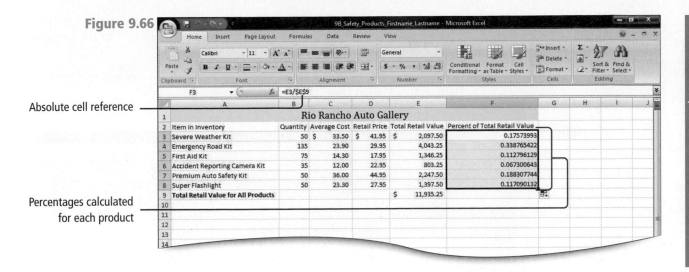

Absolute cell reference

Percentages calculated for each product

11 Click cell **F4**, examine the formula in the **Formula Bar**, and then examine the formulas for cells **F5**, **F6**, **F7**, and **F8**.

> For each formula, the cell reference for the *Total Retail Value* of each product changed relative to its row; however, the value used as the divisor—*Total Retail Value for All Products* in cell E9—remained absolute. Thus, using either relative or absolute cell references, it is easy to duplicate formulas without typing them.

12 **Save** your workbook.

Objective 10
Format Percentages and Move Formulas

A percentage is part of a whole expressed in hundredths. For example, 75 cents is the same as 75 percent of one dollar. The Percent Style button formats the selected cell as a percentage rounded to the nearest hundredth.

Excel adjusts formulas automatically if you move formulas by inserting additional rows or columns.

Activity 9.22 Formatting Cells with the Percent Style Button

1 Click cell **F3** and notice the number *0.17573993*. In the **Number group**, click the **Percent Style** button ☒.

> Your result is 18%, which is *0.17573993* rounded up to the nearest hundredth and expressed as a percentage. Percent Style displays the value of a cell as a percentage.

2 Select the range **F3:F8**, right-click over the selection, and then on the Mini toolbar, click the **Percent Style** button ☒, click the **Increase Decimal** button ☒ two times, and then click the **Center** ☰ button.

> Percent Style may not offer a percentage precise enough to analyze important financial information—adding additional decimal places

to a percentage makes data more precise. For example, with additional decimal places, Mr. Potempa can see a slight difference in the percentage of First Aid Kits and Super Flashlights.

3 Click any cell to cancel the selection, compare your screen with Figure 9.67, and then **Save** 🖫 your workbook.

Figure 9.67

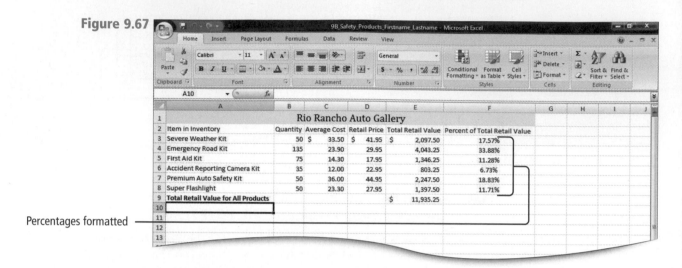

Percentages formatted

Activity 9.23 Inserting Rows in a Worksheet Containing Formulas and Wrapping Text in a Cell

You can edit formulas in the same manner as you edit text. In this activity, you will add a row for Road Trip Emergency Kits, which is another item carried by the Safety Shop, and wrap text.

1 Double-click cell **E9** and confirm that the range finder shows the formula to be the sum of cells *E3:E8*. Press Enter.

2 Click cell **E6**. On the **Home tab**, in the **Cells group**, click the **Insert button arrow**, and then from the list, click **Insert Sheet Rows**.

Another Way — **To Insert Rows**

Click the row heading and then in the Cells group, click the Insert button; or, right-click the cell, click Insert, and then click Entire row.

3 Click cell **E10**. On the **Formula Bar**, notice that the range was edited and changed to sum the newly expanded range **E3:E9**.

4 In the range **A6:D6**, type the following:

| Road Trip Emergency Kit | 35 | 67.96 | 84.95 |

5 Select the range **E5:F5** to select the two formulas above the new row, and then drag the fill handle to fill both formulas down to cells **E6** and **F6**.

6 Click cell **E10**. Move the pointer to the bottom edge of the cell until the 🔧 pointer displays, and then drag downward until cell **E11** is outlined, as shown in Figure 9.68.

Figure 9.68

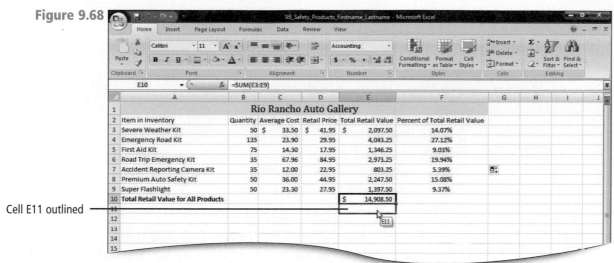

Cell E11 outlined

7 Release the mouse button, double-click cell **E11** to display the range finder, and then in cell **E11** and on the **Formula Bar**, notice that the range, **E3:E9**, did not change when you moved the formula.

If you move a formula to another cell, the cell references do not change.

8 Press Esc to cancel the range finder, and then on the **Quick Access Toolbar**, click **Undo** 🔙 to return the formula to cell **E10**.

9 In the **row heading area**, point to the lower boundary of **row 2** to display the ➕ pointer, and then drag downward until the row is **60 pixels** high.

10 Select **columns B:F**, and then from the **column heading area**, drag the right border of one of the selected columns to **80 pixels**.

11 Select the range **C2:F2**, and then in the **Alignment group**, click the **Wrap Text** button 📋.

Use the Wrap Text command to display text on multiple lines within a single cell when the column is not wide enough to display all of the cell's content.

12 Select the range **A2:F2**. In the **Font group**, click the **Bold** button B ; in the **Alignment group**, click the **Center** button ≡ and the **Middle Align** button ≡.

13 Click cell **E10**. In the **Font** group, click the **Borders button arrow** ⊞ ▾, and then from the list, click **Top and Double Bottom Border**. Click any cell to cancel the selection from cell E10.

14 **Save** 💾 your workbook, and then compare your screen with Figure 9.69.

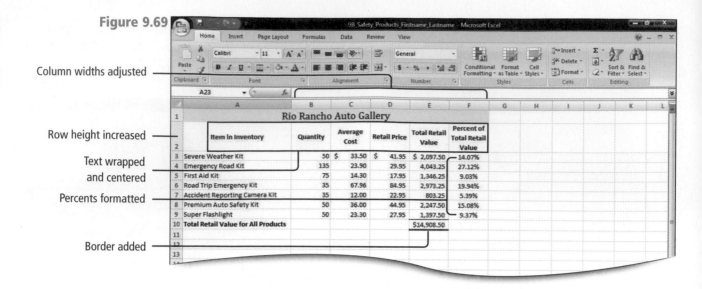

Figure 9.69

Column widths adjusted

Row height increased

Text wrapped and centered

Percents formatted

Border added

Item in Inventory	Quantity	Average Cost	Retail Price	Total Retail Value	Percent of Total Retail Value
Severe Weather Kit	50	$ 33.50	$ 41.95	$ 2,097.50	14.07%
Emergency Road Kit	135	23.90	29.95	4,043.25	27.12%
First Aid Kit	75	14.30	17.95	1,346.25	9.03%
Road Trip Emergency Kit	35	67.96	84.95	2,973.25	19.94%
Accident Reporting Camera Kit	35	12.00	22.95	803.25	5.39%
Premium Auto Safety Kit	50	36.00	44.95	2,247.50	15.08%
Super Flashlight	50	23.30	27.95	1,397.50	9.37%
Total Retail Value for All Products				$14,908.50	

Rio Rancho Auto Gallery

15 On the Ribbon, click the **Insert tab**, and then in the **Text group**, click **Header & Footer** to switch to **Page Layout view** and open the **Header area**. On the **Design tab**, in the **Navigation group**, click the **Go to Footer** button.

16 Click just above the word *Footer* to place your insertion point in the left section of the **Footer area**, and then in the **Header & Footer Elements group**, click the **File Name** button. Click any cell above the footer to exit the **Footer area** and view your file name.

17 Press Ctrl + Home to move to cell **A1** and display the upper portion of your worksheet. Click the **Page Layout tab**. In the **Page Setup group**, click the **Orientation** button, and then click **Landscape**.

18 In the **Page Setup group**, click the **Margins** button, and then at the bottom of the **Margins gallery**, click **Custom Margins**. In the **Page Setup** dialog box, under **Center on page**, select the **Horizontally** check box. Click **OK**, and then **Save**.

Objective 11
Create a Pie Chart and a Chart Sheet

Pie charts show the relationship of each part to a whole. To create a pie chart, you must select two ranges. One range contains the labels for each slice of the pie chart, and the other range contains the values that add up to a total. The two ranges must have the same number of cells and the range with the values should *not* include the cell with the total.

A legend can identify the slices of the pie by using colors, but it is usually more effective to place the labels within or close to each pie slice.

Activity 9.24 Creating a Pie Chart and a Chart Sheet

The purpose of the inventory worksheet is to determine how each item contributes to the total retail value of the inventory. To display the relationship of parts to a whole, use a pie chart. In the 9B_Safety_Products worksheet, you calculated the percent of the total in column F. This percentage can also be calculated by the Chart feature and added to the chart as a label.

1 In the lower right of your screen, on the status bar, click the **Normal** button 田 to return to **Normal view**.

2 Select the range **A3:A9** and then hold down Ctrl and select the non-adjacent range **E3:E9**—the item names and the total retail value of each item.

3 Click the **Insert tab**, and then in the **Charts group**, click **Pie**. Under **3-D Pie**, click the first chart—**Pie in 3-D**—to create the chart on your worksheet.

4 On the **Design tab**, in the **Location group**, click the **Move Chart** button. In the **Move Chart** dialog box, click the **New sheet** option button. Replace the highlighted text *Chart1* by typing **Inventory Chart** and then click **OK**.

> A **chart sheet** is created in your workbook, which is a workbook sheet that contains only a chart and is useful when you want to view a chart separately from the worksheet data. The sheet tab indicates *Inventory Chart*.

5 On the **Design tab**, in the **Chart Layouts group**, click the first layout—**Layout 1**. Right click over the text *Chart Title*, click **Edit Text**, delete the existing text, and then type **Safety Shop Inventory**

> In this layout, there is no legend and the category labels and the percentages—calculated by the chart feature—display on the pie slices. If you plan to print a chart sheet on a printer that does not print in color, it is better to label each pie slice individually rather than use a legend.

6 In the **Chart Styles group**, click the **More** button ▼, and then click **Style 5**. Click anywhere in the white area of the chart to deselect the Chart Title, and then compare your screen with Figure 9.70.

> To print on paper, the paler colors will display well. To present this chart in a PowerPoint presentation, you would likely pick one of the more vibrant styles with multiple colors.

Figure 9.70

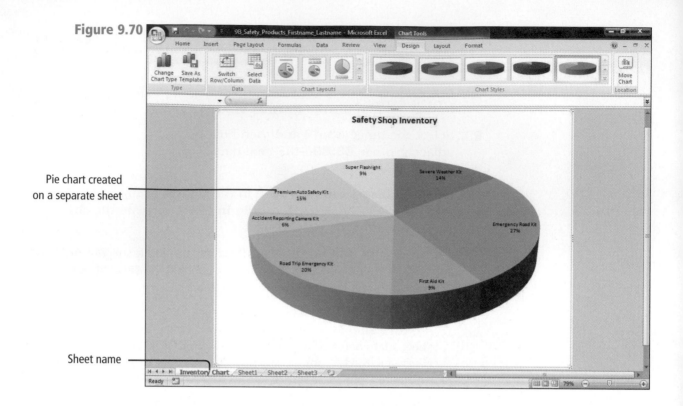

Pie chart created on a separate sheet

Sheet name

7 Click the **Insert tab**. In the **Text group**, click **Header & Footer**, and then in the **Page Setup** dialog box, click the **Custom Footer** button.

8 With the insertion point positioned in the **Left section**, click the **Insert File Name** button ⊠, and then click **OK** two times.

> Use the Page Setup dialog box in this manner to insert a footer on a chart sheet, which has no Page Layout view in which you can see the Header and Footer areas.

9 To delete the unused worksheets, click the **Sheet2 tab**, hold down Ctrl, and then click the **Sheet3 tab**.

10 Right-click over one of the selected sheet tabs, and then from the shortcut menu, click **Delete**. Be sure **Sheet1** is the active sheet, and then press Ctrl + Home to cancel the selections and make cell **A1** the active cell.

11 **Save** 🖫 your workbook. Check your *Chapter Assignment Sheet* or *Course Syllabus*, or consult your instructor, to determine if you are to submit your assignments on paper or electronically. To submit electronically, follow the instructions provided by your instructor.

12 To print, from the **Office** menu 🕮, click **Print**. In the **Print** dialog box, under **Print what**, click the **Entire workbook** option button.

13 In the lower left corner of the dialog box, click **Preview**, and notice in the status bar, *Preview: Page 1 of 2* displays.

14 Review the preview of your chart sheet, and then in the **Preview group**, click the **Next Page** button to preview the worksheet containing your data. In the **Print group**, click **Print** to print the two pages.

15 **Save** 🔲 your workbook. If you are instructed to print your formulas on Sheet1, follow the instructions in Activity 9.17 to do so, and then redisplay the worksheet by pressing ⌨Ctrl + `.

16 From the **Office** menu 🔘, click **Close**. If prompted to save changes, click **No** so that you do not save the changes that you made to print your formulas. **Close** ❎ Excel.

Objective 12
Use the Excel Help System

Excel's Help feature provides information about all of Excel's features and displays step-by-step instructions for performing many tasks.

Activity 9.25 Using the Excel Help System

Workbooks that you create in Excel 2007 can be opened in Excel 2003. In this activity, you will use the Microsoft Help feature to learn more about this feature.

1 **Start** Excel. In the upper right corner of your screen, click the **Microsoft Office Excel Help** button 🔵. Alternatively, press ⌨F1. In the displayed window, click the **Search arrow**, and then under **Content from this computer**, click **Excel Help**. In the white box on the left, type **open an Excel 2007 workbook in Excel 2003**

2 Click **Search** or press ⌨Enter. On the list of results, click **Open an Office Excel 2007 workbook in an earlier version of Excel**.

3 If you want to do so, click the **Print** button to print a copy of this information for your reference. Your name will not print.

4 On the title bar of the Excel Help window, click the **Close** button ❎ On the right side of the Microsoft Excel title bar, click the **Close** button ❎ to close Excel.

End **You have completed Project 9B** ——————————

There's More You Can Do!

Close Excel and any other open windows. Display the Start menu, click Computer, and then navigate to the student files that accompany this textbook. From the CD that came with your book, open the folder **02_theres_more_you_can_do**, locate and open the folder for this chapter. Open and print the instructions for this project, which are provided to you in Adobe PDF format.

Try IT!—Change a Chart Type

In this Try It! exercise, you will change the chart type of an existing chart from a column chart to a bar chart.

Content-Based Assessments

Summary

In this chapter, you used Microsoft Office Excel 2007 to create and analyze data organized into columns and rows and to chart and perform calculations on the data. By organizing your data with Excel, you will be able to make logical decisions and create visual representations of your data in the form of charts.

Key Terms

(Key Terms continues on the next page)

The ● symbol represents Key Terms found on the Student CD in the 02_theres_more_you_can_do folder for this chapter

Content-Based Assessments

Key Terms

(Key Terms continued)

Content-Based Assessments

Matching

Match each term in the second column with its correct definition in the first column by writing the letter of the term on the blank line in front of the correct definition.

_____ **1.** An Excel file that contains one or more worksheets.

_____ **2.** The primary document that you use in Excel to store and work with data, and which is formatted as a pattern of uniformly spaced horizontal and vertical lines.

_____ **3.** The intersection of a row and column in an Excel worksheet.

_____ **4.** An element in the Excel window that displays the value or formula contained in the active cell, and in which you can enter or edit values or formulas.

_____ **5.** The box to the left of the Formula Bar that identifies the selected cell, table, chart, or object.

_____ **6.** The user interface in Office 2007 that groups the commands for performing related tasks on tabs across the upper portion of the program window.

_____ **7.** Buttons on the right side of the status bar for viewing in Normal, Page Layout View, or Page Break Preview; also displays controls for zoom out and zoom in.

A Active cell

B Cell

C Cell content

D Cell reference

E Column headings

F Constant value

G Fill handle

H Formula

I Formula Bar

J Name Box

K Range

L Ribbon

M View options

N Workbook

O Worksheet

_____ **8.** The letters at the top of an Excel worksheet that designate the columns.

_____ **9.** Two or more selected cells on a worksheet that are adjacent or nonadjacent, and treated by Excel as a single unit for the purpose of editing.

_____ **10.** The cell, surrounded by a black border, ready to receive data or be affected by the next Excel command.

_____ **11.** The identification of a specific cell by its intersecting column letter and row number.

_____ **12.** Anything typed into a cell.

_____ **13.** Numbers, text, dates, or times of day that you type into a cell.

_____ **14.** An equation that performs mathematical calculations on values in a worksheet.

_____ **15.** The small black square in the lower right corner of a selected cell.

Fill in the Blank

Write the correct answer in the space provided.

1. A set of characters with the same design, size, and shape is called a _____.

2. A specific way in which Excel displays numbers in a cell is referred to as the _____ _____.

3. The default format that Excel applies to numbers, which has no specific characteristics except that trailing zeros to the right of a decimal point will not display, is the _____ format.

4. The data that displays in the Formula Bar is referred to as the _____ _____.

5. A formula prewritten by Excel is a _____.

6. In a formula, the address of a cell based on the relative position of the cell that contains the formula and the cell referred to is a _____ cell reference.

7. The Excel number format that applies a thousand comma separator where appropriate, inserts a fixed U.S. dollar sign aligned at the left edge of the cell, applies two decimal places, and leaves a small amount of space at the right edge of the cell to accommodate a parenthesis for negative numbers is the _____ _____ format.

8. The Excel number format that inserts thousand comma separators where appropriate, applies two decimal places, and leaves space at the right to accommodate a parenthesis for negative numbers is the _____ _____.

9. The area along the bottom of a chart that identifies the categories of data, and which is also referred to as the x-axis, is the _____ axis.

10. A numerical scale on the left side of a chart that shows the range of numbers for the data points, and also referred to as the y-axis, is the _____ axis.

11. In a chart, an explanation of the patterns or colors that are assigned to a data series that represents a category is called the _____.

12. Related data points represented by data markers in a chart, each of which has a unique color or pattern represented in the chart legend, are referred to as a _____ _____.

(Fill in the Blank continues on the next page)

Content-Based Assessments

Fill in the Blank

(Fill in the Blank continued)

13. The combination of chart elements that can be displayed in a chart such as a title, legend, labels for the columns, and the table of charted cells is referred to as the _____ _____.

14. Symbols that specify addition, subtraction, multiplication, division, percentage, and exponentiation in an Excel formula are called _____ _____.

15. A cell reference that refers to cells by their fixed position in a worksheet and which remain the same when the formula is copied is referred to as an _____ cell reference.

Content-Based Assessments

Project 9C — Service

In this project, you will apply the skills you practiced from the Objectives in Project 9A.

Objectives: 1. *Create, Save, and Navigate an Excel Workbook;* **2.** *Enter and Edit Data in a Worksheet;* **3.** *Construct and Copy Formulas, Use the Sum Function, and Edit Cells;* **4.** *Format Data, Cells, and Worksheets;* **5.** *Close and Reopen a Workbook;* **6.** *Chart Data;* **7.** *Use Page Layout View, Prepare a Worksheet for Printing, and Close Excel.*

In the following Skills Review, you will create a worksheet for Ellie Rose, Service Manager at the Rio Rancho Auto Gallery, to track weekly service revenue. Your completed worksheet will look similar to the one shown in Figure 9.71.

For Project 9C, you will need the following file:

New blank Excel workbook

You will save your workbook as 9C_Service_Firstname_Lastname

Figure 9.71

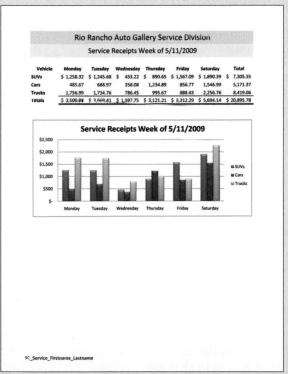

(Project 9C–Service continues on the next page)

Content-Based Assessments

Skills Review

(Project 9C–Service continued)

1. **Start** Excel. In cell **A1**, type **Rio Rancho Auto Gallery Service Division** and then press Enter. In cell **A2**, type **Service Receipts Week of 5/11/2009** and then press Enter. Display the **Save As** dialog box, navigate to your **Excel Chapter 9** folder, and then using your own first and last names, **Save** the workbook as 9C_Service_Firstname_Lastname

2. In cell **A3**, type **Vehicle** and then press Enter. Type **SUVs** and then press Enter. Type **Cars** and then press Enter. Type **Trucks** and then press Enter. In cell **A7**, type **Totals** and then press Enter.

3. In cell **B3**, type **Monday** and then press Enter. Click in cell **B3** again to make it the active cell. In the lower right corner of cell **B3**, point to the fill handle to display the ⊞ pointer, drag the fill handle to the right to cell **G3** so that the last ScreenTip that displays is *Saturday*, and then release the mouse button to fill the days of the week. In cell **H3**, type **Total** and then press Enter.

4. Press Ctrl + Home to move to cell **A1**, and then on the Ribbon, click the **Review tab**. In the **Proofing group**, click **Spelling**, and then correct any spelling errors that you may have made while typing. Beginning in cell **B4**, type the following data:

Vehicle	Monday	Tuesday	Wednesday	Thursday	Friday	Saturday
SUVs	1258.32	1245.68	453.22	890.65	1567.09	1890.39
Cars	485.67	688.97	358.08	1234.89	856.77	1546.99
Trucks	1756.99	1734.76	786.45	995.67	888.43	2256.76

5. From the **column heading area**, select **columns A:G**, and then point to the right boundary of any of the selected column letters to display the ⊞ pointer. Drag to the right until the ScreenTip indicates **75 pixels**, and then release the mouse button to resize the selected columns.

6. Point to the **row 3** heading, and then right-click to simultaneously select the row and display the shortcut menu and the Mini toolbar. From the shortcut menu, click **Insert** to insert a blank row—this will add some space between the worksheet titles and the column titles.

7. Click cell **H5**. On the **Home tab**, in the **Editing group**, click the **Sum** button, and then press Enter to enter the function—a prewritten formula. Your result is *7305.35*. Click cell **H5**, and then drag the fill handle down to cell **H7** to copy the formula. Recall that the cell references will adjust relative to their row.

8. Select the range **B5:H8**, which includes the columns to be totaled and the cells in which each total will display. Hold down Alt and then press = to enter the Sum function in cells **B8:H8**. **Save** your workbook.

9. Select the range **A1:H1**, and then on the **Home tab**, in the **Alignment group**, click the **Merge & Center** button. Select the range **A2:H2**, right-click over the selection, and then on the Mini toolbar, click the **Merge & Center** button. Both worksheet titles are centered over the worksheet.

10. Right-click cell **A1**. On the Mini toolbar, click the **Font Size arrow**, and then click **18**. Then, click the **Fill Color button arrow**, and under **Theme Colors**, in the next to last column, click the third color—**Aqua, Accent 5, Lighter 60%**.

(Project 9C–Service continues on the next page)

Content-Based Assessments

(Project 9C–Service continued)

11. Right-click cell **A2**. On the Mini toolbar, change the **Font Size** to **16**. Click the **Fill Color button arrow**, and then under **Theme Colors**, in the next to last column, click the second color— **Aqua, Accent 5, Lighter 80%**.

12. Select **rows 1** and **2**. Position the ⊞ pointer over the lower border of either of the selected row headings, and then drag down to increase the row height of both rows to **40 pixels**. Then, in the **Alignment group**, click the **Middle Align** button to center the titles vertically in the cells. Select **rows 4:8**, and then increase the row height of all of the selected rows to **24 pixels**.

13. Select the range **A4:H4**. Then, hold down Ctrl, and select the nonadjacent range **A5:A8**, so that both the column and row titles are selected. On the **Home tab**, in the **Font group**, click the **Bold** button. Select the range **A4:H4**, and then in the **Alignment group**, click the **Center** button.

14. Select the range **B5:H5**. Then, hold down Ctrl and select the nonadjacent range **B8:H8**. In the **Number group**, click the **Accounting Number Format** button to apply the format to the selected ranges. Select the range **B6:H7**, and then in the **Number group**, click the **Comma Style** button. Select the range **B8:H8**. In the **Font group**, click the **Borders button arrow**, and then click **Top and Double Bottom Border**. **Save** your workbook.

15. To chart the week's receipts by day and vehicle type, select the range **A4:G7**. On the Ribbon, click the **Insert tab**, and then in the **Charts group**, click **Column**. Under **2-D Column**, click the first chart type—**Clustered Column**. Point to the top border of the chart to display the ⬚ pointer, and then drag to position the chart so that its upper left corner is positioned inside the upper left corner of cell **A11**.

16. On the **Design tab**, in the **Chart Layouts group**, click **Layout 1**. Click in the **Chart Title**, delete the existing text, and then type **Service Receipts Week of 5/11/2009** Click in a white area slightly *inside* the chart's border to deselect the chart title, but leave the chart itself selected. On the **Design tab**, in the **Chart Styles group**, click the **More** button to display the gallery of chart styles. Click **Style 26**.

17. Click the **Layout tab**, and then, in the **Axes group**, click the **Axes** button. Point to **Primary Vertical Axis**, and then click **More Primary Vertical Axis Options**. In the **Format Axis** dialog box, in the column at the left, click **Number**. In the **Decimal places** box, change the number to **0** and then click **Close**.

18. Click any cell to deselect the chart. Click the **Insert tab**, and then in the **Text group**, click the **Header & Footer** button to switch to **Page Layout view** and open the **Header area**. In the **Navigation group**, click the **Go to Footer** button, click just above the word *Footer*, and then in the **Header & Footer Elements group**, click the **File Name** button. Click in a cell just above the footer to exit the footer area and view your file name.

19. Scroll up to view your chart. Click the chart to select it, and notice that the chart is not centered under the data in the cells. Position the pointer over the **right resize handle**, which will display the ⟷ pointer, and then drag to the right so that the right border of the chart is just inside the right border of **column H**.

(Project 9C–Service continues on the next page)

Content-Based Assessments

(Project 9C–Service continued)

20. Click any cell to deselect the chart. Click the **Page Layout tab**. In the **Page Setup group**, click the **Margins** button, and then at the bottom of the **Margins gallery**, click **Custom Margins**. In the **Page Setup** dialog box, under **Center on page**, select the **Horizontally** check box. Click **OK**, and then **Save** the changes to your workbook.

21. On the status bar, click the **Normal** button to return to **Normal view**, and then press Ctrl + Home to move to the top of your worksheet. At the lower edge of the window, click to select the **Sheet2 tab**, hold down Ctrl and click the **Sheet3 tab** to select the two unused sheets. On the **Home tab**, in the **Cells group**, click the **Delete button arrow**, and then from the list, click **Delete Sheet**.

22. **Save** the changes you have made to your workbook. Check your *Chapter Assignment Sheet* or *Course Syllabus* or consult your instructor to determine if you are to submit your assignments on paper or electronically. To submit electronically, follow the instructions provided by your instructor.

23. From the **Office** menu, point to the **Print button**, and then click **Print Preview** to check the placement of your worksheet. In the **Print group**, click the **Print** button. In the **Print** dialog box, under **Print range**, verify that the **All** option button is selected. Under **Print what**, verify that **Active sheet(s)** is selected, and then under **Copies**, verify that the **Number of copies** is **1**. Click **OK** to print your worksheet. If you are directed to submit printed formulas, refer to Activity 9.17 to do so.

24. If you printed your formulas, be sure to redisplay the worksheet by pressing Ctrl + ` . From the **Office** menu, click **Close**. If a dialog box displays asking if you want to save changes, click **No** so that you do *not* save the changes you made for printing formulas. **Exit** Excel.

 You have completed Project 9C

Content-Based Assessments

Skills Review

Project 9D — Tires

In this project, you will apply the skills you practiced from the Objectives in Project 9B.

Objectives: 8. *Design a Worksheet;* **9.** *Construct Formulas for Mathematical Operations;* **10.** *Format Percentages and Move Formulas;* **11.** *Create a Pie Chart and a Chart Sheet.*

In the following Skills Review, you will create a worksheet for Arthur Potempa, Retail Sales Manager of the Rio Rancho Auto Gallery, to track the sales of two different types of tires at the four subsidiary stores that sell only tires. Your completed worksheet will look similar to the one shown in Figure 9.72.

For Project 9D, you will need the following file:

New blank Excel workbook

You will save your workbook as 9D_Tires_Firstname_Lastname

Figure 9.72

(Project 9D–Tires continues on the next page)

Content-Based Assessments

(Project 9D–Tires continued)

1. **Start** Excel and display a new blank workbook. In cell **A1**, type **Rio Rancho Auto Gallery** and then press [Enter]. In cell **A2**, type **February Tire Sales** and then press [Enter]. Select the range **A1:A2**. In the **Font group**, click the **Font arrow**, and then click **Cambria**. Click the **Font Size arrow**, and then click **18**. Display the **Save As** dialog box, navigate to your **Excel Chapter 9** folder, and then using your own first and last names, **Save** the workbook as **9D_Tires_ Firstname_Lastname**

2. In cell **A3**, type **Store Name** and then press [Tab]. In cell **B3**, type **Standard Tires** and then press [Tab]. In cell **C3**, type **Performance Tires** and then press [Tab]. In cell **D3**, type **Total Standard Sales** and then press [Tab]. In cell **E3**, type **Total Performance Sales** and then press [Tab]. In **F3**, type **Total Tire Sales** and then press [Tab]. In cell **G3**, type **Percent of Total Sales** and then press [Enter].

3. In the **column heading area**, point to the right boundary of **column A** to display the ➕ pointer, and then drag to the right to widen the column to **120 pixels**. Select the range **A3:G3**, and then in the **Font group**, click the **Bold** button. In the **Alignment group**, click the **Wrap Text** button, click the **Center** button, and then click the **Middle Align** button. Select **columns B:G**. In the **column heading area**, point to the right boundary of any of the selected columns to display the ➕ pointer, and then drag to the right to increase the column width to **90 pixels**.

4. Select the range **A4:C6**, and then type the following data, pressing [Enter] to move from cell to cell within the selected range.

Store Name	Standard Tires	Performance Tires
Diamond Valley	42	38
Sierra Vista	26	37
Tread Works	35	40

5. In the range **A10:B11**, type the following:

Standard Price	125
Performance Price	235

6. Click cell **D4** and type **=** to begin a formula. Click cell **B4**, type ***** and then click cell **B10** to construct a formula that will multiply the number of Standard Tires sold at the Diamond Valley store by the Standard Price, which is 125. Then, press [F4] to make the reference to cell **B10** absolute so that your formula indicates *=B4*$B$10*.

Because you will copy the formula down for the other two stores, the first cell reference should change relative to each row, but the price, located in cell B10, should remain the same for each formula.

(Project 9D–Tires continues on the next page)

Content-Based Assessments

(Project 9D–Tires continued)

7. Press Enter; your result is *5250*. Select cell **D4** again, and then drag the fill handle down through cell **D6**. Check each formula to be sure that the first cell reference changed relative to the row and that the second cell reference remained absolute—in each formula referring to the price in cell **B10**.

8. In cell **E4**, construct a similar formula to calculate the total sales of Performance Tires at Diamond Valley, using the Performance Price in cell **B11**. Then, copy the formula down through cell **E6** to compute the sales of Performance Tires for the other locations.

9. In cell **F4**, type = and then use the point and click method to construct a formula to add the Total Standard Sales and the Total Performance Sales at the Diamond Valley store; your formula should indicate =D4+E4, and then click the **Enter** button on the **Formula Bar**. Your result is *14180*. With cell **F4** still selected, use the fill handle to copy the formula down to compute the Total Tire Sales for the Sierra Vista store and the Tread Works store.

10. In cell **A7**, type **Total** and then press Enter. Select the range **B4:F7**. On the **Home tab**, in the **Editing group**, click the **Sum** button to calculate totals for each column. Click any cell to deselect. Select the range **D4:F4**, and then hold down Ctrl and select the nonadjacent ranges **D7:F7** and **B10:B11**. On the **Home tab**, in the **Number group**, click **Accounting Number Format**, and then click the **Decrease Decimal** button two times to format the numbers with zero decimal places.

11. Select the range **D5:F6**, in the **Number group**, click **Comma Style**, and then click the **Decrease Decimal** button two times to format the numbers with comma separators and zero decimal places. Select the range **B7:F7**. In the **Font group**, click the **Borders button arrow**, and then from the list, click **Top and Double Bottom Border**.

12. Point to the **row 6** heading and right-click to select the row and display the shortcut menu. Click **Insert** to insert a blank row, and as you type the following data in **A6:C6**, notice that the Total in cell **B8** and cell **C8** recalculates:

Tire Factory	27	26

13. Select the range **D5:F5**, and then drag the fill handle down to fill the three formulas to the range **D6:F6**, which will calculate the sales for the Tire Factory store and recalculate the column totals.

14. Click in cell **G4**, type = click cell **F4**, type / click cell **F8**, and then press F4. Your formula =F4/$F$8 will calculate the percentage by which Diamond Valley's sales contributes to the Rio Rancho Auto Gallery's total tire sales. Press Enter; your result is *0.28713172* or approximately 29 percent. Click cell **G4**, and then use the fill handle to copy the formula down through cell **G7**. In each formula, the first cell reference will change relative to its row, and the second cell reference will remain absolute—referring to the total in cell **F8**.

15. If necessary, select the range **G4:G7**. Right-click over the selection, on the Mini toolbar, click the **Percent Style** button, click the **Center** button, and then click the **Increase Decimal** button two times. Recall that for precise information, you can increase the decimal places in a percentage.

(Project 9D–Tires continues on the next page)

Content-Based Assessments

(Project 9D–Tires continued)

16. Select the range **A1:G1**, and then on the **Home tab**, in the **Alignment group**, click **Merge & Center**. Repeat this formatting for cells **A2:G2**. Select the range **A1:A2**, click the **Fill Color arrow**, and then under **Theme Colors**, in the last column, click **Orange, Accent 6, Lighter 40%**. Right-click the **row 3** heading and insert a blank row to create space between the work-sheet titles and the column titles—recall that the formulas will be moved and adjusted accordingly. On the **Insert tab**, in the **Text group**, click the **Header & Footer** button. In the **Navigation group**, click the **Go to Footer** button. Click just above the word *Footer* in the left section of the **Footer area**, and then in the **Header & Footer Elements group**, click the **File Name** button. Click any cell just above the **Footer area** to deselect the footer and view your file name, and then press Ctrl + Home to move to the top of your worksheet.

17. Click the **Page Layout tab**. In the **Page Setup group**, click the **Orientation** button, and then click **Landscape**. Click the **Margins** button, and then at the bottom of the **Margins gallery**, click **Custom Margins**. In the **Page Setup** dialog box, under **Center on page**, select the **Horizontally** check box. Click **OK**.

18. **Save** the changes you have made. On the right edge of the status bar, click the **Normal** but-ton to return to **Normal view**. Select the range **A4:A8**, hold down Ctrl, and then select the range **F4:F8**. Click the **Insert tab**. In the **Charts group**, click **Pie**, and then under **3-D Pie**, click the first chart—**Pie in 3-D**. On the **Design tab**, in the **Location group**, click the **Move Chart** button. In the **Move Chart** dialog box, click the **New sheet** option button and replace the highlighted text *Chart1* by typing **Tire Sales Chart** Click **OK** to move the pie chart to a separate chart sheet in the workbook.

19. On the **Design tab**, in the **Chart Layouts group**, click **Layout 1**. Click the text *Total Tire Sales*, and then edit to indicate **February Tire Sales** Click inside the white area of the chart to deselect the title. In the **Chart Styles group**, click the **More** button, and then click **Style 8**.

20. To create a footer on your chart sheet, click the **Insert tab**. In the **Text group**, click the **Header & Footer** button, and then in the **Page Setup dialog box**, click the **Custom Footer** button. With the insertion point positioned in the **Left section**, click the seventh button—**Insert File Name**, and then click **OK** two times.

21. Click the **Sheet1 tab** and press Ctrl + Home to cancel the selections. Click the **Sheet2 tab**, hold down Ctrl and click the **Sheet3 tab**, right-click over the selected sheet tabs, and then click **Delete**.

22. **Save** your workbook. Check your *Chapter Assignment Sheet* or *Course Syllabus* or consult your instructor to determine if you are to submit your assignments on paper or electronically. To submit electronically, follow the instructions provided by your instructor.

23. To print, from the **Office** menu, click the **Print** button. In the **Print** dialog box, under **Print what**, click the **Entire workbook** option button. In the lower left corner of the dialog box, click **Preview**, and notice in the status bar, *Preview: Page 1 of 2* displays. Check the preview, in the **Preview group**, click the **Next Page** button, and then in the **Print group**, click **Print** to print the two pages. If you are directed to submit printed formulas, refer to Activity 9.17 to do so.

24. If you printed your formulas, be sure to redisplay the worksheet by pressing Ctrl + `. From the **Office** menu, click **Close**. If a dialog box displays asking if you want to save changes, click **No** so that you do *not* save the changes you made for printing formulas. **Exit** Excel.

End **You have completed Project 9D** _____

Excel
chapternine

Mastering Excel

Project 9E—Compensation

In this project, you will apply the skills you practiced from the Objectives in Projects 9A and 9B.

Objectives: 1. *Create, Save, and Navigate an Excel Workbook;* **2.** *Enter and Edit Data in a Worksheet;* **3.** *Construct and Copy Formulas, Use the Sum Function, and Edit Cells;* **4.** *Format Data, Cells, and Worksheets;* **7.** *Use Page Layout View, Prepare a Worksheet for Printing, and Close Excel;* **9.** *Construct Formulas for Mathematical Operations;* **10.** *Format Percentages and Move Formulas;* **11.** *Create a Pie Chart and a Chart Sheet.*

In the following Mastering Excel project, you will create a worksheet for Clint Williams, Truck Sales Manager of Rio Rancho Auto Gallery. Members of the sales staff are paid a 5 percent commission on their total sales and also receive a small expense allowance to purchase promotional items like mugs, license plate holders, and key chains to give to customers. Your completed worksheet will look similar to Figure 9.73.

For Project 9E, you will need the following file:

New blank Excel workbook

You will save your workbook as
9E_Compensation_Firstname_Lastname

Figure 9.73

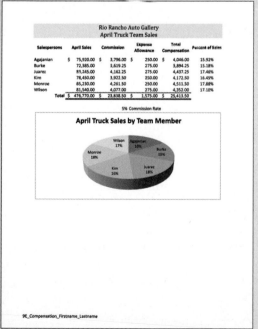

(Project 9E–Compensation continues on the next page)

Content-Based Assessments

(Project 9E–Compensation continued)

1. **Start** Excel and display a new blank workbook. In cell **A1**, type **Rio Rancho Auto Gallery** and in cell **A2**, type **April Truck Team Sales** In cell **A3**, type **Salespersons** and then press Tab. In cell **B3**, type **April Sales** In cell **C3**, type **Commission** In cell **D3**, type **Expense Allowance** In cell **E3**, type **Total Compensation** In cell **F3**, type **Percent of Sales** In your **Excel Chapter 9** folder, **Save** the workbook as **9E_Compensation_Firstname_Lastname**

2. Beginning in cell **A4**, enter the following data:

Salespersons	April Sales	Commission	Expense Allowance
Agajanian	75920		250
Burke	72385		275
Juarez	83245		275
Kim	78450		250
Monroe	85230		250
Wilson	81540		275

3. Apply the **Wrap Text** command to the range **D3:F3**. Widen all the columns to approximately **95 pixels**, and then select the column titles and apply **Bold**, **Center**, and **Middle Align**. **Merge and Center** cells **A1** and **A2** over the column titles. Select the two worksheet titles and change the **Font** to **Cambria**, the **Font Size** to **14**, and apply a **Fill Color** of **Olive Green, Accent 3, Lighter 60%**.

4. In cell **C12**, type **5%** and in cell **D12**, type **Commission Rate** In cell **C4**, construct a formula to calculate the Commission for Agajanian—April Sales times the 5% rate in cell **C12**, using absolute cell references where necessary so that you can copy the formula down. Your result is *3796*. Copy the formula down for the remaining salespersons. In cell **E4**, construct a formula to calculate Agajanian's Total Compensation by adding the Commission plus the Expense Allowance. Your result is *4046*. Copy the formula down for the remaining salespersons.

5. In cell **A10**, type **Total** Then, **Align Text Right** and apply **Bold**. Calculate totals for each of the four columns. Using financial formatting for the appropriate numbers, first apply **Comma Style**, next apply **Accounting Number Format**, and then apply a **Top and Double Bottom Border** to the total row.

6. In cell **F4**, construct a formula to calculate Agajanian's Percent of Sales by dividing Agajanian's April Sales in **B4** by Total April Sales in **B10**, using absolute cell references as necessary so that you copy the formula. Your result is *0.159238207*. Apply **Percent Style**, increase the decimal places to two, and then **Center** the percentage. Fill the formula down for the remaining salespersons.

(Project 9E–Compensation continues on the next page)

Content-Based Assessments

(Project 9E–Compensation continued)

7. Select the range of data containing the name of each salesperson and each salesperson's April Sales. **Insert** a **Pie** chart, using the **Pie in 3-D** chart type. Position the upper left corner of the chart just inside the upper left corner of cell **A13**. Apply **Chart Layout 1**, **Chart Style 5**, and as the **Chart Title**, type **April Truck Sales by Team Member**

8. **Save** your workbook. Click any cell to deselect the chart. On the **Insert tab**, in the **Text group**, click **Header & Footer** to switch to **Page Layout view** and open the **Header area**. In the **Navigation group**, click the **Go to Footer** button, click just above the word *Footer*, and then in the **Header & Footer Elements group**, click the **File Name** button. Click in a cell just above the footer to deselect the **Footer area** and view your file name.

9. Scroll up to view your chart. Select the chart, and then using the ↔ pointer, drag the right sizing handle of the chart as necessary to widen the chart so that the right border of the chart is just inside the right border of **column F**. Deselect the chart. On the **Page Layout tab**, in the **Page Setup group**, click the **Margins** button, and then at the bottom of the **Margins gallery**, click **Custom Margins**. Under **Center on page**, select the **Horizontally** check box, click **OK**, and then **Save** your workbook. Return to **Normal view** and scroll up as necessary to view the top of your worksheet. Select and delete **Sheet2** and **Sheet3**.

10. **Save** the changes to your workbook. To submit electronically, follow the instructions provided by your instructor. To print on paper, from the **Office** menu, preview and then print your worksheet. If you are directed to submit printed formulas, refer to Activity 9.17 to do so. If you printed your formulas, be sure to redisplay the worksheet by pressing Ctrl + `. **Close** your workbook. If a dialog box displays asking if you want to save changes, click **No** so that you do *not* save the changes you made for printing formulas. **Exit** Excel.

End **You have completed Project 9E** ─────────────────────────

Content-Based Assessments

Project 9F—Warranties

In this project, you will apply the skills you practiced from the Objectives in Projects 9A and 9B.

Objectives: 1. *Create, Save, and Navigate an Excel Workbook;* **2.** *Enter and Edit Data in a Worksheet;* **3.** *Construct and Copy Formulas, Use the Sum Function, and Edit Cells;* **4.** *Format Data, Cells, and Worksheets;* **7.** *Use Page Layout View, Prepare a Worksheet for Printing, and Close Excel;* **8.** *Design a Worksheet;* **9.** *Construct Formulas for Mathematical Operations;* **11.** *Create a Pie Chart and a Chart Sheet.*

In the following Mastering Excel project, you will create a workbook for Sandy Cizek, the Auto Sales Manager, which summarizes both the sales of vehicle warranties and the commissions paid on the warranties that were sold. Your completed worksheets will look similar to Figure 9.74.

For Project 9F, you will need the following file:

New blank Excel workbook

You will save your workbook as 9F_Warranties_Firstname_Lastname

Figure 9.74

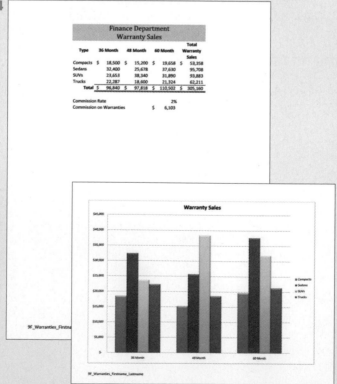

(Project 9F—Warranties continues on the next page)

Content-Based Assessments

(Project 9F—Warranties continued)

1. **Start** Excel and display a new blank workbook. In cell **A1**, type **Finance Department** and in cell **A2**, type **Warranty Sales** In cell **A3**, type **Type** and press [Tab]. In cell **B3**, type **36 Month** In cell **C3**, type **48 Month** In cell **D3**, type **60 Month** In cell **E3**, type **Total Warranty Sales** In your **Excel Chapter 9** folder, **Save** the workbook as **9F_Warranties_Firstname_Lastname**

2. In the range **A4:D7**, type the following data; if you want to do so, select the range first and use [Enter] to confine the movement of the active cell within the range.

Type	36 Month	48 Month	60 Month
Compacts	18500	15200	19658
Sedans	32400	25678	37630
SUVs	23653	38340	31890
Trucks	22287	18600	21324

3. Apply the **Wrap Text** command to cell **E3**. Format all the column titles in **row 3** with **Center**, **Middle Align**, and **Bold**. Adjust the width of **columns B:E** to **80 pixels**. **Merge and Center** the two worksheet titles over columns **A:E**, and then select and format the two titles by changing the **Font** to **Cambria**, the **Font Size** to **16**, and the **Fill Color** to **Red, Accent 2, Lighter 60%**.

4. In cell **E4**, **Sum** all the warranties sold for Compacts, and then copy the formula down for the remaining vehicle types. **Sum** the columns. In cell **A8**, type **Total** and apply **Bold** and **Align Text Right**. Using financial formatting for the appropriate numbers, first apply **Comma Style** with zero decimals, next apply **Accounting Number Format** with zero decimals, and then apply a **Top and Double Bottom Border** to the total row.

5. In cell **A10**, type **Commission Rate** and in cell **D10**, type **2%** In cell **A11**, type **Commission on Warranties** In cell **D11**, construct a formula that multiplies the Total Warranty Sales in cell **E8** by the Commission Rate in **D10**, and then apply **Accounting Number Format** with zero decimals.

6. On the **Insert tab**, in the **Text group**, click **Header & Footer** to switch to **Page Layout view**. In the **Navigation group**, click the **Go to Footer** button, click just above the word *Footer*, and then in the **Header & Footer Elements group**, click the **File Name** button. Click a cell just above the footer to deselect the **Footer area** and view your file name. On the **Page Layout tab**, display the **Margins gallery**, click **Custom Margins**, and then under **Center on page**, select the **Horizontally** check box.

7. Switch to **Normal view** and scroll to the top of your worksheet. Select the range of data that represents the types of vehicles and the warranty sales for each of the three types, including the column titles. **Insert** a **Column** chart, using the **2-D Clustered Column** chart type. Move the chart to a new sheet and name the sheet **Warranty Sales Chart** On the **Design tab**, in the **Data group**, click the **Switch Row/Column** button to display the warranty periods as the

(Project 9F—Warranties continues on the next page)

(Project 9F–Warranties continued)

categories. Apply **Chart Layout 1**, **Chart Style 26**, and change the **Chart Title** to **Warranty Sales** Deselect the chart by clicking in an area outside of the chart. To create a footer on the chart sheet, on the **Insert tab**, click the **Header & Footer** button, create a **Custom Footer** with the file name in the **Left section**.

8. Click the **Sheet1 tab** and press Ctrl + Home to cancel the selections. Select and delete **Sheet2** and **Sheet3**.

9. **Save** your workbook. To submit electronically, follow the instructions provided by your instructor. To print, from the **Office** menu, click the **Print** button. In the **Print** dialog box, under **Print what**, click the **Entire workbook** option button. In the lower left corner of the dialog box, click **Preview**, and notice in the status bar, *Preview: Page 1 of 2* displays. Check the preview, in the **Preview group**, click the **Next Page** button, and then in the **Print group**, click **Print** to print the two pages. If you are directed to submit printed formulas, refer to Activity 9.17 to do so.

10. If you printed your formulas, be sure to redisplay the worksheet by pressing Ctrl + `. From the **Office** menu, click **Close**. If a dialog box displays asking if you want to save changes, click **No** so that you do *not* save the changes you made for printing formulas. **Exit** Excel.

End You have completed Project 9F ⎯⎯⎯⎯⎯⎯⎯⎯⎯⎯⎯⎯⎯⎯⎯⎯⎯⎯⎯

Content-Based Assessments

Mastering Excel

Project 9G—Team Comparison

In this project, you will apply the skills you practiced from all the Objectives in Projects 9A and 9B.

In the following Mastering Excel project, you will create a workbook for Sandy Cizek, Auto Sales Manager, which summarizes the monthly team sales for one of the three auto sales teams at Rio Rancho Auto Gallery. Your completed worksheet will look similar to Figure 9.75.

For Project 9G, you will need the following file:

New blank Excel workbook

You will save your workbook as
9G_Team_Comparison_Firstname_Lastname

Figure 9.75

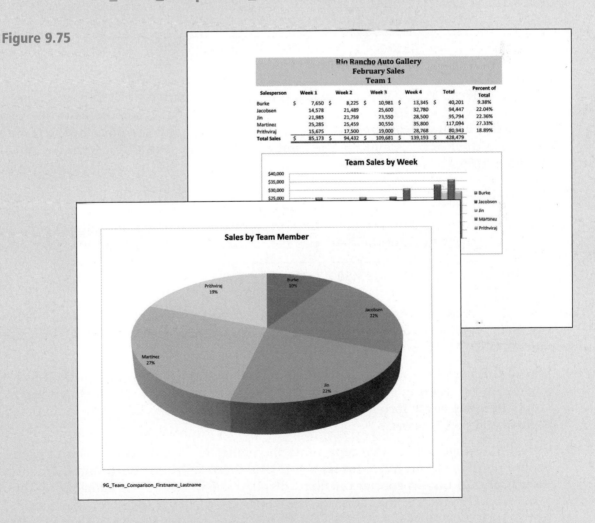

(Project 9G–Team Comparison continues on the next page)

Content-Based Assessments

(Project 9G–Team Comparison continued)

1. **Start** Excel and display a new blank workbook. In cell **A1**, type **Rio Rancho Auto Gallery** In cell **A2**, type **February Sales** In cell **A3**, type **Team 1** In cell **A4**, type **Salesperson** and then press [Tab]. In cell **B4**, type **Week 1** Select cell **B4**, and then use the fill handle to create a series in the range **B4:E4** so that *Week 2* and *Week 3* and *Week 4* display in the cells. In cell **F4**, type **Total** and then in cell **G4**, type **Percent of Total** In your **Excel Chapter 9** folder, **Save** the workbook as **9G_Team_Comparison_Firstname_Lastname**

2. In the range **A5:E8**, type the following data; if you want to do so, select the range first and use [Enter] to confine the movement of the active cell within the range.

Salesperson	Week 1	Week 2	Week 3	Week 4
Burke	7650	8225	10981	13345
Jacobsen	14578	21489	25600	32780
Jin	21985	21759	23550	28500
Prithviraj	15675	17500	19000	28768

3. Apply the **Wrap Text** command to cell **G4**. To all the column titles in **row 4**, apply the **Bold**, **Center**, and **Middle Align** commands. Adjust the width of **columns A:G** to **90 pixels**. **Merge & Center** the three worksheet titles over columns **A:G**, and then format the three titles by changing the **Font** to **Cambria**, the **Font Size** to **16**, the **Fill Color** to **Aqua, Accent 5, Lighter 40%** and applying **Bold**.

4. In cell **A9**, type **Total Sales** and format the cell with **Bold**. **Sum** the rows for each salesperson, and then **Sum** the columns for each week and for the Total. Insert a row above *Prithviraj* and enter the following data—recall that Excel will move and adjust formulas when rows are inserted. After you enter the data, use the fill handle to copy the formula from **F7** to **F8**.

Martinez	25285	25459	30550	35800

5. Using financial formatting for the appropriate numbers, first apply **Comma Style** with zero decimals, next apply **Accounting Number Format** with zero decimals, and then apply a **Top and Double Bottom Border** to the total row.

6. In cell **G5**, construct a formula to calculate the percentage by which Burke's total sales makes up the Total in cell **F10**. Use [F4] to apply absolute cell referencing where necessary. Apply **Percent Style** formatting with two decimals, and then fill the formula down to cell **G9**. **Center** the percentages.

7. Select the range of data that represents the names and each week's sales of each salesperson including the column titles. **Insert** a 2-D Clustered Column chart, and then click the **Switch Row/Column** button so that the chart displays the weeks on the category axis and the salespersons as the data points. Position the upper left corner of the chart in the upper left corner of cell **A12**.

(Project 9G–Team Comparison continues on the next page)

Excel

chapternine   ## Mastering Excel

(Project 9G–Team Comparison continued)

8. Click any cell to deselect the chart. On the **Insert tab**, click the **Header & Footer** button to switch to **Page Layout view**. Click the **Go to Footer** button, click just above the word *Footer*, and then click the **File Name** button. Click a cell just above the footer to deselect the **Footer area** and view your file name. On the **Page Layout tab**, change the **Orientation** to **Landscape**. Display the **Margins gallery**, click **Custom Margins**, and then under **Center on page**, select the **Horizontally** check box.

9. Scroll up, and then use the ⟷ pointer to resize the chart so that its right edge is even with the right side of the data. Format the chart, using **Chart Layout 1**, **Chart Style 26**, and then change the **Chart Title** to **Team Sales by Week**

10. **Save** your workbook, click any cell to deselect the chart, switch to **Normal view**, and then press Ctrl + Home to move to the top of your worksheet. Select the ranges of data that represent each salesperson's name and his or her Total for the month. **Insert** a **Pie** chart, using the **Pie in 3-D** chart type. Move the chart to a new sheet, and then name the sheet **Team Chart** Apply **Chart Layout 1**, **Chart Style 7**, and then change the **Chart Title** to **Sales by Team Member** Deselect the chart by clicking outside of the chart. To create a footer on the chart sheet, on the **Insert tab**, click the **Header & Footer** button, and then create a **Custom Footer** with the file name in the **Left section**.

11. Click the **Sheet1 tab**, and press Ctrl + Home to cancel the selections. Select and delete **Sheet2** and **Sheet3**. **Save** your workbook. Check your *Chapter Assignment Sheet* or *Course Syllabus* or consult your instructor to determine if you are to submit your assignments on paper or electronically. To submit electronically, follow the instructions provided by your instructor.

12. To print, from the **Office** menu, click the **Print** button. In the **Print** dialog box, under **Print what**, click the **Entire workbook** option button. In the lower left corner of the dialog box, click **Preview**, and notice in the status bar, *Preview: Page 1 of 2* displays. Check the preview, in the **Preview group**, click the **Next Page** button, and then in the **Print group**, click **Print** to print the two pages. If you are directed to submit printed formulas, refer to Activity 9.17 to do so.

13. If you printed your formulas, be sure to redisplay the worksheet by pressing Ctrl + `. From the **Office** menu, click **Close**. If a dialog box displays asking if you want to save changes, click **No** so that you do *not* save the changes you made for printing formulas. **Exit** Excel.

End You have completed Project 9G ——————————————————

Content-Based Assessments

Project 9H — *GO!* Fix It

In this project, you will construct a solution by applying any combination of the skills you practiced from the Objectives in Projects 9A and 9B.

For Project 9H, you will need the following file:

e09H_Accessories

You will save your workbook as
9H_Accessories_Firstname_Lastname

From the student files that accompany this textbook, locate and open the file **e09H_Accessories**, and then save the file in your chapter folder as **9H_Accessories_Firstname_Lastname**

In this project, you will edit the first draft of an Excel workbook that contains information about sales of automotive electronic accessories. The workbook was prepared for Arthur Potempa, Retail Accessories Manager of Rio Rancho Auto Gallery.

This workbook contains **ten errors** that you must find and correct. Read and examine the workbook and then edit to correct the errors that you find. Types of errors could include:

- Spelling, grammar, and punctuation errors in cells, charts, worksheet tabs, or file names.

- Errors in data entry and workbook layout. Formatting errors in text, numbers, alignment, indents and spacing, tabs, wrapping, merge and center, text direction and orientation, fonts, borders, patterns, protection, AutoFormat, conditional formatting, data sort, filter, and validation.

- Formula and function errors such as incorrect and missing formulas, error indicators and values, relative versus absolute cell referencing, What-If Analysis, Paste Special, function arguments, and Goal Seek.

- Errors in object design, layout, and formatting; for example, chart type, location, data source, elements, size, scale, positioning, pictures, and hyperlinks.

- Row and column formatting errors such as height, width, and AutoFit.

- Worksheet, tab design, and formatting errors such as missing or blank worksheets, worksheet tab colors, and locations.

- Page setup errors such as page orientation and scaling, margins and centering, headers and footers, sheet gridlines, and row and column headings.

(Project 9H–*GO!* Fix It continues on the next page)

Excel
chapternine

Mastering Excel

(Project 9H–*GO!* Fix It continued)

To complete the project you should know that in this workbook:

- Formula errors in a *range* of cells count as a *single* error.
- Cell A2 should be centered horizontally and vertically.
- Chart design should be Style 3.
- Chart title should be changed to February Sales Chart.

Save the changes you have made, add the file name to the worksheet footers, and then submit as directed.

End **You have completed Project 9H** ———————————————

Outcomes-Based Assessments

Excel
chapternine

Rubric

The following outcomes-based assessments are *open-ended assessments*. That is, there is no specific correct result; your result will depend on your approach to the information provided. Make *Professional Quality* your goal. Use the following scoring rubric to guide you in *how* to approach the problem and then to evaluate *how well* your approach solves the problem.

The *criteria*—Software Mastery, Content, Format and Layout, and Process—represent the knowledge and skills you have gained that you can apply to solving the problem. The *levels of performance*—Professional Quality, Approaching Professional Quality, or Needs Quality Improvements—help you and your instructor evaluate your result.

	Your completed project is of Professional Quality if you:	Your completed project is Approaching Professional Quality if you:	Your completed project Needs Quality Improvements if you:
1-Software Mastery	Choose and apply the most appropriate skills, tools, and features and identify efficient methods to solve the problem.	Choose and apply some appropriate skills, tools, and features, but not in the most efficient manner.	Choose inappropriate skills, tools, or features, or are inefficient in solving the problem.
2-Content	Construct a solution that is clear and well organized, contains content that is accurate, appropriate to the audience and purpose, and is complete. Provide a solution that contains no errors of spelling, grammar, or style.	Construct a solution in which some components are unclear, poorly organized, inconsistent, or incomplete. Misjudge the needs of the audience. Have some errors in spelling, grammar, or style, but the errors do not detract from comprehension.	Construct a solution that is unclear, incomplete, or poorly organized; contains some inaccurate or inappropriate content; and contains many errors of spelling, grammar, or style. Do not solve the problem.
3-Format and Layout	Format and arrange all elements to communicate information and ideas, clarify function, illustrate relationships, and indicate relative importance.	Apply appropriate format and layout features to some elements, but not others. Overuse features, causing minor distraction.	Apply format and layout that does not communicate information or ideas clearly. Do not use format and layout features to clarify function, illustrate relationships, or indicate relative importance. Use available features excessively, causing distraction.
4-Process	Use an organized approach that integrates planning, development, self-assessment, revision, and reflection.	Demonstrate an organized approach in some areas, but not others; or, use an insufficient process of organization throughout.	Do not use an organized approach to solve the problem.

Problem Solving

Project 9I—Rims

In this project, you will construct a solution by applying any combination of the skills you practiced from the Objectives in Projects 9A and 9B.

For Project 9I, you will need the following file:

New blank Excel workbook

**You will save your workbook as
9I_Rims_Firstname_Lastname**

Rio Rancho Auto Gallery stocks one brand of tire rims and in January sold 10 16-inch rims priced at $150 each, 20 18-inch rims priced at $225 each, 32 20-inch rims priced at $375 each, and 16 22-inch rims priced at $500 each. The installation fee for all rims is $50 each.

Create a spreadsheet detailing this information and include a column that calculates the Installed Price for each rim size (Price + Installation Fee) and the Total Sales for each rim size (Installed Price times Number Sold). Total the columns to calculate the total number of rims sold and the Total Sales of all rims. Add an additional column in which you create a formula that calculates the Percent of Sales that each rim size is of the Total Sales of all rim sales. Create a 3-D pie chart that compares the Total Sales generated by each rim size. Position the pie chart below the data on the worksheet.

Create a title that identifies the worksheet and apply appropriate formats to the data and the pie chart. Use borders, fill colors, and font styles and font sizes to format a professional worksheet. Add a footer that includes the file name, and center the worksheet on the page. Save the workbook as **9I_Rims_Firstname_Lastname** and submit it as directed.

End **You have completed Project 9I** _____

Outcomes-Based Assessments

Problem Solving

Project 9J — Finance

In this project, you will construct a solution by applying any combination of the skills you practiced from the Objectives in Projects 9A and 9B.

For Project 9J, you will need the following file:

New blank Excel workbook

You will save your workbook as
9J_Finance_Firstname_Lastname

In this project, you will create a worksheet for Tony Konecki, President of Rio Rancho Auto Gallery, which specifies, by quarter, the amount of credit extended to customers on vehicle purchases during the past fiscal year. The data is organized according to customer credit scores—overall, more credit was given to customers with higher credit scores. Create a worksheet with appropriate titles, and then enter the following data for Quarters 1 through 4.

Credit Score	Quarter 1	Quarter 2	Quarter 3	Quarter 4
750 or Above	350190	322489	368700	385644
700- 749	425654	496451	485200	501780
650- 699	328976	298560	316789	335679
600- 649	489561	462312	475232	490520
550- 599	182597	215600	202450	228600
Under 550	162487	175800	186532	188423

Calculate totals for each quarter and for each credit score, and then create a column chart that compares the amounts for each quarter by credit score. A chart layout that places the legend at the bottom of the chart will allow more space for the columns. Use formatting and editing techniques so that the worksheet and chart are professional and accurate. Add the file name to the footer and save the workbook as **9J_Finance_Firstname_ Lastname** Submit the project as directed.

End **You have completed Project 9J** ⸻⸻⸻

Outcomes-Based Assessments

Problem Solving

Project 9K — Service

In this project, you will construct a solution by applying any combination of the skills you practiced from the Objectives in Projects 9A and 9B.

For Project 9K, you will need the following file:

New blank Excel workbook

You will save your workbook as
9K_Service_Firstname_Lastname

In this project, you will create a worksheet for the service department to analyze the labor costs associated with different types of repairs during the current month. Create an appropriate worksheet title and then enter the following data and column headings.

Service	Hours to Complete Service	Cost for Service at Standard Rate	Number Completed During June	Total Labor Cost
Valve replacement	8		13	
Head gasket	12		12	
Transmission	15		10	
Engine replacement	15		11	
Total Labor Cost				

Two rows below the Total Labor Cost row, in column A, type **Standard Labor Rate** and in column B, type **35.75** In the Cost for Service at Standard Rate column, construct a formula to calculate the cost to complete each type of service at the standard rate. In the Total Labor Cost column, construct a formula to calculate the total labor cost for each of the services completed during the month.

Add a column to the worksheet with the column heading **Percent of Total Labor Cost** and calculate the percent that each service is of the Total Labor Cost. Create a pie chart on a separate chart sheet that compares the Total Labor Costs by Service. Add the file name to the footer in both sheets and check for spelling errors. Save the workbook as **9K_Service_Firstname_Lastname** and submit it as directed.

End You have completed Project 9K ————————————

More on your Student CD

The instructions for the following additional end-of-chapter projects are on your student CD in the folder 03_additional_end_of_chapter_projects.

Content-Based Assessments	
Project L Mastering Excel	Apply the skills you practiced in Project A.
Project M Mastering Excel	Apply the skills you practiced in Project B.
Project N Business Running Case	Apply the skills you practiced in Projects A and B while helping an entrepreneur with the daily tasks of running a business. In each chapter, this project focuses on applying the skills you have practiced in Projects A and B to a business. The project related to this business runs throughout the textbook. You will see how the Office applications relate to the day-to-day operation of a small business called Nelson Architectural Planning.

Outcomes-Based Assessments	
Project O Problem Solving	Construct a solution by applying any combination of the skills you practiced from Projects A and B.
Project P Problem Solving	Construct a solution by applying any combination of the skills you practiced from Projects A and B.
Project Q You and GO!	Construct a solution that applies to your own life by applying any combination of the skills you practiced from Projects A and B.
Project R GO! with Help	Practice using Microsoft Office's Help Feature.
Project S Group Business Running Case	Work as part of a group to apply the skills you have gained thus far to help the Bell Orchid Hotel Group achieve its business goals.

Multimedia

The following multimedia accompany this textbook:

Companion Web site *www.prenhall.com/go*	An interactive Web site designed to reinforce and test your understanding of the skills in this chapter.
AV-EDDs	In the folder in the front of this book you will find videos that demonstrate the objectives in the A and B projects in this chapter. These may help you understand how to complete the projects in this book.
Video Podcasts	In the folder in the front of this book are videos that can be played on your iPod, MP3 player, or computer. These videos demonstrate how to complete the more challenging objectives in this textbook.

chapterten

Managing Workbooks and Analyzing Data

OBJECTIVES

At the end of this chapter you will be able to:

1. Create and Save a Workbook from an Existing Workbook
2. Navigate a Workbook and Rename Worksheets
3. Enter Dates, Clear Contents, and Clear Formats
4. Move, Copy, and Paste Cell Contents
5. Edit and Format Multiple Worksheets at the Same Time
6. Create a Summary Sheet
7. Format and Print Multiple Worksheets in a Workbook

8. Design a Worksheet for What-If Analysis
9. Perform What-If Analysis
10. Compare Data with a Line Chart

OUTCOMES

Mastering these objectives will enable you to:

PROJECT 10A

Create a Summary Sheet from Multiple Worksheets

PROJECT 10B

Make Projections Using What-If Analysis

The City of Golden Grove

Golden Grove is a California city located between Los Angeles and San Diego, about 20 miles from the Pacific shore. Ten years ago the population was just over 200,000; today it has grown to over 300,000. Community leaders focus on quality and economic development in decisions about housing, open space, education, and infrastructure, making the city a model for other communities its size. The city provides many recreational and cultural opportunities with a large park system and a thriving arts community.

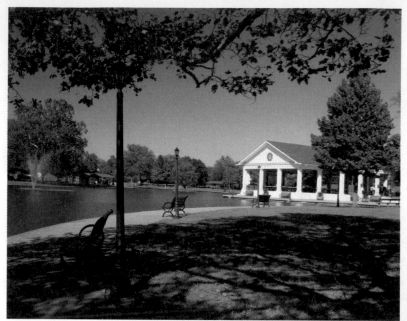

© Stan Rohrer / Courtesy of www.istockphoto.com

Managing Workbooks and Analyzing Data

Organizations typically create workbooks that contain multiple worksheets. In such a workbook, the first worksheet usually summarizes the detailed information in the other worksheets. To make it easier to work with multiple worksheets, there are techniques to enter data into multiple worksheets simultaneously by grouping the worksheets. You can also copy, and then paste information from one worksheet to another. Additional techniques for managing workbooks with multiple worksheets include naming and color coding the sheet tabs so that you can quickly locate the detailed information you are looking for.

In Excel, you can explore options by recalculating formulas that depend on other formulas. For example, you can change the interest rate in a table of loan payments to determine the amount of monthly payments based on differing interest rates.

In this chapter, you will work with workbooks that contain multiple worksheets and analyze data by making projections of future growth.

Project 10A Ticket Sales

In Activities 10.01 through 10.10, you will edit an existing Excel workbook for Judith Amaya, the Director of Arts and Parks for Golden Grove. The annual Summer Fair and Arts Festival will be held during the last week in August. During the first week in August, the city is preselling tickets at three locations in the city. The four worksheets of your completed workbook will look similar to Figure 10.1.

For Project 10A, you will need the following file:

e10A_Ticket_Sales

You will save your workbook as
10A_Ticket_Sales_Firstname_Lastname

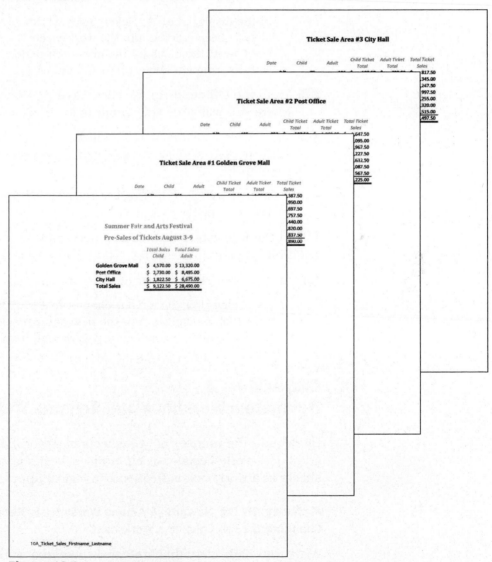

Figure 10.1
Project 10A—Ticket Sales

Objective 1
Create and Save a Workbook from an Existing Workbook

Within a workbook, individual worksheets may contain data for separate topics, locations, or periods of time related to the workbook's data. In such a workbook, it is common practice to have one worksheet that summarizes information from the other worksheets.

Activity 10.01 Creating and Saving a Workbook from an Existing Workbook

Judith has a workbook with worksheets into which she can record the number of tickets sold at the three locations during the first week in August.

1 **Start** Excel. From the **Office** menu 🏢, click **Open**. In the displayed **Open** dialog box, navigate to the student files that accompany this textbook, and then open **e10A_Ticket_Sales**.

> In the displayed e10A_Ticket_Sales workbook, some information has already been entered into the worksheets. For example, on the first worksheet, the dates for the one-week period have been entered, along with information about the ticket prices.

2 From the **Office** menu 🏢, click **Save As**. Navigate to the drive location where you will store your projects for this chapter.

3 On the **Save As** dialog box toolbar, click the **New Folder** button 🖿. With the text *New Folder* selected, type **Excel Chapter 10** and then press Enter.

> Windows creates the *Excel Chapter 10* folder and makes it the active folder in the Save As dialog box.

4 In the **File name** box, edit as necessary to indicate, using your own first and last names, **10A_Ticket_Sales_Firstname_Lastname**

5 In the lower right corner of the **Save As** dialog box, click **Save**.

> Excel saves the file in your chapter folder with the new name. The workbook redisplays, and the new name displays in the title bar. Use this technique to create a new workbook from an existing workbook.

Objective 2
Navigate a Workbook and Rename Worksheets

By default, the number of worksheets in a workbook is three. You can add additional worksheets or delete unused worksheets. Using multiple worksheets in a workbook is frequently a logical approach to arranging data.

Activity 10.02 Navigating Among Worksheets, Renaming Worksheets, and Changing the Tab Color of a Worksheet

When you have more than one worksheet in a workbook, you can *navigate* (move) among worksheets by clicking the *sheet tabs*. Sheet tabs identify each worksheet in a workbook and are located along the lower left edge of the workbook window. When you have more worksheets in the workbook than can be displayed in the sheet tab area, use the four sheet tab scrolling buttons to move sheet tabs into and out of view.

Excel names the first worksheet in a workbook *Sheet1* and each additional worksheet in order—*Sheet2*, *Sheet3*, and so on. Most Excel users rename the worksheets with names that are more meaningful. In this activity, you will navigate among three worksheets. You will also rename each worksheet and change the tab color of the sheet tabs.

1 Along the bottom of the Excel window, point to and then click the **Sheet2 tab**. Compare your screen with Figure 10.2.

> The second worksheet in the workbook displays and becomes the active worksheet. *Sheet2* displays in bold.

Figure 10.2

Sheet tabs with
Sheet2 active sheet

Sheet tab scrolling buttons

2 In cell **A1**, notice the text *Area #2*—this worksheet will contain data for Summer Fair tickets purchased at the Area #2 location. Click the **Sheet1 tab**.

> The first worksheet becomes the active worksheet, and cell A1, which is formatted with an orange background, displays *Area #1*.

3 Point to the **Sheet3 tab**, right-click, and then click **Rename**. With *Sheet3* selected, type **City Hall** and then press [Enter].

4 Point to the **Sheet1 tab**, and then double-click to select its name. Type **Golden Grove Mall** and then press [Enter]. Using either of the two methods you just practiced, rename **Sheet2** as **Post Office**

5 Right-click the **Golden Grove Mall sheet tab**. On the shortcut menu, point to **Tab Color** to display the colors associated with the workbook's theme. Under **Theme Colors**, locate and click **Purple, Accent 4, Lighter 40%**.

When the sheet is active, the tab color displays as an underline.

6 Click the **Post Office** sheet tab to make it the active sheet. On the Ribbon's **Home tab**, in the **Cells group**, click the **Format** button, and then from the displayed list, point to **Tab Color**.

7 Under **Theme Colors**, click **Aqua, Accent 5, Lighter 40%**. Using either of the two techniques you just practiced, change the **Tab Color** of the **City Hall** worksheet to **Orange, Accent 6, Lighter 40%**. Compare your screen with Figure 10.3.

Figure 10.3

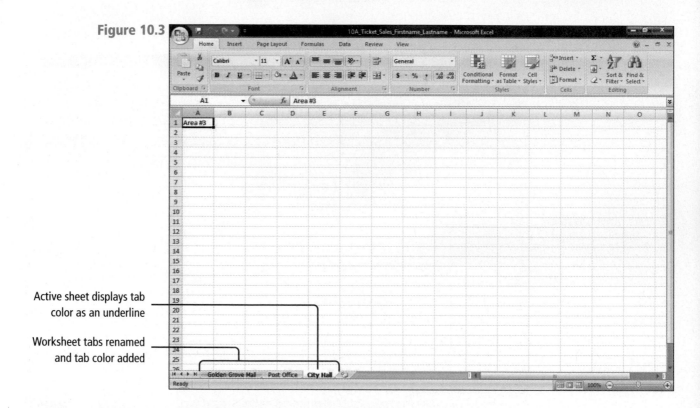

Active sheet displays tab color as an underline

Worksheet tabs renamed and tab color added

8 **Save** 🖫 the changes to your workbook.

Objective 3
Enter Dates, Clear Contents, and Clear Formats

Dates represent a type of value that you can enter in a cell. When you enter a date, Excel assigns a serial value—a number—to the date. This makes it possible to treat dates like other numbers. For example, if two cells contain dates, you can find the number of days between the two dates by subtracting the older date from the more recent date.

Activity 10.03 Entering and Formatting Dates

In this activity, you will examine the various ways that Excel can format a date that you type into a cell. Date values entered in any of the following formats will be recognized by Excel as a date:

Format	Example
m/d/yy	7/4/09
d-mmm	4-Jul
d-mmm-yy	4-Jul-09
mmm-yy	Jul-09

On your keyboard, ⊟ (the hyphen key) and ⟋ (the forward slash key) function identically in any of these formats and can be used interchangeably. You can abbreviate the month name to three characters or spell it out. You can enter the year as two digits, four digits, or even leave it off. When left off, the current year is assumed but does not display in the cell.

A two-digit year value of 30 through 99 is interpreted by the Windows operating system as the four-digit years of 1930 through 1999. All other two-digit year values are assumed to be in the 21st century. If you always type year values as four digits, even though only two digits may display in the cell, you can be sure that Excel interprets the year value as you intended. See the table in Figure 10.4 for examples.

How Excel Interprets Dates	
Date Typed As:	**Completed by Excel As:**
7/4/09	7/4/2009
7-4-98	7/4/1998
7/4	4-Jul (current year assumed)
7-4	4-Jul (current year assumed)
July 4	4-Jul (current year assumed)
Jul 4	4-Jul (current year assumed)
Jul/4	4-Jul (current year assumed)
Jul-4	4-Jul (current year assumed)
July 4, 1998	4-Jul-98
July 2009	Jul-09 (first day of month assumed)
July 1998	Jul-98 (first day of month assumed)

Figure 10.4

1 Click the **Golden Grove Mall sheet tab**. Click cell **A5** and notice that the cell indicates *8/3* (August 3). In the **Formula Bar**, notice that the full date of August 3, 2009 displays in the format *8/3/2009*.

2 With cell **A5** selected, on the Ribbon, in the **Number group**, click the **Number Format arrow**. From the bottom of the displayed menu, click **More Number Formats** to display the **Number tab** of the **Format Cells** dialog box. Compare your screen with Figure 10.5.

Under Category, *Date* is selected, and under Type, *3/14* is selected. All of the dates in Column A were formatted using this format type; that is, only the month and day display in the cell.

Figure 10.5

Format Cells dialog box
Number tab active
8/3 displays in Sample box
Date category selected
3/14 indicated as Type

3 In the displayed dialog box, under **Type**, click several other date types and watch the **Sample** area to see how applying the selected date format would format your cell. When you are finished, click the **3/14** type, and then at the bottom of the dialog box, click **OK**.

4 Click cell **A21**, type **8/10/2009** and then press Enter.

Cell A21 has no special date formatting applied, and thus displays in the default date format *8/10/2009*.

Alert!

The date does not display as 8/10/2009?

Settings in your Windows operating system determine the default format for dates. If your result is different, it is likely that the formatting of the default date was adjusted on the computer at which you are working.

5 Click cell **A21** again. Hold down Ctrl and press ; (the semicolon key) on your keyboard. Press Enter to confirm the entry.

Excel enters the current date, obtained from your computer's internal calendar, using the default date format. Ctrl + ; is a quick method to enter the current date.

6 Click cell **A21** again, type **8/10/09** and then press Enter.

> Because the year *09* is less than 30, Excel assumes a 21st century date and changes *09* to *2009* to complete the four-digit year. Typing *98* would result in *1998*. For two-digit years that you type that are between 30 and 99, Excel assumes a 20th century date.

7 Click cell **A5**, and then on the **Home tab**, in the **Clipboard group**, click the **Format Painter** button. Click cell **A21**, and notice that the date format from cell **A5** is copied to cell **A21**. **Save** your workbook.

Activity 10.04 Clearing Cell Contents and Formats

A cell has contents—a value or a formula—and a cell may also have one or more formats applied, for example bold and italic font styles, fill color, font color, and so on. You can choose to clear the contents of a cell, the formatting of a cell, or both. You can clear—delete—the contents of a selected cell in two ways: Press Del or use the Clear Contents command available both from the Editing group on the Ribbon and from a shortcut menu.

Clearing the contents of a cell deletes the value or formula typed there, but it does *not* clear formatting applied to a cell. In this activity, you will clear the contents of a cell and then clear the formatting of a cell that contains a date to see its underlying content.

1 On the **Golden Grove Mall** worksheet, click cell **A1**. On the Ribbon, in the **Editing group**, click the **Clear** button. From the displayed list, click **Clear Contents**. Click cell **A2**, and then press Delete.

> You can use either of these two methods to delete the *contents* of a cell. Deleting the contents does not, however, delete the formatting of the cell; you can see that the orange fill color format applied to the two cells still displays.

2 In cell **A1**, type **Area #1** and then on the **Formula Bar**, click the **Enter** button ✓ so that cell **A1** remains the active cell. In the **Editing group**, click the **Clear** button, and then from the displayed menu, click **Clear Formats**.

> Clearing the formats deletes formatting from the cell—the orange fill color and the bold and italic font styles—but does not delete the cell's contents.

3 Use the same technique to clear the orange fill color from cell **A2**.

4 Click cell **A5**, click the **Clear** button, and then click **Clear Formats**. In the **Number group**, notice that *General* displays as the number format of the cell.

> The box at the top of the Number group indicates the current Number format of the selected cell. Clearing the date formatting from the cell displays the date's serial number. The date, August 3, 2009, is stored as a serial number that indicates the number of days since January 1, 1900. This date is the 40,028th day since the reference date of January 1, 1900.

5 On the **Quick Access Toolbar**, click the **Undo** button to restore the date format. **Save** your workbook, and then compare your screen with Figure 10.6.

Figure 10.6

Date in Formula Bar

Orange fill color and bold italic font style cleared from cell A1

Contents and formats of cell A2 deleted

A5 reformatted as a date

Date indicated as the Number format

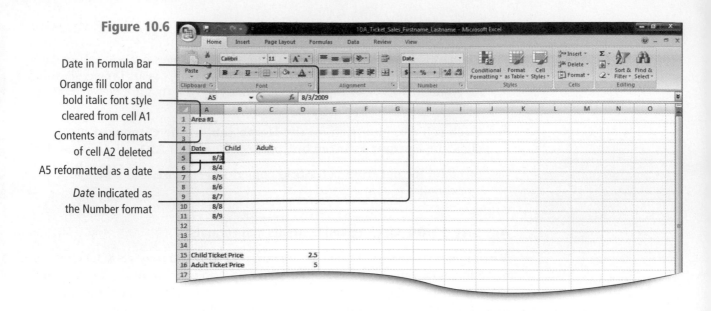

Objective 4
Move, Copy, and Paste Cell Contents

Data in cells can be copied to other cells in the same worksheet, to other sheets in the same workbook, or to sheets in another workbook. Likewise, data can be moved from one place to another. The action of placing cell contents that have been copied or moved to the Office Clipboard to another location is called **paste**.

Activity 10.05 Copying, Pasting, and Moving Cell Contents

The **Office Clipboard** is a temporary storage area maintained by your Windows operating system. When you select one or more cells, and then perform the Copy command or the Cut command, the selected data is placed on the Office Clipboard. From the Office Clipboard storage area, the data is available for pasting into other cells, other worksheets, other workbooks, and even into other Office programs.

1 On the **Golden Grove Mall** sheet, select the range **A20:A21**. Point to the upper edge of the black border surrounding the selected cells until the pointer displays. Drag upward until the ScreenTip displays *A18:A19*, as shown in Figure 10.7, and then release the mouse button to complete the move.

> Using this technique, cell contents can be moved from one location to another; this is referred to as **drag and drop**.

Figure 10.7

ScreenTip displays *A18:A19*

2 Select the range **A4:D16**.

> A range of cells identical to this one is required for the *Post Office* worksheet and the *City Hall* worksheet.

3 On the **Home tab**, in the **Clipboard group**, click the **Copy** button to place a copy of the selected cells on the Office Clipboard. Alternatively, press Ctrl + C or right-click over the selected range, and then click Copy from the shortcut menu.

> A moving border surrounds the selected range, and a message on the left side of the status bar indicates *Select destination and press ENTER or choose Paste*. These two results confirm that your selected range has been placed on the Office Clipboard.

4 At the bottom of the workbook window, click the **Post Office sheet tab** to make it the active worksheet. Click cell **A4**, and then on the **Home tab**, in the **Clipboard group**, click the **Paste** button. Alternatively, use the keyboard shortcut for Paste, which is Ctrl + V. Compare your screen with Figure 10.8.

> The selected cells from the first worksheet are copied from the Office Clipboard to the second worksheet. When pasting a range of cells, you need only select the cell in the upper left corner of the *paste area*—the target destination for data that has been cut or copied using the Office Clipboard.

Figure 10.8

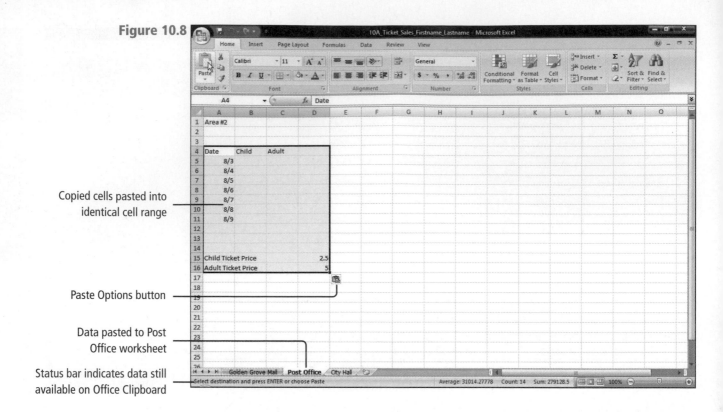

Copied cells pasted into identical cell range

Paste Options button

Data pasted to Post Office worksheet

Status bar indicates data still available on Office Clipboard

---

Note — **Pressing Enter to Complete a Paste Action**

Pressing Enter pastes the text and removes it from the Office Clipboard. Thus, if you want to paste the same text more than one time, click the Paste button so that the copied text remains available on the Office Clipboard.

---

5 In the lower right corner of the paste area, click the **Paste Options** button.

The *Paste Options button*, which displays just below your pasted selection after you perform the paste operation, displays a list of options that lets you determine how the information is pasted into your worksheet. The list varies depending on the type of content you are pasting and the program you are pasting from.

6 Click any cell to close the list and deselect the paste area. In the status bar, notice that the message still displays, indicating that your selected range remains on the Office Clipboard. Click the **City Hall sheet tab** to make it the active sheet, and then click cell **A4**. In the **Clipboard group**, click the **Paste** button.

7 On the **Home tab**, in the **Clipboard group**, click the **Clipboard Dialog Box Launcher** button, and then compare your screen with Figure 10.9.

The Clipboard task pane displays, and you can view your selection on the Clipboard. Here you can clear your selection from the Clipboard, although it is not necessary to do so.

Figure 10.9

Clipboard Dialog Box
Launcher button

Clipboard task pane

Your copied range displays

Close button

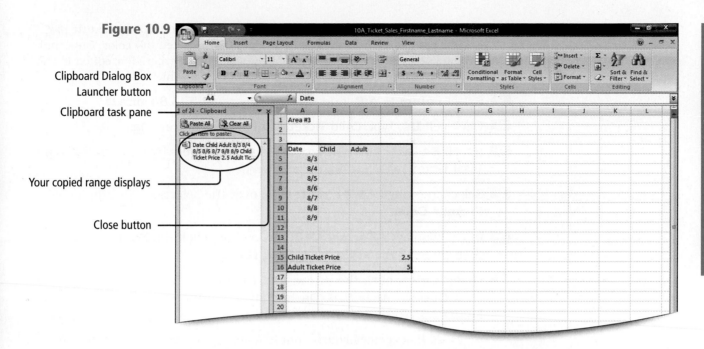

8 In the upper right corner of the **Office Clipboard task pane**, click the **Close** button ⊠ . Display the **Golden Grove Mall** sheet. Press Esc to cancel the moving border.

> The status bar no longer displays the message.

9 Save 🖬 your changes.

Objective 5
Edit and Format Multiple Worksheets at the Same Time

You can enter or edit data on several worksheets at the same time by selecting and grouping multiple worksheets. Data that you enter or edit on the active sheet is reflected in all selected sheets. If you apply color to the sheet tabs, the name of the sheet tab will be underlined in the color you selected. If the sheet tab displays with a background color, the sheet has not been selected.

Activity 10.06 Wrapping Text in a Cell in Several Worksheets at the Same Time

If you want text to appear on multiple lines within a single cell, you can format the cell so that the text wraps automatically, or you can enter a manual line break. In this activity, you will group the worksheets for the three ticket sales locations, and then format additional column titles with wrapped text on all the worksheets at the same time.

1 With the **Golden Grove Mall** worksheet as the active sheet, press Ctrl + Home to make cell **A1** the active cell. Point to the sheet tab, right-click, and then from the displayed menu, click **Select All Sheets**. At the top of your screen, look at the title bar and notice that *[Group]* displays.

All the worksheets are selected, as indicated by *[Group]* in the title bar and the sheet tab names underlined in the selected tab color. Data that you enter or edit on the active sheet will also be entered or edited in the same manner on all the selected sheets in the same cells.

2 Select **columns A:F**, and then set their width to **83 pixels**.

3 Click cell **D4**, type **Child Ticket Total** and then press Tab.

4 In cell **E4**, type **Adult Ticket Total** and then press Tab. In cell **F4**, type **Total Ticket Sales** and then press Enter.

5 Select the range **A4:F4**, right-click over the selection, and then click **Format Cells**.

6 In the displayed **Format Cells** dialog box, click the **Font tab**, and then under **Font style**, click **Bold Italic**.

7 Under **Color**, click the arrow, and then under **Theme Colors**, click **Orange, Accent 6, Darker 25%**. Compare your screen with Figure 10.10.

> Recall that commonly used font formats are also available from the Font group on the Ribbon. However, when applying multiple formats to selected cells, it is efficient to do so from the Format Cells dialog box.

Figure 10.10

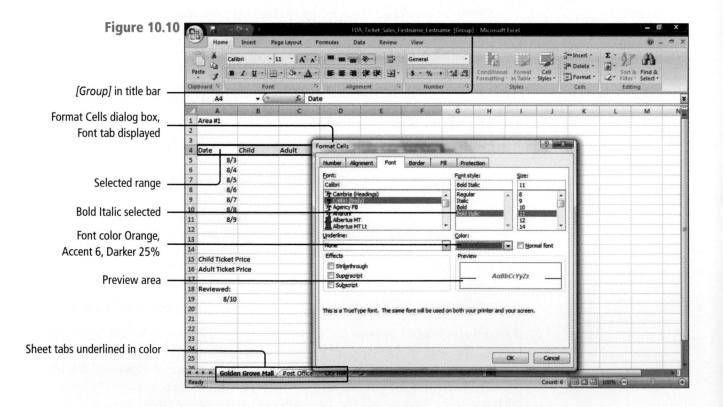

[Group] in title bar

Format Cells dialog box, Font tab displayed

Selected range

Bold Italic selected

Font color Orange, Accent 6, Darker 25%

Preview area

Sheet tabs underlined in color

8 In the **Format Cells** dialog box, click the **Alignment tab**.

> Here you can change the alignment of text in the selected range.

9 Under **Text alignment**, click the **Horizontal arrow**, and then from the displayed list, click **Center**.

10 Click the **Vertical arrow**, and then from the displayed list, click **Center**. Under **Text control**, click to select—place a check mark in—the **Wrap text** check box.

Data in the cell will wrap to fit the column width; a change in column width will automatically adjust the wrapping of the text.

Another Way

To Wrap Text or Start a New Line in a Cell

To wrap text in a cell or range of cells, select the specific cells, and then in the Alignment group, click the Wrap Text button.

To start a new line of text at a specific point in a cell, regardless of column width, double-click the cell, click the location where you want to break the line in the cell, and then press [Alt] + [Enter] to insert a line break.

11 At the bottom of the dialog box, click **OK**, and then compare your screen with Figure 10.11.

All the formats that you selected in the Format Cells dialog box are applied to the selected range of cells. Those formats that have buttons on the Ribbon are shown as being selected.

Figure 10.11
Center and Middle
Align buttons selected

Bold and Italic buttons selected

Dialog Box Launcher button

Wrap Text button selected

All formats selected in
Format Cells dialog box
applied to range

12 In the **Font group**, click the **Dialog Box Launcher** button.

The Font tab of the Format Cells dialog box displays. The most commonly used settings from this tab are displayed as buttons on the Ribbon.

13 Click **Cancel** to close the dialog box. On the Ribbon, in the **Alignment group**, click the **Dialog Box Launcher** button.

The Alignment tab of the Format Cells dialog box displays. The most commonly used settings from the Alignment tab display as buttons in the Alignment group on the Ribbon. In this manner, Excel makes frequently used commands quickly available to you on the Ribbon. To perform multiple commands, use either the Ribbon buttons or the Format Cells dialog box. To use commands that are not commonly used and thus not displayed on the Ribbon, use the Format Cells dialog box.

14 Click **Cancel** to close the dialog box. Display the **Post Office** worksheet.

> As soon as you select a single sheet, the grouping of the sheets is canceled and *[Group]* no longer displays in the title bar. Because the sheets were grouped, the same new text and formatting was applied to all of the selected sheets. In this manner, you can make the same changes to all the sheets in a workbook at one time.

15 Display the **City Hall** worksheet, and then verify that the changes have also been made to this worksheet. **Save** 🖫 your workbook.

Activity 10.07 Entering Data and Constructing Formulas on Multiple Worksheets

Recall that formulas are equations that perform calculations on values in your worksheet, and that a formula starts with an equal sign (=). Operators are the symbols with which you specify the type of calculation that you want to perform on the elements of a formula. In this activity, you will enter the number of Child and Adult tickets purchased at each of the three locations during the week of August 3, and then calculate the total sales.

1 Display the **Golden Grove Mall** worksheet as the active sheet. Verify that the sheets are not grouped—*[Group]* does *not* display in the title bar.

2 Click cell **A1**, type **Ticket Sale Area #1 Golden Grove Mall** and then click the **Enter** button ✔ on the **Formula Bar**. With cell **A1** as the active cell, change the **Font** to **Cambria**, the **Font Size** to **14**, and then apply **Bold** **B**.

> Your new typing replaces the contents of the cell.

3 Select the range **A1:F1**, and then in the **Alignment group**, click the **Merge & Center** button 🔳▾.

4 Select the range **B5:C11**, type **255** and then press ⏎. Type **350** and then press ⏎.

> Although it is not required that you do so, recall that selecting a range in this manner lets you enter columns of data by pressing ⏎ after each entry, and keeps the entries within the defined range of cells. After you type in the last selected cell in column B, which is B11, pressing ⏎ will make cell C5 the active cell.

5 Type the remaining number of tickets sold as shown in the following table, pressing ⏎ after each entry, and then compare your screen with Figure 10.12.

	Child	Adult
8/3	255	350
8/4	350	415
8/5	295	392
8/6	115	294
8/7	214	381
8/8	304	412
8/9	295	420

Figure 10.12

Worksheet title formatted

Number of tickets sold at this location entered

Typing and pressing Enter keeps data within selected range

6 Click cell **A1**, and then in the **Clipboard group**, click the **Format Painter** button. Click the **Post Office sheet tab**, and then click cell **A1** in the active sheet to apply the formatting.

7 In cell **A1**, replace *Area #2* by typing **Ticket Sale Area #2 Post Office** and then pressing Enter.

8 Select the range **B5:C11**, enter the number of tickets purchased at this location as shown in the following table, and then compare your screen with Figure 10.13.

	Child	Adult
8/3	155	252
8/4	210	314
8/5	195	296
8/6	95	198
8/7	87	283
8/8	195	320
8/9	55	36

Figure 10.13

Number of tickets sold at this location entered

---

9 Click cell **A1**, right-click, on the displayed Mini toolbar, click the **Format Painter** button, display the **City Hall** worksheet, and then click cell **A1** to copy the format.

10 In cell **A1**, replace *Area #3* by typing **Ticket Sale Area #3 City Hall** and then pressing Enter. Enter the number of tickets sold at this location by selecting the appropriate data range, and then entering the information in the following table. Compare your screen with Figure 10.14.

	Child	Adult
8/3	75	126
8/4	110	214
8/5	105	197
8/6	85	157
8/7	92	205
8/8	104	212
8/9	158	224

Figure 10.14

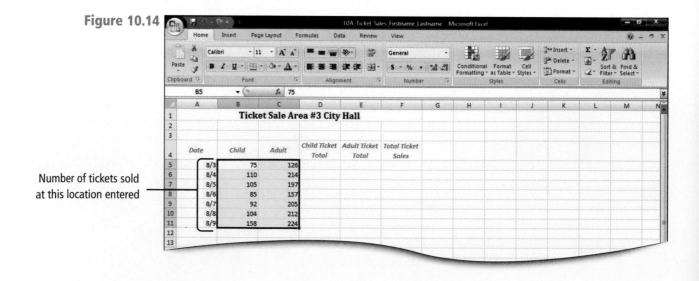

Number of tickets sold at this location entered

11 **Save** 💾 your changes. Right-click the **Golden Grove Mall sheet tab**, and then from the shortcut menu, click **Select All Sheets**.

> The first worksheet becomes the active sheet, and the worksheets are grouped. *[Group]* displays in the title bar, and the sheet tabs are underlined in the tab color to indicate they are selected as part of the group.

> Recall that when grouped, any editing or data entry that you perform on the active worksheet is *also* performed on the other selected worksheets.

12 Click cell **D5** and type = to begin a formula. Click cell **B5**, type * click cell **D15**, and then compare your screen with Figure 10.15.

> Recall that the symbols + and − and * and / are used in formulas to perform addition, subtraction, multiplication, and division. This formula will calculate the total amount from the sale of Child tickets on August 3 at the Golden Grove Mall location.

> Recall that in the General number format, trailing zeroes do not display.

Figure 10.15

Formula to multiply 255 Child tickets times price of 2.50

13 Press `F4` to make the reference to **Child Ticket Price** in cell **D15** absolute.

> Recall that when you copy formulas down to other cells in a column, the cell references change relative to the row number. For the reference to each date in column A, that is the desired result. For the cell reference to the ticket price in cell D15, the cell reference should remain the same for each date.

14 On the **Formula Bar**, click the **Enter** button ✓ to display the formula result of *637.5* and then use the fill handle to copy the formula down for the remaining dates. Compare your screen with Figure 10.16.

Figure 10.16

Sales of Child tickets
calculated for each date ————

Cell reference bar: D5   =B5*$D$15

	A	B	C	D	E	F
1			Ticket Sale Area #1 Golden Grove Mall			
2						
3						
4	Date	Child	Adult	Child Ticket Total	Adult Ticket Total	Total Ticket Sales
5	8/3	255	350	637.5		
6	8/4	350	415	875		
7	8/5	295	392	737.5		
8	8/6	115	294	287.5		
9	8/7	214	381	535		
10	8/8	304	412	760		
11	8/9	295	420	737.5		
12						
13						

15 In cell **E5**, construct a similar formula to multiply the number of **Adult** tickets sold on August 3 times the **Adult Ticket Price** in cell **D16**. Make the reference to cell **D16** absolute so that each day's sales are multiplied by the **Adult Ticket Price** in cell **D16**. Copy the formula down for the remaining dates, and then compare your screen with Figure 10.17.

Figure 10.17

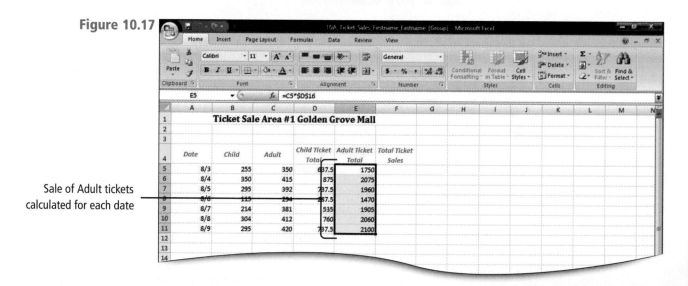

Sale of Adult tickets
calculated for each date ————

Cell reference bar: E5   =C5*$D$16

	A	B	C	D	E	F
1			Ticket Sale Area #1 Golden Grove Mall			
2						
3						
4	Date	Child	Adult	Child Ticket Total	Adult Ticket Total	Total Ticket Sales
5	8/3	255	350	637.5	1750	
6	8/4	350	415	875	2075	
7	8/5	295	392	737.5	1960	
8	8/6	115	294	287.5	1470	
9	8/7	214	381	535	1905	
10	8/8	304	412	760	2060	
11	8/9	295	420	737.5	2100	
12						
13						
14						

16 Click cell **F5**, and then in the **Editing group**, click the **Sum** button ∑▾. Notice that Excel selects all the numeric values—but not the date values—in the row.

17 To Sum only the values in **D5** and **E5**—the **Child Total** and the **Adult Total**—with your mouse, select the range **D5:E5**, and then compare your screen with Figure 10.18.

> Recall that the Sum function first looks above the selected cell for a range of numbers to sum. If no values display above the selected cell, Excel looks to the left for a range of numbers to sum. You can change the range to which you want to apply the Sum function by simply selecting the desired range.

Figure 10.18

New range selected
for the SUM function

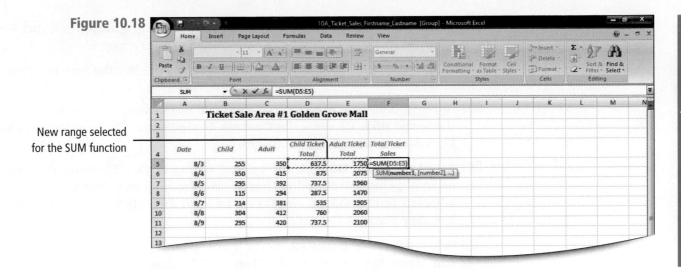

18 On the **Formula Bar**, click the **Enter** button ✔, and then copy the formula down for the remaining dates. Compare your screen with Figure 10.19.

> Because your worksheets are grouped, the calculations on the first worksheet are also being performed on the other two worksheets.

Figure 10.19

Daily totals for Child
and Adult tickets sold

19 Click cell **F12**, and then in the **Editing group**, click the **Sum** button ∑ ▾. Be sure the range **F5:F11** is selected, and then press Enter.

> Excel looks above the selected cell and proposes a range to sum. Your result is *17890*.

20 In cell **A12**, type **Totals** and then on the **Formula Bar**, click the **Enter** button ✔ to confirm the entry and keep **A12** as the active cell. Then apply the **Align Text Right** ▤ format and **Bold** **B** to the cell.

21 Select the range **B5:E12**, and then in the **Editing group**, click the **Sum** button ∑ ▾ to apply the Sum function to the range.

> Recall that selecting a range in this manner will place the Sum function in the empty cells at the bottom of each column.

22 Apply appropriate number and financial formatting as follows: Select the range **B5:C12**, click the **Comma Style** button ▾ , and then click **Decrease Decimal** ▾ two times.

23 Select the range **D6:F11** and apply **Comma Style** ▾ —leave the two decimal places displayed in these currency amounts. Select the non-adjacent ranges **D5:F5** and **D12:F12**, and then click the **Accounting Number Format** button $ ▾ .

24 Select the range **B12:F12**, in the **Font group**, click the **Borders button arrow**, and then click **Top and Double Bottom Border** to apply the common format for financial numbers. Click any blank cell to deselect, and then compare your screen with Figure 10.20.

Figure 10.20

Accounting Number Format applied

Comma Style applied

Borders applied and columns totaled

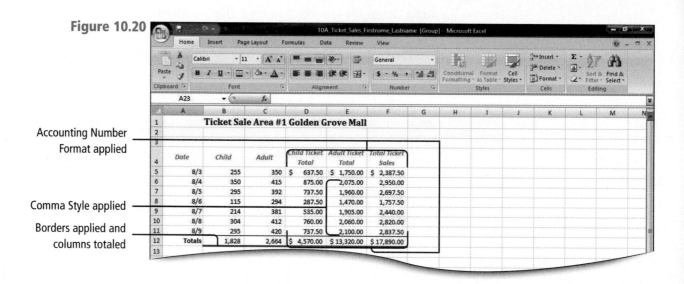

Note — Apply Comma Style First

When combining both the Comma Style and the Accounting Number Format to different ranges within a contiguous group of cells, apply Comma Style first.

25 Select the range **D15:D16**, right-click over the selection, and then on the Mini toolbar, click the **Accounting Number Format** $ ▾ button.

26 Display the **Post Office** worksheet to examine the totals, and then compare your screen with Figure 10.21.

> Because your worksheets were grouped while making the calculations, all the calculations and formatting on the first worksheet were also being performed on the other two worksheets.
>
> As soon as you select an individual sheet, as you have done here, the grouping is canceled. *[Group]* no longer displays in the title bar.

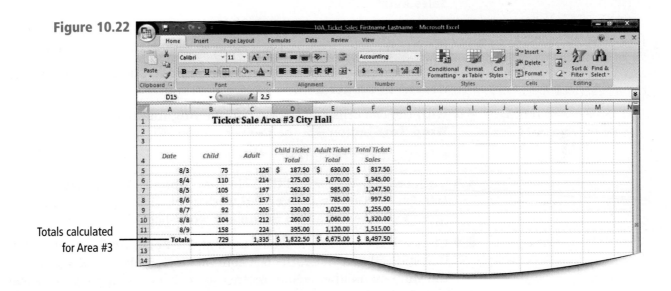

27 Display the **City Hall** worksheet to examine the totals, and then compare your screen with Figure 10.22.

> You can see that by grouping sheets and copying formulas, it is easy to make multiple calculations in Excel without typing formulas multiple times.

Figure 10.22

Totals calculated
for Area #3

28 **Save** your workbook.

Objective 6
Create a Summary Sheet

A summary sheet is a worksheet where totals from other worksheets are displayed and summarized.

Activity 10.08 Constructing Formulas that Refer to Cells in Another Worksheet

In this activity, you will insert a new worksheet in which you will place the totals from each ticket sale location's worksheet. You will construct formulas in the Summary worksheet to display the total revenue for each of the two types of tickets—Child and Adult—that will update the Summary worksheet whenever changes are made to the other worksheet totals.

1 To the right of the **City Hall** worksheet tab, click the **Insert Worksheet** button.

> A new worksheet displays with the name *Sheet1* or *Sheet2* or some other number, depending on whether the other worksheets have been renamed and how many times a new worksheet has been inserted.

2 Rename the new worksheet **Summary** and then change the **Tab Color** to **Olive Green, Accent 3, Lighter 40%**.

3 In cell **A4**, type **Golden Grove Mall** In cell **A5**, type **Post Office** and then in cell **A6**, type **City Hall**

4 Select the range **A4:A6**, right-click, and then on the Mini toolbar, change the **Font Size** to **12** and apply **Bold**. In the **column heading area**, point to the right border of **column A** to display the pointer, and then double-click to AutoFit the column.

5 In cell **B3**, type **Total Sales Child** and then in cell **C3**, type **Total Sales Adult**

6 Select the range **B3:C3**, and then right-click over the selection to display the Mini toolbar. Click **Bold**, click **Italic**, change the **Font** to **Cambria**, and then change the **Font Color** to **Orange, Accent 6, Darker 25%**.

7 With the two cells still selected, in the **Alignment group**, click the **Wrap Text** button, the **Center** button, and then click the **Middle Align** button.

8 Click cell **B4**. Type **=** and then click the **Golden Grove Mall sheet tab**. On the **Golden Grove Mall** worksheet, click cell **D12**, and then press Enter to redisplay the **Summary** worksheet.

9 Click cell **B4** to select it again. Look at the **Formula Bar** and notice that instead of a value, the cell contains a formula that is equal to the value in another cell in another worksheet. Compare your screen with Figure 10.23.

> The value in this cell is equal to the value in cell D12 of the *Golden Grove Mall* worksheet. The Accounting Number Format applied to the referenced cell is carried over. By using a formula of this type, changes in cell D12 on the *Golden Grove Mall* worksheet will be automatically updated in this *Summary* worksheet.

Figure 10.23

Cell value equal to cell D12 in the Golden Grove Mall worksheet

Column titles formatted

Accounting Number Format retained

10 Click cell **C4**. Type **=** and then click the **Golden Grove Mall sheet tab**. Click cell **E12**, and then press (Enter).

11 Use the technique you just practiced to copy the week's total for **Child** and **Adult** ticket sales for the **Post Office worksheet** and the **City Hall worksheet**. Compare your screen with Figure 10.24.

> The formulas in cells B4:C6 display the totals from the other three worksheets. Changes made to any of the other three worksheets—sometimes referred to as *detail worksheets* because the details of the information are contained there—that affect their totals will display on this Summary worksheet. In this manner, the summary worksheet accurately displays the current totals from the other worksheets.

Figure 10.24

Total Child and Adult sales from each location

12 In cell **A1**, type **Summer Fair and Arts Festival** and then **Merge & Center** the text over the range **A1:C1**. In cell **A2**, type **Pre-Sales of Tickets**

August 3-9 and then **Merge & Center** the text over the range **A2:C2**.

13 Select the two worksheet titles and change the **Font** to **Cambria**, change the **Font Color** to **Orange, Accent 6, Darker 25%**, change the **Font Size** to **14**, and apply **Bold** **B**.

14 Select **rows 1:2**. From the **row heading area**, point to the lower boundary of either selected row to display the ✛ pointer, increase the row height to **35 pixels**, and then click the **Middle Align** button ☰.

15 Select **columns B:C**, and then set the column width to **80 pixels**.

16 In cell **A7**, type **Total Sales** press Enter, and then notice that the formatting from the cell above is carried down to the new cell.

17 Select the range **B4:C7**, and then use the **Sum** button **Σ ▾** to total the two columns. Compare your screen with Figure 10.25.

> Recall that cell formatting carries over to adjacent cells unless two cells are left blank.

Figure 10.25

Worksheet titles formatted

Totals calculated for each type of ticket

	A	B	C
1	Summer Fair and Arts Festival		
2	Pre-Sales of Tickets August 3-9		
3		Total Sales Child	Total Sales Adult
4	Golden Grove Mall	$ 4,570.00	$13,320.00
5	Post Office	$ 2,480.00	$ 8,495.00
6	City Hall	$ 1,822.50	$ 6,675.00
7	Total Sales	$ 8,872.50	$28,490.00
8			
9			

18 In the **Total Sales Child column**, notice the total for the *Post Office* location is *$2,480.00* and the *Total Sales* is *$8,872.50*.

19 Display the **Post Office** worksheet, click cell **B11**, type **155** and then press Enter. Notice that the formulas in the worksheet recalculate.

20 Display the **Summary** worksheet, and notice that in the **Total Sales Child column**, both the total for the *Post Office* location and the *Total Sales* also recalculated. Compare your screen with Figure 10.26.

> In this manner, a Summary sheet recalculates any changes made in the other worksheets.

Figure 10.26

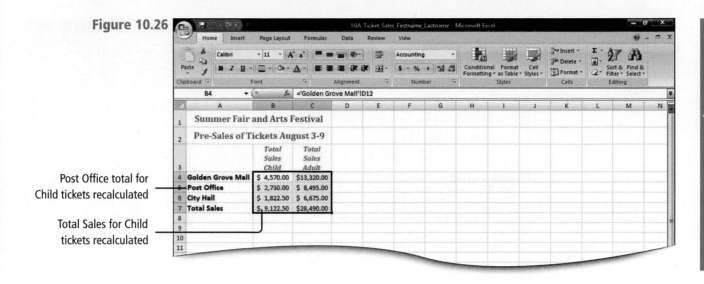

Post Office total for
Child tickets recalculated

Total Sales for Child
tickets recalculated

21 Select the range **B7:C7**, and then apply a **Top and Double Bottom** border.

22 Save 💾 your workbook.

Objective 7
Format and Print Multiple Worksheets in a Workbook

Each worksheet within a workbook can have different formatting, for example different headers or footers. If all the worksheets in the work-book will have the same header or footer, you can select all the work-sheets and apply formatting common to all of the worksheets; for example, you can set the same footer in all of the worksheets.

Activity 10.09 Moving and Formatting Worksheets in a Workbook

In this activity, you will move the Summary sheet to become the first worksheet in the workbook. Then you will format and prepare your work-book for printing. The four worksheets containing data can be formatted simultaneously.

1 Point to the **Summary sheet tab**, hold down the left mouse button to display a small black triangle—a caret—and then notice that a small paper icon attaches to the mouse pointer.

2 Drag to the left until the caret and mouse pointer are to the left of the **Golden Grove Mall sheet tab**, as shown in Figure 10.27, and then release the left mouse button.

Use this technique to rearrange the order of worksheets within a workbook.

Figure 10.27

Caret moved to the left; mouse pointer with paper icon attached

3 Be sure the **Summary** worksheet is the active sheet. Then point to its sheet tab, right-click, and then click **Select All Sheets** to display *[Group]* in the title bar. On the Ribbon, click the **Insert tab**, and then in the **Text group**, click the **Header & Footer** button.

4 In the **Navigation group**, click the **Go to Footer** button, click in the **left section** above the word *Footer*, and then in the **Header & Footer Elements group**, click the **File Name** button.

5 Click in a cell above the footer to deselect the **Footer area** and view your file name. On the Ribbon, click the **Page Layout tab**. In the **Page Setup group**, click the **Margins** button, and then at the bottom of the **Margins gallery**, click **Custom Margins**.

6 In the displayed **Page Setup** dialog box, under **Center on page**, select the **Horizontally** check box. Click **OK**, and then on the status bar, click the **Normal** button 🔲 to return to Normal view.

After displaying worksheets in Page Layout View, dotted lines display to indicate the page breaks when you return to Normal view.

7 Press Ctrl + Home to move to the top of the worksheet. Verify that *[Group]* still displays in the title bar.

Recall that by selecting all sheets, you can apply the same formatting to all the worksheets at the same time.

8 **Save** 🔲 your changes. From the **Office** menu 🔵, point to the **Print** button, and then from the displayed menu, click **Print Preview**. Alternatively, press Ctrl + F2 to display the Print Preview. Compare your screen with Figure 10.28.

With all the sheets grouped, you can view all of the sheets in Print Preview. If you do not see *Page 1 of 4* in the status bar, close the Preview, select all the sheets again, and then redisplay Print Preview.

Figure 10.28

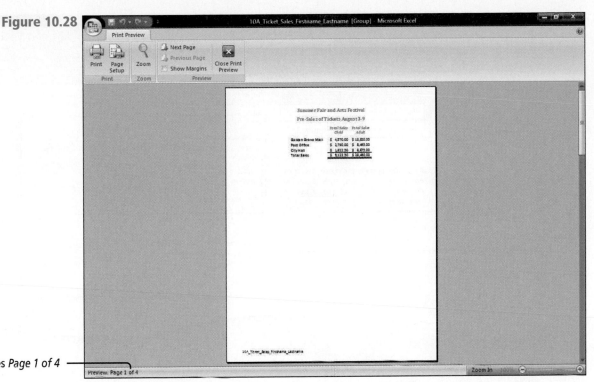

Status bar indicates *Page 1 of 4*

9 On the Ribbon, in the **Preview group**, click the **Next Page** button as necessary and take a moment to view each page of your workbook. After viewing all the worksheets, click the **Close Print Preview** button.

Activity 10.10 Printing All the Worksheets in a Workbook

1 **Save** 🖫 your workbook before printing. Check your *Chapter Assignment Sheet* or *Course Syllabus*, or consult your instructor, to determine if you are to submit your assignments on paper or electronically. To submit electronically, follow the instructions provided by your instructor.

2 Verify that the worksheets in your workbook are still grouped—*[Group]* displays in the title bar. From the **Office** menu 🔘, click the **Print** button. In the displayed **Print** dialog box, under **Print range**, verify that the **All** option button is selected.

3 Under **Print what**, verify that **Active sheet(s)** is selected. Alternatively, if your worksheets are not grouped, you can click *Entire workbook* in this dialog box to print all the worksheets in the workbook. Under **Copies**, verify that the **Number of copies** is **1**. Compare your screen with Figure 10.29.

Figure 10.29

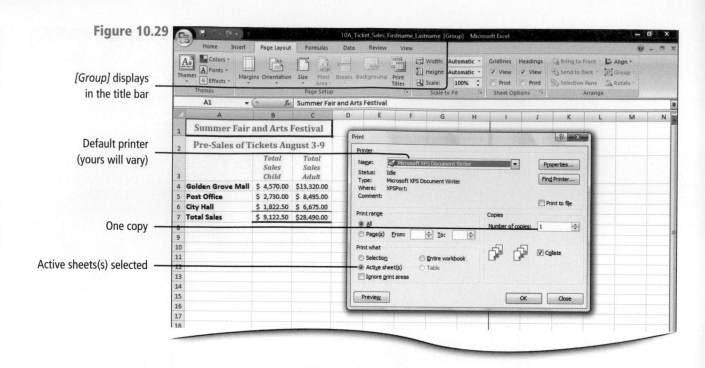

[Group] displays in the title bar

Default printer (yours will vary)

One copy

Active sheets(s) selected

4️⃣ Click **OK** to print your worksheets. Determine if you are to print formulas for any or all of the worksheets in this workbook. To print formulas, refer to Activity 9.17 in Project 9A.

5️⃣ If you printed your formulas, be sure to redisplay the worksheet by pressing Ctrl + `. From the **Office** menu 🪟, click **Close**. If you are prompted to save changes, click **No** so that you do not save the changes to the Print layout that you used for printing formulas. **Exit** Excel.

End You have completed Project 10A ⎯⎯⎯⎯⎯⎯⎯⎯

Project 10B Growth Projection

In Activities 10.11 through 10.15, you will assist Mervyn Aghazarian, the City Planner for Golden Grove, in creating a workbook to estimate future population growth based on three different growth rates. Your resulting worksheet and chart will look similar to Figure 10.30.

For Project 10B, you will need the following file:

New blank Excel workbook

You will save your workbook as
10B_Growth_Projection_Firstname_Lastname

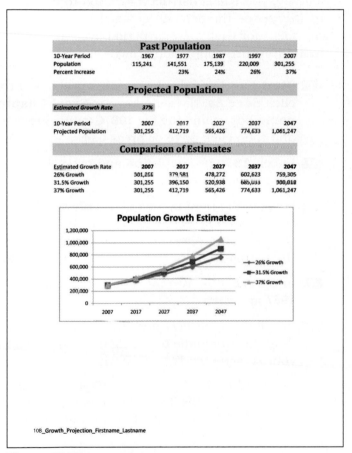

Figure 10.30
Project 10B—Growth Projection

Objective 8
Design a Worksheet for What-If Analysis

Excel recalculates; if you change the value in a cell referenced in a formula, the result of the formula is automatically recalculated. Thus, you can change cell values to see *what* would happen *if* you tried different values. This process of changing the values in cells to see how those changes affect the outcome of formulas in your worksheet is called *what-if analysis*.

Activity 10.11 Using Parentheses in a Formula

Mr. Aghazarian has the city's population figures for the past five 10-year periods. In each 10-year period, the population has increased. In this activity, you will construct a formula to calculate the *percentage rate of increase*—the percent by which one number increases over another number—for each 10-year period over the past years. From this information, future population growth can be estimated.

1 **Start** Excel and display a new workbook. From the **Office** menu 🔘, click **Save As**. Navigate to your **Excel Chapter 10** folder, in the **File name** box, name the file **10B_Growth_Projection_Firstname_Lastname** and then click **Save** or press Enter.

2 In cell **A3**, type **Population** and press Enter. In cell **A4**, type **Percent Increase** and press Enter.

3 Point to the right boundary of **column A** to display the ✛ pointer, and then double-click to AutoFit the column to accommodate its longest entry. Alternatively, on the Home tab, in the Cells group, click the Format button, and then click AutoFit Column Width.

4 In cell **A2**, type **10-Year Period** and then press Tab. In cell **B2**, type **1967** and then press Tab.

5 In cell **C2**, type **1977** and then press Tab. Select the range **B2:C2**, drag the fill handle to the right through cell **F2**, and then compare your screen with Figure 10.31.

By establishing a pattern of 10-year intervals with the first two cells, you can use the fill handle to continue the series. The Auto Fill feature will do this for any pattern that you establish with two or more cells.

Figure 10.31

Pattern used to fill 10-year periods to create column titles

Row titles entered

6 Click cell **A1**. Type **Past Population** and press Enter. Select the range **A1:F1**, and then right-click to display the Mini toolbar. Click the **Merge & Center** button ⊞▾, apply **Bold** B, change the **Font** to **Cambria**, and then change the **Font Size** to **18**.

7 Beginning in cell **B3**, and then pressing Tab to move across the row, enter the following values for the population in the years listed:

1967	1977	1987	1997	2007
115241	141551	175139	220009	301255

8 Select the range **B3:F3**, right-click, on the Mini toolbar, click **Comma Style** ▸, and then **Decrease Decimal** .00→.0 two times.

9 Click cell **C4**. Being sure to include the parentheses, type **=(c3-b3)/b3** and then press Enter. Click cell **C4**. In the **Number group**, click the **Percent Style** button % , and then examine the formula in the **Formula Bar**.

> The mathematical formula to calculate the percentage rate of population increase from 1967 to 1977 is **rate = amount of increase/base**.
>
> First, determine the *amount of increase* by subtracting the **base**—the starting point represented by the 1967 population—from the 1977 population. Thus, the *amount of increase* = 141,551 − 115,241 or 26,310. Between 1967 and 1977, the population increased by 26,310 people. In the formula, this calculation is represented by *c3-b3*.
>
> Second, calculate the *rate*—what the amount of increase (26,310) represents as a percentage of the base (1967's population of 115,241). Determine this by dividing the amount of increase (26,310) by the base (115,241). Thus, 26,310 divided by 115,241 is equal to 0.22830416 or, when rounded to a percent—23%.

10 In the **Formula Bar**, locate the parentheses enclosing *C3-B3*.

> Excel follows a set of mathematical rules called the **order of operations**, which has four basic parts:
>
> - Expressions within parentheses are processed first.
> - Exponentiation, if present, is performed before multiplication and division.
> - Multiplication and division are performed before addition and subtraction.
> - Consecutive operators with the same level of precedence are calculated from left to right.

11 Click cell **D4**, type **=** and then by typing or using a combination of typing and clicking cells to reference them, construct a formula similar to the one in cell **C4** to calculate the rate of increase in population from 1977 to 1987. Compare your screen with Figure 10.32.

> Recall that the first step is to determine the *amount of increase*—1987 population minus 1977 population—and then to write the calculation so that Excel performs this operation first; that is, place it in parentheses.
>
> The second step is to divide the result of the calculation in parentheses by the *base*—the population for 1977.

Figure 10.32

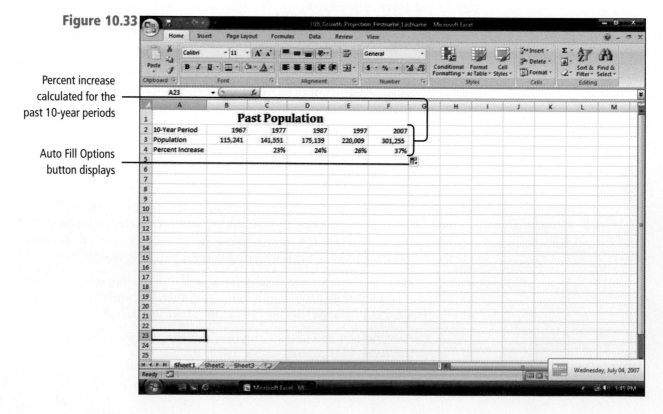

Formula to calculate percent increase from 1977 to 1987

	A	B	C	D	E	F	G
1	**Past Population**						
2	10-Year Period	1967	1977	1987	1997	2007	
3	Population	115,241	141,551	175,139	220,009	301,255	
4	Percent Increase		23%	=(d3-c3)/c3			

12 Press [Enter], and then format cell **D4** with the **Percent Style** %. Your result is *24%*.

13 With cell **D4** selected, drag the fill handle to the right through cell **F4**. Click any empty cell to cancel the selection, **Save** 🖫 your workbook, and then compare your screen with Figure 10.33.

Because this formula uses relative cell references—that is, for each year, the formula is the same but the values used are relative to the formula's location—you can copy the formula in this manner. For example, the result for 1987 uses 1977 as the base, the result for 1997 uses 1987 as the base, and the result for 2007 uses 1997 as the base.

The formula results show the percent of increase for each 10-year period between 1967 and 2007. You can see that in each 10-year period, the population has grown as much as 37%—between 1997 and 2007—and as little as 23%—between 1967 and 1977.

Figure 10.33

Percent increase calculated for the past 10-year periods

Auto Fill Options button displays

	A	B	C	D	E	F	G
1	**Past Population**						
2	10-Year Period	1967	1977	1987	1997	2007	
3	Population	115,241	141,551	175,139	220,009	301,255	
4	Percent Increase		23%	24%	26%	37%	

Use of Parentheses in a Formula

When writing a formula in Excel, use parentheses to communicate the order in which the operations should occur. For example, to average three test scores of 100, 50, and 90 that you scored on three different tests in a class, you would add the test scores and then divide by the number of test scores in the list. If you write this formula as =100+50+90/3, the result would be 180, because Excel would first divide 90 by 3 and then add 100+50+30. Excel would do so because the order of operations states that multiplication and division are calculated *before* addition and subtraction.

The correct way to write this formula is =(100+50+90)/3. Excel will add the three values, and then divide the result by 3, or 240/3 resulting in a correct average of 80. Parentheses play an important role in assuring that you get the correct result in your formulas.

Activity 10.12 Formatting as You Type

You can format numbers as you type them. When you type numbers in a format that Excel recognizes, Excel automatically applies that format to the cell. Recall that once applied, cell formats remain with the cell, even if the cell contents are deleted. In this activity, you will format cells by typing the numbers with percent signs and use Format Painter to copy text (non-numeric) formats.

1 In cell **A6**, type **Projected Population** and then press Enter. Click cell **A1**. On the **Home tab**, in the **Clipboard group**, click the **Format Painter** button , and then click cell **A6**.

> The format of cell A1 is *painted* or applied to cell A6, including the merging and centering of the text across cells A6:F6.

2 In cell **A8**, type **Estimated Growth Rate** and then press Enter. AutoFit **column A** to accommodate the new longer entry.

3 In cell **A10**, type **10-Year Period** and then in cell **A11**, type **Projected Population**

4 In cell **B10**, type **2007** and then press Tab. In cell **C10**, type **2017** and then press Tab.

5 Select the range **B10:C10**, and then drag the fill handle through cell **F10** to extend the pattern of years to *2047*. Compare your screen with Figure 10.34.

Figure 10.34

New title entered and formatted

Row and column titles entered

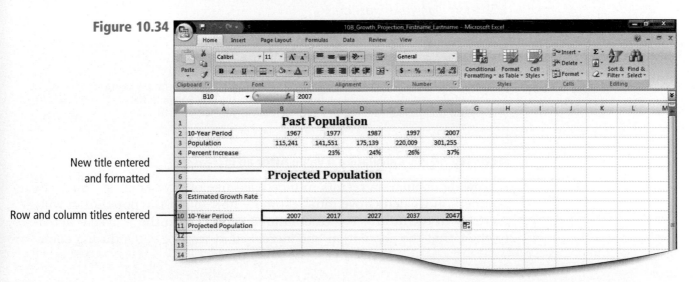

6 Click cell **B11**, and then in the **Number group**, notice that the format indicates *General*. Including the comma, type **301,255**

7 On the **Formula Bar**, click the **Enter** button ☑ to keep the cell active, and then in the **Number group**, notice that the format changed to *Number*. Then, press ⌨Delete⌨, and in the **Number group**, notice that the *Number* format is still indicated.

Recall that deleting the contents of a cell does not delete the cell's formatting.

8 *Without* typing a comma, in cell **B11**, type **301255** and then press ⌨Enter⌨.

The comma is inserted even though you did not type it. When you type a number and include a formatting symbol such as a comma, dollar sign, or percent sign, Excel applies the format to the cell. Thus, if you delete the contents of the cell and type in the cell again, the format you established remains applied to the cell. This is referred to as ***format as you type***.

9 Examine the format of the value in cell **B11**, and then compare it to the format in cell **B3** where you used the Comma Style button to format the cell. Notice that the number in cell **B11** is flush with the right edge of the cell, but the number in cell **B3** leaves a small space on the right edge.

When you type commas as you enter numbers, Excel applies the *Number* format, which does *not* leave a space at the right of the number for a closing parenthesis in the event of a negative number. This is different from the format that is applied when you use the *Comma Style* button on the Ribbon or Mini toolbar, as you did for the numbers entered in row 3. Recall that the Comma Style format applied from either the Ribbon or the Mini toolbar leaves space on the right for a closing parenthesis in the event of a negative number.

10 In cell **B8**, type **26%** and then on the **Formula Bar**, click **Enter** ☑. Then, press ⌨Delete⌨ and *without* typing a percent sign, type **26**, and then press ⌨Enter⌨.

The percent sign is inserted even though you did not type it—this is another example of the *format as you type* feature.

11 Select the range **A8:B8**, and then apply **Bold** ⒝ and **Italic** ⒤.

12 **Save** 💾 your workbook.

More Knowledge — Percentage Calculations

When you type a percentage into a cell—for example *26%*—the percentage format, without decimal points, displays in both the cell and the Formula Bar. Excel will, however, use the decimal value of *0.26* for actual calculations.

Activity 10.13 Calculating a Value After an Increase

A growing population results in increased use of city services. Thus, city planners in Golden Grove must estimate how much the population will increase in the future. The calculations you made in the previous activity show that the population has increased at varying rates during each

10-year period, ranging from a low of 23% to a high of 37% per 10-year period.

Population data from the state and surrounding areas suggests that future growth will trend closer to that of the recent past. To plan for the future, Mr. Aghazarian wants to prepare three forecasts of the city's population based on the percentage increases in 1997, in 2007, and for a percentage increase halfway between the two, that is, for 26%, 31.5%, and 37%. In this activity, you will calculate the population that would result from a 26% increase.

1 Click cell **C11**. Type **=b11*(100%+b8)** and then on the **Formula Bar**, click the **Enter** button ✓. Compare your screen with Figure 10.35.

> This formula calculates what the population will be in the year 2017 assuming an increase of 26% over 2007's population. The mathematical formula to calculate a value after an increase is **value after increase = base × percent for new value**.
>
> First, establish the *percent for new value*. The **percent for new value = base percent + percent of increase**. The *base percent* of 100% represents the base population and the *percent of increase* in this instance is 26%. Thus, the population will equal 100% of the base year plus 26% of the base year. This can be expressed as 126% or 1.26. In this formula, you will use 100% + the rate in cell B8, which is 26%, to equal 126%.
>
> Second, enter a reference to the cell that contains the *base*—the population in 2007. The base value resides in cell B11—301,255.
>
> Third, calculate the *value after increase*. Because in each future 10-year period the increase will be based on 26%—an absolute value located in cell B8—this cell reference can be formatted as absolute with the use of dollar signs.

Figure 10.35

Absolute reference to cell B8

2 With cell **C11** as the active cell, drag the fill handle to copy the formula to the range **D11:F11**.

3 Click cell **B11**, click the **Format Painter** 🖌 button, and then select the range **C11:F11**. Click an empty cell to cancel the selection, and then compare your screen with Figure 10.36.

This formula uses a relative cell address—B11—for the *base*; the population in the previous 10-year period is used in each of the formulas in cells D11:F11 as the *base* value. Because the reference to the *percent of increase* in cell B8 is an absolute reference, each *value after increase* is calculated with the value from cell B8.

The population projected for 2017—*379,581*—is an increase of 26% over the population in 2007. The projected population in 2027—*478,272*—is an increase of 26% over the population in 2017 and so on.

Figure 10.36

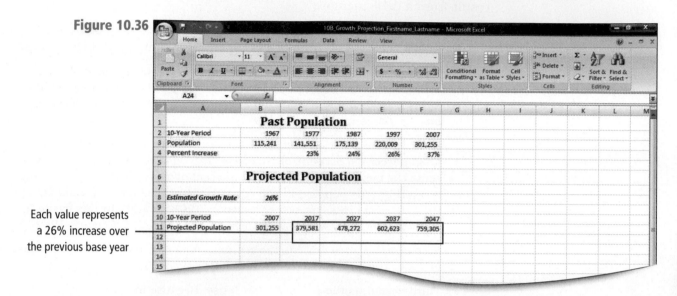

Each value represents a 26% increase over the previous base year

4 **Save** 💾 your workbook.

Workshop

Calculating Percent Increase or Decrease

The basic formula for calculating an increase or decrease can be done in two parts. First determine the percent by which the base value will be increased or decreased, and then add or subtract the results to the base. The formula can be simplified by using (1+amount of increase) or (1−amount of decrease), where 1 represents the whole, rather than 100%. Thus, the formula used in Step 1 of Activity 10.13 could also be written =b11*(1+b8), or =(b11*b8)+b11.

Objective 9
Perform What-If Analysis

If a formula depends on the value in a cell, you can see what effect it will have if you change the value in that cell. Then, you can copy the value computed by the formula and paste it into another part of the worksheet where it can be compared and charted. This can be done for multiple formulas.

Activity 10.14 Performing What-If Analysis and Using Paste Special

Mr. Aghazarian can see that a growth rate of 26% in each 10-year period will result in a population of almost 760,000 people by 2047. The city planners will likely ask him what the population might be if population grows at the highest rate (37%) or at a rate that is halfway between the 1997 and 2007 rates (31.5%).

Because the formulas are constructed to use the growth rate displayed in cell B8, Mr. Aghazarian can answer these questions quickly by entering different percentages into that cell. To keep the results of each set of calculations so they can be compared, you will paste the results of each what-if analysis into another area of the worksheet.

1 In cell **A13**, type **Comparison of Estimates** and then press Enter. Click cell **A6**, click **Format Painter** 🖌, and then click cell **A13**.

2 Select the range **A8:B8**, right-click to display the Mini toolbar, click the **Fill Color button arrow** 🎨, and then under **Theme Colors**, apply **Olive Green, Accent 3, Lighter 40%**.

3 Click cell **A1**, hold down Ctrl, and then click cells **A6** and **A13**. In the **Font group**, click the **Fill Color** button 🎨 to apply the same fill color to these titles.

> Recall that the Fill Color button retains its most recent color.

4 In the range **A15:A18**, type the following row titles:

Estimated Growth Rate
26% Growth
31.5% Growth
37% Growth

5 Select the range **B10:F10**. On the **Home tab**, in the **Clipboard group**, click the **Copy** 📋 button, click cell **B15**, and then in the **Clipboard group**, click the **Paste** button.

> Recall that when pasting a group of copied cells to a target range, you need only select the first cell of the range.

6 Select the range **B11:F11**, click **Copy** 📋, click cell **B16**, and then click the **Paste** button. Click cell **C16**, and notice on the **Formula Bar** that the *formula* was pasted into the cell. Compare your screen with Figure 10.37.

> This is *not* the desired result. The actual *calculated values*—not the formulas—are needed in the range B16:F16.

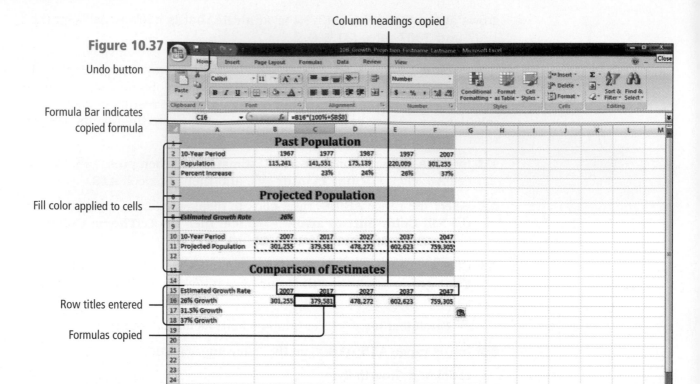

Figure 10.37

Undo button

Formula Bar indicates copied formula

Fill color applied to cells

Row titles entered

Formulas copied

Status bar indicates copied cells on Office Clipboard

Column headings copied

C16   =B16*(100%+$B$8)

	A	B	C	D	E	F
1	**Past Population**					
2	10-Year Period	1967	1977	1987	1997	2007
3	Population	115,241	141,551	175,139	220,009	301,255
4	Percent Increase		23%	24%	26%	37%
5						
6	**Projected Population**					
7						
8	*Estimated Growth Rate*	26%				
9						
10	10-Year Period	2007	2017	2027	2037	2047
11	Projected Population	301,255	379,581	478,272	602,623	759,305
12						
13	**Comparison of Estimates**					
14						
15	Estimated Growth Rate		2007	2017	2027	2037	2047
16	26% Growth	301,255	379,581	478,272	602,623	759,305
17	31.5% Growth					
18	37% Growth					
19						

7 On the **Quick Access Toolbar**, click the **Undo** button. With the range **B11:F11** still copied to the Clipboard—as indicated by the message in the status bar and the moving border—in the **Clipboard group**, click the **Paste button arrow**. From the displayed menu, click **Paste Special**.

8 In the displayed **Paste Special** dialog box, under **Paste**, click the **Values and number formats** option button.

> The *Paste Special* dialog box offers various options for the manner in which you can paste the contents of the Office Clipboard. The *Values and number formats* command pastes the *calculated values* that result from the calculation of formulas into other cells—along with the formatting applied to the copied cells.

9 In the displayed **Paste Special** dialog box, click **OK**. Click cell **C16**. Notice on the **Formula Bar** that the cell contains a value, not a formula. Press [Esc] to cancel the moving border and then compare your screen with Figure 10.38.

> The calculated estimates based on a 26% growth rate are pasted along with their formatting.

Figure 10.38

Formula Bar indicates the value —

Calculated value pasted —

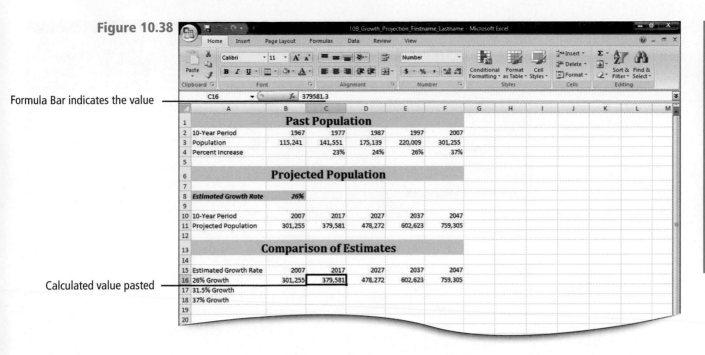

10. Click cell **B8**. Type **31.5** and then watch the values in **C11:F11** recalculate as, on the **Formula Bar**, you click the **Enter** button ✓.

> The value *31.5%* is halfway between 26% and 37%—the growth rates from the two most recent 10-year periods. Although the cell may display 32%, you can see that the underlying value is 31.5%.

11. Select the range **B11:F11**, and then press Ctrl + C, which is the keyboard shortcut for the Copy command. Click cell **B17**. In the **Clipboard group**, click the **Paste button arrow**, and then click **Paste Special**.

12. In the **Paste Special** dialog box, click the **Values and number formats** option button, and then click **OK**.

13. In cell **B8**, type **37** and then press Enter. Notice that the projected values in **C11:F11** are recalculated.

14. Using the skills you just practiced, copy the range **B11:F11**, and then paste the **values and number formats** of the copied range to the range **B18:F18**.

15. Press Esc to cancel the moving border, and then click an empty cell to cancel the selection. In **rows 15:18**, notice that the data and titles are arranged in simple rows and columns in adjacent cells for convenient charting. Compare your screen with Figure 10.39.

> With this information, Mr. Aghazarian can answer several what-if questions about the future population of the city and provide a range of population estimates based on the rates of growth over the past 10-year periods.

Figure 10.39

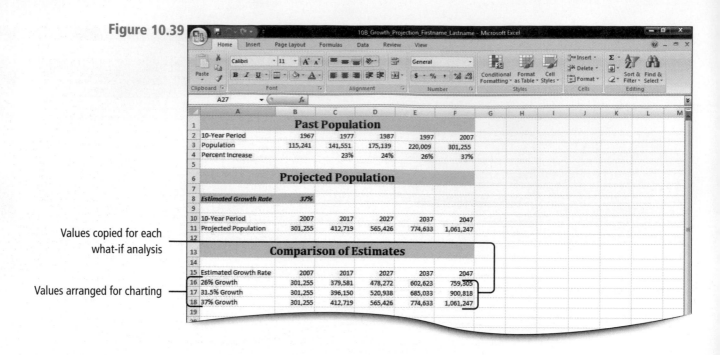

Values copied for each what-if analysis

Values arranged for charting

16 Save 💾 your workbook.

Another Way ──── **To Display the Paste Special Dialog Box**
Right-click over the target area, and then from the shortcut menu, click Paste Special. In many instances, using this method shortens the distance your mouse must travel in order to select an option from this dialog box.

Objective 10
Compare Data with a Line Chart

A *line chart* displays trends over time. Time is displayed along the bottom axis and the data point values are connected with a line. If you want to compare more than one set of values, each group is connected by a different line. The curves and directions of the lines make trends obvious to the reader.

Activity 10.15 Creating a Line Chart

In this activity, you will chart the values that represent the three different possible rates of population growth for Golden Grove. The 10-year periods will form the categories of time along the bottom of the chart and each set of values corresponding to a different growth rate will be represented by a line.

1 Select the range **B15:F15** and apply **Bold** B.

2 Select the range **A16:F18**. On the **Insert tab**, in the **Charts group**, click the **Line** button. From the displayed gallery of line charts, in the second row, point to the first chart type to display the ScreenTip *Line with Markers* as shown in Figure 10.40.

Figure 10.40

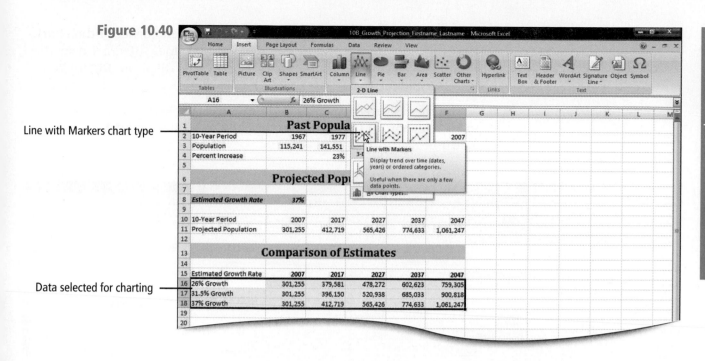

Line with Markers chart type

Data selected for charting

3 Click the **Line with Markers** chart type to create the chart as an embedded chart in the worksheet.

4 By using the 🔓 pointer, move the upper left corner of the chart just inside the upper left corner of cell **A20**. Then, scroll down so that you can view both the data and the chart on your screen. Compare your screen with Figure 10.41.

The chart still requires appropriate time labels along the category axis.

Figure 10.41

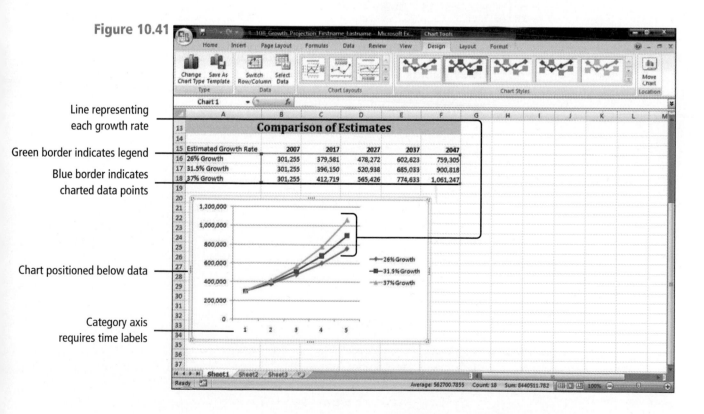

Line representing each growth rate

Green border indicates legend

Blue border indicates charted data points

Chart positioned below data

Category axis requires time labels

5 Be sure the chart is still selected. In the lower left corner of the chart, point to where the vertical and horizontal axis lines intersect near the *0* until the ScreenTip *Horizontal (Category) Axis* displays. Right-click and click **Select Data**.

6 On the right side of the displayed **Select Data Source** dialog box, under **Horizontal (Category) Axis Labels**, locate the **Edit** button, as shown in Figure 10.42.

Figure 10.42

Select Data Source dialog box

Edit button to edit labels on the category axis

Category (X) axis requires labels to identify each 10-year period

7 In the right column, click the **Edit** button. Drag the title bar of the **Axis Labels** dialog box to the right of the chart as necessary so that it is not blocking your view of the data, and then select the range **B15:F15**. Compare your screen with Figure 10.43.

Figure 10.43

Range of years surrounded
by moving border

Axis Labels dialog box

Range selected with
absolute references

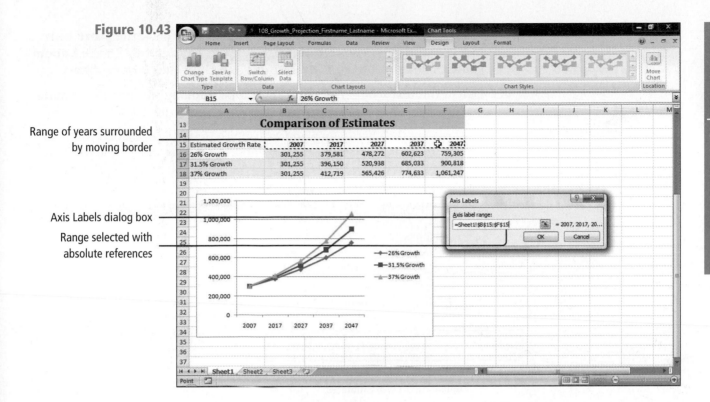

8 In the **Axis Labels** dialog box, click **OK**, and notice that in the
right column, the years display as the category labels. Click **OK** to
close the **Select Data Source** dialog box. Compare your screen with
Figure 10.44.

Figure 10.44

Three rows of data
charted as three lines

Years display as
category labels

9 On the **Design tab**, in the **Chart Styles group**, click the **More** button ▼, and then click **Style 10**. Click the **Layout tab**. In the **Labels group**, click the **Chart Title** button, and then click **Above Chart**.

10 Delete the text *Chart Title*, and then type **Population Growth Estimates** as the chart title. Compare your screen with Figure 10.45.

> Based on the chart, city planners can see that the population will probably double between now and 2037 and could more than triple between now and 2047.

Figure 10.45

11 Click any cell to deselect the chart. Click the **Insert tab**, and then in the **Text group**, click **Header & Footer** to switch to **Page Layout View** and open the **Header area**.

12 In the **Navigation group**, click the **Go to Footer** button, click just above the word *Footer*, and then in the **Header & Footer Elements group**, click the **File Name** button. Click in a cell just above the footer to exit the **Footer area** and view your file name.

13 Scroll up and to the left as necessary to view your chart. Click the chart to select it, and notice that the chart is not centered under the data in the cells. Position the pointer over the **right resize handle** to display the ⟷ pointer, and then drag to the right so that the right border of the chart is just inside the right border of **column F**.

14 Click any cell to deselect the chart. Click the **Page Layout tab**. In the **Page Setup group**, click the **Margins** button, and then at the bottom of the **Margins gallery**, click **Custom Margins**.

15 In the displayed **Page Setup** dialog box, under **Center on page**, select the **Horizontally** check box. Click **OK** to close the dialog box, and then **Save** 🖫 the changes to your workbook.

16 On the status bar, click the **Normal** button 🔳 to return to Normal view, and then press Ctrl + Home to move to the top of your worksheet.

17 At the lower edge of the window, click to select the **Sheet2 tab**, hold down Ctrl, and then click the **Sheet3 tab** to select the two unused sheets. Right-click over the selected sheet tabs, and then on the displayed shortcut menu, click **Delete**.

18 **Save** 🖫 the changes you have made to your workbook. Check your *Chapter Assignment Sheet* or *Course Syllabus* or consult your instructor to determine if you are to submit your assignments on paper or electronically. To submit electronically, follow the instructions provided by your instructor.

19 Press Ctrl + F2 to display the **Print Preview** to check the placement of your worksheet. In the **Print group**, click the **Print** button. In the displayed **Print** dialog box, click **OK** to print your worksheet. If you are directed to submit printed formulas, refer to Activity 9.17 to do so.

20 If you printed your formulas, be sure to redisplay the worksheet by pressing Ctrl + '. From the **Office** menu 🔘, click **Close**. If the dialog box displays asking if you want to save changes, click **No** so that you do *not* save the changes you made for printing formulas. **Exit** Excel.

End **You have completed Project 10B** ⎯⎯⎯⎯⎯⎯⎯⎯⎯⎯⎯⎯⎯

There's More You Can Do!

Close Excel and any other open windows. Display the Start menu, click Computer, and then navigate to the student files that accompany this textbook. In the folder **02_theres_more_you_can_do**, locate and open the folder for this chapter. Open and print the instructions for this project, which are provided to you in Adobe PDF format.

Try IT! 1 — Change the Office Theme in an Excel Workbook

In this Try It! exercise, you will change an Office theme in an Excel workbook.

Content-Based Assessments

Summary

In this chapter, you created and saved a workbook from an existing workbook, renamed worksheets, and color-coded worksheet tabs. You examined and practiced the various ways that Excel formats numbers in a worksheet. You moved, copied, and pasted cell contents using the Office Clipboard. Workbooks frequently contain multiple worksheets, and when they do, a Summary sheet is often included to summarize the data on the individual worksheets. You practiced grouping worksheets to enter and format data simultaneously on multiple worksheets, and then created a summary worksheet to summarize the data.

What-if analysis is used to determine what would happen to one value if another value changes. In this chapter, you used a what-if analysis process to project future trends, and then created a line chart to visually represent those trends.

Key Terms

The ● symbol represents Key Terms found on the Student CD in the 02_theres_more_you_can_do folder for this chapter.

Content-Based Assessments

Matching

Match each term in the second column with its correct definition in the first column. Write the letter of the term on the blank line to the left of the correct definition.

_____ **1.** To move within a document or workbook.

_____ **2.** The labels along the lower border of the worksheet window that identify each worksheet.

_____ **3.** The action of placing cell contents that have been copied or moved to the Office Clipboard to another location.

_____ **4.** A temporary storage area maintained by your Windows operating system.

_____ **5.** A method of moving or copying the content of selected cells in which you point to the selection and then drag it to a new location.

_____ **6.** The target destination for data that has been cut or copied using the Office Clipboard.

_____ **7.** A button that displays in the lower right corner of a pasted selection and that displays a list of options that lets you determine how the information is pasted into your worksheet.

_____ **8.** Within a workbook of multiple worksheets, a worksheet that contains the details of information summarized on a summary worksheet.

_____ **9.** The process of changing the values in cells to see how those changes affect the outcome of formulas in your worksheet.

_____ **10.** The percent by which one number increases over another.

_____ **11.** The mathematical formula to calculate a rate of increase.

_____ **12.** The starting point when you divide the amount of increase by it to calculate the rate of increase.

_____ **13.** The mathematical rules for performing multiple calculations within a formula.

_____ **14.** The Excel feature by which a cell takes on the formatting of the number typed into the cell.

_____ **15.** The formula for calculating the value after an increase by multiplying the original value—the base—by the percent for new value.

A Base

B Detail worksheet

C Drag and drop

D Format as you type

E Navigate

F Office Clipboard

G Order of operations

H Paste

I Paste area

J Paste Options

K Percent rate of increase

L Rate = amount of increase/base

M Sheet tabs

N Value after increase = base × percent for new value

O What-if analysis

Content-Based Assessments

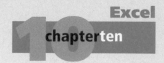
Fill in the Blank

Write the correct answers in the space provided.

1. When a worksheet is active, its tab color displays as an _____.

2. When you enter a date, Excel assigns a _____ value to the date, which makes it possible to treat dates like other numbers for the purpose of calculating the number of days between two dates.

3. A two-digit year value of 30 through 99 is interpreted by the Windows operating system as the four-digit years 1930 through _____.

4. The keyboard shortcut Ctrl + ; enters the _____ _____, which is obtained from your computer's internal calendar.

5. Clearing the contents of a cell does not clear the _____ of a cell—for example, fill color applied to the cell.

6. You can view selections stored on the Office Clipboard by displaying its _____ _____ from the Dialog Box Launcher in the Clipboard group.

7. According to the order of operations for formulas, the first expressions calculated are those within _____.

8. According to the order of operations, _____ and division are performed before addition and subtraction.

9. According to the order of operations, consecutive operators with the same level of _____ are calculated from left to right.

10. The symbol used to indicate the multiplication operation is the _____ symbol.

11. In the formula *percent for new value = base percent + percent of increase*, the base percent is usually _____ %.

12. When pasting a group of copied cells to a target range, you need only select the _____ cell of the target range.

13. The chart type that displays trends over time and that connects data point values with a line is called a _____ chart.

14. In the formula *=(B3-C4)*D3* the mathematical operation that is performed first is _____.

15. When copying the formula *=(B3-B4)*$A$2* to the right, the formula in column C would be _____.

Content-Based Assessments

Project 10C — Permit Sales

In this project, you will apply the skills you practiced from the Objectives in Project 10A.

Objectives: 1. *Create and Save a Workbook from an Existing Workbook;* **2**. *Navigate a Workbook and Rename Worksheets;* **3**. *Enter Dates, Clear Contents, and Clear Formats;* **4**. *Move, Copy, and Paste Cell Contents;* **5**. *Edit and Format Multiple Worksheets at the Same Time;* **6**. *Create a Summary Sheet;* **7**. *Format and Print Multiple Worksheets in a Workbook.*

In the following Skills Review, you will edit a workbook for the Golden Grove Parks and Recreation Director to summarize the sales of weekly and daily campground permits for the three city campgrounds in the month of June. The four worksheets of your completed workbook will look similar to those shown in Figure 10.46.

For Project 10C, you will need the following file:

e10C_Permit_Sales

**You will save your workbook as
10C_Permit_Sales_Firstname_Lastname**

Figure 10.46

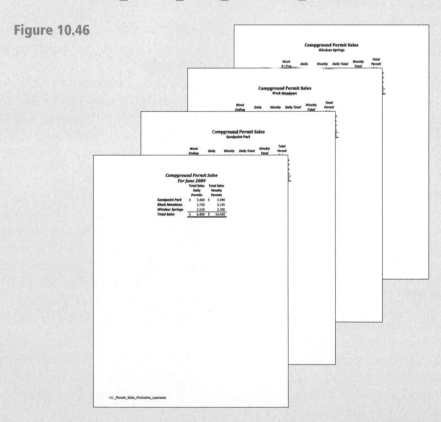

(**Project 10C–Permit Sales continues on the next page**)

Content-Based Assessments

Skills Review

(Project 10C–Permit Sales continued)

1. **Start** Excel. From the **Office** menu, click **Open**, and then navigate to the student files that accompany this textbook. Locate, select, and then open the file **e10C_Permit_Sales**. **Save** the file in your **Excel Chapter 10** folder as **10C_Permit_Sales_Firstname_Lastname** Take a moment to examine the data in each of the three worksheets.

2. Point to the **Sheet1 tab**, and then double-click to select its name. Type **Sandpoint Park** and then press ⏎ to rename the sheet. Right-click the **Sandpoint Park sheet tab**, point to **Tab Color** to display the colors associated with the workbook's theme. Under **Theme Colors**, click **Purple, Accent 4, Lighter 40%**.

3. Point to the **Sheet2 tab**, right-click, and then click **Rename**. Type **Black Meadows** and then press ⏎ to rename the sheet. On the **Home tab**, in the **Cells group**, click the **Format** button, and then point to **Tab Color**. Under **Theme Colors**, click **Aqua, Accent 5, Lighter 40%**.

4. Using either of the two techniques you just practiced, change the name of the **Sheet3 tab** to **Windsor Springs** and then change the **Tab Color** to **Orange, Accent 6, Lighter 40%**.

5. Display the **Sandpoint Park** worksheet, and then select the range **A13:D14**. On the **Home tab**, in the **Clipboard group**, click the **Copy** button to place a copy of the selected cells on the Office Clipboard.

6. Click the **Black Meadows sheet tab** to make it the active worksheet. Click cell **A13**, and then on the **Home tab**, in the **Clipboard group**, click the **Paste** button. Click the **Windsor Springs sheet tab** to make it the active worksheet, and then click cell **A13**. In the **Clipboard group**, click the **Paste** button. Click the

Sandpoint Park sheet tab to make it the active worksheet, and then press Esc to cancel the moving border.

7. Right-click the **Sandpoint Park sheet tab**, and then click **Select All Sheets** to group the sheets—*[Group]* displays in the title bar. Select the range **A5:A8**. On the **Home tab**, in the **Number group**, click the **Number Format arrow**, at the bottom, click **More Number Formats**, under **Category**, click **Date**, and then under **Type**, click **3/14** and click **OK**. The date format for the selected range of cells is changed for all three worksheets.

8. With the worksheets still grouped, click cell **D4**, type **Daily Total** and then press Tab. In cell **E4**, type **Weekly Total** and then press Tab. In cell **F4**, type **Total Permit Sales** and then press ⏎.

9. Select the range **A4:F4**, right-click, and then click **Format Cells**. Click the **Font tab**, and then under **Font style**, click **Bold Italic**. Click the **Alignment tab**. Under **Text alignment**, click the **Horizontal arrow**, and then click **Center**. Click the **Vertical arrow**, and then click **Center**. Under **Text control**, select the **Wrap text** check box. Click **OK**.

10. With the worksheets still grouped, select the range **A1:F1**, and then in the **Alignment group**, click the **Merge & Center** button. Change the **Font** to **Cambria**, the **Font Size** to **14**, and then apply **Bold**. Select the range **A2:F2**, right-click, and then on the Mini toolbar, click the **Merge & Center** button, change the **Font Size** to **12**, and apply **Bold**.

11. With the worksheets still grouped, click cell **D5** and construct a formula to calculate the total sales of *Daily* permits for the week ending June 6 as follows: type **=** to

(Project 10C–Permit Sales continues on the next page)

Content-Based Assessments

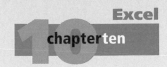
(Project 10C–Permit Sales continued)

begin a formula, click cell **B5**, type * click cell **D13**, and then press F4 to make the reference to cell **D13** absolute. On the **Formula Bar**, click the **Enter** button. Your result is *340*. Use the fill handle to copy the formula down for the remaining dates.

12. In cell **E5**, construct a similar formula to multiply the number of *Weekly* permits sold during the week of June 6 in cell **C5** times the *Weekly Permit Price* in cell **D14**. Make the reference to cell **D14** absolute so that each week's sales are multiplied by the *Weekly Permit Price* in cell **D14**. Your result is *585*. Copy the formula down for the remaining dates.

13. Click cell **A9**, and then apply **Align Text Right** and **Bold**. Select the range **B5:E9**, and then in the **Editing group**, click the **Sum** button to sum each column.

14. With the worksheets still grouped, select the range **D5:F9**, and then in the **Editing group**, click the **Sum** button to sum the rows for *Total Permit Sales* for each week.

15. With the worksheets still grouped, select the nonadjacent ranges **B5:C9** and **D6:F8**, and then apply the **Comma Style** with **zero decimal places**. Select the nonadjacent ranges **D5:F5** and **D9:F9**, and then apply **Accounting Number Format** with **zero decimal places**. Select the range **B9:F9**, in the **Font group**, click the **Borders button arrow**, and then click **Top and Double Bottom Border**. Select **columns B:F**, and then set the width to **70 pixels**.

16. Click the **Black Meadows sheet tab**, and then verify that the formulas and formatting that you applied in Steps 7 through 15 were applied to the worksheet—recall that selecting an individual worksheet

ungroups the sheets. Click the **Windsor Springs sheet tab**, and then verify that the formulas and formatting that you applied in Steps 7 through 15 were applied.

17. **Save** your workbook. To the right of the **Windsor Springs** worksheet tab, click the **Insert Worksheet** button. Rename the new worksheet **Summary** and then change the **Tab Color** to **Olive Green, Accent 3, Lighter 40%**. In cell **A4**, type **Sandpoint Park** In cell **A5**, type **Black Meadows** In cell **A6**, type **Windsor Springs** In cell **A7**, type **Total Sales** Select the range **A4:A7**, change the **Font Size** to **12**, and then apply **Bold** and **Italic**. **AutoFit column A**.

18. In cell **B3**, type **Total Sales Daily Permits** and then in cell **C3**, type **Total Sales Weekly Permits** Select the two cells, and then in the **Alignment group**, click the **Wrap Text** button and the **Center** button. In the **Font group**, click **Bold**.

19. Click cell **B4**. Type = and then click the **Sandpoint Park sheet tab**. On the **Sandpoint Park** worksheet, click cell **D9**, and then press Enter to create a formula that references the *Daily Total Sales* for *Sandpoint Park*.

20. Click cell **C4**. Type = and then click the **Sandpoint Park sheet tab**. Click cell **E9**, and then press Enter to create a formula that references the *Weekly Total Sales* for *Sandpoint Park*. Then, use the same technique to copy the totals for *Daily* and *Weekly* permit sales for the **Black Meadows worksheet** and the **Windsor Springs worksheet**.

21. In cell **A1**, type **Campground Permit Sales** and then **Merge & Center** the text over the range **A1:C1**. Change the **Font** to **Cambria**, the **Font Size** to **14**, and apply

(Project 10C–Permit Sales continues on the next page)

(Project 10C–Permit Sales continued)

Bold and **Italic**. In cell **A2**, type **For June 2009** and then use **Format Painter** to apply the format from cell **A1**.

22. Select the range **B4:C7**, click the **Sum** button to total the two columns. Format the range **B5:C6** with **Comma Style** and **zero decimal places**. Format the nonadjacent ranges **B4:C4** and **B7:C7** with the **Accounting Number Format** and **zero decimal places**. Apply a **Top and Double Bottom** border to the range **B7:C7**.

23. Point to the **Summary sheet tab**, hold down the left mouse button to display a small black caret symbol, and then drag to the left until the caret is positioned to the left of the **Sandpoint Park sheet tab**; release the left mouse button to make the Summary sheet the first sheet in the workbook.

24. Be sure the **Summary** worksheet is the active sheet. Then point to its sheet tab, right-click, and click **Select All Sheets** to display *[Group]* in the title bar. Click the **Insert tab**, and then in the **Text group**, click the **Header & Footer** button. In the **Navigation group**, click the **Go to Footer** button, click in the **left section** above the word *Footer*, and then in the **Header & Footer Elements group**, click the **File Name** button.

25. Click in a cell above the footer to deselect the **Footer area** and view your file name. Click the **Page Layout tab**. In the **Page Setup group**, click the **Margins** button, and then at the bottom of the **Margins gallery**, click **Custom Margins**. In the

displayed **Page Setup** dialog box, under **Center on page**, select the **Horizontally** check box. Click **OK**, and then on the status bar, click the **Normal** button. Press Ctrl + Home to move to the top of the worksheet. Verify that *[Group]* still displays in the title bar.

26. **Save** your workbook. Check your *Chapter Assignment Sheet* or *Course Syllabus*, or consult your instructor, to determine if you are to submit your assignments on paper or electronically. To submit electronically, follow the instructions provided by your instructor.

27. From the **Office** menu, point to the **Print arrow**, and then from the displayed menu, click **Print Preview**. At the top of the screen, click the **Next Page** button as necessary to view and check each page of your workbook.

28. Click the **Print** button. Under **Print range**, verify that the **All** option button is selected. Under **Print what**, click **Active sheet(s)** (assuming your worksheets are still grouped) and then under **Copies**, verify that the **Number of copies** is **1**. Click **OK** to print your workbook. Determine if you are to print formulas for any or all of the worksheets in this workbook. To print formulas, refer to Activity 9.17 in Project 9A.

29. If you printed your formulas, be sure to redisplay the worksheet by pressing Ctrl + `. From the **Office** menu, click **Close**. If you are prompted to save changes, click **No**. **Exit** Excel.

End **You have completed Project 10C** _____

Content-Based Assessments

Skills Review

Project 10D — Property Tax

In this project, you will apply the skills you practiced from the Objectives in Project 10B.

Objectives: 8. *Design a Worksheet for What-If Analysis;* **9**. *Perform What-If Analysis;* **10**. *Compare Data with a Line Chart.*

In the following Skills Review, you will create a worksheet for the Controller of Golden Grove to forecast property tax revenue for the next 10 years. Your completed worksheet will look similar to the one shown in Figure 10.47.

For Project 10D, you will need the following file:

New blank Excel workbook

**You will save your workbook as
10D_Property_Tax_Firstname_Lastname**

Figure 10.47

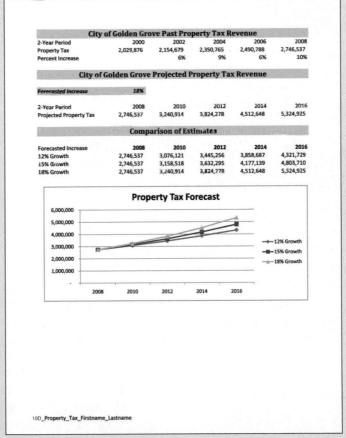

(Project 10D–Property Tax continues on the next page)

Excel

chapterten

Skills Review

(Project 10D–Property Tax continued)

1. **Start** Excel and display a new workbook. In cell **A1**, type **City of Golden Grove Past Property Tax Revenue** and then press [Enter]. Adjust the width of **column A** to **155 pixels**. Select the range **A1:F1**, right-click, and then on the Mini toolbar, apply **Bold**, change the **Font** to **Cambria**, change the **Font Size** to **14**, and click the **Merge & Center** button. From the **Office** menu, click **Save As**, navigate to your **Excel Chapter 10** folder, in the **File name** box, name the file **10D_Property_Tax_Firstname_Lastname** and then click **Save**.

2. In cell **A2**, type **2-Year Period** In cell **B2**, type **2000** and then press [Tab]. In cell **C2**, type **2002** and then press [Tab]. Select the range **B2:C2**, and then drag the fill handle to the right through cell **F2** to enter years through *2008*.

3. In cell **A3**, type **Property Tax** and then press [Enter]. In cell **A4**, type **Percent Increase** and then press [Enter]. Beginning in cell **B3** and pressing [Tab] to move across the row, enter the following values for property tax revenue in the years listed:

2000	2002	2004	2006	2008
2029876	2154679	2350765	2490788	2746537

4. Select the range **B3:F3**, and then right-click over the selection. On the Mini toolbar, apply the **Comma Style**, and then click **Decrease Decimal** two times to apply **zero decimal places**.

5. Click cell **C4**. Type **=(c3-b3)/b3** and then press [Enter] to calculate the *Percent Increase* from the year 2000 to the year 2002. Point to cell **C4** and right-click, and then on the Mini toolbar, click the **Percent Style** button. Your result is *6%*.

6. Click cell **D4**, type = and then by either typing, or using a combination of typing

and clicking cells to reference them, construct a formula similar to the one in cell **C4** to calculate the rate of increase in property tax from 2002 to 2004. Press [Enter], and then format cell **D4** with the **Percent Style**. With cell **D4** selected, drag the fill handle to the right through cell **F4** to calculate the property tax *Percent Increase* for each 2-year period.

7. In cell **A6**, type **City of Golden Grove Projected Property Tax Revenue** and then press [Enter]. Click cell **A1**. On the **Home tab**, in the **Clipboard group**, click the **Format Painter** button, and then click cell **A6**.

8. In cell **A8**, type **Forecasted Increase** and then press [Enter]. In cell **A10**, type **2-Year Period** and then in cell **A11**, type **Projected Property Tax** In cell **B10**, type **2008** and then press [Tab]. In cell **C10**, type **2010** and then press [Enter]. Select the range **B10:C10**, and then drag the fill handle through cell **F10** to extend the pattern of years to **2016**.

9. **Save** the changes you have made to your workbook thus far. In cell **B8**, type **12%** and then press [Enter]. Select the range **A8:B8**, right-click, and then on the Mini toolbar, click **Bold** and **Italic**.

10. In cell **B11**, type = click cell **F3**, and then press [Enter] to create a formula that references the 2008 Property Tax collected by the city.

11. Click cell **C11**. Type **=b11*(100%+b8)** and then on the **Formula Bar**, click the **Enter** button to create a formula that calculates the city's projected property tax revenue based on a forecasted increase of 12%. With cell **C11** as the active cell, drag the fill handle to copy the formula to **D11:F11**. Click cell **B11**, click the **Format Painter** button, and then select the range **C11:F11** to copy the formatting.

(Project 10D–Property Tax continues on the next page)

Content-Based Assessments

(Project 10D–Property Tax continued)

12. In cell **A13**, type **Comparison of Estimates** and then press Enter. Click **A6**, click the **Format Painter** button, and then click cell **A13**. Select the range **A8:B8**, right-click to display the Mini toolbar, click the **Fill Color button arrow**, and then under **Theme Colors**, click **Aqua, Accent 5, Lighter 40%**. Click cell **A1**, and then hold down Ctrl and click **A6** and **A13**. In the **Font group**, click the **Fill Color** button to apply the same fill color to these titles.

13. In cells **A15:A18**, type the following row titles:
Forecasted Increase
12% Growth
15% Growth
18% Growth

14. Select the range **B10:F10**. On the **Home tab**, in the **Clipboard group**, click the **Copy** button, click cell **B15**, and then in the **Clipboard group**, click the **Paste** button.

15. Select the range **B11:F11**, and then click **Copy**. Click cell **B16**, and then in the **Clipboard group**, click the **Paste button arrow**. From the displayed menu, click **Paste Special**. In the displayed **Paste Special** dialog box, under **Paste**, click the **Values and number formats** option button. Click **OK** to paste the values in the cells rather than the formulas.

16. Press Esc to cancel the moving border. Click cell **B8**. Type **15** and then press Enter to recalculate the values in cells **C11:F11** for a 15% increase.

17. Select the range **B11:F11**, and then press Ctrl + C to copy the selection. Click cell **B17**. In the **Clipboard group**, click the **Paste button arrow**, and then click **Paste Special**. In the **Paste Special** dialog box, click the **Values and number formats** option button, and then click **OK**.

18. In cell **B8**, change the **Forecasted Increase** to **18** and press Enter. Using the skills you just practiced, copy the values and number formats in the range **B11:F11** to the range **B18:F18**. Press Esc to cancel the moving border.

19. **Save** the changes you have made thus far. Select the range **B15:F15** and apply **Bold**.

20. Select the range **A16:F18**. On the **Insert tab**, in the **Charts group**, click the **Line** button. Click the **Line with Markers** chart type to create the chart as an embedded chart in the worksheet. Drag to position the upper left corner of the chart slightly inside the upper left corner of cell **A20**.

21. Along the lower portion of the chart, point to any of the category axis numbers such as *1* or *2* to display the ScreenTip. *Horizontal (Category) Axis* displays. Then, right-click, and from the displayed shortcut menu, click **Select Data**. On the right side of the displayed **Select Data Source** dialog box, under **Horizontal (Category) Axis Labels**, click the **Edit** button. Drag the title bar of the **Axis Labels** dialog box to the right of the chart as necessary so that it is not blocking your view of the data, and then select the range **B15:F15**. Click **OK** two times so that the years display on the horizontal axis.

22. On the **Design tab**, in the **Chart Styles group**, click the **More** button, and then click **Style 2**. Click the **Layout tab**. In the **Labels group**, click the **Chart Title** button, and then click **Above Chart**. Delete the text *Chart Title*, and then type **Property Tax Forecast**

23. Click any cell to deselect the chart. Click the **Insert tab**, and then in the **Text group**, click **Header & Footer**. In the **Navigation**

(Project 10D–Property Tax continues on the next page)

Content-Based Assessments

Excel
chapterten   Skills Review

(Project 10D–Property Tax continued)

group, click the **Go to Footer** button, click just above the word *Footer*, and then in the **Header & Footer Elements group**, click the **File Name** button. Click in a cell just above the footer to exit the **Footer area** and view your file name.

24. Scroll up to view your chart, click an edge of the chart to select it, position the pointer over the right resize handle to display the ⟷ pointer, and then drag to the right so that the right border of the chart is just inside the right border of **column F**.

25. Click any cell to deselect the chart. Click the **Page Layout tab**. In the **Page Setup group**, click the **Margins** button, and then at the bottom of the **Margins gallery**, click **Custom Margins**. In the displayed **Page Setup** dialog box, under **Center on page**, select the **Horizontally** check box. Click **OK** to close the dialog box.

26. On the status bar, click the **Normal** button to return to Normal view, and then press Ctrl + Home to move to the top of your worksheet. At the lower edge of the window, click to select the **Sheet2 tab**, hold down Ctrl, and then click the **Sheet3 tab** to

select the two unused sheets. Right-click, and then click **Delete** to delete the unused sheets.

27. **Save** the changes you have made to your workbook. Check your *Chapter Assignment Sheet* or *Course Syllabus* or consult your instructor to determine if you are to submit your assignments on paper or electronically. To submit electronically, follow the instructions provided by your instructor.

28. From the **Office** menu, point to the **Print button arrow**, and then click **Print Preview** to check the placement of your worksheet. In the **Print group**, click the **Print** button. In the displayed **Print** dialog box, click **OK** to print your worksheet. If you are directed to submit printed formulas, refer to Activity 9.17 in Project 9A to do so.

29. If you printed your formulas, be sure to redisplay the worksheet by pressing Ctrl + `. From the **Office** menu, click **Close**. If the dialog box displays asking if you want to save changes, click **No** so that you do *not* save the changes you made for printing formulas. **Exit** Excel.

End **You have completed Project 10D**

Content-Based Assessments

Mastering Excel

Project 10E — Operations Costs

In this project, you will apply the skills you practiced from the Objectives in Projects 10A and 10B.

Objectives: 1. *Create and Save a Workbook from an Existing Workbook;* **2.** *Navigate a Workbook and Rename Worksheets;* **3.** *Enter Dates, Clear Contents, and Clear Formats;* **4.** *Move, Copy, and Paste Cell Contents;* **5.** *Edit and Format Multiple Worksheets at the Same Time;* **6.** *Create a Summary Sheet;* **7.** *Format and Print Multiple Worksheets in a Workbook.* **10.** *Compare Data with a Line Chart.*

In the following Mastering Excel assessment, you will edit a workbook that summarizes and charts the operations costs of Golden Grove's Public Works Department. The department's three divisions are Contract Administration, Engineering, and Street Services. Your completed workbook will look similar to Figure 10.48.

For Project 10E, you will need the following file:

e10E_Operations_Costs

You will save your workbook as
10E_Operations_Costs_Firstname_Lastname

Figure 10.48

(Project 10E–Operations Costs continues on the next page)

(Project 10E–Operations Costs continued)

1. **Start** Excel and from your student files, open **e10E_Operations_Costs**. **Save** the workbook in your **Excel Chapter 10** folder as **10E_Operations_Costs_Firstname_Lastname**

2. Rename the **Sheet1 tab** as **Contract Administration** and then change its **Tab Color** to **Purple, Accent 4, Lighter 40%**. Rename **Sheet2** as **Engineering** and then change its **Tab Color** to **Aqua, Accent 5, Lighter 40%**. Rename **Sheet3** as **Street Services** and then change its **Tab Color** to **Orange, Accent 6, Lighter 40%**.

3. Point to the **Contract Administration** sheet tab, right-click, and then select all of the sheets so that they are grouped. **Merge and Center** the titles in **A1** and **A2** over **columns A:E**. In cell **A3**, type **12/31/2009** and then apply the **03/14/01** date format to the cell. **Merge and Center** cell **A3** over **columns A:E**, and then change the **Font Size** to **16**. Select the range **A1:A3**, and then apply a **Fill Color** of **Red, Accent 2, Lighter 40%**.

4. With the worksheets still grouped, in **row 5**, apply **Wrap Text** formatting to the column titles, and then apply **Bold** and **Italic**. **Center** the column titles.

5. With the worksheets still grouped, sum the columns and then sum the rows. Beginning with **Comma Style**, apply appropriate financial formatting using **zero decimal places**, and then change the width of **column A** to **110 pixels**. Select cell **A10** and **Clear Formats** so that the text is aligned at the left and not bold.

6. Ungroup the worksheets and verify that the formulas and formatting applied in Steps 3 through 5 were applied to the **Engineering** and **Street Services** sheets. Insert a new worksheet and **Rename** it **Summary** Change the **Tab Color** to **Olive Green, Accent 3, Lighter 40%**.

7. Display the **Contract Administration** worksheet. Select and **Copy** the range **A1:A3**, and then **Paste** the selection to the **Summary** worksheet in cell **A1**. In the **Summary** worksheet, click cell **A2**, and then type **Public Works Summary**

8. Display the **Contract Administration** worksheet. **Copy** the range **A6:A9**, **Paste** the selection to the **Summary** worksheet in cell **A6**, and then in the **Summary** worksheet, adjust the width of **column A** to **110 pixels** and the width of **columns B:E** to **100 pixels**. In cell **A10**, type **Total** and notice that the italic emphasis will carry forward from the cell above.

9. In cell **B5**, type **Contract Administration** In cell **C5**, type **Engineering** In cell **D5**, type **Street Services** In cell **E5**, type **Total Center** and apply **Wrap Text** formatting to the column titles in **row 5**, apply **Bold**, and then apply **Middle Align**.

10. **Save** the changes you have made to your workbook thus far. In the **Summary** worksheet, in cell **B6**, create a formula that references the **Contract Administration** worksheet *Quarter 1 Total Direct Costs* in cell **E6**. Fill the formula down through **B9** to create formulas that reference the remaining quarter's *Total Direct Costs*. Create similar formulas for the **Engineering** and **Street Services** quarterly *Total Direct Costs*. Sum the columns and then sum the rows. Beginning with **Comma Style**, apply appropriate financial formatting using **zero decimal places**.

11. Select the range **A5:D9**, and then insert a line chart using the **Line with Markers** chart type. Position the upper left corner of the chart inside the upper left corner of cell **A12**. Apply **Chart Style 10**, and then add the **Chart Title Public Works Costs** in the **Above Chart** position. From the

(Project 10E–Operations Costs continues on the next page)

Content-Based Assessments

(Project 10E–Operations Costs continued)

status bar, click the **Page Layout View** button, widen the chart to display attractively below the data, and then click any cell to deselect the chart. **Move** the **Summary** worksheet so that it is the first sheet in the workbook.

12. Group the worksheets, insert a footer with the **File Name** on the left, and then center the worksheets **Horizontally**. Return to **Normal** view and display the upper portion of the worksheet.

13. Save your workbook, and then examine your grouped worksheets in **Print Preview**.

Print or submit electronically as directed. If the worksheets are grouped, all the worksheets will print. If the worksheets are not grouped, click Entire workbook to print all the sheets. Determine if you are to print formulas for any or all of the worksheets in this workbook. To print formulas, refer to Activity 9.17 in Project 9A.

14. If you printed your formulas, be sure to redisplay the worksheet by pressing Ctrl + `. From the **Office** menu, click **Close**. If you are prompted to save changes, click **No**. **Exit** Excel.

End **You have completed Project 10E** _____

Mastering Excel

Project 10F—Venue Revenue

In this project, you will apply the skills you practiced from the Objectives in Projects 10A and 10B.

Objectives: 3. *Enter Dates, Clear Contents, and Clear Formats;* **8.** *Design a Worksheet for What-If Analysis;* **9.** *Perform What-If Analysis;* **10.** *Compare Data with a Line Chart.*

In the following Mastering Excel assessment, you will complete a workbook for the Director of Conventions, Culture, and Leisure, which shows revenue estimates for city-owned venues for conventions, cultural events, and leisure activities and their associated parking structures. Your resulting worksheet and chart will look similar to Figure 10.49.

For Project 10F, you will need the following file:

New blank Excel workbook

You will save your workbook as
10F_Venue_Revenue_Firstname_Lastname

Figure 10.49

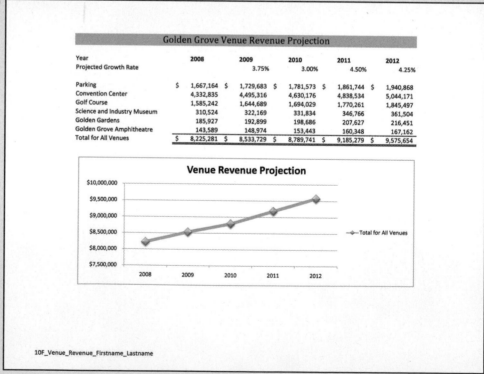

(Project 10F–Venue Revenue continues on the next page)

Excel
chapterten

Mastering Excel

(Project 10F–Venue Revenue continued)

1. **Start** Excel and display a new blank workbook. **Save** the workbook in your **Excel Chapter 10** folder as **10F_Venue_Revenue_Firstname_Lastname**

2. In cell **A1**, type **Golden Grove Venue Revenue Projection** and then **Merge and Center** the title across cells **A1:F1**. Change the **Font** to **Cambria**, the **Font Size** to **16**, and then apply the **Olive Green, Accent 3 Fill Color**. In cell **A3**, type **Year** In the range **B3:F3**, create a pattern of years from 2008 through 2012. Format the years with **Bold** and **Center**.

3. In cell **A4**, type **Projected Growth Rate** In the range **C4:F4**, type the following percentages: **3.75%** and **3.0%** and **4.5%** and **4.25%**

4. Widen **column A** to **200 pixels** and widen columns **B:F** to **100 pixels**. In the range **A6:B11**, enter the following data:

Parking	1667164
Convention Center	4332835
Golf Course	1585242
Science and Industry Museum	310524
Golden Gardens	185927
Golden Grove Amphitheatre	143589

5. In cell **C6**, construct a formula that calculates the year *2009* revenue for *Parking* assuming an increase of 3.75% (the rate in cell C4) over the previous year. That is, multiply the base value in cell **B6** times 100% plus the value in cell **C4**. Place the second expression in parentheses so that addition is performed first, and make the reference to the value in **C4** absolute so that you can copy this formula down column C. In cell **D6**, for the year *2010*, construct a similar formula using the previous year's revenue and the rate in cell **D4**. Construct similar formulas for the years

2011 and *2012* using the previous year's revenue and the projected growth rate for the year indicated. **Copy** the formulas in **row 6** down through **row 11**.

6. In cell **A12**, type **Total for All Venues** and then in **row 12**, sum the values in **columns B:F**. Beginning with **Comma Style**, apply appropriate financial formatting with **zero decimal places**.

7. **Save** the changes you have made to your workbook thus far. Using the data in the range **A12:F12**, insert a line chart using the **Line with Markers** chart type, and then apply **Chart Style 29**. Edit the data source so that the **Horizontal (Category) Axis** uses the years in the range **B3:F3** as the labels. Change the chart title to **Venue Revenue Projection** Position the upper left corner of the chart inside the upper left corner of cell **A14**.

8. Click any cell to deselect the chart. Change the **Orientation** to **Landscape**, and then center the worksheet on the page **Horizontally**. Insert a footer with the **File Name** on the left side. Widen the chart so that it displays attractively under the data. Deselect the chart, return to **Normal** view, display the top of the worksheet, and then delete the unused sheets in the workbook.

9. **Save** your workbook, and then examine your worksheet in **Print Preview**. **Print** or submit electronically as directed. To print formulas, refer to Activity 9.17 in Project 9A.

10. If you printed your formulas, be sure to redisplay the worksheet by pressing [Ctrl] + [`]. From the **Office** menu, click **Close**. If you are prompted to save changes, click **No**. **Exit** Excel.

End **You have completed Project 10F**

Excel
chapterten

Mastering Excel

Project 10G — Analysis

In this project, you will apply the skills you practiced from all the Objectives in Projects 10A and 10B.

Objectives: 1. *Create and Save a Workbook from an Existing Workbook;* **2.** *Navigate a Workbook and Rename Worksheets;* **3.** *Enter Dates, Clear Contents, and Clear Formats;* **4.** *Move, Copy, and Paste Cell Contents;* **5.** *Edit and Format Multiple Worksheets at the Same Time;* **6.** *Create a Summary Sheet;* **7.** *Format and Print Multiple Worksheets in a Workbook;* **8.** *Design a Worksheet for What-If Analysis;* **9.** *Perform What-If Analysis;* **10.** *Compare Data with a Line Chart.*

In the following Mastering Excel assessment, you will complete a workbook for the Director of Parks and Recreation, which shows departmental expenses for the three departments reporting to the director. Your resulting worksheet and chart will look similar to Figure 10.50.

For Project 10G, you will need the following file:

e10G_Analysis

You will save your workbook as 10G_Analysis_Firstname_Lastname

Figure 10.50

(Project 10G–Analysis continues on the next page)

Mastering Excel

(Project 10G–Analysis continued)

1. **Start** Excel, and then from your student files, open the file **e10G_Analysis**. Rename **Sheet1** as **Recreation** and then change the **Tab Color** to **Blue, Accent 1, Lighter 40%**. Rename **Sheet2** as **Parks** and then change the **Tab Color** to **Red, Accent 2, Lighter 40%**. Rename **Sheet3** as **Community Outreach** and then change the **Tab Color** to **Olive Green, Accent 3, Lighter 40%**. **Save** the workbook in your **Excel Chapter 10** folder as 10G_Analysis_ Firstname_Lastname

2. Display the **Recreation** worksheet, and then group the three worksheets. Select the range **A1:A2**, change the **Font** to **Cambria**, the **Font Size** to **16**, apply **Bold**, and then apply a **Fill Color** of **Aqua, Accent 5, Lighter 40%**. **Merge & Center** the two worksheet titles across the ranges **A1:D1** and **A2:D2**. Select the years in the range **B4:D4** and apply **Bold**, and **Center alignment**. Select the **Salaries** data in the range **B5:D5**, apply **Accounting Number Format** with **zero decimal places**, and then select the range **A5:D5** and apply **Bold** and **Italic**. Use **Format Painter** to copy the formatting from cell **A5** to cell **A7** and to cell **A14**.

3. Verify that the worksheets are still grouped, and then in **row 14**, sum each year's data for *Expenses*. Apply **Bold** and **Italic** to the totals. Beginning with **Comma Style** and using **zero decimal places**, apply appropriate financial formatting to the *Expenses* data, *without* a Top and Double Bottom Border. Instead, to the range **B14:D14**, apply only a **Top Border**.

4. Ungroup the worksheets and verify that the formatting and editing changes that you made in Steps 2 and 3 were applied to all three worksheets. On the **Recreation** worksheet, **Copy** the text in cell **A16**, and then **Paste** it to the same location in the

Parks worksheet and **Community Outreach** worksheet.

5. Display the **Recreation** worksheet and press [Esc] to cancel the moving border. Group the three worksheets. In cell **B16**, construct a formula that adds the *2008 Salaries* in cell **B5** and the *2008 Total Expenses* in cell **B14**. Fill the formula across the remaining two years, and then with the range **B16:D16** still selected, apply a **Bottom Double Border**. Select the range **A16:D16**, and then apply **Bold** and **Italic**.

6. With the worksheets still grouped, in cell **A18**, type Total Departmental Increase In cell **C18**, construct a formula that calculates the percent increase of the *Total Departmental Increase* for *2009* from *2008*. Your result is *0.003307521*, an increase of less than 1%. Apply **Percent Style** formatting with **two decimal places** for a result of *0.33%*. Copy the formula to the right for the year 2010; in this year, the percentage increase was more significant—*8.27%*. To the range **A18:D18**, apply **Bold**, **Italic**, and a **Fill Color** using **Aqua, Accent 5, Lighter 40%**.

7. With the worksheets still grouped, in cell **A20**, type Projected Budget Years 2010 – 2012 and then use **Format Painter** to copy the format from cell **A1** to cell **A20**. In cell **A22**, type Forecasted Increase In cell **A24**, type Year and in cell **A25**, type Forecasted Total Budget Apply **AutoFit** to **column A**. In the range **B24:D24**, enter a pattern of years from 2010 through 2012, and then **Center** and **Bold** the years. In cell **B22**, type 8.5% which will display as *8.50%*. To the range **A22:B22**, apply **Bold** and **Italic**.

8. With the worksheets still grouped, in cell **B25**, construct a formula that references

(Project 10G–Analysis continues on the next page)

(Project 10G–Analysis continued)

cell **D16**—the *Total Department* expenses for *2010*. In cell **C25**, construct a formula that calculates the *Forecasted Total Budget* for *2011* based on the 8.5% increase in cell **B22**. Be sure to make the reference to cell **B22** absolute. (The result might display as being too wide for the cell.) **Copy** the formula to cell **D25**, and then use **Format Painter** to copy the formatting from cell **B25** to the range **C25:D25**.

9. **Save** the changes you have made thus far. **Insert** a new worksheet, rename the worksheet **Summary** and then change the **Tab Color** to **Orange, Accent 6, Lighter 40%**. In cell **A1**, type **Golden Grove Parks and Recreation** In cell **A2**, type **Forecast Summary** In cell **A3**, type **Years 2010 to 2012** In the range **B5:D5**, enter the years **2010** and **2011** and **2012** Apply **Bold** and **Center** to the years. In the range **A6:A9**, enter the row titles **Recreation** and **Parks** and **Community Outreach** and **Total** Widen **column A** to **230** pixels. Widen columns **B:D** to **95** pixels.

10. **Merge & Center** each of the three worksheet titles across **columns A:D**, and then change the **Font** to **Cambria**, the **Font Size** to **16**, and apply a **Fill Color** of **Aqua, Accent 5, Lighter 40%**.

11. In cell **B6**, enter a formula that references the **Forecasted Total Budget** for **2010** from cell **B25** in the **Recreation** worksheet. Fill the formula across through cell **D6**, and then construct similar formulas for the **Forecasted Total Budget** amounts from the **Parks** worksheet and the **Community Outreach** worksheet. Calculate totals for each year in **row 9**. Beginning with **Comma Style**, apply appropriate financial formatting to the data with **zero decimal places**.

12. **Save** your changes. Using the data in the range **A6:D8**, insert a line chart using the **Line with Markers** chart type. Position the upper left corner of the chart inside the upper left corner of cell **A11**, apply **Chart Style 2**, and then edit the data source so that the **Horizontal (Category) Axis** displays the years in the range **B5:D5**. Insert a chart title in the **Above Chart** position with the text **Three-Year Budget Forecast**

13. Click any cell to deselect the chart. Move the **Summary** worksheet to become the first worksheet in the workbook, and then group the worksheets. Center the worksheets in the workbook **Horizontally** on the page. Insert a footer on the left side with the **File Name**. Ungroup the worksheets. Adjust the width of the chart so that it is slightly inside the right boundary of **column D** to display attractively below the data. Return to **Normal** view, deselect the chart, and display the top of the worksheet.

14. **Save** your workbook, and then examine your worksheets in **Print Preview**. **Print** or submit electronically as directed. If the worksheets are grouped, all the worksheets will print. If the worksheets are not grouped, click **Entire workbook** to print all the sheets. Determine if you are to print formulas for any or all of the worksheets in this workbook. To print formulas, refer to Activity 9.17 in Project 9A.

15. If you printed your formulas, be sure to redisplay the worksheet by pressing Ctrl + `. From the Office menu, click **Close**. If you are prompted to save changes, click No. **Exit** Excel.

End **You have completed Project 10G**

Content-Based Assessments

Mastering Excel

Project 10H — *GO!* Fix It

In this project, you will construct a solution by applying any combination of the skills you practiced from the Objectives in Projects 10A and 10B.

The Golden Grove City Council has maintained the same pool pass fee structure for the past six years. It has asked staff to provide information on attendance and receipts, to see if an increase in fees is warranted. Your task is to review and correct a draft workbook containing this information and to make revenue projections.

For Project 10H, you will need the following file:

e10H_Pool_Passes

**You will save your workbook as
10H_Pool_Passes_Firstname_Lastname**

From the student files that accompany this textbook, open the file **e10H_Pool_Passes**, and then save the file in your chapter folder as **10H_Pool_Passes_Firstname_Lastname**

This workbook contains five errors that you must find and correct. Read and examine the document, and then edit to correct the errors that you find. Types of errors could include:

- Spelling, grammar, and punctuation errors in cells, charts, worksheet tabs, or file names.

- Errors in data entry and workbook layout. Formatting errors in text, numbers, alignment, indents and spacing, tabs, wrapping, merge and center, text direction and orientation, fonts, borders, patterns, protection, AutoFormat, conditional formatting, data sort, filter, and validation.

- Formula and function errors such as incorrect and missing formulas, error indicators and values, relative versus absolute cell referencing, What-If Analysis, Paste Special, function arguments, and Goal Seek.

- Errors in object design, layout, and formatting, for example chart type, location, data source, elements, size, scale, positioning, pictures, and hyperlinks.

- Row and column formatting errors such as height, width, and AutoFit.

- Worksheet, tab design, and formatting errors such as missing or blank worksheets, worksheet tab colors, and locations.

- Page setup errors such as page orientation and scaling, margins and centering, headers and footers, sheet gridlines, and row and column headings.

(Project 10H–*GO!* Fix It continues on the next page)

Content-Based Assessments

Mastering Excel

(Project 10H–*GO!* Fix It continued)

To complete the project you should know:

- In your finished workbook, the grand total in Cell E36 on the Summary worksheet should be $6,193,765.

- It is efficient to work from the last worksheet to the first when looking for errors.

- Formula errors and omissions in a range of cells count as a single error.

- A chart title should be inserted above the chart, entitled *Revenue from Pool Passes 2003–2008* and formatted as Verdana, 18 pt bold.

- All the workbook pages should be centered horizontally.

Save the changes you have made, add the file name to the footers, and then submit as directed.

 You have completed Project 10H

Outcomes-Based Assessments

Rubric

The following outcomes-based assessments are *open-ended assessments*. That is, there is no specific correct result; your result will depend on your approach to the information provided. Make *Professional Quality* your goal. Use the following scoring rubric to guide you in *how* to approach the problem and then to evaluate *how well* your approach solves the problem.

The *criteria*—Software Mastery, Content, Format and Layout, and Process—represent the knowledge and skills you have gained that you can apply to solving the problem. The *levels of performance*—Professional Quality, Approaching Professional Quality, or Needs Quality Improvements—help you and your instructor evaluate your result.

	Your completed project is of Professional Quality if you:	Your completed project is Approaching Professional Quality if you:	Your completed project Needs Quality Improvements if you:
1-Software Mastery	Choose and apply the most appropriate skills, tools, and features and identify efficient methods to solve the problem.	Choose and apply some appropriate skills, tools, and features, but not in the most efficient manner.	Choose inappropriate skills, tools, or features, or are Inefficient in solving the problem.
2-Content	Construct a solution that is clear and well organized, contains content that is accurate, appropriate to the audience and purpose, and is complete. Provide a solution that contains no errors of spelling, grammar, or style.	Construct a solution in which some components are unclear, poorly organized, inconsistent, or incomplete. Misjudge the needs of the audience. Have some errors in spelling, grammar, or style, but the errors do not detract from comprehension.	Construct a solution that is unclear, incomplete, or poorly organized; contains some inaccurate or inappropriate content; and contains many errors of spelling, grammar, or style. Do not solve the problem.
3-Format and Layout	Format and arrange all elements to communicate information and ideas, clarify function, illustrate relationships, and indicate relative importance.	Apply appropriate format and layout features to some elements, but not others. Overuse features, causing minor distraction.	Apply format and layout that does not communicate information or ideas clearly. Do not use format and layout features to clarify function, illustrate relationships, or indicate relative importance. Use available features excessively, causing distraction.
4-Process	Use an organized approach that integrates planning, development, self-assessment, revision, and reflection.	Demonstrate an organized approach in some areas, but not others; or, use an insufficient process of organization throughout.	Do not use an organized approach to solve the problem.

Outcomes-Based Assessments

Excel

chapter ten

Problem Solving

Project 10I — Fire Stations

In this project, you will construct a solution by applying any combination of the skills you practiced in the Objectives covered in Projects 10A and 10B.

> **For Project 10I, you will need the following file:**

New blank Excel workbook

You will save your workbook as
10I_Fire_Stations_Firstname_Lastname

The City of Golden Grove has approved a bond measure for the construction of three new fire stations. Using the information provided, create a workbook that the City Controller can present to the City Council that details construction costs covered by the bond measure. Design your workbook so that the data for each fire station is on a separate worksheet. First, group the sheets to apply formatting and type the row and column titles that will be the same across all sheets; this will help you avoid unnecessary typing and formatting. Then, ungroup the sheets, include the fire station location at the top of each worksheet, and type the costs into each sheet. To type the costs, it may be helpful to select the range first so that the movement of the insertion point is confined to the range.

Grand Avenue Fire Station Costs	Land	Design	Construction
Phase 1	13840320	343900	2209384
Phase 2	1102984	230098	3384950
Phase 3	1920384	119739	6937409

South Edison Fire Station Costs	Land	Design	Construction
Phase 1	1866428	459320	1938400
Phase 2	293040	664739	6790474
Phase 3	288730	193804	8498502

Hill Street Fire Station Costs	Land	Design	Construction
Phase 1	394058	484927	1849023
Phase 2	1293846	559680	7593084
Phase 3	129800	583920	5890503

(Project 10I–Fire Stations continues on the next page)

Excel

chapterten

Problem Solving

(Project 10I–Fire Stations continued)

For all of the worksheets, calculate totals for each Phase (rows) and for each type of cost (columns). Insert a worksheet that summarizes, for each fire station, the total costs by type of cost (Land, Design, and Construction). Sum the columns. On each worksheet, use borders, fill colors, and font styles and sizes to create a professional worksheet. Add a footer to each worksheet that includes the file name and center the worksheets on the page. Save the workbook as **10I_Fire_Stations_ Firstname_Lastname** and submit it as directed.

 You have completed Project 10I ——————————

Outcomes-Based Assessments

Problem Solving

Project 10J—Water Usage

In this project, you will construct a solution by applying any combination of the skills you practiced in the Objectives covered in Projects 10A and 10B.

For Project 10J, you will need the following file:

New blank Excel workbook

You will save your workbook as
10J_Water_Usage_Firstname_Lastname

Golden Grove is a growing community and the City Council has requested an analysis of future water needs. In this project, you will create a worksheet for the Department of Water and Power that contains data regarding past residential water usage and that forecasts water usage in the future. Create a worksheet with the following data:

Year	2002	2004	2006	2008	2010
Water Use in Acre Feet	62500	68903	73905	76044	80342

Calculate the percent increase in water usage from 2002 to 2004, and then for 2006, 2008, and 2010. Using Project 10B as a guide, add a section to the worksheet to calculate the projected water usage for the years 2010 to 2018 in two-year increments. The 2010 amount is 80,342. Add a comparison of estimates section to the worksheet with three forecasted increases: 4%, 6%, and 9%. Include a worksheet title and use formatting and editing techniques that you practiced in this chapter so that the worksheet looks attractive and professional. Add the file name to the footer. Save the workbook as **10J_Water_Usage_Firstname_Lastname** and submit it as directed.

 End **You have completed Project 10J** _____

Outcomes-Based Assessments

Excel
chapter ten

Problem Solving

Project 10K — Schools

In this project, you will construct a solution by applying any combination of the skills you practiced in the Objectives in Projects 10A and 10B.

For Project 10K, you will need the following file:

New blank Excel workbook

You will save your workbook as
10K_Schools_Firstname_Lastname

As the city of Golden Grove grows, the school district must plan for additional students that will enroll in the elementary, middle, and high schools. In this project, you will create a workbook that contains enrollment projections for the next four years. First, create three worksheets containing the following information:

Elementary Schools	2008	2009	2010	2011	2012
Projected Increase		2%	3.5%	7%	5%
Wyndham	1350				
Warm Creek	956				
Los Serranos	1175				
Hidden Canyon	1465				
Butterfield	854				

Middle Schools	2008	2009	2010	2011	2012
Projected Increase		4.5%	5.75%	3%	3.5%
Townsend	1194				
Canyon Hills	1575				
Golden Springs	1392				

High Schools	2008	2009	2010	2011	2012
Projected Increase		6%	7.5%	4%	2.75%
Poppy Hills	2276				
Diamond Ranch	3150				

On each sheet, create formulas in the 2009 column that increase the 2008 enrollment by the Projected Increase percent. Create similar formulas for each year, increasing the previous year's enrollment by the Projected Increase percent. Calculate totals by year. Insert a line chart on each sheet with the years on the category horizontal axis. Create a summary sheet that includes the total enrollment by year for each *type* of school—Elementary Schools, Middle Schools, and High Schools—and then calculate totals for each year. Use formatting and editing techniques that you practiced in this chapter so that the workbook looks attractive and professional. Add the file name to the footer. Save the workbook as **10K_Schools_Firstname_Lastname** and submit it as directed.

End **You have completed Project 10K** ——————

Project 10K: Schools | **Excel**   443

More on your Student CD

The instructions for the following additional end-of-chapter projects are on your student CD in the folder 03_additional_end_of_chapter_projects.

Content-Based Assessments

Project L Mastering Excel

Apply the skills you practiced in Project A.

Project M Mastering Excel

Apply the skills you practiced in Project B.

Project N Business Running Case

Apply the skills you practiced in Projects A and B while helping an entrepreneur with the daily tasks of running a business.

In each chapter, this project focuses on applying the skills you have practiced in Projects A and B to a business. The project related to this business runs throughout the textbook. You will see how the Office applications relate to the day-to-day operation of a small business called Nelson Architectural Planning.

Outcomes-Based Assessments

Project O Problem Solving

Construct a solution by applying any combination of the skills you practiced from Projects A and B.

Project P Problem Solving

Construct a solution by applying any combination of the skills you practiced from Projects A and B.

Project Q You and GO!

Construct a solution that applies to your own life by applying any combination of the skills you practiced from Projects A and B.

Project R GO! with Help

Practice using Microsoft Office's Help Feature.

Project S Group Business Running Case

Work as part of a group to apply the skills you have gained thus far to help the Bell Orchid Hotel Group achieve its business goals.

Multimedia

The following multimedia accompany this textbook:

Companion Web site
www.prenhall.com/go

An interactive Web site designed to reinforce and test your understanding of the skills in this chapter.

AV-EDDs

In the folder in the front of this book you will find videos that demonstrate the objectives of the A and B projects in this chapter. These may help you understand how to complete the projects in this book.

Video Podcasts

In the folder in the front of this book are videos that can be played on your iPod, MP3 player, or computer. These videos demonstrate how to complete the more challenging objectives in this textbook.

chaptereleven

Using Functions and Tables

OBJECTIVES

At the end of this chapter you will be able to:

1. Use SUM, AVERAGE, MEDIAN, MIN, and MAX Functions
2. Use COUNTIF and IF Functions, and Apply Conditional Formatting
3. Use a Date Function
4. Freeze Panes and Create an Excel Table
5. Format and Print a Large Worksheet

6. Use Financial Functions
7. Use Goal Seek
8. Create a Data Table

OUTCOMES

Mastering these objectives will enable you to:

PROJECT 11A
Track Inventory by Using Math, Logical, and Statistical Functions and by Creating an Excel Table

PROJECT 11B
Make Financial Decisions by Using Financial Functions and What-If Analysis

Adamantine Jewelry, Inc.

Adamantine Jewelry is based in Milan, Italy, one of the world's leading centers for fashion and design. The company's designers take inspiration from nature, cultural artifacts, and antiquities to produce affordable, fashionable jewelry that is sold through major retailers around the world. With a 40-year history, the company is well respected among its retail customers and has recently expanded to online and television retailers. In addition to women's bracelets, necklaces, rings, and earrings, the company also produces sport and fashion watches for men and women.

© Paul Harris and Anne Heslope / Dorling Kindersley

Using Functions and Tables

In this chapter, you will design worksheets that use the library of formulas and procedures provided with Excel to perform specific functions. You will also use more What-If Analysis tools. Using these tools will make your worksheets valuable tools for analyzing data and making financial decisions.

Project 11A Milan Inventory

In Activities 11.01 through 11.13, you will edit a worksheet for Rose Elleni, Vice President of Production, detailing the current inventory of two product types at the Milan production facility. Your completed worksheet will look similar to Figure 11.1.

For Project 11A, you will need the following file:

e011A_Milan_Inventory

You will save your workbook as
11A_Milan_Inventory_Firstname_Lastname

Figure 11.1
Project 11A—Milan Inventory

Objective 1
Use SUM, AVERAGE, MEDIAN, MIN, and MAX Functions

A *function* is a predefined formula—a formula that Excel has already built for you—that performs calculations by using specific values in a particular order or structure.

Activity 11.01 Using the SUM, AVERAGE, and MEDIAN Functions

In this activity, you will use the SUM and AVERAGE functions to gather information about the product inventory.

1 **Start** Excel. From the student files that accompany this text, locate and open **e11A_Milan_Inventory**. From the **Office** menu 🏢, display the **Save As** dialog box, and then navigate to the location where you are storing your projects for this chapter. Create a **New Folder** named **Excel Chapter 11**.

2 In the **File name** box, type **11A_Milan_Inventory_Firstname_Lastname** and then click **Save** or press [Enter].

3 Scroll down the worksheet, and notice that the worksheet contains data related to two product types—*Bracelets* and *Earrings*—and then for each product type, information regarding the *Quantity in Stock*, *Style#*, *Retail Price*, *Gemstone*, and *Metal* is included.

4 In cell **A1**, type **Milan Facility: Inventory Status of Product Types Bracelets and Earrings** and in cell **A2** type **As of June 30, 2009 Merge and Center** 🔲 ▾ each worksheet title across columns **A:L**. Format both titles with **Bold** 🅱 , change the **Font** to **Cambria**, change the **Font Size** to **16**, and then apply a **Fill Color** 🎨 ▾ of **Dark Blue, Text 2, Lighter 60%**.

5 In cell **A4**, type **Total in Stock** In cell **A5**, type **Average Price** In cell **A6**, type **Median Price** Click cell **B4**. Click the **Formulas tab**, and then in the **Function Library group**, click the **AutoSum** button. Compare your screen with Figure 11.2.

> The **SUM function** that you have used is a predefined formula that adds all the numbers in a selected range of cells.

Figure 11.2

AutoSum button ———

Function Library group ———

Formulas tab selected ———

SUM function started in cell ———

Worksheet titles formatted ———

6 With the insertion point blinking in the function, select the range **A12:A66**, dragging down as necessary, and then press Enter. Scroll up to view the top of your worksheet, and notice your result in cell **B4**, *1657*.

7 Click cell **B4**, look at the **Formula Bar**, and then compare your screen with Figure 11.3.

> The values in parentheses are the ***arguments***—the values that an Excel function uses to perform calculations or operations. In this instance, the argument consists of the values in the range A12:A66.

Figure 11.3

SUM function in Formula Bar

Number of Bracelets in stock

Argument in parentheses

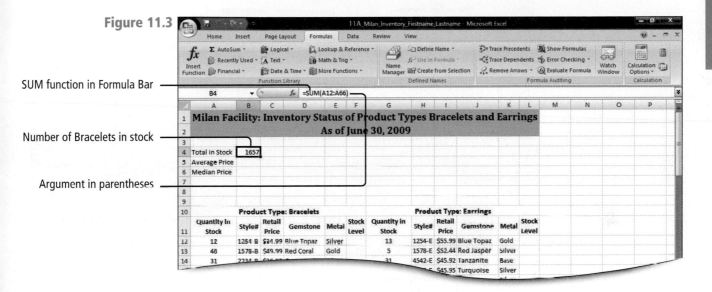

8 Click cell **B5**. In the **Function Library group**, click the **More Functions** button, point to **Statistical**, in the list, point to **AVERAGE**, and then compare your screen with Figure 11.4.

> ***Statistical functions*** are prewritten formulas that analyze a group of measurements.

Figure 11.4

More Functions button

Statistical category

List of Statistical functions

AVERAGE ScreenTip

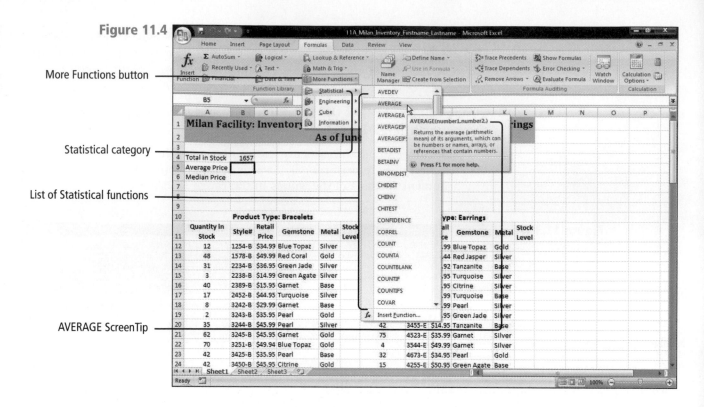

9. Click **AVERAGE**, and then if necessary, drag the title bar of the **Function Arguments** dialog box down and to the right so you can view the **Formula Bar** and cell **B5**.

> The Function Arguments dialog box for the AVERAGE function displays. The ***AVERAGE function*** is a formula that adds a group of values, and then divides the result by the number of values in the group.
>
> In the cell, the Formula Bar, and the dialog box, Excel proposes to average the value in cell B4. Recall that Excel functions will propose a range if data is above or to the left of a selected cell. Because you want to average the values in the range C12:C66—and *not* cell B4—you must edit the proposed range.

10. In the **Function Arguments** dialog box, click in the **Number1** box to display the insertion point. Delete the existing text, type **c12:c66** and then compare your screen with Figure 11.5.

> The result displays in the dialog box.

Figure 11.5

Formula Bar displays
function and argument

Function Arguments dialog
box for AVERAGE function

Range of cells to average

Result displays

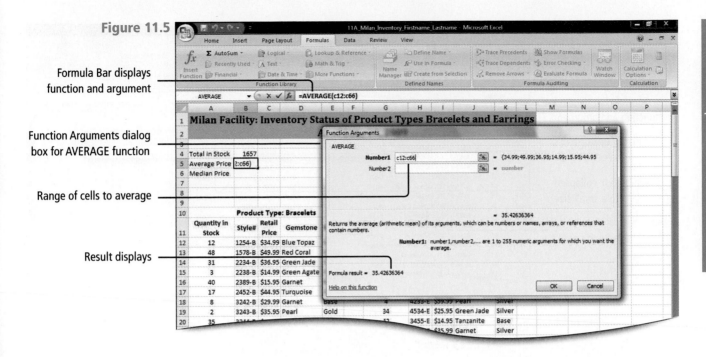

[▣] In the **Function Arguments** dialog box, click **OK**.

The result indicates that the average Retail Price of all Bracelets
is *$35.43*.

[▣] Click cell **B6**. In the **Function Library group**, click the **More
Functions** button, display the list of **Statistical** functions, scroll
down as necessary, and then click **MEDIAN**.

The *MEDIAN function* is a statistical function commonly used to
describe a group of data—you have likely seen it used to describe the
price of houses in a particular geographical area. The MEDIAN function
finds the *middle value* that has as many values *above* it in the group as
are *below* it. It differs from AVERAGE in that the result is not affected
as much by a single value that is greatly different from the others.

[▣] In the **Function Arguments** dialog box, to the right of the **Number1**
box, click the **Collapse Dialog** button [▣]—the square with the
red arrow.

The dialog box collapses to a small size containing only space for the
first argument. Now you can see more of your worksheet data.

[▣] Select the range **C12:C66**, and then compare your screen with
Figure 11.6.

Figure 11.6

Formula Bar displays
function and argument

Collapsed dialog box displays
selected range

Dialog box collapsed
to a small size

Selected range surrounded by
a moving border

15 Press Enter.

The dialog box expands to its original size and the selected range displays as the argument in the Number1 box. When entering arguments into a Function Arguments dialog box, you can either select the range of cells in this manner, or type the range into the argument box.

16 In the lower right corner of the **Function Arguments** dialog box, click **OK**. Save your workbook.

Your result is *$35.95*—in the range of prices, $35.95 is the middle value. Half of all Bracelet products are priced *above* $35.95 and half are priced *below* $35.95.

17 Select the range **A4:A6**, right-click over the selection, and then click **Copy**. Point to cell **G4**, right-click, and then click **Paste**. Press Esc to cancel the moving border.

18 Scroll to the bottom of your worksheet and notice that the **Earrings** product type ends in **row 61**. Then, in cell **H4**, use the technique you just practiced to **SUM** the total number of **Earrings** in stock.

19 In cell **H5**, use the **AVERAGE** function to display the average **Retail Price** of the **Earrings** product type. In cell **H6**, use the **MEDIAN** function to display the median value of the **Retail Price** for **Earrings**.

20 Select cells **B4** and **H4**, apply **Comma Style** with **zero decimal places**, click any cell to deselect, and then compare your screen with Figure 11.7.

Figure 11.7

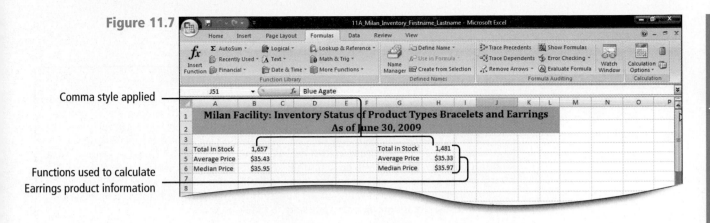

Comma style applied

Functions used to calculate
Earrings product information

21 **Save** 💾 your workbook.

Activity 11.02 Using the MIN and MAX Functions

The **MIN function** determines the smallest value in a selected range of values. The **MAX function** determines the largest value in a selected range of values.

1 In cell **A7**, type **Lowest Price** and then in cell **A8**, type **Highest Price**

2 Click cell **B7**. On the **Formulas tab**, in the **Function Library group**, click the **More Functions** button, display the list of **Statistical** functions, scroll as necessary, and then click **MIN**.

3 At the right end of the **Number1** box, click the **Collapse Dialog** button 📷, select the range **C12:C66**, and then press Enter. Click **OK**.

> The lowest retail price in the Bracelets product group is $14.95.

4 In cell **B8**, using a similar technique, insert the **MAX** function to determine the highest **Retail Price** in the **Bracelets** product type.

> The highest Retail Price in the Bracelets product type is $65.95.

5 Copy the range **A7:A8** and paste it in cell **G7**. Then in cells **H7** and **H8**, use the **MIN** and **MAX** functions to calculate the lowest and highest **Retail Price** for products in the **Earrings** product type. Compare your screen with Figure 11.8.

Figure 11.8

MIN and MAX functions
used to calculate lowest
and highest prices

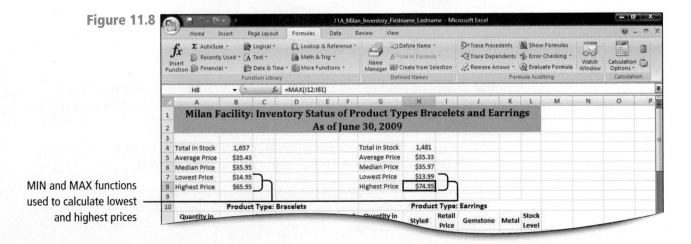

6 **Save** 🖫 your workbook.

Another Way

To Insert a Function

There are several ways to begin a function in Excel. Because the functions are grouped into categories such as *Financial*, *Logical* and so on, it is efficient to locate and insert functions from the Function Library. You can also click the Insert Function button on the Formula Bar; or, type = in the cell, type the first letter of the function, and then select the function from the list that displays. This feature is called *Formula AutoComplete*. You can also copy a similar function from another cell and edit the arguments within the cell or on the Formula Bar. Finally, you can access the Insert Function dialog box by selecting Insert Function from any of the displayed menus in the Function Library group or by pressing ⬆Shift + F3.

Activity 11.03 Moving Data, Adding Borders, and Rotating Text

Recall that you can select and move a range of cells containing formulas or functions. Use borders to emphasize a range of cells and to draw the reader's eye to a specific portion of a worksheet. Similarly, use rotated text to draw attention to data on your worksheet.

1 Select the range **A4:B8**. Point to the right edge of the selected range to display the 🔏 pointer, and then compare your screen with Figure 11.9.

Figure 11.9

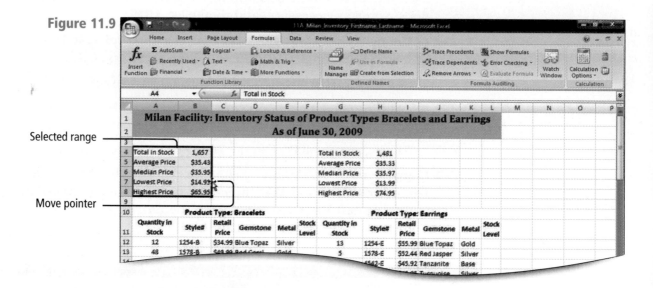

Selected range

Move pointer

2 Drag the selected range to the right until the ScreenTip displays *C4:D8*, and then release the mouse button. Select **columns C:D**, and then apply **AutoFit** to adjust the column widths.

3 By using the same technique, move the range **G4:H8** to the range **I4:J8**. Select **columns I:J**, and then apply **AutoFit**.

4 Select the nonadjacent ranges **C4:D8** and **I4:J8**, right-click to display the Mini toolbar, and then apply **Bold** **B** and a **Thick Box Border** 🔲 ▾.

5 In cell **A6**, type **Bracelets** Select the range **A5:A7**, right-click over the selection, and then click **Format Cells**. In the **Format Cells** dialog box, click the **Alignment tab**. Under **Text control**, select the **Merge cells** check box.

6 In the upper right portion of the dialog box, under **Orientation**, point to the **red diamond**, and then drag the diamond upward until the **Degrees** box indicates **30**. Alternatively, type the number of degrees directly into the Degrees box. Compare your screen with Figure 11.10.

Figure 11.10

Format Cells dialog box

Range of cells moved and formatted

Orientation set to 30 degrees

Merge cells selected

7 In the lower right corner of the **Format Cells** dialog box, click **OK**. With the merged cell still selected, display the Mini toolbar, change the **Font Size** to **12**, and then apply **Bold** and **Italic**.

8 On the **Home tab**, in the **Alignment group**, apply **Center** alignment and **Middle Align**.

9 In cell **G5**, type **Earrings** Point to the merged cell **A5** and right-click. On the Mini toolbar, click the **Format Painter** button, and then click cell **G5** to copy the formatting. Compare your screen with Figure 11.11.

Figure 11.11

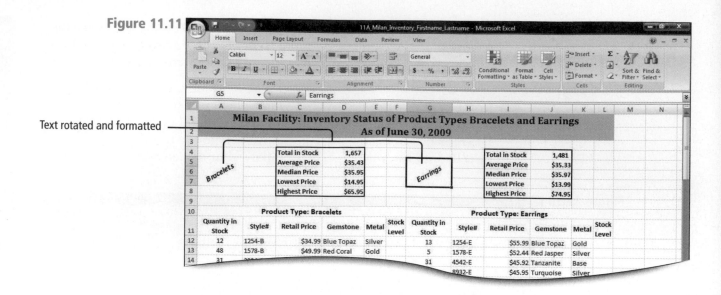

Text rotated and formatted

10 Save 💾 your workbook.

Objective 2
Use COUNTIF and IF Functions, and Apply Conditional Formatting

Recall that statistical functions analyze a group of measurements. Another group of Excel functions, referred to as *logical functions*, test for specific conditions. Logical functions typically use conditional tests to determine whether specified conditions—called *criteria*—are true or false.

Activity 11.04 Using the COUNTIF Function

The *COUNTIF function* counts the number of cells within a range that meet the given condition—the criteria that you provide. The COUNTIF function has two arguments—the range of cells to check and the criteria.

Adamantine's pearl bracelets and earrings will be featured on an upcoming segment of a TV shopping channel in Italy. In this activity, you will use the COUNTIF function to determine the number of pearl styles currently available in inventory.

1 From the **row heading area**, point to **row 10**, right-click, and then click **Insert**. Press F4 two times to repeat the last action and thus insert three blank rows.

2 Click cell **D4**, look at the **Formula Bar**, and then notice that the arguments of the **SUM** function adjusted and refer to **rows 15:69**.

The referenced range updates to A15:A69 after you insert the three new rows. In this manner, Excel adjusts the cell references in a formula relative to their new locations.

3 In cell **A10**, type **Pearl Styles Available** and then press Enter. Copy cell **A10**, and then paste it to cell **G10**. Press Esc to cancel the moving border.

4 Click cell **A11**. On the **Formulas tab**, in the **Function Library group**, click the **More Functions** button, and then display the list of **Statistical** functions. Click **COUNTIF**.

Recall that the COUNTIF function counts the number of cells within a range that meet the given condition.

5 In the **Range** box, click the **Collapse Dialog** button ![icon], select the range **D15:D69**, and then press Enter. Click in the **Criteria** box, type **Pearl** and then compare your screen with Figure 11.12.

Figure 11.12

Function displays in Formula Bar

Function Arguments dialog box

Criteria indicated as *Pearl*

Range indicated as *D15:D69*

6 In the lower right corner of the **Function Arguments** dialog box, click **OK**.

Five different styles of Pearl bracelets are available to feature on the TV show.

7 Using the technique you just practiced, in cell **G11**, count the number of **Pearl** styles available in the **Earrings** product type.

Ten different styles of Pearl earrings are available to feature on the TV show.

8 Select cells **A11** and **G11**, and then on the **Home tab**, in the **Alignment group**, click the **Align Text Left** button ![icon].

9 **Save** ![icon] your workbook.

Activity 11.05 Using the IF Function and Applying Conditional Formatting

A *logical test* is any value or expression that can be evaluated as being true or false. The *IF function* uses a logical test to check whether a condition is met, and then returns one value if true, and another value if false. For example, *C8=100* is an expression that can be evaluated as true or false. If the value in cell C8 is equal to 100, the expression is true. If the value in cell C8 is not 100, the expression is false.

In this activity, you will use the IF function to determine the inventory stock levels and determine if more products should be ordered.

1 Click cell **F15**. On the **Formulas tab**, in the **Function Library group**, click the **Logical** button, and then in the list, click **IF**. If necessary, drag the title bar of the **Function Arguments** dialog box up so that you can view **row 15** on your screen.

2 With the insertion point in the **Logical_test** box, click cell **A15**, and then type **<40**

> This logical test will look at the value in cell A15, the value of which is *12*, and then determine if the number is less than 40. The expression *<40* includes the < *comparison operator*, which means *less than*. Comparison operators compare values.

3 Take a moment to examine the table in Figure 11.13 for a list of comparison operator symbols and their definitions.

Comparison Operators

Comparsion Operators	Symbol Definition
=	Equal to
>	Greater than
<	Less than
>=	Greater than or equal to
<=	Less than or equal to
<>	Not equal to

Figure 11.13

4 Press Tab to move the insertion point to the **Value_if_true** box, and then type **Order**

> If the result of the logical test is true—the Quantity in Stock is less than 40—the cell will display the text *Order* indicating that additional product must be ordered.

5 Press Tab to move the insertion point to the **Value_if_false** box, type **OK** and then compare your dialog box with Figure 11.14.

> If the result of the logical test is false—the Quantity in Stock is *not* less than 40—then Excel will display *OK* in the cell.

Figure 11.14

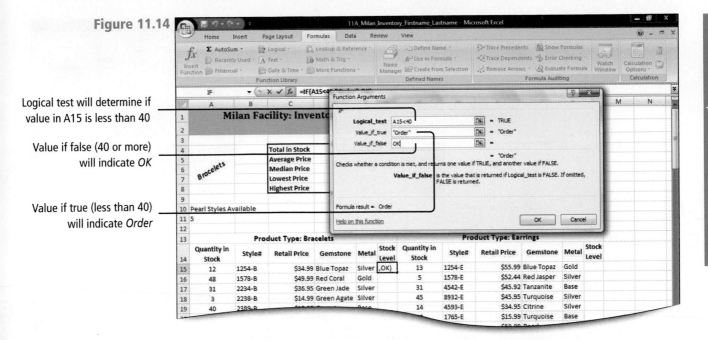

Logical test will determine if value in A15 is less than 40

Value if false (40 or more) will indicate *OK*

Value if true (less than 40) will indicate *Order*

6 Click **OK** to display the result *Order* in cell **F15**. Then, using the fill handle, copy the function down through cell **F69**. Look at cell **A19**, and then look at cell **F19** and notice that the **Stock Level** is indicated as *OK*.

> The comparison operator indicated <40 (less than 40) and thus a value of *exactly* 40 is indicated as OK.

7 Click cell **L15**, and then using the technique you just practiced and a quantity *less than* 40, conduct a logical test on the quantities of **Earrings** in stock. Then, scroll to the upper portion of your worksheet, click cell **L15**, look at the **Formula Bar**, and then compare your screen with Figure 11.15.

Note — Copying Functions

You can also copy the function in cell F15 to cell L15 and the cell references will adjust accordingly.

Figure 11.15

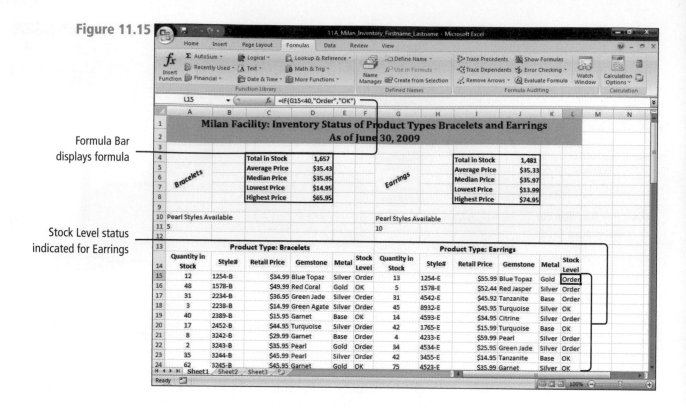

Formula Bar
displays formula

Stock Level status
indicated for Earrings

The spreadsheet shows:

Title rows:
Milan Facility: Inventory Status of Product Types Bracelets and Earrings
As of June 30, 2009

Formula Bar: L15 = `=IF(G15<40,"Order","OK")`

Bracelets		Earrings	
Total in Stock	1,657	Total in Stock	1,481
Average Price	$35.43	Average Price	$35.33
Median Price	$35.95	Median Price	$35.97
Lowest Price	$14.95	Lowest Price	$13.99
Highest Price	$65.95	Highest Price	$74.95

Pearl Styles Available: 5

Pearl Styles Available: 10

Product Type: Bracelets / Product Type: Earrings

Quantity in Stock	Style#	Retail Price	Gemstone	Metal	Stock Level	Quantity in Stock	Style#	Retail Price	Gemstone	Metal	Stock Level
12	1254-B	$34.99	Blue Topaz	Silver	Order	13	1254-E	$55.99	Blue Topaz	Gold	Order
48	1578-B	$49.99	Red Coral	Gold	OK	5	1578-E	$52.44	Red Jasper	Silver	Order
31	2234-B	$36.95	Green Jade	Silver	Order	31	4542-E	$45.92	Tanzanite	Base	Order
3	2238-B	$14.99	Green Agate	Silver	Order	45	8932-E	$45.95	Turquoise	Silver	OK
40	2389-B	$15.95	Garnet	Base	OK	14	4593-E	$34.95	Citrine	Silver	Order
17	2452-B	$44.95	Turquoise	Silver	Order	42	1765-E	$15.99	Turquoise	Base	OK
8	3242-B	$29.99	Garnet	Base	Order	4	4233-E	$59.99	Pearl	Silver	Order
2	3243-B	$35.95	Pearl	Gold	Order	34	4534-E	$25.95	Green Jade	Silver	Order
35	3244-B	$45.95	Pearl	Silver	Order	42	3455-E	$14.95	Tanzanite	Base	OK
62	3245-B	$45.95	Garnet	Gold	OK	75	4523-E	$35.99	Garnet	Silver	OK

8 **Save** your workbook.

Activity 11.06 Applying Conditional Formatting Using Custom Formats and Data Bars

A *conditional format* changes the appearance of a cell range based on a condition—a criteria. If the condition is true, the cell range is formatted based on that condition; if the condition is false, the cell range is *not* formatted based on the condition. In this activity, you will use conditional formatting as another way to draw attention to the Stock Level of products.

1 Select the range **F15:F69**. On the **Home tab**, in the **Styles group**, click the **Conditional Formatting** button. In the list, point to **Highlight Cells Rules**, and then click **Text that Contains**.

2 In the **Text That Contains** dialog box, with the insertion point blinking in the first box, type **Order** In the second box, click the **arrow**, and then in the list, click **Custom Format**.

> The Format Cells dialog box displays. Here you can select any combination of formats to apply to the cell if the condition is true. The custom format that you specify will be applied to any cell in the selected range if it contains the specific text *Order*.

3 In the **Format Cells** dialog box, on the **Font tab**, under **Font style**, click **Bold Italic**. Click the **Color arrow**, and then under **Theme Colors**, click **Dark Blue, Text 2, Darker 25%**. In the lower right corner of the **Format Cells** dialog box, click **OK**. Compare your screen with Figure 11.16.

> Within the selected range, if the cell meets the condition of containing *Order*, the font color will change to Bold Italic, Dark Blue, Text 2 Darker 25%.

Figure 11.16

Text That Contains dialog box

Only cells with the text *Order* will be formatted

Custom Format indicated

4 In the **Text That Contains** dialog box, click **OK** to apply the conditional formatting.

5 Select the range **A15:A69**. In the **Styles group**, click the **Conditional Formatting** button. In the list, point to **Data Bars**, and then in the **gallery**, click **Orange Data Bar**.

> A **data bar** provides a visual cue to the reader about the value of a cell relative to other cells. The length of the data bar represents the value in the cell. A longer bar represents a higher value and a shorter bar represents a lower value. Data bars are useful to quickly identify higher and lower numbers within a large group of data, such as very high or very low levels of inventory.

6 Using the techniques you just practiced, apply the same conditional formatting to the *Stock Level* column for the **Earrings** product type, and then apply the same data bars to indicate the *Quantity of Stock* in inventory. Press [Ctrl] + [Home] to make cell **A1** the active cell, and then compare your screen with Figure 11.17.

Figure 11.17

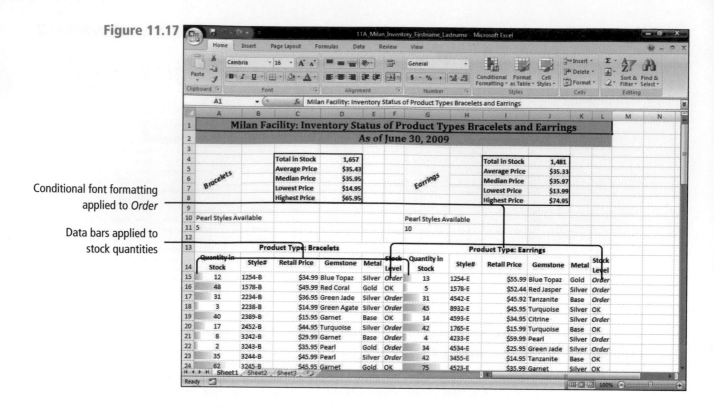

Conditional font formatting applied to *Order*

Data bars applied to stock quantities

7 **Save** 💾 your workbook.

More Knowledge — Use Format Painter to Copy Conditional Formatting

You can also use Format Painter to apply the same conditional formatting from one range of cells to another.

Activity 11.07 Using Find and Replace

The ***Find and Replace*** feature searches the cells in a worksheet—or in a selected range—for matches, and then replaces each match with a replacement value of your choice.

Because a quality grade of Tanzanite was not readily available for manufacturing, the pieces listed as having the gemstone Tanzanite were actually set with Peridot. In this activity, you will replace all occurrences of *Tanzanite* with *Peridot*.

1 To the left of the **Formula Bar**, click in the **Name Box**, type **d15:d69,j15:j64** and then press Enter. Alternatively, select the nonadjacent ranges of Gemstones with your mouse.

> The range of cells that contains the gemstone names for both product types is selected. Restrict the find and replace operation to a specific range if there is a possibility that the name occurs elsewhere in the worksheet.

2 On the **Home tab**, in the **Editing group**, click the **Find & Select** button, and then click **Replace**.

3 In the **Find and Replace** dialog box, in the **Find what** box, type **Tanzanite** In the **Replace with** box type **Peridot** and then compare your screen with Figure 11.18.

462 **Excel** | Chapter 11: Using Functions and Tables

Figure 11.18

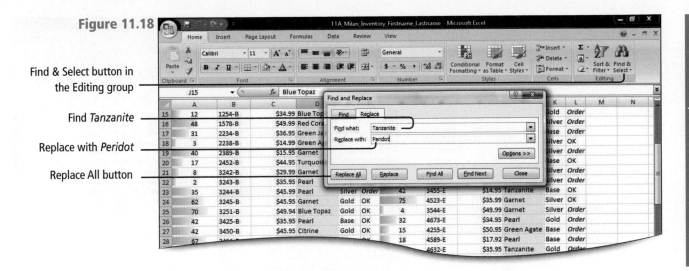

Find & Select button in the Editing group

Find *Tanzanite*

Replace with *Peridot*

Replace All button

---

4 Click the **Replace All** button. In the message box, notice that *12 replacements* were made, and then click **OK**. In the lower right corner of the **Find and Replace** dialog box, click the **Close** button. Click any cell to deselect the ranges.

5 **Save** 🖫 your workbook.

Objective 3
Use a Date Function

Excel can obtain the date and time from the computer's calendar and clock and display this information on your worksheet.

Activity 11.08 Using the NOW Function

The *NOW function* retrieves the date and time from your computer's calendar and clock and inserts the information into the selected cell. The result is formatted as a date and time, rather than in the sequential number that Excel uses for dates. This feature is useful to date stamp a worksheet to record when it was last edited.

1 Scroll down to view **row 71**. Click cell **A71**, type **Last Edited by Rose Elleni** and then press Enter.

2 With cell **A72** as the active cell, on the **Formulas tab**, in the **Function Library group**, click the **Date & Time** button. In the list of functions, click **NOW**. Compare your screen with Figure 11.19.

Figure 11.19

Function Arguments
dialog box for
NOW function

No specific arguments
for this function

3 Take a moment to read the description in the **Function Arguments** dialog box, and notice that this result is *Volatile*.

The Function Arguments dialog box displays a message indicating that this function does not require an argument. It also states that this function is **volatile**, meaning the date and time will not remain as entered, but rather the date and time will be updated each time you open this workbook.

4 In the **Function Arguments** dialog box, click **OK** to close the dialog box to display the current date and time in cell **A72**.

5 **Save** your workbook.

Note — NOW Function Recalculates When the Workbook Opens

The NOW function places a sequential number in the cell that corresponds to the date and time at the moment. The NOW function updates this number each time the workbook is opened. If you open a workbook with the NOW function in it and then close the workbook, you will see a message that asks if you want to save the changes. The change to which this message refers is the new date that has been inserted by the NOW function. With the workbook open, you can force the NOW function to update by pressing [F9], for example, to update the time.

Objective 4
Freeze Panes and Create an Excel Table

By freezing or splitting panes, you can view two areas of a worksheet and lock rows and columns in one area. When you freeze panes, you select the specific rows or columns that you want to remain visible when scrolling in your worksheet.

To analyze a group of related data, you can convert a range of cells to an **Excel table**. An Excel table is a series of rows and columns that contains related data that is managed independently from the data in other rows and columns in the worksheet.

Activity 11.09 Freezing and Unfreezing Panes

In a large worksheet, if you scroll down more than 25 rows or scroll beyond column O (the exact row number and column letter varies, depending on your screen resolution), you will no longer see the top rows of your worksheet where identifying information about the data is usually placed. You will likely find it easier to work with your data if you can always view the identifying row or column titles.

The ***Freeze Panes*** command enables you to select one or more rows or columns and freeze (lock) them into place. The locked rows and columns become separate panes. A ***pane*** is a portion of a worksheet window bounded by and separated from other portions by vertical or horizontal bars.

1 Press Ctrl + Home to make cell **A1** the active cell. Scroll down until **row 40** displays at the top of your screen, and notice that all of the identifying information in the column titles is out of view.

2 Press Ctrl + Home again, and then select **row 15**. Click the **View tab**, and then in the **Window group**, click the **Freeze Panes** button. In the list, click **Freeze Panes**. Click any cell to deselect the row, and then notice that a line displays along the upper border of **row 15**.

> By selecting row 15, the rows above—rows 1 through 14—are frozen (locked) in place and will not move as you scroll down the worksheet.

3 Watch the row numbers below **row 14**, and then begin to scroll down to bring **row 40** into view again. Compare your screen with Figure 11.20.

> Rows 1:14 remain frozen in place and the remaining rows of data continue to scroll. Use this feature when you have long or wide worksheets.

Figure 11.20

Freeze Panes button in Window group

Freeze Panes command freezes rows 1-14

Row 40 in view

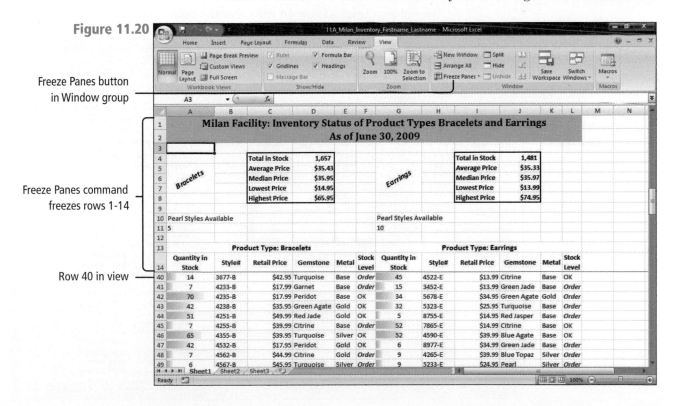

4 In the **Window group**, click the **Freeze Panes** button, and then click **Unfreeze Panes** to unlock all rows and columns.

5 **Save** 💾 your workbook.

> **More Knowledge — Freeze Columns or Freeze Both Rows and Columns**
>
> You can freeze columns that you want to remain in view on the left. Select the column to the right of the column(s) that you want to remain in view while scrolling to the left, and then click the Freeze Panes command. You can also use the command to freeze both rows and columns; click a *cell* to freeze the rows *above* the cell and the columns to the *left* of the cell.

Activity 11.10 Sorting and Filtering in an Excel Table

Recall that an Excel table is a series of rows and columns with related data that can be managed independently from the data in other rows and columns. For example, in your 11A_Milan_Inventory workbook, you have data for two product types—*Bracelets* and *Earrings*.

To manage several groups of data, you can insert more than one table in the same worksheet. In Activities 11.10 and 11.11, you will create an Excel table for each of the two product types, and then work with each set of data independently of the other.

1 Press Ctrl + Home to make cell **A1** the active cell. Be sure that you have applied the Unfreeze Panes command—no rows on your worksheet are locked.

2 Select the range **A14:F69**. Click the **Insert tab**, and then in the **Tables group**, click the **Table** button. In the **Create Table** dialog box, if necessary, click to select the **My table has headers** check box, and then compare your screen with Figure 11.21.

The column titles in row 14 will form the table headers.

Figure 11.21

Create Table dialog box

Column titles will form table headers

Range of data selected

Check box selected

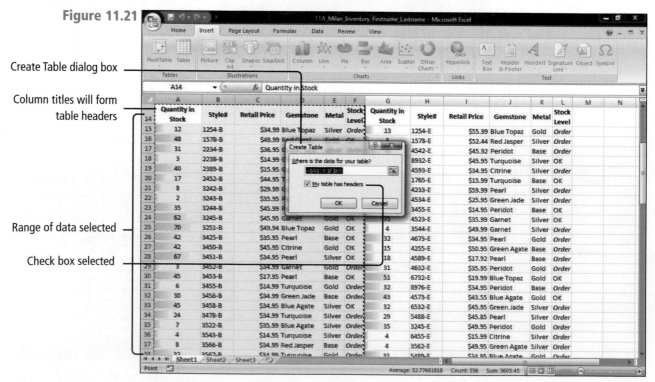

3 In the **Create Table** dialog box, click **OK**. With the range still selected, on the Ribbon notice that the **Table Tools** are active. On the **Design tab**, in the **Table Styles group**, click the **More** button ⏷, and then under **Light**, locate and click **Table Style Light 16**.

4 Press [Ctrl] + [Home] to make cell **A1** the active cell and to cancel the selection, and then compare your screen with Figure 11.22.

> Sorting and filtering arrows display in the table's header row. You can sort tables in ascending or descending order or by color. You can filter tables to show only the data that meets the criteria that you specify, or you can filter by color.

Figure 11.22

Sorting and filtering arrows in header row

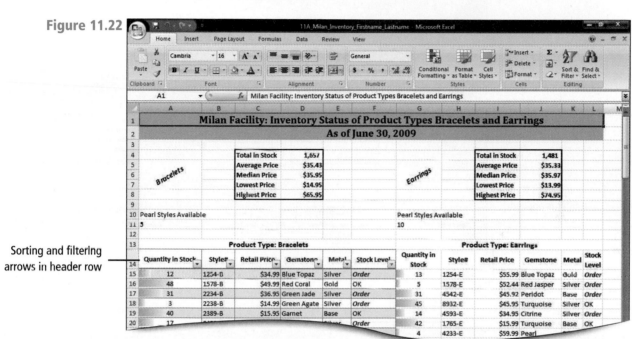

5 In the header row of the table, click the **Retail Price arrow**, and then from the menu, click **Sort Smallest to Largest**. Next to the arrow, notice the small **up arrow** indicating the sort.

> The rows in the table, which includes only columns A:F, are sorted from the lowest retail price to highest retail price. Cells in the same rows in columns G:L are not affected by the sort because the table feature isolates the table cells and treats them independently of other cells outside of the table.

6 In the header row of the table, click the **Gemstone arrow**. From the menu, click **Sort A to Z**. Next to the arrow, notice the small **up arrow** indicating an ascending (A to Z) sort.

> The rows in the table are sorted alphabetically by Gemstone.

7 Click the **Gemstone arrow** again, and then sort from **Z to A**.

> The rows in the table are sorted in reverse alphabetic order by Gemstone name, and the small arrow points downward, indicating a descending (Z to A) sort.

8 Click the **Gemstone arrow** again. On the menu, click the **(Select All)** check box to clear all the check boxes. Click to select only the **Pearl** check box, and then click **OK**. Compare your screen with Figure 11.23.

Only the rows containing *Pearl* in the Gemstone column display, and the remaining rows are hidden from view. A small funnel in the Gemstone arrow indicates that a filter is applied to the data in the table. Additionally, the row numbers display in blue to indicate that some rows are hidden from view. A filter hides the entire row in the worksheet.

Figure 11.23

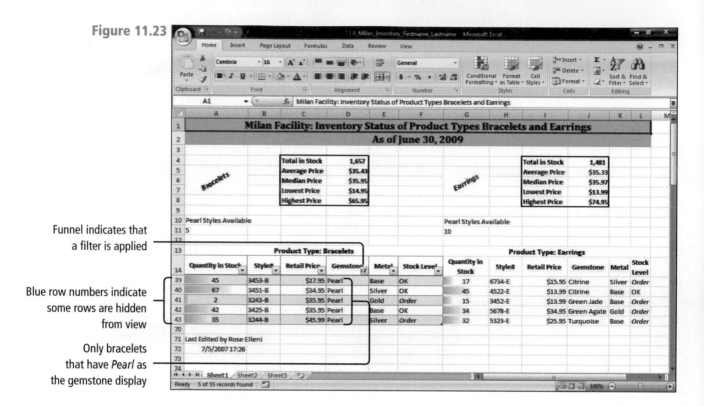

Funnel indicates that a filter is applied

Blue row numbers indicate some rows are hidden from view

Only bracelets that have *Pearl* as the gemstone display

9 Click any cell in the table so that the table is selected. On the Ribbon, click the **Design tab**, and then in the **Table Style Options group**, click to select the **Total Row** check box.

Total displays in cell A70, and in cell F70, the number 5 indicates that five rows are currently displayed.

10 Click cell **A70**, click the **arrow** that displays to the right of cell A70, and then in the list, click **Sum**.

Excel sums only the visible rows in Column A, and indicates that *191* bracelets containing the Gemstone *Pearl* are in stock. In this manner, you can use an Excel table to quickly find information about a group of data.

11 Click cell **A11**, type **Five styles, 191 total in stock** and then press `Enter`.

12 In the table header row, click the **Gemstone arrow**, and then on the menu, click **Clear Filter From "Gemstone"**.

All the rows in the table redisplay. The Z to A sort on Gemstone remains in effect.

13 Click the **Metal arrow**, click the **(Select All)** check box to clear all the check boxes, and then click to select the **Gold** check box. Click **OK**. Click the **Gemstone arrow**, click the **(Select All)** check box to clear all the check boxes, and then click the **Red Coral** check box. Click **OK**, and then compare your screen with Figure 11.24.

> By applying multiple filters, Rose can quickly determine that among the Bracelets product type, four styles have a Red Coral gemstone in a Gold setting and there are 117 total in stock.

Figure 11.24

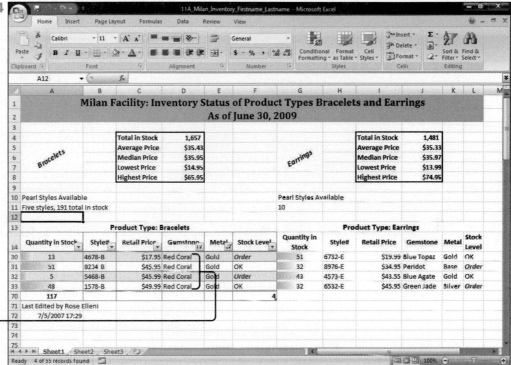

Four bracelet styles have *Red Coral* as *Gemstone* and *Gold* as *Metal*

14 Click the **Gemstone arrow**, and then click **Clear Filter from "Gemstone"**. Use the same technique to remove the filter from the **Metal** column.

15 In the table header row, click the **Style# arrow**, and then click **Sort A to Z**, which will apply an ascending sort to the *Style#* column.

16 **Save** 💾 your workbook.

Activity 11.11 Inserting a Second Table in a Worksheet

In this activity, you will format the product information for *Earrings* as a table.

1 Select the range **G14:L64**. On the **Insert tab**, in the **Tables group**, click the **Table** button. Be sure the **My table has headers** check box is selected, and then click **OK**.

2 In the **Table Styles group**, click the **More** button ▼, and then under **Light**, click **Table Style Light 18**. Press Ctrl + Home, and then compare your screen with Figure 11.25.

Figure 11.25

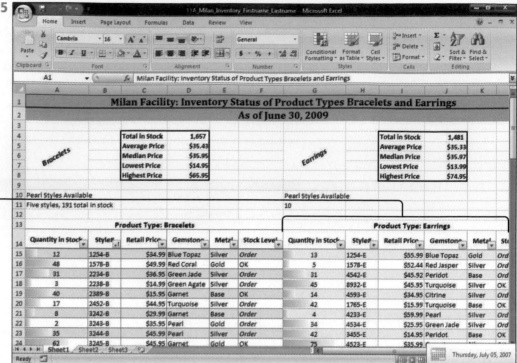

Second table inserted in the worksheet

In the worksheet title bar: 11A_Milan_Inventory_Firstname_Lastname - Microsoft Excel

Cell A1 contents: Milan Facility: Inventory Status of Product Types Bracelets and Earrings

Milan Facility: Inventory Status of Product Types Bracelets and Earrings
As of June 30, 2009

Bracelets

Total in Stock	1,657
Average Price	$35.43
Median Price	$35.95
Lowest Price	$14.95
Highest Price	$65.95

Earrings

Total in Stock	1,481
Average Price	$35.33
Median Price	$35.97
Lowest Price	$13.99
Highest Price	$74.95

Pearl Styles Available
Five styles, 191 total in stock

Pearl Styles Available
10

Product Type: Bracelets

Quantity in Stock	Style#	Retail Price	Gemstone	Metal	Stock Level
12	1254-B	$34.99	Blue Topaz	Silver	Order
48	1578-B	$49.99	Red Coral	Gold	OK
31	2234-B	$36.95	Green Jade	Silver	Order
3	2238-B	$14.99	Green Agate	Silver	Order
40	2389-B	$15.95	Garnet	Base	OK
17	2452-B	$44.95	Turquoise	Silver	Order
8	3242-B	$29.99	Garnet	Base	Order
2	3243-B	$35.95	Pearl	Gold	Order
35	3244-B	$45.99	Pearl	Silver	Order
62	3245-B	$45.95	Garnet	Gold	OK

Product Type: Earrings

Quantity in Stock	Style#	Retail Price	Gemstone	Metal	Sto
13	1254-E	$55.99	Blue Topaz	Gold	Ord
5	1578-E	$52.44	Red Jasper	Silver	Ord
31	4542-E	$45.92	Peridot	Base	Ord
45	8932-E	$45.95	Turquoise	Silver	OK
14	4593-E	$34.95	Citrine	Silver	Ord
42	1765-E	$15.99	Turquoise	Base	OK
4	4233-E	$59.99	Pearl	Silver	Ord
34	4534-E	$25.95	Green Jade	Silver	Ord
42	3455-E	$14.95	Peridot	Base	OK
75	4523-E	$35.99			

Sheet1 / Sheet2 / Sheet3

Thursday, July 05, 2007

Ready

3 In the **Earrings** table, in cell **J14**, click the **Gemstone arrow**, click the **(Select All)** check box to clear all the check boxes, and then click the **Pearl** check box. Click **OK**. Scroll down and to the right as necessary so that you can view the table on your screen.

In the worksheet, rows within the Earrings table that do not contain *Pearl* as the gemstone are hidden.

4 Click any cell in the **Earrings** table to select the table, click the **Design tab**, and then in the **Table Style Options group**, click to select the **Total Row** check box.

Total displays in cell G65, and in cell L65, the number *10* indicates that ten rows are currently displayed.

5 Click cell **G65**, click the **arrow** that displays to the right of cell G65, and then in the list, click **Sum**. Compare your screen with Figure 11.26.

Excel sums only the visible rows in Column G, and indicates that *309* earrings containing the Gemstone *Pearl* are in stock. Recall that in this manner, you can use an Excel table to quickly find information about a group of data.

Figure 11.26

309 total Pearl earrings in stock; 10 Pearl styles

6 Click cell **G11**, type **Ten styles, 309 total pairs in stock** and then press Enter.

7 In the table header row, click the **Gemstone arrow**, and then on the menu, click **Clear Filter From "Gemstone"** to redisplay all the rows in the table.

8 In the table header row of the **Earrings** table, click the **Style# arrow**, and then click **Sort A to Z**, which will apply an ascending sort to the **Style#** column.

9 **Save** your workbook.

Activity 11.12 Converting a Table to a Range of Data

When you are finished answering questions about the data in a table by sorting, filtering, and totaling, you no longer need the table. You can remove a table by converting it back to a normal range.

1 Click anywhere in the **Bracelets** table to activate the table and display the **Table Tools** on the Ribbon.

2 On the **Design tab**, in the **Tools group**, click the **Convert to Range** button. In the message box, click **Yes**.

The list arrows are removed from the column titles; the color and shading formats applied from the table style remain.

3 Use the technique you just practiced to convert the **Earrings** table to a range, and then compare your screen with Figure 11.27.

Figure 11.27

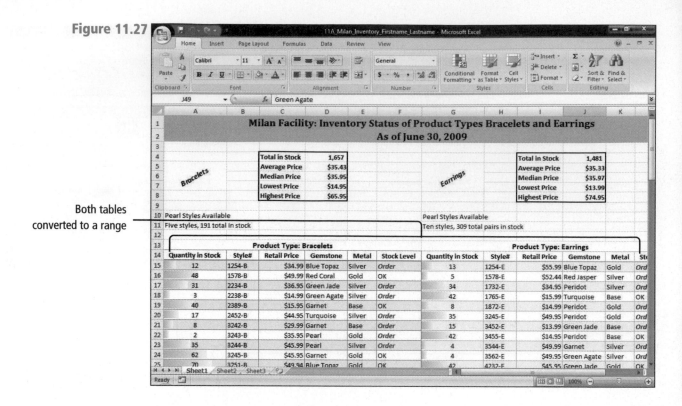

4 **Save** 🔲 your workbook.

More Knowledge — How To Remove Shading Formats From a Table

If you do not want to retain the shading and other formats applied from a table style, apply the *None* table style before converting back to a range.

Objective 5
Format and Print a Large Worksheet

A large worksheet will be too wide, too long—or both—to print on a single page. To make reading multiple printed pages easier, Excel features let you print row and column headings on each page of a worksheet.

Activity 11.13 Printing Large Worksheets

In this activity, you will adjust the column widths, change the Page Layout so that column titles display on every page, and print the worksheet.

1 Select **column C**, hold down Ctrl, select the nonadjacent **column I**, and then set their width to **90 pixels**. Select **column A**, hold down Ctrl and select columns **D**, **G**, and **J**, and then set their width to **80 pixels**.

2 Select **column B**, hold down Ctrl and select **column H**, and then set their width to **70 pixels**.

3 Select **columns E**, **F**, **K**, and **L** and set their width to **55 pixels**. Select the range **A72:B72**, right-click, click **Format Cells**, and then on the **Alignment tab** of the **Format Cells** dialog box, under **Text control**, select the **Merge cells** check box. Click **OK**.

> The merged cell is widened so that it can display the result of the NOW function that it contains.

4 Select the column titles in **Row 14**, and then on the **Home tab**, in the **Alignment group**, click the **Wrap Text** button 📋. Look at the column titles in Row 14 and either verify that the full column titles display in each cell, or if necessary, click the **Wrap Text** button again so that the full titles display.

5 Press Ctrl + Home to display the top of your worksheet.

6 On the **Insert tab**, in the **Text group**, click **Header & Footer** to switch to **Page Layout view**. In the **Navigation group**, click the **Go to Footer** button, click just above the word *Footer*, and then in the **Header & Footer Elements group**, click the **File Name** button. Click a cell just above the footer to deselect the **Footer area** and view your file name.

7 Click the **Page Layout tab**. In the **Page Setup group**, click the **Orientation** button, and then click **Landscape**. In the same group, click the **Print Titles** button. Under **Print titles**, click in the **Rows to repeat at top** box, and then at the right, click the **Collapse Dialog** button 📷. From the **row heading area**, select **rows 13:14**, and then compare your screen with Figure 11.28.

Figure 11.28

Collapsed dialog box displays the row numbers as an absolute reference

Rows 13 and 14 selected; surrounded by moving border

8 Press Enter, and then in the **Page Setup** dialog box, click the **Margins tab**. Under **Center on page**, select the **Horizontally** check box, and then click **OK**.

9 Delete the unused sheets **Sheet2** and **Sheet3**. On the right edge of the status bar, click the **Normal** button 🔲, and then press Ctrl + Home to display the top of your worksheet.

10 From the **Office** menu 🔵, point to **Print**, and then click **Print Preview**. On your screen, it is possible that the *Earrings Stock Level*

column does not display. In the **Preview Group**, click **Next Page** several times to determine if the *Stock Level column* displays on separate pages. Close the **Print Preview**.

11 If necessary, on the **Page Layout tab**, in the **Scale to Fit group**, click the **Width button arrow**, and then click **1 page**.

Excel will make the necessary adjustments to fit the worksheet columns to one page.

12 **Save** 🖫 your workbook. To submit electronically, follow the instructions provided by your instructor. To print, from the **Office** menu 🖫, point to the **Print** button, and then click **Print Preview**. In the **Preview group**, click the **Next Page** and **Previous Page** buttons as necessary to view and check each page. Be sure the two header rows and the footer display on each page, and then click the **Print** button. In the **Print** dialog box, under **Print range**, be sure that **All** is selected, and then click **OK**. If you are directed to submit printed formulas, refer to Activity 9.17 in Project 9A to do so.

13 If you printed your formulas, be sure to redisplay the worksheet by pressing Ctrl + `. From the **Office** menu 🖫, click **Close**. If a dialog box displays asking if you want to save changes, click **No** so that you do *not* save the changes you made for printing formulas. **Close** Excel.

More Knowledge — Adjust Scaling for Data that is Slightly Larger than the Printed Page

If your data is just a little too large to fit on a printed page, you can scale the worksheet to make it fit. Scaling reduces the horizontal and vertical size of the printed data to a percentage of its original size or by the number of pages that you specify. To adjust the printed output to a percentage of its actual size, for example to 80%, on the Page Layout tab, in the Scale to Fit group, click the Scale arrows to select a percentage.

End You have completed Project 11A ——————————

Project 11B New Store Loan

In Activities 11.14 through 11.19, you will create a worksheet for Wattana Dithasaro, International Sales Director, that details the loan information to purchase furniture and fixtures for a new Adamantine Jewelry store in Mexico City. Wattana plans to borrow money to pay for the new store furniture and fixtures, and then pay off the loan in monthly payments. She must decide how to arrange the loan to buy the furniture and fixtures she needs and still keep the monthly payment within her budget for new store openings. You will create a worksheet containing payments for combinations of time periods and interest rates so Wattana can identify what range of rates and time periods will meet her requirements. The worksheets of your workbook will look similar to Figure 11.29.

For Project 11B, you will need the following file:

New blank Excel workbook

You will save your workbook as
11B_New_Store_Loan_Firstname_Lastname

Loan Options for New Store in Mexico City - Rates versus Months

Amount of Loan	$350,000
Period (Months)	36
Interest Rate (per year)	7.00%

Payment Options
Number of Monthly Payments

36	42	48	54	60
9,967.73	$9,581.94	$8,544.52	$7,739.35	$7,096.74
9,947.56	$9,561.60	$8,524.00	$7,718.63	$7,075.82
9,927.41	$9,541.29	$8,503.51	$7,697.95	$7,054.94
9,907.28	$9,521.01	$8,483.05	$7,677.30	$7,034.09
9,887.18	$9,500.75	$8,462.62	$7,656.68	$7,013.28
9,867.09	$9,480.51	$8,442.21	$7,636.10	$6,992.51
9,847.04	$9,460.31	$8,421.84	$7,615.55	$6,971.78
9,827.00	$9,440.13	$8,401.50	$7,595.03	$6,951.08
9,806.98	$9,419.97	$8,381.19	$7,574.55	$6,930.42
9,786.99	$9,399.84	$8,360.90	$7,554.10	$6,909.80
9,767.02	$9,379.74	$8,340.65	$7,533.69	$6,889.21
9,747.08	$9,359.66	$8,320.43	$7,513.31	$6,868.66
9,727.15	$9,339.61	$8,300.23	$7,492.96	$6,848.15
9,707.25	$9,319.59	$8,280.07	$7,472.64	$6,827.68
9,687.37	$9,299.59	$8,259.94	$7,452.36	$6,807.24
9,667.51	$9,279.62	$8,239.83	$7,432.11	$6,786.84
9,647.68	$9,259.68	$8,219.76	$7,411.90	$6,766.48

Mexico City - New Store Loan Options

Amount of Loan	$350,000
Period (years)	3
Interest rate (per year)	7%
Payment (per month)	$10,806.98

Option #1 - Reduce the Loan

Amount of Loan	$242,898
Period (years)	3
Interest rate (per year)	7%
Payment (per month)	$7,500.00

Option #2 - Increase Years

Amount of Loan	$350,000
Period (years)	4.55
Interest rate (per year)	7%
Payment (per month)	$7,500.00

11B_New_Store_Loan_Firstname_Lastname

Figure 11.29
Project 11B—New Store Loan

Objective 6
Use Financial Functions

Financial functions perform common business calculations such as calculating a loan payment on a vehicle or calculating how much to save each month to buy something. Financial functions commonly involve a period of time such as months or years.

Activity 11.14 Designing a Loan Worksheet

1 **Start** Excel and display a new blank workbook. From the **Office** menu , display the **Save As** dialog box, navigate to your **Excel Chapter 11** folder, and then in the **File name** box, name the file **11B_New_Store_Loan_Firstname_Lastname**

2 Widen **column A** to **180 pixels** and **column B** to **100 pixels**. In the range **A2:B5**, enter the following row titles and data. Recall that you can format the numbers as you type by typing them with their symbols as shown:

Amount of Loan	$350,000
Period (years)	3
Interest rate (per year)	7%
Payment (per month)	

3 In cell **A1**, type **Mexico City - New Store Loan Options** **Merge and Center** the title in the range **A1:B1**, add a **Fill Color** of **Olive Green, Accent 3, Lighter 60%**, change the **Font** to **Cambria**, and then change the **Font Size** to **12**. Rename the worksheet tab **New Store Loan** and then **Save** your workbook. Compare your screen with Figure 11.30.

Figure 11.30

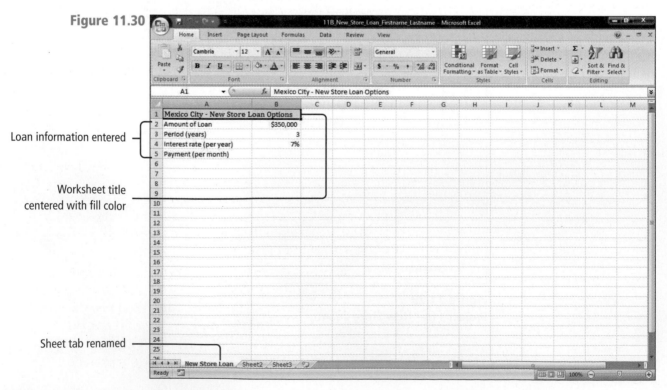

Loan information entered

Worksheet title centered with fill color

Sheet tab renamed

Activity 11.15 Inserting the PMT Financial Function

When you borrow money from a bank or a similar lending institution, the amount charged to you for your use of the borrowed money is called *interest*. Loans are typically made for a period of years, and the interest that must be paid is a percentage of the loan amount that is still owed. In Excel, this percentage is called the *rate*.

The initial amount of the loan is called the *Present value (Pv)*, which is the total amount that a series of future payments is worth now, and is also known as the *principal*. When you borrow money, the loan amount is the *present value* to the lender. The number of time periods—number of payments—is abbreviated *nper*. The value at the end of the time periods is the *Future value (Fv)*—the cash balance you want to attain after the last payment is made. The future value is usually zero for loans.

In this activity, you will calculate the monthly payments that Adamantine Jewelry will have to make to finance the purchase of the furniture and fixtures for the new store in Mexico City, the total cost of which is $350,000. You will calculate the monthly payments, including interest, for a three-year loan at an annual interest rate of 7.0%. To stay within Wattana's budget, the monthly payment must be approximately $7,500.

1 Click cell **B5**. On the **Formulas tab**, in the **Function Library group**, click the **Financial** button. Scroll down the list as necessary, and then click **PMT**.

> The Function Arguments dialog box displays. Recall that arguments are the values that an Excel function uses to perform calculations or operations.

2 If necessary, drag the **Function Arguments** dialog box to the right side of your screen so you can view **columns A:B**.

> The *PMT function* calculates the payment for a loan based on constant payments and at a constant interest rate. To complete the PMT function, first you must determine the total number of loan payment periods (months), which is 12 months × 3 years, or 36 months.

3 With your insertion point positioned in the **Rate** box, type **b4/12** Alternatively, click cell B4 and then type */12*.

> Excel will divide the annual interest rate of 7%, which is 0.070 in decimal notation, located in cell B4 by 12 (months), which will result in a *monthly* interest rate.

> When borrowing money, the interest rate and number of periods are quoted in years. The payments on a loan, however, are usually made monthly. Therefore, the number of periods, which is stated in years, and the *annual* interest rate, must be changed to a monthly equivalent in order to calculate the monthly payment amount. You can see that calculations like these can be made as part of the argument in a function.

4 Press Tab to move the insertion point to the **Nper** box. In the lower portion of the dialog box, notice that *Nper is the total number of payments for the loan* (number of periods). Type **b3*12** to have Excel convert the number of years in the loan (3) to the total number of months.

> Recall that the PMT function calculates a *monthly* payment. Thus, all values in the function must be expressed in months.

5 Press `Tab` to move to the **Pv** box, and then type **b2**

> Pv represents the present value—the amount of the loan before any payments are made—in this instance $350,000.

6 In cell **B5** and on the **Formula Bar**, notice that the arguments that comprise the PMT function are separated by commas. Notice also, in the **Function Arguments** dialog box, that the value of each argument displays to the right of the argument box. Compare your screen with Figure 11.31.

Figure 11.31

Formula displayed in Formula Bar; arguments separated by commas

Cell references entered for PMT function

Optional arguments

Argument values

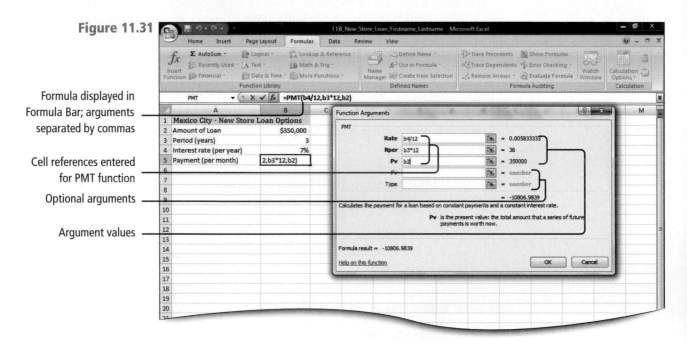

Note — Optional Arguments

The PMT function has two arguments not indicated by bold; these are optional. The Future value (Fv) argument assumes that the unpaid portion of the loan should be zero at the end of the last period. The *Type argument* assumes that the payment will be made at the end of each period. These default values are typical of most loans and may be left blank.

7 In the dialog box, click **OK**.

> The monthly payment amount, ($10,806.98), displays in cell B5. The amount displays in red and in parentheses to show that it is a negative number, a number that will be *paid out*. This monthly payment of $10,806.98 is over the budget of $7,500 per month that Wattana has in mind.

8 Click in the **Formula Bar**, and then use the arrow keys on the keyboard as necessary to position the insertion point between the equal sign and *PMT*. Type – (minus sign) to insert a minus sign into the formula, and then press `Enter`. **Save** 💾 your workbook.

> By placing a minus sign in the formula, the monthly payment amount, $10,806.98, displays in cell B5 as a *positive* number, which is more familiar and less distracting to work with.

Objective 7
Use Goal Seek

Goal Seek is a method to find a specific value for a cell by adjusting the value of one other cell. With Goal Seek, you can work backward from the desired outcome to find the input necessary to achieve your goal. If you have a result in mind, you can try different numbers in one of the cells used as an argument in the function until you get close to the answer you want. Goal Seek is one of Excel's What-If Analysis tools.

Activity 11.16 Using Goal Seek to Produce the Desired Result

Wattana knows that her budget cannot exceed $7,500 per month for the new store loan. The amount of $350,000 is necessary to purchase the furniture and fixtures to open the new store. Now she has two options—borrow less money and reduce the amount or quality of the furniture and fixtures in the store, or extend the time to repay the loan. To find out how much she can borrow for three years to stay within the budget, or how much to increase the repayment period, you will use the Goal Seek tool.

1 Click cell **B5**. On the **Data tab**, in the **Data Tools group**, click the **What-If Analysis** button, and then in the list, click **Goal Seek**. In the **Goal Seek** dialog box, in the **Set cell** box, confirm that *B5* displays.

> The cell address in this box is the cell that displays the desired result.

2 Press ⎄Tab. In the **To value** box, type the payment goal of *7500.00* and press ⎄Tab. In the **By changing cell** box, type **b2** which is the amount of the loan, and then compare your dialog box with Figure 11.32. Alternatively, you can click cell B2.

> In the By changing cell box, if you click cell B2, Excel will make the cell reference absolute.

Figure 11.32

Desired value is 7500.00

Desired result will display in B5

Cell to change to achieve desired value

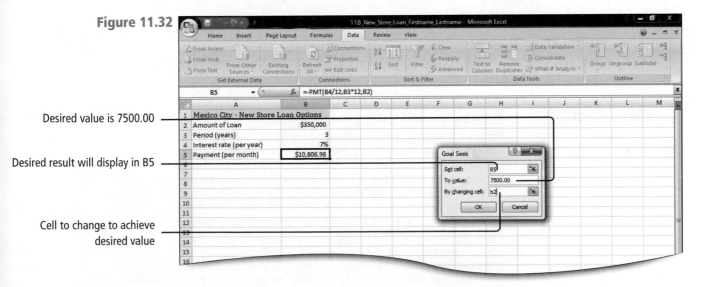

3 In the **Goal Seek** dialog box, click **OK**. In the **Goal Seek Status** dialog box, click **OK**.

Excel's calculations indicate that to achieve a monthly payment of $7,500.00 using a 3-year loan, Wattana can borrow only *$242,898*— not $350,000.

4 Click cell **A7**. Type **Option #1 - Reduce the Loan** and press Enter. Right-click cell **A7**. On the Mini toolbar, apply a **Fill Color** of **Olive Green, Accent 3, Lighter 60%**, change the **Font** to **Cambria** and the **Font Size** to **12**. **Merge and Center** the title across the range **A7:B7**.

5 Select the range **A2:B5**, right-click, and then click **Copy**. Click cell **A8**, right-click, and then click **Paste Special**. In the **Paste Special** dialog box, under **Paste**, click the **Values and number formats** option button, and then click **OK**.

Press Esc to cancel the moving border. **Save** your workbook, click anywhere to deselect, and then compare your worksheet with Figure 11.33.

Recall that with the Paste Special command, you can copy the *value* in a cell, rather than the formula, and the cell formats are retained—cell B5 contains the PMT function formula, and here you need only the value that *results* from that formula.

Figure 11.33

Values and formats pasted

Workshop

Savings Accounts—Using the Future Value Function

Another commonly used financial function, similar to the PMT function, is the Future Value function. The function has three required arguments: Rate, Nper, and Pmt. The Rate argument is the interest rate paid to you by the financial institution; the Nper is the number of periods; and Pmt is the amount you deposit into the account each period. The function also has two optional arguments—Pv and Type. The Pv argument is the amount you start with in the account. Excel assumes this is zero if you do not provide a starting amount. The Type argument assumes that the payment is made at the beginning of the time period.

For example, in the Fv Function Arguments dialog box, enter a rate of 6%/12 (6% annually divided by 12 months), enter 60 (5 years or 60 months) as the number of periods, enter 100 ($100) as the monthly deposit you will make, and enter a present value of 1500 ($1,500 opening deposit in the account). Excel will calculate that at the end of 5 years, you will have $9,000.28 in your savings account.

Activity 11.17 Using Goal Seek to Find an Increased Period

For Wattana's purchase of furniture and fixtures for the new store in Mexico City, an alternative to borrowing less money—which would mean buying fewer items or items of lesser quality—would be to increase the number of years of payments.

1 In cell **B2**, type **350000** and then press Enter to restore the original loan amount. Click cell **B5**. On the **Data tab**, in the **Data Tools group**, click the **What-If Analysis** button, and then click **Goal Seek**.

2 In the **Set cell** box, confirm that **B5** displays. press Tab. In the **To value** box, type **7500.00** and press Tab. In the **By changing cell** box, type **b3** which is the number of years for the loan. Compare your dialog box with Figure 11.34.

Figure 11.34

Value of $350,000 restored

Cell with the number of payment periods indicated as the *change* cell

3 Click **OK** two times.

Excel's calculations indicate that by making payments for 4.5 years—4.552648969—a monthly payment of $7,500.00 is achieved.

4 Click **A13**. Type **Option #2 - Increase Years** and then press Enter. Right-click cell **A7**, on the Mini toolbar, click the **Format Painter** button , and then click cell **A13** to copy the formats.

5 Select the range **A2:B5**, right-click, click **Copy** , and then click cell **A14**. Right-click, click **Paste Special**, click the **Values and number formats** option button, and then click **OK**. Press Esc to cancel the moving border.

6 Click cell **B15**, right-click to display the Mini toolbar, and then click the **Decrease Decimal** button until the number of decimal places is two. Click cell **B3**. Type **3** and then press Enter to restore the original value. Compare your worksheet with Figure 11.35.

Figure 11.35

Option 1: Reduce the amount of the loan

Option 2: Increase the number of years to pay off the loan

7 Click the **Insert tab**, and then in the **Text group**, click the **Header & Footer** button to switch to **Page Layout View** and open the **Header area**. In the **Navigation group**, click the **Go to Footer** button, click just above the word *Footer*, and then in the **Header & Footer Elements group**, click the **File Name** button. Click in a cell just above the footer to exit the **Footer area** and view your file name.

8 Click the **Page Layout tab**. In the **Page Setup group**, click the **Margins** button, and then at the bottom of the **Margins gallery**, click **Custom Margins**. In the **Page Setup** dialog box, under **Center on page**, select the **Horizontally** check box. Click **OK**, and then on the status bar, click the **Normal** button ▦. Press [Ctrl] + [Home] to move to the top of the worksheet.

9 **Save** 🖫 your workbook.

Objective 8
Create a Data Table

A *data table* is a range of cells that shows how changing certain values in your formulas affects the results of those formulas. Data tables make it easy to calculate multiple versions in one operation, and then to view and compare the results of all the different variations.

For example, banks may offer loans at different rates for different periods of time, which require different payments. Using a data table, you can calculate the possible values for each argument.

A *one-variable data table* changes the value in only one cell. For example, use a one-variable data table if you want to see how different interest rates affect a monthly payment. A *two-variable data table* changes the values in two cells—for example, you can see how both different interest rates *and* different payment periods will affect a monthly payment.

Activity 11.18 Designing a Two-Variable Data Table

Recall that the PMT function has three required arguments: Present value (Pv), Rate, and Number of periods (Nper). Because Wattana would still like to borrow $350,000 and purchase the fixtures and furniture that she has selected for the new store in Mexico City, in this data table the present value will not change. The two values that will change are the Rate and Number of periods. Possible periods will range from 24 months (2 years) to 60 months (5 years) and the Rate will vary from 8% to 6%.

1 Double-click the **Sheet2 tab**, rename it **Payment Table** and then press Enter. Right-click the **Sheet3 tab** and click **Delete**.

2 With the **Payment Table** worksheet active, widen **column A** to **165 pixels**. Widen **column B** to **80 pixels**. Select **columns C:I**, and then widen them to **85 pixels**.

3 In the range **A2:B4**, enter the following row titles and data. Recall that you format numbers as you type by typing them with their symbols as shown:

Amount of Loan	$350,000
Period (Months)	36
Interest rate (per year)	7.00%

4 Click cell **C8**. Type **24** and then press Tab. Type **30** and then press Tab.

5 Select the range **C8:D8**. Point to the fill handle, and then drag to the right through cell **I8** to fill in a pattern of months from 24 to 60 in increments of six months.

6 In cell **B9**, type **8.000%** and then press Enter. Type **7.875%** and then press Enter.

The display of both values is rounded to two decimal places.

7 Select the range **B9:B10**. Point to the fill handle, and then drag down through cell **B25** to fill in a pattern of interest rates in increments of .125 from 8.00% down to 6.00%.

8 With the range **B9:B25** still selected, right-click anywhere over the range, and then on the Mini toolbar, click the **Increase Decimal** button one time. Compare your screen with Figure 11.36.

Row 8 represents the number of monthly payments, and column B represents a range of possible annual interest rates. These two arguments will be used to calculate varying payment arrangements for a loan of $350,000.

Figure 11.36

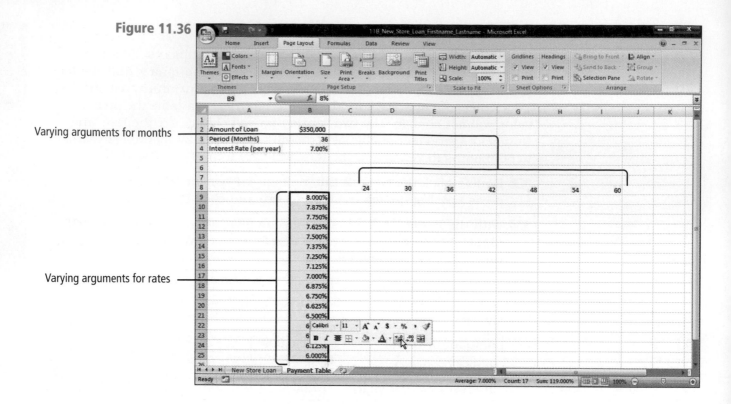

Varying arguments for months

Varying arguments for rates

9 Click cell **A1**. Type **Loan Options for New Store in Mexico City - Rates versus Months** and then press (Enter). **Merge and Center** this title across the range **A1:I1**. Change the **Font** to **Cambria**, the **Font Size** to **16**, and then apply a **Fill Color** of **Olive Green, Accent 3, Lighter 60%**.

10 Click cell **C6**. Type **Payment Options** and then press (Enter). **Merge and Center** this title across the range **C6:I6**. Change the **Font Size** to **14**, and then apply **Bold**.

11 Click cell **C7**. Type **Number of Monthly Payments** and then use the **Format Painter** to apply the format of cell **C6** to cell **C7**.

12 Click cell **A9**, type **Rates** and then press (Enter). Select the range **A9:A25**. On the **Home tab**, in the **Alignment group**, click the **Merge and Center** button, click the **Align Text Right** button, and then click the **Middle Align** button. Change the **Font Size** to **14**, and then apply **Bold**. Compare your screen with Figure 11.37.

Figure 11.37

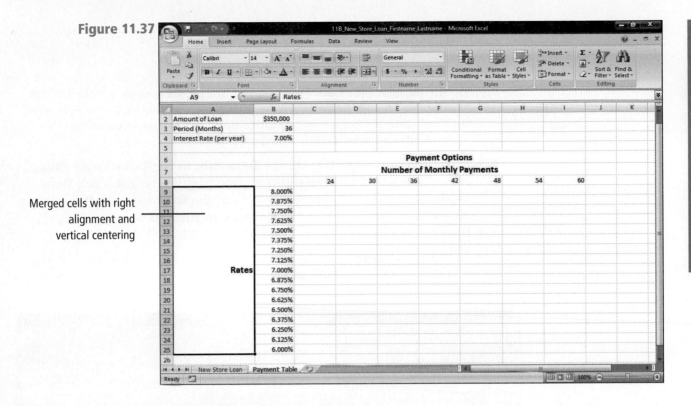

Merged cells with right alignment and vertical centering

13 **Save** 🖫 your workbook.

Activity 11.19 Using a Data Table to Calculate Options

Recall that a data table is a range of cells that shows how changing certain values in your formulas affects the results of those formulas. In this activity, you will create a table of payments for every combination of payment periods, which are represented by the column titles under *Number of Monthly Payments*, and interest rates, which are represented by the row titles to the right of *Rates*. From the resulting table, Wattana can find a combination of payment periods and interest rates that will enable her to go forward with her plan to borrow $350,000 to purchase the necessary furniture and fixtures for the new store in Mexico City.

1 Click cell **B8**, type **=** and notice that in the upper left corner of your screen, in the **Name Box**, *PMT* displays indicating the most recently used function. Click in the **Name Box** to open the **Function Arguments** dialog box for the **PMT** function. Alternatively, use one of the other methods you have practiced to insert the PMT function.

> The PMT function is entered in the upper left corner of your range of data, so that when the data table is completed, the months in row 8 and the rates in column B will be substituted into each cell's formula to fill the table with the range of months and interest rate options that are displayed.

2 In the **Rate** box, type **b4/12** to divide the interest rate per year by 12 and convert it to a monthly interest rate.

3 Press [Tab] to move the insertion point to the **Nper** box. Type **b3** and then press [Tab].

The periods in cell B3 are already stated in months and need not be changed.

4 In the **Pv** box, type **-b2** and then click **OK**.

The payment—$10,806.98—is calculated for the values in cells B2, B3, and B4. This is the same payment that you calculated on the first worksheet. Now it displays as a positive number because you entered the loan amount in cell B2 as a negative number.

5 Select the range **B8:I25**. On the **Data tab**, in the **Data Tools group**, click the **What-If Analysis** button, and then in the list, click **Data Table**. In the **Data Table** dialog box, in the **Row input cell** box, type **b3** and then press [Tab]. In the **Column input cell** box, type **b4** and then compare your screen with Figure 11.38.

The row of months will be substituted for the value in cell B3, and the column of interest rates will be substituted for the value in cell B4.

Figure 11.38

Row values substituted for months

Selected area indicates data table range

Column values substituted for interest rates

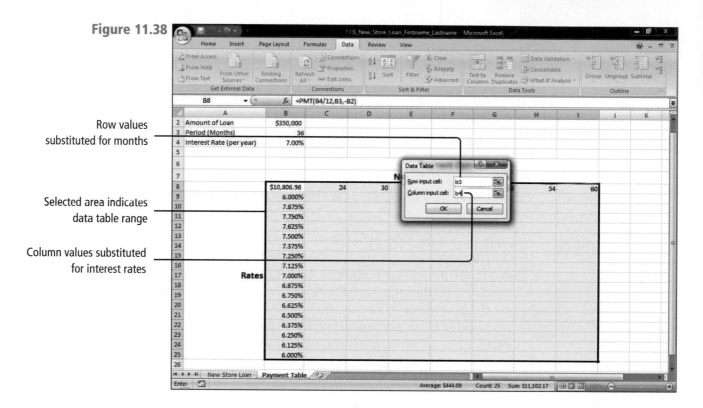

6 In the **Data Table** dialog box, click **OK**. Click cell **H21**, and then examine the formula in the **Formula Bar**. Compare your screen with Figure 11.39.

The table is filled with payment options that use the month and interest rate corresponding to the position in the table. Thus, if Wattana chooses a combination of 54 months at an interest rate of 6.5%, the monthly payment will be $7,492.96.

The data table is one of a group of Excel's What-If Analysis tools.

Figure 11.39

Period of 54 months, at 6.500% interest, results in $7,492.96 payment

7 Right-click cell **B8**, and then on the Mini toolbar, click the **Format Painter** button. Select the range **C9:I25** to apply the same format.

8 Use Ctrl to select the non-adjacent ranges **B9:B25** and **C8:I8**. Right-click over the selection, and then on the Mini toolbar, apply **Bold** and **Center**. Click anywhere to deselect the range, and then compare your worksheet with Figure 11.40.

By using a data table of payment options, you can see that Wattana must get a loan for at least 54 months (4.5 years) for any of the interest rates between 6.500% and 6.000% in order to purchase the furniture and fixtures she wants and still keep the monthly payment at approximately $7,500.

Figure 11.40

For a 54-month period, loan options in this range will be within the budget

	A	B	C	D	E	F	G	H	I	J	K
3	Period (Months)	36									
4	Interest Rate (per year)	7.00%									
5											
6							**Payment Options**				
7							**Number of Monthly Payments**				
8		$10,806.98	24	30	42	48	54	60			
9		8.000%	$15,829.55	$12,910.91	$10,967.73	$9,581.94	$8,544.52	$7,739.35	$7,096.74		
10		7.875%	$15,809.61	$12,890.88	$10,947.56	$9,561.60	$8,524.00	$7,718.63	$7,075.82		
11		7.750%	$15,789.67	$12,870.86	$10,927.41	$9,541.29	$8,503.51	$7,697.95	$7,054.94		
12		7.625%	$15,769.76	$12,850.87	$10,907.28	$9,521.01	$8,483.05	$7,677.30	$7,034.09		
13		7.500%	$15,749.86	$12,830.89	$10,887.18	$9,500.75	$8,462.62	$7,656.68	$7,013.28		
14		7.375%	$15,729.97	$12,810.93	$10,867.09	$9,480.51	$8,442.21	$7,636.10	$6,992.51		
15		7.250%	$15,710.10	$12,790.99	$10,847.04	$9,460.31	$8,421.84	$7,615.55	$6,971.78		
16		7.125%	$15,690.24	$12,771.07	$10,827.00	$9,440.13	$8,401.50	$7,595.03	$6,951.08		
17	**Rates**	7.000%	$15,670.40	$12,751.17	$10,806.98	$9,419.97	$8,381.19	$7,574.55	$6,930.42		
18		6.875%	$15,650.58	$12,731.28	$10,786.99	$9,399.84	$8,360.90	$7,554.10	$6,909.80		
19		6.750%	$15,630.77	$12,711.42	$10,767.02	$9,379.74	$8,340.65	$7,533.69	$6,889.21		
20		6.625%	$15,610.97	$12,691.57	$10,747.08	$9,359.66	$8,320.43	$7,513.31	$6,868.66		
21		6.500%	$15,591.19	$12,671.74	$10,727.15	$9,339.61	$8,300.23	$7,492.96	$6,848.15		
22		6.375%	$15,571.42	$12,651.94	$10,707.25	$9,319.59	$8,280.07	$7,472.64	$6,827.68		
23		6.250%	$15,551.67	$12,632.15	$10,687.37	$9,299.59	$8,259.94	$7,452.36	$6,807.24		
24		6.125%	$15,531.93	$12,612.37	$10,667.51	$9,279.62	$8,239.83	$7,432.11	$6,786.84		
25		6.000%	$15,512.21	$12,592.62	$10,647.68	$9,259.68	$8,219.76	$7,411.90	$6,766.48		
26											
27											

[9] Click the **Insert tab**, and then in the **Text group**, click the **Header & Footer** button to switch to **Page Layout View** and open the **Header area**. In the **Navigation group**, click the **Go to Footer** button, click just above the word *Footer*, then in the **Header & Footer Elements group**, click the **File Name** button. Click in a cell just above the footer to exit the **Footer area** and view your file name.

[10] Click the **Page Layout tab**. In the **Page Setup group**, click the **Orientation** button, and then click **Landscape**. Click the **Margins** button, and then at the bottom of the **Margins gallery**, click **Custom Margins**. In the **Page Setup** dialog box, under **Center on page**, select the **Horizontally** check box. Click **OK**, and then on the status bar, click the **Normal** button. Press Ctrl + Home to move to the top of the worksheet.

[11] **Save** your workbook. Press Ctrl + F2 to display the worksheet in **Print Preview**. To print, in the **Print group**, click the **Print** button, under **Print what**, click the **Entire workbook** option button, and then click **OK**. To submit electronically, follow your instructor's directions. Determine if you are to print formulas for any or all of the worksheets in this workbook. To print formulas, refer to Activity 9.17 in Project 9A.

[12] If you printed your formulas, be sure to redisplay the worksheet by pressing Ctrl + `. From the **Office** menu, click **Close**. If you are prompted to save changes, click **No**. **Close** Excel.

End You have completed Project 11B

There's More You Can Do!

Close Excel and any other open windows. Display the Start menu, click Computer, and then navigate to the student files that accompany this text-book. In the folder **02_theres_more_you_can_do**, locate and open the folder for this chapter. Open and print the instructions for this project, which are provided to you in Adobe PDF format.

Try IT! 1—Apply Conditional Formats by Using Color Scales, Icon Sets, and Top/Bottom Rules

In this Try It! exercise, you will use Color Scales, Icon Sets, and Top/Bottom rules to help you visualize data distribution and variation.

Content-Based Assessments

Excel
chapter eleven

Summary

Predefined formulas, referred to as functions, are available in Excel in various categories including Statistical, Logical, Date & Time, and Financial. Such functions enable you to make complex calculations without having to build the formulas yourself. Conditional formatting enables you to highlight interesting cells based on criteria, emphasize unusual values, and visualize data using Data Bars. The DATE function adds the current date to a workbook. Financial functions, along with the Goal Seek tool and data tables, are useful when making choices among various financing options.

Key Terms

The 🔘 symbol represents Key Terms found on the Student CD in the 02_theres_more_you_can_do folder for this chapter.

Content-Based Assessments

Matching

Match each term in the second column with its correct definition in the first column by writing the letter of the term on the blank line in front of the correct definition.

_____ **1.** A predefined formula—a formula that Excel has already built for you—that performs calculations by using specific values in a particular order.

_____ **2.** The values that an Excel function uses to perform calculations or operations.

_____ **3.** A statistical function that adds a group of values, and then divides the result by the number of values in the group.

_____ **4.** A statistical function that determines the smallest value in a group of values.

_____ **5.** An Excel feature which, after typing an = (equal sign) and the beginning letter or letters of a function name, displays a list of function names that match the typed letter(s), and from which you can insert the function by pointing to its name, and then pressing the Tab key or double-clicking.

_____ **6.** Conditions that you specify in a logical function.

_____ **7.** Any value or expression that can be evaluated as being _true_ or _false_.

_____ **8.** The symbols < (less than), > (greater than), and = (equal) that evaluate each field value to determine if it is the same, greater than, less than, or in between a range of values as specified by the criteria.

_____ **9.** A cell format consisting of a shaded bar that provides a visual cue to the reader about the value of a cell relative to other cells; the length of the bar represents the value in the cell—a longer bar represents a higher value and a shorter bar represents a lower value.

_____ **10.** A function within the _Date & Time_ category that retrieves the date and time from your computer's calendar and clock and inserts the information into the selected cell.

_____ **11.** A series of rows and columns in a worksheet that contains related data, and that is managed independently from the data in other rows and columns in the worksheet.

_____ **12.** A portion of a worksheet window bounded by and separated from other portions by vertical and horizontal bars.

_____ **13.** The amount charged for the use of borrowed money.

_____ **14.** The total amount that a series of future payments is worth now; also known as the principal.

_____ **15.** An Excel function that calculates the payment for a loan based on constant payments and at a constant rate of interest.

A Arguments

B AVERAGE

C Comparison operators

D Criteria

E Data Bar

F Excel table

G Formula AutoComplete

H Function

I Interest

J Logical test

K MIN

L NOW

M Pane

N PMT

O Present value

Content-Based Assessments

Fill in the Blank

Write the correct answer in the space provided.

1. The Excel function that adds all the numbers in a selected range of cells is the _____ function.

2. Prewritten formulas that analyze a group of measurements are _____ functions.

3. A statistical function commonly used to describe a group of data, and which finds the middle value in a group of values that has as many values above it in the group as are below it is the _____ function.

4. The MAX function determines the _____ value in a selected range of values.

5. Prewritten formulas that test for specific conditions, and which typically use conditional tests to determine whether specified conditions, referred to as criteria, are true or false, are _____ functions.

6. To count the number of cells within a range that meets the given condition, use the _____ function.

7. The IF function uses a logical test to check whether a condition is met, and then returns one value if true, and another value if _____.

8. A format that changes the appearance of a cell range—for example, by adding cell shading or font color—based on a condition is a _____ format.

9. The command that searches the cells in a worksheet—or in a selected range—for matches, and then replaces each match with a replacement value of your choice is called _____ _____ _____.

10. The term used to describe an Excel function that is subject to change each time the workbook is reopened; for example, when the NOW function updates itself to the current date and time each time the workbook is opened, is _____.

11. The command that enables you to select one or more rows or columns and freeze (lock) them into place as separate panes is _____ _____.

(Fill in the Blank continues on the next page)

Content-Based Assessments

Fill in the Blank

(Fill in the Blank continued)

12. The group of functions in Excel that performs common business calculations, such as calculating a loan payment on a vehicle, and that commonly involves a period of time such as months or years, are called _____ functions.

13. The value at the end of the time periods in an Excel function is known as the _____ _____.

14. One of Excel's What-If Analysis tools, which provides a method to find a specific value for a cell by adjusting the value of one other cell, is _____ _____.

15. A range of cells that shows how changing certain values in your formulas affects the results of those formulas, and that makes it easy to calculate multiple versions in one operation, is a _____ _____.

Content-Based Assessments

Project 11C—Pendants

In this project, you will apply the skills you practiced from the Objectives in Project 11A.

Objectives: 1. *Use SUM, AVERAGE, MEDIAN, MIN, and MAX Functions;*
2. *Use COUNTIF and IF Functions, and Apply Conditional Formatting;*
3. *Use a Date Function;* **4.** *Freeze Panes and Create an Excel Table;*
5. *Format and Print a Large Worksheet.*

Adamantine Jewelry creates castings, which it sells to other jewelry makers. In the following Skills Review, you will edit a worksheet for Rose Elleni, Vice President of Production, detailing the current inventory of pendant castings at the Milan production facility. Your completed worksheet will look similar to the one shown in Figure 11.41.

For Project 11C, you will need the following file:

e11C_Pendants

You will save your workbook as
11C_Pendants_Firstname_Lastname

Figure 11.41

(Project 11C–Pendants continues on the next page)

Content-Based Assessments

(Project 11C–Pendants continued)

1. **Start** Excel. From the student files that accompany this text, locate and open **e11C_Pendants**. **Save** the file in your **Excel Chapter 11** folder as **11C_Pendants_Firstname_Lastname**

2. Click cell **B4**. Click the **Formulas tab**, and then in the **Function Library group**, click the **AutoSum** button. Select the range **A12:A77**, dragging downward as necessary, and then press Enter. Right-click cell **B4**, and then apply **Comma Style** with zero decimal places.

3. Click cell **B5**. In the **Function Library group**, click the **More Functions** button, and then point to **Statistical**. Click **AVERAGE**, and then if necessary, drag the title bar of the **Function Arguments** dialog box down and to the right so you can view the **Formula Bar** and cell **B5**. In the **Function Arguments** dialog box, in the **Number1** box, delete the existing text, and then type **c12:c77** Click **OK** to calculate the average product price.

4. Click cell **B6**. In the **Function Library group**, click the **More Functions** button, display the list of **Statistical** functions, scroll down as necessary, and then click **MEDIAN**. In the **Function Arguments** dialog box, to the right of the **Number1** box, click the **Collapse Dialog** button. Select the range **C12:C77**, and then press Enter. Click **OK** to calculate the median product price.

5. Using either of the techniques that you practiced in Steps 3 and 4, in cell **B7**, insert the **MIN** function for the range **C12:C77**. In cell **B8** insert the **MAX** function for the range **C12:C77**.

6. Select the range **A4:B8**. Point to the right edge of the selected range to display the 🖑 pointer. Drag the selected range to the

right until the ScreenTip displays *C4:D8*, and then release the mouse button. Select **columns C:D**, and then apply **AutoFit** to adjust the column widths. Select the range **C4:D8**, and then apply **Bold** and a **Thick Box Border**.

7. In cell **A6**, type **Pendants** Select the range **A5:A7**, right-click over the selection, and then from the shortcut menu, click **Format Cells**. In the **Format Cells** dialog box, click the **Alignment tab**. Under **Text control**, select the **Merge cells** check box. In the upper right portion of the dialog box, under **Orientation**, point to the **red diamond**, and then drag the diamond upward until the **Degrees** box indicates *30*. Click **OK**.

8. With the cell still selected, click the **Home tab**, change the **Font Size** to **12**, and then apply **Bold** and **Italic**. In the **Alignment group**, apply **Center** alignment and **Middle Align**.

9. From the **row heading area**, point to **row 10** and right-click. From the shortcut menu, click **Insert**. Press F4 two times to insert two more rows. In cell **A10** type **Oval Styles Available:** and press Enter.

10. With cell **A11** active, on the **Formulas tab**, in the **Function Library group**, click the **More Functions** button, and then display the list of **Statistical** functions. Click **COUNTIF**. In the **Range** box, click the **Collapse Dialog** button, select the range **D15:D80**, and then press Enter. Click in the **Criteria** box, type **Oval** and then click **OK** to calculate the number of Oval pendant castings that Adamantine Jewelry has in stock.

11. Click cell **F15**. On the **Formulas tab**, in the **Function Library group**, click the **Logical** button, and then in the list, click **IF**. With

(Project 11C–Pendants continues on the next page)

(Project 11C–Pendants continued)

the insertion point in the **Logical_test** box, click cell **A15**. Type **<25** and then press [Tab] to move the insertion point to the **Value_if_true** box. Type **Order** and then press [Tab] to move the insertion point to the **Value_if_false** box. Type **OK** and then click **OK** to display the result *Order* in cell **F15**. Then, using the fill handle, copy the function down through cell **F80** to indicate the order status for each Style#.

12. Be sure the range **F15:F80** is selected. On the **Home tab**, in the **Styles group**, click the **Conditional Formatting** button. In the list, point to **Highlight Cells Rules**, and then click **Text that Contains**. In the **Text That Contains** dialog box, with the insertion point blinking in the first box, type **Order** In the second box, click the **arrow**, and then in the list, click **Custom Format**. On the **Font tab**, under **Font style**, click **Bold Italic**. Click the **Color arrow**, and then under **Theme Colors**, click **Dark Blue, Text 2, Darker 25%**. Click **OK**, and then click **OK** again to apply the formatting to the items that need to be ordered.

13. Select the range **A15:A80**. In the **Styles group**, click the **Conditional Formatting** button. In the list, point to **Data Bars**, and then in the **gallery**, click **Blue Data Bar** to visually indicate the quantity in stock for each item.

14. To the left of the **Formula Bar**, in the **Name Box**, type **e15:e80** and then press [Enter]. On the **Home tab**, in the **Editing group**, click the **Find & Select** button. From the menu, click **Replace** to display the **Find and Replace** dialog box. In the **Find what** box, type **Base** In the **Replace with** box, type **Platinum** Click the **Replace All** button, and then click **OK** to replace 16 occurrences of *Base* with *Platinum*.

Click **OK** to close the message box. **Close** the **Find and Replace** dialog box.

15. Scroll down to view **row 81**. Click cell **A81**, type **Last Edited by Rose Elleni** and then press [Enter]. With cell **A82** as the active cell, on the **Formulas tab**, in the **Function Library group**, click the **Date & Time** button. In the list of functions, click **NOW**. In the **Function Arguments** dialog box, click **OK** to close the dialog box. Adjust the width of **column A** to **127 pixels** to display the current date and time. Apply **Align Text Left** to cell **A82**.

16. **Save** your changes up to this point. Press [Ctrl] + [Home] to make cell **A1** the active cell. Select the range **A14:F80**. Click the **Insert tab**, and then in the **Tables group**, click the **Table** button. In the **Create Table** dialog box, if necessary, select the **My table has headers** check box. Click **OK** to create the table.

17. On the **Design tab**, in the **Table Styles group**, click the **More** button, and then under **Light**, click **Table Style Light 9**.

18. In the header row of the table, click the **Retail Price arrow**, and then from the menu, click **Sort Smallest to Largest** to rearrange the data so that the products display in ascending order with the lowest price item first and the highest price item last.

19. In the header row of the table, click the **Shape arrow**. From the menu, click **Sort A to Z**. Click the **Shape arrow** again. On the menu, click the **(Select All)** check box to clear all the check boxes. Then, click to select only the **Oval** check box, and then click **OK** to display only the **Oval** products.

20. Click any cell in the table so that the table is selected. On the Ribbon, click the **Design tab**, and then in the **Table Style**

(Project 11C–Pendants continues on the next page)

Content-Based Assessments

Skills Review

(Project 11C–Pendants continued)

Options group, select the **Total Row** check box. Click cell **A81**, click the **arrow** that displays, and then in the list, click **Sum** to display *683*—the total number of oval shaped pendant castings in stock. Click cell **A11**, type **Twenty different styles, 683 total in stock** and then press ⏎.

21. Click any cell in the table. On the Ribbon, click the **Design tab**, and then in the **Table Style Options group**, click the **Total Row** check box to clear it and remove the Total row from the bottom of the table. In the table header row, click the **Shape arrow**, and then on the menu, click **Clear Filter From "Shape"** to redisplay all of the products.

22. In the table header row, click the **Style#** **arrow**, and then click **Sort A to Z**, which will apply an ascending sort to the **Style#** column. In the **Tools group**, click the **Convert to Range** button. In the message box, click **Yes**.

23. Press Ctrl + Home to display the top of your worksheet. On the **Insert tab**, in the **Text group**, click **Header & Footer** to switch to **Page Layout view**. In the **Navigation group**, click the **Go to Footer** button, click just above the word *Footer*, and then in the **Header & Footer Elements group**, click the **File Name** button. Click a cell just above the footer to deselect the **Footer area** and view your file name.

24. Click the **Page Layout tab**. In the **Page Setup group**, click the **Margins** button, and then at the bottom of the **Margins**

gallery, click **Custom Margins**. In the **Page Setup** dialog box, under **Center on page**, select the **Horizontally** check box. Click **OK**, and then return the worksheet to **Normal** view. Press Ctrl + Home to move to the top of the worksheet. Delete **Sheet2** and **Sheet3**.

25. On the **Page Layout tab**, in the **Page Setup group**, click the **Print Titles** button. Under **Print titles**, click in the **Rows to repeat at top** box, and then at the right, click the **Collapse Dialog** button. From the **row heading area**, select **rows 13:14**, and then press ⏎. Click **OK**.

26. **Save** your workbook. To submit electronically, follow the instructions provided by your instructor. To print, from the **Office** menu, point to the **Print** button, and then click **Print Preview**. In the **Preview group**, click the **Next Page** and **Previous Page** buttons as necessary to view and check each page. Be sure the two header rows and the footer display on each page, and then click the **Print** button. In the **Print** dialog box, under **Print range**, be sure that **All** is selected, and then click **OK**. If you are directed to submit printed formulas, refer to Activity 9.17 in Project 9A to do so.

27. If you printed your formulas, be sure to redisplay the worksheet by pressing Ctrl + `. From the **Office** menu, click **Close**. If a dialog box displays asking if you want to save changes, click **No** so that you do *not* save the changes you made for printing formulas. **Close** Excel.

End You have completed Project 11C

Content-Based Assessments

Skills Review

Project 11D—Auto Loan

In this project, you will apply the skills you practiced from the Objectives in Project 11B.

Objectives: 6. *Use Financial Functions;* **7.** *Use Goal Seek;* **8.** *Create a Data Table.*

In the following Skills Review, you will create a worksheet for Jennifer Bernard, U.S. Sales Director, that details loan information for purchasing eight automobiles for Adamantine Jewelry sales representatives. The monthly payment for the eight automobiles cannot exceed $3,000. The two worksheets in your workbook will look similar to Figure 11.42.

For Project 11D, you will need the following file:

New blank Excel workbook

**You will save your workbook as
11D_Auto_Loan_Firstname_Lastname**

Figure 11.42

Loan Options for Automobile Purchase - Rates versus Months

Amount of Loan	$125,000
Period (months)	36
Interest rate (per year)	5.50%

Payment Options
Number of Monthly Payments

36	42	48	54	60
3,859.64	$3,364.28	$2,993.28	$2,705.20	$2,475.15
3,831.13	$3,335.58	$2,964.37	$2,676.06	$2,445.77
3,802.74	$3,307.03	$2,935.63	$2,647.11	$2,416.60
3,774.49	$3,278.63	$2,907.06	$2,618.35	$2,387.65
3,746.36	$3,250.38	$2,878.66	$2,589.79	$2,358.90
3,718.37	$3,222.28	$2,850.44	$2,561.42	$2,330.38
3,690.50	$3,194.33	$2,822.38	$2,533.24	$2,302.07
3,662.76	$3,166.54	$2,794.50	$2,505.26	$2,273.97

Adamantine Jewelry - Auto Purchase

Amount of Loan	$125,000
Period (years)	3
Interest rate (per year)	5.50%
Payment (per month)	$3,774.49

Option #1 - Reduce the Loan

Amount of Loan	$99,351
Period (years)	3
Interest rate (per year)	5.50%
Payment (per month)	$3,000.00

Option #2 - Increase Years

Amount of Loan	$125,000
Period (years)	3.86
Interest rate (per year)	5.50%
Payment (per month)	$3,000.00

11D_Auto_Loan_Firstname_Lastname

(Project 11D–Auto Loan continues on the next page)

Content-Based Assessments

Excel

chapter eleven　　**Skills Review**

(Project 11D–Auto Loan continued)

1. **Start** Excel and display a new blank workbook. From the **Office** menu, display the **Save As** dialog box, navigate to your **Excel Chapter 11** folder, and then in the **File name** box, type **11D_Auto_Loan_Firstname_Lastname** Click **Save** or press Enter.

2. Widen **column A** to **180 pixels** and **column B** to **100 pixels**. In cell **A1**, type **Adamantine Jewelry – Auto Purchase**

3. **Merge and Center** the worksheet title in the range **A1:B1**, change the **Font** to **Cambria**, the **Font Size** to **12**, and then add a **Fill Color** of **Orange, Accent 6, Lighter 40%**. Rename the worksheet tab as **Auto Loan**

4. In the range **A2:B5**, enter the following row titles and data.

Amount of Loan	$125,000
Period (years)	3
Interest rate (per year)	5.5%
Payment (per month)	

5. Click cell **B5**. On the **Formulas tab**, in the **Function Library group**, click the **Financial** button, and then click **PMT**. Drag the **Function Arguments** dialog box to the right side of your screen so you can view **columns A:B**.

6. In the **Rate** box, type **b4/12** to convert the annual interest rate to a monthly interest rate. Press Tab, and then in the **Nper** box, type **b3*12** to convert the number of years in the loan to the total number of months. Press Tab, and then in the **Pv** box, type **b2** to enter the present value of the loan. Click **OK** to create the function. In the **Formula Bar**, between the equal sign and *PMT*, type **−** (minus sign) to insert a minus sign into the formula, and then press Enter

to display the loan payment as a positive number.

7. The result of *$3,774.49* is higher than the monthly payment of $3,000 that Jennifer wants. One option is to reduce the amount of money that she is going to borrow; she can determine the maximum amount that she can borrow and still keep the payment at $3,000 by using Goal Seek. Click cell **B5**. On the **Data tab**, in the **Data Tools group**, click the **What-If Analysis** button, and then in the list, click **Goal Seek**. In the **Goal Seek** dialog box, in the **Set cell** box, confirm that *B5* displays.

8. Press Tab. In the **To value** box, type the payment goal of **3000** and then press Tab. In the **By changing cell** box, type **b2** which is the amount of the loan. Click **OK** two times. For three years at 5.5%, Jennifer can borrow only $99,351 if she maintains a monthly payment of $3,000.

9. Click cell **A7**. Type **Option #1 - Reduce the Loan** and then press Enter. Right-click cell **A1**. On the Mini toolbar, click the **Format Painter** button, and then click cell **A7** to copy the formats.

10. Select the range **A2:B5**, right-click, and then click **Copy**. Click cell **A8**, right-click, and then from the shortcut menu, click **Paste Special**. In the **Paste Special** dialog box, under **Paste**, click the **Values and number formats** option button, and then click **OK**. Press Esc to cancel the moving border.

11. In cell **B2**, type **125000** and then press Enter to restore the original loan amount. Another option that Jennifer can explore with Goal Seek is to increase the number of years over which she finances the automobiles. Click cell **B5**. On the **Data tab**, in the **Data Tools group**, click the **What-If**

(Project 11D–Auto Loan continues on the next page)

Project 11D: Auto Loan | **Excel**　　**499**

Content-Based Assessments

(Project 11D–Auto Loan continued)

Analysis button, and then click **Goal Seek**.

12. In the **Set cell** box, confirm that **B5** displays. Press [Tab]. In the **To value** box, type **3000** and then press [Tab]. In the **By changing cell** box, type **b3** which is the number of years for the loan. Click **OK** two times. Extending the loan over 3.86 years will maintain a monthly payment of $3,000 at the current interest rate.

13. Click **A13**. Type **Option #2 - Increase Years** and then press [Enter]. Use the **Format Painter** to copy the formats from cell **A7** to cell **A13**. Select the range **A2:B5**, right-click, click **Copy**, and then click cell **A14**. Right-click, click **Paste Special**, click the **Values and number formats** option button, and then click **OK**. Press [Esc] to cancel the moving border.

14. Click cell **B15**, right-click to display the Mini toolbar, and then click the **Decrease Decimal** button until the number of decimal places is two. Click cell **B3**. Type **3** and then press [Enter] to restore the original value.

15. Display the worksheet in **Page Layout** view, and then insert the **File Name** in the footer. Center the worksheet **Horizontally**, and then return the worksheet to **Normal** view. Press [Ctrl] + [Home] to move to the top of the worksheet.

16. **Save** the changes you have made thus far. To determine how variable interest rates and a varying number of payments affect the payment amount, Jennifer will set up a two-variable data table. Double-click the **Sheet2 tab**, rename it **Payment Table** and then press [Enter]. In cell **A1**, type **Loan Options for Automobile Purchase - Rates versus Months** and then press [Enter]. **Merge and Center** this title across the range

A1:I1. Change the **Font** to **Cambria**, the **Font Size** to **16**, and apply a **Fill Color** of **Orange, Accent 6, Lighter 40%**.

17. Widen **column A** to **165 pixels**. Widen **column B** to **80 pixels**. Select **columns C:I** and widen them to **85 pixels**. In the range **A2:B4**, enter the following row titles and data.

Amount of Loan	$125,000
Period (months)	36
Interest rate (per year)	5.5%

18. Click cell **C8**. Type **24** and then press [Tab]. Type **30** and then press [Tab]. Select the range **C8:D8**. Drag the fill handle to the right through cell **I8** to fill a pattern of months from 24 to 60 in increments of six months.

19. In cell **B9**, type **7.0%** and press [Enter]. Type **6.5%** and press [Enter]. Select the range **B9:B10**, and then drag the fill handle down through cell **B16** to fill a pattern of interest rates in increments of .5% from 7.00% down to 3.50%.

20. Click cell **C6**. Type **Payment Options** and then press [Enter]. **Merge and Center** this title across the range **C6:I6**. Change the **Font Size** to **14** and apply **Bold**. Click cell **C7**. Type **Number of Monthly Payments** and then use the **Format Painter** to apply the format of cell **C6** to cell **C7**.

21. Click cell **A9**, type **Rates** and then press [Enter]. Select the range **A9:A16**. On the **Home tab**, in the **Alignment group**, click the **Merge and Center** button, click the **Align Text Right** button, and then click the **Middle Align** button. Change the **Font Size** to **14** and apply **Bold**.

(Project 11D–Auto Loan continues on the next page)

Skills Review

(Project 11D–Auto Loan continued)

22. Click cell **B8**. On the **Formulas tab**, in the **Function Library group**, click the **Financial** button, and then click **PMT**. In the **Rate** box, type **b4/12** to divide the interest rate per year by 12 to convert it to a monthly interest rate. press ⟨Tab⟩, and then in the **Nper** box, type **b3** press ⟨Tab⟩. In the **Pv** box, type **-b2** and then click **OK**.

23. Select the range **B8:I16**. On the **Data tab**, in the **Data Tools group**, click the **What-If Analysis** button, and then in the list, click **Data Table**. In the **Data Table** dialog box, in the **Row input cell** box, type **b3** and then press ⟨Tab⟩. In the **Column input cell** box, type **b4** In the **Data Table** dialog box, click **OK** to create the data table.

24. Click cell **B8**, and then right-click to display the Mini toolbar. Click the **Format Painter** button. Select the range **C9:I16** to apply the same format. Select the ranges **B9:B16** and **C8:I8** and apply **Bold** and **Center**. Notice that in cell **G9**, the payment is *$2,993.28*, which is close to Jennifer's goal of a monthly payment of $3,000. At any of the interest rates, she will have to extend the loan over at least

48 months to stay within her goal of $3,000 per month.

25. Display the worksheet in **Page Layout** view, and then insert the **File Name** in the footer. Center the worksheet **Horizontally**, and set the **Orientation** to **Landscape**. Then return the worksheet to **Normal** view. Press ⟨Ctrl⟩ + ⟨Home⟩ to move to the top of the worksheet. Delete **Sheet3** from the workbook.

26. **Save** your workbook. Press ⟨Ctrl⟩ + ⟨F2⟩ to display the worksheet in **Print Preview**. To print, in the **Print group**, click the **Print** button, under **Print what**, click the **Entire workbook** option button, and then click **OK**. To submit electronically, follow your instructor's directions. Determine if you are to print formulas for any or all of the worksheets in this workbook. To print formulas, refer to Activity 9.17 in Project 9A.

27. If you printed your formulas, be sure to redisplay the worksheet by pressing ⟨Ctrl⟩ + ⟨`⟩. From the **Office** menu, click **Close**. If you are prompted to save changes, click **No**. **Close** Excel.

End **You have completed Project 11D**

Content-Based Assessments

Mastering Excel

Project 11E — Sales

In this project, you will apply the skills you practiced from the Objectives in Projects 11A and 11B.

Objectives: 1. *Use SUM, AVERAGE, MEDIAN, MIN, and MAX Functions;* **2.** *Use COUNTIF and IF Functions, and Apply Conditional Formatting;* **3.** *Use a Date Function;* **4.** *Freeze Panes and Create an Excel Table;* **5.** *Format and Print a Large Worksheet;* **7.** *Use Goal Seek.*

In the following Mastering Excel assessment, you will edit a worksheet for Jennifer Bernard, U.S. Sales Director for Adamantine Jewelry, that calculates the October sales commission and bonuses for the U.S. sales representatives. The sales representatives earn 15% commission and those whose sales exceed $20,000 per month earn a bonus of $750. The worksheet will also provide sales statistics for the month of October and will detail November sales goals. The worksheets of your workbook will look similar to Figure 11.43.

For Project 11E, you will need the following file:

e11E_Sales

You will save your workbook as 11E_Sales_Firstname_Lastname

Figure 11.43

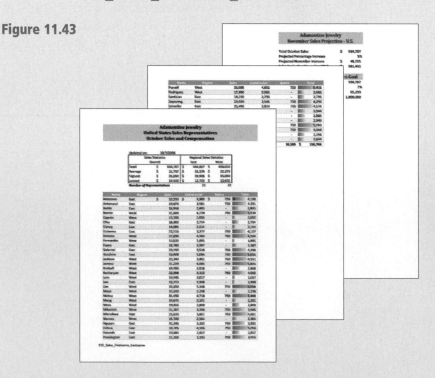

(Project 11E–Sales continues on the next page)

Content-Based Assessments

(Project 11E–Sales continued)

1. **Start** Excel, locate and open the file **e11E_Sales**, and then **Save** the file in your **Excel Chapter 11** folder as **11E_Sales_ Firstname_Lastname** Rename **Sheet1** as Sales Data In cell **C6**, enter the **NOW** function, and then on the **Home tab**, in the **Number group**, click the **Number Format arrow** and apply the **Short Date** format to the date. In cell **C9**, enter a function that sums the total sales in the range **C16:C58**. In cells **C10**, **C11**, and **C12**, use statistical functions to calculate the average sales, the highest sales, and the lowest sales.

2. In cell **D16**, construct a formula to calculate the commission on sales earned by **Anderson** by using a commission formula of *Sales times 15%*. Format the result with **Comma Style** and **zero decimal places**. Copy the formula down for each sales representative. In cell **E16**, enter an **IF** function and test whether the sales value in cell **C16** is greater than **20000**. If true, display **750** and if false, display **0** Format the result as **Comma Style**, with **zero decimal places**, and then fill the formula down for each sales representative. Those representatives who receive no bonus will display – (a minus sign) in the cell.

3. In cell **F16**, construct a formula to calculate the total compensation by adding the **Commission** and **Bonus** amounts for **Anderson**. The format of Comma Style and zero decimal places will be applied based on the reference to cell **D16**. Fill the formula down for each sales representative. With the range **F16:F58** still selected, apply **Light Blue Data Bar Conditional Formatting** to the **Total** column. In cell **D13**, enter a **COUNTIF** function to count the number of sales representatives in the **East** region. Enter a similar function in cell **E13** for the **West** region.

4. Select the range **A15:F58**, and then **Insert** a **Table** with headers. Apply **Table Style Medium 7**. In the **Name** column, **Sort** the table **A to Z**. Change the **Table Style Options** to display the **Total Row**.

5. If necessary, scroll up so that you can view **rows 1:18** on your screen. Select **row 16**, click the **View tab**. In the **Window group**, click the **Freeze Panes** button, and then click **Freeze Panes**. Scroll to bring the **Total row** at the bottom of the table closer to **row 15**—it is OK to leave three or four rows visible for visual reference. Recall that you can freeze panes in this manner to keep row titles visible while scrolling down through a large amount of data.

6. Filter the table to display only the sales representatives in the **East** region—the table will be filtered even though not all rows are in view. Click cell **C59**, and then by using the functions available from the **Total row arrow** in the **Sales** column, **Sum** the **Sales** for the **East** region. Right-click over the result, **Copy** the result, right-click over cell **D9**, click **Paste Special**, and then paste the **Values and number formats** to cell **D9**.

7. Using the same technique, and by using the **Total row arrow** in the **Sales** column, calculate the **Average** for the **East** region, and then copy and paste the **value and number format** to cell **D10**. By using the **Total row arrow** in the **Sales** column, calculate the highest and lowest sales amount for the **East** region, and paste the **values and number formats** to cells **D11** and **D12**. You can see that by freezing panes and using the shortcut menus, you can easily copy and paste values from one section of your worksheet to another without unnecessary scrolling.

(Project 11E–Sales continues on the next page)

(Project 11E–Sales continued)

8. Filter the **Sales** data for the **West** region, scroll to view the data and notice that the Freeze Panes command is still in effect. Position the **Total row** close to **row 15**. Then, by using the **Total row arrow** in the **Sales** column in the manner you did in the previous step, make similar calculations and then copy and paste the **Values and number formats** into the range **E9:E12**.

9. Clear the filter to redisplay all of the data in the table, and then in the **Total** row, **Sum** the **Sales**, **Commission**, **Bonus**, and **Total** columns. Select the four totals, right-click, and then apply **Accounting Number Format** with **zero decimal places**. Click the **View tab**, in the **Window group**, click the **Freeze Panes** button, and then click **Unfreeze Panes**. Click inside the table, and then on the **Design tab**, convert the table to a range. To the ranges **C9:E12** and **C16:F16**, apply **Accounting Number Format** with **zero decimal places**.

10. Insert a **Footer** with the **File Name** in the left section, and then **Center** the worksheet **Horizontally**. Click the **Print Titles** button and repeat **row 15** at the top of each page. Return to **Normal** view and display the top of your worksheet.

11. **Save** your work up to this point. **Rename Sheet2** as November Sales Goal In cell **A1**, type **Adamantine Jewelry** and then adjust the column width of **column A** to **220 pixels**. **Merge and Center** the title across **A1:B1**. Change the **Font** to **Cambria**, change the **Font Size** to **14**, and then add a **Fill Color** of **Orange, Accent 6, Lighter 40%**. In cell **A2**, type **November Sales Projection – U.S.** Copy the format from cell

A1 to cell **A2**. In the range **A4:B7**, enter the following data.

Total October Sales	
Projected Percentage Increase	5%
Projected November Increase	
Sales Projection November 2010	

12. Click cell **B4**, type = to begin a formula, click the **Sales Data worksheet** to make it the active sheet, click cell **C9**, and then press Enter to return to the **November Sales Goal** worksheet and reference the **Total October Sales** in cell **B4**. Format the result with **Accounting Number Format** with **zero decimal places**.

13. In cell **B6**, construct a formula to multiply the **Total October Sales** times the **Projected Percentage Increase**, and then format the result the same as cell **B4**. In cell **B7**, construct a formula to add the **Total October Sales** and the **Projected November Increase**.

14. Jennifer's sales goal for the U.S. sales representatives is $1,000,000. Use **Goal Seek** to determine the **Projected Percentage Increase** if the **Sales Projection November 2010** value is **1,000,000**. In cell **A9**, type **Increase Needed to Reach Sales Goal** and then format the cell the same as cell **A1**. **Copy** the range **A4:B7**, and then paste the **Values and number formats** to cell **A10**. In cell **B5**, reset the original value to **5%** and press Enter.

15. Insert a **Footer** in the left section with the **File Name**, and then **Center** the worksheet **Horizontally** on the page. Return to **Normal** view and display the top of the worksheet. Delete **Sheet3** from the workbook.

(Project 11E–Sales continues on the next page)

(Project 11E–Sales continued)

16. Save your workbook. **Print** the **Entire workbook** or submit electronically as directed. If you are directed to submit printed formulas, refer to Activity 9.17 in Project 9A to do so. If you printed your formulas, be sure to redisplay the worksheet by pressing Ctrl + ` . From the **Office** menu, click **Close**. If you are prompted to save changes, click **No**. **Close** Excel.

End You have completed Project 11E

Excel

chaptereleven

Mastering Excel

Project 11F — Retirement

In this project, you will apply the skills you practiced from the Objectives in Projects 11A and 11B.

Objectives: 3. *Use a Date Function;* **6.** *Use Financial Functions;* **8.** *Create a Data Table.*

In the following Mastering Excel project, you will create a data table for Rosetta Caputo, the Chief Financial Officer for Adamantine Jewelry, that she will use to consider investment alternatives for the employee benefits retirement fund. Your workbook will look similar to Figure 11.44.

For Project 11F, you will need the following file:

New blank Excel workbook

You will save your workbook as 11F_Retirement_Firstname_Lastname

Figure 11.44

(Project 11F–Retirement continues on the next page)

(Project 11F–Retirement continued)

1. **Start** Excel and display a new blank workbook. In your **Excel Chapter 11** folder, **Save** the file as **11F_Retirement_Firstname_Lastname** In cell **A1**, type **Adamantine Jewelry Retirement Fund** and then **Merge and Center** the text across **A1:L1**. Change the **Font** to **Cambria**, change the **Font Size** to **16**, and then apply a **Fill Color** of **Red, Accent 2, Lighter 40%**.

2. Copy the formatting from cell **A1** to cell **A2**. Then, in cell **A2**, enter the **NOW** function. On the **Home tab**, in the **Number group**, click the **Number Format arrow**, and then apply the **Short Date** format. In the range **A4:B8**, enter the following row titles and data and then **AutoFit column A**.

Initial Investment	$2,500,000
Rate	5%
Company Contribution	$275,000
Term	10
Future Value	

3. Click cell **B8**. Click the **Formulas tab**, and then insert the **Financial** function **FV** to calculate the future value of the retirement fund based on the data that you entered in Step 2. Complete the arguments as follows: the **Rate** is the value in cell **B5**, and **Nper** is the value in cell **B7**. **Pmt** is the amount of the **Company contribution** in cell **B6**, and **Pv** is the **Initial Investment** in cell **B4**. Click **OK**, and then edit the formula in the **Formula Bar** so that the result displays as a positive number. Format the **Future Value** with **zero decimal places**. Based on the calculations, at the end of ten years, the fund will have a value of *$7,531,157*.

4. In the range **B10:L10**, in one-year increments, use **AutoFill** to enter a series of years from **5** to **15**, indicating the term of the retirement fund. Apply a **Thick Bottom Border** to the range. Beginning in cell **A11**, enter the possible interest rates for the fund beginning with **2.5%** and increasing in increments of .5% up to 7.5%. Format the interest rates with **one decimal place**.

5. In cell **A10** type **=b8** to enter a formula that references cell **B8**. Select the range **A10:L21**, and then create a **Data Table** with a **Row input cell** that references cell **B7** and a **Column input cell** that references **B5**. Format the results in the data table with **Comma Style, zero decimal places**. You can see by the resulting data table, that the higher the interest rate that can be obtained for the investment, the higher the value of the fund will be in future years.

6. Insert a footer in the left section with the **File Name**, exit the **Footer area**, display the **Page Layout tab**, and then **Center** the worksheet **Horizontally** on the page. Change the **Orientation** to **Landscape**. In the **Scale to Fit group**, set the **Width** to **1 page** and the **Height** to **1 page** (or scale to 70%). Return to **Normal** view, display the top of the worksheet, and then delete the extra worksheets from the workbook.

7. **Save** your workbook. **Print** the worksheet, or submit electronically as directed. If you are directed to submit printed formulas, refer to Activity 9.17 in Project 9A to do so.

8. If you printed your formulas, be sure to redisplay the worksheet by pressing Ctrl + `. From the **Office** menu, click **Close**. If you are prompted to save changes, click **No**. **Close** Excel.

End You have completed Project 11F

Content-Based Assessments

Mastering Excel

Project 11G—Opals

In this project, you will apply the skills you practiced from all of the Objectives in Projects 11A and 11B.

Objectives: 1. *Use SUM, AVERAGE, MEDIAN, MIN, and MAX Functions;* **2.** *Use COUNTIF and IF Functions, and Apply Conditional Formatting;* **3.** *Use a Date Function;* **4.** *Freeze Panes and Create an Excel Table;* **5.** *Format and Print a Large Worksheet;* **6.** *Use Financial Functions;* **7.** *Use Goal Seek;* **8.** *Create a Data Table.*

In the following Mastering Excel assessment, you will edit a worksheet for Adamantine Jewelry's Chief Financial Officer, Rosetta Caputo. Adamantine Jewelry is considering the purchase of Opal Industries—a large distributor of elegant and expensive opal jewelry. The purchase includes the entire current inventory held by Opal Industries. Rosetta wants to compute the value of the Opal Industries inventory and determine which items are still in production and which items are in a warehouse. She must also explore alternatives for financing the purchase. Your completed workbook will look similar to Figure 11.45.

For Project 11G, you will need the following file:

e11G_Opals

You will save your workbook as 11G_Opals_Firstname_Lastname

Figure 11.45

(Project 11G–Opals continues on the next page)

(Project 11G–Opals continued)

1. **Start** Excel. From the student files that accompany this text, locate and open the file **e11G_Opals**, and then **Save** it in your **Excel Chapter 11** folder as 11G_Opals_Firstname_Lastname

2. In cell **B3**, insert the **NOW** function. In cell **E11**, construct a formula to calculate the **Inventory Value** of the first Style# by multiplying the **Per Item Cost to Purchase** times the **Quantity in Stock**, and then copy the formula down through **row 76**. Format the selected range with **Comma Style** and **zero decimal places**.

3. Opal Industries moves stock from the production facility to the warehouse after 20 items are produced. In cell **F11**, enter an **IF** function to test whether the **Quantity in Stock** value in cell **D11** is **greater than or equal to 20**. If true, display **In Warehouse** and if false, display **In Production** Copy the formula down through **row 76**. With the range still selected, use the **Text that Contains** conditional formatting to apply **Green Fill with Dark Green Text** to cells that contain **In Production**

4. Select the range **A10:F76**, and then **Insert** a **Table** with headers. Apply **Table Style Light 9**. Change the **Table Style Options** to display the **Total Row**. Press Ctrl + Home to deselect the table and view **row 1** on your screen. Select **row 11**, click the **View tab**, in the **Window group**, click the **Freeze Panes** button, and then click **Freeze Panes**.

5. Filter the table to display only the **Ring** products, and then scroll so that the **Total row** is closer to the column titles in **row 14**. In the **Total row**, calculate the **Sum** for the **Inventory Value** of Rings. **Copy** the result, and then in cell **C8**,

Paste the **Values and number formats**. Even though some rows are out of view, the calculation is made on the appropriate rows.

6. Repeat Step 5 for the **Pendant**, **Earrings**, and **Bracelet** products in the appropriate cells. Then clear any filters to display all of the data in the table. Click any table cell, click the **Design tab**, remove the **Total Row** from the table, and then convert the table to a range.

7. In cell **C5**, enter a function to calculate the cost to purchase the total inventory, which is the sum of the range **C8:F8**. Your result is *1,740,220*. On the **View tab**, in the **Window group**, click the **Freeze Panes** button, and then click **Unfreeze Panes**. Select cell **C11**, and then hold down Ctrl and select cell **E11**, cell **C5**, and the range **C8:F8**. To the selected cells, apply **Accounting Number Format** with **zero decimal places**. Set the width of **columns C:F** to **100 pixels**.

8. Insert a footer with the **File Name** in the left section, and then **Center** the sheet **Horizontally**. Set the **Print Titles** option to repeat **row 10** at the top of each page. Change the **Orientation** to **Landscape**, return to **Normal** view, and then display the top of your worksheet. **Save** your workbook.

9. **Copy** cell **C5**, display the **Goal** sheet, and then use **Paste Special** to paste the **Values and number formats** to cell **B2** in the **Goal** sheet. In cell **B5**, insert the **PMT** function using the data from the range **B2:B4**. Be sure that you convert the interest rate and period to reflect monthly payments by dividing the interest rate by 12 and multiplying the years by 12. Display the result as a positive number. Apply the

(Project 11G–Opals continues on the next page)

Content-Based Assessments

Mastering Excel

(Project 11G–Opals continued)

Accounting Number Format with **zero decimal places** to cell **B5**—your result is *$52,548*.

10. Rosetta prefers that the monthly payment not exceed $40,000. Use **Goal Seek** to determine the amount of money that Adamantine Jewelry can finance to keep the payment at $40,000. The interest rate and period will not change. The result is *$1,324.683.07*.

11. **Copy** the range **B2:B5**, and then paste the **Values and number formats** to cell **B8**. In cell **B2**, type **1740220** to restore the original amount.

12. Insert a footer in the left section with the **File Name**, and then **Center** the sheet **Horizontally** on the page. Display the sheet in **Normal** view, and then **Save** your workbook.

13. **Copy** cell **B8**, display the **Financing** sheet, and then in cell **B3**, paste the value and number format; this will reference the amount that Rosetta has decided to finance as the **Amount of Loan**. In cell **B7**, enter a **PMT** function using the data in the range **B3:B5**. The period is already expressed in months, but the rate is not. Be sure that the result displays as a positive number. To determine how changes in interest rates and number of payments affect the payment amount, Rosetta will set up a two-variable data table. Rosetta is exploring loan programs from 12 to 60 months in duration and at rates of 2.5% to 6.5%.

14. Select the range **B7:G16**, and then create a **Data Table** using the information in cells **B3:B5** in which the **Row input cell** is the **Period** and the **Column input cell** is the **Interest rate**. Format the data with **Comma Style** and **zero decimal** places. Format cell **B7** with **Accounting Number Format** and **zero decimal places**.

15. Select the data table results—the range **C8:G16**. Recall that Rosetta prefers a monthly payment that does not exceed $40,000. Apply **Conditional Formatting** using the **Highlight Cells Rules Less Than** option. In the **Format cells that are LESS THAN** box, type **40000** and use **Light Red Fill with Dark Red Text**. Click any cell to deselect. Rosetta can clearly see which financing rates and terms are acceptable.

16. Insert a footer in the left section with the **File Name**, and then **Center** the sheet **Horizontally** on the page. Display the sheet in **Normal** view and press [Ctrl] + [Home] to display the top of the worksheet.

17. **Save** your workbook. **Print** the **Entire workbook**, or submit electronically as directed. If you are directed to submit printed formulas, refer to Activity 9.17 in Project 9A to do so.

18. If you printed your formulas, be sure to redisplay the sheet by pressing [Ctrl] + [']. From the **Office** menu, click **Close**. If you are prompted to save changes, click **No**. **Close** Excel.

End You have completed Project 11G

Content-Based Assessments

Mastering Excel

Project 11H—*GO!* Fix It

In this project, you will construct a solution by applying any combination of the skills you practiced from the Objectives in Projects 11A and 11B.

> **For Project 11H, you will need the following file:**
>
> e11H_Ruby_Inventory
>
> **You will save your document as**
> **11H_Ruby_Inventory_Firstname_Lastname**

From the student files that accompany this textbook, open the file **e11H_Ruby_Inventory**, and then save the file in your chapter folder as **11H_Ruby_Inventory_Firstname_Lastname**

Adamantine Jewelry maintains a large stock of rubies for use in its retail business. In this project, you will edit and complete an Inventory and Reorder List and Loan Information tables.

This document contains five errors that you must find and correct. Read and examine the workbook, and then edit to correct the errors that you find. Types of errors could include:

- Spelling, grammar, and punctuation errors in cells, charts, worksheet tabs, or file names.

- Errors in data entry and workbook layout. Formatting errors in text, numbers, alignment, indents and spacing, tabs, wrapping, merge and center, text direction and orientation, fonts, borders, patterns, protection, AutoFormat, conditional formatting, data sorting, filtering, and validation.

- Formula and function errors such as incorrect and missing formulas, error indicators and values, relative vs. absolute cell referencing, What-If Analysis, Paste Special, function arguments, and Goal Seek.

- Errors in object design, layout, and formatting.

- Row and column formatting errors such as height, width, and AutoFit.

- Worksheet, tab design, and formatting errors such as missing or blank worksheets, worksheet tab colors, and locations.

- Page setup errors such as page orientation and scaling, margins and centering, headers and footers, sheet gridlines, and row and column headings.

(Project 11H–*GO!* Fix It continues on the next page)

Content-Based Assessments

Mastering Excel

(Project 11H–*GO!* Fix It continued)

To complete this project you should know:

- There are no spelling, grammar, punctuation, usage, font, font size, or border errors in the body of the worksheets.

- All the errors in the Inventory & Reorder List are in the top portion of the worksheet.

- There are no errors in the Loan Information sheet, but you must calculate the Payment in cell E13 and then create the data table.

Save the changes you have made, add the file name to the footers, and then submit as directed.

End You have completed Project 11H ————————————

Rubric

The following outcomes-based assessments are *open-ended assessments*. That is, there is no specific correct result; your result will depend on your approach to the information provided. Make *Professional Quality* your goal. Use the following scoring rubric to guide you in *how* to approach the problem, and then to evaluate *how well* your approach solves the problem.

The *criteria*—Software Mastery, Content, Format and Layout, and Process—represent the knowledge and skills you have gained that you can apply to solving the problem. The *levels of performance*—Professional Quality, Approaching Professional Quality, or Needs Quality Improvements—help you and your instructor evaluate your result.

	Your completed project is of Professional Quality if you:	Your completed project is Approaching Professional Quality if you:	Your completed project Needs Quality Improvements if you:
1-Software Mastery	Choose and apply the most appropriate skills, tools, and features and identify efficient methods to solve the problem.	Choose and apply some appropriate skills, tools, and features, but not in the most efficient manner.	Choose inappropriate skills, tools, or features, or are inefficient in solving the problem.
2-Content	Construct a solution that is clear and well organized, contains content that is accurate, appropriate to the audience and purpose, and is complete. Provide a solution that contains no errors of spelling, grammar, or style.	Construct a solution in which some components are unclear, poorly organized, inconsistent, or incomplete. Misjudge the needs of the audience. Have some errors in spelling, grammar, or style, but the errors do not detract from comprehension.	Construct a solution that is unclear, incomplete, or poorly organized; contains some inaccurate or inappropriate content; and contains many errors of spelling, grammar, or style. Do not solve the problem.
3-Format and Layout	Format and arrange all elements to communicate information and ideas, clarify function, illustrate relationships, and indicate relative importance.	Apply appropriate format and layout features to some elements, but not others. Overuse features, causing minor distraction.	Apply format and layout that does not communicate information or ideas clearly. Do not use format and layout features to clarify function, illustrate relationships, or indicate relative importance. Use available features excessively, causing distraction.
4-Process	Use an organized approach that integrates planning, development, self-assessment, revision, and reflection.	Demonstrate an organized approach in some areas, but not others; or, use an insufficient process of organization throughout.	Do not use an organized approach to solve the problem.

Outcomes-Based Assessments

Problem Solving

Project 11I — Capital Equipment

In this project, you will construct a solution by applying any combination of the skills you practiced from the Objectives in Projects 11A and 11B.

For Project 11I, you will need the following file:

New blank Excel workbook

You will save your workbook as
11I_Capital_Equipment_Firstname_Lastname

Adamantine Jewelry plans to renovate the Milan production facility. The renovation consists primarily of the purchase and installation of new capital equipment used in the production of earrings and pendants. The renovation and equipment will cost $1,500,000. Rosetta Caputo, Chief Financial Officer, is exploring financing options for the purchase of the equipment. Create a workbook with two worksheets that Rosetta can use to analyze loan payment information. In the first worksheet, enter a title in cell A1. In cells A2:A5, enter the following row titles: **Amount of Loan, Period (years), Interest Rate (per year)**, and **Payment (per month)**. In cells B2:B4, enter the loan amount, **$1,500,000**; the Period, **10** years; and the Interest rate, **6.5%**. Adjust the column widths as necessary. In B5, use the preceding data to construct a PMT function to calculate the monthly loan payment, converting the interest rate and the period to reflect monthly payments.

Marco Canaperi, the company president, has asked Rosetta to keep the loan payments below $15,000. Use Goal Seek to explore two options for reducing the loan payment, either by reducing the loan or by increasing the number of years. Arrange the worksheet so that the two loan options display similar to Project 11B in the chapter.

In the second worksheet, using your work in Project 11B as a guide, create a data table to calculate payments over 10, 15, 20, and 25 years with varying interest rates from 3.5% to 8.5% in .5% increments. In A2:B4 enter the row titles and the loan information. In C6:C7 enter titles that describe the data table. In C8:F8 enter the yearly increments. In B9:B19 enter the interest rates in .5% increments. In B8 construct the PMT function, and then create the data table. On each worksheet, apply appropriate number formatting, use borders, fill colors, and font styles and sizes to create a professional worksheet. Add a footer to each worksheet that includes the file name, center the worksheets on the page, and delete unused sheets. Save the workbook as **11I_Capital_Equipment_Firstname_Lastname** and submit it as directed.

End You have completed Project 11I

Outcomes-Based Assessments

Problem Solving

Project 11J—Commission

In this project, you will construct a solution by applying any combination of the skills you practiced from the Objectives in Projects 11A and 11B.

> **For Project 11J, you will need the following file:**
>
> e11J_Commission
>
> **You will save your workbook as**
> **11J_Commission_Firstname_Lastname**

The U.S. Sales Director for Adamantine Jewelry, Jennifer Bernard, wants a report on the December sales and compensation for the U.S. sales representatives. From your student files, open e11J_Commissions. Calculate the Commission (Commission Rate times Sales) for each sales representative, using absolute cell references as necessary. Sales representatives whose sales exceed $20,000 receive a bonus of $750. In the Bonus column, use an IF function to calculate bonuses—the value_if_true is 750 and the value_if_false is 0. Then calculate the total Compensation (Commission + Bonus) for each sales representative. Use Conditional Formatting to apply Data Bars to the Total Compensation column. In the range B8:C12, enter functions to calculate the total sales and commission, the average sales and commission, the median sales and commission, and the highest and lowest sales and commission.

Insert a table using the range of data A16:F59. Sort the table from A to Z on the Name column. Add a Total Row to the table, freeze panes if you want to do so, and then filter the table for each region. Calculate the total Sales and Commissions for each region and enter the amounts in cells F8:G11 being sure to paste the value and number format. Then, total the Sales and Commissions in F12:G12. Convert the table to a range and unfreeze panes if necessary. Use the NOW function to enter the current date in cell B5 and apply the Short Date format. Add the file name to the footer, delete unused sheets, set up for printing appropriately, including printing the table header row on each page. Save the workbook as **11J_Commission_Firstname_Lastname** and submit it as directed.

End You have completed Project 11J —————————

Outcomes-Based Assessments

Problem Solving

Project 11K — Truck Purchase

In this project, you will construct a solution by applying any combination of the skills you practiced from the Objectives in Projects 11A and 11B.

> ### For Project 11K, you will need the following file:
>
> New blank Excel workbook

You will save your workbook as
11K_Truck_Purchase_Firstname_Lastname

Rosetta Caputo, Chief Financial Officer for Adamantine Jewelry, is exploring financing options for the purchase of five new delivery trucks for the Milan production facility. The cost of the five trucks is $150,000.

Rosetta wants to look at various loan arrangements by creating a data table. In A1, enter an appropriate title for the worksheet. In A2:A4, enter the following row titles: **Amount of Loan, Period (months), Interest Rate (per year)**. In B2:B4, enter the financing data: **$150,000**; **36**; **4.5%**. In C6 fill the payment periods in six-month increments beginning with 24 and concluding with 60. In the column beginning in cell B7, create a list of varying interest rates from 4.5% to 8% in .5% increments. In B6, construct a PMT function using the data in cells B2:B4 and then create the data table. Use formatting and editing techniques that you practiced in this chapter so that the workbook looks professional and is easy to read. Add the file name to the footer, delete unused sheets, and then arrange for attractive printing. Save the workbook as **11K_Truck_Purchase_Firstname_Lastname** and submit it as directed.

End **You have completed Project 11K** ————

More on your Student CD

The instructions for the following additional end-of-chapter projects are on your student CD in the folder 03_additional_end_of_chapter_projects.

GO!
CD-ROM

Content-Based Assessments	
Project L Mastering Excel	Apply the skills you practiced in Project A.
Project M Mastering Excel	Apply the skills you practiced in Project B.
Project N Business Running Case	Apply the skills you practiced in Projects A and B while helping an entrepreneur with the daily tasks of running a business.
	In each chapter, this project focuses on applying the skills you have practiced in Projects A and B to a business. The project related to this business runs throughout the textbook. You will see how the Office applications relate to the day-to-day operation of a small business called Nelson Architectural Planning.

Outcomes-Based Assessments	
Project O Problem Solving	Construct a solution by applying any combination of the skills you practiced from Projects A and B.
Project P Problem Solving	Construct a solution by applying any combination of the skills you practiced from Projects A and B.
Project Q You and GO!	Construct a solution that applies to your own life by applying any combination of the skills you practiced from Projects A and B.
Project R GO! with Help	Practice using Microsoft Office's Help Feature.
Project S Group Business Running Case	Work as part of a group to apply the skills you have gained thus far to help the Bell Orchid Hotel Group achieve its business goals.

Multimedia

The following multimedia accompany this textbook:

Companion Web site *www.prenhall.com/go*	An interactive Web site designed to reinforce and test your understanding of the skills in this chapter.
AV-EDDs	In the folder in the front of this book you will find videos that demonstrate the objectives of the A and B projects in this chapter. These may help you understand how to complete the projects in this book.
Video Podcasts	In the folder in the front of this book are videos that can be played on your iPod, MP3 player, or computer. These videos demonstrate how to complete the more challenging objectives in this textbook.

chaptertwelve

Getting Started with Access Databases and Tables

OBJECTIVES

At the end of this chapter you will be able to:

1. Start Access and Create a New Blank Database
2. Add Records to a Table
3. Rename Table Fields in Datasheet View
4. Modify the Design of a Table
5. Add a Second Table to a Database
6. Print a Table
7. Create and Use a Query
8. Create and Use a Form
9. Create and Print a Report
10. Close and Save a Database

11. Create a Database by Using a Template
12. Organize Database Objects in the Navigation Pane
13. Create a New Table in a Database Created with a Template
14. View a Report and Print a Table in a Database Created with a Template
15. Use the Access Help System

OUTCOMES

Mastering these objectives will enable you to:

PROJECT 12A
Create a New Blank Database

PROJECT 12B
Create a Database from a Template

Texas Lakes Medical Center

Texas Lakes Medical Center is an urban hospital serving the city of Austin and surrounding Travis County, an area with a population of over one million people. Texas Lakes is renowned for its cardiac care unit, which is rated among the top ten in Texas. The hospital also offers state-of-the-art maternity and diagnostic services, a children's center, a Level II trauma center, and a number of specialized outpatient services. Physicians, nurses, scientists, and researchers from around the world come together at Texas Lakes to provide the highest quality patient care.

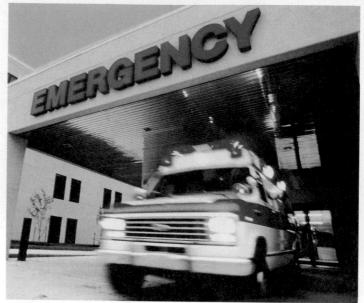
© Jeff Perkell / Photolibrary.com

Getting Started with Access Databases and Tables

Do you have a collection of belongings, such as a coin or stamp collection, a box of favorite recipes, or a stack of music CDs? Do you have an address book with the names, addresses, and phone numbers of your friends, business associates, and family members? If you collect something, chances are you have made an attempt to keep track of and organize the items in your collection.

Microsoft Office Access 2007 is a program you can use to organize a collection of related information, such as an inventory list, a list of people in an organization, or the students who are enrolled in classes in a college. Whether you use Access for personal or business purposes, it is a powerful program that enables you to organize, search, sort, retrieve, and present information in an organized manner.

Project 12A **Doctor and Patient Contact Information**

In Activities 12.01 through 12.14, you will assist June Liu, Chief Administrative Officer at Texas Lakes Medical Center, in creating a new database for tracking the contact information for doctors and patients. Using June's lists of doctors and patients, you will create an Access database to keep track of this information and to prepare a report. Your results will look similar to Figure 12.1.

For Project 12A, you will need the following file:

New blank Access database

You will save your database as
12A_Contact_Information_Firstname_Lastname

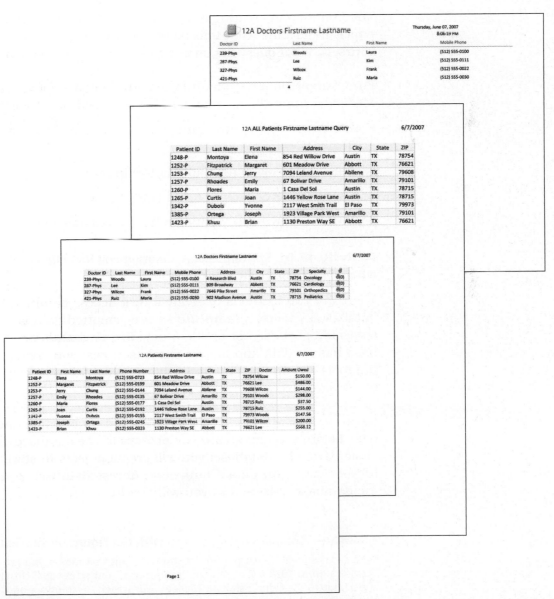

Figure 12.1
Project 12A—Contact Information

Chapter 12 | Access

Access | Chapter 12

Project 12A: Doctor and Patient Contact Information | **Access**   521

Objective 1
Start Access and Create a New Blank Database

A **database** collects and organizes **data**—facts about people, events, things, or ideas—related to a particular topic or purpose. **Information** is data that has been organized in a useful manner.

Many databases start as a simple list on paper, in a Word document, or in an Excel worksheet. As the list grows and the data becomes more difficult to keep track of, it is a good idea to transfer the data to a **database management system** (**DBMS**) such as Access.

The names and addresses of all the doctors and patients at a medical facility are an example of data that could be in a database. A database includes not only the data, but also the tools for organizing the data in a way that is useful to you.

The first step in creating a new database is to plan your database on paper. Determine what information you want to track, and then ask yourself, *What questions should this database be able to answer for me?*

For example, in a Contact Information database for the Texas Lakes Medical Center, the questions to be answered may include:

- How many doctors and patients are there at the Texas Lakes Medical Center?

- Which and how many patients live in Austin?

- Is any doctor or patient listed twice?

- Which and how many patients have a balance owed?

Activity 12.01 Starting Access, Creating and Naming a Folder, and Creating a Database from a New Blank Database

There are two methods to create a new Access database: create a new database by using a **template**—a preformatted database designed for a specific purpose—or create a new **blank database**. A blank database has no data and has no database tools; you create the data and the tools as you need them. In this activity, you will create a new blank database.

Regardless of which method you use, you must name and save the database before you can create any **objects** in the database. Objects are the basic parts of a database; you will create objects to store your data and to work with your data. Think of an Access database as a container for the database objects that you will create.

Note — Comparing Your Screen with the Figures in This Textbook

Your screen will match the figures shown in this textbook if you set your screen resolution to 1024 × 768. At other resolutions, your screen will closely resemble, but not match, the figures shown. To view your screen's resolution, on the Windows desktop, right-click in a blank area, click Personalize, and then click Display Settings.

---

1 Click the **Start** button 🔵, determine where the **Access** program is located, and then open the program. Take a moment to compare your screen with Figure 12.2 and study the parts of the Microsoft Access window described in the table in Figure 12.3.

From this Access starting point, you can open an existing database, create a new blank database, or create a new database from a template.

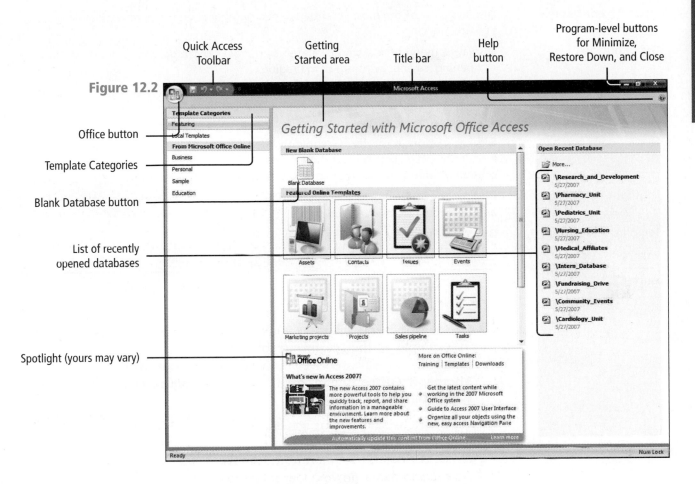

Figure 12.2

Quick Access Toolbar — Getting Started area — Title bar — Help button — Program-level buttons for Minimize, Restore Down, and Close

Office button

Template Categories

Blank Database button

List of recently opened databases

Spotlight (yours may vary)

The Access Getting Started Screen

Window Part	Description
Blank Database button	Starts a new blank database.
Getting Started area	Contains the starting point to begin a New Blank Database or view new information from Microsoft Office Online.
Help button	Displays the Access Help window.
Open Recent Database	Displays a list of the most recently opened databases on the computer at which you are working.
Office button	Displays a menu of commands related to things you can do *with* a database, such as opening, saving, printing, or managing.
Program-level buttons for Minimize, Restore Down, and Close	Minimizes, restores, or closes the Access program.
Quick Access Toolbar	Displays buttons to perform frequently used commands with a single click. Frequently used commands in Access include Save, Undo, and Redo. You can add commands that you use frequently to the Quick Access Toolbar.
Spotlight	Displays the latest online content, such as new templates, articles about Access, and tips from Microsoft's Web site.
Template Categories	Displays a list of available database templates.
Title bar	Displays the program name and the program-level buttons.

Figure 12.3

2 Decide where you will store your Access databases for this textbook—for example, in the *Documents* folder on your hard disk drive or on a removable USB flash drive. Then, in the **Getting Started with Microsoft Office Access** area, under **New Blank Database**, click **Blank Database**.

3 On the right side of your screen, to the right of the **File Name** box, click the **Browse** button [icon]. In the **File New Database** dialog box, notice the default location in the **Address bar**, which is your *Documents* folder on your hard disk drive.

> A **dialog box** is a window containing commands or that asks you to make a decision.

4 In the **File New Database** dialog box, navigate to the location where you are storing your projects for this chapter; for example, *Documents* on your hard disk drive or *LEXAR MEDIA (E:)* to store on a USB flash drive—the exact name and drive letter will vary. Then, on the toolbar, click the **New Folder** button. Type **Access Chapter 12** and press Enter. Compare your screen with Figure 12.4.

Figure 12.4

Address bar displays your new folder

File New Database dialog box

New Folder button

Other files or folder at this location may display in Content pane

Location of new folder selected in Folders List

File name box

Save as type box

Browse button

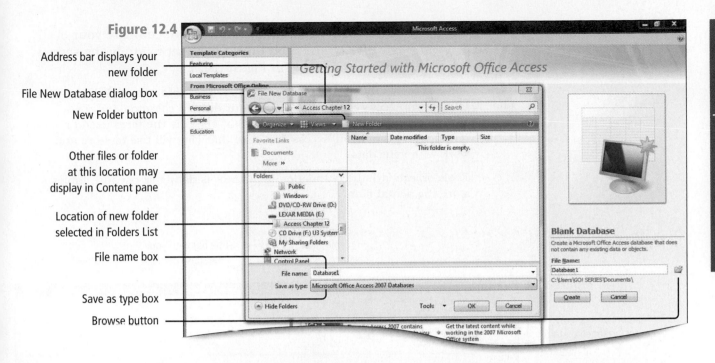

5 In the lower portion of the dialog box, in the **File name** box, select the existing text. Using your first name and last name, type **12A_Contact_Information_Firstname_Lastname** and then press Enter. Compare your screen with Figure 12.5.

> To facilitate sending your files over the Internet, in this textbook, you will save files using an underscore between words rather than a space.

Figure 12.5

.accdb file extension

File Name box with your database name

Drive and folder where your database is stored

Create button

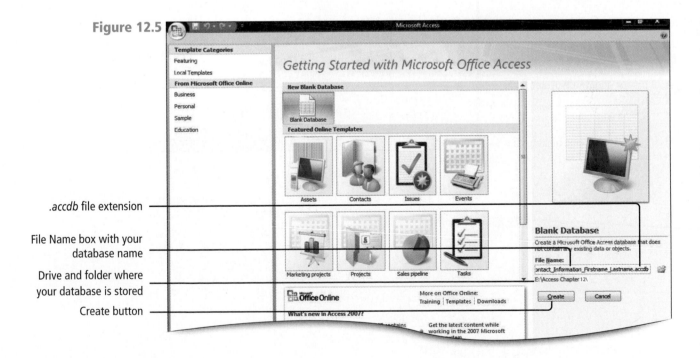

6 In the lower right corner, click the **Create** button, compare your screen with Figure 12.6, and then take a moment to study the screen elements described in the table in Figure 12.7.

> Access creates the new database and opens a *table* named *Table1*. A table is an Access object that stores your data in columns and rows, similar to an Excel worksheet. Recall that *object* is the term used to refer to the parts of an Access database that you will use to store and work with your data.
>
> Table objects are the foundation of an Access database because tables store the actual data.

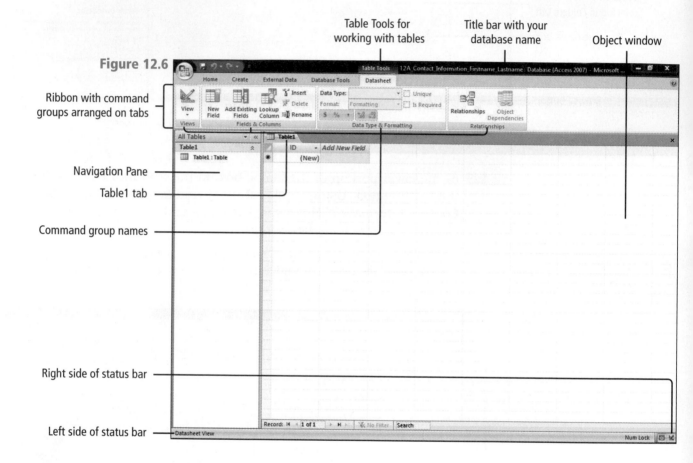

Figure 12.6

Parts of the Access Window

Window Part	Description
Command group names	Contain groups of related command buttons associated with the selected command tab.
Left side of status bar	Indicates the active view and the status of actions occurring within the database.
Navigation Pane	Displays the database objects; from here you open the database objects to display in the object window at the right.
Object window	Displays the open table object.
Ribbon with command groups arranged on tabs	Groups the commands for performing related database tasks on tabs.
Right side of status bar	Provides buttons to switch between Datasheet view and Design view.
Table Tools for working with tables	Provides tools for working with a table object; Table Tools are available only when a table is displayed.
Table1 tab	Enables you to select the table object.
Title bar with your database name	Displays the name of your database.

Figure 12.7

7 Leave your database open for the next activity.

Objective 2
Add Records to a Table

After you have saved and named the database, the next step is to plan and create the tables in which to enter your data. Recall that tables are the foundation of your database because the actual data is stored there.

Limit the data in each table to one subject. For example, think of all the data at your college; there is likely one table for student information, another table for course information, another table for classroom information, and so on.

Within each table, create as many columns as necessary so that you can break down information into the smallest usable part. For example, instead of a single column for an entire address, create a column for the street address, a column for the city name, a column for the state, and a column for the ZIP or postal code. By breaking your data into small, usable parts, you can find all of the people who live on a particular street, in a particular city, and so on.

In this project, you will create a database with two tables. One table will store the names and contact information for patients at Texas Lakes Medical Center and the other table will store the names and contact information for doctors at Texas Lakes Medical Center.

Activity 12.02 Adding Records to a Table

In a table object, each column represents a *field*. Fields describe each piece of data stored in the table. Field names display at the top of each column and can be added before or while entering data. Each row in a table represents a *record*—all of the fields of data pertaining to one person, place, thing, event, or idea. *Table design* refers to the number of fields, the names of fields, the type of content within a field—numbers or text—and other characteristics of the fields or records.

Think about buying yourself a new address book. It is not very useful until you fill it with names, addresses, and phone numbers. Likewise, a new database is not useful until you *populate* or fill a table with data. You can populate a table with records by typing data directly into the table.

In this activity, you will populate a table that stores contact information for patients at Texas Lakes Medical Center.

1 Notice the new blank table that displays in Datasheet view. Take a moment to study the elements of the table object window as shown in Figure 12.8.

> There are two ways to view a table—in *Datasheet view* or in *Design view*. Datasheet view displays the table data organized in columns and rows similar to an Excel worksheet. Design view displays the underlying design or structure of the table object.

> When you create a new blank database, only one object—a new blank table—is created. Because you have not yet named this table, the Table tab displays a default name of *Table1*. Access creates the first field and names it *ID*. In the ID field, Access assigns a unique sequential number—each number incremented by one—to each record as it is entered into the table.

Table tab   Datasheet tab

New table in Datasheet view with default table name

Figure 12.8

Navigation Pane Close button

Navigation Pane

Access creates and names first field *ID*

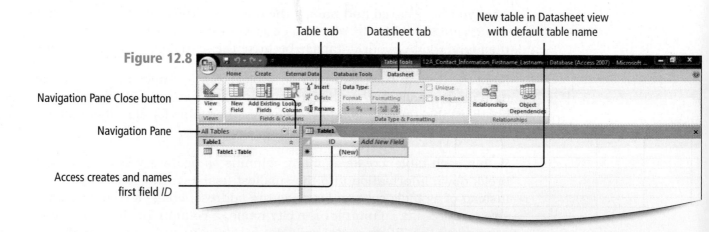

2 In the **Navigation Pane**, **click the Open/Close** button ⟨«⟩ to collapse the **Navigation Pane** into a narrow bar at the left side of your screen. Notice that you have more screen space in which to work with your table.

3 In the second column, click in the *cell*—the box formed by the intersection of a row and a column—under *Add New Field*, type **Elena** and then press Tab or Enter.

4 Click in the **ID** field. On the **Datasheet tab**, in the **Data Type & Formatting group**, click the **Data Type arrow**, and then click **Text**.

5 Type **1248-P** and then to the right of *Elena*, click in the **Add New Field** cell. Type **L** and then press Tab. Compare your screen with Figure 12.9.

> As soon as information is entered, Access assigns the name *Field1* to the field and enters an AutoNumber of 1 in the ID field, which is created automatically by Access.
>
> By default, Access creates this field for all new tables and sets the data type for the field to **AutoNumber**, which sequentially numbers each entry. Changing the ID field data type from *AutoNumber* to *Text* enables you to enter a custom patient number. As you enter data, Access assigns Field names as *Field1*, *Field2*, and so on; you can rename the fields when it is convenient for you to do so.
>
> The pencil icon ✐ in the **record selector box**—the small box at the left of a record in Datasheet view which, when clicked, selects the entire record—indicates that a new record is being entered or edited.

Field named *Field1*   First name of first patient entered

Figure 12.9

Pencil icon indicates a new record is being entered

Record selector boxes

First patient ID is *1248-P*

6 With the insertion point positioned in the fourth column, in the cell under *Add New Field*, type **Montoya** and then press Tab or Enter.

7 Type **(512) 555-0723** and then press Enter. Type **854 Red Willow Drive** and then press Tab to create *Field5*.

> Do not be concerned if the data does not completely display in the column. As you progress in your study of Access, you will adjust the column widths so that you can view all of the data.

8 Type **Austin** and then press Enter to create *Field6*. Type **TX** and then press Enter to create *Field7*.

9 Type **78754** and then press Enter to create *Field8*. Type **Wilcox** and then press Enter to create *Field9*. Type **150** and then press Enter two times. Compare your screen with Figure 12.10.

> To move across the row, you can press Tab or Enter. Pressing Tab two times moves the insertion point to the next row to begin a new record. As soon as you move to the next row, Access saves the record—you do not have to take any specific action to save the record.

Note — Correct Typing Errors

If you make a mistake while entering data, you can correct the error by using ⌫Bksp
to remove characters to the left, Delete to remove characters to the right, or by selecting the text you want to replace and typing the correct information. Press Esc to exit
out of a new record.

10 Beginning with the record for *Margaret E Fitzpatrick*, and using the
technique you just practiced, enter the contact information for three
additional patients, pressing Enter as necessary after entering the information in *Field10*. Then compare your screen with Figure 12.11.

ID	Field1	Field2	Field3	Field4	Field5	Field6	Field7	Field8	Field9	Field10
1248-P	Elena	L	Montoya	(512) 555-0723	854 Red Willow Drive	Austin	TX	78754	Wilcox	150
1252-P	Margaret	E	Fitzpatrick	(512) 555-0199	601 Meadow Drive	Abbott	TX	76621	Lee	486
1253-P	Jerry	R	Chung	(512) 555-0144	7094 Leland Avenue	Abilene	TX	79608	Wilcox	144
1257-P	Emily	A	Rhoades	(512) 555-0135	67 Bolivar Drive	Amarillo	TX	79101	Woods	298

Figure 12.11

Field 10 out of view (your
screen may vary in how many
columns are shown)

Records for four
patients entered

More Knowledge — Format for Typing Telephone Numbers in Access

Access does not require any specific format for typing telephone numbers in a database. The examples in this project use the format used in Microsoft Outlook. Using
such a format facilitates easy transfer of Outlook information to and from Access.

Objective 3
Rename Table Fields in Datasheet View

Recall that each column in a table is a *field*, and that field names display at the top of each column of the table. Recall also that each row is a *record*—all of the data pertaining to one person, place, thing, event, or idea—and that each record is broken up into smaller parts—the *fields*. Use meaningful names to name fields; for example, *Amount Owed*.

Activity 12.03 Renaming the Fields in a Table in Datasheet View

1 At the top of the second column, point to the text *Field1* to display the ⬇ pointer and click. Compare your screen with Figure 12.12.

Figure 12.12

Datasheet tab active in the Ribbon

Fields & Columns group

Rename button

Column selected

2 On the Ribbon, notice that **Table Tools** displays above the **Datasheet tab**. In the **Fields & Columns group**, click the **Rename** button, and notice that the text *Field1* is selected.

3 Type **First Name** as the field name, and then press Enter. Point to the text *Field2*, click to select the column, and then in the **Fields & Columns group**, click the **Rename** button. Type **Middle Initial** and then press Enter.

4 Point to the text *Field3* and double-click to select the text. Type **Last Name** and then press Enter. Point to the text *Field4* and then right-click. From the shortcut menu, click **Rename Column**, type **Phone Number** and then press Enter.

5 Using any of the techniques you just practiced, **Rename** the remaining fields as follows, and then compare your screen with Figure 12.13.

Field5	Address
Field6	City
Field7	State/Province
Field8	ZIP/Postal Code
Field9	Doctor
Field10	Amount Owed

Figure 12.13

Fields renamed —

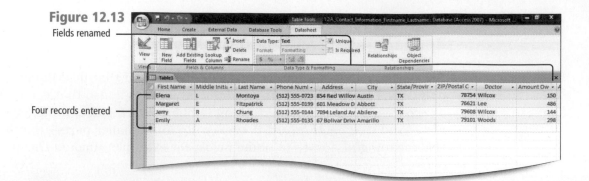

Four records entered —

Activity 12.04 Changing the Data Type of a Field in Datasheet View

Data type is the characteristic that defines the kind of data that you can type in a field, such as numbers, text, or dates. A field in a table can have only one data type. Based on the data you type into a field, Access assigns a data type, but you can change the data type if another type more accurately describes your data.

1 In any of the four records that you have entered, click in the **ID field**. On the Ribbon, on the **Datasheet tab**, in the **Data Type & Formatting group**, notice that in the **Data Type** box, *Text* displays. Compare your screen with Figure 12.14.

> Recall that the ID field was changed from *AutoNumber*, which sequentially numbers each entry, to *Text* so that a custom ID number for patients can be assigned.

Figure 12.14

Data Type box —

Text indicated as Data Type —

ID field —

Data Type & Formatting group —

Datasheet tab is active —

2 In any record, click in the **Last Name** field, and then on the **Datasheet tab**, notice that the **Data Type** indicates *Text*. Click the **Data Type arrow** to display a list of data types as shown in Figure 12.15, and then take a moment to study the table in Figure 12.16 that describes the different data types.

Figure 12.15

Data Type arrow —

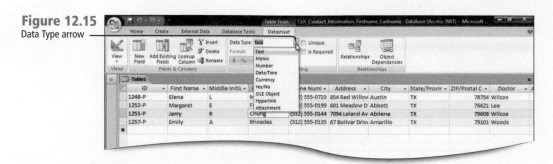

Data Types

Data Types	Description	Example
Text	Text or combinations of text and numbers; also numbers that are not used in calculations. Limited to 255 characters or length set on field, whichever is less. Access does not reserve space for unused portions of the text field. This is the default data type.	An inventory item such as a computer, or a phone number or postal code that is not used in calculations, and that may contain characters other than numbers.
Memo	Lengthy text or combinations of text and numbers up to 65,535 characters or limitations of database size.	Description of a product or information pertaining to a patient.
Number	Numeric data used in mathematical calculations with varying field sizes.	A quantity, such as 500.
Date/Time	Date and time values for the years 100 through 9999.	An order date, such as 11/10/2009 3:30 P.M.
Currency	Monetary values and numeric data that can be used in mathematical calculations involving data with one to four decimal places. Accurate to 15 digits on the left side of the decimal separator and to 4 digits on the right side. Use this data type to store financial data and when you do not want Access to round values.	An item price, such as $8.50.
Yes/No	Contains only one of two values—Yes/No, True/False, or On/Off. Access assigns *-1* for all Yes values and *0* for all No values.	Whether an item was ordered—Yes or No.
OLE Object	An object created by programs other than Access that is linked to or embedded in the table. *OLE* is an abbreviation for *object linking and embedding*, a technology for transferring and sharing information among programs.	A graphics file, such as a picture of a product, a sound file, a Word document, or an Excel worksheet stored as a bitmap image.
Hyperlink	Web or e-mail address.	An e-mail address, such as dwalker@ txlakemed.org or a Web page, such as *www.txlakemed.org.*
Attachment	Any supported type of file—images, worksheet files, documents, or charts. Similar to e-mail attachments. Preferred over OLE Object.	Same as OLE Object.
AutoNumber	Available in Design view. A unique sequential or random number assigned by Access as each record is entered and that cannot be updated.	An inventory item number, such as 1, 2, 3 or a randomly assigned employee number, such as 3852788.
Lookup Wizard	Available in Design view. Not a data type, but will display on Data Type list. Links to fields in other tables to display a list of data instead of having to manually type in the data.	Link to another field in another table.

Figure 12.16

3 Click the **Data Type arrow** again to close the list without changing the data type. In any record, click in the **Address** field, and notice that the **Data Type** box displays *Text*.

As described in the table in Figure 12.16, Access assigns a data type of *Text* to combinations of letters and numbers.

4 Scroll to the right as necessary, in any record, click in the **Amount Owed** field, and then in the **Data Type** box, notice that Access assigned a data type of *Number*.

5 Click the **Data Type arrow** to the right of *Number*, and then from the list, click **Currency**. Compare your screen with Figure 12.17.

Based on your typing of only numbers, Access determined this data type to be *Number*. However, Amount Owed refers to a monetary value, so the data type should be defined as *Currency*. With the Currency data type, Access automatically adds a U.S. dollar sign ($) and two decimal places to all of the fields in the column.

Figure 12.17

Data Type box indicates *Currency*

Amount Owed field data type changed to *Currency*

6 Scroll to the left as necessary, and in any record, click in the **ID** field.

In a database, each record should, in some way, be different from all of the other records. What is important is that the value is unique; no other record in the table will be assigned this value. You are probably familiar with unique values. For example, at your college, no two students have the same Student ID number, although they could have the same name, such as *David Michaels*.

When records in a database have *no* unique value, for example the last names in your address book, the AutoNumber data type is a useful way to automatically create a unique number so that you have a way to ensure that every record is different from the others.

7 Change the name of the **ID** field to **Patient ID**

8 In the new record row, which is indicated by an asterisk (*) in the record selector box on the left, click in the **Patient ID** field, and then type the records shown in the following list. The data in each field should be typed on one line. When you are finished, compare your screen with Figure 12.18.

Recall that you need not be concerned if the data does not completely display in the column. Also, as soon as you move to the next row, the record is saved. Correct typing mistakes using ordinary methods you have practiced in this and other programs.

Patient ID	First Name	Middle Initial	Last Name	Phone Number	Address	City	State/ Province	ZIP/Postal Code	Doctor Name	Amount Owed
1260-P	Maria	S	Flores	(512) 555-0177	1 Casa Del Sol	Austin	TX	78715	Ruiz	37.5
1265-P	Joan	M	Curtis	(512) 555-0192	1446 Yellow Rose Lane	Austin	TX	78715	Ruiz	255
1342-P	Yvonne	L	Dubois	(512) 555-0155	2117 West Smith Trail	El Paso	TX	79973	Woods	147.56
1385-P	Joseph	C	Ortega	(512) 555-0245	1923 Village Park West	Amarillo	TX	79101	Wilcox	200
1423-P	Brian	K	Khuu	(512) 555-0323	1130 Preston Way SE	Abbott	TX	76621	Lee	568.12

Figure 12.18

🔟9️⃣ On the **Quick Access Toolbar**, click the **Save** button 🔲.

> The Save As dialog box displays. Recall that a record is saved as soon as you move to another row in the table.
>
> You should give the table a more meaningful name that describes the information it contains. You can use up to 64 characters (letters or numbers), including spaces, to name a table. In the Table Name box, a suggested name of *Table1* displays and is selected—yours may differ depending on the number of tables you have attempted to create in this database.

🔟 In the **Save As** dialog box, in the **Table Name** box and using your first and last names, type **12A Patients Firstname Lastname** and then click **OK**. Notice that the table tab displays the new table name. Compare your screen with Figure 12.19.

> When you save objects within a database, it is not necessary to use underscores. Your name is included as part of the object name so that you and your instructor will be able to identify your printouts and electronic files.

Figure 12.19

Table name

> **More Knowledge — Changing the Table Name**
>
> If you type the table name incorrectly or need to change the name of a table, click the Close button ⊠ in the upper right corner of the object window to close the table. Expand the Navigation Pane, right-click the table name, and then from the shortcut menu, click Rename. The table name will display in edit mode so that you can type the new name or edit it as you would any selected text.

Objective 4
Modify the Design of a Table

When you create and populate a new table in Datasheet view, the data that you type for the first record determines the number of fields and the data type for each field in the table. This is referred to as the *table design*. Later, you may need to make changes to the design of the table by adding or deleting fields, or changing the order of the fields within a table. You can change a table in Datasheet view, but you may prefer to change the table in Design view where you have additional options.

Activity 12.05 Deleting a Field in Design View

June Liu has decided that a field for the patient's middle initial is not necessary for the 12A Patients table, so you will delete the Middle Initial field in Design view.

1 On the **Datasheet tab**, in the **Views group**, click the **View button arrow**.

> There are four common views in Access, but two that you will use often are Datasheet view and Design view. On the displayed list, Design view is represented by a picture of a pencil, a ruler, and a protractor.
>
> Datasheet view displays the table in rows and columns. When one of these icons is on the View button, clicking the View button will display the table in the view represented by the icon.

2 From the list, click **Design View**, and then take a moment to study Figure 12.20.

> Design view displays the underlying design—the structure—of the table. Each field name is listed, along with its data type. A column to add a Description—information about the data in the field—is provided.

> At the bottom of the Design view window, in the Field Properties area, you can make numerous decisions about how each individual field will look and behave. For example, you can set a specific field size.

Figure 12.20

Delete Rows button on Ribbon

Row selector box

Field Names

Data Type for each field

Field Properties area

Space to add field description

3 In the **Field Name** column, to the left of **Middle Initial**, point to the row selector box to display the ➡ pointer, and then click to select—outline in orange—the entire row.

4 On the **Design tab**, in the **Tools group**, click the **Delete Rows** button, read the message in the message box, and then click **Yes**.

> Deleting a field deletes both the field and its data; you cannot undo this action. If you change your mind after deleting the field, you must add the field back into the table and then reenter the data in that field for each record.

More Knowledge — Choosing the Proper View to Make Changes

You can make design changes in Datasheet view or Design view. Design view provides more flexibility in the types of design changes you can make, and you will become familiar with these as you progress in your study of Access.

Activity 12.06 Modifying a Field Size and Description in Design View

More than one person typically enters data into a database table. For example, at your college there are likely many Registration Assistants who enter and modify student and course information daily.

When you design your database, there are things you can do to help yourself and others to enter accurate data. Two ways to ensure accuracy are to restrict what can be typed in a field and to add descriptive information within the database itself.

1 With your table still displayed in **Design** view, in the **Field Name** column, click anywhere in the **State/Province** field name.

2 In the lower portion of the screen, under **Field Properties**, click in the **Field Size** box, select the text *255*, type **2** and then compare your screen with Figure 12.21.

> This action limits the size of the State/Province field to no more than two characters—the size of the two-letter state abbreviations provided by the United States Postal Service. **Field properties** control how the field displays and how data can be entered in the field. You can define properties for each field in the Field Properties area.

> The default field size for a text field is 255 characters. Limiting the field size property to 2 ensures that only two characters can be entered for each state. However, this does not prevent a user from entering two characters that are incorrect. A primary goal of any database is to ensure the accuracy of the data that is entered. Setting the proper data type for the field and limiting the field size are two ways to help to reduce errors.

Figure 12.21

State/Province field selected

Field Properties Field Size changed to 2

3 In the **State/Province** row, click in the **Description** box, and then type **Two-character state abbreviation**

> Descriptions for fields in a table are optional. Include a description if the field name does not provide an obvious explanation of the field. Information typed in the description area displays in the status bar of the Datasheet view when the field is active, providing additional information to individuals who are entering data.

4 In the **Amount Owed** row, click in the **Description** box, and then type **Outstanding balance**

5 On the **Quick Access Toolbar**, click the **Save** button 🖫, and then in the message box, click **Yes**.

> The message indicates that if more than two characters are currently present in the State/Province field, the data could be lost because the field was not previously restricted to two characters.

Activity 12.07 Setting a Primary Key and Saving a Table

A *primary key* is the field that uniquely identifies a record in a table. For example, in a college registration system, your Student ID number uniquely identifies you—no other student at the college has your exact student number. In the 12A Patients table, the Patient ID uniquely identifies each patient.

When you create a table, Access designates the first field as the primary key field. It is a good database design practice to establish a primary key. Doing so ensures that you do not enter the same record more than once. You can imagine the confusion if another student at your college had the same Student ID number as you do.

1 With your table still displayed in **Design** view, in the **Field Name** column, click to place your insertion point in the **Patient ID** box. To the left of the box, notice the small icon of a key, as shown in Figure 12.22.

> Access automatically designates the first field as the primary key field. However, using the Primary Key button on the Ribbon, you can set any field as the primary key.

Figure 12.22

Primary Key button

Primary Key icon

2 On the **Design tab**, in the **Views group**, notice that the **View** button contains a picture of a Datasheet, indicating that clicking the button will return you to Datasheet view. Click the **View** button; and, if prompted, click **Yes** to save the changes you have made to the design of your table.

Objective 5
Add a Second Table to a Database

Access includes a *table template*—a pre-built table format for common topics such as contacts, issues, and tasks. You can use the table template as it is or customize it to suit your needs. Using a table template is a fast way to add an additional table to your database.

Activity 12.08 Adding a Second Table to a Database

In this activity, you will add a second table to your database. The table will store contact information for the doctors at the medical center. You will use a table template that is specifically designed for contact information.

1 With your **12A Patients** table displayed in Datasheet view, on the Ribbon, click the **Create tab**. In the **Tables group**, click the **Table Templates** button, and then from the list, click **Contacts**. Compare your screen with Figure 12.23.

> A new table with predefined fields displays in the object window. Your 12A Patients table is still open—its tab is visible—but is behind the new table. The Contacts Table Template most closely matches the business need to track doctor information.

Figure 12.23

Table Templates button

12A Patients table still open

New Table1 added
with predefined fields

2 On the Ribbon, click the **Datasheet tab** to display the groups of Datasheet commands.

3 In the second column of the table, point to the **Company** field name, click to select the field, and then on the **Datasheet tab**, in the **Fields & Columns group**, click the **Delete** button. Alternatively, right-click on the selected field name, and from the shortcut menu, click Delete Column.

> You can delete fields in Design view, as you did in Activity 12.5, or you can delete fields directly in Datasheet view as you have done here.

4 Point to the **E-mail Address** field until the ⬇ pointer displays. Drag to the right to select both the **E-mail Address** field and the **Job Title** field. Right-click over the selected field names, and then from the shortcut menu, click **Delete Column**.

5 Using the techniques you have just practiced, delete the following fields: **Business Phone**, **Home Phone**, **Fax Number**, **Country/Region**, **Web Page**, and **Notes**.

> The field displaying a paper clip is the *Attachments* field. Recall that an attachment field can contain a graphics file such as a picture, a sound file, a Word document, or an Excel spreadsheet. In the future, June may use this field to attach a picture and a biography of each doctor, so do not delete it.

6 On the **Datasheet tab**, in the **Views group**, click the **View** button to switch to **Design** view. In the **Save As** dialog box, in the **Table Name** box, using your first name and last name, type **12A Doctors Firstname Lastname** and then click **OK**.

> Changes you have made to the design of the table—deleting fields—are saved, and a more meaningful table name is provided. The table displays in Design view, where the names of each field and the data types assigned to the fields display.

7 Under **Field Name**, click anywhere in the **Attachments** box. On the **Design tab**, in the **Tools group**, click **Insert Rows**. In the newly inserted field name box, type **Specialty** and then press Tab two times. In the **Description** box, type **Medical field specialty** and then compare your screen with Figure 12.24.

Figure 12.24

Table tab with new name ⎯⎯⎯⎯⎯

Description for new field ⎯⎯⎯

New field added ⎯⎯⎯⎯⎯

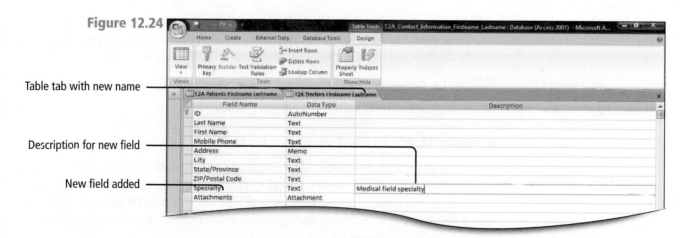

8 Under **Field Name**, click in the **ID** box. Replace the text with **Doctor ID** and then press Tab. In the **Data Type** column, click the arrow, and then from the list, click **Text**.

9 Press Tab to move to the **Description** column, and then type **Physician ID Number**

> Because the Medical Center assigns a unique ID number to each doctor, that ID number will be used as the Primary Key instead of the AutoNumber. Recall that AutoNumber is useful only when no other unique number for a record is available.

10 Under **Field Name**, click in the **State/Province** box. In the lower portion of the screen, under **Field Properties**, change the **Field Size** to **2** and then compare your screen with Figure 12.25.

Figure 12.25

Doctor ID Data Type set to *Text*

Doctor ID field name

Descriptions added for two fields

Description for Doctor ID

State/Province Field Size changed to 2

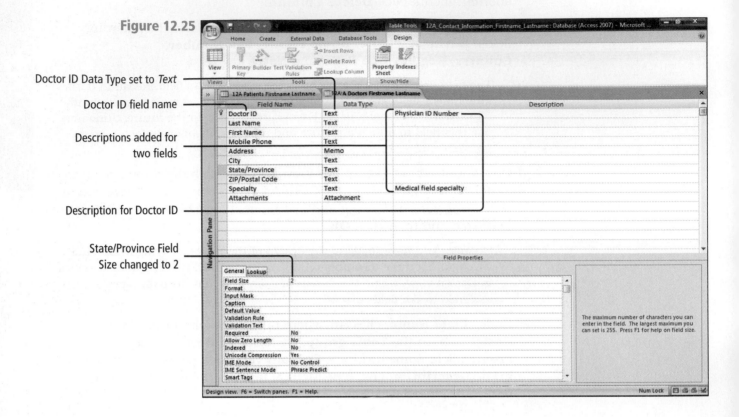

11 On the **Design tab**, in the **Views group**, click the **View** button to switch to Datasheet view—the picture of a datasheet reminds you that clicking the button will switch you to Datasheet view.

12 In the message box, click **Yes** to save the changes you have made to the design of your table.

Activity 12.09 Adding Records to a Second Table

1 With your **12A Doctors** table displayed in **Datasheet** view, beginning in the first record row under **Doctor ID**, enter the following four records. When you have entered all four records, on the **fourth record**—*Doctor ID* of *421-Phys*—click in the **Specialty** field, and then compare your screen with Figure 12.26.

> As you type in the Doctor ID field, *Physician ID Number* displays in the status bar. As you type in the Specialty field, *Medical field specialty* displays in the status bar. This description helps the person who enters the records.

Doctor ID	Last Name	First Name	Mobile Phone	Address	City	State/ Province	ZIP/Postal Code	Specialty
239-Phys	Woods	Laura	(512) 555-0100	4 Research Blvd	Austin	TX	78754	Oncology
287-Phys	Lee	Kim	(512) 555-0111	809 Broadway	Abbott	TX	76621	Cardiology
327-Phys	Wilcox	Frank	(512) 555-0022	7646 Pike Street	Amarillo	TX	79101	Orthopedics
421-Phys	Ruiz	Maria	(512) 555-0030	902 Madison Avenue	Austin	TX	78715	Pediatrics

Figure 12.26

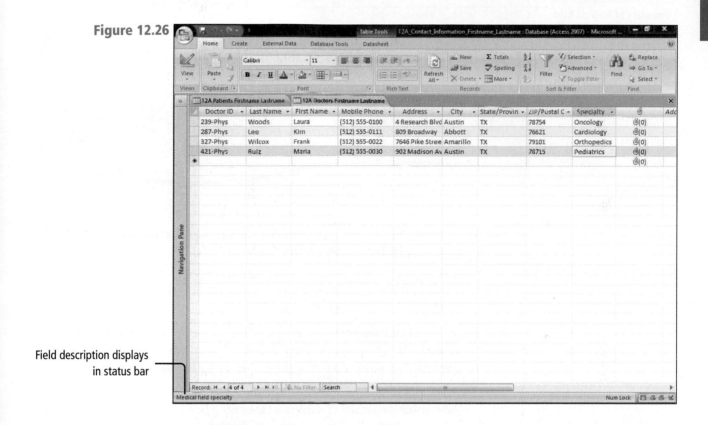

Field description displays in status bar

Objective 6
Print a Table

You can print a table, and although it will not look as professional as a printed report, there are times when you will want to do so. For example, you might need a quick reference or want to proofread the data that has been entered.

Activity 12.10 Adjusting Column Widths and Printing a Table

1 In the object window, click the tab for your **12A Patients** table.

Clicking the tabs along the top of the object window enables you to display open objects so that you can work with them.

All the columns are the same width regardless of the amount of data in the field, the field size that was set, or the length of the field name. If you print the table as currently displayed, some of the data or some of the field names may not fully display unless you adjust the column widths.

2 Change the field name of the **State/Province** field to **State** and change the name of the **ZIP/Postal Code** field to **ZIP**

3 In the field names row, point to the right boundary of the **Address** field to display the ⊕ pointer, and then compare your screen with Figure 12.27.

Figure 12.27

Pointer positioned on right boundary of Address field

Field name changed to *State*
Field name changed to *ZIP*

4 With your ⊕ pointer positioned as shown in Figure 12.27, double-click the right boundary of the **Address** field.

The column width of the Address field widens to fully display the longest entry in the field. In this manner, the width of a column can be increased or decreased to fit its contents.

5 In the field names row, point to the right border of the **City** field, and then with the ⊕ pointer, hold down the left mouse button and drag to the left to visually narrow the column width to accommodate only the widest entry in that column.

Adjusting the width of columns does not change the data stored in the table's records. It changes only the display of the data.

Another Way

To Adjust Column Widths

Select multiple columns, and then in the field names row, double-click the right boundary of any selected column to adjust all of the field widths, similar to adjusting field widths in an Excel spreadsheet. Alternatively, select one or more columns and right-click over the selection. From the shortcut menu click Column Width, and then in the Column Width dialog box, click Best Fit.

6 Using any of the techniques you have practiced or as described previously, adjust all of the column widths, and then compare your screen with Figure 12.28.

Figure 12.28

All column widths adjusted to fit longest entry in the column

Patient ID	First Name	Last Name	Phone Number	Address	City	State	ZIP	Doctor	Amount Owed	Add New
1248-P	Elena	Montoya	(512) 555-0723	854 Red Willow Drive	Austin	TX	78754	Wilcox	$150.00	
1252-P	Margaret	Fitzpatrick	(512) 555-0199	601 Meadow Drive	Abbott	TX	76621	Lee	$486.00	
1253-P	Jerry	Chung	(512) 555-0144	7094 Leland Avenue	Abilene	TX	79608	Wilcox	$144.00	
1257-P	Emily	Rhoades	(512) 555-0135	67 Bolivar Drive	Amarillo	TX	79101	Woods	$298.00	
1260-P	Maria	Flores	(512) 555-0177	1 Casa Del Sol	Austin	TX	78715	Ruiz	$37.50	
1265-P	Joan	Curtis	(512) 555-0192	1446 Yellow Rose Lane	Austin	TX	78715	Ruiz	$255.00	
1342-P	Yvonne	Dubois	(512) 555-0155	2117 West Smith Trail	El Paso	TX	79973	Woods	$147.56	
1385-P	Joseph	Ortega	(512) 555-0245	1923 Village Park West	Amarillo	TX	79101	Wilcox	$200.00	
1423-P	Brian	Khuu	(512) 555-0323	1130 Preston Way SE	Abbott	TX	76621	Lee	$568.12	

7 On the **Quick Access Toolbar**, click the **Save** button 🔲 to save the changes you have made to the table's design—changing the column widths.

If you do not save the table after making design changes, Access reminds you to save when you close the table.

8 In the upper left corner of your screen, click the **Office** button 🔵. On the menu, point to **Print**, click **Print Preview**, and then compare your screen with Figure 12.29.

Figure 12.29

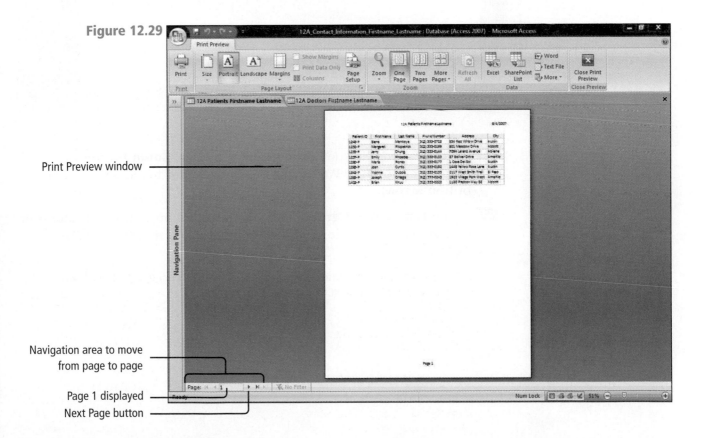

Print Preview window

Navigation area to move from page to page

Page 1 displayed

Next Page button

9 In the lower left corner of your screen, in the navigation area, click the **Next Page** ▶ button. Point to the data at the top of the page to display the 🔍 pointer, click one time to zoom in, and then compare your screen with Figure 12.30.

> The second page of the table displays the last four fields, and the display is larger. In the navigation area, the Next Page button is dimmed, indicating that there are no more pages to display. The Previous Page button is darker, indicating that a page exists before the displayed page.

Figure 12.30

Last four fields display on a second page

Previous Page button

Page 2

State	ZIP	Doctor	Amount Owed
TX	78754	Wilcox	$150.00
TX	76621	Lee	$486.00
TX	79608	Wilcox	$144.00
TX	79101	Woods	$298.00
TX	78715	Ruiz	$37.50
TX	78715	Ruiz	$255.00
TX	79973	Woods	$147.56
TX	79101	Wilcox	$200.00
TX	76621	Lee	$568.12

10 On the Ribbon, in the **Zoom group**, click the **Zoom** button to zoom back to Fit to Window view—be sure not to click the Zoom button arrow.

11 In the **Page Layout group**, click the **Margins** button. In the **Margins gallery**, point to **Wide**, and then compare your screen with Figure 12.31.

> The Wide gallery option sets top and bottom margins at 1 inch and left and right margins at .75 inch.

Figure 12.31

Margins button —

Wide gallery choice —

12 Click **Wide**. Then, in the **Page Layout group**, click the **Landscape** button.

The orientation of the printout changes, and the navigation arrows are inactive because all of the fields and all of the records display on one page. Additionally, the table name and current date display at the top of the page, and the page number displays at the bottom.

By default, Access prints in *portrait orientation*—the printed page is taller than it is wide. In *landscape orientation*, the printed page is wider than it is tall.

The change in orientation from portrait to landscape is not saved with the table. Each time you print, you must check the margins, page orientation, and other print parameters to ensure that the data will print as you intend.

Note — Headers and Footers in Access Objects

The headers and footers in Access tables and queries are controlled by default settings; you cannot add additional information or edit the information. The object name displays in the center of the header area with the date on the right—that is why adding your own name to the object name is helpful to identify your paper or electronic results. The page number displays in the center of the footer area. The headers and footers in Access reports and forms, however, are more flexible; you can add to and edit the information.

---

13 On the right side of the status bar, just to the right of the **View** buttons, drag the **Zoom** slider to the right—or click the **Zoom In** button—until you have zoomed to approximately **120%**, as shown in Figure 12.32.

To *zoom* means to increase or decrease the viewing area of the screen. Zoom in to look closely at a particular section of a document, and then zoom out to see a whole page on the screen. You can also zoom to view multiple pages on the screen.

Figure 12.32

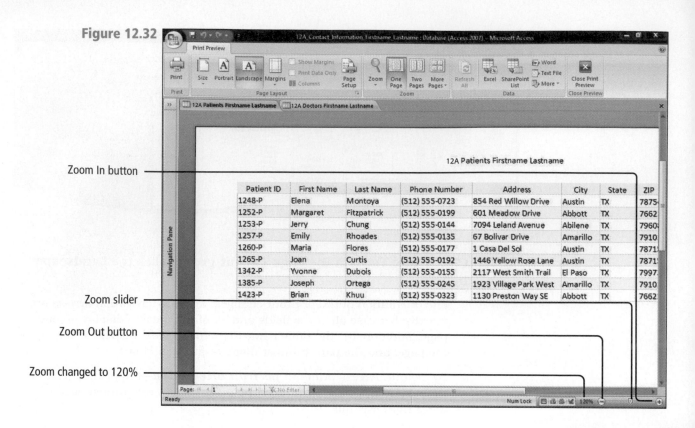

Zoom In button

Zoom slider

Zoom Out button

Zoom changed to 120%

14 Drag the **Zoom** slider to the left—or click the **Zoom Out** button—until you have zoomed to approximately **50%**, as shown in Figure 12.33.

Figure 12.33

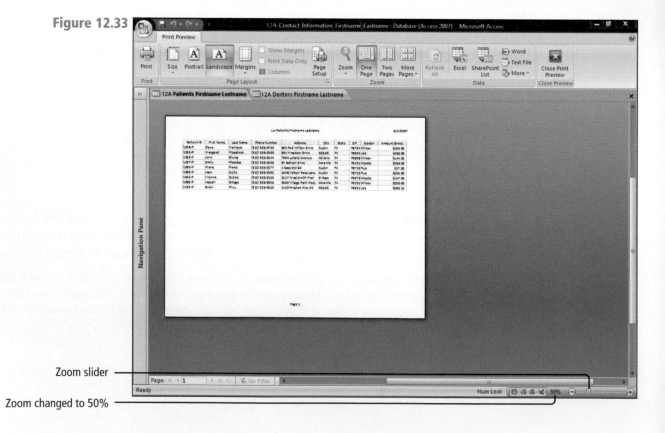

Zoom slider

Zoom changed to 50%

15 Check your *Chapter Assignment Sheet* or *Course Syllabus*, or consult your instructor, to determine whether you are to submit the printed pages that are the results of this project. If you are submitting your work on paper, on the **Print Preview tab**, in the **Print group**, click the **Print** button, and then in the **Print** dialog box, click **OK**.

16 On the Ribbon, in the **Close Preview group**, click the **Close Print Preview** button. If you are submitting your work electronically, follow the directions given by your instructor.

17 At the far right edge of the object window, click the **Close Object** button ⊠ to close the **12A Patients** table. If prompted, click Yes to save design changes.

18 With your **12A Doctors** table displayed, **Rename** the **State/Province** field to **State** and the **ZIP/Postal Code** field to **ZIP** Then, adjust all of the column widths to accommodate the longest entry in the column, including the **Attachments** column, which displays a paper clip icon.

19 Display the table in **Print Preview**. Change the **Margins** to **Wide** and the orientation to **Landscape**. Print if you are directed to do so, and then click the **Close Print Preview** button, or submit your work electronically.

20 At the far right of the object window, click the **Close Object** button ⊠. Click **Yes** to save the changes you made to the layout—changing the column widths.

> All your database objects—the *12A Patients* table and the *12A Doctors* table—are closed, and the object window is empty.

Objective 7
Create and Use a Query

A *query* is a database object that retrieves specific data from one or more database objects—either tables or other queries—and then, in a single datasheet, displays only the data you specify. Because the word *query* means *to ask a question*, think of a query as a question formed in a manner that Access can interpret.

A *select query* is one type of Access query. A select query, also called a *simple select query*, retrieves (selects) data from one or more tables or queries, displaying the selected data in a datasheet. A select query is used to create subsets of data that can be used to answer specific questions; for example, *Which patients live in Austin, TX?*

Activity 12.11 Using the Simple Query Wizard to Create a Query

The table(s) or query(ies) from which a query gets its data are referred to as the query's *data source*. In the following activity, you will create a simple select query using a *wizard*. A wizard is a feature in Microsoft Office programs that walks you step-by-step through a process.

The process involves choosing the data source, and then indicating the fields you want to include in the query result. The query—the question that you want to ask—is *What are the name, complete mailing address, and Patient ID of every patient in the database?*

1 Click the **Create tab**, and then in the **Other group**, click the **Query Wizard** button. In the **New Query** dialog box, click **Simple Query Wizard**, and then click **OK**. Compare your screen with Figure 12.34.

Figure 12.34

Simple Query Wizard dialog box

Tables/Queries arrow

Add Field button

No database objects display in object window; all are closed

2 Click the **Tables/Queries arrow**, and then click **Table: 12A Patients**.

To create a query, first choose the data source—the table(s) or query(ies) from which to select data. The name and complete mailing address of every patient is stored in the 12A Patients table.

3 Under **Available Fields**, click **Patient ID**, and then click the **Add Field** button ⟩ to move the field to the **Selected Fields** list on the right. Using the same technique, add the **Last Name** to the list. Alternatively, double-click the field name to move it to the Selected Fields list. Compare your screen with Figure 12.35.

This is the second step in creating a query—choosing the fields that you want to include in your query results.

Figure 12.35

Two fields added to
Selected Fields list

4 Using either the **Add Field** button ▶ or by double-clicking, add the
following fields to the **Selected Fields** list: **First Name**, **Address**,
City, **State**, and **ZIP**. Compare your screen with Figure 12.36.

Choosing these seven fields will give you the query result that you
want—it will answer the question, *What are the name, address, and
Patient ID of every patient in the database?*

Figure 12.36

Seven fields added to the
Selected Fields list

Next button

5 In the lower right corner, click the **Next** button. Be sure that the
option for **Detail (shows every field of every record)** is selected,
and then in the lower right corner, click the **Next** button.

6 In the **Simple Query Wizard** dialog box, click in the **What title do
you want for your query?** box. Edit as necessary so that the query
name, using your own first and last names, is **12A ALL Patients
Firstname Lastname Query** and then compare your screen with
Figure 12.37.

Figure 12.37

Name of query

Open the query to view information option selected

Finish button

7 Click **Finish**.

Access **runs** the query—performs the actions indicated in your query design by searching the table of records included in the query, finding the records that match the criteria, and then displaying the records in a datasheet—so that you can see the results. A select query *selects*—pulls out and displays—*only* the information from the data source that you requested.

In the object window, Access displays every patient record in Datasheet view, but displays only the seven fields that you included in the Selected Fields list in the Simple Query Wizard dialog box.

8 Display the query in **Print Preview**. **Print** the query, and then click the **Close Print Preview** button. Or, submit electronically as directed. Leave the query object open.

Objective 8
Create and Use a Form

A *form* is an Access object used to enter data, edit data, or display data from a table or a query. In a form, the fields are laid out in a visually attractive format on the screen, which makes working with the database more pleasant and more efficient.

One type of Access form displays only one record in the database at a time. Such a form is useful not only to the individual who performs the data entry—typing in the actual records—but also to anyone who has the job of viewing information in a database.

For example, when you visit the Records office at your college to obtain a transcript, someone displays your record on a screen. For the viewer, it is much easier to look at one record at a time, using a form, than to look at all of the student records in the database table.

Activity 12.12 Creating a Form

The Form command on the Ribbon creates a form that displays all of the fields from the underlying data source (table) one record at a time. You can use this new form immediately, or you can modify it. Records that you create or edit in a form are automatically added to or updated in the underlying table or tables.

1 In the upper right corner of the object window, click the **Close Object** button ⊠ to close the query. Then, at the top of the **Navigation Pane**, click the **Open** button ⊠.

2 In the **Navigation Pane**, notice that a table displays a datasheet icon and a query displays an icon of two overlapping datasheets. Right-click the **12A Patients** table to display a shortcut menu as shown in Figure 12.38.

Figure 12.38

Navigation Pane Close button ——

12A Patients table ——
Table icon ——
Query icon ——

Navigation Pane expanded ——

Shortcut menu ——

3 From the shortcut menu, click **Open** to display the table in the object window, and then **Close** ⊠ the **Navigation Pane** to maximize your screen space.

4 Notice that there are 10 fields in the table. Click the **Create tab**, and then in the **Forms group**, click the **Form** button. Compare your screen with Figure 12.39.

> Access creates a form based on the currently selected object—the 12A Patients table. Access creates the form in a simple top-to-bottom format, with all of the fields in the record lined up in a single column.

> The form displays in Layout view, where you can modify the design of the form. Each field displays the data for the first record in the table—*Elena Montoya*.

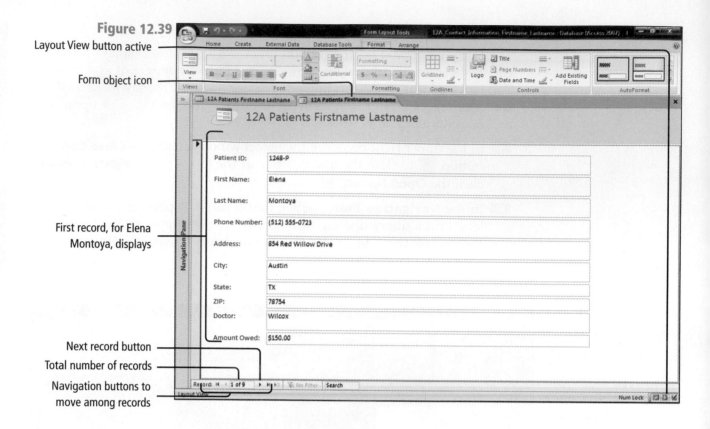

Figure 12.39

Layout View button active

Form object icon

First record, for Elena Montoya, displays

Next record button

Total number of records

Navigation buttons to move among records

5 In the lower right corner of the screen, at the right edge of the status bar, notice that the **Layout View** button ![icon] is active, indicating that the form is displayed in Layout view.

6 At the right edge of the status bar, click the **Form View** button ![icon]. Alternatively, on the Home tab, in the Views group, click the View button, which displays an icon of a form.

> In Form view, you can view the records, but you cannot change the layout or design of the form.

7 In the navigation area, click the **Next record** button ![icon] three times. The fourth record—*Emily Rhoades*—displays.

> Use the navigation buttons to scroll among the records to display any single record.

8 On the **Quick Access Toolbar**, click the **Save** button ![icon]. In the **Save As** dialog box, accept the default name for the form—*12A Patients Firstname Lastname*—by clicking **OK**. **Close** ![icon] the form object.

> The *12A Patients Firstname Lastname* table remains open.

Objective 9
Create and Print a Report

A *report* is a database object that displays the fields and records from a table or a query in an easy-to-read format suitable for printing. Create reports to summarize information in a database in a professional-looking manner.

Activity 12.13 Creating and Printing a Report

In this activity, you will create a report that lists mobile phone contact information for doctors at Texas Lakes Medical Center.

1 **Open** ≫ the **Navigation Pane**, and then open your **12A Doctors** table by double-clicking the table name or by right-clicking and clicking Open from the shortcut menu.

2 **Close** ≪ the **Navigation Pane**. Click the **Create tab**, and then in the **Reports group**, click the **Report** button. Compare your screen with Figure 12.40.

> A report displays all of the fields and all of the records in the table in a format suitable for printing. The report displays in Layout view, which means you can make quick changes to the design or layout of the report. Dotted lines indicate how the report would be broken across pages if the report were printed.

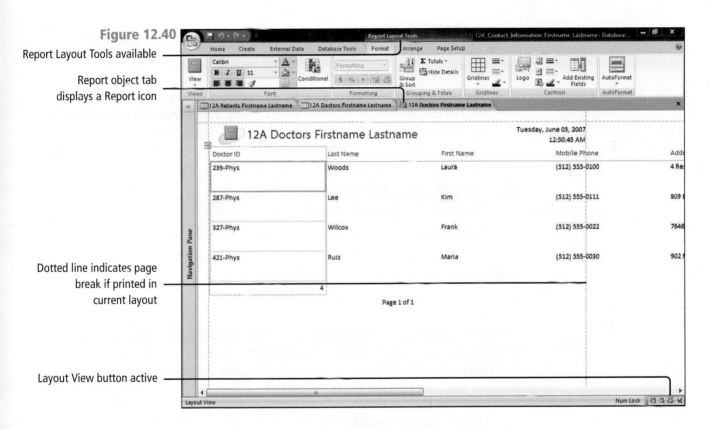

Figure 12.40

Report Layout Tools available

Report object tab displays a Report icon

Dotted line indicates page break if printed in current layout

Layout View button active

3 Scroll to the right as necessary, point to the **Address** field, right-click, and then from the shortcut menu, click **Delete**.

> The Address field and data are deleted, and the report readjusts to accommodate the deletion.

4 Use the same technique to delete the following fields in the report: **City**, **State**, **ZIP**, **Specialty**, and **Attachments**.

> This report will provide June with a quick list of each doctor and his or her ID and mobile phone number.

5 Click the **Page Setup tab**, and then in the **Page Layout group**, click the **Landscape** button. Scroll to the left, and then compare your screen with Figure 12.41.

Figure 12.41

6 If you are submitting your results from this project on paper, from the **Office** menu ⊙, point to **Print**, click **Print Preview**, and then in the **Print group**, click **Print**. In the **Print** dialog box, click **OK**, and then click the **Close Print Preview** button. To submit electronically, follow the directions provided by your instructor.

7 **Close** ☒ the report object. In the message box, click **Yes** to save the report. In the **Save As** dialog box, click **OK** to accept the report name.

8 **Close** ☒ all of the open objects, leaving the object window empty.

Objective 10
Close and Save a Database

When you close an Access table, any changes made to the records are saved automatically. If you have changed the design of the table, or have changed the layout of the Datasheet view, such as adjusting the column widths, you are prompted to save the changes. At the end of your Access session, you should close your database, and then exit Access. If the Navigation Pane is closed when you close Access, it will be closed when you reopen the database.

Activity 12.14 Closing and Saving a Database

1 Be sure that all of the objects are closed.

2 From the **Office** menu ⊙, click **Close Database**, and then at the right edge of the Access title bar, click the **Close** button ☒ to close the Access program. Alternatively, from the Office menu, click Exit Access.

End **You have completed Project 12A**

Project 12B Health Seminars

In Activities 12.15 through 12.21, you will assist June Liu, Chief Administrative Officer, by creating a database to store information about community health seminars presented by Texas Lakes Medical Center. You will use a database template that tracks event information, add seminar information to the database, and then print the results. Your printout will look similar to Figure 12.42.

For Project 12B, you will need the following file:

New Access database using the Events template

You will save your database as
12B_Health_Seminars_Firstname_Lastname

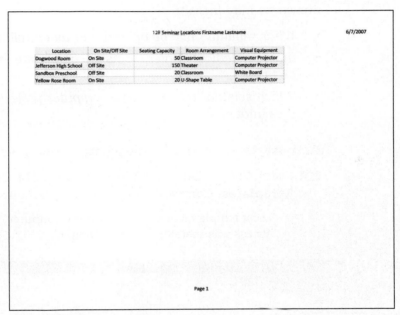

12B Seminar Locations Firstname Lastname   6/7/2007

Location	On Site/Off Site	Seating Capacity	Room Arrangement	Visual Equipment
Dogwood Room	On Site		50 Classroom	Computer Projector
Jefferson High School	Off Site		150 Theater	Computer Projector
Sandbox Preschool	Off Site		20 Classroom	White Board
Yellow Rose Room	On Site		20 U-Shape Table	Computer Projector

Page 1

Figure 12.42
Project 12B—Health Seminars

Objective 11
Create a Database by Using a Template

A database template contains pre-built tables, queries, forms, and reports to perform a specific task, such as tracking a large number of events. For example, your college may hold events such as athletic contests, plays, lectures, concerts, and club meetings. Using a predefined template, your college Activities Director could quickly create a database to manage these events.

The advantage of using a template to start a new database is that you do not have to create the objects—all you need to do is enter your data and modify the pre-built objects to suit your needs.

The purpose of the database in this project is to track the health seminars offered by Texas Lakes Medical Center. The questions to be answered may include:

- *What seminars will be offered and when will they be offered?*
- *In what Medical Center rooms or community locations will the seminars be held?*
- *Which seminar rooms have a computer projector for PowerPoint presentations?*

Activity 12.15 Creating a New Database Using a Template

1 **Start** Access. On the left, under **Template Categories**, click **Local Templates**. Compare your screen with Figure 12.43.

Local templates are stored on your computer; they were saved when Access was installed on your computer.

Figure 12.43

Local Templates

Available Local Templates

Events template

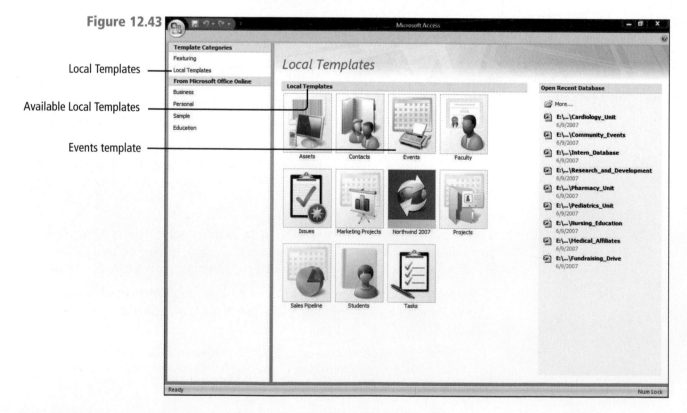

2 In the Spotlight area, under **Local Templates**, click **Events**. On the right side of the screen, to the right of the **File Name** box, click the **Browse** button 📁, and then navigate to your **Access Chapter 12** folder.

3 At the bottom of the **File New Database** dialog box, select the text in the **File name** box. Using your own information, type **12B_Health_ Seminars_Firstname_Lastname** and then press Enter.

4 On the right side of the screen, click the **Create** button.

> The *12B Health Seminars* database is created, and the database name displays in the title bar. A predesigned *form*—Event List—displays in the object window.

5 Under the Ribbon, on the **Message Bar**, check to see if a **Security Warning** displays. If a security warning does *not* display, skip the rest of this step. If a security warning displays, on the **Message Bar**, click the **Options** button. In the **Microsoft Office Security Options** dialog box, click the **Enable this content** option button, and then click **OK**. Compare your screen with Figure 12.44.

> Databases provided by Microsoft are safe to use on your computer.

Figure 12.44

Database name displays in the title bar

Form icon indicates a form object

Multiple items form prenamed as *Event List*

Total line displays by default

Activity 12.16 Building a Table by Entering Records in a Multiple Items Form

The purpose of a form is to simplify the entry of data into a table—either for you or for others who enter data. In Project 12A, you created a simple form that enabled you to display or enter records in a table one record at a time.

The Events template creates a *Multiple Items form*, a form that enables you to display or enter *multiple* records in a table, but still with an easier and more simplified layout than typing directly into the table itself.

1 Click in the first empty **Title** field. Type **Repetitive Stress Injuries** and then press Tab. In the **Start Time** field, type **3/9/09 7p** and then press Tab.

> Access formats the date and time. As you enter dates and times, a small calendar displays to the right of the field, which you can click to select a date instead of typing.

2 In the **End Time** field, type **3/9/09 9p** and then press Tab. In the **Description** field, type **Workplace Health** and then press Tab. In the **Location** field, type **Yellow Rose Room** and then press Tab three times to move to the **Title** field in the new record row. Compare your screen with Figure 12.45.

> Because the seminars have no unique value, Access uses the AutoNumber data type of the ID field to assign a unique, sequential number to each record.

Figure 12.45

First record entered

Access formats date and time

Link bar

AutoNumber creates a unique number

3 In the **Link bar**, just above the field names, click **New Event**.

> A single-record form displays, similar to the simple form you created in Project 12A.

4 Using Tab to move from field to field, enter the following record—press Tab three times to move from the **End Time** field to the **Description** field. Compare your screen with Figure 12.46.

Title	Location	Start Time	End Time	Description
First Aid for Teens	**Jefferson High School**	**3/10/09 4p**	**3/10/09 6p**	**Teen Health**

Figure 12.46

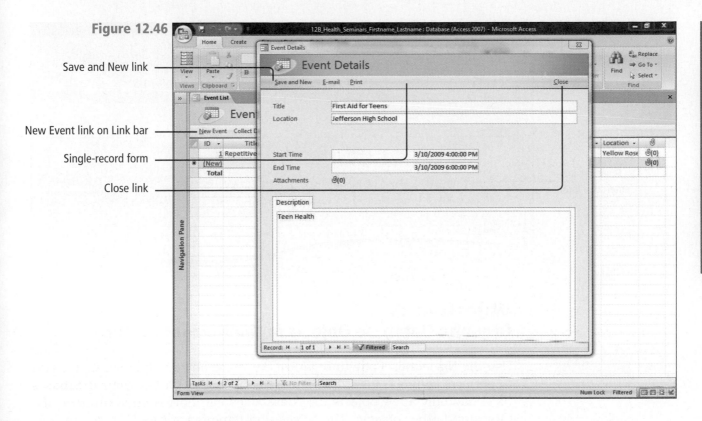

Save and New link

New Event link on Link bar

Single-record form

Close link

5 In the upper right corner of the single-record form, click **Close**, and notice that the new record displays in the Multiple Items form.

6 Using either the rows on the Multiple Items form or the New Event single-record form, enter the following records, and then compare your screen with Figure 12.47.

ID	Title	Start Time	End Time	Description	Location
3	Safety on the Job	3/18/09 2p	3/18/09 4p	Workplace Health	Yellow Rose Room
4	Nutrition for Toddlers	3/19/09 1p	3/19/09 3p	Child Health and Development	Sandbox Preschool
5	Stay Healthy While You Travel	4/6/09 9a	4/6/09 11a	Life Style and Health	Dogwood Room
6	Work Smart at Your Computer	4/8/09 11a	4/8/09 12:30p	Workplace Health	Dogwood Room
7	Be Heart Smart	4/14/09 7p	4/14/09 9p	Life Style and Health	Yellow Rose Room

Alert! **Does a single-record form open?**

In the Multiple Items form, pressing [Enter] three times at the end of a row to begin a new record may display the single-record New Event form. If you prefer to use the Multiple Items form, close the single-record form and continue entering records, using the [Tab] key to move from field to field.

Figure 12.47

Seven records
entered in form

Objective 12
Organize Database Objects in the Navigation Pane

Use the Navigation Pane to organize database objects, to open them, and to perform common tasks like renaming an object. So far, your databases have had only a few objects, but databases can have a large number of tables and other objects. The Navigation Pane is your tool for organizing database objects.

Activity 12.17 Organizing Database Objects in the Navigation Pane

The Navigation Pane groups and displays your database objects and can do so in predefined arrangements. In this activity, you will group your database objects using the *Tables and Views category*, an arrangement that groups objects by the table to which they are related. This grouping is useful because you can easily determine the underlying source table of queries, forms, and reports.

1 **Open** ⟩⟩ the **Navigation Pane**. At the top of the **Navigation Pane**, click the **Navigation arrow** ⊙. From the list, under **Navigate To Category**, click **Tables and Related Views**.

2 Click the **Navigation arrow** ⊙ to display the list again, and then under **Filter By Group**, point to **All Tables**. Compare your screen with Figure 12.48.

Figure 12.48

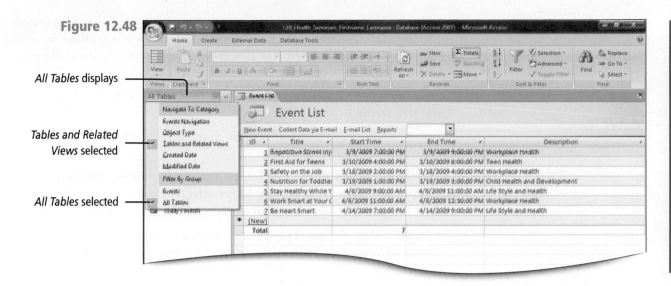

All Tables displays

Tables and Related Views selected

All Tables selected

3 Click **All Tables** to close the list, and then confirm that *Events* displays in the blue bar at the top of the **Navigation Pane**. Compare your screen with Figure 12.49.

> The icons to the left of the objects listed in the Navigation Pane indicate that the Events template created a number of objects for you—among them, one table titled *Events*, one query, two forms, and five reports. The Event List Multiple Items form, which is currently displayed in the object window, is included in the Navigation Pane. All of the objects were created using the underlying data source, which is the Events table.

Figure 12.49

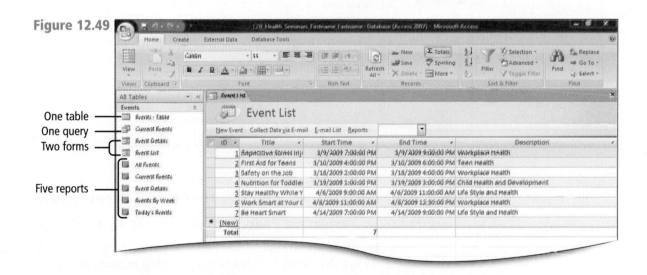

One table

One query

Two forms

Five reports

4 In the **Navigation Pane**, point to the **Events** *table*, right-click, and then click **Open**. Alternatively, double-click the table name to open it in the object window.

> The Events table is the active object in the object window. Use the Navigation Pane to open objects for use.

The seven records that you entered using the Multiple Items *form* display in the *table*. Tables are the foundation of your database because your data must be stored in a table. You can enter records directly into a table, or you can use a form to enter records.

5 In the object window, click the **Event List form tab** to bring it into view and make it the active object.

Recall that a form presents a more user-friendly screen for entering records into a table.

6 In the **Navigation Pane**, right-click the *report* named **Current Events**, and then click **Open**. Alternatively, double-click the report name to open it. Compare your screen with Figure 12.50.

An advantage of using a template to begin a database is that many objects, such as attractively formatted reports, are already designed for you.

Figure 12.50

Current Events report preformatted and designed by the template

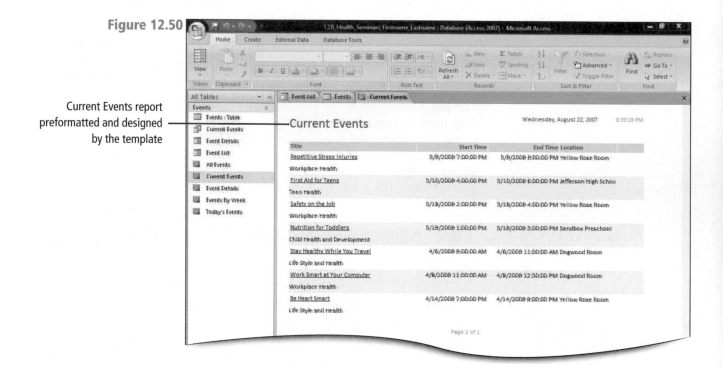

7 In the object window, **Close** ☒ the **Current Events** report.

8 From the **Navigation Pane**, open the **Events By Week** report.

In this predesigned report that came with the database template, the events are displayed by week. After entering records in the form or table, the preformatted reports are updated with the records from the table.

9 **Close** ☒ the **Events By Week** report, and then **Close** ☒ the remaining two open objects. Leave the **Navigation Pane** open.

Objective 13
Create a New Table in a Database Created with a Template

The Events database template created only one table—the *Events* table. Although the database was started from a template and contains many other objects, you can add additional objects as needed.

Create a new table in a database when you begin to see repeated information. For example, in the Events database, both the Yellow Rose Room and the Dogwood Room are listed more than one time.

Activity 12.18 Creating a New Table and Changing Its Design

June has information about the various locations where seminars are held. For example, for the Yellow Rose Room, she has information about the seating arrangements, number of seats, and audio-visual equipment.

In the Events table, three seminars are scheduled in the Yellow Rose Room and two are scheduled in the Dogwood Room. It would not make sense to store information about the rooms multiple times in the same table. It is *not* considered good database design to have duplicate information in a table.

When data in a table becomes repetitive or redundant, it is usually a signal to create a new table to contain the information about the topic. In this activity, you will create a table to track the seminar locations and the equipment and seating arrangements in each location.

1 **Close** « the **Navigation Pane** to maximize your screen space. On the Ribbon, click the **Create tab**, and then in the **Tables group**, click the **Table** button.

2 Click in the cell under **Add New Field**, type **Yellow Rose Room** and then press Tab. Type **On Site** and then press Tab.

3 Type **20** and then press Tab. Type **U-Shape Table** and then press Tab. Type **Computer Projector** and then press Tab three times. Compare your screen with Figure 12.51.

Access assigns an AutoNumber in the ID field.

Figure 12.51

New table

First record entered

Navigation Pane closed

4 Point to the text *Field1*, right-click, and then from the shortcut menu, click **Rename Column**. Type **Location** and then double-click *Field2* to select the text. Type **On Site/Off Site** and then point to and click *Field3*.

5 On the Ribbon, if necessary, click the **Datasheet tab**. In the **Fields & Columns group**, click the **Rename** button, and then type **Seating Capacity** Using any of the techniques you have just practiced, change *Field4* to **Room Arrangement** and *Field5* to **Visual Equipment**

6 In the **Views group**, click the **View** button to switch to **Design** view. In the dialog box, **Save** the table as **12B Seminar Locations Firstname Lastname** and then click **OK**.

7 In **Design** view, in the **Field Name** column, click in the **Location** box. Then, on the **Design tab**, in the **Tools group**, click the **Primary Key** button.

> The key icon moves to the left of the Location field. Recall that the Primary Key is a field that contains a unique identifier for each record. In the Seminar Locations table, the Location name is unique; no other record will have the same Location name.

8 Point to the **row selector box** for the **ID** field to display the [→] pointer, and then click to select the entire row. On the **Design tab**, in the **Tools group**, click the **Delete Rows** button. In the message box, click **Yes**.

> Because the Location name will serve as the primary key field, the ID field is no longer needed.

9 On the **Design tab**, in the **Views group**, click the **View** button, which by its icon indicates that you will return to the Datasheet view of the table. In the message box, click **Yes** to save the design changes to the table.

10 Enter the following records in the table:

Location	On Site/ Off Site	Seating Capacity	Room Arrangement	Visual Equipment
Jefferson High School	Off Site	150	Theater	Computer Projector
Dogwood Room	On Site	50	Classroom	Computer Projector
Sandbox Preschool	Off Site	20	Classroom	White Board

11 Point to the field name *Location* to display the [↓] pointer. Hold down the left mouse button, and then drag to the right to select all of the columns as shown in Figure 12.52—do *not* select the *Add New Field* column.

Figure 12.52

All the columns selected

12 Point to any of the selected field names in the top row, right-click, and then click **Column Width**. In the **Column Width** dialog box, click **Best Fit**. Alternatively, with the columns selected, in the field name row, point to the right boundary of any of the selected columns to display the ⊕ pointer, and then double-click to apply Best Fit to all of the selected columns. Notice that the widths of all of the columns are adjusted to accommodate the longest entry in the column.

13 Click in any record to cancel the selection of the columns. **Open** » the **Navigation Pane**, locate the name of your new table, and then compare your screen with Figure 12.53.

> Recall that as it is currently arranged, the Navigation Pane organizes the objects by tables and related views. The Events table is listed first, followed by its related objects, and then the Seminar Locations table is listed. Currently, no other objects were created using the Seminar Locations table.

Figure 12.53

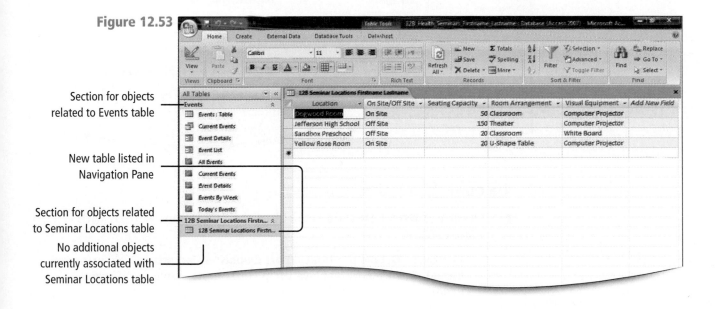

Section for objects related to Events table

New table listed in Navigation Pane

Section for objects related to Seminar Locations table

No additional objects currently associated with Seminar Locations table

14 In the object window, **Close** ☒ the **12B Seminar Locations** table, and then, in the message box, click **Yes** to save the column width layout changes. Leave the **Navigation Pane** open.

Objective 14
View a Report and Print a Table in a Database Created with a Template

Recall that an advantage to starting a new database with a template is that many report objects are already created for you.

Activity 12.19 Viewing a Report

1 From the **Navigation Pane**, open the **All Events** report. Compare your screen with Figure 12.54.

> The All Events pre-built report displays in an attractively arranged format.

Figure 12.54

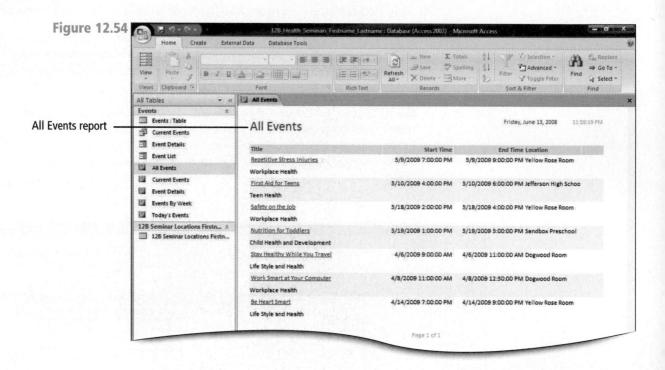

All Events report —

2 **Close** ☒ the **All Events** report.

3 Open the **Event Details** report and compare your screen with Figure 12.55.

> The Event Details pre-built report displays in an attractively arranged format. Each report displays the records in the table in different useful formats.

Figure 12.55

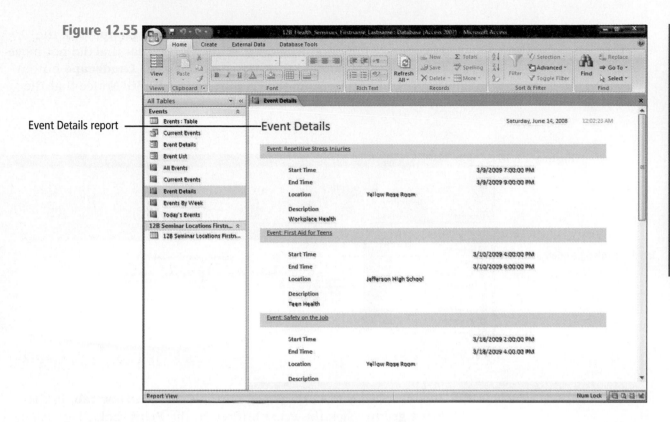

Event Details report

4 **Close** ☒ the **Event Details** report.

Activity 12.20 Printing a Table

Use the Print Preview command to determine if a table will print on one page, or if you need to adjust column widths, margins, or the orientation.

Recall that there will bc occasions when you want to print a table for a quick reference or for proofreading. For a more professional-looking format, print a report instead of the table.

1 From the **Navigation Pane**, open the **12B Seminar Locations** table. Display the **Office** menu 🔘, point to the **Print** button, and then click **Print Preview**.

> The table displays in the Print Prcview window, showing how it will look when it is printed. The name of the table and the date the table was created display at the top of the page. The navigation area at the bottom of the window displays *1* in the Pages box, and the right-pointing arrow— the Next button—is active.
>
> Recall that when you are in the Print Preview window, the navigation buttons are used to navigate from one page to the next, rather than from one record to the next.

2 In the navigation area, click the **Next Page** button ▶.

> The second page of the table displays the last field column. Whenever possible, try to print all of the fields horizontally on one page. Of course, if there are many records, more than one page may be needed to print all of the records.

3 On the **Print Preview tab**, in the **Page Layout group**, click the **Margins** button, and then click **Wide**. Notice that this did not move the last field column to the first page. Click the **Landscape** button, and then compare your screen with Figure 12.56. Notice that the entire table will print on one page.

Figure 12.56

Table in landscape orientation

4 To submit your work on paper, on the **Print Preview tab**, in the **Print group**, click the **Print** button. In the **Print** dialog box, click **OK**. In the **Close Preview group**, click the **Close Print Preview** button. To submit your work electronically, follow the directions provided by your instructor.

5 Close ✕ the **12B Seminar Locations** table, and then **Close** « the **Navigation Pane**.

6 From the **Office** menu 🔘, click **Close Database**. From the **Office** menu 🔘, click **Exit Access**.

Objective 15
Use the Access Help System

Access has a Help feature to assist you when performing a task or to get more information about a particular topic. Activate the Help feature by clicking the Help button or by pressing [F1].

Activity 12.21 Using the Access Help System

1 **Start** Access. In the upper right corner of the **Access** window, click the **Microsoft Office Access Help** button 🔘. In the **Access Help** window, click the **Search button arrow**, and then under **Content from this computer**, click **Access Help**.

Help information was stored on your computer when you installed Office. You can also obtain online help from Microsoft.

2 Click in the **Search** box, type **database design** and then press Enter. In the list, click **Database design basics**.

This information is an informative overview of how to design a database, beginning with writing your ideas on paper. This information can be printed by clicking the Print button.

3 In the upper right corner of the **Access Help** window, click the **Close** button ![X]. On the title bar for the **Getting Started** window, **Close** ![X] Access.

End **You have completed Project 12B**————————————

There's More You Can Do!

Display the Start menu, click Computer, and then navigate to the student files that accompany this textbook. In the folder **02_theres_more_you_can_do**, locate and open the folder for this chapter. Open and print the instructions for this project, which are provided to you in Adobe PDF format.

Try IT!—Convert a Database to a Different Format

In this Try It! exercise, you will convert an Access 2007 database to a database that others can view and edit in Access 2002 or Access 2003.

Content-Based Assessments

Access
chaptertwelve

Summary

Microsoft Office Access is a database management system that uses various objects—tables, forms, queries, reports—to organize a database. Data is stored in tables in which you establish fields, set the data type and field size, and create a primary key. Data from a database can be reported and printed.

Key Terms

The ● symbol represents Key Terms found on the Student CD in the 02_theres_more_you_can_do folder for this chapter.

Content-Based Assessments

Matching

Match each term in the second column with its correct definition in the first column. Write the letter of the term on the blank line in front of the correct definition.

_____ 1. An organized collection of facts about people, events, things, or ideas related to a particular topic or purpose.

_____ 2. Facts about people, events, things, or ideas.

_____ 3. Data that is organized in a useful manner.

_____ 4. The basic parts of a database, which include tables, forms, queries, reports, and macros.

_____ 5. The Access object that stores your data organized in an arrangement of columns and rows.

_____ 6. The area of the Access window that displays and organizes the names of the objects in a database, and from where you open objects for use.

_____ 7. The portion of the Access window that displays open objects.

_____ 8. A category that describes each piece of data stored in a table.

_____ 9. All of the categories of data pertaining to one person, place, thing, event, or idea.

_____ 10. The number of fields, and the type of content within each field, in an Access table.

_____ 11. The Access view that displays an object organized in a format of columns and rows similar to an Excel spreadsheet.

_____ 12. The Access view that displays the underlying structure of an object.

_____ 13. The action of filling a database table with records.

_____ 14. The characteristic that defines the kind of data that can be entered into a field, such as numbers, text, or dates.

_____ 15. An Access feature that sequentially numbers entered records creating a unique number for each field and which is useful for data that has no distinct field that is unique.

A AutoNumber

B Data

C Data type

D Database

E Datasheet view

F Design view

G Field

H Information

I Navigation Pane

J Object window

K Objects

L Populate

M Record

N Table

O Table design

Content-Based Assessments

Fill in the Blank

Write the correct word in the space provided.

1. DBMS is an acronym for _____ _____ _____.

2. A preformatted database designed for a specific purpose is a database _____.

3. A database that has no data and has no database tools, in which you create the data and the tools as you need them, is referred to as a _____ database.

4. Characteristics of a field that control how the field will display and how data can be entered in a field are known as the _____ _____.

5. The field that uniquely identifies a record in a table is the _____ _____.

6. A pre-built table format for common topics such as contacts, issues, and tasks is a _____ _____.

7. A database object that retrieves specific data from one or more tables, and then displays the specified data in Datasheet view is a _____.

8. A type of query that retrieves data from one or more tables and makes it available for use in the format of a datasheet is a _____ query.

9. The table or tables from which a query gets its data is the _____ _____.

10. A feature in Microsoft Office programs that walks you step-by-step through a process is a _____.

11. To search a table of records included in a query, find the records that match the criteria, and then display the records, _____ the query.

12. An Access object with which you can enter new records into a table, edit existing records in a table, or display existing records from a table is a _____.

13. The Access object that displays data in a formatted manner for printing and publication is a _____.

14. The Access form object in which multiple records can be entered into or displayed from a table is a _____ _____ form.

15. An arrangement of objects in the Navigation Pane in which the objects are grouped by the table to which they are related is the _____ _____ _____ category.

Content-Based Assessments

Skills Review

Project 12C — Departments

In this project, you will apply the skills you practiced from the Objectives in Project 12A.

Objectives: 1. *Start Access and Create a New Blank Database;* **2.** *Add Records to a Table;* **3.** *Rename Table Fields in Datasheet View;* **4.** *Modify the Design of a Table;* **5.** *Add a Second Table to a Database;* **6.** *Print a Table;* **7.** *Create and Use a Query;* **8.** *Create and Use a Form;* **9.** *Create and Print a Report;* **10.** *Close and Save a Database.*

In the following Skills Review, you will assist Kendall Walker, the CEO of Texas Lakes Medical Center, in creating a database to store information about the Departments and Department Directors at Texas Lakes Medical Center. Your printed results will look similar to those in Figure 12.57.

For Project 12C, you will need the following file:

New blank Access database

You will save your database as
12C_Departments_Firstname_Lastname

Figure 12.57

(Project 12C–Departments continues on the next page)

Content-Based Assessments

(Project 12C–Departments continued)

1. **Start** Access and create a new **Blank Database**. In the lower right corner, click the **Browse** button 📁, navigate to your **Access Chapter 12** folder. In the **File New Database** dialog box, name the database **12C_Departments_Firstname_Lastname** and then press ⏎. In the lower right corner, click **Create**.

2. In the **Navigation Pane**, click the **Close** button to collapse the **Navigation Pane** and maximize your screen space. Click in the first **Add New Field** box, type **Accounting** and then click in the **ID** field. To assign custom Department IDs, on the **Datasheet tab**, in the **Data Type & Formatting group**, click the **Data Type arrow**, and then click **Text**. Type **1212-D** and then click in the next **Add New Field** box to the right of *Accounting*. Complete the entry of this record and the next record as follows:

ID	Field1	Field2	Field3	Field4	Field5	Field6	Field7	Field8	Field9	Field10
1212-D	Accounting	Jennifer	R	Lee	(512) 555-0987	1 Medical Way #216	Austin	TX	78718	Duran
1233-D	Employee Benefits	Mike	M	Hernandez	(512) 555-0344	1 Medical Way #214	Austin	TX	78718	Duran

3. Point to the text *ID*, and then click to select the column. On the **Datasheet tab**, in the **Fields & Columns group**, click the **Rename** button. Type **Dept ID** and then press ⇥. Point to the text *Field1*, right-click, and then click **Rename Column**. Type **Department** and then press ⇥. Point to the text *Field2* and double-click. With the text selected, type **Director First Name** and then press ⇥. Using any of these techniques and the information in the following list, **Rename** the fields:

Field3	**Director Middle Initial**
Field4	**Director Last Name**
Field5	**Mobile Phone**
Field6	**Address**
Field7	**City**
Field8	**State**
Field9	**ZIP**
Field10	**Supervisor**

(Project 12C–Departments continues on the next page)

Content-Based Assessments

(Project 12C–Departments continued)

4. Enter the following additional records:

Dept ID	Department	Director First Name	Director Middle Initial	Director Last Name	Mobile Phone	Address	City	State	ZIP	Supervisor
1259-D	Emergency Room	Paul	S	Roberts	(512) 555-0234	1 Medical Way #212	Austin	TX	78718	Marshall
1265-D	Nursing Services	Andrea	T	McMillan	(512) 555-0233	1 Medical Way #302	Austin	TX	78718	Jones
1313-D	Finance	Beth	N	Crosby	(512) 555-0266	1 Medical Way #301	Austin	TX	78718	Duran
1355-D	Physician Services	Laura	O	Klein	(512) 555-0277	1 Medical Way #146	Austin	TX	78718	Jones
1459-D	Facilities	Mario	B	Bartello	(512) 555-0211	1 Medical Way #236	Austin	TX	78718	Santiago

5. On the **Datasheet tab**, in the **Views group**, click the **View button arrow**, and then click **Design View**. To save the changes you made to the field names and data types, and to give the table a more meaningful name, **Save** the table—using your own name—as **12C Departments Firstname Lastname** and then click **OK**.

6. In the **Field Name** column, click the **row selector box** to the left of the **Director Middle Initial** field name to select the entire row. On the **Design tab**, in the **Tools group**, click the **Delete Rows** button, read the message in the message box, and then click **Yes**. For this table, Kendall decides that having the Director's middle initial is not necessary.

7. With the table displayed in **Design** view, in the **Field Name** column, click in the **Dept ID** box. To the left of the box, notice the small icon of a key representing the primary key. Recall that the primary key is the field that uniquely identifies each individual record—no two records in the database will have the same Dept ID.

8. In the **Field Name** column, click in the **State** box, and then in the **Field Properties** area, set the **Field Size** to 2 In the **Description** column, click in the **Address** row, and then type **Include the Room number** Recall that these descriptions display in the status bar when entering records using a form, and communicate helpful information to the person entering data.

9. Click the **View** button to switch to **Datasheet** view, and then click **Yes** two times to save the changes you made to the design of the table—deleting a field, adding a description, and changing a field property.

10. With the **12C Departments** table displayed in **Datasheet** view, notice that in the **Supervisor** field, several names are repeated. Thus, it would not make sense to include information about these individuals multiple times in the same table. Recall that when you see repeated information, it is likely that an additional table should be added to the database. On the Ribbon, click the **Create tab**. In the **Tables group**, click the **Table Templates** button, and then from the list, click **Contacts**.

(Project 12C–Departments continues on the next page)

Content-Based Assessments

(Project 12C–Departments continued)

11. Click the **Datasheet tab** to display the groups of Datasheet commands. In the second column, point to the text *Company*, click to select the field, and then on the **Datasheet tab**, in the **Fields & Columns group**, click the **Delete** button.

12. **Delete** the **E-mail Address** field. With your mouse, drag to the right to select the **Business Phone** field and **Home Phone** field. Right-click over the field names, and then click **Delete Column**. **Delete** the **Fax Number** field. Then, **Delete** the fields **Country/Region**, **Web Page**, **Notes**, and **Attachments** (the field with the paper clip icon).

13. On the **Datasheet tab**, in the **Views group**, click the **View** button to switch to **Design** view. To save the changes you made to the field arrangement and to give the table a more meaningful name, **Save** the table—using your own name—as **12C Supervisors Firstname Lastname** and then click **OK**.

14. In the **Field Name** column, click the **ID** box, delete the text, and then type **Supervisor ID** Click in the **Data Type** box, click the **Data Type arrow**, and then from the list, click **Text**. Click in the **Description** box, and type **Supervisor's ID number** The medical center assigns a unique ID number to each Supervisor, which you will use as the primary key instead of the AutoNumber.

15. In the **Field Name** column, click in the **State/Province** box, and then in the **Field Properties** area, set the **Field Size** to **2** Click the **View** button to switch to **Datasheet** view, and then click **Yes** to save the changes you have made to the design of your table—changing a field name, adding a description, and changing a field property.

16. With your **12C Supervisors** table displayed in **Datasheet** view, in the new record row which is indicated by an asterisk (*) in the record selector box on the left, click in the **Supervisor ID** field, and then add the following records:

Supervisor ID	Last Name	First Name	Job Title	Mobile Phone	Address	City	State/ Province	ZIP/Postal Code
329-Sup	Duran	Brent	Controller	(512) 555-0010	1 Medical Way #400	Austin	TX	78718
347-Sup	Jones	Jordan	Director Human Resources	(512) 555-0444	1 Medical Way #402	Austin	TX	78718
417-Sup	Santiago	Francis	Operations Director	(512) 555-0031	1 Medical Way #404	Austin	TX	78718
420-Sup	Marshall	Mike	Accounting Director	(512) 555-0616	1 Medical Way #406	Austin	TX	78718

(Project 12C–Departments continues on the next page)

Content-Based Assessments

(Project 12C–Departments continued)

17. Change the field name **State/Province** to **State** and **ZIP/Postal Code** to **ZIP** Select all of the columns, and then apply **Best Fit** either by double-clicking the right border of any selected column or by displaying the shortcut menu, clicking Column Width, and then clicking Best Fit. On the **Quick Access Toolbar**, click the **Save** button to save the changes you have made to the layout of the table.

18. From the **Office** menu, point to **Print**, and then click **Print Preview**. In the **Page Layout group**, click the **Margins** button, and then click **Normal**. Click the **Landscape** button. If you are submitting paper results, click the **Print** button, and in the **Print** dialog box, click **OK**. Click the **Close Print Preview** button. To submit electronically, follow the directions provided by your instructor.

19. **Close** the **12C Supervisors** table. In the **12C Departments** table, select all of the columns, and then apply **Best Fit**. On the **Quick Access Toolbar**, click the **Save** button. From the **Office** menu, point to **Print**, and then click **Print Preview**. In the **Page Layout group**, click the **Margins** button, and then click **Normal**. Click the **Landscape** button. If you are submitting paper results, click the **Print** button, and in the **Print** dialog box, click **OK**. Click the **Close Print Preview** button. To submit electronically, follow the directions provided by your instructor.

20. **Close** the **12C Departments** table. Click the **Create tab**, and then in the **Other group**, click the **Query Wizard** button. In the **New Query** dialog box, click **Simple Query Wizard**, and then click **OK**. Click the **Tables/Queries arrow**, and then click **Table: 12C Supervisors**. Under **Available Fields**, click **Supervisor ID**, and then click the **Add Field** button to move the field to the **Selected Fields** list on the right. Add the **Last Name**, **First Name**, **Job Title**, and **Mobile Phone** fields to the **Selected Fields** list in the order specified. Recall that you can also double-click a field name to move it.

This query will answer the question *What are the Supervisor ID, name, job title, and mobile phone number of every Supervisor in the database?* Click the **Next** button. Be sure that the option **Open the query to view information** is selected. Click **Finish**. Display the query in **Print Preview**, use the default margins and orientation, **Print**, and then **Close Print Preview**. Or, submit electronically as directed.

21. **Close** your query. **Open** the **Navigation Pane**, click to select the **12C Supervisors** table. Do not open the table, just select it. **Close** the **Navigation Pane**. On the Ribbon, click the **Create tab**, and then in the **Forms group**, click the **Form** button. The form displays in Layout view, in which you can make changes to the layout of the form. Because no changes are necessary, on the **Home tab**, in the **Views group**, click the **View button arrow**, and then from the list, click **Form View**. From the **Office** menu, click **Save** to save your newly designed form, and then click **OK** to accept the default name. **Close** the form object. Recall that you typically create forms to make data entry easier for the individuals who enter new records into your database.

22. **Open** the **Navigation Pane**, locate the **12C Supervisors** table—recall that a table displays a small icon of a datasheet, a query displays a small icon of two datasheets, and a form displays a small form icon. Open the table either by double-clicking the table name or right-clicking and clicking Open. **Close** the **Navigation Pane**. On the **Create tab**, in the **Reports group**, click the **Report** button.

(Project 12C–Departments continues on the next page)

(Project 12C–Departments continued)

23. Point to the **Supervisor ID** column heading, right-click, and then click **Delete**. **Delete** the **Job Title**, **Address**, **City**, **State**, and **ZIP** fields from the report layout. From the **Office** menu, point to **Print**, and then click **Print Preview**. In the **Page Layout group**, click the **Margins** button, and then click **Wide**. Click the **Landscape** button. If you are submitting paper results, click the **Print** button. Click the **Close Print Preview** button. To submit electronically, follow the instructions provided by your instructor.

24. **Close** your **12C Supervisors** report, and then click **Yes** to save the design changes. In the **Save As** dialog box, click **OK** to save the report with the default name. If necessary, close any remaining objects and **Close** the **Navigation Pane**. From the **Office** menu, click **Close Database**. From the **Office** menu, click **Exit Access**.

End You have completed Project 12C ———————————————————

Content-Based Assessments

Skills Review

Project 12D — Benefits Fair

In this project, you will apply the skills you practiced from the Objectives in Project 12B.

Objectives: 11. *Create a Database by Using a Template;* **12.** *Organize Database Objects in the Navigation Pane;* **13.** *Create a New Table in a Database Created with a Template;* **14.** *View a Report and Print a Table in a Database Created with a Template.*

In the following Skills Review, you will assist Sharon Fitzgerald, the Human Resources Director at Texas Lakes Medical Center, in creating a database to store information about the Employee Benefits Fair at Texas Lakes Medical Center. Your printed result will look similar to Figure 12.58.

For Project 12D, you will need the following file:

New Access database using the Events template

You will save your database as
12D_Benefits_Fair_Firstname_Lastname

Figure 12.58

(Project 12D–Benefits Fair continues on the next page)

Content-Based Assessments

(Project 12D–Benefits Fair continued)

1. **Start** Access. Under **Template Categories**, click **Local Templates**, and then click **Events**. In the lower right portion of the screen, click the **Browse** button , navigate to your **Access Chapter 12** folder. **Save** the database as **12D_Benefits_Fair_Firstname_Lastname** and then press ⏎. In the lower right corner, click the **Create** button. If necessary, to the right of the Security Warning, click Options, click Enable this content, and then click OK.

2. Recall that a template opens with a pre-built Multiple Items form into which you can enter records to build a table. In the **Event List** Multiple Items form, enter the following records, pressing ⎵Tab to move across the row:

ID	Title	Start Time	End Time	Description	Location
1	Medical Plan	5/1/09 8a	5/1/09 5p	Health Benefits	Lone Star Room
2	Eye Care Plan	5/1/09 9a	5/1/09 3p	Health Benefits	Red River Room
3	Prescription Plan	5/1/09 8a	5/1/09 8p	Health Benefits	Lone Star Room
4	Pension Plan	5/1/09 10a	5/1/09 7:30p	Retirement Benefits	Capitol Room
5	Life Insurance Plan	5/1/09 1p	5/1/09 5p	Life Insurance Benefits	Blue Bird Room
6	Deferred Compensation Plan	5/1/09 10a	5/1/09 3p	Compensation Benefits	Red River Room

3. In the **Link bar**, just above the field names row, click **New Event**, and then enter the following record using the single-record form. Recall that you can also use this form to enter records into a table:

Title	Location	Start Time	End Time	Description
Dental Plan	Blue Bird Room	5/1/09 8a	5/1/09 5p	Health Benefits

4. **Close** the single-record form. **Close** the **Event List** form. **Open** the **Navigation Pane**. At the top of the **Navigation Pane**, click the **Navigation arrow**. Under **Navigate To Category**, click **Tables and Related Views**. Click the **Navigation arrow** again, and then in the **Filter By Group** section, notice that **All Tables** is selected. Recall that this arrangement organizes the database objects by the table to which they are related.

5. On the **Navigation Pane**, right-click the **Events** table, and then click **Open**—or double-click the table name to open it. This is the table that was built from the records you entered into the form. Rather than enter information about the Locations multiple times in this table, you will create another table for the Location information. **Close** the **Events** table, and then **Close** the **Navigation Pane**.

(Project 12D–Benefits Fair continues on the next page)

Content-Based Assessments

(Project 12D–Benefits Fair continued)

6. Click the **Create tab**, and then in the **Tables group**, click the **Table** button. Enter the following records, pressing ⌨Tab or ⌨Enter to move across the row. Recall that Access assigns unique numbers; your ID numbers may vary.

ID	Field1	Field2	Field3	Field4
4	Blue Bird Room	30	U-Shape Table	Computer Projector
5	Red River Room	20	Classroom	Computer Projector
6	Capitol Room	30	Classroom	Computer Projector

7. Point to the text *Field1* and click to select the column. On the **Datasheet tab**, in the **Fields & Columns group**, click the **Rename** button, and then type **Location** Point to the text *Field2*, right-click, and then click **Rename Column**. Type **Seating Capacity** Point to the text *Field3* and double-click. With the text selected, type **Room Arrangement** Using any of these techniques, **Rename** *Field4* as **Visual Equipment**

8. Enter one additional record as follows:

ID	Location	Seating Capacity	Room Arrangement	Visual Equipment
7	Lone Star Room	50	Theater	Computer Projector

9. On the **Home tab**, in the **Views group**, click the **View button arrow**, and then click **Design View**. **Save** the table as **12D Room Locations Firstname Lastname** and then click **OK**.

10. In the **Field Name** column, click in the **Location** box, and then on the **Design tab**, click the **Primary Key** button. Point to the row selector box for the **ID** field, and then click to select the entire row. On the **Design tab**, click the **Delete Rows** button, and then click **Yes**. The Location name will serve as the primary key for this table. In the **Views group**, click the **View** button, and then click **Yes** to save the changes you made to the table design.

11. In the field names row, drag across to select all of the fields (columns). Right-click over any field name, click **Column Width**, and then in the **Column Width** dialog box, click **Best Fit**.

12. **Close** the **12D Room Locations** table, and then click **Yes** to save the layout changes you made to the column widths. From the **Navigation Pane**, open the **All Events** report. Open the **Event Details** report. The pre-built reports are arranged in various useful formats. **Close** both reports.

13. From the **Navigation Pane**, open your **12D Room Locations** table. From the **Office** menu, point to **Print**, and then click **Print Preview**. If you are submitting your work on paper, on the **Print Preview tab**, in the **Print group**, click the **Print** button, and then **Close Print Preview**. To submit electronically, follow the directions provided by your instructor.

14. **Close** the **12D Room Locations** table. **Close** the **Navigation Pane**. With all of the database objects closed, from the **Office** menu, click **Close Database**. From the **Office** menu, click **Exit Access**.

End You have completed Project 12D

Content-Based Assessments

Project 12E—Gift Shop

In this project, you will apply skills you practiced from the Objectives in Projects 12A and 12B.

Objectives: 1. *Start Access and Create a New Blank Database;* **2.** *Add Records to a Table;* **3.** *Rename Table Fields in Datasheet View;* **4.** *Modify the Design of a Table;* **5.** *Add a Second Table to a Database;* **6.** *Print a Table;* **7.** *Create and Use a Query;* **8.** *Create and Use a Form;* **9.** *Create and Print a Report;* **10.** *Close and Save a Database;* **12.** *Organize Database Objects in the Navigation Pane.*

In the following Mastering Access project, you will assist Scott Williams, the Gift Shop Manager of Texas Lakes Medical Center, in creating a database to store information about gift items in the shop's inventory. Your printed results will look similar to those shown in Figure 12.59.

For Project 12E, you will need the following file:

New blank Access database

You will save your database as 12E_Gift_Shop_Firstname_Lastname

Figure 12.59

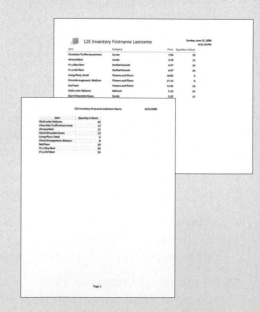

(Project 12E–Gift Shop continues on the next page)

(Project 12E–Gift Shop continued)

1. **Start** Access, create a new **Blank Database**, and then **Save** it in your **Access Chapter 12** folder as **12E_Gift_Shop_Firstname_Lastname**

2. **Close** the **Navigation Pane**. For the **ID** field, change the **Data Type** to **Text**. Enter the following records:

ID	Field1	Field2	Field3	Field4	Field5
C-1	Chocolate Truffle Assortment	Candy	7.95	Room 107	12
C-2	Almond Bark	Candy	5.79	Room 107	12
SA-1	It's a Boy Bear	Stuffed Animals	6.47	Room 107	24
SA-2	It's a Girl Bear	Stuffed Animals	6.47	Room 107	24
FP-1	Living Plant, Small	Flowers and Plants	10.83	Gift Shop Cooler	6
FP-2	Floral Arrangement, Medium	Flowers and Plants	27.15	Gift Shop Cooler	6
FP-3	Bud Vase	Flowers and Plants	11.91	Gift Shop Cooler	10
B-1	Multi-color Balloons	Balloons	5.16	Room 107	24
C-3	Giant Chocolate Kisses	Candy	5.25	Room 107	12

3. **Rename** the fields as follows:

Field1	Item
Field2	Category
Field3	Price
Field4	Storage Location
Field5	Quantity in Stock

4. Select all of the fields (columns), and then apply **Best Fit**. **Save** the table, and name it **12E Inventory Firstname Lastname** Display the table in **Print Preview**, set the margins to **Wide** and the orientation to **Landscape**. If you are submitting printed pages, click **Print**; and then **Close Print Preview**. To submit electronically, follow the directions provided by your instructor. **Close** the table and **Save** any changes.

5. **Create** a second **Table** to record the information about the storage of inventory categories. Add the following records to the new table. Recall that Access will assign unique ID numbers; yours may vary.

ID	Field1	Field2	Field3
3	Candy	Room 107	North Zone 1
4	Stuffed Animals	Room 107	South Zone 2
5	Flowers and Plants	Gift Shop Coolers	Cooler 1
6	Balloons	Room 107	East Zone 3

(Project 12E–Gift Shop continues on the next page)

(Project 12E–Gift Shop continued)

6. **Rename** *Field1* as **Category Rename** *Field2* as **Storage Location** and **Rename** *Field3* as **Location Detail** Switch to **Design** view, name the table **12E Categories Firstname Lastname** Set the **Category** field as the **Primary Key**—each category of inventory items is unique. **Delete** the **ID** field.

7. Switch to **Datasheet** view, saving the changes. Select all of the fields (columns), and then apply **Best Fit**. View the table in **Print Preview**. If you are submitting printed pages, **Print** the table, and then **Close Print Preview**. To submit electronically, follow the directions provided by your instructor. **Close** the **12E Categories** table, saving the changes to the layout.

8. **Create**, using the **Query Wizard**, a **Simple Query** based on your **12E Inventory** table. Include only the **Item** and **Quantity in Stock** fields in the query result. The query will answer the question *How many of each item do we currently have in stock?* Accept the default name. If you are submitting printed pages, **Print** the query, and then **Close** the query. To submit electronically, follow the directions provided by your instructor.

9. **Create** a **Report** based on your **12E Inventory** table. **Delete** the **ID** field and the **Storage Location** field. Display the report in **Print Preview**, set the margins to **Wide** and the orientation to **Landscape**. If you are submitting printed pages, **Print** the report. To submit electronically, follow the directions provided by your instructor. **Close** the report, **Save** the design changes, and then accept the default name. **Close** any open objects, and then **Close** the **Navigation Pane**. **Close** the **Database**, and then **Exit Access**.

End **You have completed Project 12E**

Content-Based Assessments

Mastering Access

Project 12F—Recruiting Events

In this project, you will apply skills you practiced from the Objectives in Projects 12A and 12B.

Objectives: 2. *Add Records to a Table;* **6.** *Print a Table;* **7.** *Create and Use a Query;* **10.** *Close and Save a Database;* **11.** *Create a Database by Using a Template;* **12.** *Organize Database Objects in the Navigation Pane;* **13.** *Create a New Table in a Database Created with a Template;* **14.** *View a Report and Print a Table in a Database Created with a Template.*

In the following Mastering Access project, you will assist Serge Juco, Vice President of Human Resources, in creating a database to track recruiting events that are scheduled to attract new employees to careers at the medical center. Your printed results will look similar to those shown in Figure 12.60.

For Project 12F, you will need the following file:

New Access database using the Events template

You will save your database as
12F_Recruiting_Events_Firstname_Lastname

Figure 12.60

(Project 12F–Recruiting Events continues on the next page)

Access

Mastering Access

chaptertwelve

(Project 12F–Recruiting Events continued)

1. **Start** Access and then from **Local Templates**, create a new database based on the **Events** template. In your **Access Chapter 12** folder, name the new database **12F_Recruiting_Events_ Firstname_Lastname** In the lower right corner, click the Create button. If necessary, to the right of the Security Warning, click Options, click Enable this content, and then click OK.

2. In the **Multiple Items** form, enter the following records to build the Event List table; or, if you prefer, use the New Event single record form, which is available on the Link bar:

ID	Title	Start Time	End Time	Description	Location
1	Medical Secretary	6/1/09 8a	6/1/09 8p	Administration	Austin Corporate Center
2	Cardiac Laboratory	6/2/09 8a	6/2/09 8p	Labs and Research	UT Medical School at Houston
3	Clinical Labs	6/2/09 8a	6/2/09 8p	Labs and Research	UT Medical School at Houston
4	Environmental Services	6/3/09 8a	6/4/09 8p	Administration	Austin Community Center
5	Finance	6/4/09 8a	6/4/09 8p	Administration	UT Austin McCombs School of Business
6	Information Technology	6/5/09 8a	6/5/09 8p	Administration	UT Austin McCombs School of Business
7	Medical Illustration	6/1/09 8a	6/1/09 8p	Medical Media	UT Austin Department of Art
8	Nursing	6/5/09 8a	6/5/09 8p	Nursing	UT Austin School of Nursing
9	Radiology	6/3/09 8a	6/3/09 8p	Labs and Research	UT Health Science Center at San Antonio

3. **Close** the form, and then display the **Navigation Pane**. Using the **Navigation arrow**, organize the objects by **Tables and Related Views**. Point to the **Events** table, right-click, click **Rename**, and then type **12F Recruiting Events Firstname Lastname** and press ⏎ to rename the table.

4. **Open** the **12F Recruiting Events** table; recall that the table was built by typing records into the Multiple Items form. Leave the Attachments field because Serge may decide to attach job description brochures for each event. The AutoNumber ID serves as the primary key—the unique identifier for each record. **Close** the **Navigation Pane**. Select all of the columns and apply **Best Fit**. Display the table in **Print Preview**, set the margins to **Normal** and the orientation to **Landscape**. If you are submitting paper results, **Print** and then **Close Print Preview.** Or, follow your instructor's directions for electronic submission. **Close** the table, saving the changes to the layout.

5. **Create** a new table using the **Contacts Table Template**. **Delete** the **Company** field. **Delete** the following fields: **E-mail Address**, **Business Phone**, **Home Phone**, **Fax Number**, **Country/Region**, **Web Page**, **Notes**, and **Attachments**. Click in the first **ID** field. From the

(Project 12F–Recruiting Events continues on the next page)

Content-Based Assessments

Mastering Access

(Project 12F–Recruiting Events continued)

Datasheet tab, change the **Data Type** of the **ID** field to **Text**, and then enter the following records:

ID	Last Name	First Name	Job Title	Mobile Phone	Address	City	State/Province	ZIP/Postal Code
R-01	Miller	Jason	Administration Recruiter	(512) 555-0195	1 Medical Way #401	Austin	TX	78718
R-02	Garrett	Ginny	Labs and Research Recruiter	(512) 555-0223	1 Medical Way #401	Austin	TX	78718
R-03	Yeman	Daniel	Medical Media Recruiter	(512) 555-0155	1 Medical Way #401	Austin	TX	78718
R-04	Zeja	Jonathan	Nursing Recruiter	(512) 555-0122	1 Medical Way #401	Austin	TX	78718

6. **Close** the table, **Save** the changes, and then name the table **12F Recruiters Firstname Lastname**

7. **Create**, using the **Query Wizard**, a **Simple Query** based on your **12F Recruiting Events** table. Add the appropriate fields to the query to answer the question *What are the title, location, and description of all the recruiting events?* Accept the default name for the query. **Print** and then **Close** the query.

8. From the **Navigation Pane**, open your **12F Recruiters** table. Change the name of the **ZIP/Postal Code** field to **ZIP** Select all the columns in the table and apply **Best Fit**. Display the table in **Print Preview**, set the margins to **Normal** and the orientation to **Landscape**. **Print** the table, and then **Close Print Preview**. Or, submit electronically.

9. **Close** the table, saving the layout changes. From the **Navigation Pane**, open the **All Events** report. Then, open the **Events By Week** report. Recall that one advantage of starting a database from a database template is that many objects, such as attractively arranged reports, are provided.

10. **Close** the reports and any other open objects. **Close** the **Navigation Pane**. From the **Office** menu, first **Close** the **Database**, and then **Exit Access**.

End **You have completed Project 12F** ——————————————

Content-Based Assessments

Project 12G — Facility Expansion

In this project, you will apply all the skills you practiced from the Objectives in Projects 12A and 12B.

Objectives: 1. *Start Access and Create a New Blank Database;* **2.** *Add Records to a Table;* **3.** *Rename Table Fields in Datasheet View;* **4.** *Modify the Design of a Table;* **5.** *Add a Second Table to a Database;* **6.** *Print a Table;* **7.** *Create and Use a Query;* **8.** *Create and Use a Form;* **9.** *Create and Print a Report;* **10.** *Close and Save a Database;* **11.** *Create a Database by Using a Template;* **12.** *Organize Database Objects in the Navigation Pane;* **13.** *Create a New Table in a Database Created with a Template;* **14.** *View a Report and Print a Table in a Database Created with a Template.*

In the following Mastering Access project, you will assist Jerry Lopez, the Budget Director, in creating a database to store information about the facility expansion at Texas Lakes Medical Center and in creating a separate database to store information about public events related to the expansion. Your printed results will look similar to the ones shown in Figure 12.61.

For Project 12G, you will need the following files:

New blank Access database
New Access database using the Events template

You will save your databases as
12G_Facility_Expansion_Firstname_Lastname
12G_Public_Events_Firstname_Lastname

Figure 12.61

(Project 12G–Facility Expansion continues on the next page)

Content-Based Assessments

(Project 12G–Facility Expansion continued)

1. **Start** Access, create a new **Blank Database**, and **Save** it in your **Access Chapter 12** folder as 12G_Facility_Expansion_Firstname_Lastname

2. **Close** the **Navigation Pane**. For the **ID** field, change the **Data Type** to **Text**. Enter the following records:

ID	Field1	Field2	Field3	Field4
Project-01	Lakes South Tower	Private physician practices	Glenmore Construction	30,000,000
Project-02	Lakes North Tower	Private physician practices	Glenmore Construction	30,000,000
Project-03	Lakes East Center	Specialty physician practices with outpatient services	Wright Rosen Contractors	60,000,000
Project-04	Lakes West Center	Specialty physician practices with outpatient services	Wright Rosen Contractors	60,000,000
Project-05	Lakes Conference Center	Conference and education center	Wells Construction, Inc.	10,000,000
Project-06	Lakes Acute Care Center	Emergency and acute care services	Wright Rosen Contractors	80,000,000

3. **Rename** the fields as follows:

Field1	Building Project
Field2	Description
Field3	Contractor
Field4	Budget Amount

4. For the **Budget Amount** field, change the **Data Type** to **Currency**. Apply **Best Fit** to all of the columns in the table. **Save** the table as **12G Projects Firstname Lastname** and then in **Print Preview**, set the margins to **Wide** and the orientation to **Landscape**. If you are submitting printed pages, click **Print**; and then **Close Print Preview**. Or, submit electronically as directed by your instructor. **Close** your **12G Projects** table.

5. **Create** a second **Table** to record the information about the contractors for the facility expansion. Add the following records to the new table. Recall that Access will assign unique ID numbers; your numbers may vary.

ID	Field1	Field2	Field3
3	Glenmore Construction	Bob Ballard	(512) 555-0900
4	Wright Rosen Contractors	Lisa Li	(512) 555-0707
5	Wells Construction, Inc.	Frank Levin	(512) 555-0444

(Project 12G–Facility Expansion continues on the next page)

Content-Based Assessments

Mastering Access

(Project 12G–Facility Expansion continued)

6. **Rename** the fields as follows:

Field1	Contractor
Field2	Project Manager
Field3	Phone Number

7. Switch to **Design** view, name the table **12G Contractors Firstname Lastname** Set the **Contractor** field as the **Primary Key**—each contractor name is unique. **Delete** the **ID** field. Switch to **Datasheet** view and **Save** the changes. Apply **Best Fit** to all of the columns.

8. If you are submitting printed pages, **Print** the table; or submit electronically as directed by your instructor. **Close** the **12G Contractors** table and **Save** the changes to the layout—the column widths.

9. **Create**, using the **Query Wizard**, a **Simple Query** based on your **12G Projects** table. Include only the appropriate fields to answer the question *For each Building Project, what is the Budget Amount?* Accept the default name, display the query in **Print Preview**, **Print**, and then **Close Print Preview**. Or, submit electronically as directed by your instructor. **Close** the query.

10. In the **Navigation Pane**, select your **12G Projects** table. **Create** a **Form**, and then **Close** the **Navigation Pane**. View the created form, and then **Close** the form. **Save** and accept the default name.

11. **Open** the **12G Projects** table from the **Navigation Pane**. With the table open, **Create** a **Report**. Delete the **ID** field and the **Contractor** field. Display the report in **Print Preview**, set the margins to **Wide** and the orientation to **Landscape**. If you are submitting printed pages, **Print** the report, and then **Close Print Preview**. To submit electronically, follow the directions provided by your instructor. **Close** the report, **Save** the changes, and accept the default name. **Close** any open objects and close the **Navigation Pane**. From the **Office** menu, click **Close Database**.

12. From the **Local Templates**, create a new database using the **Events template**. **Save** the database in your **Access Chapter 12** folder and name it **12G_Public_Events_Firstname_Lastname** If necessary, enable the content.

13. To build the **Events** table, enter the following records using either the displayed Multiple Items Event List form or the single-record form, which is available by clicking New Event in the Link bar:

Title	Start Time	End Time	Description	Location
Dedication	12/1/09 10a	12/1/09 11a	Building dedication ceremony	Lakes Acute Care Center
Groundbreaking	11/15/09 10a	11/15/09 11a	Groundbreaking ceremony	Lakes South Tower
Community Health Expo	11/30/09 10a	11/30/09 9p	Community Health Expo	Lakes Conference Center

(Project 12G–Facility Expansion continues on the next page)

(Project 12G–Facility Expansion continued)

14. **Close** the **Event List** form. **Open** the **Navigation Pane**, and then using the **Navigation arrow**, arrange the **Navigation Pane** by **Tables and Related Views**. From the **Navigation Pane**, point to the **Events** table and right-click. From the shortcut menu, click **Rename**, type **12G Events Table Firstname Lastname** and then press Enter. Then open the table. Recall that the table was created by entering records in the form. Change the field name **ID** to **Event ID** Delete the **Attachments** field. Select all of the columns in the table, apply **Best Fit**, and then display the table in **Print Preview**. Set the margins to **Normal** and the orientation to **Landscape**. **Print**, and then **Close Print Preview**. Or, submit electronically as directed by your instructor. **Close** the table and **Save** the changes to the layout.

15. If necessary, close the Navigation Pane and close any open objects. **Close** the **Database** and **Exit Access**.

 End **You have completed Project 12G** ————————————————

Content-Based Assessments

Project 12H — GO! Fix It

In this project, you will apply the skills you practiced from the Objectives in Projects 12A and 12B.

For Project 12H, you will need the following file:

a12H_fixit_Cardiac_Patients

You will save your database as
12H_Cardiac_Patients_Firstname_Lastname

In this project, you will edit a draft of an Access database that will be used by the Cardiac Unit nursing staff at the Texas Lakes Medical Center. From the student files that accompany this textbook, locate and make a copy of the database **a12H_Cardiac_Patients** in your **Access Chapter 12** folder. Name the copy **12H_Cardiac_Patients_Firstname_Lastname**

This database contains errors that you must find and correct. Examine the database, and then correct the errors that you find. Types of errors could include:

- Spelling, grammar, punctuation, and usage errors such as text case.

- Missing or incorrect data in tables, queries, forms, and reports such as file names, field names, types, descriptions, properties, records, and criteria.

- Table design errors such as primary key.

- Query design errors such as field, table, and show.

- Page setup errors such as margins, orientation, layout, or alignment.

Things you should know to complete this project:

- The primary key in the table should be *Patient ID*.

- Field names in the table should be properly spelled.

- Martin Harris is 68 years old.

- Both Age and Monitor Level should have a Data Type of *Text*.

- The following record is missing: Elizabeth Norton, Patient ID: 2008-0911-056, Room Number: 3006A, Age: 82, Monitor Level: 3, Attending Physician: Obester M, Secondary Physician: Ovitz J, and 2nd Physician Specialty: Gerontology.

  Add your first and last names to the name of the table. Print the table in Landscape orientation or submit your database electronically directed.

 End **You have completed Project 12H**

Outcomes-Based Assessments

Rubric

The following outcomes-based assessments are *open-ended assessments*. That is, there is no specific correct result; your result will depend on your approach to the information provided. Make *Professional Quality* your goal. Use the following scoring rubric to guide you in *how* to approach the problem and then to evaluate *how well* your approach solves the problem.

The criteria—Software Mastery, Content, Format and Layout, and Process—represent the knowledge and skills you have gained that you can apply to solving the problem. The *levels of performance*—Professional Quality, Approaching Professional Quality, or Needs Quality Improvements—help you and your instructor evaluate your result.

	Your completed project is of Professional Quality if you:	Your completed project is Approaching Professional Quality if you:	Your completed project Needs Quality Improvements if you:
1-Software Mastery	Choose and apply the most appropriate skills, tools, and features and identify efficient methods to solve the problem.	Choose and apply some appropriate skills, tools, and features, but not in the most efficient manner.	Choose inappropriate skills, tools, or features, or are inefficient in solving the problem.
2-Content	Construct a solution that is clear and well organized, contains content that is accurate, appropriate to the audience and purpose, and is complete. Provide a solution that contains no errors of spelling, grammar, or style.	Construct a solution in which some components are unclear, poorly organized, inconsistent, or incomplete. Misjudge the needs of the audience. Have some errors in spelling, grammar, or style, but the errors do not detract from comprehension.	Construct a solution that is unclear, incomplete, or poorly organized; contains some inaccurate or inappropriate content; and contains many errors of spelling, grammar, or style. Do not solve the problem.
3-Format and Layout	Format and arrange all elements to communicate information and ideas, clarify function, illustrate relationships, and indicate relative importance.	Apply appropriate format and layout features to some elements, but not others. Overuse features, causing minor distraction.	Apply format and layout that does not communicate information or ideas clearly. Do not use format and layout features to clarify function, illustrate relationships, or indicate relative importance. Use available features excessively, causing distraction.
4-Process	Use an organized approach that integrates planning, development, self-assessment, revision, and reflection.	Demonstrate an organized approach in some areas, but not others; or, use an insufficient process of organization throughout.	Do not use an organized approach to solve the problem.

Outcomes-Based Assessments

Problem Solving

Project 12I—Public Seminars

In this project, you will construct a solution by applying any combination of the skills you practiced from the Objectives in Projects 12A and 12B.

> **For Project 12I, you will need the following files:**
>
> New Access database using the Events template
> a12I_Public_Seminars (Word document)

You will save your database as
12I_Public_Seminars_Firstname_Lastname

Texas Lakes Medical Center has developed a series of public health seminars. The information about the seminars is located in your student files, in the Word document **a12I_Public_Seminars**.

Using the data in the Word document and a new database created from the Events database template, enter the data into the Multiple Items form. Each seminar will begin at 7 p.m. and end at 9 p.m. After entering the records, in the Navigation Pane, point to the name of the table that was created as a result of entering the records into the Multiple Items form, click Rename, and then name the table **12I Seminars Firstname Lastname** Open the table, apply Best Fit to the table's columns, and then display and modify the Print Preview so that that all the columns fully display on a single sheet. Print the table or submit electronically. Save the database with the name **12I_Public_Seminars_Firstname_Lastname** and then close the database.

End **You have completed Project 12I** ————————————

Outcomes-Based Assessments

Access

chaptertwelve

Problem Solving

Project 12J—Media Contacts

In this project, you will construct a solution by applying any combination of the skills you practiced from the Objectives in Projects 12A and 12B.

For Project 12J, you will need the following files:

New blank Access database
a12J_Media_Contacts (Word document)

**You will save your database as
12J_Media_Contacts_Firstname_Lastname**

The Public Relations Department at Texas Lakes Medical Center maintains a list of media contacts who receive e-mail notification when press releases regarding the Medical Center are issued. The information about the media contacts is located in your student files, in the Word document **a12J_Media_Contacts**.

Create a new blank database, and then close the default Table1. Create a new table using the Contacts table template, and then use the data in the Word document to enter the records. Delete the unneeded fields from the table. As necessary, rename fields to match those in the Word document. Change the data type of the ID field to Text, and use the IDs provided. Close the table, and save it as **12J Media Contacts Firstname Lastname** Create a report and delete the Media ID column. In Page Setup or Print Preview, use narrow margins and landscape orientation to arrange the report. Print or submit the report electronically. Close the database.

End You have completed Project 12J

Access

Problem Solving

Project 12K — Billing Rates

In this project, you will construct a solution by applying any combination of the skills you practiced from the Objectives in Projects 12A and 12B.

For Project 12K, you will need the following files:

New blank Access database
a12K_Billing_Rates (Word document)

**You will save your database as
12K_Billing_Rates_Firstname_Lastname**

Physicians at Texas Lakes Medical Center have varying billing rates. The information about the physician names and billing rates is located in your student files, in the Word document **a12K_Billing_Rates**.

Create a new blank database. Create a table with the Physician IDs and billing rates. For the rates, change data type to Currency. Apply Best Fit to the columns, save and name the table **12K Rates Firstname Lastname** and then print the table, or submit electronically as directed. From the table, create a query indicating only the Physician ID and the rate, and print or submit the query electronically. Create a second table using the Contacts table template, enter the names and phone numbers of the physicians, and delete unneeded columns. Apply Best Fit to the columns, save and name the table **12K Physicians Firstname Lastname** Print the table or submit electronically. Save the database with the name **12K_Billing_Rates_Firstname_Lastname** and then close the database.

 End **You have completed Project 12K** ————————

More on your Student CD

The instructions for the following additional end-of-chapter projects are on your student CD in the folder 03_additional_end_of_chapter_projects.

Content-Based Assessments

Project L Mastering Access	Apply the skills you practiced in Project A.
Project M Mastering Access	Apply the skills you practiced in Project B.
Project N Business Running Case	Apply the skills you practiced in Projects A and B while helping an entrepreneur with the daily tasks of running a business.
	In each chapter, this project focuses on applying the skills you have practiced in Projects A and B to a business. The project related to this business runs throughout the textbook. You will see how the Office applications relate to the day-to-day operation of a small business called Nelson Architectural Planning.

Outcomes-Based Assessments

Project O Problem Solving	Construct a solution by applying any combination of the skills you practiced from Projects A and B.
Project P Problem Solving	Construct a solution by applying any combination of the skills you practiced from Projects A and B.
Project Q You and GO!	Construct a solution that applies to your own life by applying any combination of the skills you practiced from Projects A and B.
Project R GO! with Help	Practice using Microsoft Office's Help Feature.
Project S Group Business Running Case	Work as part of a group to apply the skills you have gained thus far to help the Bell Orchid Hotel Group achieve its business goals.

Multimedia

The following multimedia accompany this textbook:

Companion Web site *www.prenhall.com/go*	An interactive Web site designed to reinforce and test your understanding of the skills in this chapter.
AV-EDDs	In the folder in the front of this book you will find videos that demonstrate the objectives of the A and B projects in this chapter. These may help you understand how to complete the projects in this book.
Video Podcasts	In the folder in the front of this book are videos that can be played on your iPod, MP3 player, or computer. These videos demonstrate how to complete the more challenging objectives in this textbook.

chapterthirteen

Sort and Query a Database

OBJECTIVES

At the end of this chapter, you will be able to:

1. Open an Existing Database
2. Create Table Relationships
3. Sort Records in a Table
4. Create a Query in Design View
5. Create a New Query from an Existing Query
6. Sort Query Results
7. Specify Criteria in a Query

8. Create a New Table by Importing an Excel Spreadsheet
9. Specify Numeric Criteria in a Query
10. Use Compound Criteria
11. Create a Query Based on More Than One Table
12. Use Wildcards in a Query
13. Use Calculated Fields in a Query
14. Group Data and Calculate Statistics in a Query

OUTCOMES

Mastering these objectives will enable you to:

PROJECT 13A
Sort and Query a Database

PROJECT 13B
Create a Database Table from an Excel Spreadsheet and Create Complex Queries

Florida Port Community College

Florida Port Community College is located in St. Petersburg, Florida, a coastal port city located near the Florida High-Tech Corridor. With 60 percent of Florida's high-tech companies and a third of the state's manufacturing companies located in the St. Petersburg and Tampa Bay areas, the college partners with businesses to play a vital role in providing a skilled workforce. The curriculum covers many areas, including medical technology, computer science, electronics, aviation and aerospace, and simulation and modeling. The college also serves the community through cultural, athletic, and diversity programs, and provides adult basic education.

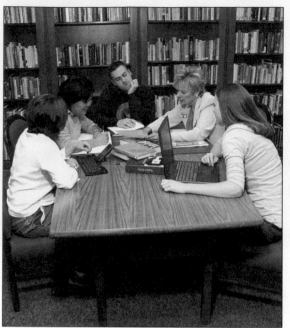

© Dennis MacDonald PhotoEdit Inc.

Sort and Query a Database

To convert data into meaningful information, the data must be manipulated in a way that you can answer questions. One question might be: *What are the names and addresses of students who are enrolled in the Business Information Technology program and who have a grade point average of 3.0 or higher?* With such information, you could send information about scholarships or internships to selected students.

Questions can be answered by sorting the data in a table or by creating a query. Queries enable you to isolate specific data in database tables by limiting the fields that display and by setting conditions that limit the records to those that match specified conditions. You can also use a query to create a new field that is calculated using one or more existing fields. In this chapter, you will sort Access database tables, and create and modify queries.

Project 13A Instructors and Courses

Florida Port Community College uses sorting techniques and queries to locate information in their databases. In Activities 13.01 through 13.13, you will assist Lydia Barwari, the Dean of Business Information Technology, in locating information about instructors and courses in the Business Information Technology Department. Your completed queries and report will look similar to those in Figure 13.1.

For Project 13A, you will need the following file:

a13A_Instructors_and_Courses

You will save your database as
13A_Instructors_and_Courses_Firstname_Lastname

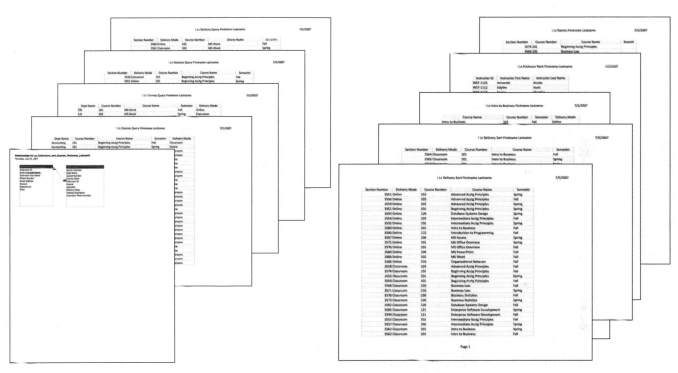

Figure 13.1
Project 13A—Instructors and Courses

Objective 1
Open an Existing Database

There are times when you might want to work with a database and still keep an original copy of the database. Like the other Microsoft Office 2007 applications, you can open a database file and save it with a new name or you can copy the original database to a new storage location and rename it before opening it.

Activity 13.01 Renaming and Opening an Existing Database

1 On the taskbar, click the **Start** button 🔵, and then on the **Start menu**, click **Computer**. Navigate to the location where you are saving your projects for this chapter.

2 On the left side of your screen, click **Organize**, and then click **New Folder**.

> A new folder is created, the words *New Folder* display highlighted in the folder's name box, and the insertion point is blinking. Recall that within Windows, highlighted text is replaced by typing new text.

3 Type **Access Chapter 13** and press Enter to rename the folder.

4 Navigate to the location where the student files that accompany this textbook are stored, and then click one time to select **a13A_Instructors_and_Courses**. Point to the selected file name, right-click, and then click **Copy**.

5 Navigate to and open the **Access Chapter 13** folder you created in Step 3. In an open area, right-click to display a shortcut menu, and then click **Paste**.

> The database file is copied to your folder and is selected.

6 Right-click the selected file name, and then from the shortcut menu, click **Rename**. As shown in Figure 13.2, and using your own first and last name, type **13A_Instructors_and_Courses_Firstname_Lastname**

Alert! **Does your system display file extensions?**

If the Windows operating system on the computer at which you are working is set to display file extensions, be sure to type the new file name in front of the extension, for example: 13A_Instructors_and_Courses_Firstname_Lastname.accdb

---

Figure 13.2

Access Chapter 13 indicated in the title bar

Your name here

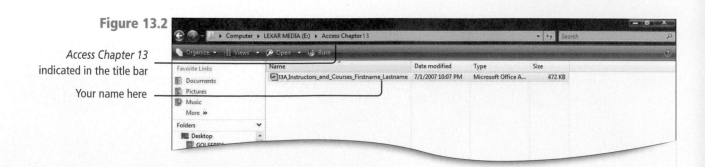

7 Press Enter to save the file with the new name. On the title bar, click **Close** ❌ to close the **Computer** window.

Alert!

Does a Confirm File Rename message display?

If the file you have copied has a Read-only property applied, a message displays to alert you when you attempt to rename the file. In the message box, click Yes to rename the file. Then, right-click the file name, and from the shortcut menu, click Properties. In the Properties dialog box, on the General tab under Attributes, click to clear the Read-only check mark. Click OK to accept the change, and then close the dialog box.

Activity 13.02 Opening an Existing Database and Resolving Security Alerts

The *Message Bar* is the area directly below the Ribbon that displays information such as security alerts when there is potentially unsafe, active content in an Office 2007 document that you open. Settings that determine which alerts display on your Message Bar are set in the Access *Trust Center*, which is an area of the Access program where you can view the security and privacy settings for your Access installation.

You may or may not be able to change the settings in the Trust Center, depending upon decisions made within your organization's computing environment. To display the Trust Center, from the Office menu, in the lower right corner click Access Options, and then click Trust Center.

1 **Start** Access. From the **Office** menu 🔘, click **Open**. In the **Open** dialog box, navigate to your **Access Chapter 13** folder.

2 Click your **13A_Instructors_and_Courses_Firstname_Lastname** database file one time to select it, and then, in the lower right corner, click the **Open** button. Alternatively, double-click the name of the database to open it.

> The database window opens, and the database name displays in the title bar.

3 On the **Message Bar**, check to see if a **Security Warning**, similar to the one shown in Figure 13.3, displays.

Figure 13.3

Database name in title bar

Security Warning message

Message Bar

Options button

4 If a security warning displays, on the **Message Bar**, click the **Options** button. In the **Microsoft Office Security Options** dialog box, click the **Enable this content** option button, and then click **OK** or press Enter.

> When working with the student files that accompany this textbook, repeat these actions each time you see this security warning. Databases provided with this textbook are safe to use on your computer.

Objective 2
Create Table Relationships

Access databases are ***relational databases*** because the tables in the database can relate—actually *connect*—to other tables through ***common fields***. Common fields are fields that contain the same data in more than one table.

After you have set up a table for each subject in your database, you must provide a way to bring that data back together again when you need to create meaningful information. To do this, place common fields in related tables, and then define table ***relationships***. A relationship is an association that you establish between two tables based on common fields. After the relationship is established, you can create a query, a form, or a report that displays information from more than one table.

Activity 13.03 Creating Table Relationships and Enforcing Referential Integrity

In this activity, you will connect a field in one table with a field in another table to create a relationship. The common field between the two tables is Instructor ID; that is, Instructor ID is the field that appears in both tables.

1 **Open** [»] the **Navigation Pane**, and at the top, click the **Navigation Pane arrow** [▾]. Look at the menu to verify that the objects are organized by **Tables and Related Views**. Click outside of the menu to close it, and then compare your screen with Figure 13.4.

> Two objects—the *13A Instructors* table and the *13A Courses* table—display in the Navigation Pane.

Figure 13.4

All Tables displays

13A Instructors Table

13A Courses Table

No objects open in the object window

2 Double-click the **13A Instructors** table and take a moment to examine its contents. Then, open the **13A Courses** table and examine its contents.

In the 13A Instructors table, *Instructor ID* is the primary key field, which ensures that each instructor will appear in the table only one time.

In the 13A Courses table, *Section Number* is the primary key. Each course's record includes the Instructor ID for the instructor who teaches the course.

Because *one* instructor can teach *many* different courses, *one* Instructor ID number can appear *many* times in the 13A Courses table. The relationship between each instructor and the courses is referred to as a ***one-to-many relationship***. This is the most common type of relationship in Access.

3 **Close** ☒ both tables and leave the **Navigation Pane** open. On the Ribbon, click the **Database Tools tab**. In the **Show/Hide group**, click the **Relationships** button to open the Relationships window and to display the **Relationship Tools tab** on the Ribbon.

4 On the **Design tab**, in the **Relationships group**, click the **Show Table** button. In the **Show Table** dialog box, in the list of table objects, click **13A Courses**, and then at the bottom of the dialog box, click **Add**.

Another Way

To Show Tables

If the Show Table dialog box does not display, on the Design tab, in the Query Setup group, click the Show Table button. Alternatively, right-click in the table area, and from the shortcut menu, click Show Table.

5 In the **Show Table** dialog box, double-click **13A Instructors** to add the table to the **Relationships** window, and then click **Close** to close the **Show Table** dialog box.

Use either technique to add a table to the Relationships window. A ***field list***—a list of the field names in a table—for each of the two table objects displays and each table's primary key is identified. Although this database currently has only two tables, larger databases can have many tables.

6 In the **13A Courses** field list, position your mouse pointer over the lower right corner of the field list to display the 🔍 pointer, and then drag down and to the right to increase the height and width of the field list until the names of each field are completely displayed.

Expanding the field list enables you to see all of the available fields, and removes the vertical scroll bar.

7 Use the 🔍 pointer to resize the **13A Instructors** field list so that all of the field names are visible. One at a time, point to the title bar of each field list and by dragging, position the expanded field lists approximately as shown in Figure 13.5.

Recall that *one* instructor can teach *many* courses. Arranging the tables in this manner on your screen displays the *one table* on the left side and the *many table* on the right side.

Recall that the primary key in each table is the field that uniquely identifies the record in each table. In the Instructors table, each instructor is uniquely identified by the Instructor ID. In the Courses table, each course section offered is uniquely identified by the Section Number.

Relationship Tools

Field list for table 13A Courses (*many table*)

Figure 13.5

Relationships tab in object window

Primary key identified in each table

Field list for table 13A Instructors (*one table*)

Instructor ID is the common field between the two tables

Note — Highlighted Field Does Not Matter

As the two field lists in the Relationships window are rearranged, the highlighted field indicates the active field list, which is the list you moved last, and the active field. This is of no consequence for completing the activity.

8 In the **13A Instructors** field list, point to **Instructor ID**, hold down the left mouse button, and then drag to the right to the **13A Courses** field list until your mouse pointer is on top of **Instructor ID** as shown in Figure 13.6. Then release the mouse button.

As you drag, a small graphic displays to indicate that you are dragging a field from one field list to another. The Edit Relationships dialog box displays.

A table relationship works by matching data in two fields—the common field. In these two tables the common field has the same name—Instructor ID. Common fields are not required to have the same names; however, they must have the same data type and field size.

Figure 13.6

Icon indicates you
are dragging the
primary key field
to another table

9 Point to the title bar of the **Edit Relationships** dialog box, and then drag the dialog box below the two field lists as shown in Figure 13.7.

Both tables include the Instructor ID field—that is the common field between the two tables. By dragging, you created the one-to-many relationship. In the Instructors table, Instructor ID is the primary key. In the Courses table, Instructor ID is referred to as the ***foreign key*** field. The foreign key is the field that is included in the related table so the field can be joined with the primary key in another table.

The field on the *one* side of the relationship is typically the primary key. Recall that *one* instructor can teach *many* courses. Thus, *one* instructor record in the Instructors table can be related to *many* course records in the Courses table.

Figure 13.7

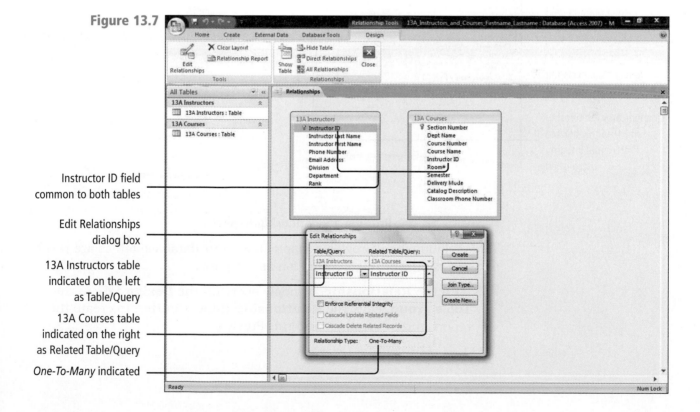

Instructor ID field
common to both tables

Edit Relationships
dialog box

13A Instructors table
indicated on the left
as Table/Query

13A Courses table
indicated on the right
as Related Table/Query

One-To-Many indicated

Another Way

To Create a Table Relationship

With the tables displayed in the Relationships window, rather than dragging one field into another field list, instead, click the Edit Relationships button on the Ribbon, click Create New, and then in the Create New dialog box, designate the Left and Right tables and fields that will create the relationship.

10 In the **Edit Relationships** dialog box, click to select the **Enforce Referential Integrity** check box.

> *Referential integrity* is a set of rules that Access uses to ensure that the data between related tables is valid. Enforcing referential integrity ensures that a course cannot be added to the 13A Courses table with the name of an instructor that is *not* included in the 13A Instructors table, ensuring that you do not have courses listed in the 13A Courses table without a corresponding instructor in the 13A Instructors table. Similarly, you cannot delete an Instructor from the 13A Instructors table if there is a course listed for that instructor in the 13A Courses table.

11 In the upper right corner of the **Edit Relationships** dialog box, click the **Create** button, and then compare your screen with Figure 13.8.

> A *join line*—the line joining two tables—displays between the two tables. On the join line, *1* indicates the *one* side of the relationship, and the infinity symbol (∞) indicates the *many* side of the relationship. These symbols display when referential integrity is enforced.

Figure 13.8

Common field in both tables

Join line connects the two common fields

Line indicates relationship and 1 and ∞ indicate referential integrity established

Activity 13.04 Printing a Relationship Report

Table relationships provide a map of how your database tables are related, and you can print this information as a report.

1 With the **Relationships** window open, on the **Design tab**, in the **Tools group**, click the **Relationship Report** button to create the report and to display it in Print Preview.

2 On the **Print Preview tab**, in the **Page Layout group**, click the **Margins** button, and then click **Normal**. Compare your screen with Figure 13.9.

Figure 13.9

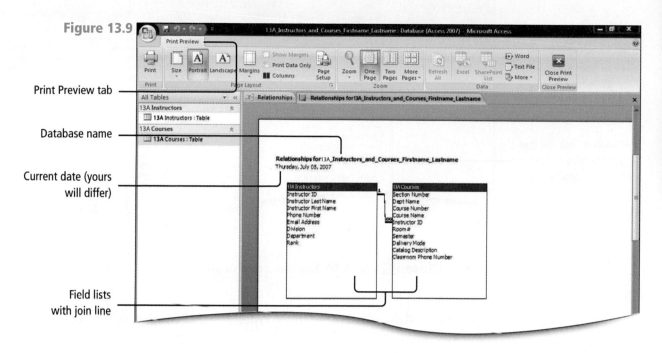

Print Preview tab

Database name

Current date (yours will differ)

Field lists with join line

3 If you are submitting your results from this project on paper, on the **Print Preview tab**, in the **Print group**, click the **Print** button. In the **Print** dialog box, click **OK**. In the **Close Preview group**, click the **Close Print Preview** button. To submit electronically, follow the directions provided by your instructor.

4 On the **Quick Access Toolbar**, click the **Save** button 🖫 to save the report. In the **Save As** dialog box, click **OK** to accept the default name.

> The report name displays in the Navigation Pane under *Unrelated Objects*. Because the report is just a map of the relationships and not a report containing actual records, it is not associated with either of the tables.

5 In the object window, **Close** ✕ the report, and then **Close** ✕ the **Relationships** window.

6 In the **Navigation Pane**, open the **13A Instructors** table. On the left side of the table, in the first record, point to the **plus sign** (+), and then click one time. If the Field List pane displays on the right side of the screen, click the Close button to remove it from the screen. Compare your screen with Figure 13.10.

> Plus signs to the left of a record in a table indicate that *related* records exist in another table. In the first record for *Julie Adeeb*, you can see that related records exist in the Courses table—she is teaching six courses. The plus sign displays because you created a relationship between the two tables using the Instructor ID field—the common field.

Figure 13.10

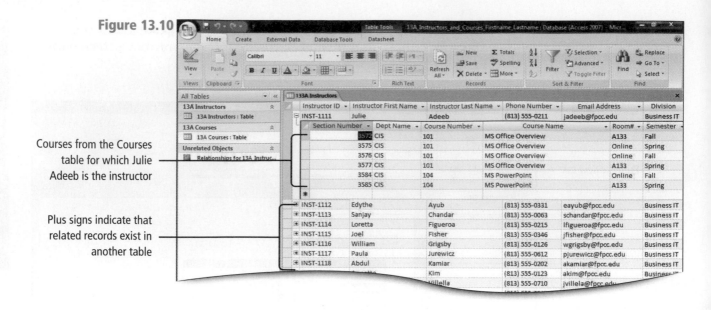

Courses from the Courses
table for which Julie
Adeeb is the instructor

Plus signs indicate that
related records exist in
another table

7 **Close** ☒ the **13A Instructors** table.

More Knowledge — Other Types of Relationships: One-to-One and Many-to-Many

There are other relationships you can create using the same process in the Relationships window. The type of relationship is determined by the placement of the primary key field. A one-to-one relationship exists between two tables when a record in one table is related to a single record in a second table. In this case, both tables use the same field as the primary key. This is most often used when data is placed in a separate table because access to the information is restricted.

You can also create a many-to-many relationship between tables, where many records in one table can be related to many records in another table. For example, many students can enroll in many courses. To create a many-to-many relationship, you must create a third table that contains the primary key fields from the tables. These primary key fields are then joined to their related fields in the other tables. In effect, you create multiple one-to-one relationships.

Objective 3
Sort Records in a Table

Sorting is the process of arranging data in a specific order based on the value in a field. For example, you could sort the names in your address book alphabetically by each person's last name, or you could sort your CD collection by the date of purchase.

Initially, records in an Access table display in the order in which they are entered into the table. After a primary key is established, the records are displayed in order based on the primary key field.

Activity 13.05 Sorting Records in a Table in Ascending or Descending Order

In the following activity, you will determine the courses in the Business Information Technology Division that will be offered each semester by sorting the data. You can sort data in either *ascending order* or *descending order*. Ascending order sorts text alphabetically (A to Z) and sorts numbers from the lowest number to the highest number. Descending order sorts text in reverse alphabetical order (Z to A) and sorts numbers from the highest number to the lowest number.

1 From the **Navigation Pane**, open the **13A Courses** table, and then **Close** « the **Navigation Pane**. Notice that the records are sorted in ascending order by Section Number, which is the primary key field.

2 In the field names row, click the **Dept Name arrow**, click **Sort A to Z**, and then compare your screen with Figure 13.11.

> To sort records in a table, click the arrow to the right of the field name in the column on which you want to sort, and then choose the sort order. After a field is sorted, a small arrow after the field name indicates its sort order. The small arrow after the field name points upward indicating an ascending sort, and in the Ribbon, the Ascending button is selected.

> The records display in alphabetical order by Dept Name. Because like names are now grouped together, you can quickly scroll the length of the table to see how many courses are offered by each department.

Figure 13.11

Ascending button selected
Small arrow indicates order in which field is sorted

Records sorted alphabetically by Dept Name

3 In the **Sort & Filter group**, click the **Clear All Sorts** button to clear all of the sorts and to return the records to the default sort order, which is by the primary key field—*Section Number*.

4 If necessary, scroll to the right, click the **Semester arrow**, and then click **Sort Z to A**.

> The records in the table are sorted by semester in reverse alphabetical order; thus *Spring* courses are listed before *Fall* courses. The small arrow in the Field name points down indicating a descending sort, and in the Ribbon, the Descending button is selected.

Activity 13.06 Sorting Records in a Table on Multiple Fields

To sort a table on two or more fields, first identify the fields that will act as the *outermost sort field* and the *innermost sort field*. The outermost sort field is the first level of sorting, and the innermost sort field is the second level of sorting. For example, you might want to sort first by the last name field, which would be the outermost sort field, and then by the first name field, which would be the innermost sort field. After you identify your outermost and innermost sort fields, sort the innermost field first, and then sort the outermost field.

Lydia Barwari, the Dean, would like to display the course names in alphabetical order by delivery mode, with online classes listed first. Access enables you to sort on two or more fields in a table.

1 On the **Home tab**, in the **Sort & Filter group**, click the **Clear All Sorts** button 🔽 to clear any sorts from the previous activity. In the **Delivery Mode** field, click any record. In the **Sort & Filter group**, click the **Descending** button 🔽.

> The records are sorted in descending alphabetical order by Delivery Mode, with Online courses listed before Classroom courses. The Delivery Mode field is the innermost sort field.

2 Point anywhere in the **Course Name** field, and then right-click. From the shortcut menu, click **Sort A to Z**. Notice the first four records in the **Course Name** column, for *Advanced Acctg Principles*, and then compare your screen with Figure 13.12.

> The records are sorted first by Course Name—the *outermost* sort field—and then within a specific Course Name grouping, the sort continues in descending alphabetical order by Delivery Mode—the *innermost* sort field. The records are sorted on multiple fields using both ascending and descending order.

Figure 13.12

Within each *Course Name*, *Online* and *Classroom* sorted in descending order

Small arrows indicate sort order in each column

Course Name column sorted in ascending order

3 In the **Sort & Filter group**, click the **Clear All Sorts** button 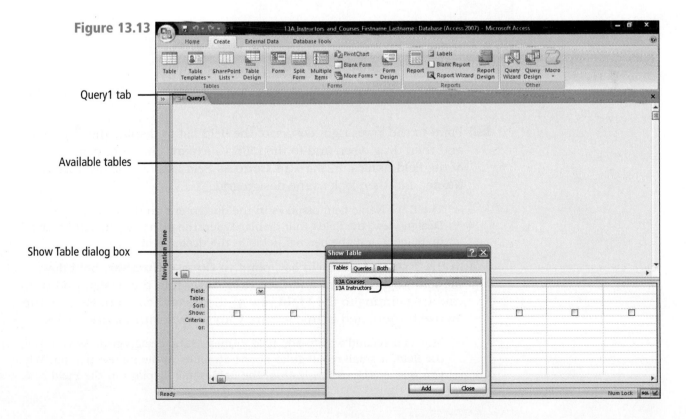. In the object window, **Close** ✕ the table. In the message box, click **No**; you do not need to save any design changes.

Objective 4
Create a Query in Design View

Recall that a *select query* is a database object that retrieves (selects) specific data from one or more tables and then displays the specified data in Datasheet view. A query answers a question such as *Which instructors are teaching CIS courses in the Fall semester?* Unless a query has already been set up to ask this question, you must create a new query.

Database users rarely need to see all of the records in all of the tables. That is why a query is so useful; it creates a subset of records according to your specifications, and then displays only those records.

Activity 13.07 Creating a New Select Query in Design View

Previously, you created a query using the Query Wizard. To create complex queries, use Query Design view instead of the Query Wizard. Recall that the table or tables from which a query selects its data is referred to as the *data source*.

1 On the Ribbon, click the **Create tab**, and then in the **Other group**, click the **Query Design** button. Compare your screen with Figure 13.13.

A new query opens in Design view and the Show Table dialog box displays, which lists all of the tables in the database.

Figure 13.13

Query1 tab

Available tables

Show Table dialog box

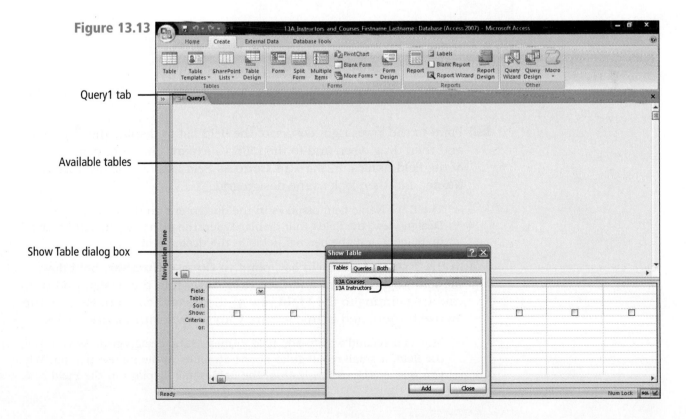

2 In the **Show Table** dialog box, click **13A Courses**, click the **Add** button, and then **Close** the **Show Table** dialog box. Alternatively, double-click a table name to add it to the Query window. Compare your screen with Figure 13.14.

A field list for the 13A Courses table displays in the upper area of the Query window. The Section Number field is the primary key field.

The Query window has two parts: the *table area* (upper area), which displays the field lists for tables that are used in the query, and the *design grid* (lower area), which displays the design of the query.

Figure 13.14

3 Point to the lower right corner of the field list to display the pointer, and then drag down and to the right to expand the field, displaying all of the field names. In the **13A Courses** field list, double-click **Dept Name**, and then look at the design grid.

The Dept Name field displays in the design grid in the Field row. In Design view, the fields that display when the query is run can be limited by placing only the desired fields in the design grid.

4 In the **13A Courses** field list, point to **Course Number**, hold down the left mouse button, and then drag down into the design grid until you are pointing to the **Field** row in the second column. Release the mouse button, and then compare your screen with Figure 13.15.

This is a second way to add field names to the design grid. As you drag the field, a small rectangular shape attaches to the mouse pointer. When you release the mouse button, the field name displays in the Field row.

Figure 13.15

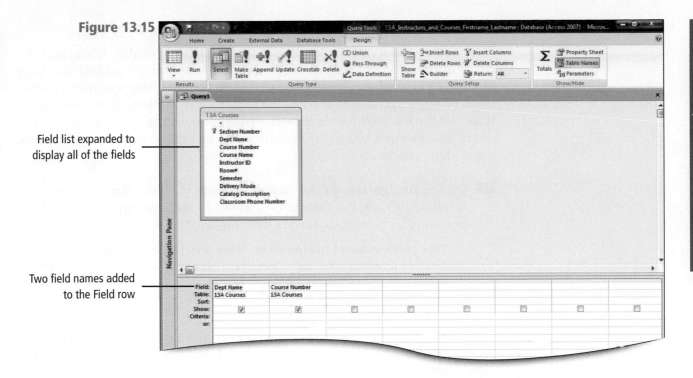

Field list expanded to
display all of the fields

Two field names added
to the Field row

---

5 In design grid, in the **Field** row, click in the third column, and then click the **arrow** that displays. From the list, click **Course Name** to add the field to the design grid, which is a third way to add a field to the design grid.

6 Using one of the techniques you practiced, add the **Semester** field to the fourth column in the design grid, and then add the **Delivery Mode** field to the fifth column in the design grid. Compare your screen with Figure 13.16.

Figure 13.16

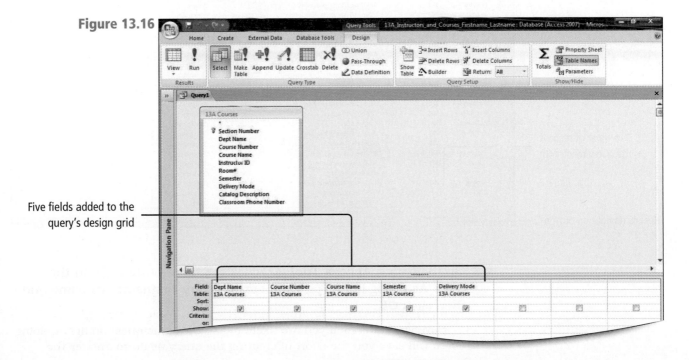

Five fields added to the
query's design grid

Activity 13.08 Running, Saving, Printing, and Closing a Query

After you create a query, you *run* it to display the results. When you run a query, Access looks at the records in the table (or tables) you have included in the query, finds the records that match the specified conditions (if any), and displays those records in a datasheet. Only the fields that you have added to the design grid display in the query results. The query always runs using the current table or tables, presenting the most up-to-date information.

1 On the **Design tab**, in the **Results group**, click the **Run** button. Alternatively, on the Design tab, in the Results group, click the View button. Compare your screen with Figure 13.17.

> This query answers the question, *What are the Dept Name, Course Number, Course Name, Semester, and Delivery Mode of all of the courses in the 13A Courses table?* A query is a subset of the records in one or more tables, arranged in Datasheet view, using the fields and conditions that you specify.

> The five fields that you specified display in columns, the records from the 13A Courses table display in rows, and navigation buttons display at the bottom of the window.

Figure 13.17

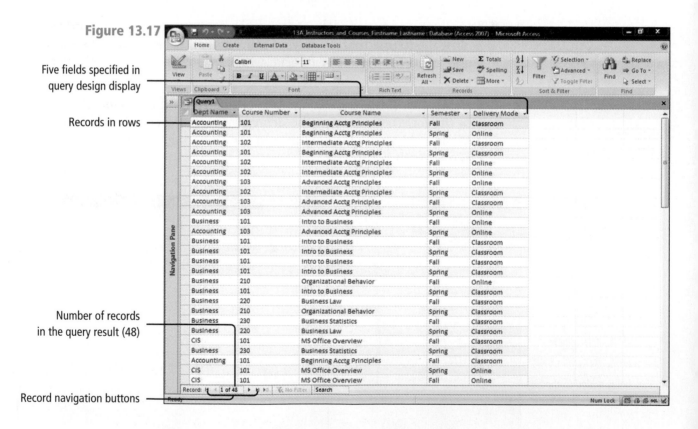

Five fields specified in query design display

Records in rows

Number of records in the query result (48)

Record navigation buttons

2 On the **Quick Access Toolbar**, click the **Save** button. In the **Save As** dialog box, type **13A Courses Query Firstname Lastname** and then click **OK**.

> Save your queries if you are likely to ask the same question again; doing so will save you the effort of creating the query again to answer the same question.

3 From the **Office** menu 🅑, point to the **Print** button, and then click **Print Preview**. In the **Page Layout group**, click the **Landscape** button. In the **Zoom group**, click the **Two Pages** button to see how the query will print on two pages. If you are printing your assignments on paper, click the **Print** button, and then in the **Print** dialog box, click **OK**. Click the **Close Print Preview** button. To submit electronically, follow the directions provided by your instructor.

> Two pages will print. Queries are created to answer questions and to create information from the data in the tables. Queries are typically created as a basis for a report. Query results can also be printed.

4 **Close** ✕ the query. **Open** 》 the **Navigation Pane**, and then compare your screen with Figure 13.18.

> The query is saved and closed. The new query name displays in the Navigation Pane under the table with which it is related—the *13A Courses* table. Only the design of the query is saved. The records still reside in the table object.
>
> Each time you open a query, Access runs it again and displays the results based on the data stored in the related table(s). Thus, the results of a query always reflect the latest information in the related table(s).

Figure 13.18

New query displays under table name with which it is associated

Objective 5
Create a New Query from an Existing Query

You can create a new query from scratch or you can open an existing query, save it with new name, and then modify the design to suit your needs. Using an existing query saves you time if your new query will use all or some of the same fields and conditions that are specified in the existing query.

Activity 13.09 Creating a New Query from an Existing Query

1 From the **Navigation Pane**, open your **13A Courses Query** by either double-clicking the name or by right-clicking and clicking Open.

> The query runs and opens in Datasheet view, displaying the records from the 13A Courses table as specified in the query design.

2 From the **Office** menu 🔘, click **Save As**. In the **Save As** dialog box, type **13A Sections Query Firstname Lastname** and then click **OK**. On the **Home tab**, in the **Views group**, click the **View** button to switch to **Design** view. Compare your screen with Figure 13.19.

A new query, based on a copy of the 13A Courses Query, is created and displays in the object window and on the Navigation Pane. The query displays in Design view.

Figure 13.19

New 13*A Sections* query in object window

New query 13*A Sections* displays in Navigation Pane

Selection bar in design grid

3 **Close** « the **Navigation Pane**. In the design grid, point to the thin gray selection bar above the **Dept Name** field name until the ⬇ pointer displays. Click to select the **Dept Name** column, and then press Delete.

The Dept Name field is removed from the design grid and the remaining four fields move to the left. This action deletes the field from the query design only—it has no effect on the underlying 13A Courses table.

4 In the gray selection bar, select the **Delivery Mode** column. In the selected column, point to the **selection bar** to display the ⬉ pointer, and then drag to the left until a dark vertical line displays on the left side of the Course Number column. Release the mouse button to position the **Delivery Mode** field in the first column.

To rearrange fields in the query design, first select the field to move, and then drag it to a new position in the design grid.

5 From the field list, add the **Section Number** field as the fifth column in the design grid. Then, select and move the **Section Number** field to the first column in the design grid. Click outside of the grid to cancel the selection, and then compare your screen with Figure 13.20.

Figure 13.20

Selection bar

Five fields in the design grid

Section Number is in the first field position

Delivery Mode is in the second field position

6 On the **Design tab**, in the **Results group**, click the **Run** button. Notice the five fields that display, and then compare your screen with Figure 13.21.

> This query answers the question, *What are the Section Number, Delivery Mode, Course Number, Course Name, and Semester of every course in the 13A Courses table?* The results of the query are a subset of the records contained in the 13A Courses table.

Figure 13.21

7 From the **Office** menu 🔘, point to the **Print** button, and then click **Print Preview**. On the **Print Preview tab**, in the **Page Layout group**, click **Landscape**. In the **Zoom group**, click the **Two Pages** button to view how your query will print on two pages.

8 If you are printing on paper, in the **Print group**, click the **Print** button. In the **Print** dialog box, click **OK**. Click the **Close Print Preview** button. To submit electronically, follow your instructor's directions.

9 **Close** ☒ the query, and in the message box, click **Yes** to save the changes to the design. **Open** ⯈ the **Navigation Pane**, and then compare your screen with Figure 13.22.

> The query is saved and closed. The new query name displays in the Navigation Pane under the related table. Recall that when you save a query, only the *design* of the query is saved; the records reside in the related table object(s).

Figure 13.22

Your 13A Sections query ————

Objective 6
Sort Query Results

You can sort the results of a query in ascending or descending order. Because the results of a query are formatted like a table in Datasheet view, the process for sorting is identical to sorting in a table; however, data in a query can also be sorted in Design view.

Activity 13.10 Sorting Query Results

In this activity, you will open an existing query, save it with a new name, and then sort the query results.

1 From the **Navigation Pane**, open your **13A Sections Query**. From the **Office** menu 🔘, click **Save As**. In the **Save As** dialog box, type **13A Delivery Sort Firstname Lastname** and then click **OK**.

> Access creates a new query, based on a copy of your 13A Sections Query.

2 **Close** ◀◀ the **Navigation Pane**, and then on the **Home tab**, in the **Views group**, click the **View** button to switch to **Design** view.

3 In the design grid, in the **Sort** row, click in the **Delivery Mode** field to display the insertion point and an arrow. Click the **Sort arrow**, and then in the list, click **Descending**. Compare your screen with Figure 13.23.

Figure 13.23

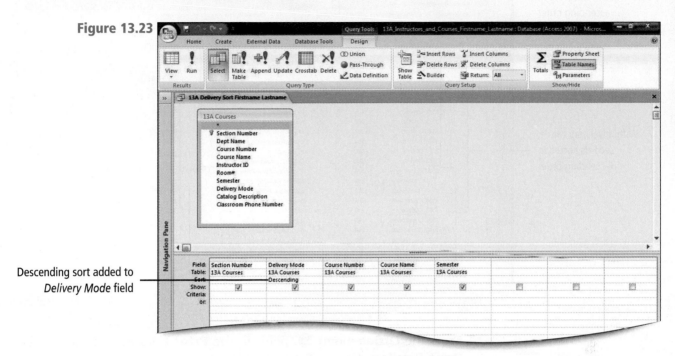

Descending sort added to *Delivery Mode* field

4 In the **Sort** row, under **Course Name**, click to display the **Sort arrow**, click the arrow, and then click **Ascending**.

5 On the **Design tab**, in the **Results group**, click the **Run** button, and then compare your screen with Figure 13.24.

Fields with a Sort designation are sorted from left to right. That is, the sorted field on the left becomes the outermost sort field, and the sorted field on the right becomes the innermost sort field. Thus, the records are sorted first in descending alphabetical order by the Delivery Mode field—the leftmost sort field. Then, within each Delivery Mode field, the Course Names are sorted in ascending alphabetical order.

Figure 13.24

Within Course Name, records sorted in ascending order

Within Delivery Mode, records sorted in descending order

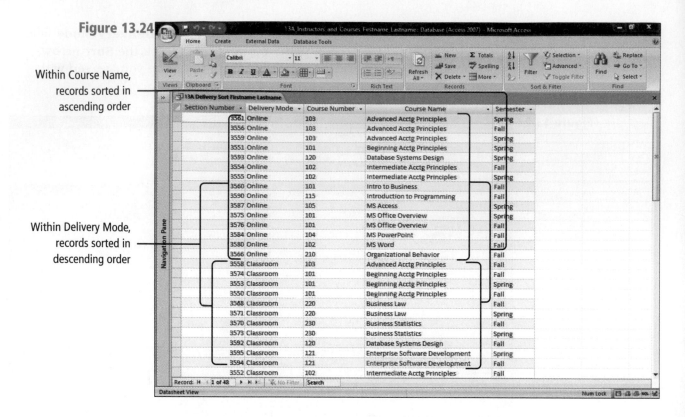

6 From the **Office** menu 😊, point to the **Print** button, and then click **Print Preview**. On the **Print Preview tab**, in the **Page Layout group**, click **Landscape**.

7 In the **Zoom group**, click the **Two Pages** button to view the layout of the pages. If you are printing on paper, in the **Print group**, click the **Print** button. In the **Print** dialog box, click **OK**. Click the **Close Print Preview** button. To submit electronically, follow your instructor's directions.

8 **Close** ☒ the query. In the message box, click **Yes** to save the changes to the query design.

More Knowledge — Sorting

If you add a sort order to the *design* of a query, it remains as a permanent part of the query design. If you use the sort buttons in the Datasheet view, it will override the sort order of the query design, and can be saved as part of the query. A sort order designated in Datasheet view will not display in the Sort row of the query design grid.

Objective 7
Specify Criteria in a Query

Queries can locate information in an Access database based on **criteria** that you specify as part of the query. Criteria are conditions that identify the specific records for which you are looking.

Criteria enable you to ask a more specific question; therefore, you will get a more specific result. For example, if you want to find out how many *Business Law* courses will be offered in the Fall and Spring semesters, limit the results to that specific course name, and then only the records that match the specified course name will display.

Activity 13.11 Specifying Text Criteria in a Query

In this activity, you will assist Lydia by creating a query to answer the question, *How many sections of Intro to Business will be offered in the Fall and Spring semesters?*

1 Be sure that all objects are closed and that the **Navigation Pane** is closed. Click the **Create tab**, and then in the **Other group**, click the **Query Design** button.

2 In the **Show Table** dialog box, **Add** the **13A Courses** table to the table area, and then **Close** the **Show Table** dialog box.

3 Expand the field list. Add the following fields to the design grid in the order given: **Course Name**, **Course Number**, **Semester**, and **Delivery Mode**.

4 In the **Criteria** row of the design grid, click in the **Course Name** field, type **Intro to Business** and then press [Enter]. Compare your screen with Figure 13.25.

> Access places quotation marks around the criteria to indicate that this is a *text string*—a sequence of characters. Use the Criteria row to specify the criteria that will limit the results of the query to your exact specifications.

Figure 13.25

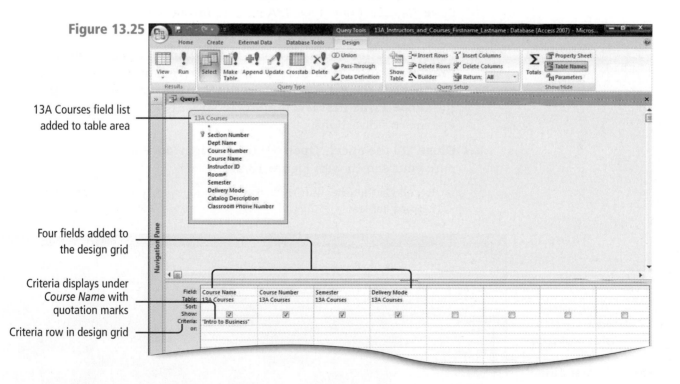

13A Courses field list added to table area

Four fields added to the design grid

Criteria displays under *Course Name* with quotation marks

Criteria row in design grid

5 **Run** the query, and then compare your screen with Figure 13.26.

Six records display that meet the specified criteria—records that have *Intro to Business* in the Course Name field.

Figure 13.26

Query result with records matching Course Name *Intro to Business* criteria

Alert!

Do your query results differ?

If you mistype the criteria, enter it under the wrong field, or make some other error, the result will display no records. This indicates that there are no records in the table that match the criteria as you entered it. If this occurs, return to the Design view and reexamine the query design. Verify that the criteria is typed on the Criteria row, under the correct field, and that there are no typing errors. Then rerun the query.

6 On the **Quick Access Toolbar**, click the **Save** button 🖫. In the **Save As** dialog box, type **13A Intro to Business Firstname Lastname** and then click **OK**.

7 From the **Office** menu 🗎, point to **Print**, and then click **Print Preview**. If you are printing your assignments on paper, in the **Print group**, click the **Print** button. In the **Print** dialog box, click **OK**. Click the **Close Print Preview** button. To submit electronically, follow your instructor's directions.

8 **Close** ✕ the query, **Open** ≫ the **Navigation Pane**, and then compare your screen with Figure 13.27.

Recall that queries in the Navigation Pane display an icon of two overlapping tables.

Figure 13.27

Queries display a distinctive icon of two tables overlapping

Four queries created based on 13A Courses table

Activity 13.12 Specifying Criteria Using a Field Not Displayed in the Query Results

So far, all of the fields that you included in the query design have also been included in the query results. It is not required to have every field in the query display in the result. In this activity, you will assist Lydia by creating a query to answer the question, *Which instructors have a rank of Professor?*

1 **Close** « the **Navigation Pane**. Click the **Create tab**, and then in the **Other group**, click the **Query Design** button.

2 From the **Show Table** dialog box, **Add** the **13A Instructors** table to the table area, and then **Close** the dialog box. Expand the field list.

3 Add the following fields, in the order given, to the design grid: **Instructor ID**, **Instructor First Name**, **Instructor Last Name**, and **Rank**.

4 In the **Sort** row, click in the **Instructor Last Name** field, click the **arrow**, and then click **Ascending**.

5 In the **Criteria** row, click in the **Rank** field, type **Professor** and then press [Enter]. Compare your screen with Figure 13.28.

When you press [Enter], the insertion point moves to the next criteria box and quotation marks are added around the text string that you entered.

Figure 13.28

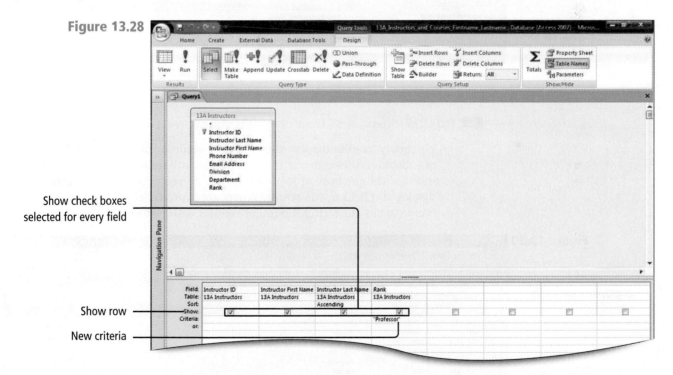

Show check boxes selected for every field

Show row

New criteria

6 In the design grid, in the **Show** row, notice that the check box is selected for every field. **Run** the query to view the result of the query.

Six records meet the criteria. In the Rank column each record displays *Professor*.

7 On the **Home tab**, in the **Views group**, click the **View** button to switch to **Design** view. In the design grid, under **Rank**, in the **Show** row, click to clear the check box, and then compare your screen with Figure 13.29.

Because it is repetitive and not particularly useful to have *Professor* display for each record in the query results, clear this check box so that the field does not display.

Figure 13.29

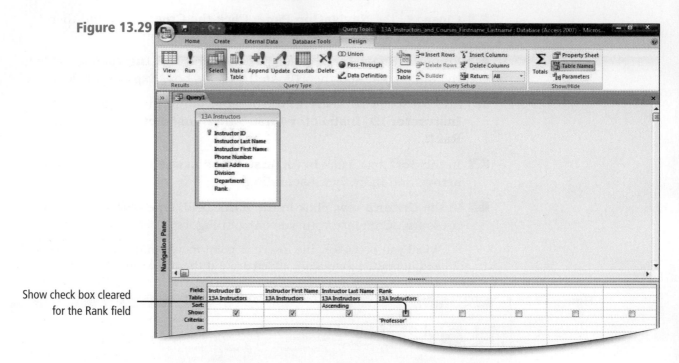

Show check box cleared
for the Rank field

8 **Run** the query, and then compare your screen with Figure 13.30.

The query results display the same six records, but the *Rank* field does not display. Although the Rank field was still included in the query criteria for the purpose of identifying specific records, it is not necessary to display the field in the result. When appropriate, clear the Show check box to avoid cluttering the query results with redundant data.

Figure 13.30

Rank field not
displayed in the result

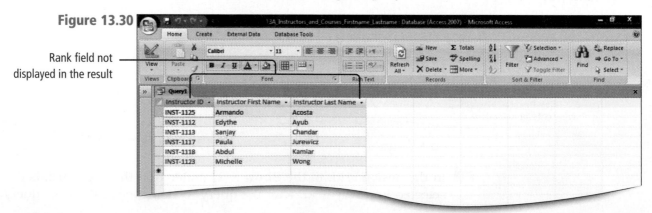

9 On the **Quick Access Toolbar**, click the **Save** button. In the **Save As** dialog box, type **13A Professor Rank Firstname Lastname** and then click **OK**.

10 From the **Office** menu ⊛, point to **Print**, and then click **Print Preview**. If you are printing your assignments on paper, in the **Print group**, click the **Print** button. In the **Print** dialog box, click **OK**. Click the **Close Print Preview** button. To submit electronically, follow your instructor's directions.

11 **Close** ✕ the query, **Open** ≫ the **Navigation Pane**, and then notice that the query is listed under the table with which it is related—the *13A Instructors* table.

Activity 13.13 Using Is Null Criteria to Find Empty Fields

Sometimes you must locate records where data is *missing*. You can locate such records by using *is null*—empty—as the criteria in a field. Additionally, you can display only the records where a value *has* been entered in a field by using *is not null* as the criteria, which will exclude records where the specified field is empty.

In this activity, you will help Lydia design a query to find out *Which course sections have not yet had a classroom assigned?*

1 **Close** ≪ the **Navigation Pane**. Click the **Create tab**, and then in the **Other group**, click the **Query Design** button. **Add** the **13A Courses** table to the table area, and then **Close** the **Show Table** dialog box. Expand the field list.

2 Add the following fields to the design grid in the order given: **Section Number**, **Course Number**, **Course Name**, and **Room#**.

3 On the **Criteria** row, click in the **Room#** field, type **Is Null** and then press Enter. Alternatively, type *is null* and Access will change the criteria to display with capital letters. Compare your screen with Figure 13.31.

> The criteria *Is Null* examines the field and looks for records that do *not* have any values entered in the Room# field, enabling you to determine which courses still need an assigned classroom.

Figure 13.31

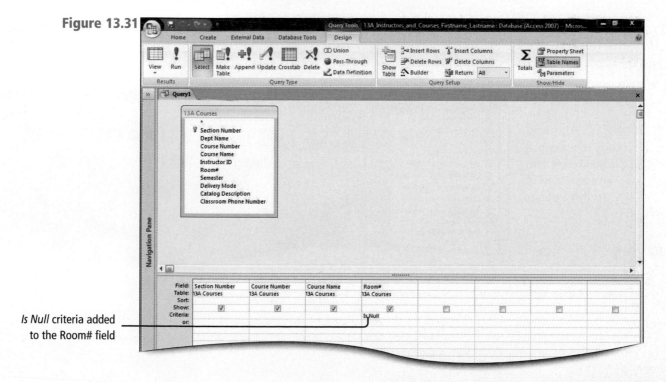

Is Null criteria added to the Room# field

4 On the **Sort** row, click in the **Course Name** field, click the **Sort arrow**, and then click **Ascending**. **Run** the query, and then compare your screen with Figure 13.32.

> Five course sections do not have a Room# assigned—the Room# field is empty. The course names are sorted in ascending (alphabetical) order.

Figure 13.32

Records sorted in ascending order by *Course Name* field

5 **Save** the query as **13A Rooms Firstname Lastname**

6 From the **Office** menu, point to **Print**, and then click **Print Preview**. If you are printing your assignments on paper, in the **Print group**, click the **Print** button. In the **Print** dialog box, click **OK**. Click the **Close Print Preview** button. To submit electronically, follow your instructor's directions.

7 **Close** the query. **Open** the **Navigation Pane**, and then compare your screen with Figure 13.33.

> Each query that you created displays under the table with which it is related. The objects display in alphabetical order.

Figure 13.33

Query objects display, in alphabetical order, with table on which they are based

8 **Close** the **Navigation Pane** and be sure that all objects are closed.

9 From the **Office** ⊙ menu, click **Close Database**, and then at the right edge of the Access title bar, click the **Close** button ❎ to close the Access program. Alternatively, from the Office menu, click Exit Access.

End **You have completed Project 13A**————————————

Project 13B **Athletes and Scholarships**

In Activities 13.14 through 13.25, you will assist Marcus Simmons, Athletic Director for Florida Port Community College, in developing and querying his Athletes and Scholarships database. In this database, Mr. Simmons tracks the scholarships awarded to student athletes. Your completed Relationship report and queries will look similar to those in Figure 13.34.

For Project 13B, you will need the following files:

a13B_Athletes_and_Scholarships
a13B_Athletes (Excel file)

You will save your database as
13B_Athletes_and_Scholarships_Firstname_Lastname

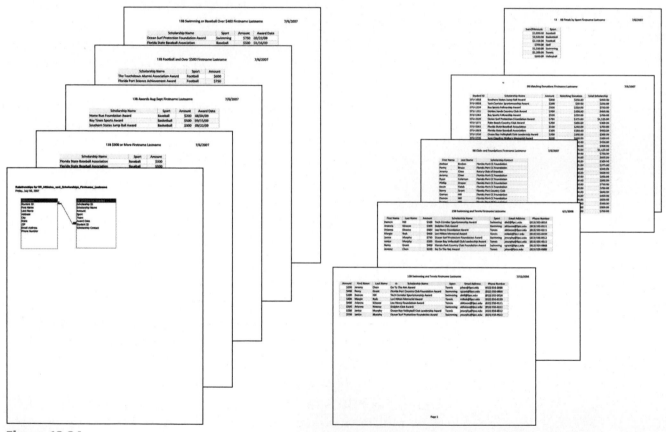

Figure 13.34

Objective 8
Create a New Table by Importing an Excel Spreadsheet

Many users of Microsoft Office track their data in an Excel spreadsheet. The sorting and filtering capabilities of Excel are useful for a simple database where all the information resides in one large Excel spreadsheet.

Excel is limited as a database management tool because it cannot support multiple tables, nor can it *relate* the information so that you can retrieve information from multiple spreadsheets using a query. However, data in an Excel spreadsheet can easily become an Access table by importing the spreadsheet because Excel's format of columns and rows is similar to that of an Access table.

Activity 13.14 Opening an Existing Database and Preparing to Import an Excel Spreadsheet

In this activity, you will open, rename, and save an existing database, and then examine an Excel spreadsheet that Mr. Simmons wants to bring into Access as a new table.

1 On the taskbar, click the **Start** button 🌐, and then click **Computer**. Navigate to the student files that accompany this textbook, and then click one time to select **a13B_Athletes_and_Scholarships**.

2 Point to the selected file name, right-click to display a shortcut menu, and then click **Copy**. Navigate to and open the **Access Chapter 13** folder you created in Project 13A. In an open area, right-click to display a shortcut menu, and then click **Paste**.

3 Right-click the selected file name, and then click **Rename**. Using your own first and last name type **13B_Athletes_and_Scholarships_Firstname_Lastname** and then press Enter to save the new file name. **Close** ❎ the **Computer** window.

4 **Start** Access. From the **Office** menu 🪟, click **Open**. In the **Open** dialog box, navigate to your **Access Chapter 13** folder, and then open the **13B_Athletes_and_Scholarships** database file.

5 On the **Message Bar**, click the **Options** button. In the **Microsoft Office Security Options** dialog box, click the **Enable this content** option button, and then click **OK**.

6 **Open** 》 the **Navigation Pane**, and then open the **13B Scholarships Awarded** table. **Close** 《 the **Navigation Pane**, and then take a moment to examine the data in the table. Compare your screen with Figure 13.35.

> In this table, Mr. Simmons tracks the names and amounts of scholarships awarded to student athletes. Students are identified only by their Student ID numbers, and the primary key is the Scholarship ID field.

Figure 13.35

Student ID of student receiving scholarship

Scholarship Name field

Amount field

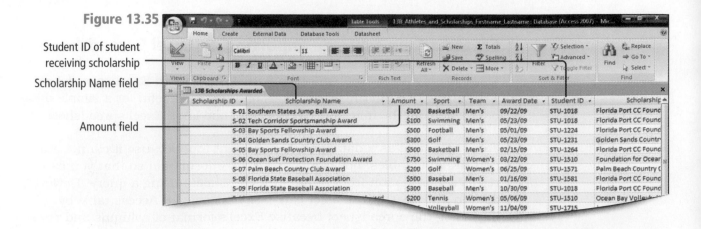

7 **Close** ⊠ the table. Click **Start** 🔘, and then locate and open **Microsoft Office Excel 2007**. In Excel, from the **Office** menu 🔘, click **Open**. Navigate to the student files for this textbook, and then open **a13B_Athletes**. Compare your screen with Figure 13.36.

> Mr. Simmons created an Excel spreadsheet to store the names, addresses, and other information of all of the student athletes.
>
> Because *one* athlete can receive *many* scholarships, Mr. Simmons can see that using Access, rather than Excel, and having two *related* tables of information, will enable him to track and query this information more efficiently.

Figure 13.36

Excel spreadsheet containing student information

Student ID field

8 In the Excel spreadsheet, notice that in **row 1**, the column titles are similar to the field names in an Access table, and that each row contains the information for one student, representing a record. From the **Office** menu 🔘, in the lower right corner of the menu, click **Exit Excel**.

Activity 13.15 Creating a New Table by Importing an Excel Spreadsheet

In this activity, you will create a new Access table by importing the Excel spreadsheet containing the names and addresses of the student athletes, create a one-to-many relationship between the new table and the 13B Scholarships Awarded table, enforce referential integrity, and then print a Relationship report.

1 **Open** **»** the **Navigation Pane**. On the Ribbon, click the **External Data tab**, and then in the **Import group**, click the **Excel button**. In the **Get External Data – Excel Spreadsheet** dialog box, to the right of the **File name** box, click **Browse**.

2 In the **File Open** dialog box, navigate to the location where the student files for this textbook are saved, and then click **a13B_Athletes**. In the lower right corner, click **Open**, and then compare your screen with Figure 13.37.

Figure 13.37

Get External Data – Excel Spreadsheet dialog box

Location of Excel file displays here (yours may vary)

Option button selected

Browse button

OK button

3 Be sure that the **Import the source data into a new table in the current database** option button is selected, and then click **OK**.

The Import Spreadsheet Wizard opens and displays the worksheet data.

4 In the upper left portion of the **Import Spreadsheet Wizard**, click to select the **First Row Contains Column Headings** check box.

The Excel data in the lower portion of the Wizard is framed, indicating that the first row of Excel column titles will become the Access table field names, and the remaining rows will become the individual records for the new Access table.

5 Click **Next**. Notice that the first column is selected, and in the upper portion of the Wizard, the **Field Name** and the **Data Type** display. Click anywhere in the **First Name** column, and then compare your screen with Figure 13.38.

Here you can review and change the field properties for each field (column).

Figure 13.38

Labels (left to right pointing into figure):
- Import Spreadsheet Wizard
- Data type of selected field identified
- Excel column titles become Field Names
- Spreadsheet data displays
- Excel rows become records
- Next button

6 Under **Field Options**, no changes should be made for any of the fields. Click **Next**.

7 In the upper portion of the Wizard, click the **Choose my own primary key** option button, and then be sure that **Student ID** displays.

> In the new table, Student ID will be the primary key. No two students have the same Student ID. By default, Access selects the first field as the primary key. If another field should be defined as the primary key, click the arrow next to the option button and then select the desired field name.

8 Click **Next**. In the **Import to Table** box, type **13B Athletes** and then click **Finish**.

9 In the **Get External Data – Excel Spreadsheet Wizard**, click **Close**.

> That is all the information the Wizard needs to import the Excel data. In the Navigation Pane, the new table displays.

10 On the Ribbon, click the **Database Tools tab**, and then in the **Show/Hide group**, click the **Relationships** button.

11 On the **Design tab**, in the **Relationships group**, click the **Show Table** button. In the **Show Table** dialog box, **Add** the **13B Athletes** table, and then **Add** the **13B Scholarships Awarded** table to the table area. **Close** the **Show Table** dialog box.

12 Expand the field lists, and then position the field lists so that the **13B Athletes** table is on the left side, allowing approximately 1 inch of space between the two field lists. Compare your screen with Figure 13.39.

> Repositioning the field lists is not required, but doing so makes it easier for you to view the field lists and the join line when creating relationships.

Figure 13.39

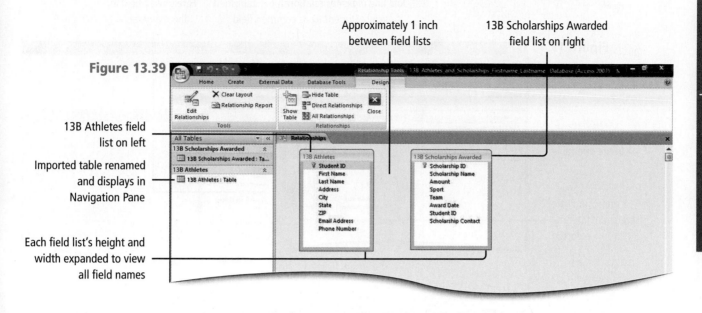

Approximately 1 inch between field lists

13B Scholarships Awarded field list on right

13B Athletes field list on left

Imported table renamed and displays in Navigation Pane

Each field list's height and width expanded to view all field names

13 In the **13B Athletes** field list, point to the **Student ID** field. Hold down the left mouse button, drag into the **13B Scholarships Awarded** field list, position the mouse pointer on top of the **Student ID** field, and then release the mouse button.

14 Point to the title bar of the **Edit Relationships** dialog box, and then drag it below the two field lists.

15 In the **Edit Relationships** dialog box, be sure that the **13B Athletes** table is displayed on the left side, that the **13B Scholarships Awarded** table is displayed on the right side, and that **Student ID** is displayed as the common field for both the *13B Athletes* and the *13B Scholarships Awarded* tables.

The two tables are related in a one-to-many relationship—*one* athlete can be awarded *many* scholarships. The common field between the two tables is the Student ID field. In the 13B Athletes table, Student ID is the primary key. In the 13B Scholarships Awarded table, Student ID is the foreign key.

16 In the **Edit Relationships** dialog box, select the **Enforce Referential Integrity** check box. Click **Create**, and then compare your screen with Figure 13.40.

The one-to-many relationship is established, and the *1* and ∞ indicate that referential integrity is enforced. Enforcing referential integrity ensures that a scholarship cannot be awarded to a student whose name is not in the 13B Athletes table. Similarly, you cannot delete a student athlete from the 13B Athletes table if there is a scholarship listed for that student in the 13B Scholarships Awarded table.

Figure 13.40

Join line indicates relationship established
using *Student ID* as common field

Foreign key field in
the *many* table

Primary key field
in the *one* table

1 and ∞ indicate
referential integrity
enforced

17 On the **Design tab**, in the **Tools group**, click the **Relationship Report** button. On the **Print Preview tab**, in the **Page Layout group**, click the **Margins button**, and then click **Normal**. If you are printing your assignments on paper, click the **Print** button, and then click **OK**. Click the **Close Print Preview button**. To submit electronically, follow your instructor's directions.

18 On the **Quick Access Toolbar**, click the **Save** button 🖫 to save the report. With the text in the **Save As** dialog box highlighted, type **13B Relationships Firstname Lastname** and then click **OK**.

19 **Close** ✕ the report and the Relationships window.

20 From the **Navigation Pane**, open the **13B Athletes** table. On the left side of the table, in the first record, click the **plus sign**.

In the first record—for *Damon Hill*—three related records exist in the 13B Scholarships Awarded table. The related records display because you created a relationship between the two tables using the Student ID field as the common field.

21 **Close** ✕ the **13B Athletes** table, and then **Close** « the **Navigation Pane**.

Objective 9
Specify Numeric Criteria in a Query

Criteria can be set for fields containing numeric data. When you design your table, set the appropriate data type for fields that will contain numbers, currency, or dates so that mathematical calculations can be performed.

Activity 13.16 Specifying Numeric Criteria in a Query

Mr. Simmons wants to know *Which scholarships are in the amount of $300, and for which sport?* In this activity, you will specify criteria in the query so that only the records of scholarships in the amount of $300 will display.

1 On the Ribbon, click the **Create tab**. In the **Other group**, click the **Query Design** button.

2 In the **Show Table** dialog box, **Add** the **13B Scholarships Awarded** table to the table area, and then **Close** the **Show Table** dialog box. Expand the field list.

3 Add the following fields to the design grid in the order given: **Scholarship Name**, **Sport**, and **Amount**.

4 Click in the **Sort** row under **Sport**, click the **Sort arrow**, and then click **Ascending**.

5 On the **Criteria** row, click in the **Amount** field, type **300** and then press Enter. Compare your screen with Figure 13.41.

> When entering currency values as criteria in the design grid, do not type the dollar sign, and include a decimal point only if you are looking for a specific amount that includes cents—for example, 300.50. Access does not insert quotation marks around the criteria because the field's data type contains numeric data.

Figure 13.41

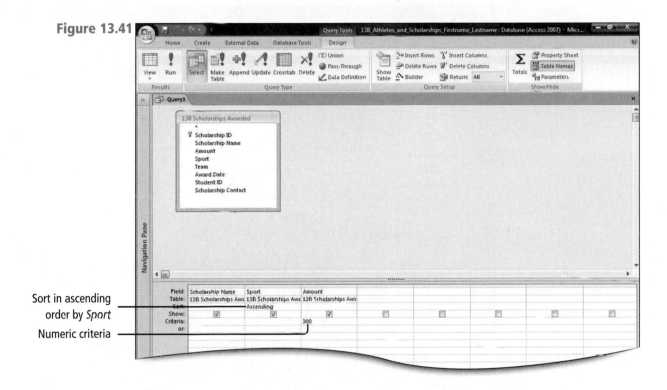

Sort in ascending order by *Sport*

Numeric criteria

6 On the **Design tab**, in the **Results group**, click the **Run** button to view the results. Alternatively, click the View button.

> Five awarded scholarships are in the exact amount of $300. In the navigation area, *1 of 5* displays to indicate the number of records that match the criteria.

7 On the **Home tab**, in the **Views group**, click the **View** button to switch to **Design** view.

Activity 13.17 Using Comparison Operators

Comparison operators are symbols that evaluate each field value to determine if it is the same (=), greater than (>), less than (<), or in between a range of values as specified by the criteria.

If no comparison operator is specified, equal (=) is assumed. For example, in the previous activity, you created a query to display only records where the *Amount* was 300. The comparison operator of = was assumed, and Access displayed only records that had entries equal to 300.

In this activity, you will specify criteria in the query to display records from the 13B Scholarships Awarded table that have scholarships that are *greater* than $300 and then to display scholarships that are *less* than $300.

1 Be sure your query is displayed in **Design view**. On the **Criteria** row, click in the **Amount** field, delete the existing criteria, type **>300** and then press Enter. Compare your screen with Figure 13.42.

Figure 13.42

Criteria with *greater than* comparison operator

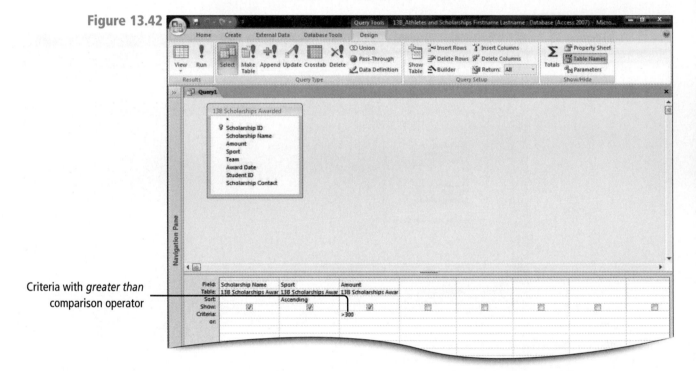

2 On the **Design tab**, in the **Results group**, click the **Run** button.

Fourteen records match the criteria for an Amount that is greater than $300. The results show the records for which the Amount is *greater than* $300, but do not display amounts that are *equal* to $300.

3 Click the **View** button to switch to **Design view**. On the **Criteria** row, under **Amount**, delete the existing criteria. Type **<300** and then press Enter. On the **Design tab**, in the **Results group**, click the **Run** button.

Eleven records display and each has an Amount less than $300. The results show the records for which the Amount is *less than* $300, but do not include amounts that are *equal to* $300.

4 Switch to **Design** view. On the **Criteria** row, click in the **Amount** field, delete the existing criteria, type **>=300** and then press [Enter].

Note — Pressing Enter After Criteria Is Added

If you press [Enter] or click in another column or row in the query design grid after you have added your criteria, you can see how Access alters the criteria so it can interpret what you have typed. Sometimes, there is no change, such as when you add criteria to a number or currency field. Other times, Access may capitalize a letter or add quotation marks or other symbols to clarify the criteria. Whether or not you press [Enter] after adding criteria does not affect the query results. It is used in this text to help you see how the program behaves.

---

5 **Run** the query, and then compare your screen with Figure 13.43.

Nineteen records display, including the records for scholarships in the exact amount of $300. The records include scholarships *equal to* or *greater than* $300. In this manner, comparison operators can be combined.

This query answers the question, *Which scholarships have been awarded in the amount of $300 or more, and for which sports?*

Figure 13.43

Records with a scholarship amount of $300 or more

Number of records that meet criteria

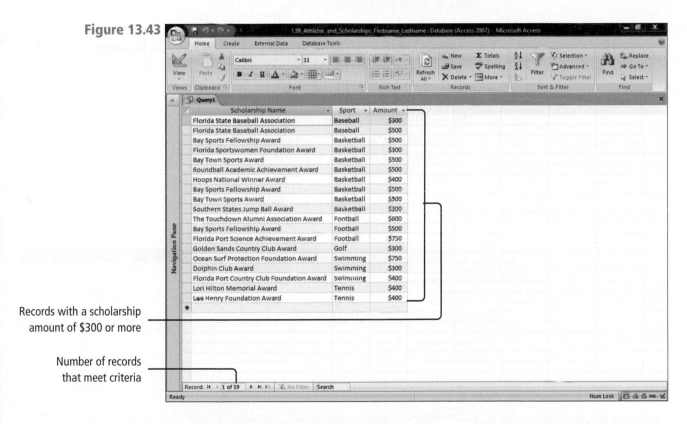

6 On the **Quick Access Toolbar**, click the **Save** button. In the **Save As** dialog box, type **13B $300 or More Firstname Lastname** and then click **OK**.

7 From the **Office** menu, point to **Print**, and then click **Print Preview**. If you are printing your assignments on paper, in the **Print group**, click the **Print** button. In the **Print** dialog box, click **OK**. Click the **Close Print Preview** button. To submit electronically, follow your instructor's directions.

8 **Close** ☒ the query. **Open** ≫ the **Navigation Pane**, and notice that the new query displays under the table from which it retrieved the records.

Activity 13.18 Using the Between … And Comparison Operator

The *Between … And operator* is a comparison operator that looks for values within a range. It is particularly useful when you need to locate records that are within a range of dates, for example, scholarships awarded between August 1 and September 30. In this activity, you will create a new query from an existing query, and then add criteria to look for values within a range of dates. The query will answer the question, *Which scholarships were awarded between August 1 and September 30?*

1 From the **Navigation Pane**, open the **13B $300 or More** query. From the **Office** menu 🏢, click **Save As**. In the **Save As** dialog box, type **13B Awards Aug-Sept Firstname Lastname** and then click **OK**.

2 **Close** ≪ the **Navigation Pane**, and then on the **Home** tab, in the **Views group**, click the **View** button to switch to **Design** view. From the **13B Scholarships Awarded** field list, add the **Award Date** as the fourth field in the design grid.

3 On the **Criteria** row, click in the **Amount** field, and then delete the existing criteria so that the query is not restricted by amount. On the **Criteria** row, click in the **Award Date** field, type **Between 08/01/09 And 09/30/09** and then press [Enter]. Notice that Access places quotation marks around the dates. Compare your screen with Figure 13.44, where the column has been widened to fully display the criteria.

> This criteria instructs Access to look for values in the Award Date field that begin with 08/01/09 and end with 09/30/09. Both the beginning and ending dates will be included in the query results. If you type the operators *Between … And* using lowercase letters, Access will capitalize the first letter of each operator.

Figure 13.44

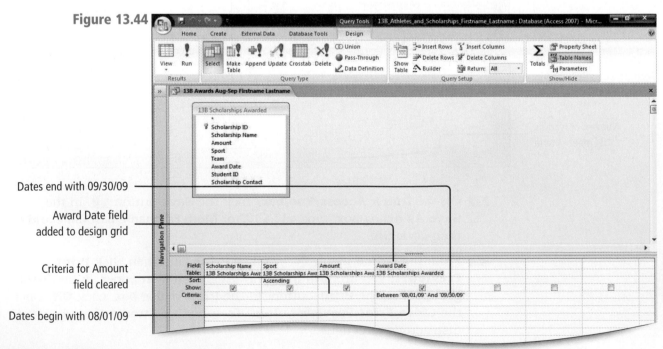

Dates end with 09/30/09

Award Date field added to design grid

Criteria for Amount field cleared

Dates begin with 08/01/09

Note — Widening Columns in the Query Grid

For a better view of your criteria, widen a column in the design grid using the same techniques that are used in a table. In the selection bar at the top of the column, point to the right border and double-click to expand the column and to fully display the contents on the criteria row. You can also drag the right border to the desired width.

4 **Run** the query and notice that three scholarships were awarded between 08/01/09 and 09/30/09.

5 From the **Office** menu 🗗, point to **Print**, and then click **Print Preview**. If you are printing your assignments on paper, in the **Print group**, click the **Print** button. In the **Print** dialog box, click **OK**. Click the **Close Print Preview** button. To submit electronically, follow your instructor's directions.

6 **Close** ✕ the query. In the message box, click **Yes** to save the changes to the query design. **Open** » the **Navigation Pane**, and notice that the new query displays under the table from which it retrieved records.

Objective 10
Use Compound Criteria

You can specify more than one condition—criteria—in a query; this is called ***compound criteria***. Compound criteria enable you to create queries that are quite specific. Two types of compound criteria used in queries are AND and OR, which are ***logical operators***. Logical operators enable you to enter criteria for the same field or different fields.

Activity 13.19 Using AND Criteria in a Query

Compound criteria use an AND condition to display records in the query results that meet *both* parts of the specified criteria. In this activity, you will help Mr. Simmons answer the question, *Which scholarships over $500 were awarded for Football?*

1 **Close** « the **Navigation Pane**. On the Ribbon, click the **Create tab**. In the **Other group**, click the **Query Design** button. **Add** the **13B Scholarships Awarded** table to the table area. **Close** the **Show Table** dialog box, and then, expand the field list.

2 Add the following fields to the design grid in the order given: **Scholarship Name**, **Sport**, and **Amount**.

3 On the **Criteria** row, click in the **Sport** field, type **Football** and then press Tab.

4 On the **Criteria** row, in the **Amount** field, type **>500** and then press Enter. Compare your screen with Figure 13.45.

> The AND condition is created by placing the criteria for both fields on the same line in the Criteria row. The results will display records that contain *Football* AND an amount greater than *$500*.

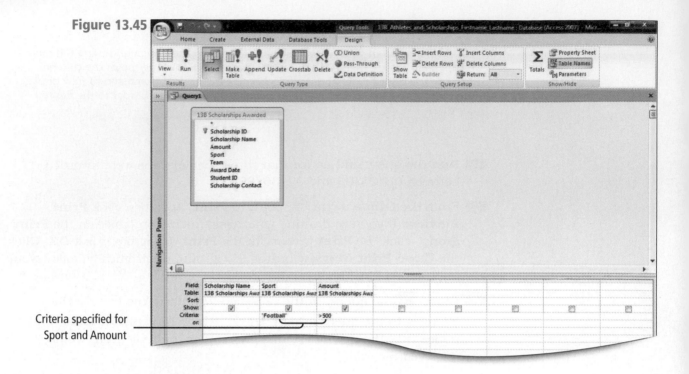

Figure 13.45

Criteria specified for Sport and Amount

5 On the **Design tab**, in the **Results group**, click the **Run** button.

Two records display that match both conditions—Football in the Sport field and greater than $500 in the Amount field.

6 **Close** ✕ the query. In the message box, click **Yes** to save changes to the query. In the **Save As** dialog box, type **13B Football and Over $500 Firstname Lastname** and then click **OK** or press Enter.

7 **Open** ≫ the **Navigation Pane**, and then click one time to select the **13B Football and Over $500** query. From the **Office** menu , point to the **Print** button and click **Print Preview**. If you are printing your assignments on paper, in the **Print group**, click the **Print** button. In the **Print** dialog box, click **OK**. Click the **Close Print Preview** button. To submit electronically, follow your instructor's directions.

8 **Close** ≪ the **Navigation Pane**.

You can print any selected object from the Navigation Pane—the object does not have to be displayed on your screen to print.

Activity 13.20 Using OR Criteria in a Query

Use the OR condition to specify multiple criteria for a single field, or multiple criteria on different fields when you want to display the records that meet either condition. In this activity, you will help Mr. Simmons answer the question, *Which scholarships over $400 were awarded in the sports of Baseball or Swimming?*

1 On the Ribbon, click the **Create tab**. In the **Other group**, click the **Query Design** button.

2 **Add** the **13B Scholarships Awarded** table and then **Close** the dialog box. Expand the field list, and then add the following four fields to the design grid in the order given: **Scholarship Name**, **Sport**, **Amount**, and **Award Date**.

3 On the **Criteria** row, click in the **Sport** field, and then type **Baseball**

4 In the design grid, on the **or** row, click in the **Sport** field, type **Swimming** and then press Enter. **Run** the query.

> The query results display seven scholarship records where the Sport is either Baseball *or* Swimming. Use the OR condition to specify multiple criteria for a single field.

5 Switch to **Design** view. Under **Sport**, on the **or** row, delete the text. Under **Sport**, click in the **Criteria** row, and then delete the existing text. Type **Swimming Or Baseball** and then on the **Criteria** row, click in the **Amount** field. Type **>400** and then press Enter. Compare your screen with Figure 13.46.

> This is an alternative way to use the OR compound operator in the Sport field. Because criteria has been entered for two different fields, Access will return the records that are Baseball *or* Swimming and that have a scholarship awarded in an amount greater than $400.

Figure 13.46

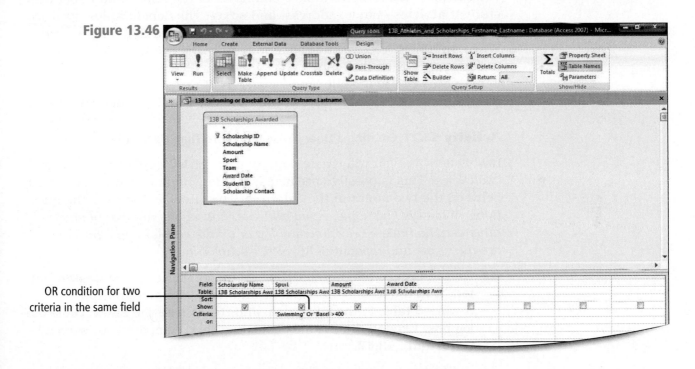

OR condition for two criteria in the same field

6 **Run** the query to display the two records that match the conditions.

7 **Close** ✕ the query. In the message box, click **Yes** to save changes to the query. In the **Save As** dialog box, type **13B Swimming or Baseball Over $400 Firstname Lastname** and then click **OK** or press Enter.

8 **Open** » the **Navigation Pane** and click one time to select the **13B Swimming or Baseball Over $400** query. From the **Office** menu ⊕, point to **Print**, and then click **Print Preview**. If you are printing your assignments on paper, in the **Print group**, click the **Print** button. In the **Print** dialog box, click **OK**. Click the **Close Print Preview** button. To submit electronically, follow your instructor's directions.

9 **Close** « the **Navigation Pane**.

Objective 11
Create a Query Based on More Than One Table

In a relational database, you can retrieve information from more than one table. Recall that each table in a relational database contains all of the records about a single topic. Tables are joined by relating the primary key field in one table to a foreign key field in another table. This common field creates a relationship, enabling you to include data from more than one table in a query.

For example, the Athletes table contains all of the information about the student athletes—name, address, and so on. The Scholarships Awarded table includes the scholarship name, amount, award date, and so on. When an athlete receives a scholarship, only the Student ID field is included with the scholarship to identify who received the scholarship. It is not necessary to include, and would result in redundant information, if any other athlete data was stored in the Scholarships Awarded table.

Activity 13.21 Creating a Query Based on More Than One Table

In this activity, you will create a query that retrieves information from two tables. This is possible because a relationship has been established between the two tables in the database. The query will answer the questions, *What are the name, email address, and phone number of student athletes who have received swimming or tennis scholarships, and what are the name and amount of his or her scholarship?*

1 On the **Create tab**, in the **Other group**, click the **Query Design** button. **Add** the **13B Athletes** table and the **13B Scholarships Awarded** table to the table area, and then **Close** the **Show Table** dialog box. Expand the two field lists, and then compare your screen with Figure 13.47.

The join line indicates the one-to-many relationship—*one* athlete can have *many* scholarships. Student ID is the common field in the two tables. In the Athletes table, Student ID is the primary key field; in the Scholarships Awarded table, Student ID is the foreign key field.

Figure 13.47

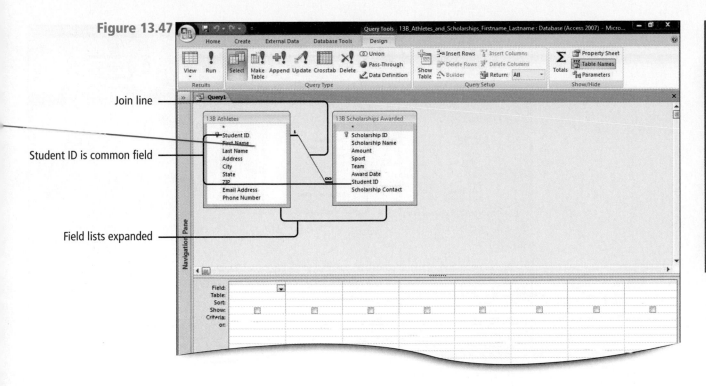

Join line

Student ID is common field

Field lists expanded

2 From the **13B Athletes** field list, add the following fields to the design grid in the order given: **First Name**, **Last Name**, **Address**, **City**, **State**, and **ZIP**.

3 On the **Sort** row, click in the **Last Name** field. Click the **Sort arrow**, and then click **Ascending** to sort the records in alphabetical order by last name.

4 From the **13B Scholarships Awarded** field list, add the following fields to the design grid in the order given: **Scholarship Name**, **Sport**, and **Amount**.

5 Click in the **Criteria** row, under **Sport**. Type **Swimming** and on the **or** row, under **Sport**, type **Tennis** and then press [Enter].

6 In the design grid, on the second row—the **Table** row—notice that for each field, the table from which the field was added is displayed. Compare your screen with Figure 13.48.

> When extracting data from multiple tables, the information on the Table row is helpful, especially when different tables may include the same field names, such as address, but different data, such as a student's address or a coach's address.

Figure 13.48

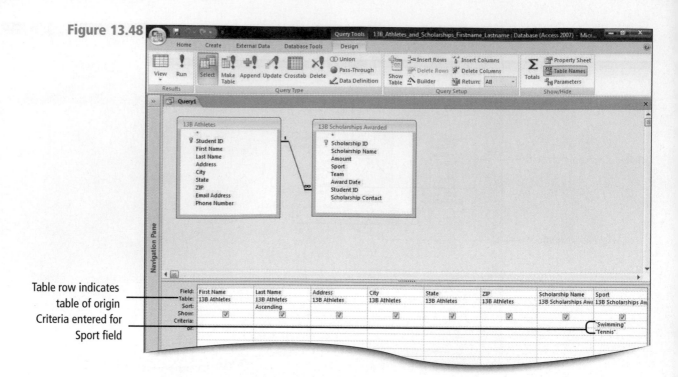

Table row indicates
table of origin
Criteria entered for
Sport field

7 **Run** the query.

> The names and addresses of eight student athletes display. Notice that the First Name and Last Name fields are included in the query results even though the common field—Student ID—was *not* included in the query design. Because Student ID is included in both tables, and a one-to-many relationship was created between the tables, you can display data from both tables in one query.

> Two students—*Arianna Kitasoe* and *Janice Murphy*—received scholarships in both Swimming and Tennis. Recall that *one* student athlete can receive *many* scholarships.

8 Switch to **Design** view. From the **13B Athletes** field list, add **Phone Number** to the design grid. In the **13B Athletes** field list, point to **Email Address**, drag it to the design grid on top of **Amount**, and then release the mouse button.

> The Email Address field is inserted to the left of the Amount field.

9 In the design grid, select, by dragging in the gray selection bar, the **Address**, **City**, **State**, and **ZIP** fields, and then press Delete.

10 In the design grid, select the **Amount** field, and then drag it to the first field position in the design grid. Click outside of the grid to cancel the selection, and then compare your screen with Figure 13.49.

> The design of the query is modified. Phone Number is added as the last field in the design grid. The Address, City, State, and ZIP fields are deleted. The Amount field is in the first position.

Figure 13.49

Seven total fields

Amount moved to first field

Phone Number added as last field

11 **Run** the query. Select all of the columns in the query results and then apply **Best Fit**—in the field heading row, point to the right boundary of any of the selected columns to display the ⊞ pointer, and then double-click.

12 On the **Quick Access Toolbar**, click the **Save** button 🔲, type **13B Swimming and Tennis Firstname Lastname** and then click **OK**. Display the query in **Print Preview**, set the **Margins** to **Normal**, and then change the orientation to **Landscape**. If you are submitting your results from this project on paper, **Print** the query and then **Close Print Preview**. To submit electronically, follow the instructions provided by your instructor.

13 **Close** ⊠ the query, **Open** ≫ the **Navigation Pane**, and notice that your new query—*13B Swimming and Tennis*—displays under *both* tables from which it retrieved records.

> In the Tables and Related Views arrangement of the Navigation Pane, any object that references a table displays with that table.

Objective 12
Use Wildcards in a Query

Wildcard characters serve as a placeholder for one or more unknown characters in the criteria. When you are unsure of the particular character or set of characters to include in criteria, use wildcard characters in place of the characters.

Activity 13.22 Using a Wildcard in a Query

Use the asterisk (*) to represent one or more characters. For example, if you use the * wildcard in the criteria Fo*, the results will return Foster,

Project 13B: Athletes and Scholarships | **Access** 649

Forrester, Forrest, Fossil, or any word beginning with *Fo*. In this activity, you will use the asterisk (*) wildcard and specify the criteria in the query to answer the question, *Which student athletes received scholarships from local Rotary Clubs, country clubs, and foundations?*

1 **Close** « the **Navigation Pane**. On the Ribbon, click the **Create tab**. In the **Other group**, click the **Query Design** button.

2 **Add** both tables to the table area, and then **Close** the **Show Table** dialog box. Expand the field lists.

3 Add the following fields to the design grid in the order given: from the **13B Athletes** table, **First Name** and **Last Name**; from the **13B Scholarships Awarded** table, **Scholarship Contact**.

4 On the **Sort** row, click under **Last Name**. Click the **sort arrow**, and then click **Ascending**.

5 On the **Criteria** row, under **Scholarship Contact**, type **Rotary*** and then press Enter.

> The wildcard character * is used as a placeholder to match one or more characters. When you press Enter, Access adds *Like* to the beginning of the criteria. This is used to compare a sequence of characters and test whether or not the text matches a pattern.

6 **Run** the query to display the three student athletes who received scholarships from Rotary Clubs.

7 Switch to the **Design** view. On the **or** row, under **Scholarship Contact**, type ***Country Club** and then press Enter.

> The * can be used at the beginning, middle, or end of the criteria. The position of the * wildcard character determines the location of the unknown characters. Here you will search for records that end in *Country Club*.

8 **Run** the query to display a total of six records.

9 Switch to **Design** view. Under **Scholarship Contact** and under **Like** "***Country Club"**, type ***Foundation*** and then press Enter. Compare your screen with Figure 13.50.

> The query will also display records that have the word *Foundation* anywhere—beginning, middle, or end—in the field. Three *OR* criteria have been included for the Scholarship Contact field—the query results will display students who have received scholarships from an organization name that begins with Rotary, that ends in County Club, or that has Foundation anywhere in the middle of the name.

Figure 13.50

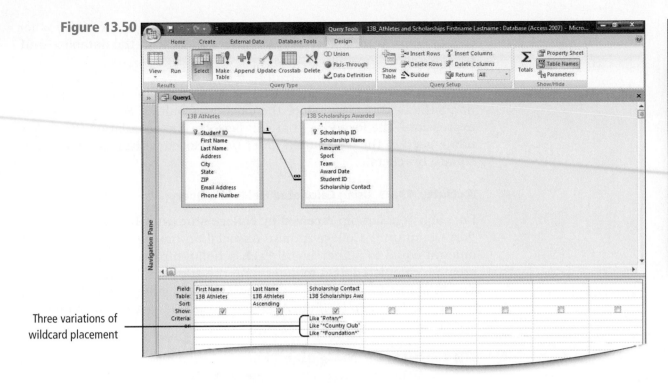

Three variations of wildcard placement

10 **Run** the query to display a total of 28 records.

Twenty-eight scholarships were awarded from a Country Club, a Rotary Club, or a Foundation.

11 On the **Quick Access Toolbar**, click the **Save** button. Name the query **13B Clubs and Foundations Firstname Lastname** and then display the results in **Print Preview**. If you are submitting paper assignments, **Print** the query results. To submit electronically, follow your instructor's directions. **Close Print Preview**.

12 **Close** ✕ the query results, and then **Open** » the **Navigation Pane**.

Because the 13B Clubs and Foundations query retrieved data from two tables, it displays below the 13B Scholarships Awarded table and the 13B Athletes table.

More Knowledge — Search for a Single Unknown Character by Using the ? Wildcard

The question mark (?) is a wildcard that is used to search for unknown single characters. For each question mark included in a criteria, any character can be inserted. For example, if you used *b?d* as a criteria, the query might locate bid, bud, bed or any three-character word beginning with *b* and ending with *d*. If *b??d* is entered as the criteria, the results could include bind, bend, bard or any four-character word beginning with *b* and ending with *d*.

Objective 13
Use Calculated Fields in a Query

Queries can create calculated values. For example, Florida Port Community College could multiply two fields together, such as Total Credit Hours and Tuition per Credit Hour to get a Total Tuition Due amount for each student without having to include a specific field for this amount in the table, which reduces the size of the database and provides more flexibility.

There are two steps to produce a calculated field in a query. First, name the field that will store the calculated values. Second, write the expression—the formula—that will perform the calculation. Each field name used in the calculation must be enclosed within its own pair of square brackets.

Activity 13.23 Using Calculated Fields in a Query

For each scholarship received by college student athletes, the Florida Port Community College Alumni Association has agreed to donate an amount equal to 50 percent of each scholarship. In this activity, you will create a calculated field to determine the additional amount each scholarship is worth. The query will answer the question, *What will the value of each scholarship be if the Alumni Association makes a matching 50% donation?*

1 Close ⟪ the **Navigation Pane**, and then click the **Create tab**. In the **Other group**, click the **Query Design** button.

2 **Add** the **13B Scholarships Awarded** table to the table area, **Close** the **Show Table** dialog box, and then expand the field list. Add the following fields to the design grid in the order given: **Student ID**, **Scholarship Name**, and **Amount**.

3 Click in the **Sort** row under **Student ID**, click the **Sort arrow**, and then click **Ascending**.

4 In the **Field** row, right-click in the first empty column to display a shortcut menu, and then click **Zoom**.

> The Zoom dialog box gives you more working space so that you can see the entire calculation as you type it. The calculation can also be typed directly in the empty Field box in the column.

5 In the **Zoom** dialog box, type **Matching Donation:[Amount]*0.5** and then compare your screen with Figure 13.51.

> The first element, *Matching Donation*, is the new field name where the calculated amounts will display. Following that is a colon (:), which separates the new field name from the expression. *Amount* is enclosed in square brackets because it is an existing field name in the 13B Scholarships Awarded table, containing the numeric data on which the calculation will be performed. Following the square brackets is an asterisk (*), which in math calculations signifies multiplication. Finally, the percentage (0.5 or 50%) displays.

Figure 13.51

Calculated value

New field name

6 In the **Zoom** dialog box, click **OK**, and then **Run** the query. Select all of the columns and apply **Best Fit**. Compare your screen with Figure 13.52.

> The query results display three fields from the 13B Scholarships Awarded table plus a fourth field—*Matching Donation*—in which a calculated amount displays. Each calculated amount equals the amount in the Amount field multiplied by 0.5.

Figure 13.52

New calculated field created (50% of Amount)

Alert!	**Does your screen differ?**
	If your calculations in a query do not work, carefully check the expression you typed. Spelling or syntax errors prevent calculated fields from working properly.

7 Notice the formatting of the **Matching Donation** field—there are no dollar signs, commas, or decimal places; you will adjust this formatting later.

8 Switch to **Design** view. On the **Field** row, in the first empty column, right-click, and then click **Zoom**.

9 In the **Zoom** dialog box, type **Total Scholarship:[Amount]+[Matching Donation]** and then click **OK**. **Run** the query to view the results. Apply **Best Fit** to the **Total Scholarship** field.

Total Scholarship is calculated by adding together the Amount field and the Matching Donation field. Each existing field name—*Amount* and *Matching Donation*—must be enclosed in separate pairs of brackets.

The Total Scholarship column includes dollar signs, commas, and decimal points, which carried over from the Amount field.

10 Switch to **Design** view. On the **Field** row, click in the **Matching Donation** field name.

11 On the **Design tab**, in the **Show/Hide group**, click the **Property Sheet** button. Alternatively, right-click the Matching Donation field name, and then click Properties.

The Property Sheet displays on the right side of your screen, where you can customize fields in a query, for example, the format of numbers in the field. The left column displays the Property name, for example, Description. To the right of the Property name is the Property setting box.

12 In the **Property Sheet**, on the **General tab**, click in the **Format** property setting box, and then click the **arrow** that displays. Compare your screen with Figure 13.53.

A list of formats for the Matching Donation field displays.

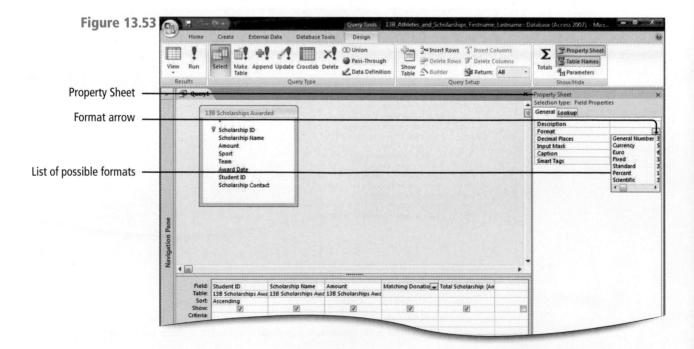

Figure 13.53

Property Sheet

Format arrow

List of possible formats

13 In the list, click **Currency**, and then **Close** the **Property Sheet**.

14 **Run** the query. Compare your screen with Figure 13.54.

> The Matching Donation column displays with currency formatting—a dollar sign, thousands comma separator, and two decimal places.

Figure 13.54

Currency format applied to all columns

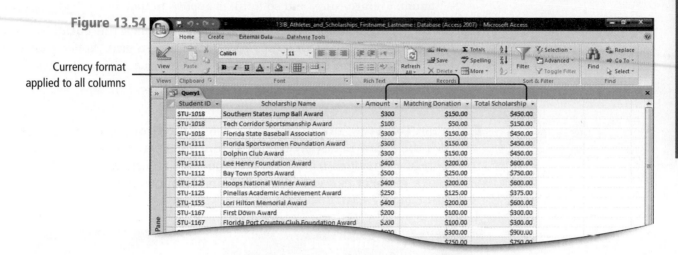

15 On the **Quick Access Toolbar**, click the **Save** button. Name the query **13B Matching Donations Firstname Lastname** and then display the query results in **Print Preview**. Change the **Orientation** to **Landscape**. If you are submitting paper assignments, **Print** the query results. **Close Print Preview**. To submit electronically, follow your instructor's directions.

16 **Close** the query.

Objective 14
Group Data and Calculate Statistics in a Query

In Access queries, you can perform statistical calculations on a group of records. Calculations that are performed on a group of records are called *aggregate functions*.

Activity 13.24 Using the MIN, MAX, AVG and SUM Functions in a Query

In this activity, you will use the minimum, maximum, average, and sum functions in a query to examine the amounts of scholarships awarded. The last query will answer the question, *What is the total dollar amount of scholarships awarded?*

1 On the Ribbon, click the **Create tab**. In the **Other group**, click the **Query Design** button.

2 Add the **13B Scholarships Awarded** table to the table area, **Close** the **Show Table** dialog box, and then expand the field list. Add the **Amount** field to the design grid.

When you want to summarize a field, include only the field you want to summarize in the query, so that the aggregate function (minimum, maximum, average, sum, and so forth) is applied to that single field.

3 On the **Design tab**, in the **Show/Hide group**, click the **Totals** button to add a **Total** row as the third row in the design grid. Notice that in the design grid, on the **Total** row, under **Amount**, *Group By* displays.

On the Total row, you select the function, such as Min, Max, Avg, or Sum, that you want to use for the field.

4 In the **Total** row, under **Amount**, click in the **Group By** box, and then click the **arrow** to display the list of functions. Access supports the aggregate functions summarized in the table shown in Figure 13.55. Take a moment to review this table, and then compare your screen with Figure 13.56.

Aggregate Functions	
Function Name	**What It Does**
Sum	Totals the values in a field
Avg	Averages the values in a field
Min	Locates the smallest value in a field
Max	Locates the largest value in a field
Count	Counts the number of records in a field
StDev	Calculates the Standard Deviation on the values in a field
Var	Calculates the Variance on the values in a field
First	Displays the First value in a field
Last	Displays the Last value in a field
Expression	Creates a calculated field that includes an aggregate function
Where	Limits records displayed to those that match a condition specified on the Criteria row

Figure 13.55

Figure 13.56

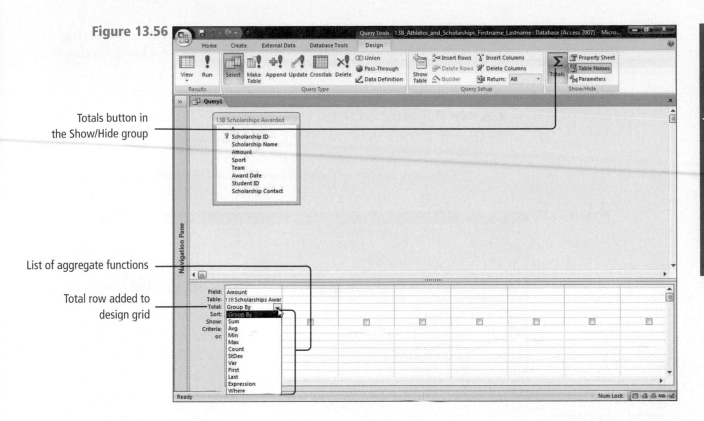

Access | Chapter 13

Totals button in
the Show/Hide group

List of aggregate functions

Total row added to
design grid

5 From the list of functions, click **Min**, and then **Run** the query. Double-click the right boundary of the new column heading to widen the column.

> Access calculates the minimum (smallest) scholarship award—*$100.00*. The field name, *MinOfAmount* displays for the calculation. This query answers the question, *What is the minimum (smallest) scholarship amount awarded?*

6 Switch to **Design** view. Using the technique you just practiced, select the **Max** function, and then **Run** the query.

> The maximum (largest) scholarship amount is *$750.00*.

7 Switch to **Design** view, select the **Avg** function, and then **Run** the query.

> The average scholarship amount awarded is *$358.33*.

8 Switch to **Design** view. Select the **Sum** function, and then **Run** the query.

> Access sums the Amount field for all of the records and displays a result of *$10,750.00*. The field name, SumOfAmount, displays. This query answers the question, *What is the total dollar amount of all the scholarships awarded?*

Activity 13.25 Grouping Data in a Query

The aggregate functions can also be used to calculate totals by groups of data. For example, if you want to group (summarize) the amount of scholarships awarded to each student, you would include the Student ID field, in addition to the Amount field, and then group all of the records for each student together to calculate a total awarded to each student. Similarly, you can calculate how much money is awarded to each sport.

1 Switch to **Design** view. Add the **Student ID** field to the design grid. On the **Total** row, under **Student ID**, notice that *Group By* displays.

> The design of this query will group—summarize—the records by StudentID and calculate a total Amount for each student.

2 **Run** the query, and then apply **Best Fit** to the fields. Click in any record to remove the selection, and then compare your screen with Figure 13.57.

> The query calculates the total amount of all scholarships for each student.

Figure 13.57

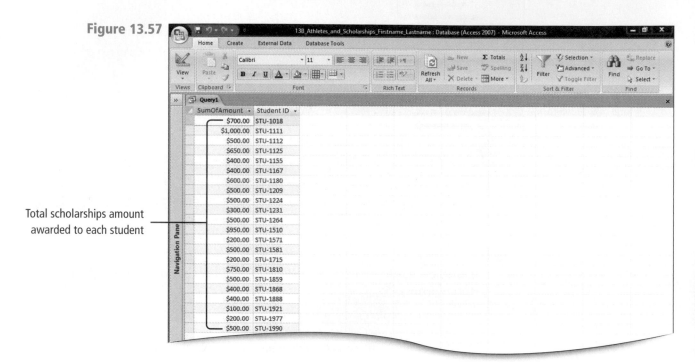

Total scholarships amount awarded to each student

3 Switch to **Design** view. In the design grid, delete the **Student ID** field, and then add the **Sport** field to the design grid. **Run** the query, and then compare your screen with Figure 13.58.

> Access summarizes the data by each sport. Basketball scholarships received the largest total Amount—*$3,500.00*.

Figure 13.58

Total scholarships amount awarded to each sport

4 On the **Quick Access Toolbar**, click the **Save** 🔲 button. Name the query **13B Totals by Sport Firstname Lastname** and then display the query results in **Print Preview**. If you are submitting paper assignments, **Print** the query results, and then **Close Print Preview**. To submit electronically, follow your instructor's directions.

5 **Close** ☒ the query, and then **Open** ⟫ the **Navigation Pane** to view the queries you have created.

6 **Close** ⟪ the **Navigation Pane**, **Close** the Database, and then **Exit** Access.

End **You have completed Project 13B** ————————————

There's More You Can Do!

Close Access and any other open windows. Display the Start menu, click Computer, and then navigate to the student files that accompany this textbook. In the folder **02_theres_more_you_can_do**, locate and open the folder for this chapter. Open and print the instructions for this project, which are provided to you in Adobe PDF format.

Try IT! 1—Password Protect Your Database

In this Try It! exercise, you will encrypt and password protect your database to conceal data and prevent unwanted users from opening your database.

Content-Based Assessments

Summary

Importing an Excel spreadsheet is an efficient way to create new tables in an Access database. Sorting data in a table reorders the records based on one or more fields and is a quick way to alphabetize records or to find the highest or lowest amount in a numeric, currency, or date field. Use queries to ask complex questions about the data in a database in a manner that Access can interpret. Save queries so they can be run as needed against current records. Use queries to limit the fields that display, add criteria to restrict the number of records in the query results, create calculated values, and include data from more than one table.

Key Terms

Content-Based Assessments

Matching

Match each term in the second column with its correct definition in the first column. Write the letter of the term on the blank line in front of the correct definition.

_____ **1.** The area directly below the Ribbon that displays information such as security alerts when there is potentially unsafe, active content in an Office 2007 document that you open.

_____ **2.** An area of the Access program where you can view the security and privacy settings for your Access installation.

_____ **3.** A type of database in which the tables in the database can relate or connect to other tables through common fields.

_____ **4.** Fields that contain the same data in more than one table.

_____ **5.** An association that is established between two tables using common fields.

_____ **6.** A relationship between two tables where one record in the first table corresponds to many records in the second table—the most common type of relationship in Access.

_____ **7.** A list of the field names in a table.

_____ **8.** The field that is included in the related table so that it can be joined to the primary key in another table for the purpose of creating a relationship.

_____ **9.** A set of rules that Access uses to ensure that the data between related tables is valid.

_____ **10.** In the Relationships window, the line joining two tables that visually indicates the related field and the type of relationship.

_____ **11.** The process of arranging data in a specific order based on the value in each field.

_____ **12.** A sorting order that arranges text in alphabetical order (A to Z) or numbers from the lowest to highest number.

_____ **13.** A database object that retrieves (selects) specific data from one or more tables and then displays the specified data in Datasheet view.

_____ **14.** When sorting on multiple fields in Datasheet view, the field that will be used for the first level of sorting.

_____ **15.** The table or tables from which a query selects its data.

A Ascending

B Common fields

C Data source

D Field list

E Foreign key

F Join line

G Message Bar

H One-to-many

I Outermost sort field

J Referential integrity

K Relational

L Relationship

M Select query

N Sorting

O Trust Center

Content-Based Assessments

Fill in the Blank

Write the correct answer in the space provided.

1. The upper pane of the Query window, which displays the field lists for tables that are used in the query is the _____ _____.

2. The lower pane of the Query window, which displays the design of the query is the _____ _____.

3. The process in which Access searches the records in the table(s) included in a query design, finds the records that match the specified criteria, and then displays those records in a datasheet is called _____.

4. Conditions that identify the specific records you are looking for are called _____.

5. Each time you open a saved query, Access _____ the query again and displays the results based on the data stored in the associated tables; thus, the results always reflect the latest information in the tables.

6. A sequence of characters, which when used in query criteria, must be matched, is referred to as a _____ _____.

7. A criteria that searches for fields that are empty is called _____ _____.

8. A criteria that searches for fields that are *not* empty is called _____ _____.

9. Symbols that evaluate each field value to determine if it is the same (=), greater than (>), less than (<), or in between a range of values as specified by the criteria are referred to as _____ _____.

10. In a _____ condition, both parts of the query must be met.

11. In a _____ condition, either part of the query must be met.

12. Multiple conditions in a query or filter are called _____ _____.

13. In a query, a character that serves as a placeholder for one or more unknown characters is a _____.

14. Calculations that are performed on a group of records are called _____ _____.

15. To locate the largest value in a group of records, use the _____ function.

Content-Based Assessments

Access

Skills Review

Project 13C—Music Department

In this project, you will apply the skills you practiced from the Objectives in Project 13A.

Objectives: 1. *Open an Existing Database;* **2.** *Create Table Relationships;* **3.** *Sort Records in a Table;* **4.** *Create a Query in Design View;* **5.** *Create a New Query from an Existing Query;* **6.** *Sort Query Results;* **7.** *Specify Criteria in a Query.*

In the following Skills Review, you will assist Pascal Sanchez, Florida Port Community College Music Director, in using his database to answer various questions about the instruments in the Music Department's inventory. Your query results will look similar to those shown in Figure 13.59.

For Project 13C, you will need the following file:

a13C_Music_Department

You will save your database as
13C_Music_Department_Firstname_Lastname

Figure 13.59

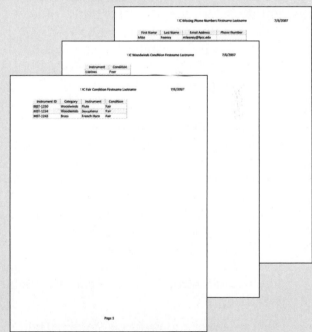

(Project 13C–Music Department continues on the next page)

Project 13C: Music Department | **Access**   663

(Project 13C–Music Department continued)

1. Navigate to the location where the student data files for this textbook are saved. Locate **a13C_Music_Department** and click one time to select the file. **Copy** and then **Paste** the file to your **Access Chapter 13** folder. **Rename** the file as **13C_Music_Department_Firstname_Lastname** and then **Start** Access. Navigate to your **Access Chapter 13** folder, open **13C_Music_Department**, and then **Enable this content**.

2. Click the **Database Tools tab**. In the **Show/Hide group**, click the **Relationships** button. On the **Design tab**, in the **Relationships group**, click the **Show Table** button. In the **Show Table** dialog box, click the **13C Student Musicians** table, and then at the bottom of the dialog box, click **Add**. Point to the **13C Instruments Inventory** table, and then double-click to add the table to the Relationships window. **Close** the **Show Table** dialog box. In each table, use the pointer to expand the field lists to display the entire table name and all of the field names.

3. In the **13C Student Musicians** field list, point to **Student ID**, hold down the left mouse button, and then drag to the right to the **13C Instruments Inventory** field list until your mouse pointer is on top of **Student ID**. Release the mouse button, and then drag the **Edit Relationships** dialog box below the two field lists. The relationship between the two tables is a one-to-many relationship; *one* student can play *many* instruments. The common field is Student ID.

4. Click to select the **Enforce Referential Integrity** check box, and then click **Create**. On the **Design tab**, in the **Tools group**, click the **Relationship Report** button. If you are submitting paper

assignments, on the **Print Preview tab**, in the **Print group**, click the **Print** button, and then click **OK**. Click **Close Print Preview**. To submit electronically, follow your instructor's directions. On the **Quick Access Toolbar**, click the **Save** button, and then in the **Save As** dialog box, click **OK** to accept the default name. **Close** all of the open objects.

5. **Open** the **Navigation Pane**, **Open** the **13C Instruments Inventory** table, and then **Close** the **Navigation Pane**. In the **Condition** field, click any record. On the **Home tab**, in the **Sort & Filter group**, click the **Descending** button to sort the records from *Poor* to *Excellent*. Point anywhere in the **Category** field, and then right-click. From the shortcut menu, click **Sort A to Z**. The records are sorted first by *Category*, the outermost sort field, and then within categories, by *Condition*, the innermost sort field. In the **Sort & Filter group**, click the **Clear All Sorts** button. **Close** the table, and then click **No**; you do not need to save the changes to the design.

6. Click the **Create tab**, and then in the **Other group**, click the **Query Design** button. From the **Show Table** dialog box, **Add** the **13C Instruments Inventory** table to the table area, and then **Close** the **Show Table** dialog box. Expand the field list.

7. In the **13C Instruments Inventory** field list, double-click **Instrument ID** to add it to the design grid. In the **13C Instruments Inventory** field list, point to **Category**, hold down the left mouse button, and then drag the field down into the design grid until you are pointing to the **Field** row in the next available column. Release the mouse button. In the **Field** row of the design grid, click in the third column, and then click the

(Project 13C–Music Department continues on the next page)

(Project 13C–Music Department continued)

arrow that displays. From the list, click **Instrument** to add this field to the design grid.

8. Using any technique, add the **Student ID** and **Condition** fields as the fourth and fifth fields in the design grid. On the **Design tab**, in the **Results group**, click the **Run** button. This query answers the question, *What are the Instrument ID, Category, Instrument, Student ID, and Condition of all of the instruments in the inventory?* On the **Quick Access Toolbar**, click the **Save** button. In the **Save As** dialog box, type **13C All Instruments Query Firstname Lastname** and then click **OK**.

9. If you are submitting paper assignments, from the **Office** menu, point to the **Print** button, click **Print Preview**, and then click the **Print** button. Click the **Close Print Preview** button. To submit electronically, follow your instructor's directions.

10. From the **Office** menu, click **Save As**. In the **Save As** dialog box, type **13C Condition Query Firstname Lastname** and then click **OK**. Recall that you can create a new query based on an existing query.

11. On the **Home tab**, in the **Views group**, click the **View** button to switch to **Design** view. In the design grid, point to the thin gray selection bar above the **Student ID** field until the ⬇ pointer displays. Click to select the **Student ID** column, and then press ⌫Delete. From the gray selection bar, select the **Instrument ID** column. Then, point to the selection bar at the top of the selected column to display the 🔁 pointer, and drag to the right to position **Instrument ID** as the fourth (last) column.

12. **Run** the query. The query results display four fields. This query answers the question,

What are the Category, Instrument, Condition, and Instrument ID of every instrument in the inventory? **Close** the query, and then click **Yes**. **Open** the **Navigation Pane** and click one time to select **13C Condition Query**. If you are submitting paper assignments, from the **Office** menu, point to the **Print** button, click **Print Preview**, and then click the **Print** button. Click the **Close Print Preview** button. To submit electronically, follow your instructor's directions.

13. **Open** the **13C All Instruments Query**. **Save** the query as **13C Instrument Sort Firstname Lastname** and then switch to **Design** view. In the design grid, delete the **Student ID** field. In the **Category** field, click in the **Sort** row, click the **Sort arrow**, and then click **Descending**. Under **Condition**, click to display the **Sort arrow**, and then click **Ascending**. **Run** the query. This query answers the question, *Within each category (with Category in descending alphabetical order), what instruments are in the inventory and what is the instrument's condition (with the condition listed in ascending alphabetic order)?* **Print** the query or submit electronically as directed. **Close** the query, and then click **Yes** to save the changes.

14. **Close** any open objects and **Close** the **Navigation Pane**. Click the **Create tab**, and then in the **Other group**, click the **Query Design** button. **Add** the **13C Instruments Inventory** table to the table area, and then expand the field list. Add the following fields to the design grid in the order given: **Instrument ID**, **Category**, **Instrument**, and **Condition**. In the design grid, on the **Criteria** row and under **Condition**, type **Fair** and then press ⏎Enter. **Run** the query. This query answers the question, *What are the Instrument ID, Category, and Instruments*

(Project 13C–Music Department continues on the next page)

Content-Based Assessments

(Project 13C–Music Department continued)

that are in Fair condition? On the **Quick Access Toolbar**, click the **Save** button. Name the query **13C Fair Condition Firstname Lastname** and then **Print** or submit the query electronically. **Close** the query.

15. **Create** a query in **Query Design View**. **Add** the **13C Instruments Inventory** table to the table area, and then expand the field list. Add the following fields to the design grid in the order given: **Category**, **Instrument**, and **Condition**. On the **Criteria** row, under **Category**, type **Woodwinds** and then press Enter. Under **Category**, in the **Show** row, click to clear the **Show** check box, and then **Run** the query. This query answers the question, *What are the conditions of the wood-wind instruments in the inventory?* Recall that if all results use the same criteria, such as Woodwinds, it is not necessary to display the data in the query results. **Save** the query with the name **13C Woodwinds Condition Firstname Lastname** and then **Print** or submit the query electronically. **Close** the query.

16. **Create** a query in **Query Design View**. **Add** the **13C Student Musicians** table to the table area, and then add the following fields to the design grid in the order given: **First Name**, **Last Name**, **Email Address**, and **Phone Number**. On the **Criteria** row, under **Phone Number**, type **Is Null** and then press Enter. On the **Sort** row, click in the **Last Name** field, click the **Sort arrow**, and then click **Ascending**. **Run** the query. This query answers the question, *For which student musicians are phone numbers missing?* **Save** the query as **13C Missing Phone Numbers Firstname Lastname** and then **Print** or submit the query electronically. **Close** the query.

17. If necessary, **Close** any open objects and be sure that the Navigation Pane is closed. From the **Office** menu, click **Close Database**, and then at the right side of the Access title bar, click the **Close** button to close the Access program. Alternatively, from the Office menu, click Exit Access.

End **You have completed Project 13C**

Content-Based Assessments

Skills Review

Project 13D—Concerts and Sponsors

In this project, you will apply the skills you practiced from the Objectives in Project 13B.

Objectives: 8. *Create a New Table by Importing an Excel Spreadsheet;* **9.** *Specify Numeric Criteria in a Query;* **10.** *Use Compound Criteria;* **11.** *Create a Query Based on More Than One Table;* **12.** *Use Wildcards in a Query;* **13.** *Use Calculated Fields in a Query;* **14.** *Group Data and Calculate Statistics in a Query.*

In the following Skills Review, you will assist Pascal Sanchez, College Music Director, in answering questions about concerts, sponsors, box office receipts, dates, and concert locations. Your query results will look similar to those shown in Figure 13.60.

For Project 13D, you will need the following files:

a13D_Concerts_Sponsors
a13D_Sponsors (Excel file)

You will save your database as
13D_Concerts_Sponsors_Firstname_Lastname

Figure 13.60

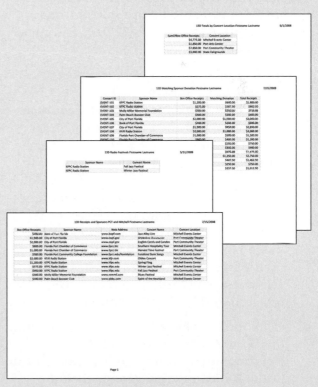

(Project 13D–Concerts and Sponsors continues on the next page)

(Project 13D–Concerts and Sponsors continued)

1. Navigate to the location where the student files for this textbook are saved. Locate **a13D_Concerts_Sponsors** and click one time to select the file. **Copy** and then **Paste** the file to your **Access Chapter 13** folder. **Rename** the file as **13D_Concerts_Sponsors_Firstname_Lastname** and then **Start** Access. Navigate to your **Access Chapter 13** folder, open **13D_Concerts_Sponsors**, and then **Enable this content**.

2. **Open** the **Navigation Pane**. On the Ribbon, click the **External Data tab**, and then in the **Import group**, click the **Excel** button. In the **Get External Data – Excel Spreadsheet** dialog box, to the right of the **File name** box, click **Browse**. Navigate to the location where the student files for this textbook are saved, and then double-click the **a13D_Sponsors** Excel file. Be sure that the **Import the source data into a new table in the current database** option button is selected, and then click **OK**.

3. In the upper portion of the **Import Spreadsheet Wizard**, click to select the **First Row Contains Column Headings** check box, and then click **Next**. Under **Field Options**, do not make any changes for the fields, and then click **Next**. In the upper portion of the Wizard, click the **Choose my own primary key** option button, and then be sure that **Sponsor ID** displays. Click **Next**. In the **Import to Table** box, type **13D Sponsors** and then click **Finish**. In the Wizard, click **Close**. The imported Excel spreadsheet becomes the second table in the database.

4. Click the **Database Tools tab**, and then in the **Show/Hide group**, click the **Relationships** button. On the **Design tab**, in the **Relationships group**, click the

Show Table button. **Add** the **13D Concerts** table, and then **Add** the **13D Sponsors** table to the table area. **Close** the **Show Table** dialog box. Expand the field lists, and then reposition the field lists so that the **13D Sponsors** field list is on the left side.

5. In the **13D Sponsors** field list, point to the **Sponsor ID** field, hold down the left mouse button, drag into the **13D Concerts** field list, position the mouse pointer on top of the **Sponsor ID** field, and then release the mouse button. In the **Edit Relationships** dialog box, click to select the **Enforce Referential Integrity** check box, and then click the **Create** button. A one-to-many relationship is established; *one* sponsor organization can sponsor *many* concerts.

6. On the **Design tab**, in the **Tools group**, click the **Relationship Report** button. If you are submitting paper assignments, on the **Print Preview tab**, click the **Print** button, click **OK**, and then click the **Close Print Preview** button. To submit electronically, follow your instructor's directions. On the **Quick Access Toolbar**, click the **Save** button, and then click **OK** to accept the default name. **Close** all open objects, and then **Close** the **Navigation Pane**.

7. Click the **Create tab**, and then in the **Other group**, click the **Query Design** button. **Add** the **13D Concerts** table to the table area, **Close** the **Show Table** dialog box, and then expand the field list. Add the following fields to the design grid in the order given: **Concert Name**, **Box Office Receipts**, and **Concert Location**. Click in the **Sort** row under **Concert Location**, click the **Sort arrow**, and then click **Ascending**. On the **Criteria** row,

(Project 13D–Concerts and Sponsors continues on the next page)

Content-Based Assessments

(Project 13D–Concerts and Sponsors continued)

under **Box Office Receipts**, type **800** and then press Enter. **Run** the query. Only one concert—*Southern Hospitality Tour*—had Box Office Receipts of exactly $800.

8. On the **Home tab**, in the **Views group**, click the **View** button to switch to **Design** view. On the **Criteria** row, under **Box Office Receipts**, delete the existing criteria, type **>800** and then press Enter. **Run** the query. Eight concerts had Box Office Receipts greater than $800. Switch to **Design** view, change the **Box Office Receipts** criteria to **<800** and then **Run** the query. Eight concerts had Box Office Receipts less than $800. Switch to **Design** view, change **Box Office Receipts** criteria to **>=800** and then **Run** the query. Nine records meet the criteria. This query answers the questions, *Which concerts had Box Office Receipts of $800 or more, what was the amount of the Box Office Receipts, and where was each concert held?* **Save** the query as **13D $800 or More Firstname Lastname Print** or submit electronically as directed.

9. From the **Office** menu, click **Save As**, type **13D Concerts Jan-Apr Firstname Lastname** and then click **OK**. Switch to **Design** view. From the **13D Concerts** field list, add **Date** to the fourth field in the design grid. On the **Criteria** row, under **Box Office Receipts**, delete the existing criteria so that the query is not restricted by receipts. Click in the **Sort** row under **Concert Location**, click the **Sort arrow**, and then click **(not sorted)**. Click in the **Sort** row under **Date**, click the **Sort arrow**, and then click **Ascending**. Click in the **Criteria** row under **Date**, type **Between 01/01/2009 And 04/30/2009** and then press Enter. **Run** the query; five records meet the criteria. This query

answers the question, *What are the name, box office receipts, location, and date, in chronological order, of concerts held between January 1, 2009, and April 30, 2009?* **Print** or submit electronically as directed. **Close** the query and click **Yes** to save the changes to the design.

10. **Create** a query in **Query Design View**. **Add** the **13D Concerts** table to the table area, and then expand the field list. Add the following fields to the design grid in the order given: **Concert Name**, **Concert Location**, and **Box Office Receipts**. On the **Criteria** row under **Concert Location**, type **Port Community Theater** and then press Tab. On the **Criteria** row under **Box Office Receipts**, type **<=1000** and then press Tab. **Run** the query; two records display. This query answers the question, *Which concerts that were held at the Port Community Theater had Box Office Receipts of $1,000 or less?* Switch to **Design** view, and then in the **Concert Location** field, clear the **Show** check box. **Run** the query. Recall that if all the records have the same criteria in one of the fields, it is not necessary to display that field in the query results. **Save** the query as **13D Port Community Theater $1000 or Less Firstname Lastname** and then **Print** or submit the query electronically. **Close** the query.

11. **Create** a query in **Query Design View**. **Add** the **13D Concerts** table to the table area, and then expand the field list. From the **13D Concerts** table, add the following fields to the design grid in the order given: **Concert Name**, **Concert Location**, **Box Office Receipts**, and **Date**. On the **Criteria** row, under **Concert Location**, type **Port Community Theater** On the **or** row, under **Concert Location**, type **Mitchell Events**

(Project 13D–Concerts and Sponsors continues on the next page)

Content-Based Assessments

(Project 13D–Concerts and Sponsors continued)

Center and then press Enter. **Run** the query. Twelve records meet the criteria. This query answers the question, *How many concerts were held at either the Port Community Theater or the Mitchell Events Center?*

12. Switch to **Design** view. On the **or** row, under **Concert Location** delete the text. On the **Criteria** row, under **Concert Location**, delete the existing text, type **Port Community Theater Or Mitchell Events Center** and then press Tab. On the **Criteria** row, under **Box Office Receipts**, type **>1000** and then press Tab. **Run** the query. Four records display. This query answers the questions, *Which concerts held at either the Port Community Theater or the Mitchell Events Center had Box Office Receipts of more than $1,000 and on what dates were the concerts held?* **Save** the query as **13D PCT or Mitchell Over $1000 Firstname Lastname** and then **Print** or submit the query electronically. **Close** the query.

13. **Create** a query in **Query Design View**, **Add** both tables to the table area, and then expand the field lists. Reposition the field lists so that **13D Sponsors** is on the left side. From the **13D Sponsors** field list, add the following fields to the design grid in the order given: **Sponsor ID**, **Sponsor Name**, and **Phone Number**. Click in the **Sort** row under **Sponsor Name**, click the **Sort arrow**, and then click **Ascending**. From the **13D Concerts** field list, add the following fields to the design grid in the order give: **Concert Name**, **Concert Location**, **Box Office Receipts**, and **Date**.

14. On the **Criteria** row, under **Concert Location**, type **Port Community Theater** and then click in the **or** row, under **Concert Location**. Type **Mitchell Events**

Center and then press Enter. **Run** the query. Twelve records display. Switch to **Design** view. From the **13D Sponsors** field list, drag **Web Address** to the design grid on top of **Phone Number**, and then release the mouse button to insert the new field to the right of **Sponsor Name**. Select the **Sponsor ID** field and then delete it.

15. In the design grid, select the **Box Office Receipts** field, and then drag it to the first field position in the grid. Delete the **Phone Number** and **Date** fields. **Run** the query. This query answers the question, *What were the box office receipts, sponsor name, sponsor Web address, concert name, and concert location of all concerts held at either the Port Community Theater or the Mitchell Events Center, sorted alphabetically by sponsor name?*

16. Select all of the columns in the query results, and then double-click any column border to apply **Best Fit**. **Save** the query as **13D Receipts and Sponsors PCT and Mitchell Firstname Lastname** and then display the query results in **Print Preview**. Change the orientation to **Landscape**, change the **Margins** to **Normal**, and then **Print** or submit the query electronically. **Close** the query, **Open** the **Navigation Pane**, and then notice that the query displays under *both* tables from which it retrieved records. **Close** the **Navigation Pane**.

17. **Create** a query in **Query Design View**, **Add** both tables to the table area, and then expand the field lists. Reposition the field lists so that **13D Sponsors** is on the left side. From the **13D Sponsors** table, add the **Sponsor Name** field to the design grid. From the **13D Concerts** table, add the **Concert Name** field to the design grid. On

(Project 13D–Concerts and Sponsors continues on the next page)

Content-Based Assessments

(Project 13D–Concerts and Sponsors continued)

the **Criteria** row, under **Sponsor Name**, type **Florida*** and then press Enter. **Run** the query and widen the **Sponsor Name** column to display all of the data. Three sponsors have names that begin with *Florida*.

18. Switch to **Design** view. On the **Criteria** row, under **Sponsor Name**, delete the text. On the **Criteria** row, under **Concert Name**, type ***Festival** and then press Enter. **Run** the query; five Concert Names end with the word *Festival*. Switch to **Design** view. On the **Criteria** row, under **Sponsor Name**, type ***Radio*** and then press Enter. **Run** the query; two records have the word *Radio* somewhere in the Sponsor Name and the word *Festival* at the end of the Concert Name. This query answers the question, *Which radio stations are sponsoring Festival-type concerts?* **Save** the query as **13D Radio Festivals Firstname Lastname** and then **Print** or submit the query electronically. **Close** the query.

19. **Create** a query in **Query Design View**. **Add** both tables to the table area, and then expand the field lists. Reposition the field lists so that **13D Sponsors** is on the left side. From the field lists, add the following fields to the design grid in the order given: **Concert ID**, **Sponsor Name**, and **Box Office Receipts**. Click in the **Sort** row under **Concert ID**, click the **Sort arrow**, and then click **Ascending**. Sponsors have indicated that they will donate an additional amount to the Music Department based on 50 percent of the Box Office Receipts. On the **Field** row, right-click in the first empty column to display a shortcut menu, and then click **Zoom**. In the **Zoom** dialog box, type **Matching Donation:[Box Office Receipts]*0.5** and then click **OK**. **Run** the query to view the new field—*Matching Donation*.

20. Switch to **Design** view. In the **Field** row, in the first empty column, right-click, and then click **Zoom**. In the **Zoom** dialog box, type **Total Receipts:[Box Office Receipts]+ [Matching Donation]** and then click **OK**. In the **Field** row, click in the **Matching Donation** field (fourth column), and then on the **Design tab**, in the **Show/Hide group**, click the **Property Sheet** button. In the **Property Sheet**, click in the **Format** property setting box, click the **arrow**, and then click **Currency**. **Close** the **Property Sheet**.

21. **Run** the query. This query answers the question, *In ascending order by Concert ID, assuming each sponsor makes a matching 50 percent donation based on each concert's Box Office Receipts, what are the Sponsor Name, Box Office Receipts, Matching Donation, and Total Receipts for each concert?* Select all of the columns, and then apply **Best Fit**. **Save** the query as **13D Matching Sponsor Donation Firstname Lastname** and then display the query results in **Print Preview**. Change the orientation to **Landscape**, and then **Print** or submit the query electronically. **Close** the query.

22. **Create** a query in **Query Design View**. **Add** the **13D Concerts** table to the table area, expand the field list, and then add the **Box Office Receipts** field to the design grid. On the **Design tab**, in the **Show/Hide group**, click the **Totals** button, which adds a *Total* row as the third row in the design grid. On the **Total** row, under **Box Office Receipts**, click in the **Group By** box, and then click the **arrow**. In the list of functions, click **Min**, and then **Run** the query. The lowest amount of Box Office Receipts for any concert was $400.00.

(Project 13D–Concerts and Sponsors continues on the next page)

Content-Based Assessments

(Project 13D–Concerts and Sponsors continued)

23. Switch to **Design** view. On the **Total** row, under **Box Office Receipts**, select the **Max** function, and then **Run** the query. The highest amount of Box Office Receipts for any concert was *$2,500.00.* Switch to **Design** view. On the **Total** row, under **Box Office Receipts**, select the **Avg** function, and then **Run** the query. The average Box Office Receipts for each concert was *$1,027.94.* Using the same technique, select the **Sum** function and then **Run** the query. The total Box Office Receipts for all the concerts was *$17,475.00.*

24. Apply **Best Fit** to the **SumOfBox Office Receipts** column. Switch to **Design** view. Add the **Sponsor ID** field to the design grid, and then **Run** the query. Concerts sponsored by *SPONSOR-101* had the largest amount of Box Office Receipts— *$4,975.00.*

25. Switch to **Design** view. In the design grid, select and delete the **Sponsor ID** field, and then add the **Concert Location** field to the design grid. **Run** the query. This query answers the question, *What are the total Box Office Receipts for each concert location?* **Save** the query as **13D Totals by Concert Location Firstname Lastname** and then **Print** or submit the query electronically. **Close** the query. From the **Office** menu, click **Close Database**, and then at the right side of the Access title bar, click the **Close** button to close the Access program. Alternatively, from the Office menu, click Exit Access.

End **You have completed Project 13D** —————————————

Content-Based Assessments

Mastering Access

Project 13E — Grants and Organizations

In this project, you will apply the skills you practiced from the Objectives in Projects 13A and 13B.

Objectives: 1. *Open an Existing Database;* **2.** *Create Table Relationships;* **4.** *Create a Query in Design View;* **5.** *Create a new Query from an Existing Query;* **6.** *Sort Query Results;* **7.** *Specify Criteria in a Query;* **8.** *Create a New Table by Importing an Excel Spreadsheet;* **9.** *Specify Numeric Criteria in a Query;* **10.** *Use Compound Criteria;* **11.** *Create a Query Based on More Than One Table;* **12.** *Use Wildcards in a Query;* **14.** *Group Data and Calculate Statistics in a Query.*

In the following Mastering Access project, you will assist Peter Donahue, Director of Grants for the college, in using his database to answer questions about public and private grants awarded to college departments. Your query results will look similar to those shown in Figure 13.61.

For Project 13E, you will need the following files:

a13E_Grants_Organizations
a13E_Organizations (Excel file)

You will save your database as
13E_Grants_Organizations_Firstname_Lastname

Figure 13.61

(Project 13E–Grants and Organizations continues on the next page)

Content-Based Assessments

(Project 13E–Grants and Organizations continued)

1. Navigate to the location where the student files for this textbook are saved. Locate **a13E_Grants_Organizations** and click one time to select the file. **Copy** and then **Paste** the file to your **Access Chapter 13** folder. **Rename** the file as **13E_Grants_Organizations_Firstname_Lastname** and then **Start** Access. Navigate to your **Access Chapter 13** folder, open **13E_Grants_Organizations**, and then **Enable this content**.

2. **Import** the **a13E_Organizations** Excel spreadsheet from the student data files that accompany this textbook into the current database. Use the first row of the spreadsheet as the column headings, and then choose the **Organization ID** field as the primary key. Name the table **13E Organizations**.

3. **Open** the **Navigation Pane**, open the database tables, and then examine their fields and records to become familiar with the data. **Close** the tables, and then **Close** the **Navigation Pane**. Create a one-to-many relationship between the **13E Organizations** table and the **13E Grants Awarded** table based on the **Organization ID** field, and then **Enforce Referential Integrity**; *one* Organization can award *many* Grants. Create a **Relationship Report**, saving it with the default name. **Print** or submit the report electronically as directed, and then **Close** all open objects.

4. **Create** a query in **Query Design** view using both tables to answer the question, *What are the Organization ID and Award Amount for grants greater than $10,000 and to what Departments (in alphabetical order) were the grants awarded?* Display the fields in the order listed in the question. Twelve records meet the criteria.

Apply **Best Fit** to the columns in the query results. **Save** the query as **13E Grants Over $10K Firstname Lastname** and then **Print** or submit the query electronically as directed. Leave the query open.

5. Create a query from the **13E Grants Over $10K** query. **Save As 13E Grants 1st Quarter Firstname Lastname** and then redesign the query to answer the question, *In chronological order by Award Date, which Grants were awarded between 01/01/2009 and 03/31/2009, from which Organization ID, for what amount, and to which Department?* Display the fields in the order listed in the question, display *only* the fields listed in the question, sort *only* on one field, and do *not* restrict the amount. Seven records meet the criteria. Apply **Best Fit** to the columns in the query results. In **Print Preview**, set the orientation to **Landscape**, and then **Print** or submit the query electronically as directed. **Close** the query, saving the design changes.

6. **Create** a query in **Query Design View**. Use the **13E Grants Awarded** table to answer the question, *What are the names of privately funded grants awarded to either the Social Science or Humanities department, on what date were they awarded, and with the largest grants listed first, for what amount?* (Hint: Open the 13E Grants Awarded table to see how the data is stored in the fields.) Display the results in the order listed in the question. Nine records meet the criteria. (Hint: If 11 records display, return to **Design** view and use the OR operator to place the department criteria on one line in the design grid.) Do *not* show the type of grant in the query results. **Save** the query as **13E Private SS and HMN Grants Firstname**

(Project 13E–Grants and Organizations continues on the next page)

Content-Based Assessments

(Project 13E–Grants and Organizations continued)

Lastname and then display the query results in **Print Preview**. Set the orientation to **Landscape**, and then **Print** or submit the query electronically as directed. **Close** the query.

7. **Create** a query in **Query Design View** using both tables to answer the question, *Which grants were awarded to either the Science or Health Technology department, for what amount, and, from which Organization Name (in alphabetical order)?* Seven records meet the criteria. Apply **Best Fit** to the columns in the query results. **Save** the query as **13E Science and Health Tech Firstname Lastname** and then display the query results in **Print Preview**. Set the orientation to **Landscape**, and then **Print** or submit the query electronically as directed. **Close** the query.

8. **Create** a query in **Query Design View** using both tables to answer the question, *Which grants were awarded from organizations that are Foundations, what is the name of the organization, what is the amount of the grant listed in descending order by amount, and what is the name and phone number of the organization contact?* (Hint: Use a wildcard in the format of **Foundation** to find organization names containing the word *Foundation*.) Fourteen records meet the criteria. Apply **Best Fit** to the columns in the query results. **Save** the query as **13E Foundation Grants Firstname Lastname** and then display the query results in **Print Preview**. Change the orientation to **Landscape**, set the **Margins** to **Normal**, and then **Print** or submit the query electronically as directed. **Close** the query.

9. **Create** a query in **Query Design View**. Using the **13E Grants Awarded** table and the **Sum** aggregate function, answer the question, *Listed from the largest amounts to the smallest, what are the total Award Amounts for each Department?* The *Humanities* Department received *$93,000.00*. Apply **Best Fit** to the columns in the query results. **Save** the query as **13E Totals by Department Firstname Lastname** and then **Print** or submit the query electronically as directed. **Close** the query, **Close** the Database, and then **Exit** Access.

End You have completed Project 13E

Content-Based Assessments

Project 13F—Events and Clients

In this project, you will apply skills you practiced from the Objectives in Projects 13A and 13B.

Objectives: 1. *Open an Existing Database;* **2.** *Create Table Relationships;* **4.** *Create a Query in Design View;* **5.** *Create a New Query from an Existing Query;* **6.** *Sort Query Results;* **7.** *Specify Criteria in a Query;* **8.** *Create a New Table by Importing an Excel Spreadsheet;* **9.** *Specify Numeric Criteria in a Query;* **10.** *Use Compound Criteria;* **11.** *Create a Query Based on More Than One Table;* **12.** *Use Wildcards in a Query;* **13.** *Use Calculated Fields in a Query;* **14.** *Group Data and Calculate Statistics in a Query.*

In the following Mastering Access project, you will assist Peter Steinmetz, Facilities Manager at the college, in using his database to answer questions about facilities that the college rents to community and private organizations. Renting the facilities at times when they are not in use for college activities requires additional funding to maintain and staff the facilities. Your query results will look similar to those shown in Figure 13.62.

For Project 13F, you will need the following files:

a13F_Events_Clients
a13F_Rental_Clients (Excel file)

You will save your database as
13F_Events_Clients_Firstname_Lastname

Figure 13.62

(Project 13F–Events and Clients continues on the next page)

Content-Based Assessments

(Project 13F–Events and Clients continued)

1. Navigate to the location where the student files for this textbook are saved. Locate **a13F_Events_Clients** and click one time to select the file. **Copy** and then **Paste** the file to your **Access Chapter 13** folder. **Rename** the file as 13F_Events_Clients_Firstname_Lastname and then **Start** Access. Navigate to your **Access Chapter 13** folder, open **13F_Events_Clients**, and then **Enable this content**.

2. **Import** the **a13F_Rental_Clients** Excel spreadsheet from the student data files that accompany this textbook into the current database. Use the first row of the spreadsheet as the column headings, and then choose the **Rental Client ID** field as the primary key. Name the table **13F Rental Clients**

3. **Open** the **Navigation Pane**, open the database tables, and then examine their fields and records to become familiar with the data. **Close** the tables, and then **Close** the **Navigation Pane**. Create a one-to-many relationship between the **13F Rental Clients** table and the **13F Events** table based on the **Rental Client ID** field, and then **Enforce Referential Integrity**; *one* Rental Client can have *many* Events. Create a **Relationship Report**, saving it with the default name. **Print** or submit the report electronically as directed, and then **Close** all open objects, saving changes if prompted.

4. **Create** a query in **Query Design View** using the 13F Events table to answer the question, *What are the Event Name, Rental Client ID, and Rental Fee for events with fees greater than or equal to $500, in ascending order by Rental Client ID, and in which Facility was the event held?* Display the fields in the order listed in the question.

    Eleven records meet the criteria. **Save** the query as **13F Fees $500 or More Firstname Lastname** and then **Print** or submit the query electronically as directed. Leave the query open.

5. **Create** a query from the **13F Fees $500 or More** query. **Save** the query as **13F Afternoon Events Firstname Lastname** and then redesign the query to answer the question, *Which Events were held in the Afternoon between 07/01/2009 and 08/31/2009, in chronological order by date, what was the Rental Fee, and what was the Event ID?* (Hint: Open the 13F Events table to see how the data is stored in the fields.) Display the fields in the order listed in the question, but do *not* display the **Time** field in the result. Do *not* restrict the result by Rental Fee. Four records meet the criteria. **Print** or submit the query electronically as directed. **Close** the query, saving design changes.

6. **Create** a query in **Query Design View** using the **13F Events** table to answer the question, *Which Events and Event Types were held in either the White Sands Music Hall or the Theater that had Rental Fees greater than $500?* Three records meet the criteria. Apply **Best Fit** to the columns in the query results. **Save** the query as **13F White Sands and Theater Over $500 Firstname Lastname** and then **Print** or submit the query electronically as directed. **Close** the query.

7. **Create** a query in **Query Design View** using both tables to answer the question, *Which Events were held on one of the sports fields, for which Renter Name, and what was the Rental Fee in order of lowest fee to highest fee?* (Hint: Use a wildcard with the word *Field*.) Five records meet the

(Project 13F–Events and Clients continues on the next page)

(Project 13F–Events and Clients continued)

criteria. Apply **Best Fit** to the columns in the query results. **Save** the query as **13F Field Usage Firstname Lastname** and then **Print** or submit the query electronically as directed. **Close** the query.

8. **Create** a query in **Query Design View**. Using the **13F Events** table and the **Sum** aggregate function, answer the question, *In descending order by total, what are the total Rental Fees for each Event Type?* Change the properties of all appropriate fields to display in **Currency** format with **0** decimal places. For a *Sports* Event Type, Rental Fees totaled *$8,900.* Apply **Best Fit** to the columns in the query results. **Save** the query as **13F Totals by Event Type Firstname Lastname** and then **Print** or submit the query electronically as directed. **Close** the query.

9. The college Alumni Association will donate money to the Building Fund in an amount based on 10 percent of total facility rental fees. **Create** a query in **Query Design View** to answer the question, *In ascending order by Event ID, what will the total of each Rental Fee be if the Alumni Association donates an additional 10 percent of each fee?* (Hint: First compute the amount of the donation and name the new field **Amount of Donation** and then calculate the new rental fee and name the new field **New Rental Fee Amount**) As necessary, change the properties of the new fields to display in **Currency** format with **0** decimal places. For *EVENT-1244,* the *Amount of Donation* is *$150* and the *New Rental Fee Amount* is $1,650. Apply **Best Fit** to the columns in the query results. **Save** the query as **13F Alumni Donation Firstname Lastname** and then **Print** or submit the query electronically as directed. **Close** the query, **Close** the Database, and then **Exit** Access.

End You have completed Project 13F

Content-Based Assessments

Mastering Access

Project 13G — Students and Scholarships

In this project, you will apply the skills you practiced from all the Objectives in Projects 13A and 13B.

Objectives: 1. *Open an Existing Database;* **2.** *Create Table Relationships;* **3.** *Sort Records in a Table;* **4.** *Create a Query in Design View;* **5.** *Create a New Query From an Existing Query;* **6.** *Sort Query Results;* **7.** *Specify Criteria in a Query;* **8.** *Create a New Table by Importing an Excel Spreadsheet;* **9.** *Specify Numeric Criteria in a Query;* **10.** *Use Compound Criteria;* **11.** *Create a Query Based on More Than One Table;* **12.** *Use Wildcards in a Query;* **13.** *Use Calculated Fields in a Query;* **14.** *Group Data and Calculate Statistics in a Query.*

In the following Mastering Access project, you will assist Diane Nguyen, director of academic scholarships, in using her database to answer questions about academic scholarships awarded to students. Your query results will look similar to those shown in Figure 13.63.

> **For Project 13G, you will need the following files:**
>
> a13G_Students_Scholarships
> a13G_Students (Excel file)

You will save your database as
13G_Students_Scholarships_Firstname_Lastname

Figure 13.63

(Project 13G–Students and Scholarships continues on the next page)

Access

chapterthirteen

(Project 13G–Students and Scholarships continued)

1. Navigate to the location where the student files for this textbook are saved. Locate **a13G_Students_Scholarships** and click one time to select the file. **Copy** and then **Paste** the file to your **Access Chapter 13** folder. **Rename** the file as 13G_Students_Scholarships_Firstname_Lastname and then **Start** Access. Navigate to your **Access Chapter 13** folder, open **13G_Students_Scholarships**, and then **Enable this content**.

2. **Import** the **a13G_Students** Excel spreadsheet from the student data files that accompany this textbook into the current database. Use the first row of the spreadsheet as the column headings, and choose the **Student ID** field as the primary key. Name the table **13G Students**

3. **Open** the **Navigation Pane**, open the two database tables, and then examine their fields and records to become familiar with the data. **Close** the tables, and then **Close** the **Navigation Pane**. Create a one-to-many relationship between the **13G Students** table and the **13G Scholarships Awarded** table based on the **Student ID** field, and then **Enforce Referential Integrity**; *one* student can have *many* scholarships. Create the **Relationship Report**, and then **Print** or submit the report electronically as directed, saving it with the default name. **Close** all open objects.

4. **Open** the **Navigation Pane**, display the **13G Students** table, and notice the **+** signs that indicate the relationships you created. **Close** the **Navigation Pane**. Perform a multiple-field sort on the table to sort students in alphabetic order by Last Name within City names that are also in alphabetical order. Remember to sort *first* by the innermost sort field. After examining the sorted table, **Clear All**

Sorts, **Close** the table, and do not save the changes.

5. **Create** a query in **Query Design View** using the **13G Scholarships Awarded** table to answer the question, *In alphabetical order by Scholarship Name, what are the Scholarship Name, Amount, and Major for scholarships greater than or equal to $500?* Display the fields in the order listed in the question. Ten records meet the criteria. **Save** the query as **13G Scholarships $500 or More Firstname Lastname** and then **Print** or submit the query electronically as directed. Leave the query open.

6. Create a query from the **13G Scholarships $500 or More** query. **Save** the query as **13G Scholarships 1st Quarter Firstname Lastname** and then redesign the query to answer the question, *In chronological order by Award Date, which scholarships were awarded between 01/01/2009 and 03/31/2009, for what amount, and what was the last name of the student?* Be sure the fields display in the order listed in the question, display *only* the fields listed in the question, do not restrict the amount, and sort only by date. Eight records meet the criteria. **Print** or submit the query electronically as directed. **Close** the query, saving the design changes.

7. **Create** a query in **Query Design View** using the **13G Scholarships Awarded** table to answer the question, *Which scholarships were awarded for either Nursing or CIS majors for amounts of more than $100, listed in descending order by amount?* Display the fields in the order listed in the question. Four records meet the criteria. (Hint: If five records display, switch to **Design** view and combine the majors on one criteria line using OR.) **Save** the query as **13G Nursing and CIS $100 Firstname Lastname** and then

(Project 13G–Students and Scholarships continues on the next page)

Content-Based Assessments

(Project 13G–Students and Scholarships continued)

Print or submit the query electronically as directed. **Close** the query.

8. **Create** a query in **Query Design View**. Use the **13G Students** table and a wild-card to answer the question, *In alphabetical order by Last Name, what are the Student ID, First Name, Last Name, and City of all students in cities that begin with the letter B?* Display the fields in the order listed in the question. Five records meet the criteria. **Save** the query as **13G Cities Firstname Lastname** and then **Print** or submit the query electronically as directed. **Close** the query.

9. **Create** a query in **Query Design View** using the **13G Students** table and all of the table's fields to answer the question, *For which students is the Address missing?* Three students are missing addresses. Apply **Best Fit** to the columns. **Save** the query as **13G Missing Addresses Firstname Lastname** and then **Print** or submit the query electronically as directed. **Close** the query.

10. **Create** a query in **Query Design View**. Use the **13G Scholarships Awarde**d table and the **Sum** aggregate function to answer the question, *In descending order by amount, what is the total scholarship amount for each Major?* Display the fields in the order listed in the question. Use the **Property Sheet** to display the sums in the **Currency** format with **0** decimal places. *History majors received $1,850 in scholarships.*

Apply **Best Fit** to the columns in the query results. **Save** the query as **13G Totals by Major Firstname Lastname** and then **Print** or submit the query electronically as directed. **Close** the query.

11. For each academic scholarship received by students, the Board of Trustees of the college will donate an amount equal to 50 percent of each scholarship. **Create** a query in **Query Design View**. Use both tables and calculated fields to answer the question, *In alphabetical order by scholarship name, and including the first and last name of the scholarship recipient, what will the value of each scholarship be if the Board of Trustees makes a matching 50 percent donation?* (Hint: First compute the amount of the donation, naming the new field **Donation** and then calculate the new scholarship value, naming the new field **New Value**) As necessary, change the properties of all the numeric fields to display in **Currency** format with **0** decimal places. For the *Bankers Association Scholarship*, the *Donation* is *$100* and the *New Value* is *$300*. Apply **Best Fit** to the columns in the query results. **Save** the query as **13G Trustee Donation Firstname Lastname** and then display the query results in **Print Preview**. Set the orientation to **Landscape**, and then **Print** or submit the query electronically as directed. **Close** the query, **Close** the Database, and then **Exit** Access.

End You have completed Project 13G

Content-Based Assessments

Project 13H — *GO!* Fix It

In this project, you will apply the skills you practiced from the Objectives in Projects 13A and 13B.

For Project 13H, you will need the following file:

a13H_Division_Social_Science

You will save your document as
13H_Division_Social_Science_Firstname_Lastname

Navigate to the location where the student files for this textbook are saved. Locate **a13H_Division_Social_Science** and click one time to select the file. **Copy** and then **Paste** the file to your **Access Chapter 13** folder. **Rename** the file as **13H_Division_Social_Science_Firstname_Lastname** and then **Start** Access. Navigate to your **Access Chapter 13** folder, open **13H_Division_Social_Science**, and then **Enable this content**.

This database contains **five errors** that you must find and correct. Examine the tables and queries in the database, and then edit to correct the errors that you find. Types of errors could include:

- Missing or incorrect data in tables, queries, forms, and reports such as file names, field names, types, descriptions, properties, records, and criteria.

- Table design errors such as primary key.

- Query design errors such as field, table, show, sort, and criteria.

- Forms design errors such as form header and footer, page header and footer, detail, and layout.

- Reports design errors such as report header and footer, page header and footer, detail, and layout.

- Page setup errors such as margins, orientation, layout, or alignment.

To complete the project, you should know:

- There is no table relationship between the Faculty table and the Course Schedule table. Create the relationship and the report; one faculty member can teach many courses.

- Examine and correct any queries that do not accurately reflect the query name. Add your first name and last name to the query name.

Print the relationship report and the four queries or submit your database as directed.

 End You have completed Project 13H

Outcomes-Based Assessments

Rubric

The following outcomes-based assessments are *open-ended assessments*. That is, there is no specific correct result; your result will depend on your approach to the information provided. Make *Professional Quality* your goal. Use the following scoring rubric to guide you in *how* to approach the problem and then to evaluate *how well* your approach solves the problem.

The *criteria*—Software Mastery, Content, Format and Layout, and Process—represent the knowledge and skills you have gained that you can apply to solving the problem. The *levels of performance*—Professional Quality, Approaching Professional Quality, or Needs Quality Improvements—help you and your instructor evaluate your result.

	Your completed project is of Professional Quality if you:	Your completed project is Approaching Professional Quality if you:	Your completed project Needs Quality Improvements if you:
1-Software Mastery	Choose and apply the most appropriate skills, tools, and features and identify efficient methods to solve the problem.	Choose and apply some appropriate skills, tools, and features, but not in the most efficient manner.	Choose inappropriate skills, tools, or features, or are inefficient in solving the problem.
2-Content	Construct a solution that is clear and well organized, contains content that is accurate, appropriate to the audience and purpose, and is complete. Provide a solution that contains no errors of spelling, grammar, or style.	Construct a solution in which some components are unclear, poorly organized, inconsistent, or incomplete. Misjudge the needs of the audience. Have some errors in spelling, grammar, or style, but the errors do not detract from comprehension.	Construct a solution that is unclear, incomplete, or poorly organized; contains some inaccurate or inappropriate content; and contains many errors of spelling, grammar, or style. Do not solve the problem.
3-Format and Layout	Format and arrange all elements to communicate information and ideas, clarify function, illustrate relationships, and indicate relative importance.	Apply appropriate format and layout features to some elements, but not others. Overuse features, causing minor distraction.	Apply format and layout that does not communicate information or ideas clearly. Do not use format and layout features to clarify function, illustrate relationships, or indicate relative importance. Use available features excessively, causing distraction.
4-Process	Use an organized approach that integrates planning, development, self-assessment, revision, and reflection.	Demonstrate an organized approach in some areas, but not others; or, use an insufficient process of organization throughout.	Do not use an organized approach to solve the problem.

Outcomes-Based Assessments

Problem Solving

Project 13I — Student Refunds

In this project, you will construct a solution by applying any combination of the skills you practiced from the Objectives in Projects 13A and 13B.

For Project 13I, you will need the following files:

a13I_Student_Refunds
a13I_Student_Refunds (Word document)

**You will save your database as
13I_Student_Refunds_Firstname_Lastname**

Start Microsoft Word, and then from your student files, open the Word document **a13I_Student_Refunds**. Use the skills you have practiced in this chapter to assist Kathy Knudsen, the Associate Dean of Student Services, in answering questions about student refunds in your database **13I_Student_Refunds_Firstname_Lastname**. Save queries that you create, include your name in the query title, and submit your queries as directed by your instructor. Record your answers to the questions in the Word document.

End You have completed Project 13I ——————————

Outcomes-Based Assessments

Access

chapter thirteen

Problem Solving

Project 13J—Leave

In this project, you will construct a solution by applying any combination of the skills you practiced from the Objectives in Projects 13A and 13B.

For Project 13J, you will need the following files:

a13J_Leave
a13J_Leave (Word document)

**You will save your database as
13J_Leave_Firstname_Lastname**

Start Microsoft Word, and then from your student files, open the Word document **a13J_Leave**. Use the skills you have practiced in this chapter to assist Gabe Stevens, the Director of Human Resources, in answering questions about employee leave time in your database **13J_Leave_Firstname_Lastname**. Save queries that you create, include your name in the query title, and submit your queries as directed by your instructor. Record your answers to the questions in the Word document.

End **You have completed Project 13J**

Outcomes-Based Assessments

Problem Solving

Project 13K — Coaches

In this project, you will construct a solution by applying any combination of the skills you practiced from the Objectives in Projects 13A and 13B.

> **For Project 13K, you will need the following files:**
>
> a13K_Coaches
> a13K_Coaches (Word document)

You will save your database as
13K_Coaches_Firstname_Lastname

Start Microsoft Word, and then from your student files, open the Word document **a13K_Coaches**. Use the skills you have practiced in this chapter to assist Marcus Simmons, the Athletic Director, in answering questions about the coaches in your database **13K_Coaches_Firstname_Lastname**. Save queries that you create, include your name in the query title, and submit your queries as directed by your instructor. Record your answers to the questions in the Word document.

End **You have completed Project 13K** ————————————————

More on your Student CD

The instructions for the following additional end-of-chapter projects are on your student CD in the folder 03_additional_end_of_chapter_projects.

Content-Based Assessments

Project L Mastering Access   Apply the skills you practiced in Project A.

Project M Mastering Access   Apply the skills you practiced in Project B.

Project N Business Running Case   Apply the skills you practiced in Projects A and B while helping an entrepreneur with the daily tasks of running a business.

In each chapter, this project focuses on applying the skills you have practiced in Projects A and B to a business. The project related to this business runs throughout the textbook. You will see how the Office applications relate to the day-to-day operation of a small business called Nelson Architectural Planning.

Outcomes-Based Assessments

Project O Problem Solving   Construct a solution by applying any combination of the skills you practiced from Projects A and B.

Project P Problem Solving   Construct a solution by applying any combination of the skills you practiced from Projects A and B.

Project Q You and GO!   Construct a solution that applies to your own life by applying any combination of the skills you practiced from Projects A and B.

Project R GO! with Help   Practice using Microsoft Office's Help Feature.

Project S Group Business Running Case   Work as part of a group to apply the skills you have gained thus far to help the Bell Orchid Hotel Group achieve its business goals.

Multimedia

The following multimedia accompany this textbook:

Companion Web site   An interactive Web site designed to reinforce and test your under-
www.prenhall.com/go   standing of the skills in this chapter.

AV-EDDs   In the folder in the front of this book you will find videos that demon-
                                     strate the objectives of the A and B projects in this chapter. These may
                                     help you understand how to complete the projects in this book.

Video Podcasts   In the folder in the front of this book are videos that can be played
                                     on your iPod, MP3 player, or computer. These videos demonstrate
                                     how to complete the more challenging objectives in this textbook.

chapter fifteen

Getting Started with Microsoft Office PowerPoint 2007

OBJECTIVES

At the end of this chapter you will be able to:

1. Open, View, and Save a Presentation
2. Edit a Presentation
3. Format a Presentation
4. Create Headers and Footers and Print a Presentation

OUTCOMES

Mastering these objectives will enable you to:

PROJECT 15A
Open, Edit, Save, and Print a Presentation

5. Create a New Presentation
6. Use Slide Sorter View
7. Add Pictures to a Presentation
8. Use the Microsoft Help System

PROJECT 15B
Create and Format a Presentation

Skyline Bakery and Cafe

Skyline Bakery and Cafe is a chain of casual dining restaurants and bakeries based in Boston. Each restaurant has its own in-house bakery, which produces a wide variety of high-quality specialty breads, breakfast sweets, and desserts. Breads and sweets are sold by counter service along with coffee drinks, gourmet teas, fresh juices, and sodas. The full-service restaurant area features a menu of sandwiches, salads, soups, and light entrees. Fresh, high-quality ingredients and a professional and courteous staff are the hallmarks of every Skyline Bakery and Cafe.

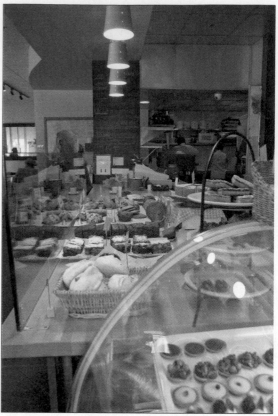

© Angus Oborn / Rough Guides / Dorling Kindersley

Getting Started with Microsoft Office PowerPoint 2007

Presentation skills are among the most important skills you will learn. Good presentation skills enhance your communications—written, electronic, and interpersonal. In our technology-enhanced world of e-mail and cellular phones, communicating ideas clearly and concisely is a critical personal skill. Microsoft Office PowerPoint 2007 is a presentation graphics software program used to create electronic slide presentations and black-and-white or color overhead transparencies. Use PowerPoint to effectively present information to your audience.

Project 15A **Expansion**

In Activities 15.01 through 15.17, you will edit and format a presentation that Lucinda dePaolo, Chief Financial Officer, created to detail the Skyline Bakery and Cafe's expansion plan. Your completed presentation will look similar to Figure 15.1.

For Project 15A, you will need the following file:

p15A_Expansion

You will save your presentation as
15A_Expansion_Firstname_Lastname

Skyline Bakery and Cafe

Expansion Plans

Mission

To provide a nutritious, satisfying, and delicious

meal experience for each of our customers in a

relaxing and temptingly aromatic environment.

Company Information

▸ **Founded in Boston by Samir Taheri in 1985**
▸ **Current locations in Massachusetts and Maine**
▸ **Expansion plans in 2009**
  ▫ Rhode Island
  ▫ Virginia
▸ **Awards received this year**
  ▫ Golden Bakery
  ▫ Cuisine Excellence

Expansion Plans

▸ **2009**
  ▫ Rhode Island and Virginia
▸ **2010**
  ▫ New Hampshire and New Jersey
▸ **2011**
  ▫ West Virginia and Ohio
▸ **2012**
  ▫ New York and Connecticut

Figure 15.1
Project 15A—Expansion

Objective 1
Open, View, and Save a Presentation

Microsoft Office PowerPoint is a ***presentation graphics software*** program that you can use to effectively present information to your audience. In the following activities, you will start Microsoft Office PowerPoint 2007, become familiar with the PowerPoint window, and then open, edit, and save an existing PowerPoint presentation.

Activity 15.01 Starting PowerPoint and Identifying Parts of the PowerPoint Window

In this activity, you will start PowerPoint and identify the parts of the PowerPoint window.

> **Note — Comparing Your Screen with the Figures in This Textbook**
>
> Your screen will match the figures shown in this textbook if you set your screen resolution to 1024 × 768. At other resolutions, your screen will closely resemble, but not match, the figures shown. To view your screen's resolution, on the Windows Vista desktop, right-click in a blank area, click Personalize, and then click Display Settings.

1 On the left side of the Windows taskbar, click the **Start** button.

2 From the **Start** menu, locate the **PowerPoint** program, and then click **Microsoft Office PowerPoint 2007**.

> The PowerPoint program may be located under All Programs or Microsoft Office or on the Start menu.

3 Take a moment to study the parts of the screen as shown in Figure 15.2 and described in the table in Figure 15.3.

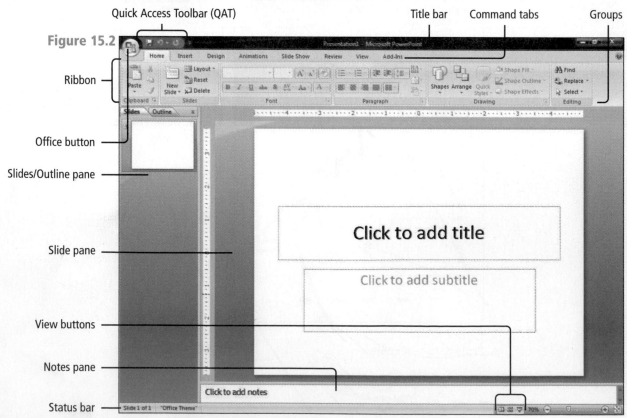

Figure 15.2

Quick Access Toolbar (QAT)   Title bar   Command tabs   Groups

Ribbon

Office button

Slides/Outline pane

Slide pane

View buttons

Notes pane

Status bar

Microsoft PowerPoint Screen Elements

Screen Element	Description
Command tab	Displays the commands most relevant for a particular task area, such as inserting, designing, and animating.
Group	Identifies related command buttons associated with the selected command tab.
Notes pane	Displays below the Slide pane and allows you to type notes regarding the active slide.
Office button	Displays a list of commands related to things you can do with a presentation, such as opening, saving, printing, or sharing.
Quick Access Toolbar (QAT)	Displays buttons to perform frequently used commands with a single click. Frequently used commands in PowerPoint include Save, Undo, and Repeat. For commands that you use frequently, you can add additional buttons to the Quick Access Toolbar.
Ribbon	Organizes commands on tabs, and then groups the commands by topic for performing related presentation tasks.
Slide pane	Displays a large image of the active slide.
Slides/Outline pane	Displays either the presentation outline (Outline tab) or all of the slides in the presentation in the form of miniature images called *thumbnails* (Slides tab).
Status bar	A horizontal bar at the bottom of the presentation window that displays the current slide number, number of slides in a presentation, Theme, View buttons, Zoom slider, and Fit slide to current window button. The status bar can be customized to include other information.
Title bar	Displays the name of the presentation and the name of the program. The Minimize, Maximize/Restore Down, and Close buttons are grouped on the right side of the title bar.
View buttons	A set of commands that control the look of the presentation window.

Figure 15.3

Alert!

Does your screen differ?

The appearance of the screen can vary, depending on settings that were established when the program was installed. For example, the Add-Ins tab may or may not display on your Ribbon. Additionally, the Quick Access Toolbar can display any combination of buttons, and may occupy its own row on the Ribbon.

Activity 15.02 Opening a Presentation

To open a presentation that has already been created in PowerPoint, use the Office button. As you edit a presentation, save your changes frequently.

1 In the upper left corner of the PowerPoint window, click the **Office** button , and then click **Open** to display the **Open** dialog box.

2 On the left side of the **Open** dialog box, in the **Navigation pane**, under **Favorite Links**, if necessary, click More, and then click Computer to view a list of the drives available to you as shown in Figure 15.4.

Your list of available drives may differ.

Figure 15.4

Your list of available drives will differ

Favorite Links

Computer

Navigation pane

3 Navigate to the location where the student files for this textbook are stored. Click **p15A_Expansion**, and then click the **Open** button or press Enter to display **Slide 1** of the presentation in the PowerPoint window.

The file name displays in the title bar at the top of the screen.

4 Look at the **Slides/Outline pane** on the left side of the window. Notice that the presentation contains four slides, and at the right side of the window, a scroll bar displays a scroll box and up- and down-pointing arrows for navigating through your presentation.

5 Below the scroll bar, locate the **Previous Slide** ⬆ and **Next Slide** ⬇ buttons as shown in Figure 15.5.

Figure 15.5

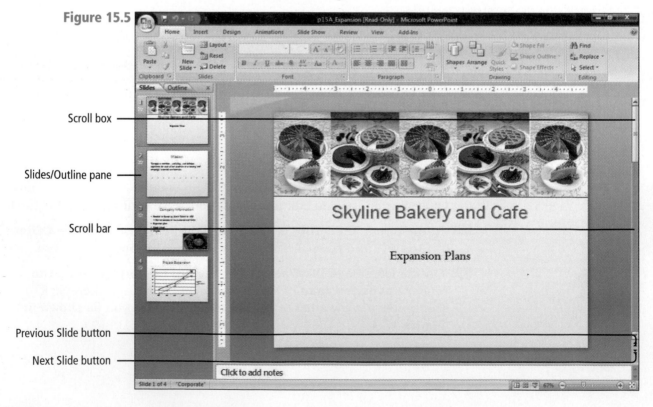

Scroll box

Slides/Outline pane

Scroll bar

Previous Slide button

Next Slide button

6 In the scroll bar, click the **Next Slide** button ⬇ three times so that each slide in the presentation displays. Then click the **Previous Slide** button ⬆ three times until **Slide 1** displays.

> When you click the Next Slide or the Previous Slide button, you can scroll through your presentation one slide at a time.

Activity 15.03 Viewing a Slide Show

When you view a presentation as an electronic slide show, the entire slide fills the computer screen, and a large audience can view your presentation if your computer is connected to a projection system.

1 On the Ribbon, click the **Slide Show tab**. In the **Start Slide Show group**, click the **From Beginning** button.

> The first slide fills the entire screen and *animation effects* display the picture, and then the title and subtitle. Animation effects introduce individual slide elements one element at a time.

Another Way

To Start a Slide Show

Press F5 to start the slide show from the beginning. You can also display the first slide you want to show, and click the Slide Show button on the lower right side of the status bar, or press ⬆Shift + F5.

2 Click the left mouse button or press Spacebar to advance to the second slide, noticing the transition as **Slide 1** moves off the screen and **Slide 2** displays.

> An animation effect stretches the graphic images across the screen from left to right.

> *Transitions* refer to the way that a slide appears or disappears during an onscreen slide show. For example, when one slide leaves the screen, it may fade or dissolve into another slide.

3 Click the left mouse button or press Spacebar and notice that the third slide displays and the slide title drops onto the screen from the top of the slide and a picture appears from the lower right corner.

4 Click again or press Spacebar and notice that the first bullet point displays. Continue to click or press Spacebar until each bullet point displays on the slide and the next slide—*Project Expansion*—displays.

5 Click or press Spacebar to display the chart, and then click or press Spacebar one more time to display a black slide.

> After the last slide in a presentation, a *black slide* displays, indicating that the presentation is over.

6 On the black slide, click the left mouse button to exit the slide show and return to **Slide 1**.

Activity 15.04 Creating Folders and Saving a Presentation

In the same way that you use file folders to organize your paper documents, your Windows operating system uses a hierarchy of electronic folders to keep your electronic files organized. Changes that you make to existing presentations, such as changing text or typing in new text, are not permanently saved until you perform a Save operation.

1 In the upper left corner of the PowerPoint window, click the **Office** button ⊙, and then click **Save As** to display the **Save As** dialog box.

2 In the **Save As** dialog box, in the **Navigation pane**, click **Computer** to view a list of the drives available to you, as shown in Figure 15.6. If you are saving your files on your hard drive, in the Navigation pane, click Documents.

Figure 15.6

Navigation pane
Click Computer

3 Navigate to the location in which you will be storing your folders and projects for this chapter—for example, a USB flash drive that you have connected, a shared drive on a network, the Documents folder on your computer's hard drive, or the drive designated by your instructor or lab coordinator.

4 In the **Save As** dialog box, on the toolbar, click the **New Folder** button. With the text *New Folder* selected, type **PowerPoint Chapter 15** as shown in Figure 15.7, and then press Enter. If the text *New Folder* is not selected, right-click the words *New Folder*, and then from the shortcut menu, click Rename and type the new folder name.

The new folder name displays in the Address Bar at the top of the Save As dialog box, indicating that the folder is open and ready to store your presentation.

Figure 15.7

Address bar ——

New Folder button ——

New folder name ——

5 In the lower portion of the **Save As** dialog box, locate the **File name** box. If necessary, select or delete the existing text, and then in the **File name** box, using your own first and last names, type **15A_Expansion_Firstname_Lastname** as shown in Figure 15.8.

Figure 15.8

Type file name with underscores ——

6 In the lower portion of the **Save As** dialog box, click the **Save** button, or press Enter.

> Windows saves your presentation with the new file name on the storage device that you selected and in the PowerPoint Chapter 15 folder. The new file name displays in the title bar.

Objective 2
Edit a Presentation

In **Normal view**, the PowerPoint window is divided into three areas—the Slide pane, the Slides/Outline pane, and the Notes pane. Changes made in the Slides/Outline pane are reflected immediately in the Slide pane and changes made in the Slide pane are reflected in the Slides/Outline pane.

Activity 15.05 Editing Slide Text

Editing is the process of adding, deleting, or changing the contents of a slide. When you click in the middle of a word or sentence and start typing, the existing text moves to the right to make space for your new keystrokes.

1 In the **Slides/Outline pane**, if necessary, click the **Slides tab** to display the slide thumbnails.

> You can use the slide thumbnails to navigate in your presentation. When you click on a slide thumbnail, the slide displays in the Slide pane.

2 In the **Slides/Outline pane**, on the **Slides tab**, click **Slide 2** to display the company's mission statement. In the paragraph with the company's mission statement, click to the left of the word *experience* as shown in Figure 15.9.

> On this slide, a red wavy underline indicates that there is a misspelled word. Do not be concerned at this time with the misspelling—you will correct it in a later activity.

Figure 15.9

3 Type **meal** and notice that as you type, the existing text moves to the right to accommodate your typing. Press Spacebar to insert a space between *meal* and *experience*.

> After you type the space, the word *meal* moves to the first line of the paragraph because there is enough space in the first line to accommodate the text.

4 In the **Slides/Outline pane**, on the **Slides tab**, click **Slide 3**. In the bulleted list, in the third line, click to the right of the word *plans* and press [Spacebar]. Type **in 2009**

5 On the **Quick Access Toolbar**, click the **Save** button 🖫 to save the changes you have made to the presentation since your last save operation.

Activity 15.06 Inserting a New Slide

To insert a new slide in a presentation, display the slide that will come before the slide that you want to insert.

1 If necessary, display **Slide 3**. On the Ribbon, click the **Home tab**.

> On the Home tab, the Slides group includes the New Slide button. The New Slide button is divided into two parts. The upper part contains the New Slide icon, which inserts a slide without displaying options; the lower part contains the words *New Slide* and a downward pointing arrow that when clicked, displays a *gallery*. The gallery—a visual representation of a command's options—displays slide layouts. *Layout* refers to the placement and arrangement of the text and graphic elements on a slide.

2 In the **Slides group**, click the lower part of the **New Slide** button to display the gallery.

Alert!

Did you insert a slide without displaying the gallery?

The New Slide button is divided into two parts. If you click the upper part, a new slide is inserted using the layout of the previous slide. To view the gallery, you must click the lower part of the New Slide button. Do not be concerned if the gallery did not display—the correct type of slide was inserted. Read Step 3, and then continue with Step 4.

3 Point to **Title and Text** as shown in Figure 15.10, and then click to insert a slide with the Title and Text layout. Notice that the new blank slide displays in the Slide pane and in the Slides/Outline pane.

> The new slide contains two *placeholders*—one for the slide title and one for content. A placeholder reserves a portion of a slide and serves as a container for text or other content, including pictures, graphics, charts, tables, and diagrams.

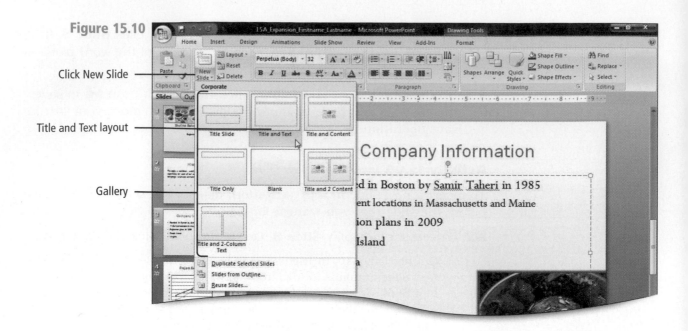

Figure 15.10

Click New Slide

Title and Text layout

Gallery

4 In the **Slide pane**, the title placeholder displays the text *Click to add title*. Click in the title placeholder. Type **Expansion Plans** and then click in the *Click to add text* content placeholder.

5 Type **2009** and then press Enter.

6 Type **Rhode Island and Virginia** and then press Enter.

7 Type **2010** and then on the **Quick Access Toolbar**, click **Save** .

Activity 15.07 Increasing and Decreasing List Levels

Text in a PowerPoint presentation is organized according to outline levels. The highest level on an individual slide is the title. ***Bulleted levels***—outline levels represented by a bullet symbol—are identified in the slides by the indentation and the size of the text.

1 If necessary, display **Slide 4**, click at the end of the last bullet point—*2010*—and then press Enter to create a new bullet.

2 Press Tab and notice that a lower level bullet point is created. Type **New Hampshire and New Jersey**

3 Click anywhere in the second bullet point—*Rhode Island and Virginia*. On the **Home tab**, in the **Paragraph group**, click the **Increase List Level** button .

4 Display **Slide 3**. Notice that the second bullet point is a lower outline level than the first bullet point.

5 Click anywhere in the second bullet point. On the **Home tab**, in the **Paragraph group**, click the **Decrease List Level** button .

> The second bullet point is at the same list level as the other bullet points on the slide.

Another Way

To Decrease List Level

You can decrease the list level of a bullet point by holding down ⇧Shift and pressing Tab.

6 You can change the outline level of more than one bullet point by first selecting all of the text whose outline level you want to change. In the fourth bullet point, position the pointer to the left of *Rhode*, hold down the left mouse button, and then drag to the right and down to select the *Rhode Island* and the *Virginia* bullet points as shown in Figure 15.11. Release the mouse button.

Dragging is the technique of holding down the left mouse button and moving over an area of text so that it is selected. When you select text, the *Mini toolbar* displays near the selection. The Mini toolbar displays buttons that are commonly used with the selected object, as shown in Figure 15.11. The Mini toolbar is semi-transparent unless you move the pointer over it. When you move the pointer away from the Mini toolbar, it disappears.

Figure 15.11

Mini toolbar

Both bullet points selected

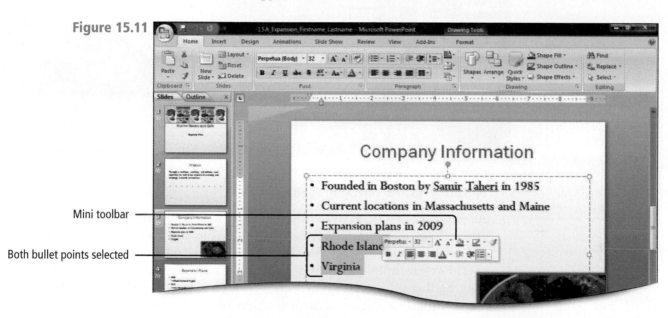

Note — **Demoting and Promoting Text**

Increasing and decreasing the list level of a bullet point is sometimes referred to as demoting and promoting text.

7 On the **Home** tab, in the **Paragraph group**, click the **Increase List Level** button.

The list level for both bulleted items increases.

8 Click at the end of the word *Virginia*. Press Enter to create a new bullet, and notice that the new bullet is indented at the same level as *Virginia*.

9 Click the **Decrease List Level** button to promote the new bullet. Type **Awards received this year** and then press Enter.

10 Click the **Increase List Level** button 📊. Type **Golden Bakery** and press [Enter]. Type **Cuisine Excellence**

11 Compare your slide with Figure 15.12. **Save** 💾 your presentation.

Figure 15.12

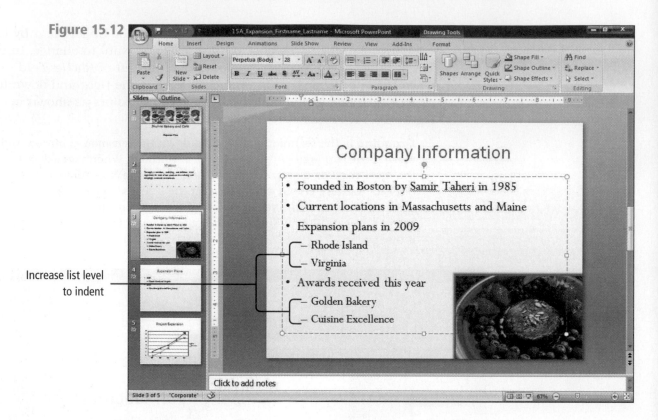

Increase list level to indent

Activity 15.08 Checking Spelling

As you type, PowerPoint compares your words to those in the PowerPoint dictionary. Words that are not in the PowerPoint dictionary are marked with a wavy red underline. Sometimes these words are correct. For example, a person's name may not be in the dictionary and may be flagged as misspelled even though it is correctly spelled. The red wavy underline does not display when the presentation is viewed as a slide show.

1 Display **Slide 2**. Notice that the word *cstomers* is flagged with a red wavy underline, indicating that it is misspelled.

2 Point to *cstomers* and right-click to display the **_shortcut menu_** with a suggested solution for correcting the misspelled word, and the Mini toolbar, as shown in Figure 15.13.

> A shortcut menu is a context-sensitive menu that displays commands and options relevant to the selected object.

Figure 15.13

Mini toolbar

Misspelled word

Suggested solution

Shortcut menu

3 From the shortcut menu, click **customers** to correct the spelling of the word.

4 Display **Slide 3** and notice that the name *Samir Taheri* is flagged as misspelled; this proper name is spelled correctly.

5 Right-click *Samir*, and then from the shortcut menu, click **Ignore All** so that every time the name *Samir* displays in the presentation, it will not be flagged as a misspelled word. Repeat this procedure to ignore the flagged word *Taheri*.

More Knowledge — Spelling Correction Options

The Ignore All option is particularly useful when proper nouns are flagged as spelling errors even when they are spelled correctly. If you are using PowerPoint 2007 on a system that you can customize—such as your home computer—you can add frequently used names and proper nouns to the PowerPoint custom dictionary by clicking the Add to Dictionary option from the shortcut menu.

6 Display each slide in the presentation and correct any spelling errors that you may have made when editing the slides.

7 **Save** your presentation.

Another Way

To Check Spelling

You can check the spelling of the entire presentation at one time. On the Ribbon, click the Review tab. In the Proofing group, click the Spelling button to display a dialog box that will select each spelling error in your presentation and provide options for correcting it.

Activity 15.09 Editing Text by Using the Thesaurus

The *Thesaurus* is a research tool that provides a list of *synonyms*—words with the same meaning—for text that you select. You can access synonyms by using either the shortcut menu or the Review tab on the Ribbon.

1 Display **Slide 2**. In the first line of the paragraph, point to the word *supply*, and then click the right mouse button to display the shortcut menu.

2 Near the bottom of the shortcut menu, point to **Synonyms** to display a list of suggested words to replace *supply*. Point to **provide** as shown in Figure 15.14, and then click to change *supply* to *provide*.

Figure 15.14

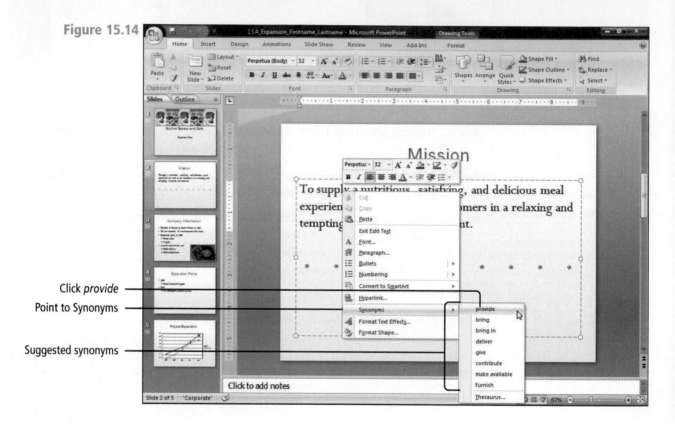

Click *provide*

Point to Synonyms

Suggested synonyms

3 **Save** your presentation.

Another Way

To Access the Thesaurus

After you select the word that you want to replace, on the Ribbon, click Review. In the Proofing group, click Thesaurus to display the Research task pane, which contains a more comprehensive list of suggested synonyms.

Activity 15.10 Adding Speaker's Notes to a Presentation

Recall that when a presentation is displayed in Normal view, the Notes pane displays below the Slide pane. The Notes pane is used to type speaker's notes that can be printed below a picture of each slide. You can refer to these printouts while making a presentation, thus reminding you of the important points that you want to discuss during the presentation.

1 Display **Slide 4**. Look at the PowerPoint window and notice the amount of space that is currently dedicated to each of the three panes—the Slides/Outline pane, the Slide pane, and the Notes pane. Locate the horizontal and vertical borders that separate the three panes.

> These narrow borders are used to adjust the size of the panes. If you decide to type speaker notes, you may want to make the Notes pane larger.

2 Point to the border that separates the **Slide pane** from the **Notes pane**. The ⬍ pointer displays, as shown in Figure 15.15.

Figure 15.15

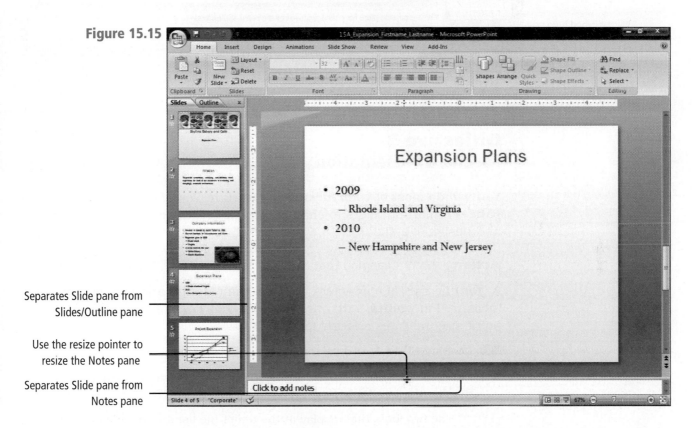

Separates Slide pane from Slides/Outline pane

Use the resize pointer to resize the Notes pane

Separates Slide pane from Notes pane

3 Press and hold down the left mouse button and drag the ⬍ pointer up approximately 1 inch, and then release the left mouse button to resize the pane.

4 With **Slide 4** displayed, click in the **Notes** pane and type **These expansion plans have been approved by the board of directors.** Compare your screen with Figure 15.16.

Figure 15.16

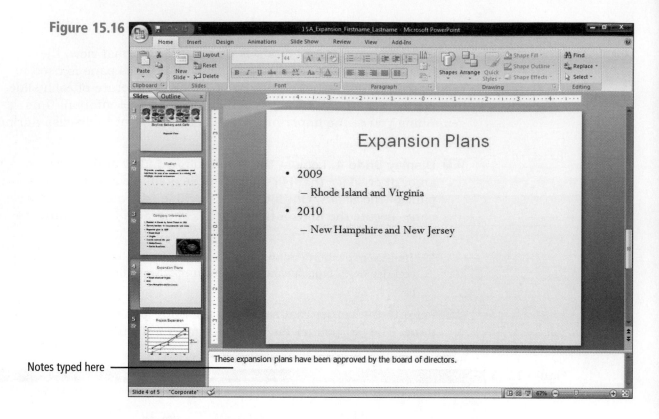

Notes typed here

These expansion plans have been approved by the board of directors.

5 **Save** 🖫 your presentation.

Objective 3
Format a Presentation

You will do most of your *formatting* work in PowerPoint in the Slide pane. Formatting refers to changing the appearance of the text, layout, and design of a slide.

Activity 15.11 Changing Font and Font Size

A *font* is a set of characters with the same design and shape. Fonts are measured in *points*, with one point equal to 1/72 of an inch. A higher point size indicates a larger font size.

1 Display **Slide 1** and select the title text—*Skyline Bakery and Cafe.*

2 Point to the Mini toolbar, and then click the **Font button arrow** to display the available fonts, as shown in Figure 15.17.

The two fonts that display at the top of the list are the fonts currently used in the presentation.

Alert! | **Did the Mini toolbar disappear?**

When you select text, the Mini toolbar displays. If you move your pointer away from the selection and into the slide area without pointing to the Mini toolbar, it may no longer display. If this happened to you, select the text again, and then point to the Mini toolbar, making sure that you do not point to another area of the slide.

Figure 15.17

Mini toolbar

Font button arrow

Selected text

List of fonts

3 Scroll the list as necessary, and then click **Book Antiqua**.

4 On the **Home tab**, in the **Font group**, click the **Font Size button arrow**, and then click **48**.

5 Select the subtitle text—*Expansion Plans*. In the **Font group**, click the **Font button arrow**. In the list, scroll as necessary, and then point to—but do not click—**Arial Black**. Compare your screen with Figure 15.18.

> *Live Preview* is a technology that shows the results of applying an editing or formatting change as you move your pointer over the results presented in a gallery. Thus, you can decide whether or not you want to apply the formatting. In this case, Live Preview displays the selected text in the Arial Black font, even though you did not click the font name. The font will change when you click the font name.

Figure 15.18

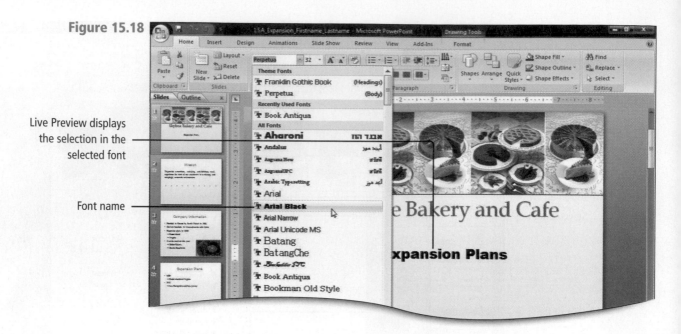

Live Preview displays
the selection in the
selected font

Font name

6 Click **Arial Black**.

7 **Save** 🖫 the changes you have made to your presentation.

Activity 15.12 Applying Font Styles

Font styles emphasize text and are a visual cue to draw the reader's eye to important text. Font styles include bold, italic, and underline.

1 On **Slide 1**, select the title *Skyline Bakery and Cafe*. On the **Home tab**, in the **Font group**, point to the **Bold** button **B** as shown in Figure 15.19, and then click to apply bold to the title.

Figure 15.19

Click the Bold button

Selected text

2 Select the subtitle—*Expansion Plans*. On the Mini toolbar, click the **Bold** button **B** , and then click the **Italic** button *I* to apply both bold and italic to the selection. Notice that on the **Home tab**, in the **Font group**, the **Bold** and **Italic** buttons are selected.

The Bold, Italic, and Underline buttons are *toggle buttons*; that is, you can click the button once to turn it on and click it again to turn it off.

3 With the subtitle still selected, on the **Home tab**, in the **Font group**, click the **Bold** button **B** to turn off the bold formatting.

4 Click **Save** 🖫.

Another Way

To Apply Font Styles

There are four methods to apply font styles:

- On the Home tab, in the Font group, click the Bold, Italic, or Underline button.

- On the Mini toolbar, click the Bold or Italic button.

- From the keyboard, use the keyboard shortcuts Ctrl+B for bold, Ctrl + I for italic, or Ctrl + U for underline.

- On the Home tab, in the Font group, click the Dialog Box Launcher to open the Font dialog box, and then click the font styles that you want to apply.

Activity 15.13 Aligning Text and Changing Line Spacing

Text alignment refers to the horizontal placement of text within a placeholder. You can align left, centered, right, or justified. When text is justified, the left and right margins are even.

1 Display **Slide 2** and click in the paragraph.

2 On the **Home tab**, in the **Paragraph group**, click the **Center** button ☰ to center align the paragraph within the placeholder.

3 In the **Paragraph group**, click the **Line Spacing** button. In the list, click **1.5** to change from single-spacing between lines to one-and-a-half spacing between lines.

4 Click **Save** 🖫.

Activity 15.14 Modifying Slide Layout

Recall that layout refers to the placement and arrangement of the text and graphic elements on a slide. PowerPoint includes predefined layouts that you can apply to your slide for the purpose of arranging slide elements. For example, a Title Slide contains two placeholder elements—the title and the subtitle. When you design your slides, consider the content that you want to include, and then choose a layout that contains elements that best display the message that you want to convey.

1 Display **Slide 4.**

2 On the **Home tab**, in the **Slides group**, click the **Layout** button to display the **Slide Layout gallery**.

The gallery displays an image of each layout and the name of each layout.

3 Point to each layout and notice that a *ScreenTip* also displays the name of the layout.

A ScreenTip is a small box, activated by holding the pointer over a button or other screen object, which displays information about a screen element.

4 Point to **Title and 2-Column Text**—as shown in Figure 15.20—and then click to change the slide layout.

The existing text displays in the placeholder on the left and a blank content placeholder displays on the right.

Figure 15.20

Slide Layout gallery

Title and 2-Column Text layout

5 Click in the placeholder on the right. Type **2011** and then press Enter. Press Tab to increase the list level. Type **West Virginia and Ohio** and then press Enter.

6 Press ⇧ Shift + Tab to decrease the list level. Type **2012** and then press Enter. Press Tab to increase the list level. Type **New York and Connecticut**

7 Click outside of the placeholder so that it is not selected, and then compare your slide with Figure 15.21.

Figure 15.21

8 **Save** [icon] your changes.

Activity 15.15 Changing the Presentation Theme

A *theme* is a set of unified design elements that provides a look for your presentation by using color, fonts, and graphics. The overall *presentation* theme may include background designs, graphics, and objects that can be customized, using one of the three additional types of themes available in PowerPoint 2007—color themes, font themes, and effect themes. Color themes include sets of colors, font themes include sets of heading and body text fonts, and the effect themes include sets of effects that can be applied to lines and other objects on your slides.

1 Click the **Design tab**. In the **Themes group**, to the right of the last theme, point to the **More** button [icon] as shown in Figure 15.22, and then click to display the **Themes gallery**.

Figure 15.22

Themes

More button

2 Under **Built-In**, *point* to several of the themes and notice that a ScreenTip displays the name of each theme and that the Live Preview feature displays how each theme will look if applied to your presentation.

The first theme that displays is the Office theme. Subsequent themes are arranged alphabetically.

3 In the first row, point to the first theme—the **Office Theme**, as shown in Figure 15.23—and then click to change the theme.

The Office Theme is applied to the entire presentation, and all text, the chart, and accent colors are updated to reflect the change.

Figure 15.23

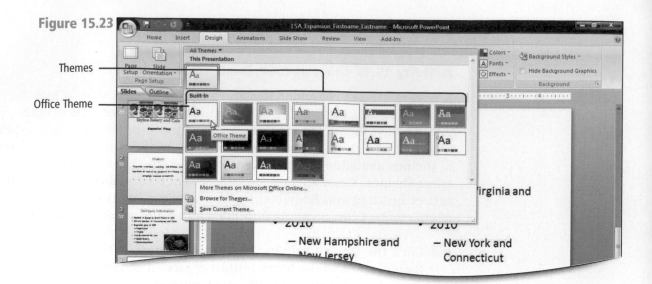

4 In the **Slides/Outline pane**, click to select **Slide 3**, and then press and hold down ⇧ Shift and click **Slide 4**. Compare your screen with Figure 15.24.

> Both slides are selected as indicated by the contrasting colors that surround the slides in the Slides/Outline pane.

Figure 15.24

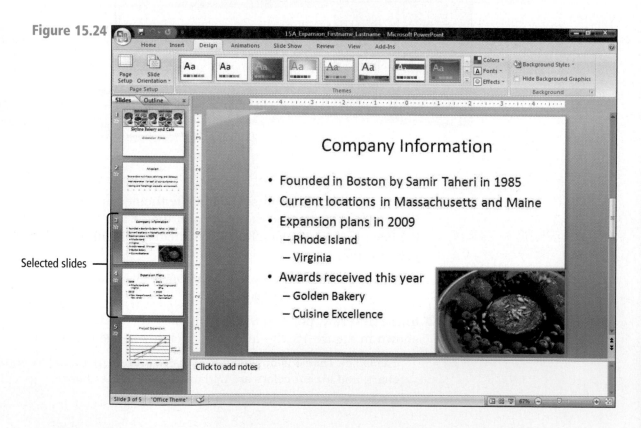

5 On the **Design tab**, in the **Themes group**, click the **More** button ▼ to display the **Themes gallery**. Under **Built-In**, in the first row, *point* to the fifth theme—**Concourse**—and then click the right mouse button to display the shortcut menu. Click **Apply to Selected Slides**.

> The Concourse Theme is applied to Slides 3 and 4.

6 **Save** 💾 your presentation.

Objective 4
Create Headers and Footers and Print a Presentation

A *header* is text that prints at the top of each sheet of *slide handouts* or *notes pages*. Slide handouts are printed images of slides on a sheet of paper. Notes pages are printouts that contain the slide image in the top half of the page and notes that you have created in the Notes pane in the lower half of the page. In addition to headers, you can create *footers*—text that displays at the bottom of every slide or that prints at the bottom of a sheet of slide handouts or notes pages.

Activity 15.16 Creating Headers and Footers

In this activity, you will add a header to the handouts and notes pages that includes the current date and a footer that includes the page number and the file name.

1 Click the **Insert tab**, and then in the **Text group**, click the **Header & Footer** button to display the **Header and Footer** dialog box.

Another Way

To Display the Header and Footer Dialog Box
On the Insert tab, in the Text group, you can click either the Date & Time button or the Slide Number button.

2 In the **Header and Footer** dialog box, click the **Notes and Handouts tab**. Under **Include on page**, select the **Date and time** check box, and as you do so, watch the Preview box in the lower right corner of the Header and Footer dialog box.

The Preview box indicates the placeholders on the printed Notes and Handouts pages. The two narrow rectangular boxes at the top of the Preview box indicate placeholders for the header text and date. When you select the Date and time check box, the placeholder in the upper right corner is outlined, indicating the location in which the date will display.

3 If necessary, click the **Update automatically** button so that the current date prints on the notes and handouts each time the presentation is printed.

4 If necessary, *clear* the **Header** check box to omit this element. Notice that in the **Preview** box, the corresponding placeholder is not selected.

5 If necessary, select the **Page number** and **Footer** check boxes, and notice that the insertion point displays in the **Footer** box. Using your own first and last names, type **15A_Expansion_Firstname_Lastname** and then compare your dialog box with Figure 15.25.

6 Click **Apply to All**. **Save** 💾 your changes.

Figure 15.25

Preview box

Notes and Handouts tab

Date and time check box selected

Update automatically selected

Header check box cleared

Page number and Footer selected

Footer text includes your first name and last name

More Knowledge — Adding Footers to Slides

You can add footers to slides by using the Slide tab in the Header and Footer dialog box. Headers cannot be added to individual slides.

Activity 15.17 Previewing and Printing a Presentation and Closing PowerPoint

1 Click the **Office** button 🔘, point to **Print** as shown in Figure 15.26, and then click **Print Preview**.

> *Print Preview* displays your presentation as it will print, based on the options that you choose. In the Print Preview window, you can click the Orientation button to change the direction in which the paper prints—landscape or portrait. You can choose whether you will print slides, handouts, note pages, or the presentation outline by clicking the Print What button.
>
> In the Print group, the Options button enables you to print your presentation in color, grayscale, or black and white.

Figure 15.26

Office button —

Print Preview —

Point to Print —

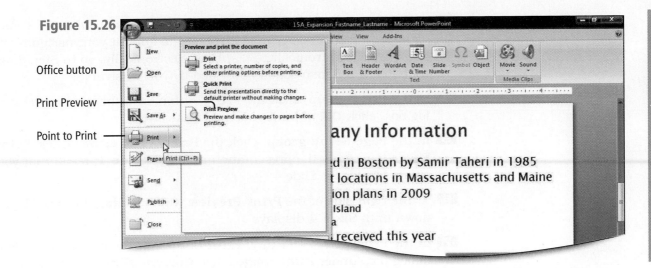

2 In the **Page Setup group**, click the **Print What arrow**, and then click **Handouts (6 Slides Per Page)** as shown in Figure 15.27. Notice that the preview of your printout changes to reflect your selection.

Figure 15.27

Print What arrow —

Handouts (6 Slides Per Page) selected —

Note — Printing Slide Handouts in Grayscale

Printing a presentation as Slides uses a large amount of ink and toner. Thus, the majority of the projects in this textbook require that you print handouts, not slides. If your system is connected to a color printer, your handouts may display in color. If you want to conserve colored ink, in the Print Group, click the Options button, point to Color/Grayscale, and then click Grayscale.

3 Check your *Chapter Assignment Sheet* or *Course Syllabus*, or consult your instructor, to determine if you are to submit your assignments on paper or electronically. To submit electronically, go to Step 8, and then follow the instructions provided by your instructor.

4 In the **Print group**, click the **Print** button, and then in the **Print** dialog box, click **OK** to print your handouts.

5 In the **Page Setup group**, click the **Print What arrow**. Click **Notes Pages** to preview the presentation notes for **Slide 1**; recall that you created Notes for Slide 4.

6 At the right side of the **Print Preview** window, drag the scroll box down until **Slide 4** displays.

7 In the **Print group**, click the **Print** button. In the middle of the **Print** dialog box, under **Print range**, click **Current slide**, and then click **OK** to print the Notes pages for Slide 4.

8 Click **Close Print Preview** to close the Print Preview window and return to the presentation.

Another Way

To Print a Presentation

Click the Office button, and then click Print to display the Print dialog box. The options that are available in Print Preview can be accessed and modified in the Print dialog box.

9 **Save** 💾 your presentation. On the right edge of the title bar, click the **Close** button ❎ to close the presentation and close PowerPoint.

Note — Changing Print Options

When you preview your presentation, check to be sure that the text displays against the slide background. If it does not, on the Print Preview tab in the Print group, click Options. Point to Color/Grayscale, and then click Color or Color (On Black and White Printer).

End You have completed Project 15A ————————

Project 15B **Overview**

In Activities 15.18 through 15.25 you will create a presentation that provides details of the Skyline Bakery and Cafe projected expansion. You will add a graphic image to the presentation, insert slides from another PowerPoint presentation, and rearrange and delete slides. Your completed presentation will look similar to Figure 15.28.

For Project 15B, you will need the following files:

p15B_Skyline
p15B_Cake
p15B_Template

You will save your presentation as
15B_Overview_Firstname_Lastname

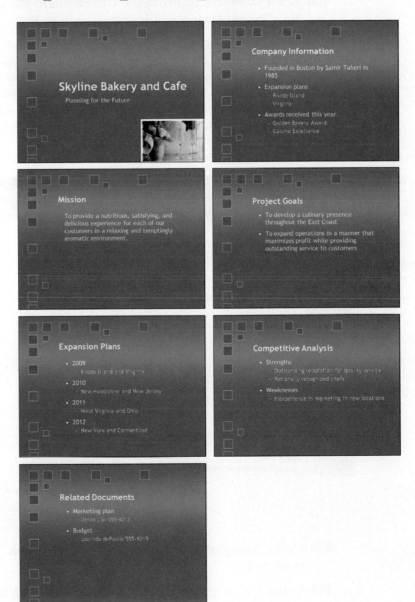

Figure 15.28
Project 15B—Overview

Objective 5
Create a New Presentation

To start a new presentation, you can use a *template* that is saved on your system or that you access from Microsoft Office Online. A template is a file that contains the styles in a presentation, including the type and size of bullets and fonts, placeholder sizes and positions, background design and fill color schemes, and theme information. You can also start a blank presentation that you can customize by adding text, background graphics, and colors.

Activity 15.18 Starting a New Presentation

In this activity, you will create a new presentation based on a template from Microsoft Office Online.

1 **Start** PowerPoint. From the **Office** menu 🔵, click **New** to display the **New Presentation** window as shown in Figure 15.29.

> At the left of the New Presentation window, a list of the Template categories installed on your system or available from Microsoft Office Online displays. The center section displays either subcategories or thumbnails of the slides in the category that you select. When you select a template, the right section displays a larger view of the selected template and sometimes additional information about the template.

Figure 15.29

New blank presentation

Template categories available from Microsoft Office Online

2 Under **Templates**, click **Installed Templates**. Click each template to preview it.

3 In the left panel under **Microsoft Office Online**, click several of the categories. Notice that as you do so, the title of the center panel changes to the name of the category that you have chosen, and in some instances, subcategories display.

Alert!

Are you unable to access the templates from Microsoft Office Online?

If you are unable to access the templates from Microsoft Office Online, the template for this project is available from your student data files. In the New Presentation window, click Cancel to close the New Presentation window. Click the Office button, and then click Open. Navigate to your student files and open the p15B_Template file. Then, skip to Step 6.

4 Under **Microsoft Office Online**, click **Presentations**, and then in the center panel, point to **Other presentations** to display the 🖑 pointer as shown in Figure 15.30.

Figure 15.30

Other presentations

Presentations

Another Way

To Locate Templates

In the New Presentation window, you can search for templates by using keywords. Click the Office button, and then click New. At the top center of the New Presentation window, type the keyword and then press Enter to view the presentation templates with the keyword that you typed.

5 Click **Other presentations**. In the center section of the New Presentation window, if necessary, scroll to display the **Project planning overview presentation** template. Click **Project planning overview presentation**, and then in the lower right corner of the window, click **Download** to access the template from Microsoft Office Online.

Alert! **Does a Microsoft window display?**

If a window displays regarding the validation of your software, click Continue. If you are unable to download the template, close all message windows and the New Presentation window. Click the Office button, and then click Open. Navigate to your student files, open the p15B_Template file, and then continue with Step 6.

6 If necessary, close any windows that display after the template is downloaded.

> The new presentation includes 11 slides with ideas for content when making a project overview presentation. You can modify the text and delete slides so that the content is specific to this presentation topic.

7 On **Slide 1**, select the text in the title placeholder—*Project Overview*—and then type **Skyline Bakery and Cafe** to replace it. Select the three lines of text in the subtitle placeholder, and then type **Planning for the Future**

8 Display **Slide 2**. Select the text *Ultimate goal of project*, and then type **To develop a culinary presence throughout the East Coast**

9 Select the remaining two bullet points on the slide, and then type to replace them with the text **To expand operations in a manner that maximizes profit while providing outstanding service to customers**

10 Display **Slide 4**. In the bulleted list, select the *Competitors* bullet point and its second-level bullet point—*You may want to allocate one slide per competitor*—and then press ⌷Delete⌷. Select *Your strengths relative to competitors*, and then type **Outstanding reputation for quality service** and then press ⌷Enter⌷. Type **Nationally recognized chefs**

11 Replace the text *Your weaknesses relative to competitors* with **Inexperience in marketing in new locations**

12 In the scroll bar, click the **Next Slide** button several times until **Slide 11** displays. Select and delete the *Post-mortem* and *Submit questions* bullet points and their subordinate bullet points. Under the *Marketing plan* bullet point, select *Location or contact name/phone*, and then type **Janet Liu/555-9012** Under the *Budget* bullet point, select *Location or contact name/phone*, and then type **Lucinda dePaolo/555-9019**

13 Click the **Office** button 🏢, and then click **Save As**. In the **Save As** dialog box, navigate to your **PowerPoint Chapter 15** folder.

14 In the **File name** box, delete any existing text, and then using your own first and last names type **15B_Overview_Firstname_Lastname** and then click **Save**.

Activity 15.19 Inserting Slides from an Existing Presentation

Presentation content is often shared among employees. Rather than re-creating slides, you can insert slides from an existing presentation into the current presentation. In this activity, you will insert slides from an existing presentation into your 15B_Overview presentation.

1 Display **Slide 1**. Click the **Home tab**, and then in the **Slides group**, click the **New Slide arrow** to display the **Slide Layout gallery** and additional options for inserting slides. Compare your screen with Figure 15.31.

Figure 15.31

New Slide arrow

Slide Layout gallery

Additional options
for inserting slides

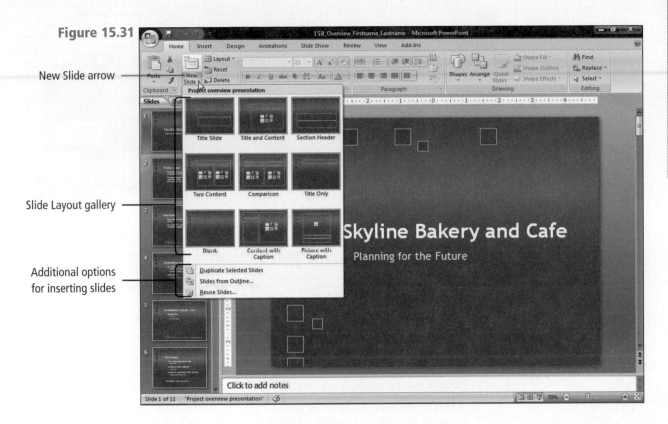

2 Below the gallery, click **Reuse Slides** to open the **Reuse Slides** task pane on the right side of the PowerPoint window.

A *task pane* enables you to enter options for completing a command.

3 In the **Reuse Slides** task pane, click the **Browse** button, and then click **Browse File**. In the **Browse** dialog box, navigate to where your student files are stored, and then double-click **p15B_Skyline**.

The slides contained in the p15B_Skyline presentation display in the Reuse Slides task pane. The title of each slide displays to the right of the slide image.

4 In the **Reuse Slides** task pane, point to **Slide 2** and notice that a zoomed image displays along with a ScreenTip with the presentation title and the slide title. Compare your screen with Figure 15.32.

Figure 15.32

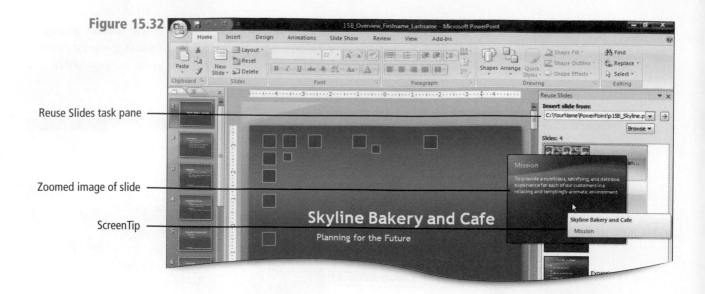

Reuse Slides task pane

Zoomed image of slide

ScreenTip

5 Click **Slide 2—Mission**—and notice that it is inserted into the current presentation after Slide 1.

The theme of the current presentation is applied to the slide that you inserted. If you want to retain the theme and other formatting from the slide that you insert, you can select the *Keep source formatting* check box at the bottom of the Reuse Slides task pane.

More Knowledge — Inserting All Slides

You can insert all of the slides from an existing presentation into the current presentation at one time. In the Reuse Slides task pane, right-click one of the slides that you want to insert, and then click Insert All Slides.

6 In your **15B_Overview** presentation, in the **Slides/Outline pane**, scroll the slide thumbnails to display **Slide 11**. Click **Slide 11** to display it in the **Slide** pane.

7 In the **Reuse Slides** task pane, click **Slide 3—Company Information**, and then click **Slide 4—Expansion Plans** to insert both slides after **Slide 11**.

Your presentation contains 14 slides.

8 In the **Reuse Slides** task pane, click the **Close** button ⊠. **Save** 🖫 your presentation.

Note — Inserting Slides

You can insert slides into your presentation in any order; remember to display the slide that will precede the slide that you want to insert.

Objective 6
Use Slide Sorter View

Slide Sorter view displays all of the slides in your presentation in miniature. You can use Slide Sorter view to rearrange and delete slides, to apply formatting to multiple slides, and to get an overall impression of your presentation.

Activity 15.20 Selecting and Deleting Slides

To select more than one slide, click the first slide that you want to select, press and hold down ⇧Shift or Ctrl, and then click another slide. Using ⇧Shift enables you to select a group of slides that are adjacent—next to each other. Using Ctrl enables you to select a group of slides that are nonadjacent (*not* next to each other). With multiple slides selected, you can move or delete them as a group.

1 Recall that the View buttons are located on the status bar in the lower right corner of the PowerPoint window. Locate the **View** buttons, and then click the **Slide Sorter** button 🔲 to display all of the slide thumbnails. Alternatively, on the Ribbon, click the View tab, and then in the Presentation Views group, click Slide Sorter.

2 Click **Slide 4** and notice that a thick outline surrounds the slide, indicating that it is selected. On your keyboard, press Delete to delete the slide.

3 Click **Slide 5**, and then hold down ⇧Shift and click **Slide 10** so that slides 5 through 10 are selected. Compare your screen with Figure 15.33.

Figure 15.33

Selected slides

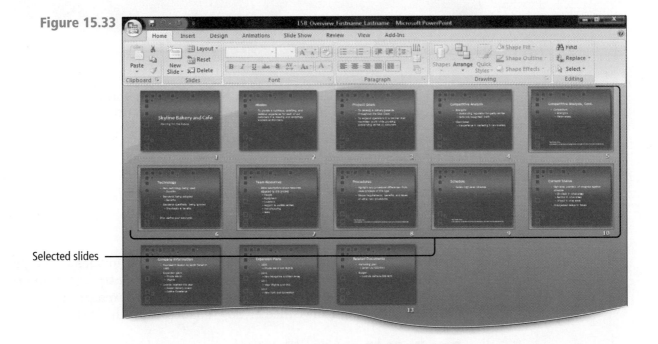

4 Press (Delete) to delete the selected slides; notice that your presentation contains seven slides.

5 **Save** 🖫 your changes.

Activity 15.21 Moving Slides

1 Click **Slide 5** to select it.

2 While pointing to **Slide 5**, press and hold down the left mouse button, and then drag the slide to the left until the vertical bar is positioned to the left of **Slide 2**, as shown in Figure 15.34. Release the left mouse button.

The slide that you moved becomes Slide 2.

Figure 15.34

Vertical bar positioned between Slides 1 and 2 to move slide to this position

Selected slide

3 Select **Slide 6**. Using the same technique that you used in Step 2, drag to position the slide between **Slides 4** and **5**.

4 In the status bar, click the **Normal** button 🔳. **Save** 🖫 your presentation.

Objective 7
Add Pictures to a Presentation

There are many sources from which you can insert images into a presentation. One type of image that you can insert is *clip art*. Clip art can include drawings, movies, sounds, or photographic images that are included with Microsoft Office or downloaded from the Web.

Activity 15.22 Inserting Clip Art

In this activity you will access Microsoft Office Online to insert a clip art image on the title slide.

1 Display **Slide 1**. Click the **Insert tab**, and then in the **Illustrations group**, click **Clip Art** to display the **Clip Art** task pane.

2 In the **Clip Art** task pane, click in the **Search for** box and type **wedding cake** so that PowerPoint can search for images that contain the keywords *wedding cake*. If a message displays to include additional clip art images from Microsoft Office online, click Yes.

3 In the **Clip Art** task pane, click the **Search in arrow**, and if necessary, select the **Everywhere** check box. Click the **Search in** arrow again to collapse the search list.

When you select the Everywhere option, *All collections* displays in the Search in box. This action instructs PowerPoint to search for images stored on your system and on the Microsoft Office Online Web site.

4 Click the **Results should be arrow**, and then click as necessary to *deselect*—clear the selection by removing the check mark—the **Clip Art**, **Movies**, and **Sounds** check boxes so that only the **Photographs** check box is selected as shown in Figure 15.35.

With the Photographs check box selected, PowerPoint will search for images that were created with a digital camera or a scanner.

Figure 15.35

wedding cake is search term

All collections selected

Photographs selected

5 In the **Clip Art** task pane, click **Go**. After a brief delay, several images display in the Clip Art task pane. Locate the image of the wedding cake shown in Figure 15.36.

Figure 15.36

Selected image ——————

Alert!

Is the wedding cake picture unavailable?

If you are unable to locate the picture for this project, it is available from your student data files. On the Insert tab, in the Illustrations group, click Picture. Navigate to your student files, and then double-click the p15B_Cake file.

6 Click the wedding cake picture to insert it in the center of Slide 1, and then notice that the Ribbon has changed and the picture is surrounded by white square and circular handles, indicating that it is selected.

Because the picture is selected, ***contextual tools*** named *Picture Tools* display and add a ***contextual tab***—*Format*—next to the standard tabs on the Ribbon as shown in Figure 15.37.

Contextual tools enable you to perform specific commands related to the selected object, and display one or more contextual tabs that contain related groups of commands that you will need when working with the type of object that is selected.

Contextual tools display only when needed for a selected object; when you deselect the object, the contextual tools no longer display. In this case, the Format contextual tab contains four groups—Adjust, Picture Styles, Arrange, and Size.

Figure 15.37

Contextual tab

Contextual tool

7 **Close** ✕ the Clip Art task pane. **Save** 💾 your changes.

Activity 15.23 Moving and Sizing Images

When an image is selected, it is surrounded by white *sizing handles* that are used to size the image. In the corners of the image, the handles are circular. When you point to a circular sizing handle, a diagonal pointer displays, indicating that you can resize the image by dragging up or down. In the center of each side of the selected image, the handles are square. When you point to a square handle, a left- and right-pointing arrow or an up- and down-pointing arrow displays. These arrows indicate the direction in which you can size the image. When you point to an image without positioning the pointer over a handle, a four-headed arrow displays, indicating that you can move the image.

1 If necessary, click to select the picture of the wedding cake so that the handles display.

2 Position the pointer anywhere over the image to display the ⬨ pointer. Drag down and to the right until the lower right corner of the picture is aligned with the lower right corner of the slide as shown in Figure 15.38. Release the mouse button.

Figure 15.38

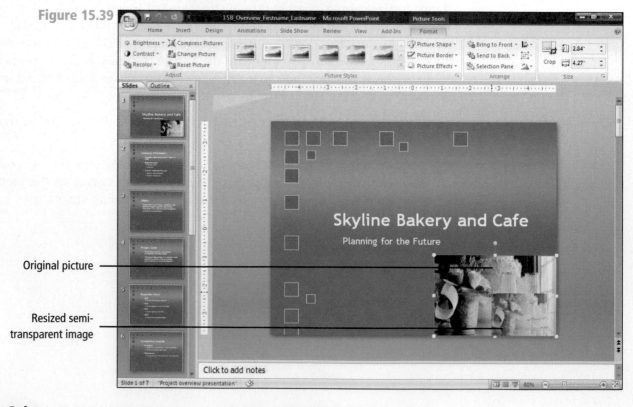

Drag to this position

3 If necessary, select the picture, and then point to the upper left circular handle to display the ▨ pointer.

4 Drag down and to the right, noticing that as you do so, a semitransparent image displays the size of the picture. Continue to drag until the semitransparent image is approximately half the height and width of the original picture as shown in Figure 15.39. Release the mouse button to size the picture.

Figure 15.39

Original picture

Resized semi-transparent image

5 **Save** 🖫 the presentation.

Workshop

Sizing a Picture
Using one of the corner sizing handles ensures that the original proportions of the image are maintained. When a top or side sizing handle is used, the picture is stretched either taller or wider, thus distorting the image.

Activity 15.24 Applying a Style to a Picture

You can use the Picture Tools Format tab to change the color and brightness of your picture; apply a shape, border, or effect; arrange multiple images; or size your picture.

1 If necessary, click the picture of the wedding cake to select it and notice that the **Picture Tools** are available.

2 On the **Format tab**, in the **Picture Styles group**, click the **More** button 🔽 to display the **Picture Styles gallery**.

3 In the gallery, point to several of the picture styles to display the ScreenTips and to use Live Preview to see the effect of the style on your picture. Then, in the first row, click **Simple Frame, White**.

4 Click on a blank area of the slide so that the picture is not selected, and then compare your slide to Figure 15.40. Make any necessary adjustments to the size and position of the picture.

Figure 15.40

Picture size adjusted and *Simple Frame, White* applied

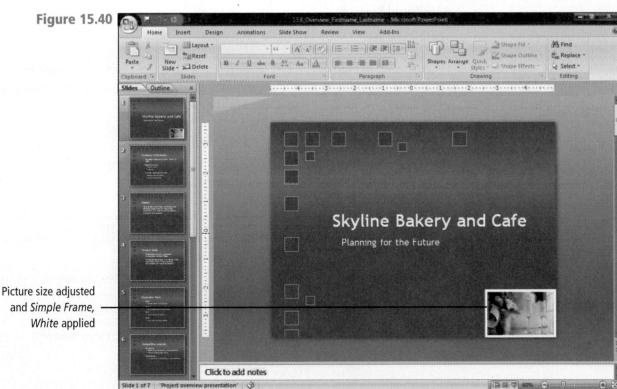

5 Click the **Insert tab**, and then, in the **Text group**, click the **Header & Footer** button to display the **Header and Footer** dialog box. Click the **Notes and Handouts tab**.

6 Under **Include on page**, click to select the **Date and time** check box, and if necessary, click the **Update automatically** button so that the current date prints on the notes and handouts each time the presentation is printed. If necessary, *clear* the **Header** check box to omit this element from your handouts.

7 Click to select the **Page number** and **Footer** check boxes, noticing that when you do so, the insertion point displays in the Footer box. Using your own first and last names, type **15B_Overview_Firstname_Lastname** and then click **Apply to All**.

8 Check your *Chapter Assignment Sheet* or *Course Syllabus* or consult your instructor to determine if you are to submit your assignments on paper or electronically. To submit electronically, go to Step 10, and then follow the instructions provided by your instructor.

9 From the **Office** menu, point to **Print**, and then click **Print Preview** to make a final check of your presentation. In the **Page Setup group**, click the **Print What arrow**, and then click **Handouts (4 Slides Per Page)**. Click the **Print** button, and then click **OK** to print the handouts—two pages will print. In the **Preview group**, click the **Close Print Preview** button.

10 **Save** the changes to your presentation, and then from the **Office** menu, click **Exit PowerPoint**.

Objective 8
Use the Microsoft Help System

PowerPoint provides a Help feature in which you can ask questions and Help will provide you with information and step-by-step instructions for performing tasks.

Activity 15.25 Accessing PowerPoint Help

In this activity, you will use the Microsoft Help feature to learn more about this feature.

1 **Start** PowerPoint. In the upper right corner of your screen, click the **Microsoft Office PowerPoint Help** button. Alternatively, press F1.

> You can browse the PowerPoint Help topics by clicking any of the listed items; or, near the top of the Help window, you can click in the search box and type a keyword to search for a specific item.

2 Near the upper left corner of the Help window, in the **Search** box, type **Printing Slides** as shown in Figure 15.41.

Figure 15.41

PowerPoint | Chapter 15

Search box

3 Press [Enter] or click **Search**. On the list of results, click **Print your slides** and then read the information that displays.

4 On the PowerPoint Help title bar, click the **Close** button ⊠.
On the right side of the title bar, click the **Close** button ⊠ to close PowerPoint.

End **You have completed Project 15B** ————————————

There's More You Can Do!

Close PowerPoint and any other open windows. Display the Start menu, click Computer, and then navigate to the student files that accompany this textbook. From the CD that came with your book, open the folder **02_theres_more_you_can_do**, locate and open the folder for this chapter. Open and print the instructions for this project, which are provided to you in Adobe PDF format.

Try IT!—Set Slide Orientation and Size

In this Try It! exercise, you will change the size and orientation of a slide.

Content-Based Assessments

Summary

In this chapter, you started PowerPoint and opened a PowerPoint presentation. You entered, edited, and formatted text in Normal view and worked with slides in Slide Sorter view; you added speaker notes; and you viewed the presentation as a slide show. Spell check was demonstrated, and you practiced how to change font style and size and add emphasis to text.

You created a new presentation, added content and clip art, and moved and deleted slides. You also added a footer to the notes and handouts pages and created a chapter folder to help organize your files. Each presentation was saved, previewed, printed, and closed. Finally, the Help program was introduced as a tool that can assist you in using PowerPoint.

Key Terms

Content-Based Assessments

Matching

Match each term in the second column with its correct definition in the first column. Write the letter of the term on the blank line in front of the correct definition.

_____ **1.** A feature that introduces individual slide elements one element at a time.

_____ **2.** The PowerPoint view in which the window is divided into three panes—the Slide pane, the Slides/Outline pane, and the Notes pane.

_____ **3.** Outline levels represented by a symbol that are identified in the slides by the indentation and the size of the text.

_____ **4.** A feature that displays buttons that are commonly used with the selected object.

_____ **5.** A context-sensitive menu that displays commands and options relevant to the selected object.

_____ **6.** The action of holding down the left mouse button and moving the mouse pointer over text to select it.

_____ **7.** A set of characters (letters and numbers) with the same design and shape.

_____ **8.** A unit of measure to describe the size of a font.

_____ **9.** A container that reserves a portion of a slide for text, graphics, and other slide elements.

_____ **10.** A slide that is inserted at the end of every slide show to indicate that the presentation is over.

_____ **11.** The changing of the appearance of the text, layout, and design of a slide.

_____ **12.** A technology that shows the results of applying an editing or formatting change as you move your pointer over the results presented in a gallery.

_____ **13.** A feature that changes the horizontal placement of text within a placeholder.

_____ **14.** Printouts that contain the slide image in the top half of the page and notes that you have created in the Notes pane in the lower half of the page.

_____ **15.** A feature that displays your presentation as it will print, based on the options that you select.

A Animation

B Black slide

C Bulleted levels

D Dragging

E Font

F Formatting

G Live Preview

H Mini toolbar

I Normal view

J Notes pages

K Placeholder

L Point

M Print Preview

N Shortcut menu

O Text alignment

Content-Based Assessments

Fill in the Blank

Write the correct word in the space provided.

1. Microsoft Office PowerPoint 2007 is a presentation _____ _____ program that you can use to effectively present information to your audience.

2. Miniature images of slides are known as _____.

3. A slide _____ controls the way in which a slide appears or disappears during an onscreen slide show.

4. The process of adding, deleting, or changing the contents of a slide is known as _____.

5. A _____ is a visual representation of a command's options.

6. The placement and arrangement of the text and graphic elements on a slide refer to its _____.

7. Tools that enable you to perform specific commands related to the selected object are _____ tools.

8. A file that contains the styles in a presentation, including the type and size of bullets and fonts, placeholder sizes and positions, background design and fill color schemes, and theme information, is known as a _____.

9. The _____ is a research tool that provides a list of synonyms for a selection.

10. Words with the same meaning are known as _____.

11. Font _____ add emphasis to text, and may include bold, italic, and underline.

12. A _____ button is one in which you can click the button once to turn it on and click it again to turn it off.

13. Text that prints at the top of a sheet of slide handouts or notes pages is known as a _____.

14. Text that displays at the bottom of every slide or that prints at the bottom of a sheet of slide handouts or notes is known as a _____.

15. The view in which all of the slides in your presentation display in miniature is _____ _____ view.

Content-Based Assessments

Skills Review

Project 15C — Hospitality

In this project, you will apply the skills you practiced from the Objectives in Project 15A.

Objectives: 1. *Open, View, and Save a Presentation;* **2.** *Edit a Presentation;* **3.** *Format a Presentation;* **4.** *Create Headers and Footers and Print a Presentation.*

In the following Skills Review, you will edit a presentation created by Shawna Andreasyan, the Human Resources Director, for new Skyline Bakery and Cafe employees. Your completed presentation will look similar to the one shown in Figure 15.42.

> ### For Project 15C, you will need the following file:
>
> p15C_Hospitality

You will save your presentation as
15C_Hospitality_Firstname_Lastname

Figure 15.42

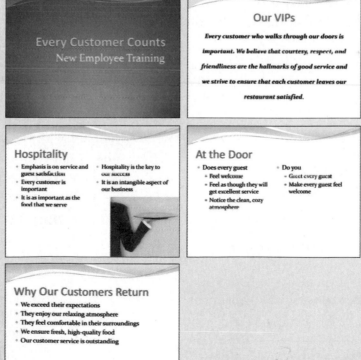

(Project 15C–Hospitality continues on the next page)

Content-Based Assessments

(Project 15C–Hospitality continued)

1. **Start** PowerPoint. Click the **Office** button, and then click **Open**. From your student files, open the file **p15C_Hospitality**. Click the **Office** button, and then click **Save As**. Navigate to your **PowerPoint Chapter 15** folder, and then using your own first and last names, **Save** the file as **15C_Hospitality_Firstname_Lastname**

2. Click the **Design tab**. In the **Themes group**, click the **More** button to display the **Themes gallery**. Under **Built-In**, locate and click the **Flow** theme to apply the theme to the entire presentation.

3. Display **Slide 2**, and then click in the paragraph. Click the **Home tab**, and then in the **Paragraph group**, click the **Center** button to center align the paragraph within the placeholder. In the **Paragraph group**, click the **Line Spacing** button, and then click **2.0** to apply double-spacing to the paragraph. Then, click in the slide title, and click the **Center** button to center align the title.

4. On **Slide 2**, select all of the text in the paragraph. Point to the Mini toolbar, and then click **Bold** and **Italic** to apply both font styles to the paragraph.

5. Display **Slide 4** and notice the red wavy underline in the last bullet point. Point to *atmoshere*, and then click the right mouse button to display the shortcut menu. Click **atmosphere** to correct the spelling of the word.

6. On **Slide 4**, in the third bullet point, right-click the word *good*, point to **Synonyms**, and then in the synonyms list, click **excellent** to use the Thesaurus to change *good* to *excellent*.

7. With **Slide 4** still displayed, on the **Home tab**, in the **Slides group**, click **Layout** to display the **Slide Layout gallery**. Click the **Two Content** layout.

8. Click in the placeholder on the right. Type **Do you** and then press Enter. Press Tab to increase the list level. Type **Greet every guest** and then press Enter. Type **Make every guest feel welcome**

9. In the placeholder at the left of **Slide 4**, select the last three bulleted items. On the **Home tab**, in the **Paragraph group**, click the **Increase List Level** button.

10. With **Slide 4** still displayed, on the **Home tab**, in the **Slides group**, click the **New Slide arrow**, and then in the **gallery**, click **Title and Content** to create a new Slide 5.

11. On **Slide 5**, click in the title placeholder, type **Why Our Customers Return** and then click in the content placeholder. Type the following five bulleted items, pressing Enter at the end of each of the first four lines to create a new bullet. Do not press Enter after the last item.

   We exceed their expectations

   They enjoy our relaxing atmosphere

   They feel comfortable in their surroundings

   We ensure fresh, high-quality food

   Our customer service is outstanding

12. With **Slide 5** displayed, click in the **Notes** pane and type **Remember that every single one of our customers is a VIP!** Make spelling corrections as necessary on the slide and in the notes.

13. Display **Slide 1** and select the subtitle text—*New Employee Training*. On the Mini toolbar, click the **Font Size button arrow**, and then change the **Font Size** to **44**.

14. Click the **Insert tab**, and then, in the **Text group**, click **Header & Footer** to display the **Header and Footer** dialog box.

15. Click the **Notes and Handouts tab**. Under **Include on page**, select the **Date and**

(Project 15C–Hospitality continues on the next page)

Content-Based Assessments

(Project 15C–Hospitality continued)

time check box and, if necessary, click the Update automatically button so that the current date prints on the notes and handouts each time the presentation is printed. If necessary, clear the Header check box to omit this element. If necessary, select the Page number and Footer check boxes, noticing that when you do so, the insertion point displays in the Footer box. Using your own first and last names, in the **Footer** box, type **15C_ Hospitality_Firstname_Lastname** and then click **Apply to All**.

16. On the Ribbon, click the **Slide Show tab**, and then in the **Start Slide Show group**, click **From Beginning**. Press [Spacebar] or click the left mouse button to advance through the presentation and view the slide show.

17. Check your *Chapter Assignment Sheet* or *Course Syllabus* or consult your instructor to determine if you are to submit your assignments on paper or electronically. To submit electronically, go to Step 20, and then follow the instructions provided by your instructor.

18. From the **Office** menu, point to **Print**, and then click **Print Preview** to make a final check of your presentation. In the **Page Setup group**, click the **Print What arrow**, and then click **Handouts (6 Slides Per Page)**. Click the **Print** button, and then click **OK** to print the handouts.

19. In the **Page Setup group**, click the **Print What arrow**, and then click **Notes Pages**. Click the **Print** button, and then in the **Print** dialog box, under **Print range**, click the **Slides** option button. In the **Slides** box, type **5** to instruct PowerPoint to print the notes pages for Slide 5. Click **OK**, and then **Close** Print Preview.

20. **Save** your presentation, and then from the **Office** menu, click **Exit PowerPoint**.

End **You have completed Project 15C** ———————————————

Content-Based Assessments

Skills Review

Project 15D — Funding

In this project, you will apply the skills you practiced from the Objectives in Project 15B.

Objectives: 5. *Create a New Presentation;* **6.** *Use Slide Sorter View;* **7.** *Add Pictures to a Presentation.*

In the following Skills Review, you will create the preliminary slides for a presentation that Lucinda dePaolo, Chief Financial Officer for Skyline Bakery and Cafe, will use to provide an overview of financial plans to a group of investors. Your completed presentation will look similar to the one shown in Figure 15.43.

For Project 15D, you will need the following files:

p15D_Background
p15D_Proposal_Template
p15D_Calculator

You will save your presentation as
15D_Funding_Firstname_Lastname

Figure 15.43

(Project 15D–Funding continues on the next page)

Content-Based Assessments

(Project 15D–Funding continued)

1. **Start** PowerPoint. From the **Office** menu, click **New** to display the **New Presentation** window. Under **Microsoft Office Online**, click **More categories** and then under **More categories**, click **Proposals**. Click the **Grant proposal** template, and then in the lower right corner of the **New Presentation** window, click **Download** to access the template from Microsoft Office Online. If a Microsoft Office window displays, click Continue. Alternatively, if you are unable to access the templates from Microsoft Office Online, the template for this project is available from your student data files. Click the Office button, and then click Open. Navigate to your student files and open the **p15D_Proposal_ Template** presentation.

2. On **Slide 1**, select the text *Organization Name*, and type **Skyline Bakery and Cafe** to replace it. Select the text that you just typed. On the Mini toolbar, click the **Font Size button arrow**, and then click **24**. Select the text in the title placeholder, and then type **Funding Proposal for Expansion**

3. Click the **Office** button, and then click **Save As**. Navigate to your **PowerPoint Chapter 15** folder, and then using your own first and last names, **Save** the file as **15D_Funding_Firstname_Lastname**

4. Scroll through the presentation to view the content suggested for a funding proposal. Notice that in **Slide 2**, an introduction and mission statement are suggested. This content exists in another presentation and can be inserted without retyping the slides.

5. Display **Slide 1**. On the **Home tab**, in the **Slides group**, click the **New Slide arrow** to display the **Slide Layout gallery** and additional options for inserting slides. At the

bottom of the gallery, click **Reuse Slides** to open the **Reuse Slides** task pane.

6. In the **Reuse Slides** task pane, click the **Browse** button, and then click **Browse File**. In the **Browse** dialog box, navigate to where your student files are stored and double-click **p15D_Background**. In the **Reuse Slides** task pane, point to either of the two slides that display and right-click. From the shortcut menu, click **Insert All Slides** to insert both slides into the presentation. **Close** the **Reuse Slides** task pane.

7. On the status bar, locate the **View** buttons, and then click the **Slide Sorter** button to display the 15 slides in the presentation. Click **Slide 4**, and then press Delete to delete the slide. Click **Slide 5**, hold down ⇧ Shift and click **Slide 7** so that slides 5 through 7 are selected. Press Delete to delete the selected slides.

8. Click **Slide 6**, hold down ⇧ Shift and click **Slide 9** so that slides 6 through 9 are selected. With the four slides still selected, hold down Ctrl, and then click **Slide 11**. Press Delete to delete the selected slides. Six slides remain in the presentation.

9. Click **Slide 3** to select it. While pointing to **Slide 3**, press and hold down the left mouse button, and then drag the slide to the left until the vertical bar is positioned to the left of **Slide 2**. Release the left mouse button to move the slide.

10. In the status bar, click the **Normal** button, and then **Save** your presentation. Display **Slide 4**, and then select the text in the content placeholder. Replace the selected text with the following two bullets:

   Build a chain of high-quality restaurants

   Build a profitable brand of recognized bakery products

(Project 15D–Funding continues on the next page)

(Project 15D–Funding continued)

11. Display **Slide 5,** change the title to **Statement of Finances** and then select the text in the content placeholder. Replace the selected text with the following bullet points, increasing and decreasing the list level as indicated:

    Current Resources
       Franchise revenue
       Restaurant sales
    Future Resources
       Stock offering

12. Click the **Insert tab**, and then in the **Illustrations group**, click **Clip Art** to display the **Clip Art** task pane. In the **Clip Art** task pane, click in the **Search for** box, delete the existing text, and then type **calculator**

13. In the **Clip Art** task pane, click the **Search in arrow**, and if necessary, click the **Everywhere** check box so that it is selected. Click the **Results should be arrow**, and then *clear* the **Clip Art**, **Movies**, and **Sounds** check boxes so that only **Photographs** is selected. Click **Go** to display the photographs of calculators.

14. Click the picture of the white calculator with a machine tape on a blue background. Check Figure 15.43 at the beginning of this project if you are unsure of the picture that you should insert. **Close** the **Clip Art** task pane. If you cannot locate the picture, on the Insert tab, in the Illustrations group, click Picture. Navigate to your student files and then double-click **p15D_Calculator**.

15. Position the pointer anywhere over the picture, and then drag to the right so that the picture is positioned approximately one-half inch from the right edge of the slide.

16. If necessary, click the picture of the calculator to select it and to activate the Picture Tools. Click the **Format tab**, and then in

the **Picture Styles group**, in the first row, click **Reflected Rounded Rectangle**.

17. Display **Slide 6**. Select the bulleted list text, and then replace it with the following bulleted items:

    Board of Directors
    National Investors Group
    East Coast Bank and Trust

18. Click the **Insert tab**, and then in the **Text group**, click **Header & Footer** to display the **Header and Footer** dialog box.

19. Click the **Notes and Handouts tab**. Under **Include on page**, select the **Date and time** check box and, if necessary, click the **Update automatically** button so that the current date prints on the notes and handouts each time the presentation is printed. If necessary, clear the **Header** check box to omit this element. Select the **Page number** and **Footer** check boxes. Using your own first and last names, in the **Footer** box, type **15D_Funding_Firstname_Lastname** and then click **Apply to All**.

20. Check your *Chapter Assignment Sheet* or *Course Syllabus* or consult your instructor to determine if you are to submit your assignments on paper or electronically. To submit electronically, go to Step 22, and then follow the instructions provided by your instructor.

21. From the **Office** menu, point to **Print**, and then click **Print Preview** to make a final check of your presentation. In the **Page Setup group**, click the **Print What arrow**, and then click **Handouts (6 Slides Per Page)**. Click the **Print** button, and then click **OK** to print the handouts. **Close** Print Preview.

22. **Save** the changes to your presentation, and then from the **Office** menu, click **Exit PowerPoint**.

 End You have completed Project 15D ⸻⸻⸻⸻⸻⸻

Content-Based Assessments

Mastering PowerPoint

Project 15E — Flyer

In this project, you will apply the skills you practiced from the Objectives in Projects 15A and 15B.

Objectives: 2. *Edit a Presentation;* **3.** *Format a Presentation;* **4.** *Create Headers and Footers and Print a Presentation;* **5.** *Create a New Presentation;* **7.** *Add Pictures to a Presentation.*

In the following Mastering PowerPoint project, you will create a single slide to be used as a flyer for the annual employee baking contest. Your completed presentation will look similar to Figure 15.44.

For Project 15E, you will need the following files:

New blank PowerPoint presentation
p15E_Cookies

**You will save your presentation as
15E_Flyer_Firstname_Lastname**

Figure 15.44

(**Project 15E–Flyer continues on the next page**)

Content-Based Assessments

(Project 15E–Flyer continued)

1. **Start** PowerPoint and begin a new blank presentation. Change the **Layout** of the title slide to the **Comparison** layout. Change the **Design** of the presentation by applying the **Oriel** theme. **Save** your presentation as **15E_Flyer_Firstname_Lastname**

2. The title of the slide is **Annual Employee Baking Contest** Change the **Font** to **Bradley Hand ITC** and the **Font Size** to **36**. Apply **Bold**, and then **Center** the title.

3. In the orange box on the left side of the slide, type **How do you participate and join the fun?** In the orange box on the right side of the slide, type **Bring your favorite yummy dessert! Center** the text in both boxes.

4. In the content placeholder on the left side of the slide, type the following bullet points:

   Bake your favorite secret recipe!
   Bring it to work on December 15!
   Our chefs will be judging all day!
   Great prizes in lots of different categories!

5. Click in the content placeholder on the right side of the slide and insert a clip art by using the keyword **cookies** Search for **Photographs** in **All collections**. Click the

picture with the star-shaped cookie on the brown background. If you cannot find the picture, insert the picture from your student files—p15E_Cookies.

6. If necessary, move the picture so that it is centered below the *Bring your favorite yummy dessert!* text. Then, apply **Picture Style—Drop Shadow Rectangle**.

7. Insert a **Footer** on the **Slide** (*not* the Notes and Handouts), that includes the file name **15E_Flyer_Firstname_Lastname** Because of the layout of this slide, the footer will display vertically on the right side of the slide.

8. Check your *Chapter Assignment Sheet* or *Course Syllabus* or consult your instructor to determine if you are to submit your assignments on paper or electronically. To submit electronically, go to Step 10, and then follow the instructions provided by your instructor.

9. Display your presentation in **Print Preview**. Because there is only one slide in the presentation, print **Slides**.

10. **Save** and **Close** your presentation.

End **You have completed Project 15E**

Content-Based Assessments

Mastering PowerPoint

Project 15F—Fresh

In this project, you will apply the skills you practiced from the Objectives in Projects 15A and 15B.

Objectives: 2. *Edit a Presentation;* **3.** *Format a Presentation;* **4.** *Create Headers and Footers and Print a Presentation;* **5.** *Create a New Presentation;* **6.** *Use Slide Sorter View;* **7.** *Add Pictures to a Presentation.*

In the following Mastering PowerPoint project, you will create a presentation that describes some of the steps taken by Skyline Bakery and Cafe to ensure the freshest possible food. Your completed presentation will look similar to Figure 15.45.

For Project 15F, you will need the following files:

New blank PowerPoint presentation
p15F_Text
p15F_Apple_Template
p15F_Vegetables
p15F_Tomato

You will save your presentation as 15F_Fresh_Firstname_Lastname

Figure 15.45

Keeping It Fresh!
Skyline Bakery and Cafe

Our Commitment
- Fresh food, unforgettable taste, served in a clean and cozy setting
- Quality ingredients selected by our discerning staff of chefs
- Cooked to perfection at all times

How We Keep It Fresh

Buyers
- Purchase by specialty
  - Patisserie chef
  - Executive chef
  - Line chef
- Continuous training
- International access

Sellers
- Must pass inspections
  - Federally regulated
- Freshest produce
- Organically fed livestock

Skyline Bakery and Cafe

ALWAYS FRESH!

(Project 15F–Fresh continues on the next page)

(Project 15F–Fresh continued)

1. **Start** PowerPoint and begin a new presentation by searching for a template with the keyword **Apple** Click the template with the three green apples. If the template is not available, from your student files, open **p15F_Apple_Template**.

2. The title of this presentation is **Keeping It Fresh!** and the subtitle is **Skyline Bakery and Cafe Save** the presentation as **15F_Fresh_Firstname_Lastname**

3. Add the two slides from the **p15F_Text** presentation. Display **Slide 3**, and then in the left bulleted list placeholder, increase the list level of the *Patisserie chef*, *Executive chef*, and *Line chef* bullet points. In the right bulleted list placeholder, increase the list level of the *Federally regulated* bullet point.

4. Add a **New Slide** with the **Title and Content** layout, and in the title placeholder, type **Our Commitment** In the bulleted list placeholder, type the following bullet points:

   Fresh food, unforgettable taste, served in a clean and cozy setting

   Quality ingredients picked by our discerning staff of chefs

   Cooked to perfection at all times

5. In **Slide Sorter** view, switch **Slides 2** and **4** so that **Slide 2** becomes the last slide and the *Our Commitment* slide becomes the second slide. Return the presentation to **Normal** view.

6. On **Slide 2**, in the second bullet point, use the shortcut menu to view **Synonyms** for the word *picked*. Change the word *picked* to **selected**.

7. Display **Slide 4**. Insert a clip art image by using the keyword **cabbage** Search for **Photographs** in **All collections**. Click the picture with many different types and colors of vegetables. Move the picture down and to the left so that it covers the apples

and is positioned in the lower left corner of the slide. If you cannot locate the picture, it is available in your student files. The file name is p15F_Vegetables.

8. Insert the vegetable picture again so that there are two copies of the same picture on the slide. Move the picture down and to the right so that it is positioned in the lower right corner of the slide.

9. Insert another clip art image, this time by using the keywords **cherry tomato** Search for **Photographs** in **All collections**. Click the picture with tomatoes that look like they are spilling out of a bowl as shown in the figure at the beginning of this project. If you cannot locate the picture, it is available in your student files—p15F_Tomato. Drag the tomato picture straight down so that it overlaps the two vegetable pictures and its bottom edge aligns with the bottom edge of the slide. Apply **Picture Style—Simple Frame**, **Black**.

10. Insert a **Header & Footer** for the **Notes and Handouts**. Include only the **Date and time updated automatically**, the **Page number**, and a **Footer** with the file name **15F_Fresh_Firstname_Lastname** and then view the slide show.

11. Check your *Chapter Assignment Sheet* or *Course Syllabus* or consult your instructor to determine if you are to submit your assignments on paper or electronically. To submit electronically, go to Step 13, and then follow the instructions provided by your instructor.

12. **Print Preview** your presentation, and then print **Handouts (4 Slides Per Page)**. If the text or pictures do not display, on the Print Preview tab, in the Print group, click Options, point to Color/Grayscale, and then click Color or Color (On Black and White Printer).

13. **Save** the changes to your presentation. **Close** the presentation.

End You have completed Project 15F —————

Content-Based Assessments

PowerPoint
chapterfifteen

Mastering PowerPoint

Project 15G — Holiday

In this project, you will apply the skills you practiced from the Objectives in Projects 15A and 15B.

Objectives: 1. *Open, View, and Save a Presentation;* **2.** *Edit a Presentation;* **3.** *Format a Presentation;* **4.** *Create Headers and Footers and Print a Presentation;* **5.** *Create a New Presentation;* **6.** *Use Slide Sorter View;* **7.** *Add Pictures to a Presentation.*

In the following Mastering PowerPoint project, you will create a presentation that details the holiday activities at Skyline Bakery and Cafe. Your completed presentation will look similar to Figure 15.46.

For Project 15G, you will need the following files:

New blank PowerPoint presentation
p15G_December
p15G_Green_Template
p15G_Coffee
p15G_Ornaments

**You will save your presentation as
15G_Holiday_Firstname_Lastname**

Figure 15.46

(Project 15G–Holiday continues on the next page)

Mastering PowerPoint

(Project 15G–Holiday continued)

1. **Start** PowerPoint and begin a new presentation by searching for the green and gold holiday template. If the template is not available, from your student files, open **p15G_Green_Template**. The title of the presentation is **Holiday Happenings** and the subtitle is **With Skyline Bakery and Cafe** Insert all of the slides from the presentation **p15G_December**. **Save** the presentation as **15G_Holiday_Firstname_Lastname**

2. On **Slide 2**, increase the list level for bullet points 2, 3, and 4 and for the last two bullet points. Change the **Layout** to **Two Content**, and then in the right placeholder insert a clip art photograph of a white coffee mug— search for **coffee**—on a green background. If you cannot find the image, it is located with your student files—p15G_Coffee.

3. Size the picture so that it is approximately as wide as the word *December* and as tall as the text in the left placeholder. Apply **Picture Style—Compound Frame**, **Black** and position the picture, using Figure 15.46 at the beginning of this project as your guide.

4. Display **Slide 3** and change the **Layout** to **Comparison**. In the *Click to add text* box on the left side of the slide, type **Traditional Elegance** and then in the box on the right side of the slide, type **Bountiful Buffet**

5. **Center** and apply an **Underline** to the text in both boxes, and then change the **Font Size** to **28**.

6. Insert a **New Slide** with the **Content with Caption** layout. In the *Click to add title* box, type **Luncheon** and then change the **Font Size** to **36**. In the text placeholder on the left side of the slide, type the following paragraph:

   Luncheons during December are reminiscent of years gone by. Join us for a pleasing array of old-fashioned festive delights, served by candlelight while holiday music plays.

7. Select the paragraph, and then change the **Font** to **Constantia** and the **Font Size** to **20**. Apply **Bold** and **Italic**, and then change the **Line Spacing** to **1.5**.

8. In the content placeholder on the right side of the slide, insert a clip art of five brightly colored glass ornaments by searching for the keyword **Ornaments** If you cannot locate the picture, the file name in your student files is p15G_Ornaments.

9. Apply **Picture Style—Reflected Bevel, Black** and use Figure 15.46 at the beginning of this project as your guide for sizing and positioning the picture.

10. Insert a **New Slide** with the **Title Slide** layout. In the title placeholder, type **Savor the Holidays** and in the subtitle placeholder type **Skyline Bakery and Cafe**

11. Move **Slide 4** so that it is between **Slides 2** and **3**. Check the presentation for spelling errors, and then view the slide show from the beginning.

12. Insert a **Header & Footer** for the **Notes and Handouts** that includes the **Date and time updated automatically**, the **Page number**, and the file name **15G_Holiday_Firstname_Lastname**

13. Check your *Chapter Assignment Sheet* or *Course Syllabus* or consult your instructor to determine if you are to submit your assignments on paper or electronically. To submit electronically, go to Step 15, and then follow the instructions provided by your instructor.

14. Display your presentation in **Print Preview**, and then print **Handouts (6 Slides Per Page)**.

15. **Save** the changes to your presentation, and then **Close** the file.

End You have completed Project 15G

Content-Based Assessments

Mastering PowerPoint

Project 15H — *GO!* Fix It

In this project, you will apply the skills you practiced from the Objectives in Projects 15A and 15B.

For Project 15H, you will need the following file:

p15H_Fundraiser

**You will save your presentation as
15H_Fundraiser_Firstname_Lastname**

In this project, you will edit a draft slide presentation by Sandra Lee, Director of Marketing for Skyline Bakery and Cafe. Sandra is requesting approval from corporate headquarters for Skyline to become the business sponsor of the Springfield Firefighters Barbecue and Auction. From the student files that accompany this textbook, open the file **p15H_Fundraiser**, and then save the file in your chapter folder as **15H_Fundraiser_Firstname_Lastname**

This presentation contains errors that you must find and correct. Read and examine the presentation, and then edit to correct the errors that you find. Types of errors could include:

- Content errors such as misspellings, missing or incorrect text, pictures, hyperlinks, or other objects.
- Font and paragraph formatting and positioning errors such as fonts, font styles, font sizing, alignment, text color, indent levels, and bullet features.
- Slide layout, orientation, design themes, backgrounds, animation and transition errors.
- Page setup errors on slides, handouts, notes and outlines such as margins, orientation, layout, alignment, headers and footers, date and time, color, grayscale, black-and-white, and sizing.

To complete the project you should know:

- There are two spelling errors.
- Ms. Lee prefers the Civic presentation theme for the presentation.
- Slide 5 bullet points should be all the same level.

Create a footer for the Notes and Handouts. Include only the date and time updated automatically, the page number, and a footer with the file name. Submit as directed.

 You have completed Project 15H ————————

Outcomes-Based Assessments

Rubric

The following outcomes-based assessments are *open-ended assessments*. That is, there is no specific correct result; your result will depend on your approach to the information provided. Make *Professional Quality* your goal. Use the following scoring rubric to guide you in *how* to approach the problem, and then to evaluate *how well* your approach solves the problem.

The *criteria*—Software Mastery, Content, Format and Layout, and Process—represent the knowledge and skills you have gained that you can apply to solving the problem. The *levels of performance*—Professional Quality, Approaching Professional Quality, or Needs Quality Improvements—help you and your instructor evaluate your result.

	Your completed project is of Professional Quality if you:	Your completed project is Approaching Professional Quality if you:	Your completed project Needs Quality Improvements if you:
1-Software Mastery	Choose and apply the most appropriate skills, tools, and features and identify efficient methods to solve the problem.	Choose and apply some appropriate skills, tools, and features, but not in the most efficient manner.	Choose inappropriate skills, tools, or features, or are inefficient in solving the problem.
2-Content	Construct a solution that is clear and well organized, contains content that is accurate, appropriate to the audience and purpose, and is complete. Provide a solution that contains no errors of spelling, grammar, or style.	Construct a solution in which some components are unclear, poorly organized, inconsistent, or incomplete. Misjudge the needs of the audience. Have some errors in spelling, grammar, or style, but the errors do not detract from comprehension.	Construct a solution that is unclear, incomplete, or poorly organized; contains some inaccurate or inappropriate content; and contains many errors of spelling, grammar, or style. Do not solve the problem.
3-Format and Layout	Format and arrange all elements to communicate information and ideas, clarify function, illustrate relationships, and indicate relative importance.	Apply appropriate format and layout features to some elements, but not others. Overuse features, causing minor distraction.	Apply format and layout that does not communicate information or ideas clearly. Do not use format and layout features to clarify function, illustrate relationships, or indicate relative importance. Use available features excessively, causing distraction.
4-Process	Use an organized approach that integrates planning, development, self-assessment, revision, and reflection.	Demonstrate an organized approach in some areas, but not others; or, use an insufficient process of organization throughout.	Do not use an organized approach to solve the problem.

Outcomes-Based Assessments

PowerPoint
chapter fifteen

Problem Solving

Project 15I — Catering

In this project, you will construct a solution by applying any combination of the skills you practiced from the Objectives in Projects 15A and 15B.

For Project 15I, you will need the following file:

New blank PowerPoint presentation

You will save your presentation as
15I_Catering_Firstname_Lastname

Using the information provided, create a presentation that contains four to six slides that Nancy Goldman, Chief Baker, can use to describe the catering services offered by Skyline Bakery and Cafe. The presentation will be used at a business expo attended by representatives of many companies that frequently host business luncheons and dinners for their clients. The presentation should include a title slide, a slide that describes why customers would be interested in Skyline Bakery and Cafe's catering services, at least two slides with sample menus, and an ending slide that summarizes the presentation. The tone of the presentation should be positive and sales oriented so that the audience is encouraged to try Skyline's catering service.

The presentation should include a theme or template that is creative and appropriate to the upbeat tone of the presentation. Use at least two different slide layouts to vary the way in which the presentation text is displayed. Search for clip art that visually represents the types of menu items described. Add the file name to the Notes and Handouts footer and check the presentation for spelling errors. Save the presentation as **15I_Catering_Firstname_Lastname** and submit it as directed.

 You have completed Project 15I ————————————

Outcomes-Based Assessments

Problem Solving

Project 15J—Picnic

In this project, you will construct a solution by applying any combination of the skills you practiced from the Objectives in Projects 15A and 15B.

For Project 15J, you will need the following file:

New blank PowerPoint presentation

You will save your presentation as
15J_Picnic_Firstname_Lastname

In this project, you will create a one-slide flyer to be distributed to employees of Skyline Bakery and Cafe advertising the upcoming employee picnic. The picnic is held every summer at a large, regional park. The tone of the flyer is fun! Use two fonts that are informal and inviting and large enough to easily read if the flyer were posted on a bulletin board. Include in the flyer a slide title that will make the employees feel welcome and excited about attending. Choose a content layout that includes multiple placeholders for the information that you need to provide. The flyer should include information on location, date, time, and types of activities. Include a picture that is reminiscent of a picnic or large outdoor gathering.

Add the file name to the footer and check the presentation for spelling errors. Save the presentation as **15J_Picnic_Firstname_Lastname** and submit it as directed.

End **You have completed Project 15J** ———————

Outcomes-Based Assessments

Problem Solving

Project 15K — Opening

In this project, you will construct a solution by applying any combination of the skills you practiced from the Objectives in Projects 15A and 15B.

For Project 15K, you will need the following file:

New blank PowerPoint presentation

You will save your presentation as
15K_Opening_Firstname_Lastname

In this project, you will create a presentation to be shown by Skyline Bakery and Cafe's Chief Executive Officer, Samir Taheri, at a Chamber of Commerce meeting. The presentation will explain the details of the company's grand opening of two new locations in Rhode Island taking place in June. The presentation should contain six to eight slides, and the first two to three slides should include background information that may be taken from the following paragraph that describes the company and the new restaurant locations.

Skyline Bakery and Cafe is a chain of casual dining restaurants and bakeries based in Boston. Each restaurant has its own in-house bakery, which produces a wide variety of high-quality specialty breads, breakfast sweets, and desserts. Breads and sweets are sold by counter service along with coffee drinks, gourmet teas, fresh juices, and sodas. The full-service restaurant area features a menu of sandwiches, salads, soups, and light entrees. Fresh, high-quality ingredients and a professional and courteous staff are the hallmarks of every Skyline Bakery and Cafe.

The new restaurants are located in outdoor lifestyle centers where many residents gather in the evening to socialize. The restaurants are opening in June, so consider a summer theme as you develop ideas about the kinds of events that the owners may host during the grand opening. Include in the presentation four slides representing four different days of events—two at each of the new locations. The Comparison and Two Content slide layouts would be very effective for these four slides. Use fonts and clip art to enhance your presentation but do not clutter the presentation with excess images or many different types of fonts. Add the date and file name to the Notes and Handouts footer and check the presentation for spelling errors. Save the presentation as **15K_Opening_Firstname_Lastname** and submit it as directed.

End **You have completed Project 15K** ————————————

More on your Student CD

The instructions for the following additional end-of-chapter projects are on your student CD in the folder 03_additional_end_of_chapter_projects.

Content-Based Assessments

Project L Mastering PowerPoint	Apply the skills you practiced in Project A.
Project M Mastering PowerPoint	Apply the skills you practiced in Project B.
Project N Business Running Case	Apply the skills you practiced in Projects A and B while helping an entrepreneur with the daily tasks of running a business.
	In each chapter, this project focuses on applying the skills you have practiced in Projects A and B to a business. The project related to this business runs throughout the textbook. You will see how the Office applications relate to the day-to-day operation of a small business called Nelson Architectural Planning.

Outcomes-Based Assessments

Project O Problem Solving	Construct a solution by applying any combination of the skills you practiced from Projects A and B.
Project P Problem Solving	Construct a solution by applying any combination of the skills you practiced from Projects A and B.
Project Q You and GO!	Construct a solution that applies to your own life by applying any combination of the skills you practiced from Projects A and B.
Project R GO! with Help	Practice using Microsoft Office's Help Feature.
Project S Group Business Running Case	Work as part of a group to apply the skills you have gained thus far to help the Bell Orchid Hotel Group achieve its business goals.

Multimedia

The following multimedia accompany this textbook:

Companion Web site *www.prenhall.com/go*	An interactive Web site designed to reinforce and test your understanding of the skills in this chapter.
AV-EDDs	In the folder in the front of this book you will find videos that demonstrate the objectives of the A and B projects in this chapter. These may help you understand how to complete the projects in this book.
Video Podcasts	In the folder in the front of this book are videos that can be played on your iPod, MP3 player, or computer. These videos demonstrate how to complete the more challenging objectives in this textbook.

chaptersixteen

Designing a PowerPoint Presentation

OBJECTIVES

At the end of this chapter you will be able to:

OUTCOMES

Mastering these objectives will enable you to:

1. Format Slide Elements
2. Insert and Format Pictures and Shapes
3. Apply Slide Transitions

PROJECT 16A
Format a Presentation

4. Reorganize Presentation Text and Clear Formats
5. Create and Format a SmartArt Graphic

PROJECT 16B
Enhance a Presentation with SmartArt Graphics

Montagna del Pattino

Montagna del Pattino was founded and built by the Blardone family in the 1950s. It has grown from one ski run and a small lodge to 50 trails, 6 lifts, a 300-room lodge, and a renowned ski and snowboard school. Luxurious condominiums on the property have ski in/ski out access. A resort store offers rental and sale of gear for enthusiasts who want the latest advances in ski and snowboard technology. A variety of quick service, casually elegant, and fine dining restaurants complete the scene for a perfect ski-enthusiast getaway.

© AGE Fotostock America, Inc.

Designing a PowerPoint Presentation

A PowerPoint presentation is a visual aid in which well-designed slides help the audience understand complex information, while keeping them focused on the message. Color is an important element that provides uniformity and visual interest. When used correctly, color enhances your slides and draws the audience's interest by creating focus. When designing the background and element colors for your presentation, use a consistent look throughout the presentation and be sure that the colors you use provide contrast so that the text is visible on the background.

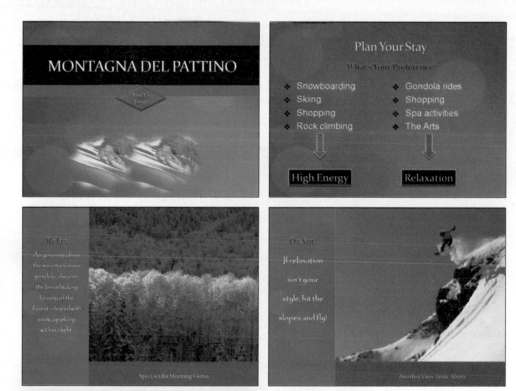

Project 16A Welcome

In Activities 16.01 through 16.13, you will edit and format a presentation that Kirsten McCarty, Director of Marketing, has created for a travel fair that introduces potential resort visitors to the types of activities available at Montagna del Pattino. Your completed presentation will look similar to Figure 16.1.

For Project 16A, you will need the following files:

p16A_Snow
p16A_Snowboard
p16A_Welcome
p16A_Winter

You will save your presentation as
16A_Welcome_Firstname_Lastname

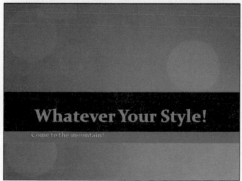

Figure 16.1
Project 16A—Welcome

Objective 1
Format Slide Elements

Recall that formatting is the process of changing the appearance of the text, layout, and design of a slide. You have practiced formatting text by changing the font and font size, and by applying bold and italic text styles. Other slide elements can be formatted, such as bulleted and numbered lists, and there are other methods that you can use to enhance text, including WordArt and the Format Painter.

Activity 16.01 Selecting Placeholder Text and Using the Repeat Key

1 **Start** PowerPoint. From your student files, **Open** the file **p16A_ Welcome**. From the **Office** menu , click **Save As**, and then click the **New Folder** button. Navigate to the location where you are saving your files, create a new folder named **PowerPoint Chapter 16** and then click **OK**. In the **File name** box, type **16A_Welcome_Firstname_ Lastname** and then click **Save** to save your file.

2 Display **Slide 2**. Click anywhere in the bulleted list on the left side of the slide and notice that the placeholder is surrounded by a dashed border, as shown in Figure 16.2.

> The dashed border indicates that you can make editing changes to the placeholder text.

Figure 16.2

Dashed border

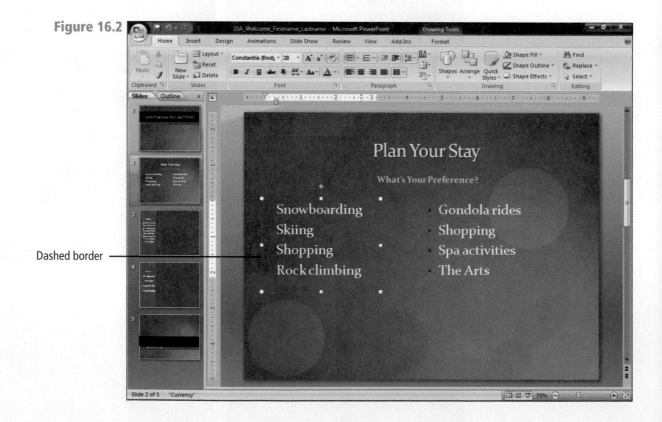

3 Point to the dashed border to display the ⬚ pointer, as shown in Figure 16.3.

Figure 16.3

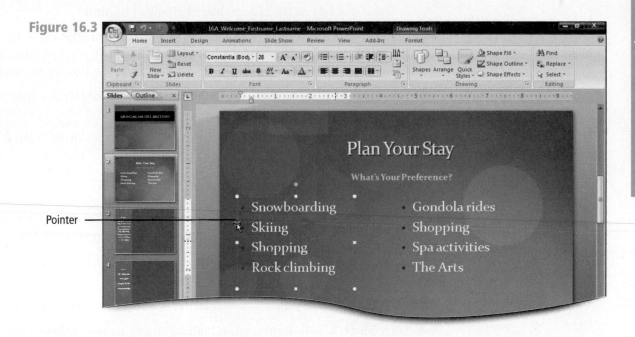

Pointer

4 With the ⬚ pointer displayed, click the mouse button one time to display the border as a solid line as shown in Figure 16.4.

When a placeholder's border displays as a solid line, all of the text in the placeholder is selected and can be formatted at one time. Thus, any formatting changes that you make will be applied to all of the text in the placeholder.

Figure 16.4

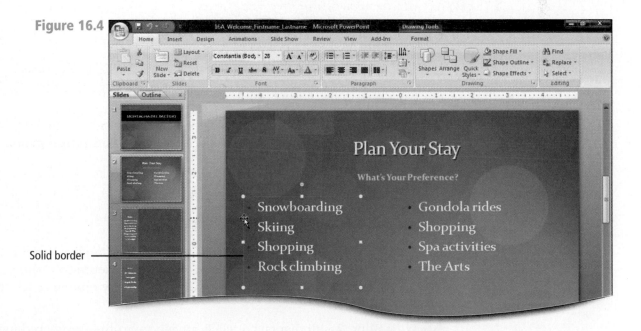

Solid border

5 With the border of the placeholder displaying as a solid line, on the **Home tab**, in the **Font group**, click the **Font button arrow**, and then click **Arial**.

All of the text in the placeholder is changed to Arial.

6 Click in the text in the bulleted list placeholder on the right side of the slide. Point to the dashed border to display the 🗘 pointer, and then click the mouse button one time so that the border is solid.

7 Press F4, which repeats the last command or keystroke that you entered.

All of the text in the placeholder on the right is formatted in Arial.

8 **Save** 🖫 your changes.

Another Way

To Repeat a Command

On the Quick Access Toolbar, click the Repeat button 🔃 to repeat the last command or keystroke that you entered.

Activity 16.02 Changing a Bulleted List to a Numbered List

1 With **Slide 2** still displayed, click anywhere in the bulleted list on the left side of the slide, and then point to its dashed border to display the 🗘 pointer. Click the dashed border so that it displays as a solid line, indicating that all of the text is selected.

2 On the **Home tab**, in the **Paragraph group**, click the **Numbering** button 🔢.

All of the bullets are converted to numbers. The color of the numbers is determined by the presentation theme.

Alert!

Did you display the Numbering gallery?

If you clicked the Numbering button arrow instead of the Numbering button, the Numbering gallery displays. Click the Numbering button arrow again to close the gallery, and then click the Numbering button to convert the bullets to numbers.

---

3 Select the bulleted list placeholder on the right side of the slide so that the border displays as a solid line. In the **Paragraph group**, click the **Numbering** button 🔢.

4 **Save** 🖫 the presentation.

Activity 16.03 Modifying the Bulleted List Style

The theme applied to your presentation includes default styles for the bulleted points in content placeholders. In this presentation, the default bullet is a blue circle. You can customize a bullet by changing its style, color, and size.

1 With **Slide 2** still displayed, click anywhere in the numbered list on the left side of the slide, and then point to its dashed border. Click

---

the dashed border so that it displays as a solid line, indicating that all of the text is selected.

2 On the **Home tab**, in the **Paragraph group**, click the **Bullets button arrow** ▤ ▾ to display the **Bullets gallery**, as shown in Figure 16.5.

The gallery displays several bullet characters that you can apply to the selection.

Figure 16.5

Bullets button arrow

Bullets gallery

Displays the Bullets and Numbering dialog box

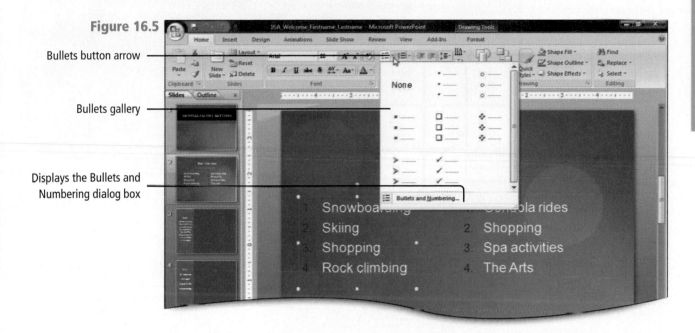

Alert! | **Did you replace the numbers with bullets?**
If you replaced the numbers with bullets, then you clicked the Bullets *button* instead of the Bullets *arrow*. Click the Bullets arrow, and then continue with Step 3.

3 At the bottom of the **Bullets gallery**, click **Bullets and Numbering**. In the displayed **Bullets and Numbering** dialog box, point to each bullet style to display its ScreenTip. Then, in the second row, click **Star Bullets**. If the Star Bullets do not display, in the second row of bullets, click the second bullet style, and then click the Reset button.

4 Below the gallery, click the **Color** button. Under **Theme Colors**, in the first row, click the first color—**Black, Background 1**. Click **OK** to apply the bullet style.

5 Click in the text in the numbered list placeholder on the right side of the slide. Point to the dashed border to display the ▤ pointer, and then click the mouse button so that the placeholder border is solid, indicating that all of the text in the placeholder can be formatted at one time.

6 Press [F4] to repeat the bullet formatting, and then compare your slide with Figure 16.6.

Figure 16.6

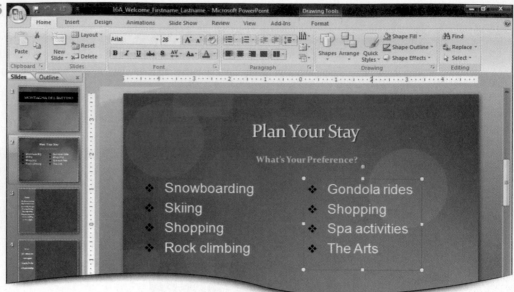

7 **Save** 💾 your changes.

More Knowledge — Using Other Symbols as Bullet Characters

Many bullets styles are available for you to insert in your presentation. In the Bullets and Numbering dialog box, click the Customize button to view additional bullet styles.

Activity 16.04 Applying WordArt Styles to Text

The **WordArt** feature applies combinations of decorative formatting to text, including shadows, reflections, and 3-D effects, as well as changing the line and **fill color** of text. A fill color is the inside color of text or of an object. You can choose from a gallery of WordArt styles to insert a new WordArt object or you can customize existing text by applying WordArt formatting.

1 Display **Slide 3**, and then select the word *Relax*. On the **Format tab**, in the **WordArt Styles group**, click the **More** button 🔽 to display the **WordArt Styles gallery**.

The WordArt Styles gallery is divided into two sections. If you choose a WordArt style in the *Applies to Selected Text* section, you must first select all of the text to which you want to apply the WordArt. If you choose a WordArt style in the *Applies to All Text in the Shape* section, the WordArt style is applied to all of the text in the placeholder or shape.

2 Point to several of the WordArt styles and notice that Live Preview displays the formatting effects on the selected word.

3 Under **Applies to Selected Text**, in the first row, click the second style—**Fill – None, Outline – Accent 2**.

The word *Relax* displays outlined in blue.

4 With the word *Relax* still selected, in the **Word Art Styles group**, click the **Text Fill button arrow** ▲▾. Under **Theme Colors**, in the first row, click the first color—**Black, Background 1**, and then compare your slide with Figure 16.7.

Figure 16.7

5 Display **Slide 5**. Click the **Insert tab**, and then in the **Text group**, click the **WordArt** button. In the **gallery**, click the first WordArt style in the first row—**Fill – Text 2, Outline – Background 2**.

> In the center of your slide, a WordArt placeholder displays *Your Text Here*. Text that you type will replace this text and the placeholder will expand to accommodate the text. The WordArt is surrounded by sizing handles with which you can adjust its size by using the same technique you practiced when sizing clip art.

6 Type **Whatever Your Style!** to replace the WordArt placeholder text.

7 Look at the Slide pane and verify that the horizontal ruler displays above the slide and that the vertical ruler displays to the left of the slide. If the rulers do not display, on the Ribbon, click the View tab, and then in the Show/Hide group, click to select the Ruler check box.

8 Point to the WordArt border to display the 🔀 pointer. Using Figure 16.8 as a guide, drag down and to the left approximately 1 inch to move the WordArt.

Figure 16.8

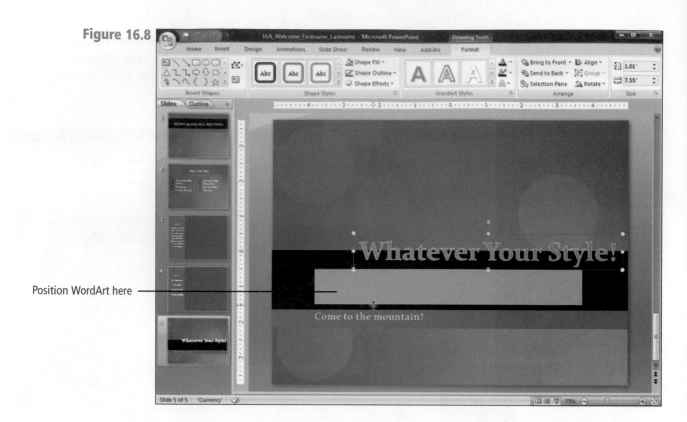

Position WordArt here

9 **Save** 🖫 the presentation.

Activity 16.05 Using Format Painter

Format Painter copies *formatting* from one selection of text to another. Use Format Painter to ensure formatting consistency in your presentation.

1 Display **Slide 3**, and then select the word *Relax*. On the **Home tab**, in the **Clipboard group**, *double-click* the **Format Painter** button 🖌, and then move your pointer anywhere into the Slide pane. Compare the pointer on your screen with the one shown in Figure 16.9.

> The pointer displays with a small paintbrush attached to it, indicating that Format Painter is active.

Figure 16.9

Format Painter pointer

2 In the **Slides/Outline** pane, click **Slide 4** to display it. Drag the ▲I pointer over the slide title—*Or Not!*

The WordArt formatting is applied to the title on Slide 4.

3 Display **Slide 2**. Drag the Format Painter pointer over the text **What's Your Preference?**, and then click the **Format Painter** button 🖋 one time to turn off the Format Painter.

4 **Save** 🖫 the presentation.

Alert!

> **Were you unable to use Format Painter more than one time?**
>
> When the Format Painter button is clicked one time instead of double-clicked, you can only use it to apply formatting to one selection. If you were only able to use Format Painter once, repeat Steps 1, 3, and 4.

Objective 2
Insert and Format Pictures and Shapes

PowerPoint 2007 provides a number of options for adding pictures and shapes to your presentation. You can draw lines, arrows, stars and banners, and a number of other basic shapes including ovals and rectangles. You can add text to a shape that you create and position it anywhere on a slide, and you can fill a shape with a picture. After you create a shape, you can add 3-D, glow, bevel effects, and shadows, or you can apply a predefined *Shape Style* that includes a combination of formatting effects.

Activity 16.06 Inserting a Picture Using a Content Layout

Many of the slide layouts in PowerPoint 2007 are designed to accommodate digital pictures that you have stored on your system or on a portable storage device.

1 Display **Slide 3**, which is formatted with the Content and Caption layout.

In the center of the large Content placeholder on the right side of the slide, the *Insert Picture from File* button displays.

2 In the center of the content placeholder, click the **Insert Picture from File** button 📷 to open the **Insert Picture** dialog box. Navigate to the location in which your student files are stored, and then double-click **p16A_Winter**. Alternatively, click p16A_Winter, and then click Insert.

The picture fills the entire placeholder.

3 Display **Slide 4**. Using the technique you practiced in **Step 2**, insert the picture **p16A_Snowboard**, and then compare your slide with Figure 16.10.

Figure 16.10

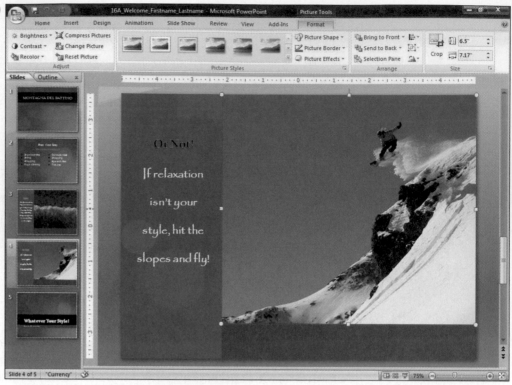

4. **Save** the presentation.

Workshop

Using Pictures Effectively in a Presentation

Large photographic images add impact to a presentation and help the audience visualize the message you are trying to convey.

Activity 16.07 Changing the Size and Shape of a Picture

Recall that you can resize a picture by dragging the sizing handles. Alternatively, you can use the Picture contextual tools to specify a picture's height and width. You can also modify a picture by changing its shape.

1. Display **Slide 1**. Click the **Insert tab**, and then in the **Illustrations group**, click **Picture**. Navigate to your student files, and then double-click **p16A_Snow**.

   The picture displays in the center of your slide and the Picture Tools contextual tab displays on the Ribbon.

2. On the **Format tab**, in the **Size group**, notice that the height of the picture is *5.34* inches and the width of the picture is *6.68* inches, as shown in Figure 16.11.

Figure 16.11

Picture height

Picture width

Inserted picture

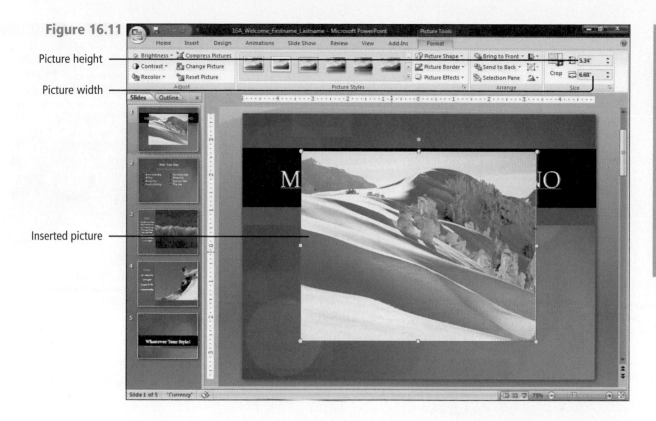

3 On the **Format tab**, in the **Size group**, click in the **Shape Height box** ⌖ 2″ ↕ so that 5.34 is selected. Type **3** and then press Enter. Notice that the height of the picture is resized to 3 inches and the width is also resized.

> When you change the height of a picture, the width adjusts proportionately unless you type a new size in the Width box.

4 If necessary, select the picture. On the **Format tab**, in the **Picture Styles group**, click the **Picture Shape** button to display a gallery of shapes that you can apply to the picture. Under **Basic Shapes**, in the third row, click the third to last shape—**Cloud**.

5 Point to the picture to display the ⌖ pointer and then drag straight down so that the bottom edge of the cloud touches the bottom of the slide. Compare your slide with Figure 16.12.

Figure 16.12

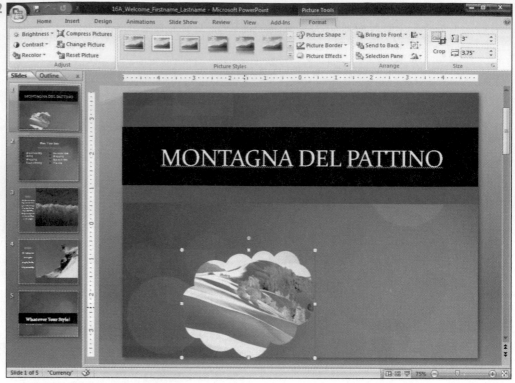

6 **Save** your presentation.

> **More Knowledge** — **Moving an Object by Using the Arrow Keys**
>
> You can use the directional arrow keys on your keyboard to move a picture, shape, or other object in small increments. Select the object so that its outside border displays as a solid line. Then on your keyboard, hold down the Ctrl key and press the directional arrow keys to move the selected object precisely.

Activity 16.08 Inserting and Positioning a Text Box

One way that you can customize a slide layout is by adding a *text box*. A text box is an object with which you can position text anywhere on a slide. When you create a text box, the *insertion point*—a blinking vertical line that indicates where text will be inserted—displays inside the text box, indicating that you can begin to type.

1 Display **Slide 4**. Click the **Insert tab**, and then in the **Text group**, click the **Text Box** button. In the slide, move the pointer below the picture as shown in Figure 16.13.

Figure 16.13

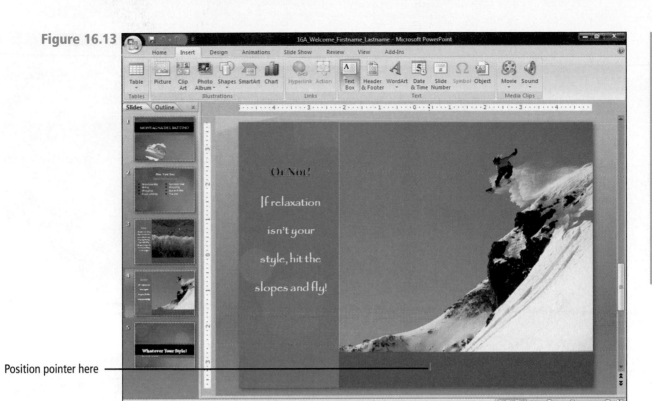

Position pointer here ──────────────

2 Click one time to create a narrow rectangular text box. Type **Another View From Above** and notice that as you type, the width of the text box expands to accommodate the text.

Alert!

Does the text that you type in the text box display vertically, one character at a time?

If you move the pointer when you click to create the text box, PowerPoint sets the width of the text box and does not widen to accommodate the text. If this happened to you, your text may display vertically instead of horizontally or it may display on two lines. Point to the center right sizing handle and drag to the right so that the text box is approximately 3 inches wide. When you finish typing the text, adjust the width of the text box as necessary so that all of the text displays on one line.

3 Compare your slide with Figure 16.14 and if necessary, use the 🏃 pointer to adjust the size and position of the text box.

Do not be concerned if your text box does not match Figure 16.14 exactly. In a later activity, you will practice using the Align tools to position slide elements precisely.

4 Display **Slide 3**. On the **Insert tab**, in the **Text group**, click the **Text Box** button. Click to create a text box in approximately the same position as the one that you created on Slide 4. Type **Spectacular Morning Vistas** and then click in a blank area of the slide.

Figure 16.14

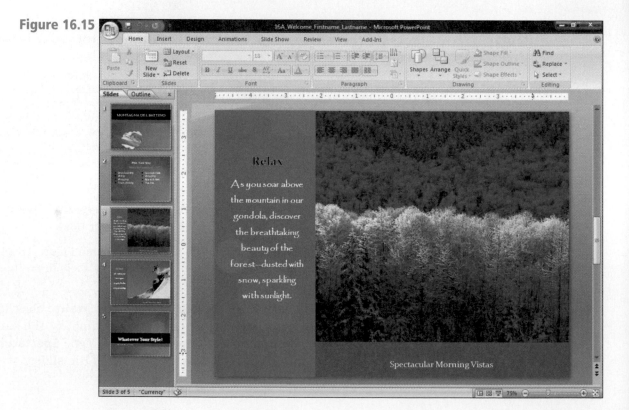

Position text box here ———————— Another View From Above

5 Compare your slide with Figure 16.15, and if necessary, re-select the text box, and use the pointer or Ctrl + any arrow key to adjust the position of the text box.

Figure 16.15

6 **Save** 🖫 the presentation.

More Knowledge — Formatting a Text Box

You can format the text in a text box by using the same techniques that you use to format text in any other placeholder. For example, you can change fonts, font styles, and font sizes, and you can apply WordArt styles to the text in a text box.

Activity 16.09 Inserting, Sizing, and Positioning Shapes

Shapes include lines, arrows, stars and banners, ovals and rectangles and other basic forms that can be used to illustrate an idea, a process, or a workflow. Shapes can be sized and moved using the same techniques that you use to size and move clip art images.

1 Display **Slide 1**, and then verify that the rulers display. If the rulers do not display, on the View tab, in the Show/Hide group, select the Ruler check box.

2 Click the **Insert tab**, and then in the **Illustrations group**, click the **Shapes** button to display the **Shapes gallery**. Under **Basic Shapes**, in the first row, click the seventh shape—**Diamond**.

3 Move the pointer into the slide until the ⊞ pointer—called the *crosshair pointer*—displays, indicating that you can draw a shape. Notice that when you move the ⊞ pointer into the slide, *guides*—vertical and horizontal lines—display in the rulers to give you a visual indication of the pointer's position so that you can draw a shape.

4 Move the ⊞ pointer so that the guides are positioned at approximately **1 inch to the left of zero on the horizontal ruler** and **1 inch above zero on the vertical ruler**, as shown in Figure 16.16.

Figure 16.16

Guide on horizontal ruler

Guide on vertical ruler

Crosshair pointer

5 Hold down the left mouse button, and then drag down and to the right so that the guide displays at **1 inch to the right of zero on the horizontal ruler** and at **zero on the vertical ruler**. Release the mouse button to draw the diamond.

The Drawing Tools contextual tab displays on the Ribbon.

6 On the **Format tab**, in the **Size group**, look at the **Shape Height** $\boxed{\downarrow}$ 2" $\boxed{}$ and **Shape Width** $\boxed{}$ 2.67" $\boxed{}$ boxes. If necessary, change the **Height** to **1** and the **Width** to **2** and then click on the diamond to change its size and to keep the diamond selected. Compare your slide with Figure 16.17. If necessary, use $\boxed{\text{Ctrl}}$ + any arrow key to position the diamond correctly.

Figure 16.17
Shape Height is 1″

Shape Width is 2″

7 Save 🖫 your presentation.

Another Way

To Insert a Shape
On the Home tab, in the Drawing group, click the Shapes button.

Activity 16.10 Adding Text to Shapes

Shapes can serve as a container for text. After you add text to a shape, you can change the font and font size, apply font styles, and change text alignment.

1 On **Slide 1**, if necessary, click the diamond so that it is selected. Text can be typed in a shape when the shape is selected.

2 Type **Visit Today!** Notice that the text wraps to two lines and is centered.

3 Point to the left of the word *Today*, and then click so that the insertion point displays to the left of the word. Type **Us** and press $\boxed{\text{Spacebar}}$, and then click outside of the shape.

The text wraps to three lines and extends slightly outside of the diamond. The diamond shape is not large enough to accommodate the amount of text that you have typed.

4 Select the text *Visit Us Today!* On the **Home tab**, in the **Font group**, click the **Decrease Font Size** button A˅ to change the font size to **16**. Click outside of the shape.

The text displays on two lines and fits within the diamond shape.

5 Compare your slide with Figure 16.18. **Save** 💾 the presentation.

Figure 16.18

Text displays on two lines

MONTAGNA DEL PATTINO

Activity 16.11 Applying Shape and Picture Styles and Effects

Shapes and pictures can be formatted using a variety of effects, including 3-D, glow, bevel, and shadows. These effects soften the outer edges of a shape or image. Shapes can also be formatted by changing the inside fill color and the outside line color. Predefined combinations of these styles are available in the Shape Styles, Quick Styles, and Picture Styles galleries.

1 On **Slide 1**, select the diamond, and then click the **Format tab**. In the **Shape Styles group**, click the **Shape Fill** button, and then point to several of the theme colors and watch as Live Preview changes the inside color of the diamond.

2 Point to **Gradient** to display the **Gradient Fill gallery**. Under **Dark Variations**, in the second row, click the second variant—**From Center**.

A *gradient fill* is a color combination in which one color fades into another. The diamond is filled with a blue gradient in which the outer points of the diamond are light and the center of the diamond is a darker color.

3 In the **Shape Styles group**, click the **Shape Outline** button, and then point to **Weight**. Click **6 pt** and notice that a thick outline surrounds the diamond.

4 With the diamond still selected, in the **Shape Styles group**, click the **Shape Effects** button. Point to **Bevel**, and then under **Bevel**, in the first row, click the last bevel—**Cool Slant**.

The Cool Slant bevel applies a three-dimensional effect to the diamond.

5 Select the snow picture in the shape of a cloud. Click the **Format tab**, and then in the **Picture Styles group**, click **Picture Effects**. Point to **Soft Edges**, and then click the second to last effect—**25 Point**—to blur and soften the edges of the picture, giving it a more cloudlike effect.

6 Click on a blank part of the slide so that no objects are selected, and then compare your slide with Figure 16.19.

Figure 16.19

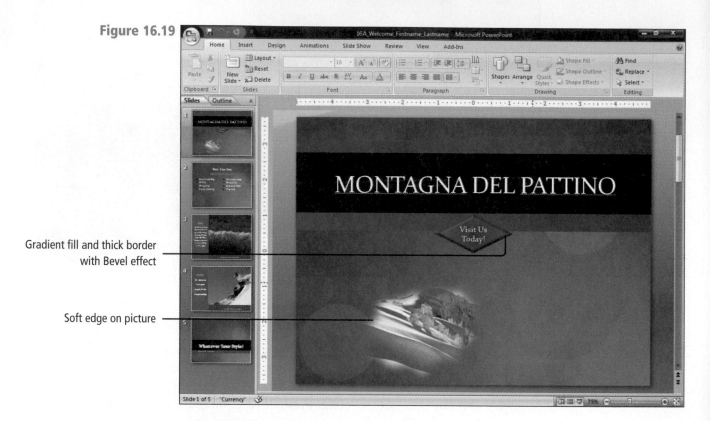

Gradient fill and thick border with Bevel effect

Soft edge on picture

7 **Save** 💾 your presentation.

More Knowledge — Applying a Quick Style or Shape Style to a Shape or Placeholder

You can format an object such as a shape, text box, or placeholder quickly by using one of the predefined Quick Styles or Shape Styles. Quick Styles and Shape Styles apply combinations of edges, shadows, line styles, gradients, and 3-D effects to the selected object. To apply a Quick Style, select the object, and then on the Home tab, click Quick Styles to display the gallery. To apply a Shape Style, select the object, and then on the Format tab, in the Shape Styles group, click the More button to display the gallery.

Activity 16.12 Duplicating and Aligning Objects

You can duplicate an object by using a keyboard shortcut. You can align objects by dragging the object to another position on the slide or by using the Ribbon.

1 On **Slide 1**, select the picture. Press and hold down Ctrl, and then press D one time. Release Ctrl.

> A duplicate of the picture overlaps the original picture and the duplicated image is selected.

2 Point to the duplicated image to display the 🔓 pointer. Drag the duplicated image up and to the right so that its left edge overlaps the right edge of the picture, using Figure 16.20 as a guide.

Figure 16.20

Duplicated picture overlaps original picture

3 Display **Slide 2**. Click the **Insert tab**, and then in the **Illustrations group**, click the **Shapes** button to display the **Shapes gallery**.

4 Under **Block Arrows**, in the first row, click the fourth arrow—**Down Arrow**. Position the ⊞ pointer at approximately **3 inches to the left of zero on the horizontal ruler** and at **1 inch below zero on the vertical ruler**, as shown in Figure 16.21.

Figure 16.21

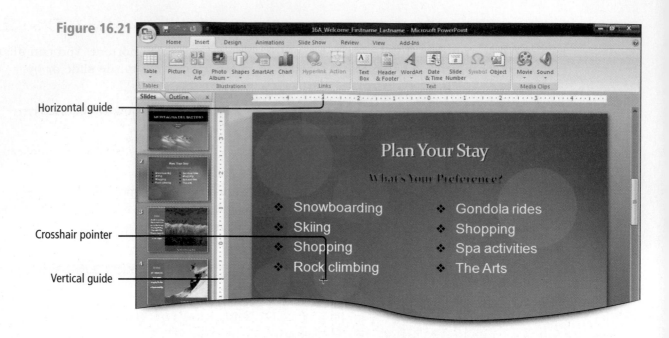

Horizontal guide

Crosshair pointer

Vertical guide

5 Drag approximately **1/2 inch to the right** and **1 inch down** to create the arrow and to display the **Drawing Tools contextual tab**. Check the size of the shape by looking at the **Format tab** in the **Size group**. If necessary, adjust the size of the arrow to a height of 1 inch and a width of 0.5 inch.

6 With the arrow selected, on the **Format tab**, in the **Shape Styles group**, click the **More** button ⬇. In the last row, click the second effect—**Intense Effect – Accent 1**.

7 With the arrow still selected, hold down Ctrl, and then press D to duplicate the arrow. Drag the new duplicate arrow to the right so that the arrow is positioned below the text on the right of the slide at approximately **2 inches to the right of zero on the horizontal ruler**.

8 With the arrow on the right selected, hold down ⇧ Shift, and then click the arrow on the left so that both arrows are selected. Release ⇧ Shift, click the **Format tab**, and then in the **Arrange group**, click the **Align** button. Click **Align Selected Objects**.

> The Align Selected Objects option aligns the objects that you select relative to each other. The Align to Slide option aligns objects with the edges of the slide determining placement.

9 On the **Format tab**, in the **Arrange group**, click the **Align** button, and then click **Align Top**.

> With the two arrows selected, the lower arrow moves up so that its top edge is aligned with the top edge of the higher arrow. Thus, the tops of the two arrows are positioned at the same location on the vertical ruler. Compare your slide with Figure 16.22.

Figure 16.22

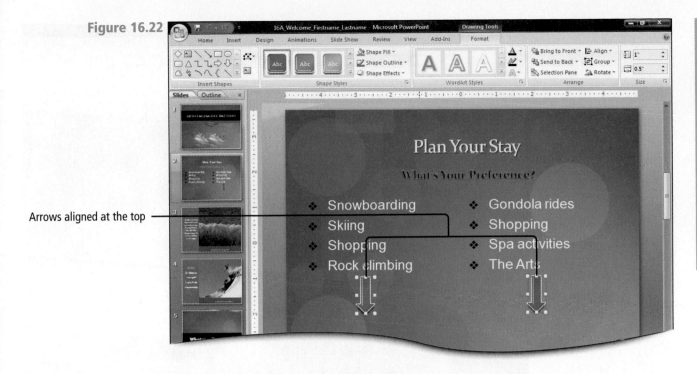

Arrows aligned at the top

10 Click the **Insert tab**, and then in the **Text group**, click **Text Box**. Position the pointer at approximately **4 inches to the left of zero on the horizontal ruler** and at **2.5 inches below zero on the vertical ruler**. Click one time to create a text box.

11 Type **High Energy** and then select the text that you typed. On the Mini toolbar, click the **Font Size button arrow**, and then click **32**. Click **Center** ☰. If the text box does not expand to accommodate the text, use the center right sizing handle to widen the text box.

12 Click the **Format tab**, and then in the **Shape Styles group**, click the **More** button ▼. In the last row, click the first style—**Intense Effect – Dark 1**.

13 Point to the outer edge of the text box to display the ⬚ pointer and then click to select the text box. Hold down (Ctrl), and then press (D) to duplicate the text box. Drag the duplicated text box to the right so that it is positioned below the arrow on the right side of the slide.

14 Select the text *High Energy*, and then type **Relaxation** to replace the text.

15 Use the (⇧ Shift) key to select the two text boxes—*High Energy* and *Relaxation*. On the **Format tab**, in the **Arrange group**, click the **Align** button. Click **Align Top** to align the top edges of the two text boxes, and then click anywhere on the slide so that none of the objects are selected.

16 Click the bulleted list placeholder on the left side of the slide. Hold down (⇧ Shift) and click the arrow on the left and the *High Energy* text box so that all three objects are selected, as shown in Figure 16.23.

Figure 16.23

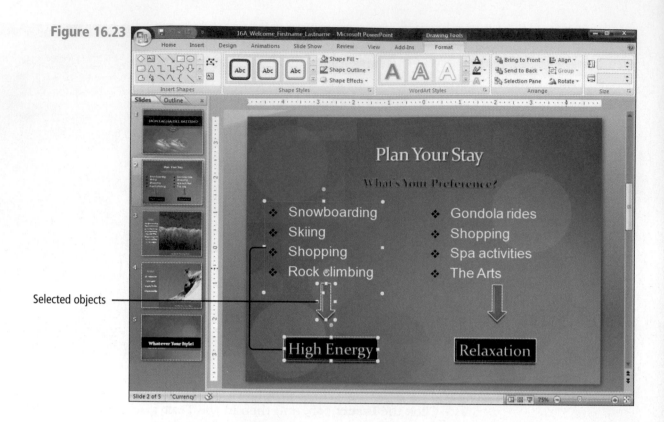

Selected objects

17 Release the ⇧Shift key. On the **Format tab**, in the **Arrange group**, click the **Align** button. Click **Align Selected Objects**. Click the **Align** button again, and then click **Align Center**.

The three objects are aligned at their center points.

18 Using the technique you just practiced, **Align Center** the placeholder, arrow, and text box on the right side of the slide.

19 **Save** 🖫 the presentation.

Objective 3
Apply Slide Transitions

Recall that a slide transition controls the way that a slide appears or disappears during an onscreen slide show. For example, when one slide leaves the screen, it may fade or dissolve into another slide. You can choose from a variety of transitions, and you can control the speed and method with which the slides advance during a presentation.

Activity 16.13 Applying Slide Transitions to a Presentation

In this activity, you will add slide transitions to all of the slides in the presentation.

1 If necessary, display the slide thumbnails, and then display **Slide 1**.

2 Click the **Animations tab**. In the **Transition to This Slide group**, click the **More** button ⤓ to display the **Transitions gallery** as shown in Figure 16.24.

The slide transitions are categorized in six groups—No Transition, Fades and Dissolves, Wipes, Push and Cover, Stripes and Bars, and Random. You may need to scroll the gallery to view all of the transitions. The pictures illustrate the type of transition and the arrows indicate the direction in which the slide moves.

Figure 16.24

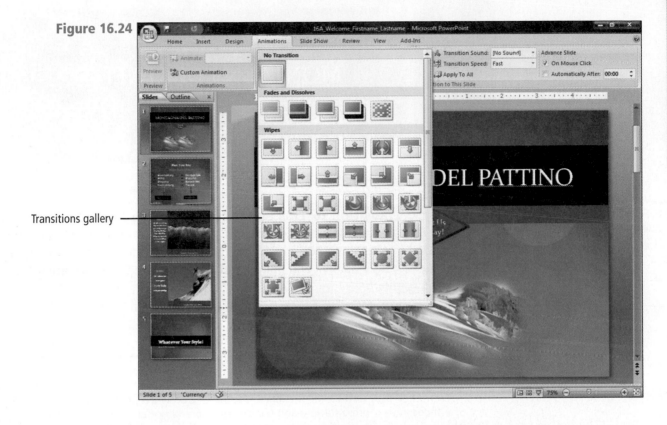

Transitions gallery

3 Point to several of the transitions to view the Live Preview of the transition effects and to display the ScreenTip with the transition name. Under **Wipes**, locate and then click the **Box Out** transition.

4 In the **Transition to This Slide group**, click the **Transition Speed arrow**, and then click **Medium**.

5 In the **Transition to This Slide group**, under **Advance Slide**, verify that **On Mouse Click** is selected. If it is not, click the On Mouse Click check box, as shown in Figure 16.25.

The On Mouse Click option enables you to control when the slide will advance to the next slide. During the slide show, you can click the mouse button or press Spacebar to advance the presentation.

Figure 16.25

Box Out transition
selected

Medium speed

On Mouse Click selected

6 In the **Transition to This Slide group**, click the **Apply To All** button so that the medium speed Box Out transition is applied to all of the slides in the presentation. Notice that in the Slides/Outline pane, a star displays below each slide number, indicating that a transition was applied.

Workshop

Applying Transitions

You can apply more than one type of transition in your presentation by displaying the slides one at a time, and then clicking the transition that you want to apply instead of clicking the Apply To All button. However, using too many different transitions in your presentation may distract the audience. Choose one basic transition to use on most of the slides in your presentation, and use one or two additional transitions if you feel that a particular slide would display more effectively with a different transition.

7 Click the **Slide Show tab**. In the **Start Slide Show group**, click the **From Beginning** button, and then view your presentation, clicking the mouse button to advance through the slides. When the black slide displays, click the mouse button one more time to display the presentation in Normal view.

8 Create a **Header & Footer** for the **Notes and Handouts**. Include only the **Date and time updated automatically**, the **Page number**, and a **Footer** with the file name **16A_Welcome_Firstname_Lastname**

9 Check your *Chapter Assignment Sheet* or *Course Syllabus* or consult your instructor to determine if you are to submit your assignments on paper or electronically. To submit electronically, go to Step 11, and then follow the directions provided by your instructor.

10 Display your presentation in **Print Preview**, and then print **Handouts (6 Slides Per Page)**.

11 **Save** and then **Close** the presentation.

End You have completed Project 16A

Project 16B Itinerary

In Activities 16.14 through 16.22, you will edit a presentation that Kirstin McCarty, Director of Marketing, has created that includes itineraries and contact information for resort guests. You will move and copy text, and you will create diagrams that will illustrate different types of itineraries. Your completed presentation will look similar to Figure 16.26.

For Project 16B, you will need the following files:

p16B_Itinerary
p16B_Reservations_Director
p16B_Ski_Lodge_Director
p16B_Spa_Director
p16B_Tour_Director

You will save your presentation as
16B_Itinerary_Firstname_Lastname

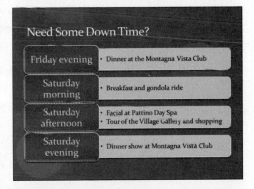

Figure 16.26
Project 16B—Itinerary

Objective 4
Reorganize Presentation Text and Clear Formats

When you select text or objects and then perform the Copy command or the Cut command, the selection is placed on the *Office Clipboard*—a temporary storage area maintained by your Microsoft Office program. From the Office Clipboard storage area, the object is available to *paste* into other locations, including other Office programs.

Activity 16.14 Moving and Copying Text

The *Cut* command removes selected text or graphics from your presentation and moves the selection to the Office Clipboard. Then from the Office Clipboard, you can paste the selection to a new location. The *Copy* command duplicates a selection and places it on the Office Clipboard.

1 **Start** PowerPoint and from your student files, **Open p16B_Itinerary**. **Save** the file in your **PowerPoint Chapter 16** folder as 16B_Itinerary_Firstname_Lastname

2 Display **Slide 2**, and then on the **Home tab**, in the **Slides group**, click the **New Slide arrow**. In the displayed **gallery**, click **Title and Content**. If you inserted a slide without displaying the gallery, on the Home tab, in the Slides group, click Layout, and then click Title and Content.

3 In the title placeholder, type **High Energy Weekend?**

4 Display **Slide 4**, and then select all of the text in the bulleted list placeholder. On the **Home tab**, in the **Clipboard group**, click the **Copy** button ⧉. Alternatively, hold down Ctrl, and then press C.

5 Display **Slide 3**, and then click in the content placeholder. In the **Clipboard group**, click the **Paste** button to copy the selection to **Slide 3**. Alternatively, hold down Ctrl, and then press V.

Below the pasted text an additional bullet and a button may display, as shown in Figure 16.27. This is the Paste Options button that provides three options for formatting pasted text.

Figure 16.27

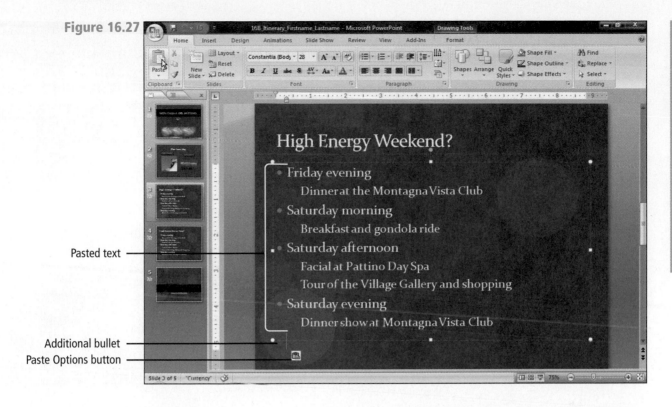

Pasted text

Additional bullet

Paste Options button

6 Point to the **Paste Options** button so that an arrow displays to its right, and then click the arrow to display the formatting options. Be sure that **Use Destination Theme** is selected so that the formatting of Slide 3 is applied to the pasted text.

Use Destination Theme applies the format of the slide to which you pasted the text to the selection, and *Keep Text Only* removes all formatting from the selection.

> **Note — Removing the Paste Options Button**
> You do not need to click the Paste Options button arrow every time you paste a selection. The default setting is *Use Destination Theme*. Thus, you need only click the arrow if you want to apply a different option. The Paste Options button will remain on the screen until you perform another action.

7 Click outside of the button menu to close it. If necessary, use ⌫Bksp or Delete to delete any extra bullets at the bottom of the pasted text.

8 In the second bullet point, replace the text *Montagna Vista Club* with **Summit Clubhouse** In the fourth bullet point, replace *gondola ride* with **2-mile hike**

9 Under *Saturday afternoon*, select both of the subordinate level bullet points, and then type **Skiing or snowboarding** to replace both of the selected bullet points. Select the last bullet point on the slide, and then replace it with **Party at Summit Clubhouse**

10 Click outside the content placeholder, and then compare your slide with Figure 16.28. Make spelling and layout corrections as necessary.

Figure 16.28

11 Display **Slide 2**. Click the WordArt text at the bottom of the slide—*Whatever Your Style*, and then click its dashed boundary box so that it displays as a solid line, indicating that all of the text is selected.

12 In the **Clipboard group**, click the **Cut** button 📋. Alternatively, hold down ⌃Ctrl, and then press ⌊X⌋.

> The text is removed from the slide and is stored on the Office Clipboard.

13 Display **Slide 5**. In the **Clipboard group**, click the **Paste** button to move the selection to the bottom of the last slide. Point to the edge of the pasted text to display the 🔀 pointer, and then drag up to position the text in the center of the black rectangle.

14 **Save** 💾 the presentation.

More Knowledge — Using Drag-and-Drop Text Editing

Another method to move text is the ***drag-and-drop*** technique, which uses the mouse to drag selected text from one location to another. To use drag-and-drop text editing, select the text you want to move, and then position the pointer over the selected text to display the 🔀 pointer. Drag the text to the new location. A vertical line attached to the pointer enables you to see exactly where the text will be pasted.

Activity 16.15 Copying Multiple Selections by Using the Office Clipboard

The Office Clipboard can store up to 24 selections that you have cut or copied, and each one can be pasted multiple times. Additionally, groups of items on the Office Clipboard can be pasted all at one time.

1 Display **Slide 1**. On the **Home tab**, in the lower right corner of the **Clipboard group**, click the **Dialog Box Launcher** 🖿 to display the Clipboard task pane on the left side of the PowerPoint window.

2 In the **Clipboard** task pane, check to see if any items display. Compare your screen with Figure 16.29.

> When the Office Clipboard is empty, *Clipboard empty* displays in the task pane. If items have been cut or copied, they will display on the Office Clipboard. In Figure 16.29, the WordArt text that was cut in the previous Activity displays. You may or may not have items displayed on the Office Clipboard, depending on its last use.

Figure 16.29

Dialog Box Launcher button ——

Items on Clipboard display here ——

Clipboard task pane ——

3 At the top of the **Clipboard** task pane, click the **Clear All** button to delete any items that are stored on the Office Clipboard.

4 Click in the slide title, and then click its dashed border so that it displays as a solid line. In the **Clipboard group**, click the **Copy** button 🖿, and then notice that a boxed object displays in the Clipboard task pane.

> The box appears to be empty, because the text is white and the Clipboard task pane uses a white background. Although the letters are not visible, they are still there.

5 At the bottom of the slide, three copies of the same picture display. Click any one of the three pictures to select it. In the **Clipboard group**, click the **Copy** button 🖿, and then notice that the object displays on the Office Clipboard as the first item, and the previous item that you copied moves down.

> You have a collection of two objects for copying.

6 Display **Slide 5**. In the **Clipboard** task pane, click **Paste All** to paste both objects to Slide 5.

> The objects are pasted in the same location from which they were copied.

7 Drag the picture to the upper right corner of the slide.

8 Click the pasted text so that its dashed border displays. Point to the dashed border to display the pointer. Using Figure 16.30 as a guide, hold down ⇧Shift, and then drag the pasted text down approximately one inch.

Pressing ⇧Shift while dragging constrains the text box so that it does not move off center, thus allowing for precision placement.

Figure 16.30

Drag picture here

Drag text here

9 In the **Clipboard** task pane, click the **Clear All** button to delete the two selections from the Office Clipboard. **Close** × the task pane.

10 Save the presentation.

> **More Knowledge — Pasting and Deleting Single Items from the Office Clipboard**
>
> When you point to an item on the Office Clipboard, a down arrow displays to its right. Click the arrow to display a menu with two options—Paste and Delete. You can paste and delete individual items from the Office Clipboard using this menu.

Activity 16.16 Undoing and Redoing Changes

PowerPoint remembers each change that you make so that you can undo them if you change your mind or perform an action by mistake. You can change your mind again and reverse an undo by using the Redo command.

1 Display **Slide 3**. In the fourth bullet point, select the words *2-mile*, and then type **Mountain Falls** to replace the selected words.

2 On the **Quick Access Toolbar**, click the **Undo** button.

2-mile displays on the slide.

3 On the **Quick Access Toolbar**, click the **Redo** button.

Mountain Falls displays in the slide.

4 **Save** the presentation.

Alert!

Did you repeat an action instead of redo an action?

The Redo button is context-sensitive—it changes depending upon the action that you have performed. Before you click Undo, the Redo button displays as the Repeat button. Recall that the Repeat button repeats the last command or keystroke. In order to activate the Redo button, you must first Undo a command.

Activity 16.17 Clearing Formatting from a Selection

After applying multiple formats to a selection of text, you may decide that the selection is best displayed without the formats that you applied. You can clear formatting from a selection and return it to its default font and font size, and you can remove styles that have been applied.

1 Display **Slide 5** and notice that the text *Come to the Mountain* does not display well against the background.

2 Select *Come to the Mountain*, and then on the **Home tab**, in the **Font group**, click the **Clear All Formatting** button. Click in a blank area of the slide.

The text is restored to its original formatting and contrasts with the background, making it easier to read.

3 **Save** the presentation.

Workshop

Creating Contrast on a Slide

Contrast is an important element of slide design because it helps in distinguishing text and objects from the slide background. Be sure that the font color that you choose contrasts with the background so that your audience can easily read the text. For example, if your background is dark, choose a light-colored font. If your background is light, choose a dark-colored font.

Objective 5
Create and Format a SmartArt Graphic

A ***SmartArt graphic*** is a designer-quality visual representation of information that you can create by choosing from among many different layouts to communicate your message or ideas effectively. SmartArt graphics can illustrate processes, hierarchies, cycles, lists, and relationships. You can include text and pictures in a SmartArt graphic, and you can apply colors, effects, and styles that coordinate with the presentation theme.

Activity 16.18 Creating a SmartArt Diagram by Using a Content Layout

When you create a SmartArt graphic, it is a good idea when choosing a layout to consider the message that you are trying to convey. The table in Figure 16.31 describes types of SmartArt layouts and suggested purposes.

Microsoft PowerPoint SmartArt Graphic Types	
Graphic Type	**Purpose of Graphic**
List	Shows nonsequential information.
Process	Shows steps in a process or timeline.
Cycle	Shows a continual process.
Hierarchy	Shows a decision tree or displays an organization chart.
Relationship	Illustrates connections.
Matrix	Shows how parts relate to a whole.
Pyramid	Shows proportional relationships with the largest component on the top or bottom.

Figure 16.31

1 Display **Slide 4**, and then on the **Home tab**, in the **Slides group**, click the **New Slide** button to add a slide with the **Title and Content** layout. In the title placeholder, type **Contact Information** and then **Center** ▤ the title. Notice that in addition to adding text to this slide, you can insert a SmartArt graphic by clicking the Insert SmartArt Graphic button ▦ in the center of the slide, as shown in Figure 16.32.

Figure 16.32

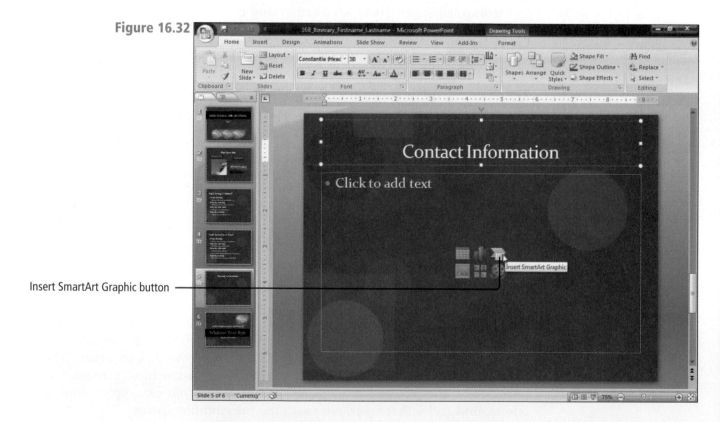

Insert SmartArt Graphic button

2 In the center of the slide, click the **Insert SmartArt Graphic** button ▦ to open the **Choose a SmartArt Graphic** dialog box.

The dialog box is divided into three sections. The left section lists the diagram types. The center section displays the diagrams according to type. The third section displays the selected diagram, its name, and a description of its purpose and how text displays.

Another Way

To Insert a SmartArt Graphic

On the Insert tab, in the Illustrations group, click the SmartArt button.

3 Explore the types of diagrams available by clicking on several and reading their descriptions. Then, on the left side of the **Choose a SmartArt Graphic** dialog box, click **Hierarchy**. In the center section in the second row, click the last diagram—**Hierarchy List**—and then click **OK** to create a hierarchical diagram surrounded by a thick border, indicating the area that the diagram will cover on the slide. Notice that on the Ribbon, the SmartArt contextual tools display two tabs—Design and Format, as shown in Figure 16.33.

The hierarchical diagram displays with two upper level shapes and two subordinate level shapes under each upper level shape. You can type text directly into the shapes or you can type text in the Text pane. The Text pane is displayed by clicking the Text pane tab on the left side of the SmartArt graphic border. Depending on your software settings, the Text pane may be displayed.

Figure 16.33

SmartArt Design and Format tabs

Upper level shapes

Text pane tab

Diagram border

Subordinate level shapes

Note — **Displaying and Closing the Text Pane**

On the Ribbon, in the SmartArt Tools group, click the Design tab. In the Create Graphic group, click the Text Pane button to toggle the Text pane on and off.

4 In the diagram, click in the dark red box on the left, and then type **Day Spa** Click in the box below it, and then type **Patricia Reeves** Click in the box below Patricia's name, and then type **555-0921**

> The text is resized and when necessary, wraps to two lines in order to fit into each shape. When text is typed into additional shapes, the text in all shapes at the same level adjusts to the same size.

5 On the right side of the diagram, enter the following information in the boxes, and then click in a blank area of the slide. Compare your slide with Figure 16.34.

Ski Lodge

Victor Blardone

555-0563

Figure 16.34

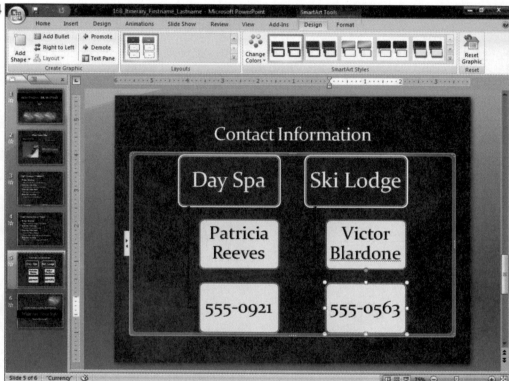

6 **Save** 💾 the presentation.

Activity 16.19 Adding and Removing Shapes in a Diagram

If a diagram does not have enough shapes to illustrate a concept or display the relationships, you can add more shapes.

1 Click in the shape that contains the text *Ski Lodge*. In the SmartArt Tools, click the **Design tab**. In the **Create Graphic group**, click the **Add Shape arrow**, and then click **Add Shape After** to insert an upper level shape to the right of the *Ski Lodge* shape. Type **Tours**

Alert! **Did you add a shape below the Ski Lodge shape?**

If you clicked the Add Shape button instead of the arrow, the new shape displays below the phone number shape. Click Undo to delete the shape, and then repeat Step 1, being sure to click the Add Shape arrow.

2 On the **Design tab**, in the **Create Graphic group**, click the **Add Shape** button.

> When an upper level shape is selected and the Add Shape button is clicked, a lower level shape is added.

3 Type **Terry Anderson** and then click the **Add Shape** button. Type **555-0987** and then click the **Add Shape** button.

> An additional shape is added below the phone number. You can promote the shape so that it is at the same level as the Day Spa, Ski Lodge, and Tours shapes.

4 On the **Design tab**, in the **Create Graphic group**, click the **Promote** button to create a fourth, upper level shape. Type **Reservations** and notice that the text in all of the upper level shapes is resized. Add a shape, type **Anthony Johnson** and then add one more shape. Type **555-0547**

5 On the **Design tab**, in the **Create Graphic group**, click the **Add Shape** button to create an extra shape below Anthony Johnson's phone number.

6 Press Delete to delete the shape, and then click on a blank area of the slide. Compare your slide with Figure 16.35.

Figure 16.35

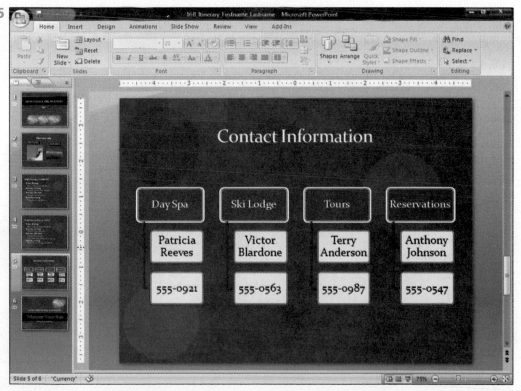

7 **Save** 🖫 the presentation.

More Knowledge — Deleting Shapes that Contain Text

To delete a shape that contains text, you must click its border. If you click the shape without clicking the border, you will delete text instead of the shape. When you delete an upper level shape that has subordinate shapes with text, the first subordinate shape is promoted to an upper level shape.

Activity 16.20 Changing the Diagram Type and Size

When you are creating a diagram, remember that it is important to choose the layout and type that provides the best visual representation of your information. In this activity, you will change the diagram type to one that includes placeholders for pictures of each contact person.

1 Click anywhere in the diagram. In the SmartArt Tools, click the **Design tab**. In the **Layouts group**, click the **More** button 🔽, and then click **More Layouts** to display the **Choose a SmartArt Graphic** dialog box.

2 On the left side of the dialog box, click **List**, and then click **Horizontal Picture List**, as shown in Figure 16.36. Click **OK**.

The diagram is converted and contains shapes at the top of each group to insert pictures.

Figure 16.36

Horizontal Picture List

3 In the shape above the *Day Spa* information, click the **Insert Picture From File** button 🖾. Navigate to your student files, and then double-click **p16B_Spa_Director** to insert the picture of Patricia

Reeves. Repeat this process in each of the three remaining shapes by inserting the files **p16B_Ski_Lodge_Director**, **p16B_Tour_Director**, and **p16B_Reservations_Director**.

Alert!

Did you move a shape when inserting a picture?

If you move the mouse when you click the Insert Picture from File button in one of the diagram shapes, the shape may move. If this happens, click the Undo button to reposition the shape. Then click the Picture button, making sure that you hold the mouse steady.

4 Notice that the shapes that contain the pictures are wider than they are tall, and thus distort the pictures. You can adjust the size of all of the pictures at one time by sizing the SmartArt graphic.

5 The border surrounding a diagram contains sizing handles in the shape of three small circles in the corners and at the center of each side. You can use these sizing handles to size the diagram. Point to the center-right sizing handle to display the ⟷ pointer, as shown in Figure 16.37.

Figure 16.37

Pointer positioned over sizing handle

6 Hold down the mouse button and drag to the left, noticing that as you do so the + pointer displays, as does a semitransparent rectangle that indicates the size of the SmartArt graphic. Continue to drag to the left until the pointer and semitransparent rectangle display between the Tours and Reservations shapes, as shown in Figure 16.38. Release the mouse button to size the diagram.

Figure 16.38

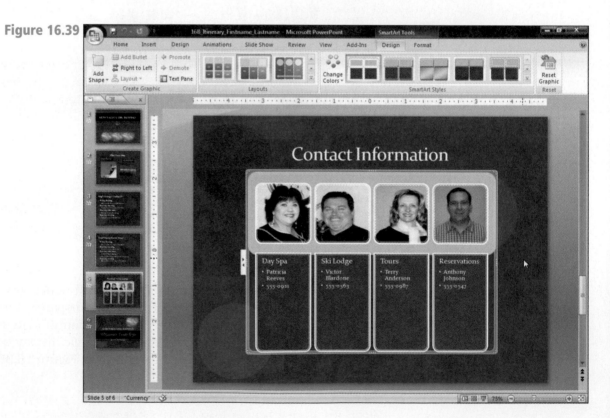

Crosshair pointer and transparent rectangle indicate new size of diagram

7 Point to the border surrounding the diagram to display the ⬚ pointer, and then drag to the right to center the diagram.

8 Compare your slide with Figure 16.39, and then **Save** 🖫 your presentation.

Figure 16.39

Alert! —— **Did only a part of the diagram move?**

Individual parts of a SmartArt diagram, such as text and picture shapes, can be moved. Be sure that when you move the diagram that you are pointing to the border that surrounds the SmartArt graphic and not to an individual element. If you inadvertently moved a portion of the diagram instead of the entire diagram, click the Undo button and then repeat Step 7.

Activity 16.21 Creating a SmartArt Diagram from Bullet Points

You can convert an existing bulleted list into a SmartArt diagram. In this activity, you will convert the bulleted lists on Slides 3 and 4 to list diagrams.

1 Display **Slide 3**. Right-click anywhere in the bulleted list placeholder to display the shortcut menu. Point to **Convert to SmartArt**, and at the bottom of the **gallery**, click **More SmartArt Graphics**.

2 In the **Choose a SmartArt Graphic** dialog box, click **List**. In the first row, point to each SmartArt graphic so that the ScreenTips display, and then click **Vertical Box List**. Click **OK**.

> The entire bulleted list is converted to a diagram. It is not necessary to select all of the text in the bulleted list. By clicking in the list, PowerPoint converts all of the bullet points to the selected diagram.

3 Display **Slide 4**, and then click anywhere in the bulleted list place-holder. On the **Home tab**, in the **Paragraph group**, click the **Convert to SmartArt Graphic** button.

4 At the bottom of the gallery, click **More SmartArt Graphics**. In the **Choose a SmartArt Graphic** dialog box, click **List**, and then use the ScreenTips to locate **Vertical Block List**. Click **Vertical Block List**, and then click **OK** to convert the bulleted list to a SmartArt graphic.

5 **Save** the presentation.

Activity 16.22 Changing the Color and Style of a Diagram

SmartArt Styles are combinations of formatting effects that you can apply to diagrams. If you change the layout of a diagram, the SmartArt Style is applied to the new layout, as are any color changes that you have made.

1 Display **Slide 5** and click on the diagram. Click the **Design tab**. In the **SmartArt Styles group**, click the **Change Colors** button to display the color gallery.

> The colors that display are coordinated with the presentation theme.

2 Under **Accent 1**, click the last style—**Transparent Gradient Range - Accent 1**—to change the color scheme of the diagram.

3 On the **Design tab**, in the **SmartArt Styles group**, click the **More** button to display the **SmartArt Styles gallery**. Point to several of the styles to display the Live Preview of their effects on the diagram. Then, under **3-D**, in the first row, click the first style—**Polished**. Click in a blank area of the slide, and then compare your slide with Figure 16.40.

Figure 16.40

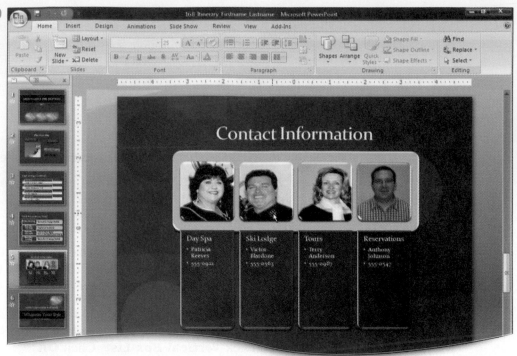

4 Display **Slide 3** and click on the diagram. Click the **Design tab**. In the **SmartArt Styles group**, click the **More** button ⬇ to display the **SmartArt Styles gallery**. Under **3-D**, in the first row, click the second style—**Inset**.

5 Display **Slide 4**. By using the technique you practiced in Step 4, under **Best Match for Document**, apply the last style—**Intense Effect**.

6 Click the **Slide Show tab**. In the **Start Slide Show group**, click **From Beginning**, and then view your presentation, clicking the mouse button to advance through the slides. When the black slide displays, click the mouse button one more time to display the presentation in Normal view.

7 Create a **Header and Footer** for the **Notes and Handouts**. Include only the **Date and time updated automatically**, the **Page number**, and a **Footer** with the file name 16B_Itinerary_Firstname_Lastname

8 Check your *Chapter Assignment Sheet* or *Course Syllabus* or consult your instructor to determine if you are to submit your assignments on paper or electronically. To submit electronically, go to Step 10, and then follow the directions provided by your instructor.

9 Display your presentation in **Print Preview**, and then print **Handouts (6 Slides Per Page)**.

10 **Save** 💾, and then **Close** the presentation.

End **You have completed Project 16B** ⸺⸺⸺⸺⸺

There's More You Can Do!

Close PowerPoint and any other open windows. Display the Start menu, click Computer, and then navigate to the student files that accompany this textbook. From the CD that came with your book, open the folder **02_theres_more_you can_do**, locate, and open the folder for this chapter. Open and print the instructions for this project, which are provided to you in Adobe PDF format.

Try IT! 1—Prepare a Presentation for Remote Delivery

In this Try It! exercise, you will prepare a presentation for remote delivery by compressing images and packaging the presentation for CD.

Content-Based Assessments

Summary

In this chapter, you formatted a presentation by changing the bullet style and by applying WordArt styles to text. You copied formatting by using Format Painter and you also copied text and objects using the Office Clipboard. You enhanced your presentations by inserting, sizing, and formatting shapes, pictures, and SmartArt diagrams. You gave your presentation a finished look by applying transitions to your slides, resulting in a professional-looking presentation.

Key Terms

Content-Based Assessments

Matching

Match each term in the second column with its correct definition in the first column. Write the letter of the term on the blank line in front of the correct definition.

_____ **1.** A feature that applies combinations of decorative formatting to text, including shadows, reflections, and 3-D effects, and that changes the line and fill color of text.

_____ **2.** The inside color of text or an object.

_____ **3.** A feature that copies formatting from one selection of text to another, ensuring formatting consistency in your presentation.

_____ **4.** A combination of formatting effects that includes 3-D, glow, and bevel effects and shadows that can be applied to shapes.

_____ **5.** An object that is used to position text anywhere on the slide.

_____ **6.** The pointer that indicates that you can draw a shape.

_____ **7.** Vertical and horizontal lines that display in the rulers to give you a visual indication of the pointer position so that you can draw a shape.

_____ **8.** A blinking vertical line that indicates where text will be inserted.

_____ **9.** A color combination in which one color fades into another.

_____ **10.** The way a slide appears or disappears during an onscreen slide show.

_____ **11.** The action of placing text or objects that have been copied or moved from one location to another location.

_____ **12.** A temporary storage area maintained by your Microsoft Office program.

_____ **13.** The action of moving a selection by dragging it to a new location.

_____ **14.** A designer-quality visual representation of your information that you can create by choosing from among many different layouts to effectively communicate your message or ideas.

_____ **15.** Combinations of formatting effects that are applied to diagrams.

A Crosshair pointer

B Drag-and-drop

C Fill color

D Format Painter

E Gradient fill

F Guides

G Insertion point

H Office Clipboard

I Paste

J Shape Styles

K SmartArt graphic

L SmartArt Styles

M Text box

N Transition

O WordArt

Content-Based Assessments

Fill in the Blank

Write the correct word in the space provided.

1. When you click the dashed border of a placeholder, it displays as a _____ line.

2. To repeat the last command or text that you entered, press the _____ function key.

3. To copy formatting to multiple selections, _____ Format Painter.

4. To horizontally or vertically position selected objects on a slide relative to each other, use the _____ tools.

5. When you apply slide transitions, you can control the _____ and the method with which the slides advance during the presentation.

6. The Clipboard can store up to _____ selections that you have cut or copied.

7. You can reverse an Undo by using the _____ command.

8. To show nonsequential information, use a _____ diagram.

9. To show steps in a process or timeline, use a _____ diagram.

10. To show a continual process, use a _____ diagram.

11. To show a decision tree or create an organization chart, use a _____ diagram.

12. To illustrate connections, use a _____ diagram.

13. To show how parts relate to a whole, use a _____ diagram.

14. To show proportional relationships with the largest component on the top or bottom, use a _____ diagram.

15. When you are creating a diagram, choose the layout and type that provides the best _____ representation of your information.

Content-Based Assessments

Skills Review

Project 16C — Snowboarding

In this project, you will apply the skills you practiced from the Objectives in Project 16A.

Objectives: 1. *Format Slide Elements;* **2**. *Insert and Format Pictures and Shapes;* **3**. *Apply Slide Transitions.*

In the following Skills Review, you will edit a presentation created by Dane Richardson, the Director of Ski and Snowboard Instruction, that describes the snowboarding events and services available at Montagna del Pattino. Your completed presentation will look similar to the one shown in Figure 16.41.

For Project 16C, you will need the following files:

p16C_Board
p16C_Hillside
p16C_Silhouette
p16C_Snowboarding

You will save your presentation as
16C_Snowboarding_Firstname_Lastname

Figure 16.41

(Project 16C–Snowboarding continues on the next page)

Content-Based Assessments

(Project 16C–Snowboarding continued)

1. **Start** PowerPoint, and then from your student data files, **Open p16C_Snowboarding**. Click the **Office** button, and then click **Save As**. Navigate to your **PowerPoint Chapter 16** folder and using your own first and last names, **Save** the file as **16C_Snowboarding_Firstname_Lastname**

2. Display **Slide 1** and select the title text. On the **Format tab**, in the **WordArt Styles group**, click the **More** button to display the **WordArt gallery**. Under **Applies to All Text in the Shape**, in the last row, click the last style—**Fill – Accent 1, Metal Bevel, Reflection**.

3. Click the **Insert tab**, and then in the **Illustrations group**, click **Picture**. Navigate to the location where your student files are stored, and then double-click **p16C_Silhouette** to insert the picture in the middle of the slide.

4. With the picture selected, click the **Format tab**. In the **Size group**, click in the **Shape Height** box, and then type **4** Click on the picture to change its size, and then point to the picture to display the 🕂 pointer. Drag the picture up and to the left so that its upper left corner aligns with the upper left corner of the white rounded rectangle.

5. With the picture still selected, in the **Picture Styles group**, click **Picture Effects**. Point to **Soft Edges**, and then click **50 Point** to blur the edges of the image.

6. Display **Slide 2**, and then click in the bulleted list placeholder. Point to the dashed border so that the 🕂 pointer displays, and then click so that the border displays as a solid line, indicating that all of the text in the placeholder is selected. On the **Home tab**, in the **Paragraph group**, click

the **Bullets button arrow** to display the **Bullets gallery**, and then click **Arrow Bullets**.

7. Display **Slide 3**, and then select the bulleted list placeholder on the right side of the slide so that its solid border displays. Press F4 to repeat the bullet formatting that you applied in the previous step. If you have entered another action before pressing F4 and the bullet formatting does not repeat, click the Bullets button arrow, and then apply the Arrow Bullets style.

8. On **Slide 3**, in the placeholder on the left of the slide, in the second row of buttons, click the first button—**Insert Picture from File**. From your student files, double-click **p16C_Hillside**. In the **Picture Styles group**, click the **Picture Shape** button. Under **Basic Shapes**, in the third row, click the fourth shape—**Folded Corner**. In the **Picture Styles group**, click the **Picture Effects** button, point to **Glow**, and then under **Glow Variations**, in the third row, click the first effect—**Accent color 1, 11 pt glow**.

9. Click in the bulleted list placeholder on the right, and then click its border so that it displays as a solid line, indicating that all of the text is selected. On the **Home tab**, in the **Font group**, apply **Italic**, and then, in the **Paragraph group**, click the **Line Spacing** button. Click **2.0**. **Save** your presentation.

10. Display **Slide 4** and verify that the rulers display. If the rulers do not display, on the View tab, in the Show/Hide group, select the Ruler check box. Click the **Insert tab**, and then in the **Illustrations group**, click the **Shapes** button to display the **Shapes gallery**.

(Project 16C–Snowboarding continues on the next page)

Content-Based Assessments

(Project 16C–Snowboarding continued)

11. Under **Block Arrows**, in the first row, click the fourth arrow—**Down Arrow**. Position the crosshair pointer at approximately **2.5 inches to the left of zero on the horizontal ruler** and at **2 inches above zero on the vertical ruler**.

12. Drag approximately 0.5 inch to the right and 1 inch down to create the arrow. Check the size of the shape by looking at the **Format tab** in the **Size group**. If necessary, adjust the size of the arrow to a Height of **1** and a Width of **0.5**.

13. With the arrow selected, on the **Format tab**, in the **Shape Styles group**, click the **More** button. In the last row, click the second style—**Intense Effect – Accent 1**.

14. With the arrow still selected, hold down `Ctrl`, and then press `D` to duplicate the arrow. Point to the new arrow, and then drag to the right so that the arrow is positioned above the text on the right of the slide at approximately **2 inches to the right of zero on the horizontal ruler**.

15. With the arrow on the right selected, press `⇧ Shift`, and then click the arrow on the left so that both arrows are selected. On the **Format tab**, in the **Arrange group**, click the **Align** button. Click **Align Selected Objects** to align the objects that you selected relative to each other. On the **Format tab**, in the **Arrange group**, click the **Align** button, and then click **Align Top**.

16. Click the **Insert tab**, and then in the **Text group**, click **Text Box**. Position the pointer at approximately **3 inches to the left of zero on the horizontal ruler** and at **3 inches above zero on the vertical ruler**. Click to create a text box, and then type **Gear** Select the text that you typed, and then on the **Home tab**, in the **Font group**, click the **Font Color arrow** and then click

White, Background 1. Change the **Font Size** to **24**, and then click on a blank area of the slide.

17. Click the **Insert tab**, and then in the **Text group**, click **Text Box**. Position the pointer at approximately **1 inch to the right of zero on the horizontal ruler** and at **3 inches above zero on the vertical ruler**. Click to create a text box, and then type **Accessories**

18. Select the text that you typed, and then on the **Home tab**, in the **Font group**, click the **Font Color button arrow**, and then click **White, Background 1**. Change the **Font Size** to **24**.

19. Use the `⇧ Shift` key to select the two text boxes—*Gear* and *Accessories*. Click the **Format tab**, and then in the **Arrange group**, click the **Align** button. Click **Align Top** to align the top edges of the two text boxes, and then click anywhere on the slide so that none of the objects are selected. **Save** your presentation.

20. Click the bulleted list placeholder on the left side of the slide. Hold down `⇧ Shift` and then click the arrow on the left and the *Gear* text box so that all three objects are selected. On the **Format tab**, in the **Arrange group**, click the **Align** button. Click **Align Selected Objects**. Click the **Align** button again, and then click **Align Center**.

21. Using the technique you just practiced, align center the placeholder, arrow, and text box on the right side of the slide. **Save** your presentation.

22. Display **Slide 5**. In the placeholder on the left side of the slide, click the **Insert Picture from File** button, and then navigate to your student files. Double-click

(Project 16C–Snowboarding continues on the next page)

Content-Based Assessments

Skills Review

(Project 16C–Snowboarding continued)

p16C_Board. On the **Format tab**, in the **Picture Styles group**, click the **Picture Effects** button, and then point to **Glow**. In the last row, click the first glow effect— **Accent color 1, 18 pt glow**.

23. On **Slide 5**, select the slide title. On the **Home tab**, in the **Clipboard group**, click the **Format Painter** button. Display **Slide 3**, and then drag the pointer over the title to apply the font, font size, and shadow effects from the title on **Slide 5** to the title on **Slide 3**.

24. Click the **Animations tab**. In the **Transition to This Slide group**, click the **More** button, and then under **Wipes**, in the first row, click the third transition— **Wipe Right**. In the **Transition to This Slide group**, click the **Apply To All** button. Click the **Slide Show tab**. In the **Start Slide Show group**, click **From Beginning**, and then view your presentation, clicking the mouse button to advance from slide to slide.

25. Create a **Header and Footer** for the **Notes and Handouts**. Include only the **Date and time updated automatically**, the **Page number**, and a **Footer** with the file name **16C_Snowboarding_Firstname_Lastname**

26. Check your *Chapter Assignment Sheet* or *Course Syllabus* or consult your instructor to determine if you are to submit your assignments on paper or electronically. To submit electronically, go to Step 28, and then follow the instructions provided by your instructor.

27. From the **Office** menu, point to the **Print arrow**, and then click **Print Preview** to make a final check of your presentation. In the **Page Setup group**, click the **Print What arrow**, and then click **Handouts (6 Slides Per Page)**. Click the **Print** button, and then click **OK** to print the handouts.

28. **Save** the changes to your presentation, and then **Close** the file.

End **You have completed Project 16C** ─────────────

Content-Based Assessments

PowerPoint
chaptersixteen

Skills Review

Project 16D — Lessons

In this project, you will apply the skills you practiced from the Objectives in Project 16B.

Objectives: 4. *Reorganize Presentation Text and Clear Formats;* **5**. *Create and Format a SmartArt Graphic.*

In the following Skills Review, you will edit a presentation created by Dane Richardson, the Director of Ski and Snowboard Instruction, that describes the snowboarding lessons for children at Montagna del Pattino. Your completed presentation will look similar to the one shown in Figure 16.42.

For Project 16D, you will need the following files:
p16D_Cara
p16D_Dane
p16D_Lessons
p16D_Marty

You will save your presentation as 16D_Lessons_Firstname_Lastname

Figure 16.42

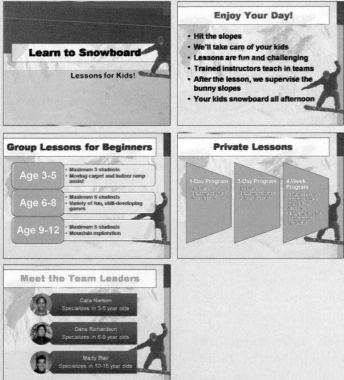

(Project 16D–Lessons continues on the next page)

Content-Based Assessments

chaptersixteen   ## Skills Review

(Project 16D–Lessons continued)

1. **Start** PowerPoint, and then from your student files, **Open p16D_Lessons**. Click the **Office** button, and then click **Save As**. Navigate to your **PowerPoint Chapter 16** folder, and then using your own first and last names, **Save** the file as 16D_Lessons_Firstname_Lastname

2. Display **Slide 3**. On the **Home tab**, in the **Clipboard group**, click the **Dialog Box Launcher** to display the Clipboard task pane. In the **Clipboard** task pane, click the **Clear All** button. Select the slide title—*Private Lessons*. In the **Clipboard group**, click the **Cut** button to move the title to the Office Clipboard.

3. Display **Slide 4**. Select the title, and then on the **Home tab**, in the **Clipboard group**, click the **Cut** button to move the title to the Office Clipboard.

4. With **Slide 4** still displayed and the insertion point blinking in the title placeholder, in the **Clipboard** task pane, click **Private Lessons** to paste the item to the title placeholder.

5. Display **Slide 3**, and then click in the title placeholder. In the **Clipboard** task pane, click **Group Lessons for Beginners** to paste the item to the title placeholder. In the **Clipboard** task pane, click **Clear All**, and then **Close** the Clipboard task pane.

6. On **Slide 3**, right-click in the bulleted list placeholder to display the shortcut menu, and then point to **Convert to SmartArt**. In the first row, click the second graphic—**Vertical Block List**.

7. Click in the blank, fourth shape, and then press [Delete] to delete the extra shape. **Save** your presentation.

8. Click the **Design tab**. In the **SmartArt Styles group**, click the **Change Colors** button. Under **Primary Theme Colors**, click the third color set—**Dark 2 Fill**. In the **SmartArt Styles group**, click the **More** button. Under **3-D**, in the first row, click the third style—**Cartoon**.

9. Display **Slide 4**, and then click in the bulleted list placeholder. On the **Home tab**, in the **Paragraph group**, click the **Convert to SmartArt Graphic** button, and then click **More SmartArt Graphics**. Click **List**, and then in the fifth row, click **Trapezoid List**. Click **OK** to create a diagram with four shapes. Click in the blank, fourth shape, and then press [Delete] to delete the extra shape. In the **SmartArt Tools Design tab**, click the **Change Colors** button, and then under **Primary Theme Colors**, click the third color—**Dark 2 Fill**.

10. Click the **Home tab**. In the **Slides group**, click the **New Slide** button to insert a slide with the **Title and Content** layout. Click in the title placeholder, and then type Meet the Team Leaders

11. In the content placeholder, click the **Insert SmartArt Graphic** button. In the fourth row, click the second graphic—**Vertical Picture Accent List**, and then click **OK**. Click in the first **Text** shape, type Cara Nielsen and then press [Enter]. Type Specializes in 3–5 year olds

12. In the second shape, type Dane Richardson and then press [Enter]. Type Specializes in 6–9 year olds

13. In the third shape, type Marty Blair and then press [Enter]. Type Specializes in 10–15 year olds and then **Save** your presentation.

14. Click the **Design tab**. In the **SmartArt Styles group**, click the **Change Colors** button. Scroll the color list, and then under **Accent 4**, click the second color

(Project 16D–Lessons continues on the next page)

886   **PowerPoint** | Chapter 16: Designing a PowerPoint Presentation

Content-Based Assessments

Skills Review

(Project 16D–Lessons continued)

set—**Colored Fill - Accent 4**. In the **SmartArt Styles group**, click the **More** button. Under **Best Match for Document**, click the last style—**Intense Effect**.

15. To the left of Cara Nielsen's information, in the circle shape, click the **Insert Picture From File** button. Navigate to your student files, and then double-click **p16D_Cara** to insert the picture. Repeat this process for the remaining two circles, inserting the files **p16D_Dane** and **p16D_Marty**.

16. Click the **Slide Show tab**. In the **Start Slide Show group**, click **From Beginning**, and then view your presentation, clicking the mouse button to advance from slide to slide. Create a **Header and Footer** for the **Notes and Handouts**. Include only the **Date and time updated automatically**, the **Page number**, and a **Footer** with the file name **16D_Lessons_Firstname_Lastname**

17. Check your *Chapter Assignment Sheet* or *Course Syllabus* or consult your instructor to determine if you are to submit your assignments on paper or electronically. To submit electronically, go to Step 19, and then follow the instructions provided by your instructor.

18. From the **Office** menu, point to the **Print arrow**, and then click **Print Preview** to make a final check of your presentation. In the **Page Setup group**, click the **Print What arrow**, and then click **Handouts (6 Slides Per Page)**. Click the **Print** button, and then click **OK** to print the handouts. **Close** Print Preview.

19. **Save** the changes to your presentation, and then from the **Office** menu, click **Exit PowerPoint**.

End **You have completed Project 16D**

Content-Based Assessments

Project 16E — Packages

In this project, you will apply the skills you practiced from the Objectives in Projects 16A and 16B.

Objectives: 1. *Format Slide Elements;* **2.** *Insert and Format Pictures and Shapes;* **3.** *Apply Slide Transitions;* **5.** *Create and Format a SmartArt Graphic.*

In the following Mastering PowerPoint project, you will edit a presentation that Kirsten McCarty, Director of Marketing, will be showing at a travel fair to highlight the vacation packages offered at Montagna del Pattino. Your completed presentation will look similar to Figure 16.43.

For Project 16E, you will need the following files:

p16E_Fireworks

p16E_Mountain

p16E_Packages

p16E_Ski_Lift

p16E_Sunset

You will save your presentation as
16E_Packages_Firstname_Lastname

Figure 16.43

(Project 16E–Packages continues on the next page)

(Project 16E–Packages continued)

1. **Start** PowerPoint, and then from your student files, **Open p16E_Packages. Save** your presentation as **16E_Packages_ Firstname_Lastname**

2. Display **Slide 2**, and then change the bulleted list to **Numbering**. Insert a **Basic Shape Bevel** at **1 inch to the right of zero on the horizontal ruler** and at **0.5 inch below zero on the vertical ruler**. Size the bevel so that its **Height** is **1.3** inches and its **Width** is **3** inches. In the bevel, type **We'll customize your package; just call for reservations! Center** the text.

3. Select the shape so that its outer border is solid, and then duplicate the shape by using Ctrl + D. Drag the new shape down so that it almost touches the bottom of the slide. Replace the text with **Book two packages in one year; get a free weekend stay!**

4. Select both shapes, and then **Arrange** the shapes, using **Align Left** so that the left edges of the two shapes align. Apply a **Shape Style** found in the third row, **Light 1 Outline, Colored Fill – Accent 1** to both shapes.

5. Display **Slide 3**. In the placeholder on the left side of the slide, use the **Insert Picture from File** button in the placeholder to insert from your student files **p16E_Ski_Lift**. Change the **Picture Shape** under **Basic Shapes** to **Parallelogram**, and then apply the first **Reflection** effect—**Tight Reflection, touching**.

6. Display **Slide 4**, and then add a **New Slide** with the **Comparison** layout. Type and **Center** the title **Fifth Night Free Package** In the caption box on the left, type **Stay an extra day** and then in the caption box on the right, type **Enjoy the evening view Center** both captions, and then in the content placeholder on the left, type the following bullet points:

Accommodations at the Summit Lodge Book four nights, stay for free on the fifth Complimentary breakfast every morning

7. Select the placeholder so that its outer edge displays as a solid line, and then change the **Line Spacing** to **1.5** and the **Font Size** to **20**. With the placeholder border displayed as a solid line, the change is applied to all of the text.

8. In the placeholder on the right side of the slide, use the **Insert Picture from File** button in the placeholder to insert from your student files **p16E_Sunset**. Apply the second **Glow Picture Effect** in the second row—**Accent color 2, 8 pt glow**. **Save** the presentation.

9. Add a **New Slide** to the presentation with the **Content with Caption** layout. The slide title is **Fourth of July Celebration Package Center** the title and increase the **Font Size** to **24**. Remove the **Bold** formatting. In the text placeholder on the left of the slide, type **Stay Fourth of July weekend at the Summit Lodge and receive preferred seating at the evening fireworks show and complimentary tickets for four to our barbecue**

10. Change the **Font Size** of the text that you typed to **16**, and then change the **Line Spacing** to **2.5**. **Center** the text and apply **Italic**. In the placeholder on the right side of the slide, use the **Insert Picture from File** button to insert **p16E_Fireworks** from your student files.

11. Add a **New Slide** with the **Title and Content** layout. The slide title is **Summer Festivals** In the content placeholder, use the **SmartArt Graphic** button to insert a **List** graphic found in the fifth row—**Table List**. Apply the **3-D Powder SmartArt Style** to the graphic.

(Project 16E–Packages continues on the next page)

Content-Based Assessments

Mastering PowerPoint

(Project 16E–Packages continued)

12. In the long rectangular box at the top of the SmartArt graphic, type **Stay For Any Weekend Festival** and then select the text. On the **Format tab**, display the **WordArt Styles** gallery. In the first row of WordArt styles, apply **Fill – White, Outline – Accent 1** to the selection. In the three remaining boxes, type the following points, one in each box from left to right.

Free admission to festival
Complimentary lunch
Free parking or free trolley ride to event

13. Display **Slide 8**. Click the **Insert Picture from File** button in the placeholder and insert from your student files **p16E_ Mountain**. Apply the second **Reflection** effect in the first row—**Half Reflection, touching**.

14. Display **Slide 2**, and then select the title. Change the **Font** to **Tahoma**. Use the **Format Painter** to apply the formatting to the titles on **Slides 3**, **4**, and **7**.

15. In the **Transitions** gallery, under **Wipes**, apply the **Uncover Left-Up** transition, and then change the **Transition Speed** to **Medium** for all of the slides. View the **Slide Show** from the beginning.

16. Create a **Header and Footer** for the **Notes and Handouts**. Include only the **Date and time updated automatically**, the **Page number**, and a **Footer** with the file name **16E_Packages_Firstname_Lastname** using your own first and last name.

17. Check your *Chapter Assignment Sheet* or *Course Syllabus* or consult your instructor to determine if you are to submit your assignments on paper or electronically. To submit electronically, go to Step 19, and then follow the instructions provided by your instructor.

18. Display your presentation in **Print Preview**, and then print **Handouts (4 Slides Per Page)**.

19. **Save** your presentation, and then **Close** the file.

End **You have completed Project 16E**

Content-Based Assessments

Mastering PowerPoint

Project 16F—Family

In this project, you will apply the skills you practiced from the Objectives in Projects 16A and 16B.

Objectives: 2. *Insert and Format Pictures and Shapes;* **3**. *Apply Slide Transitions;* **4**. *Reorganize Presentation Text and Clear Formats;* **5**. *Create and Format a SmartArt Graphic.*

In the following Mastering PowerPoint project, you will create a presentation based on the activities that the Gillis family enjoyed while spending a day at Montagna del Pattino. Your completed presentation will look similar to Figure 16.44.

For Project 16F, you will need the following files:

New blank PowerPoint presentation
p16F_Baby
p16F_Group

p16F_Memories
p16F_Snowflake
p16F_Winner

You will save your presentation as 16F_Family_Firstname_Lastname

Figure 16.44

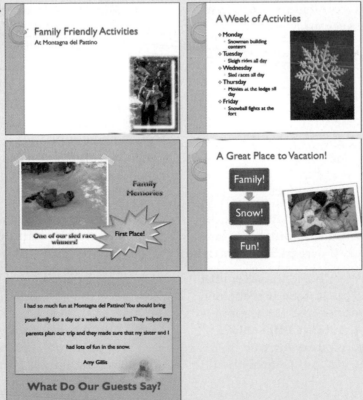

(Project 16F–Family continues on the next page)

Content-Based Assessments

(Project 16F–Family continued)

1. **Start** PowerPoint, and then begin a new blank presentation. Apply the **Solstice** theme. In the **Themes group**, click the **Theme Colors** button, and then click the fifth color theme under **Built-In—Civic**. **Save** the file as 16F_Family_Firstname_Lastname

2. The title of this presentation is **Family Friendly Activities** and the subtitle is **At Montagna del Pattino** From your student files, insert the **p16F_Group** picture. Adjust the picture **Height** to **4.5** and the **Width** to **3**. Drag the picture to the lower right corner of the slide. Change the picture shape to **Bevel**, and then apply a **Soft Edges Picture Effect** of **10 Point**.

3. Add a **New Slide** with the **Two Content** layout, and then in the title placeholder, type **A Week of Activities** In the content placeholder on the left, type the following bullet points, increasing and decreasing the list level as necessary:

   Monday
     Snowman building contests
   Tuesday
     Sleigh rides all day
   Wednesday
     Sled races
   Thursday
     Movies at the lodge
   Friday
     Snowball fights at the fort

4. In the placeholder on the right, click the **Insert Picture from File** button. From your student files, insert **p16F_Snowflake**.

5. Add a **New Slide** with the **Picture with Caption** layout. In the title placeholder, type **Family Memories** and then apply **WordArt Style Gradient Fill – Black, Outline – White, Outer Shadow**. Increase the **Font Size** to **32** and **Center** the title.

6. In the Picture placeholder, from your student files insert **p16F_Winner**. In the caption box below the picture, type **One of our sled race winners!** In the slide title, select the word *Family*, and then use **Format Painter** to apply the WordArt style to the caption. **Center** the caption and change the **Line Spacing** to **1.0**.

7. On the **Insert tab**, display the **Shapes gallery**. Under **Stars and Banners**, in the first row, click the second shape—**Explosion 2**. Draw a shape that extends from **zero on the horizontal** and **vertical rulers** to **4 1/2 inches to the right of zero on the horizontal ruler** and **3 inches below zero on the vertical ruler**.

8. In the explosion shape, type **First Place!** and then change the **Font Size** to **28**. Display the **Shape Styles gallery**, and then in the fourth row apply **Subtle Effect – Accent 1**. Apply the **Bevel Shape Effect Soft Round**—the second effect in the second row.

9. Add a **New Slide** with the **Two Content** layout, and then in the title placeholder, type **A Great Place to Vacation!** In the content placeholder on the left, insert the **Vertical Process SmartArt** graphic. In the first box, type **Family!** In the second box, type **Snow!** In the last box, type **Fun!** Apply **SmartArt Style 3-D Polished** to the graphic.

10. In the placeholder on the right of the slide, from your student files, insert the picture **p16F_Memories**. Apply **Picture Style Rotated, White**, and then apply the **Glow Picture Effect—Accent color 1, 5 pt glow**.

11. Add a **New Slide** with the **Comparison** layout, and then in the title placeholder at the bottom of the slide, type **What Do Our**

(Project 16F–Family continues on the next page)

Content-Based Assessments

Mastering PowerPoint

(Project 16F–Family continued)

Guests Say? Click in the white placeholder at the top left of the slide, hold down ⬆Shift and click the white placeholder at the top right to select both placeholders. **Delete** both placeholders.

12. Click in the placeholder on the left, and then type **I had so much fun at Montagna del Pattino! You should bring your family for a day or a week of winter fun! They helped my parents plan our trip and they made sure that my sister and I had lots of fun in the snow.** Press Enter, and then type **Amy Gillis**

13. In the placeholder on the right, use the **Insert Picture from File** button to insert from your student files **p16F_Baby**. Change the shape of the picture to the **32-Point Star**, and then apply the **Soft Edges 50 Point Picture Effect** so that the baby almost appears to be crawling on the slide. Drag the picture to the right so that the points of the stars and its border box align with the right edge of the slide.

14. With the picture selected, press ⬆Shift, and then click the slide title to select both the picture and the title. On the **Drawing Tools Format tab**, in the **Arrange group**, click **Align**, and then click **Align Bottom** to align the bottom edges of the two objects. The baby displays slightly above the word *Say.*

15. Select the text in the bulleted list placeholder, and then on the **Home tab**, click the **Bullets** button to toggle the bullets off. **Center** all of the text in the placeholder. Point to the placeholder's right-center sizing handle and drag to the right to **4.5**

inches to the right of zero on the horizontal ruler to resize the placeholder. Apply the **Shape Style** found in the fourth row—**Subtle Effect – Accent 3**, and then change the **Line Spacing** of the text to **2.0**.

16. Display **Slide 2**, and then click in the first bullet point—*Monday*. Change the Bullet style to **Star Bullets**. Use F4 or Format Painter to apply the same bullet style to each bullet point that includes a day of the week. In the fourth bullet point, **Copy** the words *all day* to the end of the sixth and eighth bullet points after the words *races*, and *lodge*.

17. Apply the **Box In** transition and change the **Transition Speed** to **Medium**. Click **Apply To All**, and then view the slide show from the beginning.

18. Create a **Header & Footer** for the **Notes and Handouts**. Include only the **Date and time updated automatically**, the **Page number**, and a **Footer** with the file name **16F_Family_Firstname Lastname**

19. Check your *Chapter Assignment Sheet* or *Course Syllabus* or consult your instructor to determine if you are to submit your assignments on paper or electronically. To submit electronically, go to Step 21, and then follow the instructions provided by your instructor.

20. Display your presentation in **Print Preview**, and then print **Handouts (6 Slides Per Page)**.

21. **Save** changes to your presentation, and then **Close** the file.

End **You have completed Project 16F**

Content-Based Assessments

PowerPoint
chaptersixteen

Mastering PowerPoint

Project 16G—Summer

In this project, you will apply the skills you practiced from all the Objectives in Projects 16A and 16B.

Objectives: 1. *Format Slide Elements;* **2**. *Insert and Format Pictures and Shapes;* **3**. *Apply Slide Transitions;* **4**. *Reorganize Presentation Text and Clear Formats;* **5**. *Create and Format a SmartArt Graphic.*

In the following Mastering PowerPoint Assessment, you will edit a presentation that Kirsten McCarty, Director of Marketing, will be showing at a travel fair describing the summer activities at Montagna del Pattino. Your completed presentation will look similar to Figure 16.45.

For Project 16G, you will need the following files:

p16G_Art   p16G_Fireworks
p16G_Balloons   p16G_Summer

You will save your presentation as
16G_Summer_Firstname_Lastname

Figure 16.45

(Project 16G–Summer continues on the next page)

Content-Based Assessments

Mastering PowerPoint

(Project 16G–Summer continued)

1. **Start** PowerPoint, and then from your student files **Open** the file **p16G_Summer**. **Save** the presentation as 16G_Summer_Firstname_Lastname

2. On **Slide 2**, apply a **WordArt Style—Gradient Fill – Accent 6, Inner Shadow** found in the fourth row—to the title, and then decrease the **Font Size** to **32**. Select the bulleted list placeholder so that its border displays as a solid line, and then display the **Bullets and Numbering** dialog box. Change the bullet style to the third style in the first row of the Bullets gallery—**Hollow Round Bullets**. Change the bullet **Color** to the first color under **Standard Colors—Dark Red**.

3. On **Slide 2**, display the **Shapes** gallery. Under **Basic Shapes**, insert the fifth shape in the second row—**Frame**. Position the pointer at **1.5 inches to the right of zero on the horizontal ruler** and at **1.5 inches above zero on the vertical ruler**. Draw the shape with a **Height** of **1.5** and a **Width** of **3.25**, using the **Format tab** to adjust the size as necessary. In the frame, type **Reservations recommended at least two months in advance** Apply **Italic** and **Center** the text.

4. Duplicate the frame shape, and then drag the duplicated shape down so that it is approximately 0.5 inch below the first shape. Align the left edges of the shapes, and then in the second shape, replace the text with **Check out our Stay and Play packages for special discounts** On the **Format tab**, click the **Shape Fill arrow**, and then under **Standard Colors**, click the first color—**Dark Red**. Use F4 to repeat the fill color formatting to the other frame shape.

5. Display **Slide 3**. In the placeholder on the right, from your student files, insert the picture **p16G_Art**. Change the **Picture**

Shape to a **Rounded Rectangle**. Apply the fourth **Glow Effect** in the first row—**Accent color 4, 5 pt glow**.

6. Display **Slide 4**. Select the title, and then in the **Font group**, click the **Clear All Formatting** button to remove the WordArt formatting from the selection.

7. On **Slide 4**, convert the existing content placeholder text to a **Process** SmartArt—**Alternating Flow**. Click in the *Mile 10* shape, and then in the **Create Graphic group**, click **Add Shape**. In the gray box, type **Finish** and then in the brown box, type **Summit Lodge**

8. Change the color of the SmartArt to the first **Accent 1** color—**Colored Outline - Accent 1**, and then apply **3-D Style Powder**.

9. Display **Slide 5**. Select the *Fireworks Display* text, and then apply the second **Word Art Style** in the first row. Change the **Text Fill** color to **Dark Red**. Use the **Format Painter** to apply the same formatting to the *Hot Air Balloon Race* text. In the placeholder on the left, insert from your student files the picture **p16G_Fireworks**. Apply the **Glow Picture Effect Accent color 2, 8 pt glow**.

10. In the placeholder on the right, insert from your student files the picture **p16G_Balloons**. Apply the **Soft Edges Picture Effect 5 Point**. Size the picture to a **Height** of **2.5** and a **Width** of **3.75** and then drag the picture up so that its top edge is positioned at **1 inch above zero on the vertical ruler**. It should *not* align with the fireworks picture.

11. Insert a 4-inch-wide **Text Box** positioned at **zero on the horizontal ruler** and at **2 inches below zero on the vertical ruler**.

(Project 16G–Summer continues on the next page)

Content-Based Assessments

PowerPoint
chaptersixteen   **Mastering PowerPoint**

(Project 16G–Summer continued)

Type **Color lights up the sky in July and August. Join us for both events and enjoy a barbecue, carnival rides, and music.** Apply the second **WordArt Style—Fill – None, Outline – Accent 2**, and then change the **Text Fill** to **Dark Red**. Apply **Italic**, and then change the **Font Size** to **16**. **Center** the text.

12. Use ⇧Shift to select the text box that you created in Step 11, the balloon picture, and the *Hot Air Balloon Race* text box. **Align Center** the three objects. (Hint: Use the Drawing Tools Format tab).

13. In the first row of the **Wipes** transitions, apply the **Wedge Transition** to all of the slides in the presentation, and then view the slide show.

14. Create a **Header & Footer** for the **Notes and Handouts**. Include only the **Date and time updated automatically**, the **Page number**, and a **Footer** with the file name **16G_Summer_Firstname_Lastname**

15. Check your *Chapter Assignment Sheet* or *Course Syllabus* or consult your instructor to determine if you are to submit your assignments on paper or electronically. To submit electronically, go to Step 17, and then follow the instructions provided by your instructor.

16. Display your presentation in **Print Preview**, and then print **Handouts (6 Slides Per Page)**.

17. **Save** any changes to your presentation, and then **Close** the presentation.

End **You have completed Project 16G**

Content-Based Assessments

Mastering PowerPoint

Project 16H — *GO!* Fix It

In this project, you will apply the skills you practiced from the Objectives in Projects 16A and 16B.

For Project 16H, you will need the following files:

p16H_SkiFest

p16H_Skier

You will save your document as
16H_SkiFest_Firstname_Lastname

In this project, you will edit a draft slide presentation being prepared for Dane Richardson, Director of Ski and Snowboard Instruction at Montagna del Pattino, to advertise their Monster Mogul SkiFest to skiers. From the student files that accompany this textbook, open the file **p16H_SkiFest**, and then save the file in your chapter folder as **16H_SkiFest_Firstname_Lastname**

This presentation contains errors that you must find and correct. Read and examine the document, and then edit to correct the errors that you find. Types of errors could include:

- Spelling, grammar, punctuation, and usage errors such as text case, subject-verb agreement, and meaning.

- Content errors such as missing or incorrect data, text, pictures, hyperlinks, or other objects.

- Font and paragraph formatting and positioning errors such fonts, font styles, font sizing, alignment, text color, indent levels, and bullet features.

- Slide layout, orientation, design themes, backgrounds, animation and transition errors.

- Image or object formatting and positioning errors on tables, illustrations, links, text, and media clips relating to color, lines, size, scale, styles, layout, positioning, and control.

- Page setup errors on slides, handouts, notes and outlines such as margins, orientation, layout, alignment, headers and footers, date and time, color, grayscale, black and white, and sizing.

To complete the project, you should know that:

- Mr. Richardson wants an additional photo on Slide 1, resized to a height of 3.75 and a width of 5, and positioned in the upper right section of the slide. Use the **p16H_Skier** photo from your student files.

(Project 16H–*GO!* Fix It continues on the next page)

(Project 16H–*GO!* Fix It continued)

- On all of the slides with time periods, correct as necessary to use a consistent format for the times; for example *4:00 pm*.

- There are some errors in bullet styles.

- On Slide 7, Mr. Richardson wants the phrase **Don't Miss It!** in the slide using the WordArt style Fill - Accent 2, Matte Bevel positioned centered below the date.

Create a footer for the Notes and Handouts. Include only the date and time updated automatically, the page number, and a footer with your name included. Submit as directed, using four slides per page.

End **You have completed Project 16H**

Outcomes-Based Assessments

Rubric

The following outcomes-based assessments are *open-ended assessments*. That is, there is no specific correct result; your result will depend on your approach to the information provided. Make *Professional Quality* your goal. Use the following scoring rubric to guide you in *how* to approach the problem and then to evaluate *how well* your approach solves the problem.

The *criteria*—Software Mastery, Content, Format and Layout, and Process—represent the knowledge and skills you have gained that you can apply to solving the problem. The *levels of performance*—Professional Quality, Approaching Professional Quality, or Needs Quality Improvements—help you and your instructor evaluate your result.

	Your completed project is of Professional Quality if you:	Your completed project is Approaching Professional Quality if you:	Your completed project Needs Quality Improvements if you:
1-Software Mastery	Choose and apply the most appropriate skills, tools, and features and identify efficient methods to solve the problem.	Choose and apply some appropriate skills, tools, and features, but not in the most efficient manner.	Choose inappropriate skills, tools, or features, or are inefficient in solving the problem.
2-Content	Construct a solution that is clear and well organized, contains content that is accurate, appropriate to the audience and purpose, and is complete. Provide a solution that contains no errors of spelling, grammar, or style.	Construct a solution in which some components are unclear, poorly organized, inconsistent, or incomplete. Misjudge the needs of the audience. Have some errors in spelling, grammar, or style, but the errors do not detract from comprehension.	Construct a solution that is unclear, incomplete, or poorly organized; contains some inaccurate or inappropriate content; and contains many errors of spelling, grammar, or style. Do not solve the problem.
3-Format and Layout	Format and arrange all elements to communicate information and ideas, clarify function, illustrate relationships, and indicate relative importance.	Apply appropriate format and layout features to some elements, but not others. Overuse features, causing minor distraction.	Apply format and layout that does not communicate information or ideas clearly. Do not use format and layout features to clarify function, illustrate relationships, or indicate relative importance. Use available features excessively, causing distraction.
4-Process	Use an organized approach that integrates planning, development, self-assessment, revision, and reflection.	Demonstrate an organized approach in some areas, but not others; or, use an insufficient process of organization throughout.	Do not use an organized approach to solve the problem.

Outcomes-Based Assessments

Problem Solving

Project 16I — Adult Lessons

In this project, you will construct a solution by applying any combination of the skills you practiced from the Objectives in Projects 16A and 16B.

For Project 16I, you will need the following file:

New blank PowerPoint presentation

You will save your presentation as
16I_Adult_Lessons_Firstname_Lastname

Using the information provided, create a presentation that contains four to six slides that Dane Richardson, Director of Ski and Snowboard Instruction, can use to describe the adult ski and snowboard lessons offered at Montagna del Pattino. The presentation will be used as a part of a larger presentation on resort activities to be shown to an audience of varying skiing abilities at a regional ski and snowboard convention.

The resort offers Adult Group Lessons that are comprised of individuals with similar skill levels. Two-hour group lessons include equipment. Private lessons, which are one-on-one instruction geared toward an individual's skill level and preferences, are also available. The resort offers 8-week programs, which are group lessons for those who prefer more in-depth, ongoing instruction. The resort also offers several specialty lessons. The Ladies Only group lessons are geared specifically toward women and participants are encouraged to bring a friend. The Backcountry Adventure is a chance for advanced skiers to explore lesser-known areas of the resort. Finally, the Racing Camps are for recreational skiers seeking to fine-tune their skills, and feature gate running and on-hill training.

Use the techniques that you learned in this chapter to insert and format graphics to visually enhance your presentation. The tone of the presentation should be positive and encouraging so that the audience—regardless of skill level—will be interested in visiting the resort and attending the Ski and Snowboard School. Add the file name to the Notes and Handouts footer and check the presentation for spelling errors. Save the presentation in your PowerPoint Chapter 16 folder as **16I_Adult_Lessons_Firstname_Lastname** and submit it as directed.

You can find many appropriate images available to Office users. To access these images, click the Insert tab, and then from the Illustrations group, click the Clip Art button. In the Clip Art task pane, type a key word—such as *ski*—in the *Search for* box. You can specify the image type (clip art or photographs) and where to search. The largest variety of photographs can be found by including Web Collections in the *Search in* box. You can also use images from earlier projects in this chapter, or images from your personal collection.

End You have completed Project 16I

Outcomes-Based Assessments

Problem Solving

Project 16J — Festivals

In this project, you will construct a solution by applying any combination of the skills you practiced from the Objectives in Projects 16A and 16B.

For Project 16J, you will need the following file:

New blank PowerPoint presentation

**You will save your presentation as
16J_Festivals_Firstname_Lastname**

In this project, you will create a presentation that Justin Mitrani, Hotel Manager, is creating as part of a collection of presentations given to guests on CDs. The presentation describes the seasonal festivals and events held at Montagna del Pattino. The events that are sponsored at the resort include a Celtic Festival, a Chili Cook-Off, and a Country Music Festival. The tone of the presentation should be fun and interesting so that guests will be encouraged to return to the resort during the events. Research these types of events on the Internet to develop content and use a SmartArt graphic to highlight the dates of the festivals. Include pictures and shapes that are relevant to the events, and format the pictures using the techniques that you learned in this chapter. (See the note at the end of Project 16I for hints about locating images.) Add the file name to the Notes and Handouts footer and check the presentation for spelling errors. Save the presentation in your PowerPoint Chapter 16 folder as **16J_Festivals_Firstname_Lastname** and submit it as directed.

End **You have completed Project 16J** ——————————

Outcomes-Based Assessments

Problem Solving

Project 16K — Orientation

In this project, you will construct a solution by applying any combination of the skills you practiced from the Objectives in Projects 16A and 16B.

> **For Project 16K, you will need the following file:**
>
> New blank PowerPoint presentation

You will save your presentation as
16K_Orientation_Firstname_Lastname

In this project, you will create an orientation presentation consisting of four to six slides to be used by Justin Mitrani, Hotel Director for Montagna del Pattino. This presentation will be used to introduce new employees to the resort and to the importance of customer service. Begin the presentation with slides that include information about the resort. You can summarize from the following information, and you can expand upon this information by researching mountain ski resorts.

Montagna del Pattino was founded and built by the Blardone family in the 1950s. It has grown from one ski run and a small lodge to 50 trails, 6 lifts, a 300-room lodge, and a renowned ski and snowboard school. Luxurious condominiums on the property have ski in/ski out access. A resort store offers rental and sale of gear for enthusiasts who want the latest advances in ski and snowboard technology. A variety of quick service, casually elegant, and fine dining restaurants complete the scene for a perfect ski-enthusiast getaway.

Include at least two slides that describe why customer service and hospitality are important at the resort. Guests who return year after year are impressed by the friendly attitude and helpfulness of the staff and the cleanliness of the facilities. Stress the importance of greeting guests and making them feel at home, thus exemplifying the family-friendly atmosphere that is a hallmark of the resort. Use a process SmartArt graphic to illustrate how hospitality and customer service lead to satisfied guests.

The tone of this presentation is informative and should include examples of how customer service is provided on a daily basis. Keep this in mind when choosing a theme, diagrams, bullet styles, and pictures. (See the note at the end of Project 16I for hints about locating images.) Add the date and file name to the Notes and Handouts footer and check the presentation for spelling errors. Save the presentation in your PowerPoint Chapter 16 folder as **16K_Orientation_Firstname_Lastname** and submit it as directed.

End **You have completed Project 16K** ―――――――

More on your Student CD

The instructions for the following additional end-of-chapter projects are on your student CD in the folder 03_additional_end_of_chapter_projects.

Content-Based Assessments

Project L Mastering PowerPoint   Apply the skills you practiced in Project A.

Project M Mastering PowerPoint   Apply the skills you practiced in Project B.

Project N Business Running Case   Apply the skills you practiced in Projects A and B while helping an entrepreneur with the daily tasks of running a business.

In each chapter, this project focuses on applying the skills you have practiced in Projects A and B to a business. The project related to this business runs throughout the textbook. You will see how the Office applications relate to the day-to-day operation of a small business called Nelson Architectural Planning.

Outcomes-Based Assessments

Project O Problem Solving   Construct a solution by applying any combination of the skills you practiced from Projects A and B.

Project P Problem Solving   Construct a solution by applying any combination of the skills you practiced from Projects A and B.

Project Q You and GO!   Construct a solution that applies to your own life by applying any combination of the skills you practiced from Projects A and B.

Project R GO! with Help   Practice using Microsoft Office's Help Feature.

Project S Group Business Running Case   Work as part of a group to apply the skills you have gained thus far to help the Bell Orchid Hotel Group achieve its business goals.

Multimedia

The following multimedia accompany this textbook:

Companion Web site
www.prenhall.com/go

An interactive Web site designed to reinforce and test your understanding of the skills in this chapter.

AV-EDDs

In the folder in the front of this book you will find videos that demonstrate the objectives of the A and B projects in this chapter. These may help you understand how to complete the projects in this book.

Video Podcasts

In the folder in the front of this book are videos that can be played on your iPod, MP3 player, or computer. These videos demonstrate how to complete the more challenging objectives in this textbook.

chapter seventeen

17

Enhancing a Presentation with Animation, Tables, and Charts

OBJECTIVES

At the end of this chapter you will be able to:

OUTCOMES

Mastering these objectives will enable you to:

---

1. Customize Slide Backgrounds and Themes

2. Animate a Slide Show

PROJECT 17A

Customize a Presentation

---

3. Create and Modify Tables

4. Create and Modify Charts

PROJECT 17B

Present Data with Tables and Charts

Select National Properties

Select National Properties is a diversified real estate company that develops, builds, manages, and acquires a wide variety of properties nationwide. Among the company's portfolio of properties are shopping malls, mixed-use town center developments, high-rise office buildings, office parks, industrial buildings and warehouses, multifamily housing developments, educational facilities, and hospitals. Residential developments are mainly located in and around the company's hometown, Chicago; commercial and public buildings in the portfolio are located nationwide. The company is well respected for its focus on quality and commitment to the environment and economic development of the areas where it operates.

© Rob Crandall Stock Connection

Enhancing a Presentation with Animation, Tables, and Charts

Recall that a presentation theme applies a consistent look to a presentation. You can customize a presentation by modifying the theme and by applying animation to slide elements, and you can enhance your presentations by creating tables and charts that help your audience understand numeric data and trends just as pictures and diagrams help illustrate a concept. The data that you present should determine whether a table or a chart would most appropriately display your information. The charts most commonly used in PowerPoint presentations are bar, column, line, and pie. Styles applied to your tables and charts unify these slide elements by complementing your presentation theme.

Project 17A New Homes

In Activities 17.01 through 17.08, you will edit and format a presentation that Shaun Walker, President of Select National Properties, has created for a City Council meeting that describes a proposed residential development. Your completed presentation will look similar to Figure 17.1.

For Project 17A, you will need the following files:

p17A_Bedroom
p17A_Community
p17A_Family_Room
p17A_New_Homes

You will save your presentation as
17A_New_Homes_Firstname_Lastname

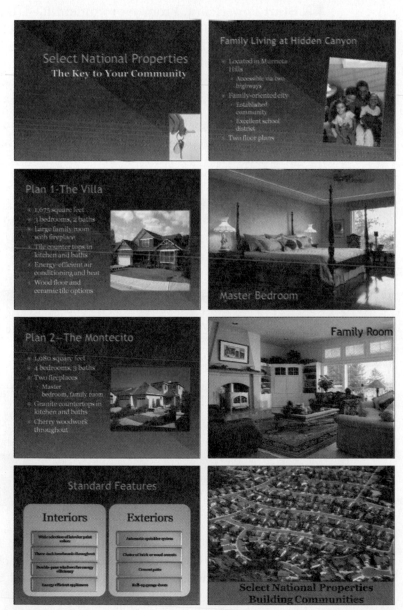

Figure 17.1
Project 17A—New Homes

Objective 1
Customize Slide Backgrounds and Themes

You have practiced customizing presentations by applying themes with unified design elements, backgrounds, and colors that provide a consistent look in your presentation. You can further customize a slide by changing the background color, applying a background style, or inserting a picture on the slide background.

Activity 17.01 Applying a Background Style

Recall that the presentation theme is a coordinated, predefined set of colors, fonts, lines, and fill effects. In this activity, you will open a presentation in which the Verve theme is applied, and then you will change the theme colors for the entire presentation and the background style for the first slide.

1 **Start** PowerPoint. From your student files, **Open** the file **p17A_New_Homes**. From the **Office** menu 🖫 , click **Save As**, and then click the **New Folder** button. Navigate to the location where you are saving your solution files, create a folder with the name **PowerPoint Chapter 17** and then click **OK**. In the **File name** box, type **17A_New_Homes_Firstname_Lastname** and then click **Save** to save your file.

2 Click the **Design tab**, and then in the **Themes group**, click the **Colors** button. Click **Trek** to change the theme color for the entire presentation.

3 With **Slide 1** displayed, on the **Design tab**, in the **Background group**, click the **Background Styles** button to display the **Background Styles gallery**, as shown in Figure 17.2.

> A *background style* is a slide background fill variation that combines theme colors in different intensities.

Figure 17.2

Background Styles gallery —

4 Point to each of the background styles to use Live Preview to view the style on **Slide 1**. Then, in the first row, *right-click* **Style 2** to display the shortcut menu. Click **Apply to Selected Slides**.

> The background style is applied to Slide 1.

5 **Save** 🖫 your presentation.

More Knowledge — Applying Background Styles to All Slides in a Presentation

You do not need to display the shortcut menu to apply a background style to all of the slides in a presentation. Click the background style that you want to apply and the style will be applied to all of the slides in the presentation.

Activity 17.02 Hiding Background Graphics

Slide themes and backgrounds often contain graphic elements that display on slides with various layouts. In the Verve theme applied to this presentation, the background includes a triangle and a line that intersect near the lower right corner of the slide. Sometimes the background graphics interfere with the slide content. When this happens, you can hide the background graphics.

■1 Display **Slide 6** and notice that on this slide, you can clearly see the triangle and line on the slide background.

> You cannot delete these objects because they are a part of the slide background; however, you can hide them.

■2 Display **Slide 5**. On the **Design tab**, in the **Background group**, click to select the **Hide Background Graphics** check box, and then compare your slide with Figure 17.3.

> The background objects no longer display behind the SmartArt diagram.

Figure 17.3

Hide Background
Graphics check
box selected

3 Display **Slide 1**. On the **Design tab**, in the **Background group**, select the **Hide Background Graphics** check box to toggle the graphics off.

4 Click the **Hide Background Graphics** check box again to toggle the graphics on.

5 **Save** 🖫 the presentation.

Activity 17.03 Formatting a Slide Background with a Picture

You can insert a picture on a slide background so the image fills the entire slide.

1 Display **Slide 3**, and then click the **Home tab**. In the **Slides group**, click the **New Slide arrow**, and then click the **Title Only** layout.

2 Click the **Design tab**. In the **Background group**, click the **Hide Background Graphics** check box, and then click the **Background Styles** button. Below the displayed gallery, click **Format Background**.

> The Format Background dialog box displays, providing options for customizing slide backgrounds.

3 If necessary, on the left side of the dialog box, click **Fill**. On the right side of the dialog box, under **Fill**, click the **Picture or texture fill** option button as shown in Figure 17.4, and then notice that on the slide background, a textured fill displays.

Figure 17.4

Fill selected

Picture or texture fill option button selected

Your background may differ

4 Under **Insert from**, click the **File** button to display the **Insert Picture** dialog box. Navigate to your student files, and then click **p17A_Bedroom**. Click **Insert**.

> The picture displays on the background of Slide 4.

5 In the **Format Background** dialog box, under **Stretch options**, verify that the **Left**, **Right**, **Top**, and **Bottom Offsets** are set to **0%** and make changes as necessary. Compare your dialog box with Figure 17.5.

> The Stretch options enable you to control the way in which the picture displays on the slide background by cropping portions of the picture and then stretching it to fit on the background. Setting the Offsets to 0% ensures that the slide background is formatted with the original picture in its entirety.

Figure 17.5

Picture displays on slide background

Set all Offsets to 0%

6 Click **Close** and notice that the picture has been applied to the slide background.

> When a picture is applied to the slide background using the Format Background option, the picture is not treated as an object. Thus, you cannot move it or size it.

7 Click in the title placeholder, type **Master Bedroom** and then notice that the background picture does not provide sufficient contrast with the text to display the title effectively.

8 Point to the outer edge of the title placeholder so that the 🔀 pointer displays. Drag the title placeholder down and to the left so that its lower left corner aligns with the lower left corner of the slide. Release the mouse button, and then compare your slide with Figure 17.6.

> The brown background of the floor provides good contrast for the title text.

Figure 17.6

Workshop

Overlaying Text on a Picture

When you insert a picture on a slide background, it is a good idea to choose a picture that has a solid area in which you can overlay a text box or title. For example, in the picture that you inserted on Slide 4, the lower left corner has a brown area that provides good contrast for light-colored text. When the picture that you choose does not contain a solid area, you can create one by filling the text box with color.

9 Display **Slide 5**, and then insert a **New Slide** with the **Title Only** layout.

10 On the **Design tab**, in the **Background group**, select the **Hide Background Graphics** check box, and then click the **Background Styles** button. Click **Format Background**.

11 Under **Fill**, click the **Picture or texture fill** option button. Under **Insert from**, click **File**. Navigate to your student files, click **p17A_Family_Room**, and then click **Insert**. Under **Stretch options**, if necessary change the **Left**, **Right**, **Top**, and **Bottom Offsets** to **0%**. **Close** the **Format Background** dialog box to format the slide background with the picture.

12 In the title placeholder, type **Family Room** Select the text, and then on the Mini toolbar, click the **Font Color button arrow** to display the **Theme Colors gallery**. In the first row, click the first color, **Black**, **Background 1**. On the Mini toolbar, click the **Align Text Right** button.

13 Point to the outer edge of the placeholder to display the pointer, and then drag the placeholder up and to the right so that its upper right corner aligns with the upper right corner of the slide. Compare your slide with Figure 17.7.

Figure 17.7

14 Display **Slide 8**. Using the process that you practiced in **Step 11**, on the background of **Slide 8**, insert the picture **p17A_Community**.

> The background does not provide sufficient contrast for the slide title to be easily read. You can apply a Shape Style to the title placeholder so that the text is visible.

15 Click in the title placeholder, and then click the **Format tab**. In the **Shape Styles group**, click the **More** button ▾. In the second row of the **Shape Styles gallery**, click the third style—**Colored Fill – Accent 2**.

16 Point to the outer edge of the placeholder to display the 🕀 pointer, and then drag the placeholder down so that its bottom edge aligns with the bottom of the slide. Click outside of the placeholder, and then compare your slide with Figure 17.8.

Figure 17.8

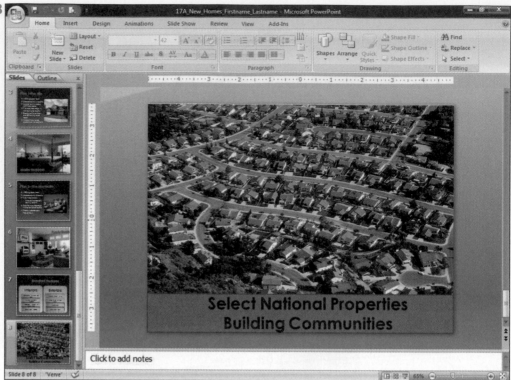

17 **Save** 📙 your presentation.

Activity 17.04 Applying a Background Fill Color and Resetting a Slide Background

1 Display **Slide 1**, and then click the **Design tab**. In the **Background group**, click the **Background Styles** button, and then click **Format Background**.

2 In the **Format Background** dialog box, if necessary, click the Solid fill option button, and then click the **Color** button 🖌️ ▾. Under **Theme Colors**, in the last row, click the second color—**Black, Text 1, Lighter 5%**. Click **Close**.

> The solid fill color is applied to the slide background.

3 On the **Design tab**, in the **Background group**, click the **Background Styles** button. Below the gallery, click **Reset Slide Background**.

> After making many changes to a slide background, you may decide that the original theme formatting is the best choice for displaying the text and graphics on a slide. The Reset Slide Background feature restores the original theme formatting to a slide.

4 **Save** 📙 the presentation.

Activity 17.05 Modifying Font Themes

Every presentation theme includes a *font theme* that determines the font applied to two types of slide text—headings and body. The *Headings font* is applied to slide titles and the *Body font* is applied to all other text. Sometimes the heading and body fonts are the same, but are different sizes. In other font themes, the heading and body fonts are different. When you apply a new font theme to the presentation, the text on every slide is updated with the new heading and body fonts.

1 If necessary, display **Slide 1**. Click anywhere in the title placeholder. Click the **Home tab**, and then in the **Font group**, click the **Font button arrow**. Notice that at the top of the Font list, under **Theme Fonts**, *Century Gothic (Headings)* and *Century Gothic (Body)* display as shown in Figure 17.9.

Figure 17.9

Theme fonts ——

2 Click anywhere on the slide to close the Font list.

3 Click the **Design tab**, and then in the **Themes group**, click the **Fonts** button.

> This list displays the name of each font theme and the pair of fonts in the theme. The first and larger font in each pair is the Headings font and the second and smaller font in each pair is the Body font.

4 Scroll the **Theme Fonts** list and notice that the last theme—*Verve*—is selected as shown in Figure 17.10.

Figure 17.10

Current font theme ——

5 Point to several of the themes and watch as Live Preview changes the title and subtitle text. Click the **Urban** theme, and then scroll through the slides in the presentation, noticing that the font changes have been applied to every slide.

6 **Save** 💾 your presentation.

Objective 2
Animate a Slide Show

Animation effects are used to introduce individual slide elements so that the slide can progress one element at a time. When used correctly, animation effects focus the audience's attention, providing the speaker with an opportunity to emphasize important points using the slide element as an effective visual aid.

Activity 17.06 Applying Entrance Effects

Entrance effects are animations that bring a slide element onto the screen.

1 Display **Slide 1**. Click the **Animations tab**, and then in the **Transition to This Slide group**, click the **More** button 🔽. Under **Wipes**, click the transition that contains four arrows pointing inward toward a center box—**Box In**. Click the **Transition Speed arrow**, and then click **Medium**. Click the **Apply To All** button.

2 Display **Slide 2**, and then click the bulleted list placeholder. In the **Animations group**, click the **Custom Animation** button. At the top of the displayed **Custom Animation** task pane, click the **Add Effect** button, and then point to **Entrance**. Compare your screen with Figure 17.11.

A list of the most recently used animation effects displays. At the bottom of the list, the *More Effects* option displays.

Figure 17.11

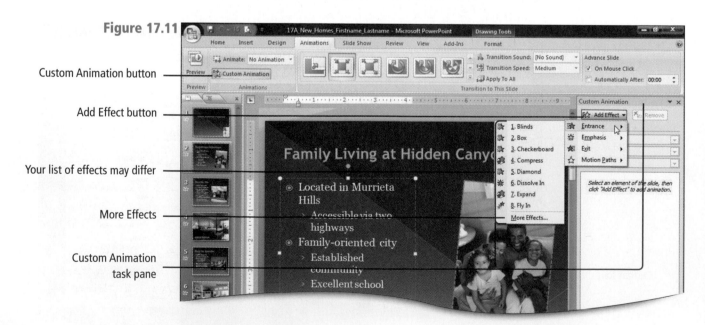

Custom Animation button

Add Effect button

Your list of effects may differ

More Effects

Custom Animation task pane

3 Click **More Effects** to display the **Add Entrance Effect** dialog box. Scroll through the list to view the *Basic, Subtle, Moderate,* and *Exciting* entrance effects.

4 At the bottom of the **Add Entrance Effect** dialog box, if necessary, click to select the Preview Effect check box. Click several of the effects in each of the four categories to view the animation.

5 Under **Basic**, click **Blinds**, and then click **OK**. Compare your screen with Figure 17.12.

The numbers *1, 2,* and *3* display to the left of the bulleted list placeholder, indicating the order in which the bullet points will display. For example, the first bullet point and its subordinate bullet are both numbered *1.* Thus, both will display at the same time.

In the task pane, the ***custom animation list*** indicates that an animation effect has been applied to the selected item. The custom animation list displays the animation sequences for a slide. The mouse image next to item 1 in the custom animation list indicates that the animation will display the bulleted list placeholder text when the left mouse button is clicked or when the Spacebar is pressed. Below item 1, a button with two downward-pointing arrows displays. This is the *Click to expand contents* button, which when clicked, displays the animation for bullet points 1, 2, and 3.

Figure 17.12

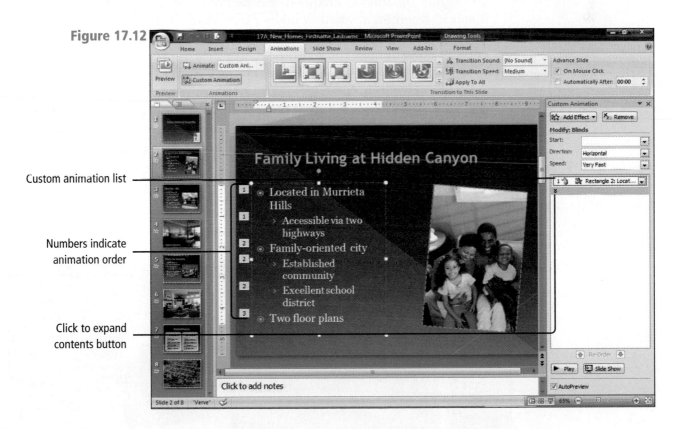

Custom animation list

Numbers indicate animation order

Click to expand contents button

6 Select the picture. In the **Custom Animation** task pane, click the **Add Effect** button, point to **Entrance**, and then click **More Effects**. In the **Add Entrance Effect** dialog box, under **Basic**, click **Dissolve In**, and then click **OK**.

The task pane displays item number 4 in the custom animation list, and the number 4 also displays on the slide next to the picture. These numbers display only when the Custom Animation task pane is open.

7 At the bottom of the task pane, click the **Play** button.

For the active slide only, the slide transition and each animation display. Additionally, the task pane indicates the number of seconds that elapse with each animation. This is a good way to test the animations you have applied to a single slide, without switching to Slide Show view.

8 **Save** 🖫 the presentation.

More Knowledge — Removing Animation Effects

You can remove animation that you have applied to a slide element by clicking the element in the Custom Animation task pane, and then clicking the Remove button. If you have applied an animation effect to a slide element, and then change your mind and decide to apply a different one, be sure to remove the animation that you do not want to use. Otherwise, when you view your slide show, all of the animation effects will display one after another.

Activity 17.07 Setting Effect and Timing Options

Use *effect options* to change the direction of an animation effect, play a sound when an animation takes place, control the levels of text that display, or control how text displays when the next animation sequence occurs. For example, after you have discussed a bullet point, you can click the mouse button to display the next point and dim the previous point, thus keeping the audience focused on the new bullet point.

1 With **Slide 2** displayed, click in the bulleted list placeholder. If necessary, display the Custom Animation task pane by clicking the Custom Animation button, in the Animations group.

2 In the **custom animation list**, notice that item 1 is selected and a downward-pointing arrow displays to the right of the item. In the **custom animation list**, click the **item 1 arrow**, and then point to **Effect Options**, as shown in Figure 17.13.

Figure 17.13

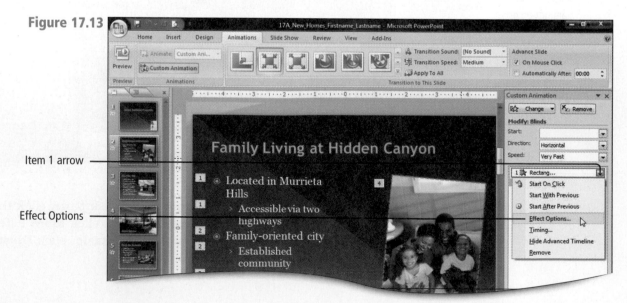

Item 1 arrow

Effect Options

3 Click **Effect Options** to display the **Blinds** dialog box.

When you click the Effect Options command, the dialog box that displays is named according to the applied animation.

4 In the **Blinds** dialog box, click the **Effect tab**. Under **Enhancements**, click the **After animation arrow**.

Use the After animation options to choose how the text will display after it is animated and you click the mouse button. The default—*Don't Dim*—keeps the text onscreen without any changes. You can dim the text by choosing a color that blends with the slide background, or you can hide the text so that it does not display at all.

5 In the row of colors, click the **fifth color**, as shown in Figure 17.14, and then click **OK** to apply the effect option.

Figure 17.14

After animation arrow

Fifth color selected

6 Select the picture. Near the top of the **Custom Animation** task pane, under **Modify: Dissolve In**, click the **Start arrow** to display three options—On Click, With Previous, and After Previous.

The *On Click* option begins the animation sequence for the selected slide element when the mouse button is clicked or the [Spacebar] is pressed. The *With Previous* option begins the animation sequence at the same time as the item preceding it in the custom animation list. The *After Previous* option begins the animation sequence for the selected slide element immediately after the completion of the previous animation or transition.

7 Click **After Previous**. In the **Custom Animation** task pane, under **Modify: Dissolve In**, click the **Speed arrow**, and then click **Fast**. Compare your task pane with Figure 17.15.

Figure 17.15

Start option

Speed

8 At the bottom of the **Custom Animation** task pane, click **Play** to view the animation applied to the slide.

9 Display **Slide 4**, and then click in the title placeholder. In the **Custom Animation** task pane, click **Add Effect**, and then point to **Entrance**. Click **More Effects**. Under **Basic**, click **Fly In**, and then click **OK**.

10 In the **Custom Animation task pane**, click the **Start arrow**, and then click **After Previous** so that the title displays immediately after the slide transition. If necessary, click the Direction arrow, and then click From Bottom. In the **Custom Animation** task pane, click **Play** to view the animation applied to the slide.

11 Display **Slide 6**, and then click in the title placeholder. In the **Custom Animation** task pane, click **Add Effect**, and then point to **Entrance**.

Recall that the Animation Effects list displays the most recently applied animations.

12 In the **Animation Effects list**, click **Fly In**. Click the **Start arrow**, and then click **After Previous**. Click the **Direction arrow**, and then click **From Top**. In the **Custom Animation** task pane, click **Play** to view the animation applied to the slide.

13 **Close** ☒ the **Custom Animation** task pane, and then **Save** 🖫 the presentation.

Workshop

Applying Animation Effectively

It is not necessary to animate every item on every slide in your presentation. Too much animation can distract your audience by focusing their attention on what the presentation is going to do instead of the message that you are trying to convey. Remember, the purpose of animation is to draw attention to important text and graphics!

Activity 17.08 Applying Animation to a SmartArt Graphic

The most efficient way to animate a SmartArt graphic is to use one of the choices in the Animate list. You can modify your animation choice by using the Custom Animation task pane.

1 Display **Slide 7**, and then click anywhere in the *Interiors/Exteriors* SmartArt graphic to select it.

2 On the **Animations tab**, in the **Animations group**, click the **Animate arrow** to display the Animate list, as shown in Figure 17.16.

Figure 17.16

Animate arrow

Animate list

3 Point to several of the **Animate** options and watch as Live Preview displays the animation effects.

4 Under **Wipe**, click **By level at once**.

> *By level at once* animates all shapes at the same level at the same time. In this case, the light-colored Interiors and Exteriors boxes will display at the same time, and then all of the gold boxes will display.

5 Click the **Slide Show tab**. In the **Start Slide Show group**, click **From Current Slide** to view the animation on Slide 7. Press [Spacebar] to advance through the SmartArt animation effects. After the animations for Slide 7 are complete, press [Esc] to end the slide show and return to the presentation.

6 In the **Start Slide Show group**, click **From Beginning**, and then view your presentation, clicking the mouse button to advance through the slides. Notice the animation that is applied to each slide, and then when the black slide displays, click the mouse button one more time to display the presentation in **Normal** view.

7 Insert a **Header & Footer** for the **Notes and Handouts**. Include the **Date and time** updated automatically, the **Page number**, and a **Footer** with the file name 17A_New_Homes_Firstname_Lastname

8 Check your *Chapter Assignment Sheet* or *Course Syllabus* or consult your instructor to determine if you are to submit your assignments on paper or electronically. To submit electronically, go to Step 10, and then follow the instructions provided by your instructor.

9 Display your presentation in **Print Preview**. If the pictures on the background of Slides 4, 6, and 8 do not display, set the Print Preview to display in Color. Print **Handouts (4 Slides Per Page)**.

10 **Save** the changes to your presentation, and then **Close** the presentation.

More Knowledge — Showing Selected Slides During a Slide Show

When you are delivering a presentation, you can right-click to display the shortcut menu and then point to Go to Slide to view a list of the slides in the presentation. Then click the slide that you want to display.

End You have completed Project 17A

Project 17B Developments

In Activities 17.09 through 17.14, you will add a table and two charts to a presentation that Shaun Walker, President of Select National Properties, is creating to apprise investors of the status of several new residential developments. Your completed presentation will look similar to Figure 17.17.

For Project 17B, you will need the following file:

p17B_Developments

**You will save your presentation as
17B_Developments_Firstname_Lastname**

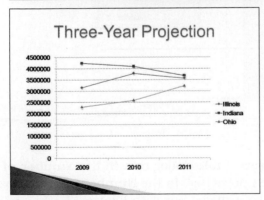

Figure 17.17
Project 17B—Developments

Objective 3
Create and Modify Tables

A *table* is a format for information that organizes and presents text and data in columns and rows. The intersection of a column and row is a *cell* and is the location in which you type text in a table.

Activity 17.09 Creating a Table

Here are several ways to insert a table: Use the Draw Table pointer, which is useful when the rows and columns contain cells of different sizes. Or insert a slide with a Content Layout and then click the Insert Table button. Or click the Insert tab and then click Table. In this Activity, you will use a Content Layout to create a table.

1 **Start** PowerPoint, from your student files open **p17B_Developments**, and then **Save** the presentation in your **PowerPoint Chapter 17** folder as **17B_Developments_Firstname_Lastname**

2 With **Slide 1** displayed, on the **Home tab**, in the **Slides group**, click the **New Slide** button to insert a slide with the **Title and Content** layout. In the title placeholder, type **Residential Development Status** and then **Center** the title.

3 In the content placeholder, click the **Insert Table** button to display the **Insert Table** dialog box, as shown in Figure 17.18.

In the Insert Table dialog box, you can enter the number of columns and rows that you want the table to contain.

Figure 17.18

Insert Table dialog box

Insert Table button

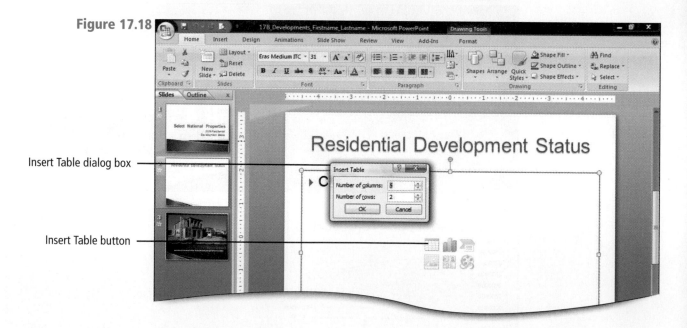

4 In the **Insert Table** dialog box, in the **Number of columns** box, type **3** and then press Tab. In the **Number of rows** box, type **2** and then compare your dialog box with Figure 17.19.

Figure 17.19

3 columns
2 rows

Click **OK** to create a table with three columns and two rows. Notice that the insertion point is blinking in the upper left cell of the table.

> The table extends from the left side of the content placeholder to the right side and the three columns are equal in width. By default, a style is applied to the table.

With the insertion positioned in the first cell of the table, type **Illinois** and then press Tab.

> Pressing Tab moves the insertion point to the next cell in the same row. If the insertion point is positioned in the last cell of a row, pressing Tab moves the insertion point to the first cell of the next row.

Alert!

Did you press Enter instead of Tab?

In a table, pressing Enter creates another line in the same cell. If you press Enter by mistake, you can remove the extra line by pressing ←Bksp.

With the insertion point positioned in the second cell of the first row, type **Indiana** and then press Tab. Type **Ohio** and then press Tab to move the insertion point to the first cell in the second row. Compare your table with Figure 17.20.

Figure 17.20

Text inserted in table

Insertion point

8 With the insertion positioned in the first cell of the second row, type **Hidden Canyon** and then press Enter to create a second line in the cell.

9 Type **250 new homes** and then press Tab. Type **Sienna Estates** and then press Enter to create a second line in the cell.

10 Type **325 new homes** and then press Tab. Type **Vineyard View** and then press Enter.

11 Type **285 new homes** and then press Tab to insert a new blank row.

When the insertion point is positioned in the last cell of a table, pressing Tab inserts a new blank row at the bottom of the table.

12 In the first cell of the third row, type **September 2010** and then press Tab. Type **April 2011** and then press Tab. Type **December 2010** and then compare your table with Figure 17.21.

Figure 17.21

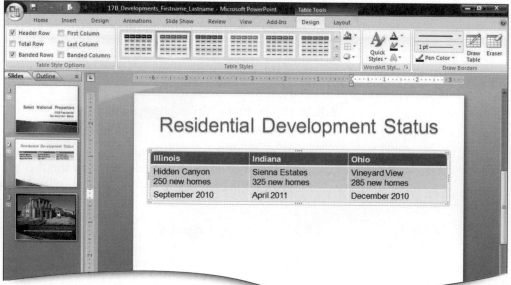

Alert!

Did you add an extra row to the table?

Recall that when the insertion point is positioned in the last cell of the table, pressing Tab inserts a new blank row. If you inadvertently inserted a blank row in the table, on the Quick Access Toolbar, click Undo.

13 **Save** 💾 your presentation.

Activity 17.10 Modifying the Layout of a Table

You can modify the layout of a table by inserting or deleting rows and columns, changing the alignment of the text in a cell, adjusting the height and width of the entire table or selected rows and columns, and by merging multiple cells into one cell.

1 Click in any cell in the first column, and then click the **Layout tab**. In the **Rows & Columns group**, click the **Insert Left** button.

A new first column is inserted and the width of the columns is adjusted so that all four columns are the same width.

2 Click in the first cell in the *second row*, and then type **Development**

3 Click in the first cell in the third row, type **Project Completion** and then compare your table with Figure 17.22.

Figure 17.22

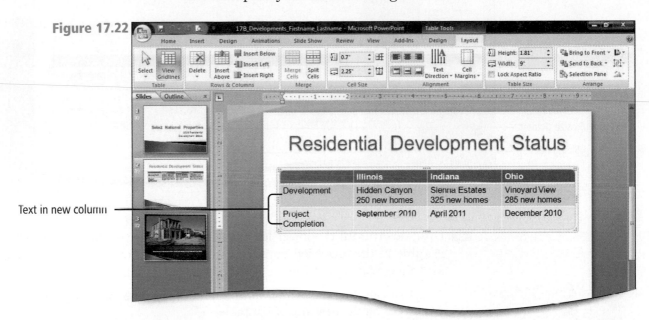

Text in new column ——

4 With the insertion point positioned in the third row, on the **Layout tab**, in the **Rows & Columns group**, click the **Insert Above** button to insert a new third row. In the first cell type **Percent Sold** and then press [Tab]. Type the remaining three entries, pressing [Tab] to move from cell to cell: **75%** and **50%** and **65%**

More Knowledge — Deleting Rows and Columns

To delete a row or column from a table, click in the row or column that you want to delete. Click the Layout tab, and then in the Rows & Columns group, click Delete. In the displayed list, click Delete Columns or Delete Rows.

5 At the center of the lower border surrounding the table, point to the four dots—the sizing handle—to display the ⬍ pointer, as shown in Figure 17.23.

Figure 17.23

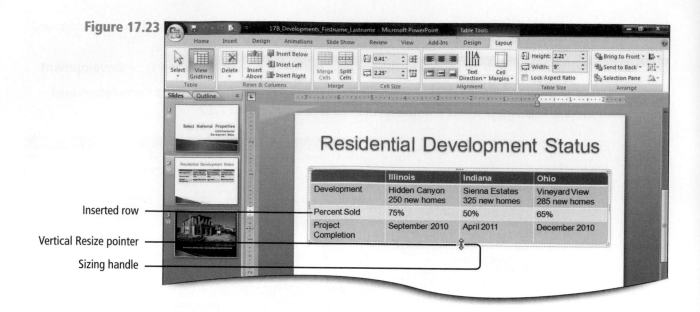

Inserted row ——————

Vertical Resize pointer ——————

Sizing handle ——————

6 Drag down until the lower left corner of the table outline touches the graphic in the lower left corner of the slide as shown in Figure 17.24, and then release the mouse button to size the table.

> When you drag the pointer down, an outline of the table displays, indicating the new size of the table.

Figure 17.24

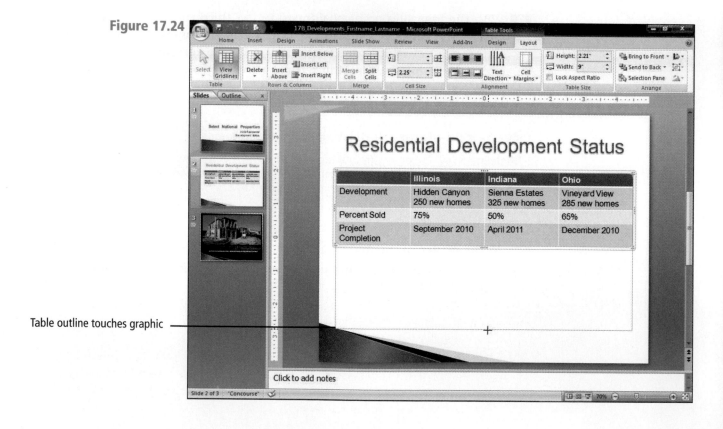

Table outline touches graphic ——————

Click in the first cell of the table. On the **Layout tab**, in the **Cell Size group**, click the **Distribute Rows** ⊞ button.

> The Distribute Rows command adjusts the height of the rows in the table so that they are equal.

8 On the **Layout tab**, in the **Table group**, click **Select**, and then click **Select Table**. In the **Alignment group**, click the **Center** button ≣, and then click the **Center Vertically** button ≣.

> All of the text in the table is centered horizontally and vertically within the cells.

9 Compare your table with Figure 17.25, and then **Save** 🖫 your presentation.

Figure 17.25

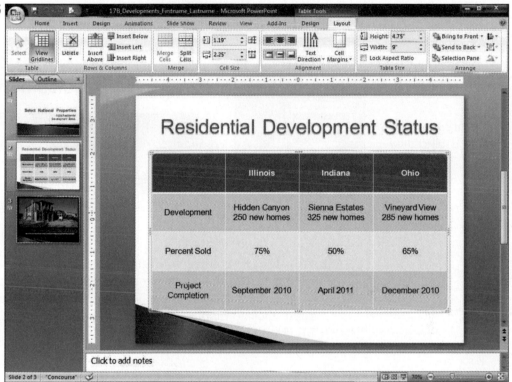

Activity 17.11 Modifying a Table Design

You can modify the design of a table by applying a **table style**. A table style formats the entire table so that it is consistent with the presentation theme. There are color categories within the table styles—Best Match for Document, Light, Medium, and Dark.

1 Click in any cell in the table. In the **Table Tools**, click the **Design tab**, and then in the **Table Styles group**, click the **More** button ⊽. In the displayed **Table Styles gallery**, point to several of the styles to view the Live Preview of the style.

2 Under **Best Match for Document**, click the second button— **Themed Style 1 – Accent 1**—to apply the style to the table.

3 On the **Design tab**, in the **Table Style Options group**, clear the **Banded Rows** check box. Notice that each row except the header row displays in the same color.

> The check boxes in the Table Style Options group control where Table Style formatting is applied.

4 Select the **Banded Rows** check box.

5 Move the pointer outside of the table so that is positioned to the left of the first row in the table to display the ➡ pointer, as shown in Figure 17.26.

Figure 17.26

Right-pointing Row Select arrow

6 With the ➡ pointer pointing to the first row in the table, click the mouse button to select the entire row so that you can apply formatting to the selection. Move the pointer into the selected row, and then right-click to display the Mini toolbar and shortcut menu. On the Mini toolbar, change the **Font Size** to **28**.

More Knowledge — Selecting Columns

To select an entire column, position the pointer above the column that you want to select to display the ⬇ pointer, and then click to select the column.

---

7 Verify that the first row is still selected. Click the **Design tab**, and then in the **Table Styles group**, click the **Effects** button ⬜▾. Point to **Cell Bevel**, and then under **Bevel**, click the first bevel—**Circle**.

> The Bevel effect is applied to the first row in the table.

8 Click in a blank area of the slide, and then compare your slide with Figure 17.27. **Save** ⬜ the presentation.

Figure 17.27

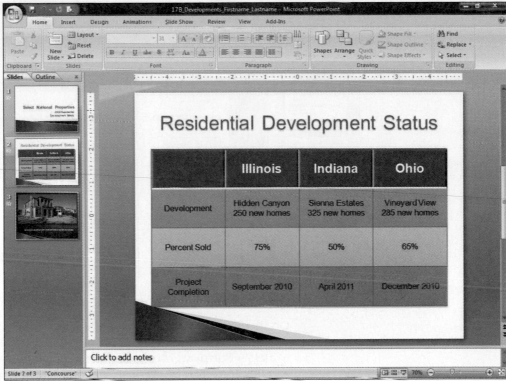

Objective 4
Create and Modify Charts

A *chart* is a graphic representation of numeric data. A chart is usually easier to understand than a table of numbers. Commonly used chart types include bar and column charts, pie charts, and line charts. A chart that you create in PowerPoint is stored in an Excel worksheet that is incorporated into the PowerPoint file.

Activity 17.12 Creating a Column Chart and Applying a Chart Style

A *column chart* is useful for illustrating comparisons among related numbers. In this activity, you will create a column chart that compares the quarterly 2009 revenue generated by the Residential Development Sector of Select National Properties.

1 Display **Slide 3**, and then add a **New Slide** with the **Title and Content** layout. In the title placeholder, type **2009 Revenue** and then **Center** the title.

2 In the content placeholder, click the **Insert Chart** button to display the **Insert Chart** dialog box. In the dialog box, scroll down to view the types of charts that you can insert in your presentation, and then on the left side of the dialog box, if necessary, click Column.

3 Point to the first chart to display the ScreenTip *Clustered Column*, and then click. Compare your screen with Figure 17.28.

Figure 17.28

Clustered Column chart

▣ Click **OK**, and then compare your screen with Figure 17.29.

On the left side of your screen, the PowerPoint window displays a column chart. On the right side of your screen, a Microsoft Office Excel worksheet displays containing vertical columns and horizontal rows. A cell is identified by the intersecting column letter and row number, which forms the *cell reference*.

The worksheet contains sample data in a data range outlined in blue, from which the chart in the PowerPoint window is generated. You can include additional data by dragging the lower right corner of the data range, and you can replace the sample data to update the chart. The column headings—*Series 1*, *Series 2*, and *Series 3* display in the chart *legend* and the row headings—*Category 1*, *Category 2*, *Category 3*, and *Category 4*—display as *category labels*. The legend identifies the patterns or colors that are assigned to the categories in the chart. The category labels display along the bottom of the chart to identify the categories of data.

Figure 17.29

Legend data

Category label data

Excel window with
sample data

PowerPoint window
with sample chart

Category labels

Legend

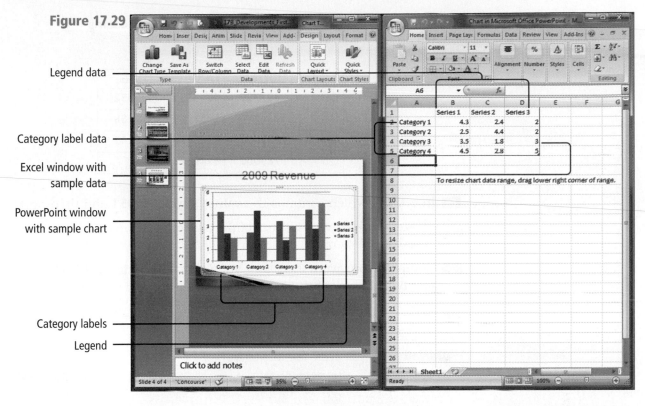

5 In the Excel window, click in cell **B1**, which contains the text *Series 1*. Type **Illinois** and then press Tab to move to cell **C1**.

> The legend in the PowerPoint chart is updated to reflect the change in the Excel worksheet.

6 In cell **C1**, which contains the text *Series 2*, type **Indiana** and then press Tab to move to cell **D1**, which contains the text *Series 3*. Type **Ohio** and then press Tab. Notice that cell **A2**, which contains the text *Category 1*, is selected. Compare your screen with Figure 17.30.

> The blue box outlining the range of cells defines the area in which you are entering data. When you press Tab in the rightmost cell, the first cell in the next row becomes the active cell.

Figure 17.30

Column headings

Cell A2 selected

Legend updated
to reflect Excel data

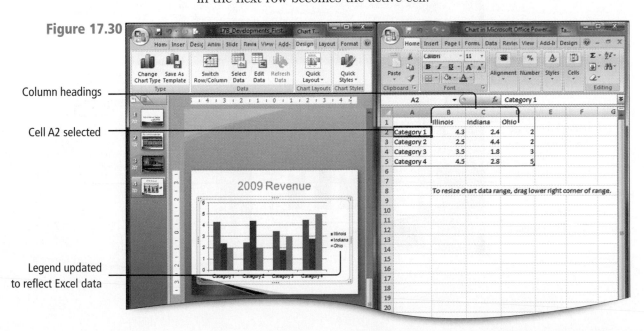

7 Beginning in cell **A2**, type the following data, pressing [Tab] to move from cell to cell.

	Illinois	Indiana	Ohio
Qtr 1	857300	453228	639852
Qtr 2	1235750	563214	741258
Qtr 3	987653	852147	632145
Qtr 4	789000	674982	

8 In cell **D5**, which contains the value *5*, type **753951** and then press [Enter].

Pressing [Enter] in the last cell of the blue outlined area maintains the existing data range.

9 Compare your worksheet and your chart with Figure 17.31. Correct any typing errors by clicking in the cell that you want to change, and then retype the data.

Alert!

Did you press [Tab] after the last entry?

If you pressed [Tab] after entering the data in cell D5, you expanded the chart range. In the Excel window, click Undo.

Each of the twelve cells containing the numeric data that you entered is a ***data point***—a value that originates in a worksheet cell. Each data point is represented in the chart by a ***data marker***—a column, bar, area, dot, pie slice, or other symbol in a chart that represents a single data point. Related data points form a ***data series***; for example, there is a data series for *Illinois*, *Indiana*, and *Ohio*. Each data series has a unique color or pattern represented in the chart legend.

Figure 17.31

Outlined area does not include Row 6

Data markers (columns) represent each data point

Data entered in worksheet

Pattern for each data series defined in legend

10 In the **Excel window**, click the **Office** button 🏶 , and then click **Close**.

You are not prompted to save the Excel worksheet because the work-sheet data is a part of the PowerPoint presentation. When you save the presentation, the Excel data is saved with it.

More Knowledge — Editing the Chart Data After Closing Excel

You can redisplay the Excel worksheet and make changes to the data after you have closed Excel. In PowerPoint, click the chart to select it, and then on the Design tab in the Data group, click Edit Data to redisplay the Excel worksheet.

---

11 If necessary, click on the chart so that it is selected. In the **Chart Tools**, click the **Design tab**, and then in the **Chart Styles group**, click the **More** button ⯆ .

12 In the displayed **Chart Styles gallery**, notice that the chart styles are numbered sequentially and ScreenTips display the style numbers. Click **Style 20** to apply the style to the chart.

13 **Save** 🖫 your presentation.

Activity 17.13 Deleting Chart Data and Changing the Chart Type

To analyze and compare annual data over a three-year period, an additional chart must be inserted. Recall that there are a number of different types of charts that you can insert in a PowerPoint presentation. After you create a chart, you can easily change the chart type. In this activity, you will create a column chart and then change it to a line chart.

1 With **Slide 4** displayed, add a **New Slide** with the **Title and Content** layout. In the title placeholder, type **Three-Year Projection** and then **Center** 🗒 the title.

2 In the content placeholder, click the **Insert Chart** button 📊 . In the displayed **Insert Chart** dialog box, click the first **Column** chart—**Clustered Column**—and then click **OK**.

3 In the displayed Excel worksheet, click in cell **B1**, which contains the text *Series 1*. Type **Illinois** and then press `Tab`. Type **Indiana** and then press `Tab`. Type **Ohio** and then press `Tab`.

4 Beginning in cell **A2**, type the following data, pressing `Tab` to move from cell to cell. If you make any typing errors, click in the cell that you want to change, and then retype the data.

	Illinois	Indiana	Ohio
2009	3156951	4238714	2289746
2010	3786521	4095372	2589674
2011	3569782	3679850	3226915

5 In the Excel window, position the pointer over **row heading 5** so that the ➡ pointer displays as shown in Figure 17.32.

Figure 17.32

Column headings

Years

Select Row pointer

6 With the ➡ pointer displayed, click the *right* mouse button to select the row and display the shortcut menu as shown in Figure 17.33.

Figure 17.33

Selected row

Shortcut menu

7 From the shortcut menu, click **Delete** to delete the extra row from the worksheet.

> The data in the worksheet contains four columns and four rows and the blue outline defining the chart data range is resized. You must delete columns and rows that you do not want to include in the chart. You can add additional rows and columns by typing column and row headings and then entering additional data. When data is typed in cells adjacent to the chart range, the range is resized to include the new data.

More Knowledge — Deleting Columns

To delete a worksheet column, position the pointer over the column letter that you want to select so that the ↓ pointer displays. Right-click to select the column and display the shortcut menu. Click Delete.

8 **Close** ⊠ the Excel window.

9 If necessary, select the chart, and then in the **Chart Tools**, click the **Design tab**. In the **Type group**, click **Change Chart Type**. Under **Line**, click the fourth chart type—**Line with Markers**—and then click **OK**.

> The column chart is converted to a *line chart*. A line chart is ideal for this data because line charts show trends over time.

10 In the **Chart Styles group**, click the **More** button ⊽. In the displayed **Chart Styles gallery**, click **Style 26**, and then compare your slide with Figure 17.34.

Figure 17.34

11 **Save** 🖫 your presentation.

Activity 17.14 Animating a Chart

1 Display **Slide 4**, and then click the column chart to select it.

2 Click the **Animations tab**, and then in the **Animations group**, click the **Animate arrow** to display the Animate list as shown in Figure 17.35.

Figure 17.35

Animate arrow

Animate list

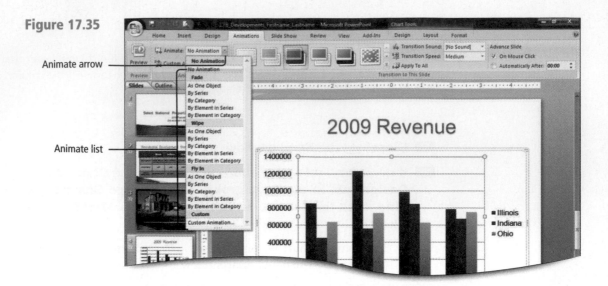

3 Point to several of the **Animate** options to view the Live Preview of the animation effects. Then, under **Wipe**, click **By Category**.

In this chart, the *By Category* option animates the column data markers by *Qtr*.

4 Click the **Slide Show tab**. In the **Start Slide Show group**, click **From Current Slide** to view the animation on Slide 4. Press Spacebar to display the legend and labels. Press Spacebar again to display the *Qtr 1* data.

5 Continue to press Spacebar to advance through the remaining animation effects. After the animations for Slide 4 are complete, press Esc to end the slide show and return to the presentation.

6 Create a **Header & Footer** for the **Notes and Handouts**. Include the **Date and time updated automatically**, the **Page number**, and a **Footer** with the file name **17B_Developments_Firstname_Lastname**

7 Check your *Chapter Assignment Sheet* or *Course Syllabus* or consult your instructor to determine if you are to submit your assignments on paper or electronically. To submit electronically, go to Step 8, and then follow the instructions provided by your instructor.

8 Display your presentation in **Print Preview**, and then print **Handouts (6 Slides Per Page)**.

9 **Save** and then **Close** your presentation.

End **You have completed Project 17B** ━━━━━━

There's More You Can Do!

Close PowerPoint and any other open windows. Display the Start menu, click Computer, and then navigate to the student files that accompany this text-book. In the folder **02_theres_more_you_can_do**, locate and open the folder for this chapter. Open and print the instructions for this project, which are provided to you in Adobe PDF format.

Try IT!—Compress Pictures

In this Try It! exercise, you will compress pictures in a presentation in order to reduce file size.

Content-Based Assessments

Summary

In this chapter, you formatted a presentation by applying background styles, inserting pictures on slide backgrounds, and by changing the theme fonts. You enhanced your presentation by applying animation effects and by changing effect and timing options. You practiced creating tables to present information in an organized manner and you used charts to visually represent data.

Key Terms

Content-Based Assessments

Matching

Match each term in the second column with its correct definition in the first column. Write the letter of the term on the blank line in front of the correct definition.

_____ **1.** A slide background fill variation that combines theme colors in different intensities.

_____ **2.** A theme that determines the font applied to two types of slide text—headings and body.

_____ **3.** The font applied to slide titles.

_____ **4.** The font applied to all slide text except titles.

_____ **5.** Effects used to introduce individual slide elements so that the slide can progress one element at a time.

_____ **6.** Animations that bring a slide element onto the screen.

_____ **7.** A list that indicates the animation effects applied to slide items.

_____ **8.** Animation options that include changing the direction of an effect and playing a sound when an animation takes place.

_____ **9.** A format for information that organizes and presents text and data in columns and rows.

_____ **10.** The intersection of a column and row.

_____ **11.** Formatting applied to an entire table so that it is consistent with the presentation theme.

_____ **12.** A graphic representation of numeric data.

_____ **13.** A type of chart used to compare data.

_____ **14.** A combination of the column letter and row number identifying a cell.

_____ **15.** A chart element that identifies the patterns or colors that are assigned to the categories in the chart.

A Animation effects

B Background style

C Body font

D Cell

E Cell reference

F Chart

G Column chart

H Custom animation list

I Effect options

J Entrance effects

K Font theme

L Headings font

M Legend

N Table

O Table style

Content-Based Assessments

Fill in the Blank

Write the correct word in the space provided.

1. To help an audience understand numeric data and trends, insert a
   _____ or a _____ on a slide.

2. The charts most commonly used in PowerPoint presentations are
   _____, _____, _____, and _____.

3. When the background graphics interfere with slide content, you can
   _____ the background graphics.

4. When you insert a picture on a slide background, it is a good idea
   to choose a picture that has a _____ area in which you can
   overlay a text box or title.

5. When you apply a new font theme to the presentation, the text on every
   slide is updated with the new _____ and _____ fonts.

6. Animation effects focus the audience's attention, providing the speaker
   with an opportunity to emphasize an important point using the slide
   element as an effective _____ _____.

7. The most efficient method of animating a SmartArt graphic is to use
   one of the choices in the _____ _____.

8. When you are delivering a presentation, to view a list of the slides in
   the presentation, display the shortcut menu, and then point to
   _____ _____ _____.

9. You can modify the layout of a table by inserting or deleting
   _____ and _____.

10. The document matching styles provide the best choices for coordi-
    nating the table with the presentation _____.

11. When you create a chart in PowerPoint, the chart data is stored in a
    _____ worksheet.

12. In a chart, categories of data are identified by _____
    _____.

13. A chart value that originates in a worksheet cell is a _____
    _____.

14. A group of related data points is a _____ _____.

15. A column, bar, area, dot, pie slice, or other symbol in a chart that
    represents a single data point is a _____ _____.

Content-Based Assessments

Project 17C — Seniors

In this project, you will apply the skills you practiced from the Objectives in Project 17A.

Objectives: 1. *Customize Slide Backgrounds and Themes;* **2.** *Animate a Slide Show.*

In the following Skills Review, you will edit a presentation created by Marla Rodriguez, the Marketing Director for Select National Properties, which describes a new real estate development in Illinois. Your completed presentation will look similar to the one shown in Figure 17.36.

For Project 17C, you will need the following files:

p17C_Seniors
p17C_Walkway

You will save your presentation as
17C_Seniors_Firstname_Lastname

Figure 17.36

(Project 17C–Seniors continues on the next page)

Content-Based Assessments

chapterseventeen Skills Review

(Project 17C–Seniors continued)

1. **Start** PowerPoint. From your student files, **Open** the file **p17C_Seniors**. From the **Office** menu, click **Save As**, and then navigate to your **PowerPoint Chapter 17** folder. In the **File name** box, type **17C_Seniors_ Firstname_Lastname** and then click **Save** to save your presentation.

2. Click the **Design tab**, and then in the **Themes group**, click the **More** button to display the **Themes gallery**. Under **Built-In**, in the first row, click **Civic**. In the **Themes group**, click the **Colors** button, and then click **Office** to change the theme color for the entire presentation. In the **Background group**, click the **Background Styles** button to display the **Background Styles gallery**. In the second row, right-click **Style 7**. From the displayed shortcut menu, click **Apply to Selected Slides** to apply the style to **Slide 1**.

3. Display **Slide 2**. On the **Design tab**, in the **Background group**, click the **Background Styles** button to display the **Background Styles gallery**. In the last row, right-click **Style 11**, and then click **Apply to Selected Slides** to apply the style to **Slide 2**.

4. With **Slide 2** displayed, click the **Home tab**. In the **Slides group**, click the **New Slide arrow**, and then click the **Title Only** layout to create a new Slide 3. In the title placeholder, type **Take a Stroll Around the Lake** Click the **Design tab**, and then in the **Background group**, click the **Hide Background Graphics** check box so that the background graphics do not display.

5. In the **Background group**, click the **Background Styles** button, and then click **Format Background**. In the displayed **Format Background** dialog box, if necessary, on the left side of the dialog box, click **Fill**. On the right side of the dialog box,

under **Fill**, click the **Picture or texture fill** option button.

6. Under **Insert from**, click the **File** button. In the displayed **Insert Picture** dialog box, navigate to the location where your student files are located, and then click **p17C_Walkway**. Click **Insert**, and then under **Stretch options**, if necessary, change the **Left**, **Right**, **Top** and **Bottom Offsets** to **0%** and then click **Close** to close the **Format Background** dialog box.

7. If necessary, click in the title placeholder. Click the **Format tab**, and then in the **Shape Styles group**, click the **Shape Fill** button. In the last row, click the fourth color—**Dark Blue, Text 2, Darker 50%** so that the text displays against the background.

8. Point to the outer edge of the placeholder to display the ⬚ pointer, and then drag the placeholder down so that its bottom edge aligns with the bottom of the slide. Point to the center, right sizing handle to display the ↔ pointer. Drag to the right so that the right side of the placeholder touches the right edge of the slide. Point to the center, left sizing handle to display the ↔ pointer. Drag to the left so that the left side of the placeholder touches the left edge of the slide.

9. Display **Slide 5**, and then select the subtitle text. On the **Home tab**, click the **Font Color button arrow**. Under **Theme Colors**, in the first row, click the seventh color—**Olive Green, Accent 3**. Click the **Design tab**. In the **Background group**, click the **Background Styles** button, and then click **Format Background**. In the **Format Background** dialog box, if necessary, click the **Solid fill** option button, and then click the **Color** button. Under

(Project 17C–Seniors continues on the next page)

Content-Based Assessments

(Project 17C–Seniors continued)

Theme Colors, in the last row, click the fourth color—**Dark Blue, Text 2, Darker 50%**. Click **Close**.

10. Display **Slide 1**. On the **Design tab**, in the **Themes group**, click the **Fonts** button. Click the first font theme—**Office**—and then scroll through the slides in the presentation, noticing that the font changes have been applied to every slide.

11. Click the **Animations tab**, and then in the **Transition to This Slide group**, click the **More** button. Under **Wipes**, click **Box Out**. Click the **Transition Speed arrow**, and then click **Medium**. Click the **Apply To All** button.

12. Display **Slide 2**, and then click the bulleted list placeholder. In the **Animations group**, click the **Custom Animation** button. At the top of the displayed **Custom Animation** task pane, click the **Add Effect** button, and then point to **Entrance**. Click **More Effects** to display the **Add Entrance Effect** dialog box.

13. At the bottom of the **Add Entrance Effect** dialog box, if necessary, select the Preview Effect check box. Under **Basic**, click **Blinds**, and then click **OK**. In the **Custom Animation** list, click the **item 1 arrow**, and then click **Effect Options** to display the **Blinds** dialog box.

14. In the **Blinds** dialog box, click the **Effect tab**. Under **Enhancements**, click the **After animation arrow**. In the row of colors, click the **fifth color**, and then click **OK** to apply the effect option.

15. Select the picture. In the **Custom Animation** task pane, click the **Add Effect** button, point to **Entrance**, and then click **More Effects**. In the displayed **Add Entrance Effect** dialog box, under

Basic, click **Dissolve In**, and then click **OK**.

16. Near the top of the **Custom Animation** task pane, under **Modify: Dissolve In**, click the **Start arrow**, and then click **After Previous** to display the picture immediately after the last bulleted item displays. In the **Custom Animation** task pane, under **Modify: Dissolve In**, click the **Speed arrow**, and then click **Fast**.

17. Display **Slide 3**, and then click in the title placeholder. In the **Custom Animation** task pane, click **Add Effect**, and then point to **Entrance**. Click **More Effects**. Under **Basic**, click **Fly In**, and then click **OK**. In the **Custom Animation task pane**, click the **Start arrow**, and then click **After Previous** to display the title immediately after the slide transition. If necessary, click the **Direction arrow**, and then click **From Bottom**. **Close** the task pane.

18. Display **Slide 4**, and then select the **SmartArt graphic**. On the **Animations tab**, in the **Animations group**, click the **Animate arrow** to display the Animate list. Under **Wipe**, click **By level at once**.

19. Click the **Slide Show tab**. In the **Start Slide Show group**, click **From Beginning**, and then view your presentation, clicking the mouse button to advance through the slides. Notice the animation that is applied to each slide, and then when the black slide displays, click the mouse button one more time to display the presentation in Normal view.

20. Create a **Header & Footer** for the **Notes and Handouts**. Include only the **Date and time updated automatically**, the **Page number**, and a **Footer** with the file name 17C_Seniors_Firstname_Lastname

(Project 17C–Seniors continues on the next page)

Content-Based Assessments

Skills Review

(Project 17C–Seniors continued)

21. Check your *Chapter Assignment Sheet* or *Course Syllabus* or consult your instructor to determine if you are to submit your assignments on paper or electronically. To submit electronically, go to Step 23, and then follow the instructions provided by your instructor.

22. Display your presentation in **Print Preview**, and then print **Handouts (6 Slides Per Page)**.

23. **Save** the changes to your presentation, and then **Close** the presentation.

 You have completed Project 17C

Content-Based Assessments

Skills Review

Project 17D — Commercial Developments

In this project, you will apply the skills you practiced from the Objectives in Project 17B.

Objectives: 3*. Create and Modify Tables;* **4***. Create and Modify Charts.*

In the following Skills Review, you will add a table and two charts to a presentation that Shaun Walker, President of Select National Properties, is creating to apprise investors of the status of several new commercial developments. Your completed presentation will look similar to the one shown in Figure 17.37.

For Project 17D, you will need the following file:

p17D_Commercial_Developments

You will save your presentation as
17D_Commercial_Developments_Firstname_Lastname

Figure 17.37

(Project 17D–Commercial Developments continues on the next page)

Content-Based Assessments

(Project 17D–Commercial Developments continued)

1. **Start** PowerPoint and from your student files, **Open p17D_Commercial_ Developments**. **Save** the presentation in your **PowerPoint Chapter 17** folder as 17D_Commercial_Developments_Firstname_ Lastname

2. With **Slide 1** displayed, on the **Home tab**, in the **Slides group**, click the **New Slide** button to insert a slide with the **Title and Content** layout. In the title placeholder, type **Commercial Development Status** and then **Center** the title.

3. In the content placeholder, click the **Insert Table** button. In the **Insert Table** dialog box, in the **Number of columns** box, type **4** and then press Tab. In the **Number of rows** box, type **2**. Click **OK** to create a table with four columns and two rows.

4. Click in the second cell of the first row— the first cell will remain blank. Type **Illinois** and then press Tab. With the insertion point positioned in the third cell of the first row, type **New York** and then press Tab. Type **New Jersey** and then press Tab to move the insertion point to the first cell in the second row.

5. With the insertion point positioned in the first cell of the second row, type **Project** and then press Tab. Type **Select Commercial Properties** and then press Tab. Type **National Developments** and then press Tab. Type **New Jersey Real Estate Division** and then press Tab to insert a new blank row.

6. In the first cell of the third row, type **Expansion Plan** and then press Tab. Type **January 2010** and then press Tab. Type **June 2011** and then press Tab. Type **October 2010**

7. With the insertion point positioned in the third row, click the **Layout tab**. In the

Rows & Columns group, click the **Insert Above** button to insert a new third row. In the first cell of the newly inserted row, type **Percent Occupied** and then press Tab. Type the remaining three entries, pressing Tab to move from cell to cell: **85%, 72%** and **91%**

8. If necessary, on the View tab, in the Show/Hide group, select the Ruler check box so that the Ruler displays. At the center of the lower border surrounding the table, point to the four dots—the sizing handle—to display the ⬍ pointer. Drag down so that the bottom edge of the table is aligned at approximately **3 inches below zero on the vertical ruler**.

9. Click in the first cell of the table. On the **Layout tab**, in the **Cell Size group**, click the **Distribute Rows** button so that the four rows are equal in height. In the **Table group**, click **Select**, and then click **Select Table**. In the **Alignment group**, click the **Center** button, and then click the **Center Vertically** button.

10. In the **Table Tools**, click the **Design tab**, and then in the **Table Styles group**, click the **More** button. Under **Light**, in the second row, click the first style—**Light Style 2**.

11. Move the pointer outside of the table so that is positioned to the left of the first row to display the ➡ pointer. Click so that the entire row is selected. Move the pointer into the selected row, and then right-click to display the Mini toolbar and shortcut menu. On the Mini toolbar, change the **Font Size** to **24**.

12. With the first row still selected, in the **Table Tools** click the **Design tab**. In the **Table Styles group**, click the **Effects**

(Project 17D–Commercial Developments continues on the next page)

Content-Based Assessments

(Project 17D–Commercial Developments continued)

button. Point to **Cell Bevel**, and then under **Bevel**, click the first bevel—**Circle**.

13. Display **Slide 3**, and then insert a **New Slide** with the **Title and Content** layout. In the title placeholder, type **2009 Revenue** and then **Center** the title. In the content placeholder, click the **Insert Chart** button. In the **Insert Chart** dialog box, point to the first chart to display the ScreenTip *Clustered Column*, and then if necessary, select it. Click **OK**.

14. In the Excel window, click in cell **B1**, which contains the text *Series 1*. Type **Illinois** and then press (Tab) to move to cell **C1** containing the text *Series 2*. Type **New York** and then press (Tab) to move to cell **D1**. Type **New Jersey**

15. Click in cell **A2**, and then type the data from the following table, pressing (Tab) to move from cell to cell. Be sure that you press (Enter) after the last entry—*1753840*—not (Tab).

	Illinois	New York	New Jersey
Qtr 1	1657305	1453230	1039855
Qtr 2	1434850	1563360	1141290
Qtr 3	1887640	1852175	1632785
Qtr 4	2286730	1974930	1753840

16. **Close** the Excel window. If necessary, select the chart. In the **Chart Tools**, click the **Design tab**, and then in the **Chart Styles group**, click the **More** button. In the **Chart Styles gallery**, click **Style 26**. On the **Animations tab**, in the **Animations group**, click the **Animate arrow**. In the **Animate list**. Under **Wipe**, click **As One Object**.

17. With **Slide 4** displayed, insert a **New Slide** with the **Title and Content layout**. In the title placeholder, type **Three-Year Projection** and then **Center** the title. In the content placeholder, click the **Insert Chart** button. In the **Create Chart** dialog box, under **Line**, click **Line with Markers**, and then click **OK**.

18. In the Excel worksheet, click in cell **B1**. Type **Illinois** and then press (Tab). Type **New York** and then press (Tab). Type **New Jersey** and then press (Tab).

19. Beginning in cell **A2**, enter the projected revenue for each state and each year as shown in the following table. If you make any typing errors, click in the cell that you want to change, and then retype the data.

	Illinois	New York	New Jersey
2009	4236950	5138726	3289728
2010	4896525	5395318	3589622
2011	5289862	5569857	4026935

20. Position the pointer over **row heading 5** to display the ➡ pointer. Click the right mouse button to select the row. From the shortcut menu, click **Delete** to delete the extra row from the worksheet.

21. **Close** the Excel window. In the **Chart Tools**, click the **Design tab**. In the **Chart Styles group**, click the **More** button. In the **Chart Styles gallery**, click **Style 26**.

22. Create a **Header & Footer** for the **Notes and Handouts**. Include only the **Date and time updated automatically**, the **Page number**, and a **Footer** with the file name 17D_Commercial_Developments_Firstname_Lastname

(Project 17D–Commercial Developments continues on the next page)

Content-Based Assessments

Skills Review

(Project 17D–Commercial Developments continued)

23. Check your *Chapter Assignment Sheet* or *Course Syllabus* or consult your instructor to determine if you are to submit your assignments on paper or electronically. To submit electronically, go to Step 25, and then follow the instructions provided by your instructor.

24. Display your presentation in **Print Preview**, and then print **Handouts (6 Slides Per Page)**.

25. **Save** the changes to your presentation, and then **Close** the presentation.

End You have completed Project 17D

Content-Based Assessments

PowerPoint
chapterseventeen | **Mastering PowerPoint**

Project 17E — Restaurants

In this project, you will apply the skills you practiced from the Objectives in Projects 17A and 17B.

Objectives: 1. *Customize Slide Backgrounds and Themes;* **2**. *Animate a Slide Show;* **3**. *Create and Modify Tables;* **4**. *Create and Modify Charts.*

In the following Mastering PowerPoint project, you will edit a presentation that the president of Select National Properties will make to the National Restaurant Owners Association proposing new restaurant construction in the city of Monroe Heights. Your completed presentation will look similar to Figure 17.38.

For Project 17E, you will need the following files:

New blank PowerPoint presentation
p17E_Tables

You will save your presentation as
17E_Restaurants_Firstname_Lastname

Figure 17.38

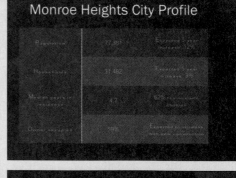

(Project 17E–Restaurants continues on the next page)

Content-Based Assessments

(Project 17E–Restaurants continued)

1. **Start** PowerPoint and begin a new blank presentation. In the title placeholder, type **Presentation to the National Restaurant Owners Association** and then in the subtitle placeholder, type **Select National Properties Save** the presentation in your **PowerPoint Chapter 17** folder as 17E_Restaurants_Firstname_Lastname

2. Apply the **Technic** theme to the presentation, and then change the **Theme Colors** to **Solstice**. Hide the background graphics, and then display the **Format Background** dialog box. Use the **Picture or texture fill option** to insert the **p17E_Tables** picture on the slide background. Verify that the **Stretch options Offsets** are set to **0%**.

3. Click in the title placeholder, and then on the **Format tab**, click the **Shape Fill** button. In the first row of colors, apply the **Brown, Background 2** fill to the title placeholder. In the **Size group**, change the **Height** to **1.5** and the **Width** to **10** and then **Center** the text. Move the title placeholder so that its lower edge aligns with the lower edge of the slide and the left and right edges of the slide and placeholder also align.

4. Click in the subtitle placeholder, and then change the **Shape Fill** color to **Black, Background 1**. Adjust the **Height** to **1.0** and the **Width** to **10** and then **Center** the text and change the **Font Size** to **28**. Drag the subtitle placeholder down so that its lower edge aligns with the top edge of the title placeholder and the left and right edges of the slide and placeholder also align.

5. Insert a **New Slide** with the **Title and Content** layout. Hide the background graphics on this slide.

6. In the title placeholder, type **Monroe Heights City Profile** and then **Center** the title. In the content placeholder, insert a table with **3 columns** and **4 rows**. Type the following table text:

Population	77,381	Expected 5-year increase: 12%
Households	31,482	Expected 5-year increase: 3%
Median years in residence	4.7	62% families with children
Owner occupied	59%	Expected to increase with new construction

7. If necessary, display the Ruler, and then adjust the size of the table so that its lower edge aligns at approximately **3 inches below zero on the vertical ruler**. Select the table, and then **Center** the text horizontally and vertically in the cells. Click **Distribute Rows** so that all of the rows are the same height.

8. Change the table **Design** by changing the **Table Style Options** so that only the **Banded Rows** and **First Column** check boxes are selected. In the **Tables Styles gallery**, under **Dark**, apply **Dark Style 1 – Accent 5**.

9. Add a slide with the **Two Content** layout. In the title placeholder, type **Increased Demand for New Restaurants in Monroe Heights** and then **Center** the title.

10. On **Slide 3**, hide the background graphics. In the placeholder on the left, insert a **SmartArt** graphic. In the **Choose a Smart Graphic** dialog box, click **Pyramid**, click the last pyramid graphic—**Segmented Pyramid**—and then click **OK**.

(Project 17E–Restaurants continues on the next page)

Content-Based Assessments

Mastering PowerPoint

(Project 17E–Restaurants continued)

11. In the top triangle shape, type **Large family base** and then click in the center triangle. Type **Clientele from nearby cities** and then click in the lower left triangle. Type **New theaters** and then click in the lower right triangle. Type **New retail outlets**

12. On the **SmartArt Tools**, click the **Design tab**, and then click **Change Colors**. Under **Colorful**, click the last color set—**Colorful Range – Accent Colors 5 to 6**. In the **SmartArt Styles group**, under **3-D**, apply the fourth effect—**Powder**.

13. In the placeholder on the right, type the following bullet points.

Vibrant economic climate
Growing population
Community loyal to local merchants
Close to major suburbs
Small number of restaurants relative to population

14. Insert a **New Slide** with the **Title and Content** layout. In the title placeholder, type **Current Number of Establishments** and then **Center** the title.

15. In the content placeholder, insert a **Clustered Column** chart. In the **Excel** worksheet, type the following data, deleting extra columns and rows as necessary:

	2008	2009	2010
Retail	28	35	43
Fast Food	8	8	12
Restaurants	10	12	17

16. **Close** Excel, and then apply **Style 3** to the chart. Use the **Animate** list to apply the **Wipe By Category** animation.

17. Apply the **Wipe Down** transition, and then change the **Transition Speed** to **Medium**. Apply the transition setting to all of the slides in the presentation.

18. Display **Slide 3**, and then select the **SmartArt graphic**. Use the **Animate list** to apply the **Fade As One Object** animation. Click the bulleted list placeholder, and then use the **Custom Animation** task pane to apply the **Blinds Entrance Effect**. View the slide show from the beginning.

19. Create a **Header & Footer** for the **Notes and Handouts**. Include only the **Date and time updated automatically**, the **Page number**, and a **Footer** with the file name **17E_Restaurants_Firstname_Lastname**

20. Check your *Chapter Assignment Sheet* or *Course Syllabus* or consult your instructor to determine if you are to submit your assignments on paper or electronically. To submit electronically, go to Step 22, and then follow the instructions provided by your instructor.

21. Display your presentation in **Print Preview**, and then print **Handouts (4 Slides Per Page)**.

22. **Save** the changes to your presentation, and then **Close** the presentation.

End **You have completed Project 17E**

Content-Based Assessments

Mastering PowerPoint

Project 17F—Town Centers

In this project, you will apply the skills you practiced from the Objectives in Projects 17A and 17B.

Objectives: 1. *Customize Slide Backgrounds and Themes;* **2**. *Animate a Slide Show;* **4**. *Create and Modify Charts.*

In the following Mastering PowerPoint Assessment, you will edit a presentation that Randall Thomas, Select National Properties Chief Executive Officer, has created to explain the growth of mixed-use town centers in large cities. Your completed presentation will look similar to Figure 17.39.

For Project 17F, you will need the following files:

New blank PowerPoint presentation
p17F_Definition

You will save your presentation as
17F_Town_Centers_Firstname_Lastname

Figure 17.39

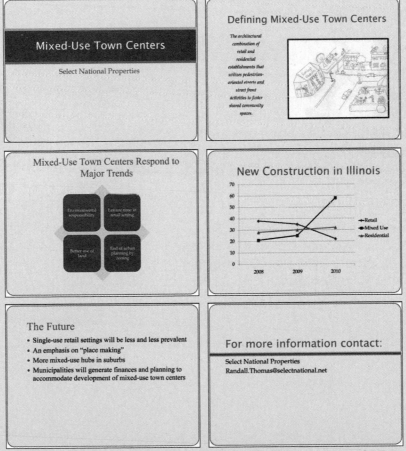

(Project 17F–Town Centers continues on the next page)

Content-Based Assessments

(Project 17F–Town Centers continued)

1. **Start** PowerPoint and begin a new blank presentation. In the title placeholder, type **Mixed-Use Town Centers** In the subtitle placeholder, type **Select National Properties** and then **Save** the file in your **PowerPoint Chapter 17** folder as **17F_Town_Centers_Firstname_Lastname**

2. Apply the **Equity** theme to the presentation, and then apply **Background Style 2**. Apply the **Apex Fonts Theme** which consists of the *Lucida Sans* and *Book Antiqua* fonts.

3. From your student files, insert all of the slides from the **p17F_Definition** file. (*Hint:* click the **New Slide arrow**, and then click **Reuse Slides**). Display **Slide 2**, and then click in the text on the left side of the slide. Apply the **Compress Entrance Effect. Start** the effect **After Previous**, and change the **Speed** to **Medium**.

4. With **Slide 2** still displayed, move the picture so that its lower edge aligns at **2.5 inches below zero**.

5. Display **Slide 3**. Select the SmartArt graphic, and then use the **Animate** list to apply the **Wipe**, **One by one** animation. Apply the **Wipe Left** transition, and then set the **Transition Speed** to **Fast**. Apply the transition settings to all of the slides in the presentation.

6. With **Slide 3** still displayed, insert a **New Slide** with the **Title and Content** layout. In the title placeholder, type **New Construction in Illinois** and then **Center** the title. In the content placeholder, insert a **Line with**

Markers chart, and then enter the following data in the **Excel** worksheet:

	Retail	Mixed Use	Residential
2008	38	21	28
2009	35	25	30
2010	22	58	32

7. Delete the unused row, and then **Close** Excel. Apply **Chart Style 18**, and then view the slide show from the beginning of the presentation.

8. Create a **Header & Footer** for the **Notes and Handouts**. Include only the **Date and time updated automatically**, the **Page number**, and a **Footer** with the file name **17F_Town_Centers_Firstname_Lastname**

9. Check your *Chapter Assignment Sheet* or *Course Syllabus* or consult your instructor to determine if you are to submit your assignments on paper or electronically. To submit electronically, go to Step 11, and then follow the instructions provided by your instructor.

10. Display your presentation in **Print Preview**, and then print **Handouts (6 Slides Per Page)**.

11. **Save** the changes to your presentation, and then **Close** the presentation.

End **You have completed Project 17F**

Content-Based Assessments

Mastering PowerPoint

Project 17G—Clients

In this project, you will apply the skills you practiced from all the Objectives in Projects 17A and 17B.

Objectives: 1. *Customize Slide Backgrounds and Themes;* **2**. *Animate a Slide Show;* **3**. *Create and Modify Tables;* **4**. *Create and Modify Charts.*

In the following Mastering PowerPoint Assessment, you will edit a presentation that Randall Thomas, Select National Properties Chief Executive Officer will present to a group of prospective clients. Your completed presentation will look similar to Figure 17.40.

For Project 17G, you will need the following files:

p17G_Clients
p17G_Building

You will save your presentation as
17G_Clients_Firstname_Lastname

Figure 17.40

(Project 17G–Clients continues on the next page)

(Project 17G–Clients continued)

1. **Start** PowerPoint. From your student files, **Open** the file **p17G_Clients. Save** the file in your **PowerPoint Chapter 17** folder as **17G_Clients_Firstname_Lastname**

2. Apply **Background Style 8** to all of the slides in the presentation, and then change the **Fonts Theme** to **Equity**. Under **Wipes**, apply the **Split Vertical Out** transition to all of the slides in the presentation.

3. Display **Slide 3**, and then in the content placeholder, insert a **SmartArt** graphic. In the **Choose a SmartArt Graphic** dialog box, insert the **Process** type graphic—**Funnel**. On the **Design tab**, in the **Create Graphic group**, click the **Text Pane** button to display the text pane. Type the following text in each of the four bullet points:

    Integrity
    Trust
    Loyalty
    Success

4. **Close** the text pane. Apply the **Fade As One Object** animation to the SmartArt graphic.

5. With **Slide 3** displayed, insert a **New Slide** with the **Title Slide** layout. In the title placeholder, type **Quality** and then in the subtitle placeholder, type **Large enough to meet all your needs; small enough to give your project the attention it deserves. Center** the title and subtitle text.

6. With **Slide 4** still displayed, hide the background graphics, and then on the **Background**, insert a picture from your student files—**p17G_Building**. Before closing the **Format Background** dialog box, verify that the **Stretch options Offsets** are set to **0%**.

7. Drag the title placeholder up so that the top edge of the placeholder aligns with the top edge of the slide and the word *Quality* is centered at the intersection of the two buildings. Select the word *Quality*, and then change the **Font Color** to **Black, Background 1**.

8. Select the subtitle placeholder, and then change the **Shape Fill** color to **Black, Background 1**. Size the placeholder so that it extends from the left edge to the right edge of the slide, and then drag the placeholder down so that its lower edge aligns with the lower edge of the slide.

9. Display **Slide 6**, and then in the content placeholder, insert a **Clustered Column** chart. In the **Excel** worksheet, enter the following data:

	2009	2010	2011
Commercial	318	402	435
Housing	122	257	305
Non-profit	216	268	322

10. Delete the unused row in the worksheet, and then **Close** Excel. Apply chart **Style 42**, and then from the **Animate** list, apply the **Fade By Category** animation.

(Project 17G–Clients continues on the next page)

Content-Based Assessments

Mastering PowerPoint

(Project 17G–Clients continued)

11. Display **Slide 7**, and then in the content placeholder, insert a **Table** with **3 columns** and **4 rows**. Type the following text in the table:

Service	Number	Location
Development	Over 15 million square feet	Throughout Midwest
Property Management	Over 40 properties	Illinois and Indiana
Current Construction	5 million square feet	Illinois and Maine

12. If necessary, display the Ruler. Size the table so that its lower edge aligns at approximately **1 inch below zero on the vertical ruler**. Distribute the rows, and then **Center** the text horizontally and vertically. In the **Tables Styles gallery**, apply **Dark Style 1 – Accent 1**. Select the entire table, and then change the **Font Size** to **28**. With the table still selected, apply the **Circle, Cell Bevel** effect.

13. Display **Slide 8**, and then select the title placeholder. Display the **Custom Animation** task pane, and then apply the **Blinds Entrance Effect. Start** the animation **After Previous**, and then change the **Speed** to **Fast**. Apply the same animation effect and settings to the subtitle, and then view the slide show from the beginning.

14. Create a **Header & Footer** for the **Notes and Handouts**. Include only the **Date and time updated automatically**, the **Page number**, and a **Footer** with the file name 17G_Clients_ Firstname_Lastname

15. Check your *Chapter Assignment Sheet* or *Course Syllabus* or consult your instructor to determine if you are to submit your assignments on paper or electronically. To submit electronically, go to Step 17, and then follow the instructions provided by your instructor.

16. Display your presentation in **Print Preview**, and then print **Handouts (4 Slides Per Page)**.

17. **Save** the changes to your presentation, and then **Close** the presentation.

End **You have completed Project 17G** ——————————————————

Content-Based Assessments

Mastering PowerPoint

Project 17H — *GO!* Fix It

In this project, you will apply the skills you practiced from the Objectives in Projects 17A and 17B.

For Project 17H, you will need the following files:

p17H_Kid_Fun_Nursery_School
p17H_Vacant_Lot

**You will save your presentation as
17H_Kid_Fun_Nursery_School_Firstname_Lastname**

In this project, you will edit a presentation that is being made to the Kid Fun Nursery School board of directors. Select National Properties is bidding on the development and construction of a new nursery school and two sites are under consideration. SNP had its architects develop energy-efficient buildings. From your student files, open the file **p17H_Kid_Fun_Nursery_School**, and then save the file in your chapter folder as **17H_Kid_Fun_Nursery_School_Firstname_Lastname**

This presentation contains errors that you must find and correct. Read and examine the document, and then edit to correct the errors that you find. Types of errors could include:

- Spelling, grammar, punctuation, and usage errors such as text case, subject-verb agreement, and meaning.

- Content errors such as missing or incorrect data, text, pictures, hyperlinks, or other objects.

- Font and paragraph formatting and positioning errors such as fonts, font styles, font sizing, alignment, text color, indent levels, and bullet features.

- Slide layout, orientation, design themes, backgrounds, animation and transition errors.

- Image or object formatting and positioning errors on tables, illustrations, links, text, and media clips relating to color, lines, size, scale, styles, layout, positioning, and control.

- Page setup errors on slides, handouts, notes and outlines such as margins, orientation, layout, alignment, headers and footers, date and time, color, grayscale, black and white, and sizing.

(Project 17H–*GO!* Fix It continues on the next page)

Content-Based Assessments

(Project 17H–*GO!* Fix It continued)

To complete the project, you should:

- Apply the **Wipe Left** transition to all of the slides in the presentation.

- On **Slide 2**, add and format the background with the picture **p17H_ Vacant_Lot** from your student files, hide the background graphics, and set all of the **Stretch options offsets** to **0**.

- On **Slide 6**, format the sun graphic with **Colored Outline, Accent 2** shape style. Animate the graphic using the entrance effect **Exciting Swivel** with **Very Slow speed**.

- Create a footer for the **Notes and Handouts**. Include only the **Date and time updated automatically**, the page number, and a footer with your name included. Submit as directed, using 6 slides per page.

End You have completed Project 17H ————————————

Outcomes-Based Assessments

Rubric

The following outcomes-based assessments are *open-ended assessments*. That is, there is no specific correct result; your result will depend on your approach to the information provided. Make *professional Quality* your goal. Use the following scoring rubric to guide you in *how* to approach the problem and then to evaluate *how well* your approach solves the problem.

The *criteria*—Software Mastery, Content, Format and Layout, and Process—represent the knowledge and skills you have gained that you can apply to solving the problem. The *levels of performance*—Professional Quality, Approaching Professional Quality, or Needs Quality Improvements—help you and your instructor evaluate your result.

	Your completed project is of Professional Quality if you:	Your completed project is Approaching Professional Quality if you:	Your completed project Needs Quality Improvements if you:
1-Software Mastery	Choose and apply the most appropriate skills, tools, and features and identify efficient methods to solve the problem.	Choose and apply some appropriate skills, tools, and features, but not in the most efficient manner.	Choose inappropriate skills, tools, or features, or are inefficient in solving the problem.
2-Content	Construct a solution that is clear and well organized, contains content that is accurate, appropriate to the audience and purpose, and is complete. Provide a solution that contains no errors of spelling, grammar, or style.	Construct a solution in which some components are unclear, poorly organized, inconsistent, or incomplete. Misjudge the needs of the audience. Have some errors in spelling, grammar, or style, but the errors do not detract from comprehension.	Construct a solution that is unclear, incomplete, or poorly organized; contains some inaccurate or inappropriate content; and contains many errors of spelling, grammar, or style. Do not solve the problem.
3-Format and Layout	Format and arrange all elements to communicate information and ideas, clarify function, illustrate relationships, and indicate relative importance.	Apply appropriate format and layout features to some elements, but not others. Overuse features, causing minor distraction.	Apply format and layout that does not communicate information or ideas clearly. Do not use format and layout features to clarify function, illustrate relationships, or indicate relative importance. Use available features excessively, causing distraction.
4-Process	Use an organized approach that integrates planning, development, self-assessment, revision, and reflection.	Demonstrate an organized approach in some areas, but not others; or, use an insufficient process of organization throughout.	Do not use an organized approach to solve the problem.

Outcomes-Based Assessments

Problem Solving

Project 17I—Coral Ridge

In this project, you will construct a solution by applying any combination of the Objectives found in Projects 17A and 17B.

> **For Project 17I, you will need the following file:**
>
> New blank PowerPoint presentation

You will save your presentation as
17I_Coral_Ridge_Firstname_Lastname

Select National Properties has developed a new housing development in the suburbs of Chicago. Randall Thomas, CEO, will be making a presentation on the new community to prospective home buyers. The development— Coral Ridge—consists of 55 homes with two different floor plans. The first floor plan—The Oakmont—includes 1,700 square feet and has 3 bedrooms and 2 baths. There is a fireplace in the family room and the kitchen and bathrooms have tile countertops. The second floor plan—The Seneca—has 1,925 square feet with 4 bedrooms and 2 baths. There are fireplaces in the master bedroom and in the family room, and the bathrooms and kitchens have granite countertops. The community has an excellent school district and is accessible by major highways.

Create a presentation with six slides that describes the community and the development. Apply a design template of your choice, change the background style on at least one slide, and include a picture on the background of one slide. Using the information in the preceding paragraph, insert a slide with a table that compares the two floor plans. Apply slide transitions and animation. Add the file name to the Notes and Handouts footer and check the presentation for spelling errors. Save the presentation as **17I_Coral_Ridge_Firstname_Lastname** and submit it as directed.

Note: You can find many appropriate images available to Office users. To access these images, click the Insert tab, and then from the Illustrations group, click the Clip Art button. In the Clip Art task pane, type a key word—such as *construction*—in the *Search for* box. You can specify the image type (clip art or photographs) and where to search. The largest variety of photographs can be found by including Web Collections in the *Search in* box. You can also use images from earlier projects in this chapter, or images from your personal collection.

End **You have completed Project 17I** ——————————

Outcomes-Based Assessments

Problem Solving

Project 17J — Land Development

In this project, you will construct a solution by applying any combination of the Objectives found in Projects 17A and 17B.

For Project 17J, you will need the following file:

New blank PowerPoint presentation

You will save your presentation as
17J_Land_Development_Firstname_Lastname

Select National Properties owns several land parcels in the growing community of Lake Monahan. The Chief Financial Officer, Morgan Bannon-Navarre, is creating a presentation for the members of the Lake Monahan Real Estate Association that describes the available parcels located in three areas of the city: North, South, and Central. Create a presentation with four to six slides describing the community and the parcels using the following information.

The City of Lake Monahan is a vacation destination for many out-of-state families. The lake provides opportunities for water sports, fishing, and boating. Select National Properties invested in the city by purchasing several land parcels approximately 15 years ago and is now ready to develop and sell the parcels.

In your presentation, insert one slide with a picture on the slide background that depicts the lake. (See the note at the end of project 17I for ideas on locating images.) Insert a slide titled **Available Parcels** and use the data below to create a table describing the parcels.

	North	South	Central
2008	$22,300	$55,675	$41,375
2009	$32,500	$62,420	$45,850
2010	$45,000	$68,000	$52,000

Insert a slide with the title **Average Parcel Price** and then insert an appropriate chart using the following data:

	North	South	Central
Parcels	10	15	18
Size	.75 acres	1.2 acres	1.05 acres
Price	$45,000	$68,000	$52,000

(Project 17J–Land Development continues on the next page)

Outcomes-Based Assessments

chapterseventeen

Problem Solving

(Project 17J–Land Development continued)

Use formatting and animation techniques that you learned in this chapter to create a professional presentation. Add the file name to the Notes and Handouts footer and check for spelling errors. Save the presentation as **17J_Land_Development_Firstname_Lastname** and submit it as directed.

End **You have completed Project 17J** —————————

Outcomes-Based Assessments

chapterseventeen

Problem Solving

Project 17K — Renovation

In this project, you will construct a solution by applying any combination of the Objectives found in Projects 17A and 17B.

For Project 17K, you will need the following files:

New blank PowerPoint presentation
p17K_Scaffold
p17K_Scaffold2

**You will save your presentation as
17K_Renovation_Firstname_Lastname**

Select National Properties' Vice President of Construction, Michael Wentworth, is presenting the status of The Lincoln Plaza—a large renovation project—to the project investors. Use the following information to create a presentation with at least four slides, including a table and a chart.

The Lincoln Plaza consists of three 10-story buildings on the perimeter of a large courtyard. The renovation is taking place in three overlapping phases: Exteriors that are 75 percent complete with an expected completion date of September 2009; Interior Infrastructure that is 55 percent complete with an expected completion date of June 2010; and Courtyard Enhancements that is 35 percent complete with an expected completion date of December 2010. The cost of each phase in millions is estimated as follows:

	Exterior	Interior	Courtyard
Labor	22.6	33.8	5.25
Materials	36.9	48.7	12.6

Apply an appropriate design and background style, and change the Fonts Theme. Format the background of one slide using one of the pictures provided with your student files—p17K_Scaffold or p17K_Scaffold2. Apply chart and table styles and slide transitions and animation. Add the file name to the Notes and Handouts footer and check for spelling errors. Save the presentation as **17K_Renovation_Firstname_Lastname** and submit it as directed.

End You have completed Project 17K ────────────

More on your Student CD

The instructions for the following additional end-of-chapter projects are on your student CD in the folder 03_additional_end_of_chapter_projects.

Content-Based Assessments

Project L Mastering PowerPoint	Apply the skills you practiced in Project A.
Project M Mastering PowerPoint	Apply the skills you practiced in Project B.
Project N Business Running Case	Apply the skills you practiced in Projects A and B while helping an entrepreneur with the daily tasks of running a business.
	In each chapter, this project focuses on applying the skills you have practiced in Projects A and B to a business. The project related to this business runs throughout the textbook. You will see how the Office applications relate to the day-to-day operation of a small business called Nelson Architectural Planning.

Outcomes-Based Assessments

Project O Problem Solving	Construct a solution by applying any combination of the skills you practiced from Projects A and B.
Project P Problem Solving	Construct a solution by applying any combination of the skills you practiced from Projects A and B.
Project Q You and GO!	Construct a solution that applies to your own life by applying any combination of the skills you practiced from Projects A and B.
Project R GO! with Help	Practice using Microsoft Office's Help Feature.
Project S Group Business Running Case	Work as part of a group to apply the skills you have gained thus far to help the Bell Orchid Hotel Group achieve its business goals.

Multimedia

The following multimedia accompany this textbook:

Companion Web site *www.prenhall.com/go*	An interactive Web site designed to reinforce and test your understanding of the skills in this chapter.
AV-EDDs	In the folder in the front of this book you will find videos that demonstrate the objectives of the A and B projects in this chapter. These may help you understand how to complete the projects in this book.
Video Podcasts	In the folder in the front of this book are Videos that can be played on your iPod, MP3 player, or computer. These videos demonstrate how to complete the more challenging objectives in this textbook.

Glossary

Absolute cell reference A cell reference that refers to cells by their fixed position in a worksheet; an absolute cell reference remains the same when the formula is copied.

Accounting Number format The Excel number format that applies a thousand comma separator where appropriate, inserts a fixed U.S. dollar sign aligned at the left edge of the cell, applies two decimal places, and leaves a small amount of space at the right edge of the cell to accommodate a parenthesis for negative numbers.

Active cell The cell, surrounded by a black border, ready to receive data or be affected by the next Excel command.

Active window The window in which the mouse pointer movements, commands, or text entry occur when two or more windows are open.

Adaptive A feature where menus adapt to the way you work by displaying the commands you most frequently use.

Address bar Displays the path of the current file or folder; also, in Internet Explorer, displays the address of the active Web page.

Adjacent ranges Cell ranges that are next to each other.

Adjustment handle A handle on a selected object that can be used to drag parts of an object into various positions.

Adware Spyware that tracks a user's Internet browsing and installs malicious cookies.

Aero See Windows Aero.

Aggregate functions Calculations that are performed on a group of records.

All Programs Command at the bottom of the Start menu that takes you to all available programs on your computer.

Alignment The placement of paragraph text relative to the left and right margins

American Psychological Association (APA) style One of two commonly used styles for formatting research papers.

Anchor A symbol that indicates to which paragraph an object is attached.

AND condition A condition in which only records where both specified values are present in the selected fields.

Animated banner A series of rotating or changing text and images embedded within the Web page.

Animation effects Effects used to introduce individual slide elements so that the slide can progress one element at a time.

Antispyware software A program that protects a computer from malicious software designed to threaten privacy and confidentiality.

Antivirus software A program that protects a computer from malicious codes such as viruses, worms, and Trojan horses.

Application software Programs with which you accomplish tasks such as word processing, photo editing, or sending email, and use the computer in a productive manner.

Appointment A calendar activity occurring at a specific time and day that does not require inviting other people.

Appointment area A one-day view of the current day's calendar entries.

Archive To back up files and store them somewhere other than the main hard drive.

Arguments The values that an Excel function uses to perform calculations or operations.

Arithmetic logic unit (ALU) Part of the CPU that performs all the arithmetic and logic functions for the computer; handles addition, subtraction, multiplication, and division, and also makes logical and comparison decisions.

Arithmetic operator The symbols +, −, *, /, %, and ^ used to denote addition, subtraction (negation), multiplication, division, percentage, and exponentiation in an Excel formula.

Arrow keys The keys at the lower right section of the keyboard, used to move the insertion point within the program window.

Ascending order A sorting order that arranges text in alphabetical order (A to Z) or numbers from the lowest to highest number.

Aspect ratio The relationship of an object's height to its width; if locked, changing either the height or width will resize the object proportionally.

Audio port A port that connects audio equipment to the sound card of a computer to facilitate the exchange of data.

Auto fill An Excel feature that extends values into adjacent cells based on the values of selected cells.

AutoComplete (Excel) A feature that speeds your typing and lessens the likelihood of errors; if the first few characters you type in a cell match an existing entry in the column, Excel fills in the remaining characters for you.

AutoComplete (Word) A feature that assists in your typing by suggesting words or phrases.

AutoCorrect (Excel) A feature that assists in your typing by automatically correcting and formatting some text as you type; for example Excel compares your typing to a list of commonly mistyped words and when it finds a match, it substitutes the correct word.

AutoCorrect (Word) A feature that corrects common typing and spelling errors as you type, for example changing *teh* to *the*.

AutoFormat As You Type A Word feature that anticipates formatting based on what you type.

AutoNumber An Access feature that sequentially numbers entered records creating a unique number for each record; useful for data that has no distinct field that could be considered unique.

AutoSum Another term for the Sum function.

AutoText A Word feature with which you can create shortcuts to quickly insert long phrases with just a few keystrokes.

AVERAGE function A pre-written formula that adds a group of values and then divides the result by the number of values in the group.

Background style A slide background fill variation that combines theme colors in different intensities.

Backup tape drive A storage device used to save data to tapes resembling audiocassettes.

Banner area The screen area that displays important calendar information including **Day**, **Week**, and **Month** view buttons.

Base The starting point when you divide the amount of increase by it to calculate the rate of increase.

Between. . . And operator A comparison operator that looks for values within a range.

Bibliography A term used to describe a list of referenced works in a report or research paper, also referred to as Works Cited, Sources, or References, depending upon the report style.

Black slide A slide that displays at the end of a slide presentation indicating the end of the slide show.

Blank database A database that has no data and has no database tools; you create the data and the tools as you need them.

Blank form In Outlook, a lined page added to the printout of the Card print style that you can use to manually list new contacts.

Blank Report tool An Access feature with which you can create a report from scratch by adding the fields you want in the order you want them to appear.

Bluetooth Wireless technology that uses radio waves to transmit data over short distances, and often used with mobile devices.

Body font A font that is applied to all slide text except titles.

Boot The process of starting up a computer.

Boot process See Boot.

Bound The term used to describe objects and controls that are based on data that is stored in tables.

Building block Pre-formatted content that you can add to your document, such as cover pages, pull quotes, and letterheads.

Bulleted levels Outline levels identified by a symbol.

Bulleted list A list of items with each item introduced by a symbol such as a small circle or check mark—useful when the items in the list can be displayed in any order.

Bullets Text symbols such as small circles or check marks used to introduce items in a list.

Burn The process of recording data to optical media such as a CD or DVD.

Bus topology A networking configuration in which all devices are connected to a central high-speed cable called the bus or backbone.

Calculated controls Controls whose source of data is an expression—typically a formula—rather than a field.

Card Style In Outlook, a print style which displays the name and address information alphabetically by last name.

Cascade To display the open windows on the desktop so that they line up in a diagonal line from the upper left corner of the screen downward.

Category axis The area along the bottom of a chart that identifies the categories of data; also referred to as the x-axis.

Category labels The labels that display along the bottom of a chart to identify the categories of data; Excel uses the row titles as the category names.

Cathode-ray tube (CRT) A picture tube device used in a monitor, similar to a television.

CD A compact disc—an optical storage device used to store data, and which can be read-only or read-write.

CD burner An optical storage device capable of reading data from and writing data to a CD.

CD drive A storage device used to read and, possibly, write data to CD.

CD-R Another name for a CD-ROM disc.

CD-ROM The acronym for Compact Disc-Read Only Memory; an optical storage device used to permanently store data and from which you can read and open files.

CD-RW A compact disc that can be reused to read and save files.

Cell (Access) The box formed by the intersection of a row and a column in a datasheet.

Cell (Excel) The small box formed by the intersection of a column and a row.

Cell address Another name for a cell reference.

Cell content Anything typed into a cell.

Cell reference The identification of a specific cell by its intersecting column letter and row number.

Center alignment Text centered between the left and right margin.

Central processing unit (CPU) The part of the computer responsible for controlling all the commands and tasks the computer performs, acting as the brain of the computer.

Chart (Excel) The graphic representation of data in a worksheet; data presented as a chart is usually easier to understand than a table of numbers.

Chart A graphic representation of numeric data.

Chart layout The combination of chart elements that can be displayed in a chart such as a title, legend, labels for the columns, and the table of charted cells.

Chart Layouts gallery A group of predesigned chart layouts that you can apply to an Excel chart.

Chart sheet A workbook sheet that contains only a chart and is useful when you want to view a chart separately from the worksheet data.

Chart style The overall visual look of a chart in terms of its graphic effects, colors, and backgrounds; for example, you can have flat or beveled columns, colors that are solid or transparent, and backgrounds that are dark or light.

Chart Styles gallery A group of predesigned chart styles that you can apply to an Excel chart.

Chart types Various chart formats used in a way that is meaningful to the reader; common examples are column charts, pie charts, and line charts.

Citation A list of information about a reference source, usually including the name of the author, the full title of the work, the year of publication, Web address, and other publication information.

Click To press the left mouse button one time.

Click and type pointer The text select (I-beam) pointer with various attached shapes that indicate which formatting will be applied when you double-click—such as a left-aligned, centered, or right-aligned.

Client In a client/server network, this is the computer most people interact with to request information from the server and to perform many of the tasks that can be accomplished with a computer.

Client/server network A network consisting of client and server computers; often used in businesses.

Clip art Graphic images included with the Microsoft Office program or obtained from other sources.

Clip art (PowerPoint) Images included with Microsoft Office or downloaded from the Web that can make your presentation more interesting and visually appealing; drawings, movies, sounds, or photographic images that are included with Microsoft Office or downloaded from the Web.

Clipboard A temporary storage area in Windows that stores the most recently copied item.

Clock speed A measurement of how quickly a CPU processes data, an indication of a CPU's processing power.

Close button A shortcut button in a title bar that closes a window or a program.

Collapse button A small minus (−) button to the left of a folder that you click to hide the items in that folder.

Collect and paste The process of collecting a group of graphics or selected text blocks, and then pasting them into a document at any time; the Office Clipboard holds up to 24 items, and the Office Clipboard task pane displays a preview of each item.

Color scales Visual guides that help you understand data distribution and variation.

Column A vertical group of cells in a worksheet.

Column chart A chart in which the data is arranged in columns and which is useful for showing data changes over a period of time or for illustrating comparisons among items.

Column heading The letter that displays at the top of a vertical group of cells in a worksheet; beginning with the first letter of the alphabet, a unique letter or combination of letters identifies each column.

Comma style The Excel number format that inserts thousand comma separators where appropriate, applies two decimal places, and leaves space at the right to accommodate a parenthesis for negative numbers.

Command bar Area at the top of a window that includes the toolbar, menu bar, address bar, and search pane.

Comment A note that can be added to a Word document from the Review tab; comments are not generally printed.

Comments area In Outlook, the area in the lower half of the Appointments form and Task form where you can enter information not otherwise specified in the form.

Common fields Fields that contain the same data in more than one table.

Communication or organizational software A program such as Microsoft Outlook, used to send and retrieve email and manage day-to-day tasks.

Comparison operators Symbols that evaluate each field value to determine if it is the same (=), greater than (>), less than (<), or in between a range of values as specified by the criteria.

Complimentary closing A parting farewell in a business letter.

Compound criteria Multiple conditions in a query or filter.

Compress Reduce the size of a file or combine several files into one.

Computer A programmable electronic device that can input, process, output, and store data.

Computer fluent The term used to describe a person who understands the capabilities and limitations of computers and knows how to use computer technology to accomplish tasks.

Computer icon An icon that represents the computer on which you are working, and that provides access to the drives, folders, and files on your computer.

Conditional format A format that changes the appearance of a cell range—for example by adding cell shading or font color—based on a condition; if the condition is true the cell range is formatted based on that condition, and if the condition is false the cell range is *not* formatted based on the condition.

Connectivity port A port that enables a computer to be connected to other devices or systems, such as networks, modems, and the Internet.

Constant value Numbers, text, dates, or times of day that you type into a cell.

Contact A person or organization about whom you can save information such as street and e-mail addresses, telephone and fax numbers, Web page addresses, birthdays, and pictures.

Content pane Displays files and folders stored in the disk drive or folder that is currently selected in the Navigation pane.

Context-sensitive command A command associated with activities in which you are engaged; often activated by right-clicking a screen item.

Contextual tabs Tabs that are added to the Ribbon when a specific object, such as a chart, is selected, and that contain commands relevant to the selected object.

Contextual tools Sets of commands added to the Ribbon when a specific object is selected and which enable you to perform specific commands related to the selected object; contextual tools display only when needed and no longer display after the object is deselected.

Control Objects on a form or report that display data, perform actions, and let you view and work with information.

Control keys Special keys, such as Ctrl, Alt, or Esc, used to increase keyboard functionality or provide shortcuts.

Control layout The grouped arrangement of controls on a form or report.

Control unit The part of the CPU responsible for obtaining instructions from the computer's memory; the control unit interprets the instructions and executes them, thereby coordinating the activities of all the other computer components.

Cookie A small text file containing information that identifies a visitor to a Web site.

Copy A command that duplicates a selection and places it on the Clipboard.

Copyright Laws that protect the rights of authors of original works, including text, art, photographs, and music.

COUNTIF function A statistical function that counts the number of cells within a range that meet the given condition—the criteria that you provide.

CPU See Central processing unit.

Criteria (Access) Conditions that identify the specific records you are looking for.

Criteria (Excel) Conditions that you specify in a logical function.

Crosshair pointer The pointer that indicates that you can draw a shape.

CRT See Cathode-ray tube.

Curly quote A decorative quotation mark, with curved lines instead of the straight lines found in straight quotes.

Custom animation list A list that indicates the animation effect applied to slide items.

Cut (PowerPoint) A command that removes selected text or graphics from your presentation and moves the selection to the Clipboard.

Cut (Word) The command to remove selected text from a document and move it to the Office Clipboard.

Daily Style In Outlook, a print style that prints the appointments for the currently displayed day.

Daily Task List In Outlook, an abbreviated list of current tasks stored in the Tasks folder.

Data Words, numbers, sounds, or pictures that represent facts about people, events, things, or ideas.

Data (Access) Facts about people, events, things, or ideas.

Data (Excel) Text or numbers in a cell.

Data bar A cell format consisting of a shaded bar that provides a visual cue to the reader about the value of a cell relative to other cells; the length of the bar represents the value in the cell—a longer bar represents a higher value and a shorter bar represents a lower value.

Data entry The action of typing the record data into a database.

Data marker A column, bar, area, dot, pie slice, or other symbol in a chart that represents a single data point; related data points form a data series.

Data point A value that originates in a worksheet cell and that is represented in a chart by a data marker.

Data series Related data points represented by data markers; each data series has a unique color or pattern represented in the chart legend.

Data source (Word) A list of variable information, such as names and addresses, that is merged with a main document to create customized form letters or labels.

Data source The table or tables from which a query selects its data.

Data table A range of cells that shows how changing certain values in your formulas affects the results of those formulas, and which makes it easy to calculate multiple versions in one operation.

Data type The characteristic that defines the kind of data that can be entered into a field, such as numbers, text, or dates.

Database An organized collection of facts about people, events, things, or ideas related to a particular topic or purpose.

Database software Programs, such as Microsoft Access, used to store and organize large amounts of data and perform complex tasks such as sorting and querying to generate specialized reports.

Datasheet view The Access view that displays an object organized in a format of columns and rows similar to an Excel spreadsheet.

Date control A control on a form or report that inserts the current date each time the form or report is opened.

Date line The first line in a business letter.

Date Navigator In Outlook, a one-month view of the calendar that you can use to display specific days in a month.

DBMS An acronym for database management system.

Dedicated server A computer that is assigned to handle one specific task on a network.

Denial of service (DoS) An attack caused when a large number of computers attempt to access a Web site at the same time, effectively overloading it and causing it to shut down.

Descending order A sorting order that arranges text in reverse alphabetical (Z to A) order or numbers from the highest to the lowest number.

Deselect The action of canceling a selection.

Design grid The lower pane of the Query window, which displays the design of the query.

Design view The detailed structured view of a form or report, and the view in which some tasks must be performed; only the controls, and not the data, are visible in this view.

Desktop The basic screen from which Windows and programs are run, and which consists of program icons, a taskbar, a Start button, and a mouse pointer.

Desktop background The picture, pattern, or color that displays on the desktop.

Desktop computer A class of microcomputer, such as a PC or a Mac.

Detail section The section of a form or report that displays the records from the underlying table or query.

Details pane Displays details about the drive, folder, or file selected in the Content pane.

Dialog box A box that asks you to make a decision about an individual object or topic.

Dialog Box Launcher A small icon that displays to the right of some group names on the Ribbon, and which opens a related dialog box or task pane providing additional options and commands related to that group.

Digital camera A type of camera that saves photographs in a digital format rather than on film.

Digital Video Interface (DVI) port A port used to connect an LCD monitor to a computer in order to use a pure digital signal.

Digital video recorder A device used to record video in digital format directly to a hard drive, without the need for videotape.

Dimmed An icon or menu object is gray and faded, indicating that the icon or menu object is not currently available.

Display screen See Monitor.

Displayed value The data that displays in a cell.

Double-click Press the left mouse button two times in rapid succession, using caution not to move the mouse.

Document Information Panel The area of the screen just below the Ribbon that displays document properties.

Document properties The detailed information about a document that can help you identify or organize your files, including author name, title, and keywords.

Document window The Word window that displays the active document.

Dot leader A series of dots preceding a tab.

Dot matrix An impact printer, useful for printing multipage forms.

Dot pitch The diagonal distance between adjacent pixels, measured in millimeters and that is used to determine image quality for monitors.

Dots per inch (dpi) A measurement of printer resolution.

Double-click The action of clicking the left mouse button twice in rapid succession while keeping the mouse still.

Downloading The action of requesting and copying a file or program from a remote server, such as a Web server, and saving it on your local computer or storage device.

Draft view A simplified view of a document that does not show graphics, margins, headers, or footers.

Drag Move the mouse pointer while holding down the left mouse button, and then release at the appropriate time.

Drag and drop The action of moving a selection by dragging it to a new location.

Drag and drop (Excel) A method of moving or copying the content of selected cells in which you point to the selection and then drag it to a new location.

Drag and drop (Word) A technique by which you can move selected text from one location in a document to another—best used with text that will be moved a short distance, such as on the same screen.

Dragging The technique of holding down the left mouse button and moving over an area of text in order to select it.

Drawing canvas A work area for creating and editing complex figures created using the drawing tools.

Drawing object A graphic object, including shapes, diagrams, lines, and circles.

Drive An area of storage that is formatted with the Windows file system and that has a drive letter such as C.

Dual-boot A system with two different operating systems installed, giving the user the option to boot the computer using either one.

Dual-core A CPU that includes two microprocessors on a single integrated circuit. See also Multicore.

DVD A digital video (or versatile) disc—an optical storage device used to store data, and which can be read-only or read-write.

DVD drive A storage device used to read and, possibly, write data to DVD.

DVI port See Digital Video Interface (DVI) port.

E-Mail Account A unique address that you can use to receive and send e-mail.

Edit (Word) The action of making changes to the text or format of a document.

Edit (Excel) The action of making changes in a worksheet or workbook.

Edit mode A Windows mode that enables you to change the name of a file or folder, and works the same in all Windows applications.

Editing (PowerPoint) The process of adding, deleting, or changing the contents of a slide.

Effect options Animation options that include changing the direction of an effect and playing a sound when an animation takes place.

Em dash The word processing name for a long dash in a sentence, and which marks a break in thought, similar to a comma but stronger.

Embedded chart A chart that displays as an object within a worksheet.

Embedded computers Components of larger products, devices that perform pre-defined tasks using specially programmed processors.

Enclosure An additional document included with a letter.

Endnotes In a report or research paper, references placed at the end of the chapter containing the reference.

Enhanced ScreenTip A ScreenTip for a button that has more information than just the name, sometimes including a link to the topic in the Help system.

Entrance effects Animations that bring a slide element onto the screen.

Ethernet port A port, slightly larger than a telephone jack, that can transmit data at speeds up to 1,000 megabits per second (Mbps) and is usually used to connect to a cable modem or a network.

Excel table A series of rows and columns in a worksheet that contains related data, and that is managed independently from the data in other rows and columns in the worksheet.

Expand button A small plus (+) button to the left of a folder that you click to display the items in that folder.

Expand Formula Bar button An Excel window element with which you can increases the height of the Formula Bar for the purpose of displaying lengthy cell content.

Expand horizontal scroll bar button A button with which you can increase the width of the horizontal scroll bar.

Favorites Center An area in Internet Explorer that lets you manage your favorites list, the history list, and the feeds list.

Field A category that describes each piece of data stored in a table.

Field list A list of the field names in a table.

Field properties Characteristics of a field that control how the field will display and how the data can be entered in the field.

File Data that you save and store on a drive, such as a Word document or a PowerPoint presentation.

File extension The characters to the right of the period in a file name, and that tell the computer the program to use to open the file; extensions can be displayed or hidden.

Fill color (Excel) The background color a cell.

Fill color The inside color of text or an object.

Fill handle The small black square in the lower right corner of a selected cell.

Filter By Form An Access command that filters the records in a form based on one or more fields, or based on more than one value in the same field.

Filter By Selection An Access command that retrieves only the records that contain the value in the selected field.

Filtering The process of displaying only a portion of the total records (a subset) based on matching a specific value.

Financial functions Prewritten formulas that perform common business calculations such as calculating a loan payment on a vehicle or calculating how much to save each month to buy something; financial functions commonly involve a period of time such as months or years.

Find and Replace (Excel) A command that searches the cells in a worksheet—or in a selected range—for matches and then replaces each match with a replacement value of your choice.

Firewall See Personal firewall.

FireWire port A port used to send data at rates up to 800 megabits per second (Mbps), frequently used for digital cameras or digital video recorders.

Flash drive A small, portable, digital storage device that connects to a computer's USB port; also called a thumb drive, jump drive, or USB drive.

Flash memory Portable, nonvolatile memory, that uses electronic, solid-state circuitry.

Flat panel See Liquid crystal display.

Flat screen A type of screen used in CRT monitors, and which differs from flat panel monitors.

Flip 3D A three-dimensional visual representation that enables you to flip through the windows that are open.

Floating object An object or graphic that can be moved independently of the surrounding text.

Floppy disk drive (or floppy drive) The original storage device for a microcomputer, which enables portable, permanent storage on floppy disks.

Folder Storage area, represented on the screen by a picture of a paper file folder, used to store files or other folders.

Folders list Part of the Navigation pane that displays the drive and folder structure on the computer.

Font A set of characters with the same design and shape.

Font size The size of characters in a font measured in points; there are 72 points in an inch, with 10 or 11 points being a typical font size.

Font style Formatting emphasis such as bold, italic, and underline.

Font theme A theme that determines the font applied to two types of slide text—headings and body.

Footer (PowerPoint) Text that displays at the bottom of every slide or that prints at the bottom of a sheet of slide handouts or notes pages.

Footer (Word) A reserved area for text and graphics that displays at the bottom of each page in a document or section of a document.

Footers (Excel) Text, graphics, or page numbers that print at the bottom of every page of a worksheet.

Footnotes In a report or research paper, references placed at the bottom of a report page containing the source of the reference.

Foreign key The field that is included in the related table so that it can be joined to the primary key in another table for the purpose of creating a relationship.

Form A window for displaying and collecting information.

Form (Access) An Access object with which you can enter new records into a table, edit existing records in a table, or display existing records from a table.

Form footer Information at the bottom of the screen in Form view that is printed after the last detail section on the last page.

Form header Information, such as a form's title, which displays at the top of the screen in Form view, and that is printed at the top of the first page when records are printed as forms

Form tool The Access tool that creates a form with a single mouse click, and that includes all the fields from the underlying data source (table or query).

Format as you type The Excel feature by which a cell takes on the formatting of the number typed into the cell.

Format Painter (Excel) An Excel feature with which you can copy the formatting of a specific cell to other cells.

Format Painter (PowerPoint) A feature that copies formatting from one selection of text to another, thus ensuring formatting consistency in your presentation.

Format Painter (Word) A Word tool with which you can copy the formatting of specific text, or of a paragraph, to text in another location in the document.

Formatting (Excel) The process of specifying the appearance of cells and the overall layout of a worksheet; accomplished through various commands on the Ribbon, many of which are also available using shortcut menus or keyboard shortcuts.

Formatting (PowerPoint) Changing the appearance of the text, layout, and design of a slide.

Formatting marks Characters that display on the screen, but do not print, indicating where the Enter key, the Spacebar, and the Tab key were pressed; also called nonprinting characters.

Formatting text The process of establishing the overall appearance of text in a document.

Formula An equation that performs mathematical calculations on values in a worksheet.

Formula AutoComplete An Excel feature which, after typing an = (equal sign) and the beginning letter or letters of a function name, displays a list of function names that match the typed letter(s), and from which you can insert the function by pointing to its name and pressing the Tab key or double-clicking.

Formula Bar An element in the Excel window that displays the value or formula contained in the active cell; here you can also enter or edit values or formulas.

Frames Separate areas of content placed closely together so they will display as one unified Web page with or without any visible demarcation lines between them.

Freeze Panes A command that enables you to select one or more rows or columns and freeze (lock) them into place; the locked rows and columns become separate panes.

Full Screen Reading view A view that displays easy-to-read pages that fit on the screen.

Function A predefined formula—a formula that Excel has already built for you—that performs calculations by using specific values in a particular order.

Function key The keys, numbered F1 through F12, located above the numeric keys on a keyboard that have different functions depending upon the software program in use.

Future value The value at the end of time periods in an Excel function; the cash balance you want to attain after the last payment is made—usually zero for loans.

Fv The abbreviation for *future value* in various Excel functions.

Gadget A dynamic program—such as a clock, a stock market ticker, or a weather window—that displays on the desktop, usually in the Windows Sidebar.

Gadget controls A set of tools that include a Move button in the shape of eight small dots, an Options button in the shape of a wrench, and a Close button.

Gallery An Office 2007 feature that displays a list of potential results; it shows the results of commands rather than just the command name.

General format The default format that Excel applies to numbers; the general format has no specific characteristics—whatever you type in the cell will display, with the exception that trailing zeros to the right of a decimal point will not display.

Gigabyte (GB) Approximately one billion bytes; a unit of measure for memory and storage space.

Gigahertz (GHz) One billion hertz; hertz is the unit of measure for processor speed.

Goal Seek One of Excel's What-If Analysis tools that provides a method to find a specific value for a cell by adjusting the value of one other cell.

Gradient fill A color combination in which one color fades into another.

Graphic A picture, clip art image, chart, or drawing object.

Graphical user interface (GUI) A computer interface that shows documents as they will look in their final form and uses icons to represent programs.

Group A set of command buttons related to the Ribbon tab that is currently selected.

Group footer Displays the field label by which the summarized data has been grouped.

Group header Information printed at the beginning of each new group of records, for example the group name.

Group, Sort, and Total pane A pane that opens at the bottom of your screen in which you can control how information is sorted and grouped in a report; provides the most flexibility for adding or modifying groups, sort orders, or totals options on a report.

GUI See Graphical user interface.

Guided help In the Windows Help and Support dialog box, a help technique that walks you through a process step-by-step.

Guides Vertical and horizontal lines that display in the rulers to give you a visual indication of where the crosshair pointer is positioned so that you can draw a shape.

Handheld computers See Personal digital assistant.

Hanging indent An indent style in which the first line of a paragraph extends to the left of the remaining lines, and that is commonly used for bibliographic entries.

Hard copy Data or information retrieved from a computer and printed.

Hard drive A large disk drive inside your computer, also referred to as a Local Disk.

Hardware The computer memory, disk drive space, attached devices such as printers and scanners, and the central processing unit (CPU).

Header (PowerPoint) Text that displays at the top of every slide or that prints at the top of a sheet of slide hand-outs or notes pages.

Header (Word) A reserved area for text and graphics that displays at the top of each page in a document or section of a document.

Headers (Excel) Text, graphics, or page numbers that print at the top of every page of a worksheet.

Headings font The font that is applied to slide titles.

Help button A button at the far right of the Ribbon tabs that you click to display the program's Help window.

History A feature of Internet Explorer that tracks recently visited Web pages and sites.

Home page The Web page that displays every time you start Internet Explorer.

Horizontal scroll bar The bar at the bottom of a window that enables you to move left and right to view information that extends beyond the left and right edges of the screen.

Horizontal window split box A small box with which you can split the document into two horizontal views of the same document.

Hyperlink Text that you click to go to another location in a document, another document, or a Web site; the text is a different color (usually blue) than the surrounding text, and commonly underlined.

Hyperlinks Text, buttons, pictures, or other objects displayed on Web pages that, when clicked, access other Web pages or display other sections of the active page.

Hyperthreading Technology that allows a CPU to emulate multiple processors, improving processing power and speed.

Icon A graphic representation of an object that you can click to open that object.

Icon set A collection of icons such as arrows, flags, bars, or circles that annotate and classify data into three to five categories separated by a threshold value.

IF function A logical function that uses a logical test to check whether a condition is met, and then returns one value if true, and another value if false.

Impact A type of printer that resembles a typewriter; a key and ink ribbon are used to imprint a character on paper.

Inbox In Outlook, the folder that stores e-mail.

Indenting A format for text in which lines of text are moved relative to the left and right margins, for example, moving the beginning of the first line of a paragraph to the right or left of the rest of the paragraph.

Information Data that has been organized in a useful manner.

Information processing cycle The cycle composed of the four basic computer functions: input, process, output, and storage.

Ink-jet Type of printer that uses a special nozzle and ink cartridges to distribute liquid ink on the surface of the paper.

Inline object An object or graphic inserted in a document that acts like a character in a sentence.

Innermost sort field When sorting on multiple fields in datasheet view, the field that will be used for the second level of sorting.

Input The act of entering data into a computer.

Input devices Computer hardware used to enter data and instructions into a computer; examples include the keyboard, mouse, stylus, scanner, microphone, and digital camera.

Insert mode The mode in which text moves to the right to make space for new keystrokes.

Insert Worksheet button Located on the row of sheet tabs, a sheet tab that, when clicked, inserts an additional worksheet into the workbook.

Insertion point A blinking vertical line that indicates where text or graphics will be inserted.

Inside address The address block under the date in a business letter.

Interest The amount charged for the use of borrowed money.

Internet control key Usually found at the top of a keyboard, this type of key can be used for various Internet-related activities including opening a Web browser and sending email.

Internet Explorer 7.0 A software program that allows you to view the contents of the World Wide Web.

Internet Service Provider (ISP) A company that provides an Internet connection through a regular telephone line, a special high-speed telephone line, or a cable.

IrDA port A port enabling data transmission through the use of infrared light waves; the devices sharing data require a clear line of site with no visual obstructions.

Is Not Null A criteria that searches for fields that are not empty.

Is Null A criteria that searches for fields that are empty.

Items An element of information in Outlook, such as a message, a contact name, a task, or an appointment.

Join line In the Relationships window, the line joining two tables that visually indicates the related field and the type of relationship.

Joysticks Input devices used to control actions and movement within computer games.

Justified alignment Text aligned on both the left and right margins.

Key logger A software program or hardware device that records every keystroke made on the computer.

Keyboard The hardware device used to input typed data and commands into a computer.

Keyboard shortcut A combination of keys on the keyboard that perform a command.

Label control A control on a form or report that contains descriptive information, typically a field name.

LAN See Local area network.

Landscape orientation A page orientation in which the printed page is wider than it is tall.

Laser A type of printer that uses a drum, static electricity, and a laser to distribute dry ink or toner on the surface of the paper.

Layout (PowerPoint) The placement and arrangement of the text and graphic elements on a slide.

Layout selector A small symbol that displays in the upper left corner of a selected control layout, and with which you can move the entire group of controls.

Layout view The Access view in which you can make changes to a form or to a report while the form is running—the data from the underlying record source displays.

LCD See Liquid crystal display.

Leader characters Characters that form a solid, dotted, or dashed line that fills the space preceding a tab stop.

Left aligned The cell format in which characters align at the left edge of the cell; this is the default for text entries and is an example of formatting information stored in a cell.

Left alignment Text aligned at the left margin, leaving the right margin uneven.

Left pane In the My Computer window, a pane at the left that displays information and commonly used tools.

Legend A chart element that identifies the patterns or colors that are assigned to the categories in the chart.

Line chart A chart type that displays trends over time; time displays along the bottom axis and the data point values are connected with a line.

Line spacing The distance between lines of text in a paragraph.

Link Select pointer The mouse pointer displaying as a pointing hand as you point to an item that links to another Web page.

Linux An open-source operating system based on the UNIX operating system developed for mainframe computers.

Liquid crystal display (LCD) Technology used in flat panel monitors, resulting in thinner and lighter monitors.

Live Preview A technology that shows the result of applying an editing or formatting change as you move your pointer over the results presented in a gallery.

Local area network (LAN) A network in which the nodes are located within a small geographic area.

Local disk A large disk drive inside your computer, also referred to as a hard disk.

Logical functions Pre-written formulas that test for specific conditions, and which typically use conditional tests to determine whether specified conditions, referred to as criteria, are true or false.

Logical operators (Access) The criteria of AND and OR used to enter criteria for the same field or different fields; AND requires that both conditions be met and OR requires that either condition be met.

Logical test Any value or expression that can be evaluated as being true or false.

Mac OS The operating system designed specifically for Apple's Mac computers.

Magnetic A type of storage process using magnetized film to store data; used by media such as floppy disks or Zip disks.

Mail merge A Word feature that joins a main document and a data source to create customized letters or labels.

Main document The document that contains the text or formatting that remains constant in a mail merge.

Mainframe A large computer capable of performing more than one task at the same time and supporting many users simultaneously.

Manual column break An artificial end to a column to balance columns or to provide space for the insertion of other objects.

Manual line break The action of ending a line, before the normal end of the line, without creating a new paragraph; this is useful, for example, if your paragraph style includes space before or after paragraphs and you want to begin a new line without the space.

Margins The space between the text and the top, bottom, left, and right edges of the paper.

MAX function A statistical function that determines the largest value in a group of values.

Maximize To increase the size of a window to fill the screen.

MEDIAN function A statistical function commonly used to describe a group of data, and which finds the middle value in a group of values that has as many values above it in the group as are below it.

Megabyte (MB) Approximately one million bytes; a unit of measure for memory and storage space.

Megahertz (MHz) One million hertz; hertz is the unit of measure for processor speed.

Memo Style In Outlook, a print style that prints a single item on a single page and provides detailed information about that item.

Menu A list of commands within a category.

Menu bar The bar beneath the title bar that lists the names of menu categories.

Message Bar The area directly below the Ribbon that displays information such as security alerts when there is potentially unsafe, active content in an Office 2007 document that you open.

Message header In Outlook, the basic information about an e-mail message such as the sender's name, the date sent, and the subject.

Metadata Information about a file, such as tags, a title, a rating, the file name, and the file size.

MFD See Multifunction device.

Microcomputer The computer most users are familiar with, ranging in size from large desktop systems to handheld devices.

Microphones Input devices used to digitally record sound.

Microprocessor chip See Central processing unit.

Microsoft Exchange Server An e-mail based communications server for businesses and organizations.

Microsoft Windows The operating system found on most microcomputers.

MIDI port Musical Instrument Digital Interface port used to connect electronic musical instruments to a system.

MIN function A statistical function that determines the smallest value in a group of values.

Mini toolbar A small toolbar containing frequently used formatting commands, and sometimes accompanied by a shortcut menu of other frequently used commands, which displays as a result of right-clicking a selection or of selecting text.

Mini toolbar (Excel) A small toolbar containing frequently used formatting commands and which displays as a result of right-clicking or selecting cells; the toolbar fades when you move the mouse away and dismisses itself when you click outside of the toolbar.

Minimize Removing the window from the screen without closing it; minimized windows can be reopened by clicking the associated button in the taskbar.

Mobile devices Lightweight, portable computing devices such as PDAs, smartphones, and handheld computers.

Modem port A port that connects to a standard telephone line, usually used to connect to the Internet or a local network, with a maximum speed of 56 kilobits per second (Kbps).

Modern Language Association (MLA) style One of two commonly used styles for formatting research papers.

Monitor (or display screen) A common output device that displays text, graphics, and video.

Monitor port A port used to connect a monitor to a computer's graphic processing unit, located on the motherboard or video card.

Motherboard A large printed circuit board located in the system unit to which all other boards are connected; the motherboard contains the central processing unit (CPU), the memory (RAM) chips, and expansion card slots.

Mouse An input device used to enter commands and user responses into a computer.

Mouse pointer The arrow, I-beam, or other symbol that shows the location or position of the mouse on your screen. Also called the pointer.

Multicore A CPU that includes more than two microprocessors on a single integrated circuit. See also Dual-core.

Multifunction device (MFD) A device that has more than one purpose, often combining input and output capabilities.

Multimedia control key Usually found at the top of a keyboard, this type of key can be used to control or mute speaker volume.

Multimedia projectors Output devices used to display information on a screen for viewing by an audience.

Multiple items form A form in which multiple records can be entered into or displayed from a table.

Multitask The action of performing more than one task at the same time.

Name Box An element of the Excel window that displays the name of the selected cell, table, chart, or object.

Navigate To move within a document or workbook.

Navigation pane The pane on the left side of the Computer or Windows Explorer window that contains Personal folders and the Folders list.

Navigation Pane (Access) The area of the Access window that displays and organizes the names of the objects in a database; from here you open objects for use.

Navigation Pane (Outlook) The area on the left side of the Outlook window that provides quick access to Outlook's components.

Network A group of two or more computers (or nodes) connected to share information and resources.

Network icon An icon that represents the network to which your computer is attached, and that provides access to the drives, folders, and files on your network.

Network topology The layout and structure of a computer network.

Node Any object connected to a network—may be a computer or a peripheral device.

Non-breaking hyphen A special type of hyphen that will not break at the end of a line and is useful for telephone numbers in which you normally do not want the number to be placed on two separate lines by the word wrap feature.

Non-breaking space A special type of space inserted between two words that results in treating the two words as one, and thus forcing both words to wrap even if the second word would normally wrap to the next line.

Nonadjacent ranges Cell ranges that are not next to each other.

Nonimpact A type of printer that does not actually touch the paper.

Nonprinting characters Characters that display on the screen, but do not print, indicating where the Enter key, the Spacebar, and the Tab key were pressed; also called formatting marks.

Nonvolatile Permanent storage, as in read only memory (ROM); data remains even when power is shut down.

Normal view (PowerPoint) The view in which the PowerPoint window is divided into three areas: the Slides/Outline pane, the Slide pane, and the Notes pane.

Normal view (Excel) A screen view that maximizes the number of cells visible on your screen and keeps the column letters and row numbers close to the columns and rows.

Notebook computer Also known as a laptop, this microcomputer is smaller than a desktop and designed to be portable.

Notes area In Outlook, a blank area of the Contact form that can be used for any information about the contact that is not otherwise specified in the form.

Notes pages Printouts that contain the slide image in the top half of the page and speaker's notes in the lower half of the page.

Notification area Area on the right side of the taskbar that keeps you informed about processes that are occurring in the background, such as antivirus software, network connections, and other utility programs. It also displays the time.

NOW function A function within the *Date & Time* category that retrieves the date and time from your computer's calendar and clock and inserts the information into the selected cell.

Nper The abbreviation for *number of time periods* in various Excel functions.

Number format A specific way in which Excel displays numbers in a cell.

Numbered lists A list of items with each item introduced by a consecutive number to indicate definite steps, a sequence of actions, or chronological order.

Numeric keypad A bank of keys on a keyboard with which you can input numbers, it is located on the right side of a keyboard and is similar to an adding machine or calculator.

Object window The portion of the Access window that displays open objects.

Objects The basic parts of a database, which includes tables, forms, queries, reports, and macros.

Office button The large button to the left of the Quick Access Toolbar that displays a list of commands related to things you can do *with* a workbook, such as opening, saving, printing, or sharing.

Office Clipboard A temporary storage area maintained by your Microsoft Office program.

Office Clipboard (Word) A temporary storage area that holds text or graphics that has been cut or copied, and that can subsequently be placed in another location in the document or in another Office program.

Offline Your status when you are not connected to a network or to the public Internet.

OLE An abbreviation for *object linking and embedding*, a technology for transferring and sharing information among applications.

One-to-many relationship A relationship between two tables where one record in the first table corresponds to many records in the second table—the most common type of relationship in Access.

One-variable data table A data table that changes the value in only one cell.

Online Your status when you are connected to your organization's network or to the public Internet.

Open-source Software whose code is made available for developers to modify and use as they wish, usually available at no cost.

Operating system A set of instructions that coordinates the activities of your computer; Microsoft Windows XP is an operating system.

Operating system (OS) System software that controls the way in which a computer system functions, including the management of hardware, peripherals, and software; Microsoft Windows XP is an operating system.

Operators The symbols with which you can specify the type of calculation you want to perform in an Excel formula.

Optical A type of storage process using a laser to read and write data; used by media such as CDs and DVDs.

OR condition A condition in which only records where one of two values is present in the selected field.

Order of operations The mathematical rules for performing multiple calculations within a formula.

OS See Operating system.

Outermost sort field When sorting on multiple fields in datasheet view, the field that will be used for the first level of sorting.

Outline view A document view that shows headings and subheadings, which can be expanded or collapsed.

Outlook Today In Outlook, a summary view of your schedule, tasks, and e-mail for the current day.

Output To retrieve data or information from a computer.

Output devices Computer hardware used to retrieve processed data and information from a computer; examples include the monitor, printer, and speakers.

P2P network See Peer-to-peer network.

Page footer Information printed at the end of every page in a report; used to print page numbers or other information that you want to appear at the bottom of every report page.

Page header (Access) Information printed at the top of every page of a report.

Page Layout view A screen view in which you can use the rulers to measure the width and height of data, set margins for printing, hide or display the numbered row headings and the lettered column headings, and change the page orientation; this view is useful for preparing your worksheet for printing.

Page number control A control on a form or report that inserts the page numbers of the pages when displayed in Print Preview or when printed.

Page orientation (Excel) The position of your printed worksheet on paper—either portrait or landscape.

Paint A program included with Vista in which graphics are created or edited.

Pane A portion of a worksheet window bounded by and separated from other portions by vertical and horizontal bars.

Parallel port A port used to connect a printer to a computer, and which sends data in groups of bits at speeds of up to 500 kilobits per second (Kbps).

Parenthetical reference In the MLA report style, references placed in parenthesis within the report text that include the last name of the author or authors, and the page number in the referenced source.

Paste The action of placing text or objects that have been copied or moved from one location to another location.

Paste (Excel) The action of placing cell contents that have been copied or moved to the Office Clipboard to another location.

Paste area The target destination for data that has been cut or copied using the Office Clipboard.

Paste Options button (Excel) A button that displays in the lower right corner of a pasted selection and that displays a list of options that lets you determine how the information is pasted into your worksheet; the list varies depending on the type of content you are pasting and the program you are pasting from.

Paste Special A dialog box that offers various options for the manner in which you can paste the contents of the Office Clipboard into one or more cells; for example, you can paste the calculated result of a formula rather than the actual formula.

PDA See Personal digital assistant.

Peer-to-peer (P2P) network A network in which each node can communicate directly with every other node, and which is often used for home and small business networks.

Percent for new value = base percent + percent of increase The formula for calculating a percentage by which a value increases by adding the base percentage—usually 100%—to the percent increase.

Percent rate of increase The percent by which one number increases over another.

Peripheral A hardware device connected to a computer, but not located within the system unit, such as a monitor, printer, or mouse.

Permanent memory Memory used by storage devices to retain data and information.

Personal digital assistant (PDA) Also known as a handheld computer, a small device that enables a user to carry digital information.

Personal folders The top part of the Navigation pane that displays folders associated with the current user.

Personal firewall A software program or hardware device designed to prevent unauthorized access to a computer.

Personal information manager In Outlook, a feature that enables you to electronically store and manage information about contacts, appointments, and tasks.

Phishing Email that masquerades as an authentic entity such as a bank or credit card company, requesting confidential information.

Picture element A point of light measured in dots per square inch on a screen; sixty-four pixels equals 8.43 characters, which is the average number of digits that will fit in a cell using the default font.

Pie chart A type of chart that shows the relationship of each part to a whole.

Pinned programs area An area at the top of the Start menu that is reserved for programs that you want to display permanently, although you can also delete programs from this area.

Pixel An abbreviated name for picture element.

Placeholder A slide element that reserves a portion of a slide and serves as a container for text, graphics, and other slide elements.

PMT function An Excel function that calculates the payment for a loan based on constant payments and at a constant rate of interest.

Point (noun) A measurement of the size of a font; there are 72 points in an inch, with 10–12 points being the most commonly used font size.

Point (verb) The action of moving the mouse pointer over something on the screen.

Point and click method The technique of constructing a formula by pointing to and then clicking cells; this method is convenient when the referenced cells are not adjacent to one another.

Pointer See mouse pointer.

Pointing Positioning the tip of the pointer in the center of an icon or other screen object.

Pop-up blocker A command on the Tools menu that stops or allows pop-ups to display as you browse the Internet.

Pop-ups Small windows that display on your screen without you actually requesting them as your browse the Internet.

Populate The action of filling a database table with records.

Port An interface through which external devices are connected to the computer.

Portals Home pages that act as launching sites to other Web pages, for example containing links to access frequently visited sites, up-to-the-minute news, weather reports, and maps and directories.

Portrait orientation A page orientation in which the printed page is taller than it is wide.

Present value The total amount that a series of future payments is worth now; also known as the principal.

Presentation graphics software A program used to effectively present information to an audience.

Presentation software A program used to create dynamic slideshows and generate speaker notes and audience handouts.

Primary key The field that uniquely identifies a record in a table—for example, a Student ID number at a college.

Principal Another term for present value.

Print Layout view A view of a document that looks like a sheet of paper, and which displays margins, headers, footers, and graphics.

Print Preview A feature that displays information as it will print based on the options that you select.

Print styles A combination of paper and page settings that determines the way items print.

Printer An output device used to generate hard copy.

Process The term used to describe the action of a computer when it converts data into information.

Program A set of instructions used by a computer to perform certain tasks.

Program tab A tab on the Ribbon that replaces the standard set of tabs when you switch to certain authoring modes or views, such as Print Preview.

Program-level buttons Buttons at the far right of the title bar that minimize, restore, or close the program.

Property sheet A list of characteristics—properties —for controls on a form or report in which you can make precision changes to each property associated with the control.

Protocol A set of rules for transferring data over the Internet.

Pt. An abbreviation for point.

Pv The abbreviation for *present value* in various Excel functions.

Query A database object that retrieves specific data from one or more tables and then displays the specified data in datasheet view.

Quick Access Toolbar A small toolbar in the upper left corner of the program window that displays buttons to perform frequently used commands with a single click.

Quick Launch toolbar An area to the right of the Start button that contains shortcut icons for commonly used programs.

RAM See Random access memory.

Random Access Memory (RAM) A computer's temporary storage space or short-term memory and stored on chips located on the motherboard; measured in megabytes (MB) and gigabytes (GB).

Range Two or more selected cells on a worksheet that are adjacent or nonadjacent; because the range is treated as a single unit, you can make the same change, or combination of changes, to more than one cell at a time.

Range finder An Excel feature that outlines cells in color to indicate which cells are used in a formula; useful for verifying which cells are referenced in a formula or for quickly positioning the insertion point within the cell to perform editing directly in the cell.

Rate In the Excel PMT function, the term used to indicate the interest rate for a loan.

Rate = amount of increase/base The mathematical formula to calculate a rate of increase.

RE Commonly used to mean *in regard to* or *regarding*.

Read Only Memory (ROM) A set of memory chips located on the motherboard that stores data and instructions that cannot be changed or erased; it holds all the instructions the computer needs to start up.

Reading Pane In Outlook, a window in which you can preview an e-mail message without actually opening it.

Recognizer A purple dotted underscore beneath a date or address indicating that the information could be placed into another Microsoft Office application program such as Outlook.

Record All of the categories of data pertaining to one person, place, thing, event, or idea.

Record selector The bar on the left side of a form with which you can select the entire record.

Record selector box The small box at the left of a record in datasheet view which, when clicked, selects the entire record.

Record source The tables or queries that provide the underlying data for a report.

Recycle Bin A storage area for files that have been deleted. Files can be recovered from the Recycle Bin or permanently removed.

References Within a report or research paper, a notation to indicate information that has been taken from another source; also in APA style, the title on the page that lists the sources used in the document.

Referential integrity A set of rules that Access uses to ensure that the data between related tables is valid.

Refresh rate The speed at which the pixels are reilluminated, measured in cycles per second and expressed as hertz (Hz).

Relational database A type of database in which the tables in the database can relate or connect to other tables through common fields.

Relationship An association that is established between two tables using common fields.

Relative cell reference In a formula, the address of a cell based on the relative position of the cell that contains the formula and the cell referred to.

Reminder A small dialog box that displays in the middle of the Outlook screen that is used to remind you of a pending appointment or task.

Report A database object that summarizes the fields and records from a table, or from a query, in an easy-to-read format suitable for printing.

Report footer Information printed once at the end of a report; use to print report totals or other summary information for the entire report.

Report header Information printed once at the beginning of a report; used for logos, titles, and dates.

Report tool The Access feature that creates a report with one mouse click, and which displays all the fields and records from the record source that you choose—a quick way to look at the underlying data.

Report Wizard An Access feature with which you can create a report by answering a series of questions; Access designs the report based on your answers.

Resolution The measurement used to assess the clarity of an image on a monitor; determined by pixel density.

Restore Using the Restore Down button to return a window to the size it was before it was maximized.

Restore point A record created by Windows XP for all of a computer's system settings.

Ribbon (Outlook) The area along the top of an Outlook form that contains frequently needed commands.

Ribbon The user interface in Office 2007 that groups the commands for performing related tasks on tabs across the upper portion of the program window.

Rich Text Format A universal document format that can be read by nearly all word processing programs, and that retains most text and paragraph formatting.

Right alignment Text aligned on the right margin, leaving the left margin uneven.

Right-click Click the right mouse button to activate a shortcut menu.

Ring (or token-ring) topology A networking configuration in which all devices are set up in a circular layout; data flows in a circular fashion, in one direction only.

ROM See Read only memory.

Root folder The first folder from which all other folders branch.

Rotate handle A handle on a selected image that can be dragged to rotate the image to any angle.

Rounding A procedure in which you determine which digit at the right of the number will be the last digit displayed and then increase it by one if the next digit to its right is 5, 6, 7, 8, or 9.

Row A horizontal group of cells in a worksheet.

Row headings The numbers along the left side of an Excel worksheet that designate the row numbers.

Ruler (Word) Displays the location of paragraph margins, indents, and tab stops for the selected paragraph.

Run The process in which Access searches the records in the table(s) included in a query design, finds the records that match the specified criteria, and then displays those records in a datasheet; only the fields that have been included in the query design display.

S-video port A port used to connect ancillary video equipment, such as a television or projector to a computer.

Salutation The greeting line of a business letter.

Sans serif font A font with no lines or extensions on the ends of characters.

Scanners Input devices used to convert hard copy documents or images into digital files.

Screen (or window) In a graphical user interface, the rectangular box that contains the program displayed on the monitor.

Screen saver A picture or animation that displays on your screen after a set period of computer inactivity.

ScreenTip A small box, activated by holding the pointer over a button or other screen object, that displays the name of a screen element.

Scroll box The box in the vertical and horizontal scroll bars that can be dragged to reposition the document on the screen.

Scroll box (Excel) The box in the vertical and horizontal scroll bars that can be dragged to reposition the worksheet on the screen.

Scroll wheel A feature on some mouse pointing devices; rolling the wheel enables you to quickly move a page up or down within a window.

Scrolling The action of moving a pane or window vertically (up or down) or horizontally (side to side) to bring unseen areas into view.

Search box A box in which you type a search word or phrase.

Search Engines Software programs that search for keywords in files and documents or other Web sites found on the Internet.

Search folder Retains all of the search conditions you specified during your search, and re-creates the search every time you click the search folder.

Section bar A gray bar in a form or report that identifies and separates one section from another; used to select the section and to change the size of the adjacent section.

Sectors Wedge-shaped sections of a hard disk drive, each measured from the center point to the outer edge.

Select (Excel) Highlighting, by clicking or dragging with your mouse, one or more cells so that the selected cells can be edited, formatted, copied, or moved; selected cells are indicated by a dark border.

Select All box A box in the upper left corner of the worksheet grid that selects all the cells in a worksheet.

Select Query A database object that retrieves (selects) specific data from one or more tables and then displays the specified data in datasheet view.

Selecting text Highlighting text so that it can be formatted, deleted, copied, or moved.

Separator character A character used to identify column placement in text; usually a tab or a comma.

Serial port A type of port that sends data one bit at a time at speeds of up to 115 kilobits per second (Kbps).

Series A group of things that come one after another in succession; for example, January, February, March, and so on.

Serif A font design that includes small line extensions on the ends of the letters to guide the eye in reading from left to right.

Server In a client/server network, the computer that manages shared network resources and provides access to the client computer when requested.

Shape Style A combination of formatting effects that includes 3-D, glow, and bevel effects and shadows.

Shapes Drawing objects including lines, arrows, stars and banners, and ovals and rectangles that are used to help convey a message by showing process and by containing text.

Sheet tab The labels along the lower border of the workbook window that identify each worksheet.

Sheet tab scrolling buttons Buttons to the left of the sheet tabs used to display Excel sheet tabs that are not in view; used when there are more sheet tabs than will display in the space provided.

Shortcut menu A context-sensitive menu that displays commands and options relevant to the selected object.

Shortcut menu A menu activated by placing the pointer over an object and clicking the right mouse button.

Simple select query Another name for a select query.

Sizing handle A small square or circle in the corners and the middle of the sides of a graphic that can be used to increase or decrease the size of the graphic.

Sizing handles (Access) The small boxes around the edge of a control indicating the control is selected and that can be adjusted to resize the selected control.

Slide handouts Printed images of more than one slide on a sheet of paper.

Slide Sorter View A view useful for rearranging slides in which all of the slides in the presentation display as thumbnails.

Small caps A font effect, usually used in titles, that changes lowercase text into capital (uppercase) letters using a reduced font size.

SmartArt graphic A designer-quality visual representation of your information that you can create by choosing from among many different layouts to effectively community your message or ideas.

SmartArt Styles Combinations of formatting effects that are applied to diagrams.

Smartphones Cell phones with additional computing capabilities or the ability to access the Internet.

Soft copy Data or information displayed on a monitor.

Software patches Quick software fixes provided to resolve an error found in program code until a software update can be issued.

Software updates Small, downloadable software modules that repair errors identified in commercial program code.

Sorting The process of arranging data in a specific order based on the value in each field.

Sources A term used to describe a list of referenced works in a report or research paper, also referred to as Works Cited, Bibliography, or References, depending upon the report style.

Spam Junk or unsolicited email.

Speakers Output devices that allow the user to hear any auditory signals the computer sends.

Spin box A small box with an upward- and downward-pointing arrow that lets you move rapidly through a set of values by clicking.

Spin box arrows The upward- and downward-pointing arrows in a spin box.

Split bar The gray bar that indicates the location of the border between two Word windows.

Sponsored links Web sites that pay to be prominently displayed as results at a search engine site.

Spotlight The area in the opening Access program screen that displays content from Microsoft's Web site.

Spreadsheet Another name for a worksheet.

Spreadsheet software A program with which you perform calculations and numerical analyses.

Spyware Software designed to capture personal and confidential information that resides on a computer and then send it elsewhere.

Stacked All of the open windows display on the screen.

Star topology A flexible and frequently used network configuration for businesses, in which nodes connect to a central communication device known as a switch.

Start button The button on the left side of the taskbar that is used to start programs, change system settings, find Windows help, or shut down the computer.

Start menu A menu that enables you to access the programs on your computer, and also enables you to change the way Windows operates, to access and configure your network, and to get help and support when it is needed.

Statistical functions Pre-written formulas that analyze a group of measurements.

Status area Another name for the notification area on the right side of the taskbar.

Status bar The area along the lower edge of the program window that displays, on the left side, the current mode, page number, and document information, and on the right side, displays buttons to control how the window looks.

Status bar (Word) A horizontal bar at the bottom of the document window that displays, on the left side, the page and line number, word count, and the Proof button. On the right side, displays buttons to control the look of the window. The status bar can be customized to include other information.

Storage To retain data or information for future use.

Straight quote A quotation mark that uses straight, rather than curved, lines.

Style A set of formatting characteristics—such as line spacing, space after paragraphs, font, and font style—that can be applied to text, paragraphs, tables, or lists.

Styles Formats for paragraphs stored in one shortcut command.

Stylus An input device used to write on a tablet computer or PDA.

Subject line The line following the subject line in a business letter that states the purpose of the letter.

Submenu A second-level menu activated by selecting a menu option.

Subpoint Secondary-level information in a SmartArt graphic.

Subset A portion of the total records available.

Suite A collection of application software programs developed by the same manufacturer, bundled together and sold at a price that is usually less than the cost of purchasing each program individually.

SUM function A predefined formula that adds all the numbers in a selected range of cells.

Supercomputer A large, powerful computer typically devoted to specialized tasks.

Synonyms Words with the same meaning as a selected word.

System software The set of programs that enables a computer's hardware devices and program software to work together; it includes the operating system and utility programs.

System tray Another name for the notification area on the right side of the taskbar.

System unit The tower, box, or console that contains the critical hardware and electrical components of a computer.

Tab order The order in which the insertion point moves from one field to the next in a form when you press the Tab key.

Tab stop Specific locations on a line of text, marked on the Word ruler, to which you can move the insertion point by pressing the Tab key; used to align and indent text.

Table A format for information that organizes and presents text and data in columns and rows.

Table (Access) The Access object that stores your data organized in an arrangement of columns and rows.

Table area The upper pane of the Query window, which displays the field lists for tables that are used in the query.

Table design The number of fields, and the type of content within each field, in an Access table.

Table Style In Outlook, a format that lists the contents of a folder on a single page and provides limited information about each item.

Table style (Excel) A predefined set of formatting characteristics, including font, alignment, and cell shading.

Table style (PowerPoint) Formatting applied to an entire table so that it is consistent with the presentation theme.

Table template A pre-built table format for common topics such as contacts, issues, and tasks.

Tables and Views category An arrangement of objects in the Navigation Pane in which the objects are grouped by the table to which they are related.

Tablet computer A portable computer that features a screen that swivels and can be written on using advanced handwriting recognition software.

Tabs A feature of Internet Explorer 7.0 that allows multiple Web pages to be displayed at the same time without opening multiple browsers.

Tags Custom file properties such as names, places, and descriptions that are added to files to enable you to categorize and find files more quickly.

Task A personal or work-related activity that you want to track until it is complete.

Task Pane In Outlook, a pane, usually below the appointment area, that can be used to schedule tasks.

Taskbar Displays the Start button and the name of any open documents. The taskbar may also display shortcut buttons for other programs.

Template The horizontal placement of text within a placeholder.

Template (Access) A pre-formatted database designed for a specific purpose.

Text box A movable, resizable container for text or graphics.

Text box control The graphical object on a form or report that displays the data from the underlying table or query; a text box control is known as a bound control because its source data comes from a table or a query.

Text format A universal document format that retains text and paragraph marks, but does not support any text or paragraph formatting.

Text string A sequence of characters, which when used in query criteria, much be matched.

Text wrapping The manner in which text displays around an object.

Theme A predefined set of colors, fonts, lines, and fill effects that look good together and that can be applied to your entire document or to specific items

Theme (Excel) A predefined set of colors, fonts, lines, and fill effects that look good together and that can be applied to your entire workbook or to specific items—for example to a chart or table.

Thesaurus A research tool that provides a list of synonyms.

Three-color scale Compares a range of cells by using a gradation of three colors; the shades represent higher, middle, or lower values.

Thumb drive A small storage device that plugs into a computer USB port; also called a USB drive or a flash drive.

Thumbnail A miniature representation of the contents of a picture file.

Thumbnails (PowerPoint) Miniature images of each slide.

Title bar Displays the program icon, the name of the document, and the name of the program. The Minimize, Maximize/Restore Down, and Close buttons are grouped on the right side of the title bar.

To-Do Bar A pane, usually along the right edge of the Outlook window, which provides quick access to daily tasks.

To-Do List pane In Outlook, a pane that displays an area to type a new task and a flag for each task.

Toggle button A button that can be turned on by clicking it once, and then turned off by clicking it again.

Toggle key A keyboard key that switches on or off each time it is pressed.

Token-ring topology See Ring topology.

Toolbar A row of buttons that activate commands, such as Undo or Bold, with a single click of the left mouse button.

Toolbars Rows of buttons, usually located under a menu bar, from which you can perform commands using a single click.

Top-level point The main text points in a SmartArt graphic.

Top/Bottom Rules A set of rules that enable you to apply conditional formatting to the highest and lowest values in a range of cells; for example, you can identify the top 5 selling products or the top 25 salaries in a personnel analysis.

Topology See Network topology.

Track Changes A Word tool that provides a visual indication of deletions, insertions, and formatting changes in a document.

Tracks Concentric circles on a hard disk drive.

Transitions The manner in which a slide appears or disappears during an onscreen slide show.

Trojan horse A program that appears to be useful or desirable, but acts maliciously in the background after installation.

Trust Center (Access) An area of the Access program where you can view the security and privacy settings for your Access installation.

Two-color scale Compares a range of cells by using a gradation of two colors.

Two-variable data table A data table that changes the values in two cells.

Type argument An optional argument in the PMT function that assumes that the payment will be made at the end of each time period.

Unbound control A term used to describe a control that does not have a source of data.

Underlying formula The formula entered in a cell and visible only on the Formula Bar.

Underlying value The data that displays in the Formula Bar.

Uniform Resource Locator (URL) The unique address used to locate a Web page or Web site.

Universal serial bus (USB) port A versatile port used to connect a wide array of peripheral devices to a computer.

USB drive A small storage device that plugs into a computer USB port; also called a thumb drive or a flash drive.

User interface The features of a computer operating system that enable you to interact with the computer.

Utility program A component of system software, typically a small program used to perform routine maintenance and housekeeping tasks for the computer.

Value Another name for constant value.

Value after increase = base x percent for new value Formula for calculating the value after an increase by multiplying the original value—the base—by the percent for new value (see the *Percent for new value* formula).

Value axis A numerical scale on the left side of a chart that shows the range of numbers for the data points; also referred to as the Y-axis.

Vertical scroll bar The bar at the right side of a window that enables you to move up and down to view information that extends beyond the top and bottom of the screen.

Vertical window split box A small box on the vertical scroll bar with which you can split the window into two vertical views of the same document.

View options (Word) Area on the right side of the status bar that contains buttons for viewing the document in Print Layout, Full Screen Reading, Web Layout, Master Document Tools, or Draft views, and also displays controls to Zoom Out and Zoom In.

View options Buttons on the right side of the status bar for viewing in normal, page layout view, or page break preview; also displays controls for zoom out and zoom in.

Views Ways to look at similar information in different formats and arrangements

Virus Malicious code or program, usually installed on a computer without the user's knowledge or permission.

Volatile Temporary storage, as in random access memory (RAM); data is erased when power is shut down.

Volatile (Excel) A term used to describe an Excel function that is subject to change each time the workbook is reopened; for example, the NOW function updates itself to the current date and time each time the workbook is opened.

WAN See Wide area network.

Web browser Software that enables you to use the Web and navigate from page to page and site to site.

Web Layout view A document view that shows how the document would look if viewed with a Web browser.

Web page A document on the World Wide Web that displays as a screen with associated links, frames, pictures, and other features of interest.

Web site A group of related Web pages published to a specific location on the World Wide Web.

Welcome Center By default, a window that displays every time you start your computer, and displays links to a number of topics, including upgrading Windows, connecting to the Internet, adding new users, and taking advantage of special offers from Microsoft.

What-if analysis The process of changing the values in cells to see how those changes affect the outcome of formulas in your worksheet.

Wide area network (WAN) A network composed of local area networks connected over long distances.

Wildcard A character, such as an asterisk, that can be used to match any number of characters in a file search.

Wildcard character In a query, a character that serves as a placeholder for one or more unknown characters in your criteria.

Window A box or screen that displays information or a program.

Window name The name of the window or program, displayed in the status bar or title bar.

Windows An operating system that coordinates the activities of a computer.

Windows Aero The Vista user interface that features a three-dimensional look, with transparent window frames, live previews of open windows, and multiple color schemes. Aero is an acronym for **A**uthentic, **E**nergetic, **R**eflective, **O**pen.

Windows Explorer A program that enables you to create and manage folders, and manage copy, move, sort, and delete files.

Windows Sidebar An area on the right side of the screen that displays useful Gadgets, such as a clock, a stock market ticker, or a weather map.

Wireless network A network that connects using radio waves instead of wires or cable.

Wizard A feature in Microsoft Office programs that walks you step by step through a process.

Word document window Displays the active document.

Word processing software A program used to create and edit written documents such as papers, letters, and resumes.

WordArt A feature that applies combinations of decorative formatting to text, including shadows, reflections, and 3-D effects, as well as changing the line and fill color of text.

WordPad A simple word processing program that comes with Windows Vista.

Wordwrap The feature that moves text from the right edge of a paragraph to the beginning of the next line as necessary to fit within the margins.

Work week A calendar option that shows only the weekdays, Monday through Friday.

Workbook An Excel file that contains one or more worksheets.

Workbook-level buttons Buttons at the far right of the Ribbon tabs used to minimize or restore a displayed workbook.

Works Cited A term used to describe a list of referenced works placed at the end of a research paper or report when using the MLA Style.

Worksheet The primary document that you use in Excel to store and work with data, and which is formatted as a pattern of uniformly spaced horizontal and vertical lines.

Worksheet grid The area of the Excel window that displays the columns and rows that intersect to form the cells of the worksheet.

Worm A program that is able to replicate and spread from computer to computer without human interaction.

Writer's identification The name and title of the author of a letter, placed near the bottom of the letter, under the complimentary closing.

X-axis Another name for the category axis.

Y-axis Another name for the value axis.

Zip drive A magnetic storage device used to save and retrieve data on Zip disks.

Zombie A computer that is controlled remotely and can be used to help spread viruses, spyware, and spam.

Zoom The action of increasing or decreasing the viewing area of the screen.

Index

The CD symbol represents Index entries found on the CD (see CD file name for page numbers).

Cut command
  PowerPoint 2007, 862
  Word 2007, 86
cutting text in documents (Word 2007), 85–87

D

data
  charts (PowerPoint 2007), deleting, 935–937
  databases (Access 2007)
    definition, 522
    grouping queries, 657–659
    inserting, 528–530
  multiple worksheets (Excel 2007), inserting, 386–393
  tables (Access 2007), 527
    populating, 528
  worksheets (Excel 2007), 282
    data bars, 460–462
    displayed values, 292, 294
    inserting, 285–290
    inserting into cell ranges, 329–330
    moving, 454–456
    scaling, 474
data bars
  applying conditional formatting, 460–462
  definition, 461
data markers (charts), 315, 934
data points (charts), 315, 934
data series (charts), 315, 934
data sources, 549
  creating select queries, 615–617
  selecting for query creation, 550
data tables, 482–488
  calculating options, 485–488
  definition, 482
  one-variable data tables, 482
  two-variable data tables, 482–485
data types
  Attachment, 533
  AutoNumber, 529, 532–534
  changing in Datasheet view, 532–536
  Currency, 533
  Date/Time, 533
  Hyperlink, 533
  Lookup Wizard, 533
  Memo, 533
  Number, 533
  OLE Object, 533
  Text, 529, 532–534
  Yes/No, 533
database management systems (DBMS), definition, 522
databases (Access 2007)
  blank, 522
  closing, 556
  comparison operators, 640–642
  creating, 526–527, 558–559
  data
    definition, 522
    inserting, 528–530
  database management systems (DBMS), definition, 522
  definition, 522
  folders, creating, 524–525
  forms, creating, 552–554
  importing worksheets into, 633–638
  names, 559, 604–605, 633–634

  objects, 522
    footers, 547
    headers, 547
    Navigation Pane (Access 2007), 562, 567
    organizing in Navigation Pane, 562–564
    saving, 535
    Tables and Views category, 562
  opening, 604–606, 633–634
  password protecting, ● Chapter 13, Try It!
  queries. *See* queries
  referential integrity, 606–610
  relational databases, definition, 606
  reports
    All Events, 568
    creating, 554–556
    Event Details, 568–569
    printing, 554–556
    relationship reports, 610–612
    viewing, 568–569
  saving, 556, 633–634
    with different formats, ● Chapter 12, Try It!
  tables, 526–527
    adding, 540–542
    adding records, 528–530, 542–543, 695–697
    columns, 527, 543–549
    creating by entering records into Multiple Items form, 559–561
    creating by importing worksheets, 635–638
    creating queries based on multiple tables, 646–649
    creating relationships, 606–610
    creating with new designs, 565–568
    data, 527
    deleting records with forms, 697–698
    fields. See fields (database tables)
    foreign key, 609
    join lines, 610
    names, 536
    previewing, 569
    primary key, 539–540, 566
    printing, 543–549, 569–570
    saving, 539–540
    showing, 607
    sorting records, 612–613
    sorting records on multiple fields, 614–615
  templates
    definition, 522
    local templates, 558
Datasheet view (Access 2007), 528, 536–537
  changing data types, 532–536
  naming fields (databases), 531
Date and Time dialog box (Word 2007), 105
Date format (Excel 2007), 305
date line (letters), definition, 6
Date/Time data type, 533
dates
  inserting into documents (Word 2007), 104–105
  worksheets (Excel 2007)
    formats, 377–379
    formatting, 377–379
    inserting, 377–379
    NOW function, 463–464
    as values, 376
DBMS (database management systems), definition, 522
decimal places, Decrease Decimal button (Excel 2007), 306
Decrease Decimal button (Excel 2007), 306
Decrease List Level button (PowerPoint 2007), 783